P9-BBT-591

Walking in
SPAIN

Miles Roddis
Nancy Frey & Jose Placer
Matthew Fletcher
John Noble

LONELY PLANET PUBLICATIONS
Melbourne • Oakland • London • Paris

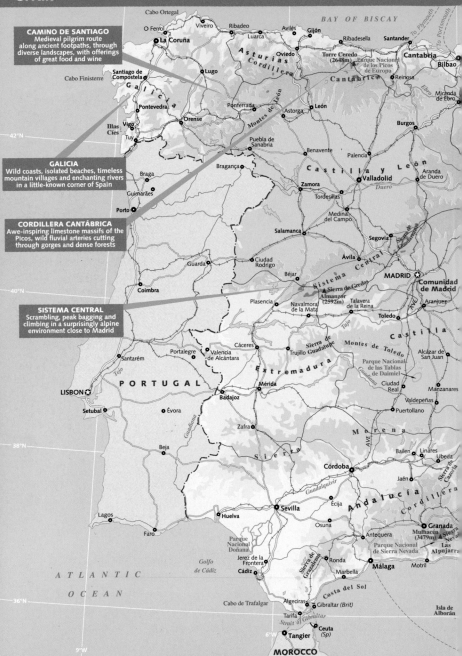

SPAIN

CAMINO DE SANTIAGO
Medieval pilgrim route along ancient footpaths, through diverse landscapes, with offerings of great food and wine

GALICIA
Wild coasts, isolated beaches, timeless mountain villages and enchanting rivers in a little-known corner of Spain

CORDILLERA CANTÁBRICA
Awe-inspiring limestone massifs of the Picos, wild fluvial arteries cutting through gorges and dense forests

SISTEMA CENTRAL
Scrambling, peak bagging and climbing in a surprisingly alpine environment close to Madrid

BAY OF BISCAY
To Plymouth
To Portsmouth

Cabo Ortegal
O Ferrol
Viveiro
Ribadeo
Avilés
Gijón
Ribadesella
Santander
La Coruña
Luarca
Oviedo
Torre Ceredo (2648m)
Parque Nacional de los Picos de Europa
Cantabria
Bilbao
Asturias Cordillera
Cantábrica
Reinosa
Santiago de Compostela
Lugo
Miranda de Ebro
Cabo Finisterre
Galicia
Ponferrada
Astorga
León
Burgos
Pontevedra
Orense
Montes de León
Castilla y León
Puebla de Sanabria
Benavente
Palencia
Aranda de Duero
Illas Cíes
Vigo
Tuy
Bragança
Zamora
Tordesillas
Valladolid
Duero
Braga
Guimarães
Medina del Campo
Segovia
Porto
Salamanca
Sistema de Guadarrama
Guarda
Ciudad Rodrigo
Ávila
MADRID
Comunidad de Madrid
Béjar
Sistema Central
Sierra de Gredos
Almanzor (2592m)
Coimbra
Plasencia
Navalmoral de la Mata
Talavera de la Reina
Aranjuez
AVE
Toledo
Castilla
PORTUGAL
Cáceres
Sierra de Guadalupe
Montes de Toledo
Alcázar de San Juan
Santarém
Portalegre
Valencia de Alcántara
Trujillo Guadalupe
Parque Nacional de las Tablas de Daimiel
Extremadura
Guadiana
Ciudad Real
Manzanares
LISBON
Mérida
Valdepeñas
Setúbal
Badajoz
Puertollano
Évora
Zafra
Morena
AVE
Bailén
Linares
Úbeda
Beja
Sierra
Córdoba
Jaén
Sierra de Cazorla
Lagos
Huelva
Sevilla
Guadalquivir
Andalucía
Cordillera
Faro
Osuna
Écija
Granada
Mulhacén (3479m)
Sierra Nevada
Parque Nacional Doñana
Antequera
Parque Nacional de Sierra Nevada
Las Alpujarras
ATLANTIC OCEAN
Golfo de Cádiz
Jerez de la Frontera
Ronda
Marbella
Málaga
Motril
Costa del Sol
Cádiz
Sierra de Grazalema
Cabo de Trafalgar
Algeciras
Gibraltar (Brit)
Isla de Alborán
Tarifa
Strait of Gibraltar
Ceuta (Sp)
Tangier
MOROCCO

42°N
40°N
38°N
36°N
9°W
6°W

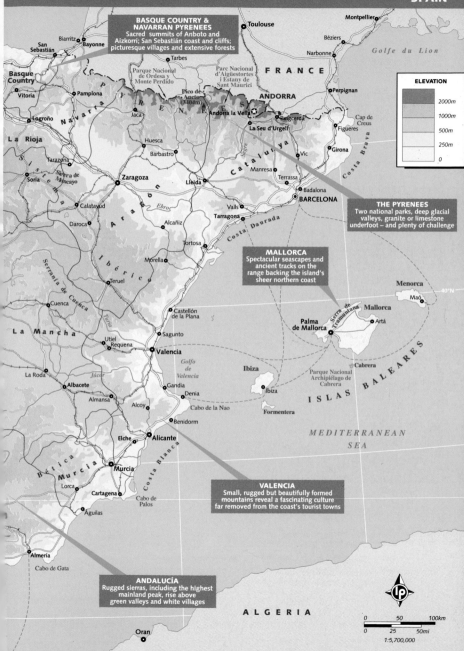

SPAIN

BASQUE COUNTRY & NAVARRAN PYRENEES
Sacred summits of Anboto and Aizkorri; San Sebastián coast and cliffs; picturesque villages and extensive forests

THE PYRENEES
Two national parks, deep glacial valleys, granite or limestone underfoot – and plenty of challenge

MALLORCA
Spectacular seascapes and ancient tracks on the range backing the island's sheer northern coast

VALENCIA
Small, rugged but beautifully formed mountains reveal a fascinating culture far removed from the coast's tourist towns

ANDALUCÍA
Rugged sierras, including the highest mainland peak, rise above green valleys and white villages

ELEVATION

2000m
1000m
500m
250m
0

FRANCE

Montpellier
Toulouse
Béziers
Narbonne
Golfe du Lion
Biarritz
Bayonne
San Sebastián
Perpignan
Tarbes
Parc National d'Aigüestortes i Estany de Sant Maurici
ANDORRA
Andorra la Vella
Puigcerdà
La Seu d'Urgell
Cap de Creus
Figueres
Costa Brava
Girona
Vic
Manresa
Terrassa
Badalona
BARCELONA
Tarragona
Costa Daurada

Parque Nacional de Ordesa y Monte Perdido
Pico de Aneto (3404m)
Basque Country
Vitoria
Pamplona
Jaca
Logroño
Navarra
La Rioja
Huesca
Barbastro
Lleida
Sistema
Tarazona
Sierra de Moncayo
Soria
Zaragoza
Aragón
Calatayud
Daroca
Alcañiz
Ebro
Valls
Ibérica
Morella
Teruel
Tortosa

Serranía de Cuenca
Cuenca
La Mancha
Utiel
Requena
Castellón de la Plana
Sagunto
Valencia
Golfo de Valencia
La Roda
Albacete
Júcar
Almansa
Alcoy
Gandia
Denia
Cabo de la Nao
Benidorm
Elche
Alicante
Bética
Murcia
Lorca
Cartagena
Cabo de Palos
Águilas
Almería
Cabo de Gata
Costa Blanca

Menorca
Maó
40°N
Mallorca
Artá
Palma de Mallorca
Sierra de Tramuntana
Ibiza
Ibiza
Formentera
Cabrera
Parque Nacional Archipiélago de Cabrera
ISLAS BALEARES

MEDITERRANEAN SEA

ALGERIA
Oran

0   50   100km
0   25   50mi
1:5,700,000

Walking in Spain
3rd edition – April 2003
First published – May 1990

Published by
Lonely Planet Publications Pty Ltd ABN 36 005 607 983
90 Maribyrnong St, Footscray, Victoria 3011, Australia

Lonely Planet Offices
Australia Locked Bag 1, Footscray, Victoria 3011
USA 150 Linden St, Oakland, CA 94607
UK 10a Spring Place, London NW5 3BH
France 1 rue du Dahomey, 75011 Paris

Photographs
Many of the images in this guide are available for licensing from
Lonely Planet Images.
w www.lonelyplanetimages.com

Main front cover photograph
Cliff-top houses in Ronda, Andalucía (Simeone Huber, Getty Images)

Small front cover photograph
Walking from Sóller to Sa Calobra, Mallorca (Ingrid Roddis)

ISBN 1 74059 245 X

Contents

2 Contents

The Walks	Duration	Difficulty	Season
Sistema Central			
Alta Ruta de Gredos	5 days	moderate–demanding	June or Sept
Covacha Walk	3 days	moderate–demanding	June or Sept
Sierra de Candelario	2 days	moderate	June/Sept
Valle de la Fuenfría	6½–7½ hours	easy–moderate	May–June or Sept
Cuerda Larga	3 days	moderate	May–June or Sept
The Pyrenees			
The Pyrenean Traverse	23 days	moderate–demanding	mid-June–Sept
Basses de les Salamandres	3¾–4¼ hours	moderate	May–Oct
Estanys de Siscaró	4–4½ hours	moderate	May–Oct
Pic de l'Estanyó	6½–7½ hours	demanding	June–Sept
Estany Llong	5½–6 hours	easy–moderate	June–Sept
Refugi de Colomina	2 days	moderate–demanding	June–Sept
Port de Ratera d'Espot	4½–5 hours	moderate	June–Sept
Frontier Ridge	3½ hours	easy–moderate	June–Sept
Lago de Cregüeña	5–5½ hours	moderate	June–Sept
Basque Country & Navarran Pyrenees			
Gorbeia Traverse	7–8 hours	moderate–demanding	May–Oct
Urkiola: Anboto Ridge	5½–6 hours	demanding	May–Oct
Around Aizkorri	2 days	moderate–demanding	July–Sept
San Sebastián to Hondarribia	2 days	moderate	year-round
GR11: Elizondo to Roncesvalles	2 days	moderate–demanding	July–Sept
Cordillera Cantábrica			
Costa Naviega	6–6½ hours	easy–moderate	year-round
Ruta de los Lagos	6½–7½ hours	moderate	July–Sept
Ruta de las Brañas	5 hrs	moderate–demanding	July–Sept
Besaya-Saja Traverse	2 days	moderate	May–Sept
Picos de Europa Circuit	9 days	demanding	July–Sept

The Walks	Duration	Difficulty	Season
Galicia			
Monte Pindo	5–6 hours	moderate–demanding	May–Oct
Spindrift Walk	2 days	easy–moderate	year-round
Illa Do Faro	2–2½ hours	easy–moderate	June–Sept
Illa Monte Agudo	2–2½ hours	easy	June–Sept
Ancares Ridge	5½–7 hours	moderate–demanding	June–Oct
Piornedo Loop	4½–5½ hours	moderate	June–Oct
Devesa da Rogueira Loop	6–7 hours	moderate–demanding	June–Oct
Río Lor Meander	3 days	moderate	June–Oct
Valencia			
Els Ports Loop	6 days	moderate	Apr–June
Ruta La Marina Alta	4 days	moderate	Mar–May
Serra de Bérnia Traverse	9–10½ hours	demanding	Mar–May
Mallorca			
Monestir de Sa Trapa	4–4½ hours	easy–moderate	Feb–May
Sóller to Deià	3–4 hours	easy	Oct–May
Barranc de Biniaraix & Embassament de Cúber	3½–4 hours	easy–moderate	Feb–May
Valldemossa Loop	5¼–5¾ hours	moderate	Feb–May
Sóller to Sa Calobra	6¼–7¼ hours	moderate	Feb–May
Torrent de Pareis	4–4½ hours	moderate–demanding	May–Sept
Andalucía			
Sierra de Cazorla Loop	6½ hours	easy–moderate	Apr–June/Sept–Oct
Barranco del Guadalentín	5 hours	easy–moderate	Apr–June/Sept–Oct
Río Borosa	6–7 hours	easy–moderate	Apr–June/Sept–Oct
Alpujarras Tour	5 days	moderate	Apr–June/Sept–Oct
Sierra Nevada Traverse	3 days	moderate–demanding	July–early Sept
Cabo de Gata Coast	3 days	easy–moderate	Mar–June/Sept–Oct
Grazalema Loop	6 hours	easy–moderate	May–June/Sept–Oct
Benamahoma to Zahara de la Sierra	5 hours	easy	May–June/Sept–Oct
Camino de Santiago			
Camino Francés	30 days	moderate–demanding	May–June/Sept–Oct

The Maps

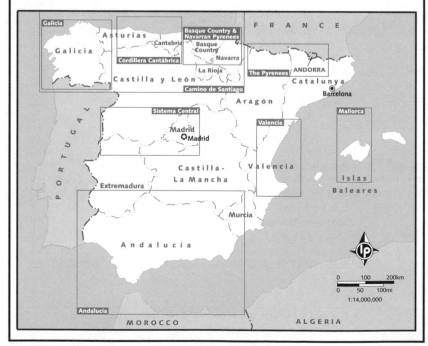

The Authors

Miles Roddis

Over 25 years, Miles has lived, worked and walked in eight countries, including Laos, Iran, Egypt, Jordan and Sudan. Spain was also one of those countries and he and his wife Ingrid bought a tatty old flat in the Barrio del Carmen, Valencia's oldest and most vibrant quarter. Now renovated, this shoebox-sized apartment is their principal home, the place to which they retreat to recover wind and write up.

Miles has contributed to Lonely Planet's *Africa on a Shoestring*, *West Africa*, *Read This First: Africa*, *Lonely Planet Unpacked*, *France*, *Italy*, *Spain*, *Valencia & the Costa Blanca*, *Canary Islands*, *Western Europe*, *Mediterranean Europe*, *Europe on a Shoestring*, *Walking in Britain* and *Walking in France*.

Matthew Fletcher

As a child Matt spent his holidays in rainy English seaside resorts developing a skill for passing on random facts to innocent tourists. He now travels worldwide doing much the same and has contributed to Lonely Planet's *Walking in Spain*, *Walking in Australia*, *Morocco*, *Kenya*, *East Africa*, *West Africa* and *Tonga*. For *Lonely Planet Unpacked* and *Lonely Planet Unpacked Again* he was stranded in a Madagascan swamp and had a dingo steal his breakfast.

Nancy Frey & Jose Placer

Nancy and Jose met while in the Pyrenees. Nancy was researching why thousands of people walk the medieval Camino de Santiago pilgrimage across Spain's north for her doctoral dissertation in cultural anthropology (at the University of California, Berkeley, 1996). The six-year project developed in her book, *Pilgrim Stories: On and Off the Road to Santiago*. Jose was coming from the Alps after abandoning his law career, and had decided to walk the Camino, back home to Santiago de Compostela. He's enjoyed the heights of many European countries, North Africa, the Middle East and Nancy's native California. Since their fateful encounter they've not stopped walking together. They run their own company, On Foot In Spain, and lead educational walking tours to the Iberian Peninsula's most enchanting hidden corners. They live in Galicia and have an adorable son, Jacob.

John Noble

John Noble grew up at the bottom of a hill called Sawley Old Brow in the Ribble valley on the edge of England's Pennines, and has been walking up, down, over and along hills and valleys ever since. Pendle Hill, home of the Lancashire Witches, was the first summit he conquered (*en famille*, at an age too early to remember). Numerous school trips up the hills of England's Lake District ingrained the habit. Studies and jobs in flat places like Surrey, Cambridge and London never had a chance of lasting long, and John soon took to perusing the bumpier parts of the world, from Mexican volcanoes to the donkey trails of Zanskar, on foot whenever time permitted. The steep streets of the Andalucian hill village he now calls home are the ideal springboard for exploring many wonderfully rugged bits of southern Spain.

FROM THE AUTHORS

Miles Roddis Special thanks to mountain guides Miguel Motes in Benasque and Jacinto Verdaguer – plus all the cheerful team in Canillo's tourist office. Also to Joan Torres (Grup d'Excursió Mallorqui) and Gerard Gimenez (Casa del Parc, Parc Nacional d'Aigüestortes i Estany de Sant Maurici). Tourist office staff Magdalena Mayor (Sóller), Raimunda Jordan (Port de Sóller), Javier Soler (Tavascan) and Natalia (Torla) and *refugio* wardens Angi (Vall Ferrera), Sergi (Colomers), Chema (Angel Orus) and Javier Abajo (Respomuso) who went out of their way to help.

Reader Omer Rotem sent in a particularly detailed and much appreciated updating email about the Pyrenees. The Cazcarra family of Viadós, Mercedes and Jose-Luis of Camping Los Vives (Saravillo) and David Wilcock were all pinpricks of light on one of my darkest nights.

The most and best of thanks to Ingrid, on the trail, in the tent, at the stove and behind the wheel and the man. Oh, how I missed you when you missed me!

Matthew Fletcher Thanks to Clare for walking/staying with me, Miles and Ingrid for putting us up in Valencia, Tommy Minor et al for leading me astray many times in Madrid and putting up with smelly gear in your living room, Pete Green and Bando for company in the Sierra de Guadarrama (more than one day next time eh boys?) and finally to all the staff I hassled in *refugios*, bus stations and tourist information offices across Valencia and the Sistema Central.

Nancy Frey & Jose Placer Many thanks to Miles for a fine coordinating job and to Andrew for his understanding. Special thanks go to our anonymous walking companions who love and tend their mountains and shared them with us; Lela and Lelo for taking care of Jacob when he was unable to join us on the trails; Dindindin for keeping us going; and above all, to Cobo, for being our patient lamb.

John Noble Special thanks to Mariano Cruz, Inger and Sepp, Epifania, and David and Emma for their kind welcomes and generous assistance in Las Alpujarras. *¡Hasta pronto!* And to Isabella for spotting a crucial red-and-white paint mark on the Monte de Pampaneira. And above all to Simba the stray dog who followed me over the mountain to Trevélez, around Cabo de Gata, around Cazorla and Grazalema, then back home to become part of the family.

This Book

A dedicated team of authors tirelessly walked the mountains, gorges, ridges, beaches and villages of Spain to research this new edition. Miles Roddis was the coordinating author and wrote the introductory chapters, The Pyrenees, Mallorca and Travel Facts. Matthew Fletcher wrote Sistema Central and Valencia. Nancy Frey and Jose Placer collaborated on Basque Country & Navarran Pyrenees, Cordillera Cantábrica, Galicia and Camino de Santiago. John Noble wrote Andalucía.

From the Publisher

Back in LP's Melbourne office was an equally dedicated (though considerably less suntanned) crew. Editing was coordinated by Marg Toohey, with assistance from David Andrew, Melanie Dankel, Sally Dillon, Victoria Harrison, Evan Jones and Nick Tapp. Cartographic work was done by Karen Fry, Jarrad Needham, Adrian Persoglia, Tessa Rottiers, Jacqui Nguyen and Andrew Smith. The language chapter was polished by Quentin Frayne. The colour pages were created by Indra Kilfoyle. Layout/design was handled by Steven Cann. The illustrations were rounded up by Pepi Bluck. The climate charts were compiled by Csanad Csutoros. The project was managed by Glenn van der Knijff and the entire process was overseen by Lindsay Brown and Andrew Bain.

Thanks

Many thanks to the travellers who used the last edition and wrote to us with helpful hints, advice and interesting anecdotes.

James Blair, Kim Brown, Murray Brown, Joan Burton, Donald Chaikin, Brendan Donnelly, Lynton Eames, Fiona Gell, Mark Harding, Marjorie Hayes, Oren Melamud, Ian Mitchell, Eran Nevo, Hendrik Roesel, Philippa Rollin, Omar Rotem, Sara Schneider, Paul Shewry, Nicole Smith, Raf Vermeyen, Roy Wiesner, Adrian Wright

Grateful acknowledgment is made to Instituto Geográfico Nacional-Centro Nacional de Información Geográfica (IGN) and Centro Geográfico del Ejército (SGE) for reproduction permission of the contour maps.

Walk Descriptions

This book contains 51 walk descriptions ranging from day trips to a 30-day walk, plus suggestions for side trips and alternative routes. Each walk description has a brief introduction outlining the natural and cultural features you may encounter, plus information to help you plan your walk – transport options, level of difficulty, time frame and any permits required.

Day walks are often circular and are located in areas of uncommon beauty. Multiday walks include information on camp sites, *refugios* (mountain huts or refuges), hostels or other accommodation and where you can obtain water and supplies.

Times & Distances

These are provided only as a guide. Times are based on actual walking time and do not include stops for snacks, taking photographs, rests or side trips. Be sure to factor these in when planning your walk. Distances are provided but should be read in conjunction with altitudes. Significant elevation changes can make a greater difference to your walking time than lateral distance. In most cases, the daily stages can be varied.

Level of Difficulty

Grading systems are always arbitrary. However, having an indication of the grade may help you choose between walks. Our authors use the following grading guidelines:

Easy – a walk on flat terrain or with minor elevation changes usually over short distances on well-travelled routes with no navigational difficulties.
Moderate – a walk with challenging terrain, often involving longer distances and steep climbs.
Demanding – a walk with long daily distances and difficult terrain with significant elevation changes; may involve challenging route-finding and high-altitude or glacier travel.

True Left & True Right

The terms 'true left' and 'true right', used to describe the bank of a stream or river, sometimes throw readers. The 'true left bank' simply means the left bank as you look downstream.

Maps

Our maps are based on the best available references, often combined with GPS data collected in the field. They are intended to show the general route of the walk and should be used in conjunction with maps suggested in the walk description.

Maps may contain contours or ridge lines in addition to major watercourses, depending on the available information. These features build a three-dimensional picture of the terrain, allowing you to determine when the trail climbs and descends. Altitudes of major peaks and passes complete the picture by providing the actual extent of the elevation changes.

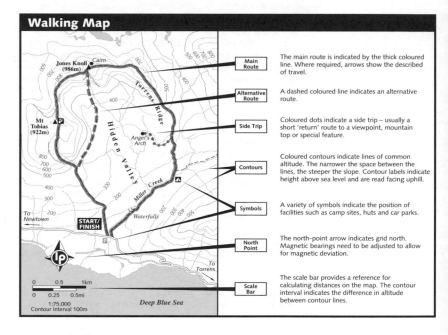

Walking Map

Main Route	The main route is indicated by the thick coloured line. Where required, arrows show the described of travel.
Alternative Route	A dashed coloured line indicates an alternative route.
Side Trip	Coloured dots indicate a side trip – usually a short 'return' route to a viewpoint, mountain top or special feature.
Contours	Coloured contours indicate lines of common altitude. The narrower the space between the lines, the steeper the slope. Contour labels indicate height above sea level and are read facing uphill.
Symbols	A variety of symbols indicate the position of facilities such as camp sites, huts and car parks.
North Point	The north-point arrow indicates grid north. Magnetic bearings need to be adjusted to allow for magnetic deviation.
Scale Bar	The scale bar provides a reference for calculating distances on the map. The contour interval indicates the difference in altitude between contour lines.

Route Finding

While accurate, our maps are not perfect. Inaccuracies in altitudes are commonly caused by air-temperature anomalies. Natural features such as river confluences and mountain peaks are in their true position, but the location of villages and trails may not always be so. This could be because a village is spread over a hillside, or the size of the map does not allow for detail of the trail's twists and turns. However, by using several basic route-finding techniques, you will have few problems following our descriptions:

1. Always be aware of whether the trail should be climbing or descending.
2. Check the north-point arrow on the map and determine the general direction of the trail.
3. Time your progress over a known distance and calculate the speed at which you travel in the given terrain. You can then determine with reasonable accuracy how far you have travelled.
4. Watch the path – look for boot prints and other signs of previous passage.

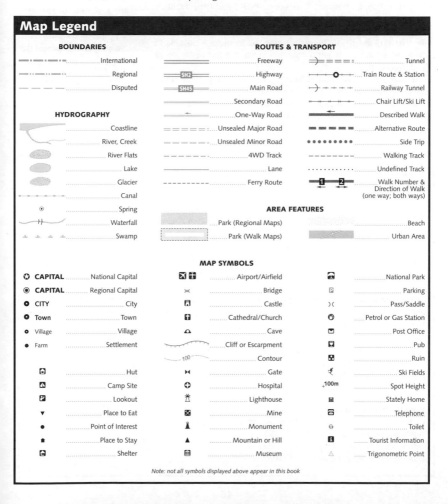

Map Legend

BOUNDARIES

━ ┉ ━ ┉ ━	International
━ ┉┉ ━ ┉ ━	Regional
━ ━ ━ ━ ━	Disputed

HYDROGRAPHY

	Coastline
	River, Creek
	River Flats
	Lake
	Glacier
	Canal
⊙	Spring
⌣⊬⌣	Waterfall
⩜ ⩜ ⩜ ⩜	Swamp

ROUTES & TRANSPORT

	Freeway
SH2	Highway
SH45	Main Road
	Secondary Road
	One-Way Road
= = = = =	Unsealed Major Road
	Unsealed Minor Road
━ ━ ━ ━	4WD Track
	Lane
━ ━ ━ ━	Ferry Route

⇒═ ═ ═ ═	Tunnel
┝━●━┥	Train Route & Station
┥ ┿ ┿ ┿ ┿	Railway Tunnel
┝┿┿┿┿┿┥	Chair Lift/Ski Lift
	Described Walk
▬ ▬ ▬ ▬	Alternative Route
● ● ● ● ● ●	Side Trip
━ ━ ━ ━	Walking Track
· · · · · ·	Undefined Track
◀**1**▶ ◀**2**▶	Walk Number & Direction of Walk (one way; both ways)

AREA FEATURES

	Park (Regional Maps)
	Park (Walk Maps)
	Beach
	Urban Area

MAP SYMBOLS

✪ **CAPITAL**	National Capital
◉ **CAPITAL**	Regional Capital
● **CITY**	City
● **Town**	Town
● Village	Village
● Farm	Settlement
🏠	Hut
⛺	Camp Site
🅵	Lookout
▼	Place to Eat
●	Point of Interest
■	Place to Stay
🅶	Shelter

✈ 🛦	Airport/Airfield
≍	Bridge
🏰	Castle
✝	Cathedral/Church
⌂	Cave
⌒	Cliff or Escarpment
⌒100	Contour
⋈	Gate
✛	Hospital
🛉	Lighthouse
⊠	Mine
🛉	Monument
▲	Mountain or Hill
🏛	Museum

🏞	National Park
🅿	Parking
)(	Pass/Saddle
⊖	Petrol or Gas Station
▣	Post Office
🍺	Pub
▣	Ruin
⛷	Ski Fields
₊100m	Spot Height
🏛	Stately Home
☎	Telephone
⊙	Toilet
🅸	Tourist Information
△	Trigonometric Point

Note: not all symbols displayed above appear in this book

Foreword

ABOUT LONELY PLANET GUIDEBOOKS

The story begins with a classic travel adventure: Tony and Maureen Wheeler's 1972 journey across Europe and Asia to Australia. There was no useful information about the overland trail then, so Tony and Maureen published the first Lonely Planet guidebook to meet a growing need.

From a kitchen table, Lonely Planet has grown to become the largest independent travel publisher in the world, with offices in Melbourne (Australia), Oakland (USA), London (UK) and Paris (France).

Today Lonely Planet guidebooks cover the globe. There is an ever-growing list of books and information in a variety of media. Some things haven't changed. The main aim is still to make it possible for adventurous travellers to get out there – to explore and better understand the world.

At Lonely Planet we believe travellers can make a positive contribution to the countries they visit – if they respect their host communities and spend their money wisely. Since 1986 a percentage of the income from each book has been donated to aid projects and human rights campaigns, and, more recently, to wildlife conservation.

Although inclusion in a guidebook usually implies a recommendation we cannot list every good place. Exclusion does not necessarily imply criticism. In fact there are a number of reasons why we might exclude a place – sometimes it is simply inappropriate to encourage an influx of travellers.

UPDATES & READER FEEDBACK

Things change – prices go up, schedules change, good places go bad and bad places go bankrupt. Nothing stays the same. So, if you find things better or worse, recently opened or long-since closed, please tell us and help make the next edition even more accurate and useful.

Lonely Planet thoroughly updates each guidebook as often as possible – usually every two years, although for some destinations the gap can be longer. Between editions, up-to-date information is available in our free, monthly email bulletin *Comet* ([W] www.lonelyplanet.com/newsletters). You can also check out the *Thorn Tree* bulletin board and *Postcards* section of our website, which carry unverified, but fascinating, reports from travellers.

Tell us about it! We genuinely value your feedback. A well-travelled team at Lonely Planet reads and acknowledges every email and letter we receive and ensures that every morsel of information finds its way to the relevant authors, editors and cartographers.

Everyone who writes to us will find their name listed in the next edition of the appropriate guidebook. The very best contributions will be rewarded with a free guidebook.

We may edit, reproduce and incorporate your comments in Lonely Planet products such as guidebooks, websites and digital products, so let us know if you don't want your comments reproduced or your name acknowledged.

How to contact Lonely Planet:
Online: [e] talk2us@lonelyplanet.com.au, [W] www.lonelyplanet.com
Australia: Locked Bag 1, Footscray, Victoria 3011
UK: 10a Spring Place, London NW5 3BH
USA: 150 Linden St, Oakland, CA 94607

Introduction

Spain receives more than 50 million visitors annually. So why, when the greatest joys of walking are tramping alone or in congenial company, choose to walk in Spain?

For a start, a high proportion of tourism is confined to the Mediterranean coastal belt and star urban attractions such as Seville, Barcelona and Madrid. Head for the hills and it's possible to spend the whole day scarcely seeing another walker.

If you're staying in a coastal holiday resort, those hills aren't far away. In the Valencia chapter are walks a mere bus ride from Benidorm. Several of our Andalucía trails are within striking distance of the Costa del Sol and all the walks on Mallorca are easily accessible from a beachside base.

Spain's spectacular national parks, such as the Picos de Europa in Asturias, Ordesa y Monte Perdido in Aragón or Aigüestortes i Estany de Sant Maurici in the Catalan Pyrenees, pull in visitors by the thousand. Yet walk no more than a kilometre from the car park and you'll have the magnificent scenery almost to yourself.

For this new, revised edition, we've re-tramped every metre of the walks listed in the table (pp4–7), from the hands-in-pockets family half-day outings to challenging sorties lasting several weeks. We've also added quite a few new walks featuring spectacular scenery.

Spain's most significant geographical feature is the Pyrenees, the mountain chain that demarcates the frontier with France and was for a long time a physical and psychological barrier to the rest of Europe. But now that Spain is a fully fledged member of

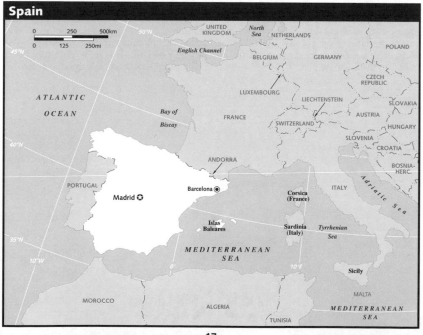

17

the EU (European Union) the border posts at the passes are no longer staffed.

A wonderfully varied and demanding resource for walkers, the Pyrenees range demands exploration by foot, from the green, misty mountains of the Basque Country to the challenge of the Catalan mountains, into which the tiny, independent state of Andorra protrudes. We describe a three- to four-week traverse from Andorra to the heart of the Aragonese Pyrenees.

The Picos de Europa, west of the Pyrenean isthmus, are as gentle or as challenging as you care to make them. Within the Sierra Nevada, Europe's most southerly ski area in winter and a destination for release from the heat of the Andalucian plains in summer, rises Mulhacén, at 3479m the highest point in peninsular Spain. In the same region, the Sierra de Alpujarras and Sierra de Cazorla are both excellent bases for walking holidays.

But great walks don't necessarily demand mountains. Galicia, with its own Atlantic mix of mist and greenness, recalls the west coast of Ireland and other Celtic fringes, even down to the bagpipes. And in eastern Andalucía on the Mediterranean shore, there's a fine three-day coastal trail leading to the Cabo de Gata.

Spain is crisscrossed by threads of ancient pilgrim ways, of which the best known is the Camino de Santiago (Way of St James). Its most famous variant, the Camino Francés, crosses the French border at the pass of Roncesvalles and finishes at the cathedral in Santiago de Compostela. Nowadays it's travelled year-round as much by lay folk walking their history as by bona fide pilgrims.

The enjoyment continues once you've pulled your boots off. As you'd expect from Western Europe's second-largest country, the sheer variety of Spain's scenery, vegetation and terrain is mirrored in the diversity of its people, food, customs, domestic architecture and wines.

This book gives plenty of accommodation options for all budgets, as well as tips on the gear and equipment you need and advice on navigation and safety.

Even tiny villages in Spain can offer clean, simple, reasonably priced rooms. In popular mountain areas such as the Pyrenees, Picos de Europa and Sierra Nevada, there's a network of *refugios* (mountain huts or refuges) and the climate makes summer camping with a lightweight tent a pleasure – but make it a strong one: mountain storms, when they rage, can be powerful. But they're usually brief and the sun will soon peek through again.

Facts about Spain

HISTORY

As a Mediterranean nation, Spain's early history was marked by incursions: Celts and Iberians followed by Phoenicians, Carthaginians and Greeks, each of whom established coastal settlements. Then came other, longer-term settlers: the Romans, Visigoths and Muslims. To Spain's short Atlantic coast, ships later brought unheard-of treasure from Spain's colonies in the Americas.

For centuries the Pyrenees were a barrier, isolating the Iberian peninsula from the mainstream of European thought and social development. In the last century, the Spanish Civil War was a bloody rehearsal for WWII and the fight against fascism. Contemporary Spain, by contrast, is among the vanguard of European Union (EU) countries pressing for closer integration.

20,000-8000 BC – Magdalenian hunting culture prevails in northern Spain.

1500 BC – The Iberians begin to arrive, probably from North Africa.

1200-600 BC – The Phoenicians, sailing from present-day Lebanon, establish coastal settlements.

1000-500 BC – Celts, originally from Central Europe, settle, bringing iron technology and merging with the Iberians in the central *meseta* (high tableland).

600 BC – The Greeks begin trading and establishing coastal colonies.

230 BC – The Carthaginians, from Carthage near contemporary Tunis, establish Barcelona, and Carthago Nova, today's Cartagena.

218 BC – Rome defeats Carthage and begins a 600-year occupation of the Iberian peninsula. (today's Spain and Portugal), renaming the Spanish part Hispania.

3rd century AD – Christianity spreads throughout Hispania.

5th century – The Visigoths, a Germanic tribe, overrun most of the Iberian peninsula.

711 – The Muslims invade from North Africa and remain the dominant force in the peninsula for nearly 600 years.

722 – Christian forces are victorious at Covadonga, in contemporary Asturias – the first battle in the long Reconquista (Reconquest) of the peninsula.

10th century – 'Al-Andalus' (Andalucía) reaches its cultural and political zenith under the independent Caliphate of Córdoba.

1031 – The unified caliphate fragments into as many as 20 *taifas*, or small emirates.

1137 – In the north, Aragón and Catalunxya (Cataluña in Spanish) unite to form the powerful new Kingdom of Aragón.

1230s – Jaume I of Aragón recaptures the Balearic Islands, then Valencia.

1236 – Córdoba falls to Fernando III of Castilla.

1248 – Fernando III recovers Seville.

1469 – The marriage of Isobel I of Castilla and Fernando II of Aragón unites their kingdoms.

1492 – The fall of Granada, the last Muslim stronghold. Fernando and Isobel order the expulsion of all Jews who refuse baptism. They fund Cristóbal Colón (Christopher Columbus), who 'discovers' the New World (the Americas).

1502 – Muslims are ordered to convert to Christianity or leave. Those who convert and stay are known as Moriscos.

1519 – Carlos I of Spain, when only 19, inherits the Hapsburg territories in Austria and is elected Holy Roman Emperor (thus becoming Carlos V in that line).

1521–31 – In the New World, Hernán Cortés conquers the Aztec empire in contemporary Mexico while Francisco Pizarro overthrows the Inca empire in present-day Peru.

1556 – Carlos abdicates in favour of his son, Felipe II.

1588 – Felipe II's Armada Invencible (Invincible Armada) is destroyed by storm and the English fleet.

1609 – The Moriscos are expelled.

1618–48 – The Thirty Years' War signals the end of Spain's role as a European power.

1805 – The British defeat of a combined Spanish-French fleet at Trafalgar ends Spanish sea power and heralds the loss of its American colonies.

1808–14 – The French Emperor Napoleon nominates his brother Joseph as King José I of Spain, sparking the Spanish War of Independence (Peninsular War).

1813 – Chile, Colombia, Paraguay and Uruguay, taking advantage of the war, declare their independence.

1833–39 – The first of three Carlist Wars is held, fighting over who should succeed to the throne.

1835 – The Desamortización decree suppresses religious orders and confiscates their property.

1873 – The First Republic lasts a mere 11 months.
late 19th century – Strong Basque and Catalan separatist movements emerge.
1898 – Defeated in the Spanish-American War, Spain loses Cuba, Puerto Rico and the Philippines, its last overseas colonies.
1923–29 – General Miguel Primo de Rivera rules as a relatively benign dictator, with the concurrence of the king, Alfonso XIII.
1931–36 – The Second Republic. Alfonso XIII abdicates. Universal suffrage is introduced.
1936 – The Popular Front, a left-wing coalition, wins the general election. Elements of the army mutiny, sparking the Spanish Civil War (1936–39). Nationalists are pitted against Republicans and an estimated 350,000 Spaniards die.
1939–40 – An estimated 100,000 people are executed by the victorious Nationalist forces or die in prison.
1939–75 – General Francisco Franco, the Nationalist commander, is dictator.
1953 – In return for the right to establish military bases in Spain the USA grants the country massive aid. Economic recovery begins, aided by remittances from emigre Spanish workers and the advent of mass tourism.
1975 – King Juan Carlos I, Franco's nominated successor, takes the throne.
1977 – A new constitution declares Spain a parliamentary monarchy with no official religion.
1982–96 – Spain is governed by the Partido Socialista Obrera Español (PSOE), a centre-left party headed by Felipe González.
1983 – The country is divided into 17 Comunidades Autónomas or Autonomous Regions, each with a high degree of local control. Even so, ETA (Euzkadi ta Azkatasuna), the Basque terrorist organisation continues its campaign of violence.
1986 – Spain joins the EU.
1996 – The centre-right Partido Popular (PP), led by José María Aznar, assumes power, ushering in several years of economic prosperity.
2000 – The PP is re-elected, this time with an absolute majority; Spain, as a signatory to the Schengen Convention, abolishes checks at its frontiers with France and Portugal.

For a more detailed treatment of Spanish history, consult Lonely Planet's *Spain*.

History of Walking

Until relatively recently, walking in Spain was primarily a utilitarian activity – to get from A to B. The Pyrenees, for example, today regarded as a magnificent resource for walkers, were for centuries the preserve of shepherds and hunters; they were seen as an

---

The Colourful Count

The most eccentric of early walking pioneers was the half-French, half-Irish Count Henry Patrick Marie Russell-Killough, who bagged 16 first ascents of Pyrenean peaks. Among his many idiosyncrasies, he rented a sizeable hunk of the Vignemale massif in the Aragonese Pyrenees for the princely sum of one French franc a year and proceeded to haul himself to its summit 33 times, the last ascent in his 70th year.

When rather more spry, the count marked one successful climb by having an impromptu grave dug on the summit in which he asked his guides to bury him up to the neck. He excavated a number of caves in the mountain's lower slopes and lived in one for long periods between mountain walks. He was famous, too, for hosting dinner parties on the fringes of a glacier. Elegant Persian carpets were spread out and laden with fine food and wine carried up from the valley by a retinue of servants.

❀ ❀ ❀ ❀ ❀ ❀ ❀ ❀ ❀ ❀ ❀ ❀ ❀

---

obstacle – a natural frontier separating Spain from the rest of Europe. The few passes leading into France were trodden mainly by merchants and smugglers, people walking to reach a goal, not walking for its own sake.

The Camino de Santiago (Way of St James) pilgrim route was always the exception. Walking the Way was considered to confer just as much merit as arriving at the goal. Every year, between 500,000 and two million pilgrims would make the journey on foot from all corners of Europe to Santiago de Compostela in Galicia. Its cathedral, believers say, houses the tomb of Santiago (St James) the apostle, and a pilgrimage to Santiago ranked in its time with one to Rome or Jerusalem. Nowadays, it's not only the faithful who make the journey. Many undertake the route for its own sake, staying at the ancient *hospitales* (wayside guesthouses) which mark the Way – or more accurately Ways (see the Camino de Santiago chapter, p328).

Walking simply for pleasure was the preserve of the leisured and wealthy. However, many first-recorded ascents of the highest peaks were by surveyors or natural scientists, for whom the walk was merely the means to a greater end. It was, for example, the French botanist and geologist Louis-François Ramond de Carbonnières who, at the end of the 18th century, made the first known attempt to conquer the Glaciar de Maladeta in the Aragonese Pyrenees. A Russian officer, Platon de Tchihatcheff, was the first to scale the nearby Pico de Aneto in 1842. Similarly, it was as late as 1904 that the Spanish aristocrat El Marqués de Villaviciosa, Don Pedro Pidal, became the first to conquer El Naranjo de Bulnes in the Picos de Europa – guided by local shepherd Gregorio Pérez, who must have wondered what all the fuss was about.

Charles Packe was both a gentleman and a scholar. A member of the English landed gentry, his meticulously researched *Guide to the Pyrenees*, first published in 1862, was the standard text for many years.

Nowadays, most major towns have an association of walking and climbing aficionados. The first walking group to be established in Spain was the Centre Excursionista de Catalunya (CEC), founded in Barcelona in 1876 and still going strong.

GEOGRAPHY

Spain and Portugal share the roughly square-shaped Iberian Peninsula. Separated from France by the Pyrenees mountains and from Africa by less than 25km of sea across the Strait of Gibraltar, it's the continent's second highest country after Switzerland, with more than a third of its area above 800m. Spread over 505,000 sq km, it's also Western Europe's second-largest country after France.

Spain is probably Europe's most geographically diverse country, with coastline on two seas and land ranging from the near-deserts of eastern Andalucía in the south to the deep coastal inlets of Galicia in the northwest; from the sunbaked uplands of Castilla-La Mancha in the centre to the rugged, snowcapped Pyrenees.

The bombardment of names in this section may be a bit overwhelming unless you're familiar with Spain. If so, flick to the colour country map at the front of the book, where you'll find the main features illustrated.

Meseta

At the centre of the peninsula spreads the *meseta*, a bleak tableland 400 to 1000m above sea level. Occupying some 40% of the country, it embraces most of Castilla y León, Castilla-La Mancha and Extremadura.

Apart from a handful of towns (including the capital city, Madrid), it's sparsely populated, with numbers still declining as the agricultural population of this harsh terrain continues to migrate to more hospitable areas. Grain is the most popular crop, though there are also vineyards producing the strong reds of La Mancha plateau, while huge olive groves stretch across the south; Extremadura, in the west, boasts extensive pastures.

A land of boundless but unvarying horizons, boiling summers and harsh winters, it's not the stuff of great walking. However, there are some enticing mountain chains running through and around the *meseta*.

Mountains

The Sierra de Gredos, to the west of Madrid, and the Sierra de Guadarrama, to its north, both rise above 2400m. Cleaving through the *meseta*, they form part of the Sistema Central mountain range, which runs from northeast of Madrid to the Portuguese border.

Mountain chains enclose the *meseta* on all sides except the west, where the terrain slopes more gently towards and then across Portugal.

At the northern limit of the *meseta*, Cordillera Cantábrica runs from near the Atlantic Ocean almost to the Basque Country, isolating central Spain from the Bay of Biscay (Mar Cantábrico). It rises above 2500m in the spectacular Picos de Europa, one of Spain's most popular walking areas. In the northwest, the more modest Montes de León and their offshoots cut off Galicia from the *meseta*.

The Sistema Ibérico runs from La Rioja in the west to southern Aragón, varying from plateaus and high moorland to deep gorges and eroded rock formations as in the Serranía de Cuenca. The southern boundary of the *meseta* is marked by the wooded Sierra Morena, which runs across northern Andalucía.

Spain's highest mountains lie at or near its edges. The Pyrenees mark 400km of border with France, from the Mediterranean to the

Bay of Biscay, with stubby fingers reaching southwards into Navarra, Catalunya and Aragón and foothills extending west into the Basque Country. Aragón and Catalunya boast numerous 3000m peaks, the highest being Aragón's Pico de Aneto (3404m).

Across southern and eastern Andalucía stretches the Cordillera Bética, a rumpled mass of ranges that includes mainland Spain's highest peak, Mulhacén (3479m), in the Sierra Nevada, and an unusual spur radiating north, the Sierra de Cazorla. This same system continues east into Murcia and southern Valencia, dips under the Mediterranean, then re-emerges as the Balearic islands of Ibiza and Mallorca. On Mallorca it rises to over 1400m in the Serra de Tramuntana.

Lowlands

Five lower-lying areas spread around and between the mountains of Spain.

Fertile Catalunya, in the northeast, is mainly ranges of lower hills. The Ebro basin, between the Sistema Ibérico to its south and the Cordillera Cantábrica and Pyrenees to its north, supports wine production in La Rioja, grain crops in Navarra and vegetables in eastern Aragón. Other less watered parts of Aragón, by contrast, are near-desert.

The soil of Galicia in the northwest is poor and farming difficult. The green, hilly terrain, from which people sailed in their thousands to seek a new life in the Americas, resembles other Celtic lands of emigration such as Ireland or Brittany. There's some great walking to be had along its deeply incised coastal inlets.

The coastal areas of Valencia and Murcia in the east are dry plains transformed by irrigation into green *huertas* (market gardens and orchards). Similar areas farther south, around Almería in eastern Andalucía, where there's much less inland water to be tapped, are virtually desert and have provided the location for many a 'spaghetti Western'.

The Río Guadalquivir basin, stretching across Andalucía between the Sierra Morena and Cordillera Bética, is another fertile zone, producing, in particular, grain, olives and citrus fruit. Its delta, like that of the Río Ebro, is one of Europe's great bird sanctuaries.

Rivers

Spain has five major rivers: the Ebro, Duero (Douro), Tajo (Tejo), Guadiana and Guadalquivir, each draining a different basin between the mountains. They and their tributaries provide much of Spain's water and hydropower.

The Ebro, the largest in volume, is the only one flowing eastwards, entering the Mediterranean in southern Catalunya. In its delta, rice paddies flourish and provide a resting place for migratory birds flying the north–south corridor between Europe and Africa.

The other four empty into the Atlantic. The Duero drains the northern half of the *meseta*, then continues across Portugal as the Douro. The Tajo and Guadiana drain the southern *meseta*. The Tajo continues west across Portugal to Lisbon as the Tejo, while the Guadiana turns south into the Golfo de Cádiz. The Guadalquivir meanders across the middle of Andalucía.

GEOLOGY

The Iberian Peninsula was an early transatlantic traveller before finally settling down in its present position, separated from the main European landmass by the Pyrenees in the north and from Africa by the Strait of Gibraltar to the south.

On the grand timescale, it's like a plate that spun between the continental tables of Europe, Africa and America. In Palaeozoic times, the bedrock crashed into America, at about the level of present-day Newfoundland.

In Triassic times, when the Atlantic Ocean rose, the three prototype mountain chains became islands surrounded by accumulating sediment. The whole mass tore free from the American continent and drifted slowly eastwards again to graft itself onto Europe.

Erosion over the millenniums was intense; by the Jurassic period, the giant mountains were all but rubbed out and the landmass was once again a vast plain with little relief. By Cretaceous times, it had eased itself away from the European continent, rotating slowly on its axis and leaving behind a vast cavity – the Bay of Biscay.

In the Palaeocene era, as the Iberian plate smashed into the Europe and Africa

Signs of a Glacial Past

Several of Spain's finest walks, especially in the Pyrenees, are through landscapes substantially shaped by glaciers. As a glacier flows downhill its weight of ice and snow creates a distinctive collection of landforms, many of which are preserved once the ice has vanished or retreated (as it is doing in Spain's few remaining high-mountain glaciers).

The most obvious is the *U-shaped valley* (1), gouged out by the glacier as it moves downhill, often with one or more bowl-shaped *cirques* or *corries* (2) at its head. Cirques are found along high mountain ridges or at mountain passes or *cols* (3). Where an alpine glacier – which flows off the upper slopes and ridges of a mountain range – has joined a deeper, more substantial valley glacier, a dramatic *hanging valley* (4) is often the result. Hanging valleys and cirques commonly shelter hidden alpine lakes or *tarns* (5). The thin ridge, which separates adjacent glacial valleys, is known as an *arête* (6).

As a glacier grinds its way forward it usually leaves long, *lateral moraine* (7) ridges along its course – mounds of debris either deposited along the flanks of the glacier or left by sub-ice streams within its heart. At the end – or snout – of a glacier is the *terminal moraine* (8), the point where the giant conveyor belt of ice drops its load of rocks and grit. Both high up in the hanging valleys and in the surrounding valleys and plains, *moraine lakes* (9) may form behind a dam of glacial rubble.

The plains that surround a glaciated range may feature a confusing variety of moraine ridges, mounds and outwash fans – material left by rivers flowing from the glaciers. Perched here and there may be an *erratic* (10), a rock carried far from its origin by the moving ice and left stranded when the ice melted (for example, a granite boulder dumped in a limestone landscape).

View of area before glacier's retreat

KATE NOLAN

landmasses once again, large-scale folding took place. Today's major mountain chains reared up and the peninsula took on its approximate present shape.

There's still movement. Though it's unlikely to throw you off balance, the coastline of Galicia is dropping a few centimetres each year, while the Mediterranean shore is rising correspondingly.

The oldest rock is on the *meseta*. Occupying much of central Spain, this high plateau is composed mostly of igneous and metamorphic materials. The Pyrenees, also formed early, have, in addition to their east–west axial range, more recent chains flanking them to north and south, known as the Prepirineos, or the pre-Pyrenees.

In the west of Spain and much of Portugal, the most common rock is igneous, commonly granite, supplemented by metamorphic forms such as slate, schist and gneiss. In central and southern areas, limestone predominates, while inland from the Mediterranean coast and in the Ebro basin are mostly clays and marls.

In the Mediterranean, the Balearic islands were thrust up when the African plate burrowed under the more static European one.

CLIMATE

The *meseta* and Ebro basin have a continental climate: scorching in summer, cold in winter and dry. Madrid, for example, regularly freezes in winter but roasts in summer temperatures well above 30°C. Locals describe the weather as *nueve meses de invierno y tres de infierno* (nine months of winter and three of hell). The northern *meseta* and much of the Ebro basin are even drier, with only around 300mm of rain a year. Most of inland Andalucía bakes in high summer, with temperatures of 35°C and above. The compensation comes with its milder winters.

The western Pyrenees and the Cordillera Cantábrica block the moisture-laden airstreams from the Atlantic Ocean, bringing moderate temperatures and heavy rainfall (three or four times Madrid's) to the north and northwest coasts. Even in high summer you can be drenched.

The Mediterranean coast and Balearic Islands get little more rain than Madrid, while

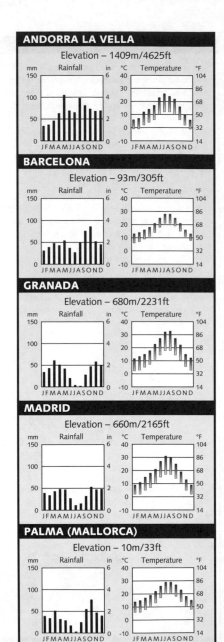

What Storm?

To calculate how far you are from the eye of a storm in metres, multiply by 340 (sound travels at 340m per second) the number of seconds between a flash of lightning and the thunderclap that follows.

✦✦✦✦✦✦✦✦✦✦✦✦✦

the semi-desert regions of Murcia and Amería on the southern Mediterranean shores can be even hotter than the capital in summer. By contrast, the whole coast enjoys mild winters.

In general, you can rely on pleasant or hot temperatures just about everywhere from April to early November (plus March in the south, but minus a month at either end on the north and northwest coasts). Andalucía has plenty of warm, sunny days right through winter. In July and August, temperatures can be unpleasant – even unbearable – anywhere inland unless you're up high. At this time Spaniards abandon their cities in droves for the coast and mountains.

In Galicia, be prepared for drizzle and mist at any time. Other northwest regions – Asturias, Cantabria and the provinces of the Basque Country – are similarly damp and lush, their climate determined by supersaturated clouds borne in from the Atlantic Ocean by the dominant winds. In the Pyrenees too, where summer storms can be spectacular, rain, often intense but usually shortlived, can fall at any time.

Snowfalls in Spain's high mountains can start as early as September and some snow lasts year-round on the highest peaks. Even key passes for walkers, such as the Coll de Mulleres in the Pyrenees or the road over the Sierra Nevada in Andalucía, may have a residue of snow well into July.

ECOLOGY & ENVIRONMENT

Humans have been shaping Spain's environment ever since hunter-gatherers scattered their first seeds and assumed a more sedentary life as cultivators of the land. Large-scale environmental changes are far from a late-20th-century phenomenon. It was the Romans who first began to hack away at the

country's woodlands, which until then had covered as much as half of the *meseta*.

Over the ensuing 2000 years, further deforestation along with overcultivation of the land and overgrazing (notably by flocks of several thousand sheep) has brought about substantial topsoil erosion. Most of the 300 sq km delta of the Río Ebro, for example – today a vital staging post for migratory birds and a fertile area for rice paddies – has been formed by deposits of topsoil sluiced down from the *meseta* over the past 600 years. Environmental change isn't always negative and one area's loss can be another's gain.

Spain generally supports a varied, often low-tech and mostly healthy agriculture. By European standards, the country is sparsely populated and most of its people live in towns and cities, reducing their impact on the countryside. There's still lots of wilderness and plenty of unpolluted wild land to roam. However, Spain has particular environmental problems, some imposed by nature and others the result of human negligence.

Spain shares the problem of unpredictable and often deficient rainfall with its southern Mediterranean neighbours. Drought is perhaps its most serious environmental problem. Last striking seriously in the early 1990s, it brought seasonal water rationing to 10 million people. To combat this, reservoirs cover a higher proportion of Spain than any other country in the world.

Water means money and is a hot political issue. In 2000 the government attempted to develop a cohesive, pan-Spain, long-term water policy. The key element of its Plan Hidrologico Nacional (National Water Plan) was to double the amount of water diverted from the Río Ebro, which flows across the north of the country, to serve agriculture in Mediterranean coastal regions. That would mean one billion cubic metres a year would be diverted and inhabitants of the Ebro region poured on to the streets in protest at the prospect of their water being channelled away. Environmentalists had objections too. The plan is still bogged down in controversy.

Another particular consequence for walkers is that in areas of high rainfall, which are confined mostly to the north coast and the

Pyrenees, just about every upland lake has been dammed, as a source of water and for electricity. Purists get uptight about the artificially induced changes in water levels and the impact upon the high mountain environment, but they reduce Spain's dependency on nuclear or fossil fuels, and are small scale and relatively unintrusive. Not so, however, the ugly tubes that channel the water from the heights and scar many a hillside.

The tunnels that have been bored through the Pyrenees are a more negative implant. Again, the motive is laudable: to reduce Spain's isolation and to increase trans-frontier contact with France. But there's a palpable difference between valleys that have tunnel connection with France, such as the heavily commercialised Valle de Bielsa, and those that retain their original identity.

The opening of the new Somport Tunnel through the Pyrenees was delayed many times. The tunnel and EU-aided project have been pushed through despite tenacious opposition from ecologists. The fear is that the 9km tunnel and the widening of its approach roads, and consequent increase in traffic, will not only disfigure France's beautiful Vallée d'Aspe but also adversely affect the remaining half-dozen Pyrenean bears, who prowl thereabouts, as well as various species of eagle and other birds.

The soil of much of Spain is unyielding and impoverished. As everywhere, farmers supplement its deficiencies by adding fertilisers and increase its yield by using pesticides. This may be fine for the farmer, but problems are created downstream as the chemicals leech out. In the Albufera, a freshwater lake south of Valencia, fish and eels die every so often due to contamination upstream. The slow accumulation of toxic chemicals is not the only problem; in 1998 the fragile wetlands of the Parque Nacional de Doñana in Andalucía were assailed by an industrial spill of acids and heavy metals.

Intensive agriculture in the form of *invernaderos* (huge plastic greenhouses) is unsightly and tends to drive out indigenous plants. However, a more pressing problem is excessive irrigation, which can lead to a lowering of the water table.

All the above can be justified – and is, energetically – as a way of ensuring rural life continues. Less defensible, but just as ingrained in local culture, is hunting, an almost exclusively male preserve. The words *coto privado de caza* (private hunting area) daubed on rocks are a familiar sign and over 1.25 million shooting licences are issued annually. Birds are shot out of the sky, limed (caught in sticky bird-lime smeared on tree branches), netted and trapped, and older hunters especially resent limits on catches set for hunting and fishing seasons. Even though many species are now protected, poaching or winking at the law is commonplace and strict enforcement in Spain's vast countryside is impossible.

Despite all the human odds stacked against them, in some areas species such as wild boar and red deer have recovered to the point where they are now legally culled. The Spanish ibex, a kind of mountain goat, was almost extinct by 1900 but protection since then has raised its numbers to around 10,000.

The private car remains one of Spain's principal polluters. There are ecological movements in major cities, but the car rules. Politicians bend to the voting power of the car lobby, and the arteries of most large towns are clogged with traffic.

However, in popular walking areas there are signs of change. For example, in summer, the peak visiting season, you can now only enter the Parque Nacional de Ordesa y Monte Perdido on foot or by bus. Similarly, private-vehicle access to the Parque Posets-Maladeta in Aragón, one of Spain's newest protected areas, is restricted to between 8pm and 8am.

More generally, controls and legislation are beginning to bite as environmental awareness increases. The PSOE government, in power from 1982 to 1996, made environmental pollution a crime and spurred on a range of actions by regional governments, which now have responsibility for most environmental matters. In 1981 Spain had just 35 environmentally protected areas, covering 2200 sq km. Today there are more than 400, embracing more than 25,000 sq km.

[Continued on page 33]

WATCHING WILDLIFE

Many of the walking areas we describe are a treasure-trove for botanists and birdwatchers (see Books, pp47–8, for some useful field guides). Spring, even in those regions that are brown and arid for most of the year, is spectacular with wildflowers. Spain is on one of the main corridors for birds migrating between Europe and Africa, so if you manage to time your visit to coincide with the twice-yearly fly-past, you'll spot plenty of birds of passage as well as several endemic species you'll never see elsewhere.

Walkers stand a very good chance of seeing **chamois** and **ibex**. However, many of the larger mammals, as elsewhere in Europe's wilder regions, have been shot, poisoned and starved to near-extinction. There are, nevertheless, **wild boar** and a very few **brown bears** clinging on precariously in the north. You'll be lucky, however, to hear even the distant howl of one of the estimated 2000 surviving **wolves**.

Flora

In mainland Spain and the Balearic Islands around 8000 of Europe's 9000 plant species grow. Of these, 2000 are unique to the Iberian Peninsula (plus, in some instances, North Africa). There's such diversity and abundance because the last Ice Age did not blanket the entire peninsula so plants that were frozen to death and extinction farther north managed to survive in Spain.

High- & Medium-Altitude Plants

Spain's many mountain areas claim much of the variety. The Pyrenees have about 150 unique species and even the much smaller Sierra Nevada in Andalucía has around 60. When the snows melt, the zones above the tree line bloom with small rock-clinging, ground-hugging plants.

Among the prettiest and most common of mountain plants is the **gentian**. The trumpet gentian is a deeper blue than the smaller, star-shaped spring gentian. Look out too for the great yellow gentian, its flowers arranged in bunches along the tall, single stem.

In spring, you'll come across whole fields of **poet's narcissus** (also called **pheasant's eye narcissus**). Like the gentians, its flowers are disproportionately large compared to the foliage in order to entice pollinating insects, which are much rarer at higher altitudes.

While many **orchids** flourish in damper, shadier woodlands, the alpine meadows of the Picos de Europa are a particularly rich area for these exotic flowers, boasting as many as 40 different species.

Purple gentian

The white (which can just as often be mauve) **crocus** is one of the first flowers to push through the matted grass, still damp from snowmelt. In the brief high-mountain summer and well into autumn, the leafless crocus offers patches of pink or white colour.

Rhododendron and **azalea** are colourful, low-level shrubs growing at most to knee height.

Mountain Forests

On the cooler mountains of northern Spain, three kinds of conifer are dominant. Branches of the **silver fir** (*abeto blanco*), so named because of the silvery colour of the underside of its needles, poke out almost at right angles. Often mixing it with beeches, or in stands of its own, its needles are set along side branches in two or three dense bunches. The long, tight cylindrical cones with a blunt top are a good identifier. With its flaking red bark the **Scots pine** (*pino albar*) – more accurately called the *pi roig*, or red pine, in Catalan – has needles in pairs and an egg-shaped cone that tapers to a point. Toughest of all, more of a loner and surviving as high as 2300m, where other varieties can't hold root, the **mountain** or **black pine** (*pino negro*) is recognisable by its grey-black bark. Sparse on the windward side and more abundant to the lee, it's usually quite stunted in height because of the difficult conditions it endures. In more favourable conditions, however, it can grow taller than 30m.

Lowland Forests

Mixed evergreen and deciduous forests sprinkle the lowlands and *meseta* (high tableland of central Spain). Many contain two useful evergreen oaks. With a particularly hard wood at its core, the thick, lightweight bark of the **cork oak** (*alcornoque*) is stripped every nine years for cork. The **holm** or **ilex oak** (*encina*) is harvested for making charcoal. It also grows acorns, which are gobbled up by pigs whose fate is to become *jamon ibérico*, a particularly fine ham that's gobbled up in turn by humans. Although of the oak family, its shiny, evergreen leaves often have small, holly-like spines.

Where the tree cover is scattered, the mix of woodland and pasture is known as *dehesa*. Occurring mostly in the southwestern *meseta* and parts of Galicia and Andalucía, *dehesas* are bright with wildflowers in early summer.

The solitary **umbrella pine** (*pino piñonero*) has a large spreading top and edible nuts, prized in cooking; it grows near the coast.

Pyrenean oak and some of Europe's finest and most extensive forests of **beech** (*haya*) cover the lower slopes of the damp mountains in northern Spain.

The Last of the Pyrenean Goats

The Pyrenean goat (*bucardo*), has been hunted and harried into extinction. Once flourishing throughout the Pyrenees and Cordillera Cantábrica, its long history is confirmed in Palaeolithic cave paintings. Its last retreat was the Parque Nacional de Ordesa y Monte Perdido, where a tiny herd endured. But on 6 January 2001, a tree fell on the last surviving *bucardo*. Attempts at cloning failed and the world is now another species the poorer.

Scrub & Steppe

Where there's no woodland or agriculture, the vegetation is often scrub, called *matorral* or *montebajo*, or steppe.

Scrub is quick to colonise where trees fail to take, have been logged long ago or have been wiped out by more recent forest fire. Herbs such as **lavender** *(lavanda)*, **rosemary** *(romero)*, **sage** *(salvia)* and **thyme** *(tomillo)* scent the air. In the south of the country and on Mallorca, shrubs of the prickly **rockrose** family abound. In the north and inland from the Mediterranean, **gorse** *(aliaga)*, low **juniper** bushes *(enebro)*, varieties of **heather** *(brezo)* and the **strawberry tree** *(madroño)* predominate. If the soil is acid there may also be **broom** *(retama)*. **Asphodels, orchids, gladioli,** and **irises** may flower beneath these shrubs, which themselves can be quite colourful in spring.

Steppe is the result of overgrazing or occurs naturally where the climate is hot and very dry. Much of the Ebro valley and Castilla-La Mancha are steppe, as is the almost desert-like Cabo de Gata in Andalucía. These areas too blossom with colour after rain.

Fauna
Mammals

Spain's wild terrain has allowed the survival of several species that have died out in many other countries – though the numbers of some are now perilously small. Many of Spain's wild mammals are nocturnal and you need to be both dedicated and lucky to track them down.

In 1900 Spain had about 2000 **brown bears** *(oso pardo)*. Today, it's estimated that only 60 to 80 survive in the Picos de Europa and farther west in the Cordillera Cantábrica, and a handful, if that, remain in the Pyrenees. Though hunting or killing bears has been banned for over 30 years, numbers have failed to increase since the mid-1980s despite conservation programs costing well over €1 million. Bear experts complain that local administrations give low priority to bear conservation – a contentious issue that arouses fierce opposition from many shepherds and landowners. The Pyrenean population is effectively extinct (although the French are attempting to boost numbers by importing bears from Slovenia) while the Cantabrian bears are seriously threatened. Hunting, poisoning (accidental and deliberate) and loss of habitat are the main reasons for the perhaps terminal decline in Spain of these shy creatures.

Equally threatened, primarily by hunting, **wolves** *(lobos)* are, by contrast, on the increase. From a population of about 500 in 1970, there are now over 1000 wolves in Spain. Their heartland is the mountains of Galicia and northwestern Castilla y León, but

Brown bear

in recent years small groups have travelled huge distances to settle within 100km of Madrid. There are also a few farther south, in Andalucía's Sierra Morena. Though heavily protected, they're still regarded as an enemy by many country people, and in some parts of the country wolf-hunting licences are still issued. Farmers complain that they have to wait far too long for compensation when wolves kill livestock.

Things look altogether better for the **Spanish ibex** (cabra montés). The males of this stocky, high-mountain goat species sport distinctive, long horns. The ibex spends summer hopping agilely around high crags and descends to pastures in winter. Almost hunted to extinction by 1900, the ibex was protected by royal decree a few years later (though it's still subject to controlled hunting today). There may now be around 20,000 in the country, the main populations being in the Sierra de Gredos (see the boxed text 'The Gredos Ibex', p68) and Andalucía's Sierra de Cazorla. Sadly, its Pyrenean cousin (see the boxed text 'The Last of the Pyrenean Goats', p29) is no more.

Unique to the Iberian Peninsula and smaller than the lynx of northern Europe, the **Iberian** or **pardel lynx** (lince ibérico) is the world's most endangered feline. Its numbers have been reduced to probably about 400 in Spain and under 50 in Portugal because of hunting and a decline in the number of rabbits, its staple food. Now stringently protected, it lives in wild southern and western woodlands, primarily in Andalucía.

You'll probably see traces of devastation from the indiscriminate snuffling of **wild boar** (jabalí), though you'll be lucky to spot one since they're mainly nocturnal. They're not at all uncommon, and favour thick woods and marshes – especially those within striking distance of farmers' root crops.

Red (ciervo), **roe** (corzo) and **fallow** (gamo) **deer** graze in forests and all types of woodland.

Chamois (rebeco), by contrast, live up high near the tree line of the Pyrenees and Cordillera Cantábrica, descending to pastures in winter. Since they live in such wide-open country, you stand a very good chance of spotting a family browsing. They resemble a smaller, shorter-horned version of the ibex but are actually a member of the antelope family.

With only a little more luck, you may spot a **red squirrel** (ardilla), bounding through the mountain forests or scattering its discarded nut shells on you from above.

Birds of Prey

Around 25 species of birds of prey, some of them summer visitors from Africa, breed in Spain. You'll often see them circling or hovering above the mountains or *meseta*.

Although still officially threatened, the **lammergeier** or **bearded vulture** is slowly recovering in the high Pyre-

Marmots

The reintroduction of the marmot (marmota) is an example of positive human intervention. Having become extinct in the Pyrenees, marmots were successfully brought from the Alps, where they thrive, in the 1950s.

The first re-colonisers were let loose on the French side of the Pyrenees. But, being no respecters of man-made frontiers, they soon established themselves on Spanish slopes around boulder fields and rocky areas, where they live in family groups. Hibernators, their body temperature can drop to 10°C and their heartbeat to as low as five pulses per minute. Adults can weigh up to 8kg – a hearty dinner for the golden eagle, their public enemy number one.

Look out for – or rather listen out for their distinctive whistle since the lookout they always post will probably spot you first.

KATE NOLAN

Lammergeier

nees, where there are about 55 breeding pairs, and is being reintroduced in its other Spanish habitat, the Sierra de Cazorla. Poisoned food and furtive hunting have been the bird's main threats. Its Spanish name, *quebrantahuesos* (bone smasher) reflects its habit of dropping bones from on high onto rocks so it can pick at the marrow. You can recognise it by the long bristles on its chin and its majestic 2m-plus wingspan.

The **black vulture** *(buitre negro)*, a veritable winged monster, is Europe's largest bird of prey and Spain's few hundred pairs are probably the world's biggest population. Its strongholds are Mallorca and parts of Extremadura, western Andalucía and Castilla-La Mancha.

Another emblematic bird, the **Spanish imperial eagle** *(águila imperial)* remains one of Europe's rarest birds of prey, having been almost killed off by hunting and a decline in the rabbit population. Its white shoulders distinguish it from other imperial eagles. Around 100 pairs remain in southwest Spain, the Pyrenees and Cantabria. Poisoned bait put out by farmers and illicit hunters is its greatest threat.

There are also other notable large birds of prey, which you're much more likely to spot if you're walking in high mountain regions. The **golden eagle** *(águila real)*, with its square tail and splayed, upwardly turned wingtips, can soar for hours. The **griffon vulture** *(buitre leonado)* roosts on crags and cliff edges, and is the only member of the vulture family of any size that's relatively light in colour. Other significant features are its dark tail and wing tips. The **Egyptian vulture** *(alimoche)*, unlike the golden eagle and griffon vulture, which live year-round in Spain, is a smaller, summer visitor. Black and white with a wedge-shaped tail and bare yellowish skin on its head and throat, it's relatively easy to identify.

Smaller birds of prey include the **kestrel** *(cernícalo)* and **buzzard** *(ratonero* – literally 'mouse catcher'), both of which are fairly common, the **sparrowhawk** *(gavilán)*, various **harriers** *(aguiluchos)*, and the acrobatic **red kite** *(milano real)* and **black kite** *(milano negro)*. You'll find many of them around deciduous or lowland woods and forests. Black kites are fairly common too over open ground near marshes and scavenging around rubbish dumps.

Water Birds

Spain is a haven for numerous water birds, thanks to some large wetland areas. Most famous and important of these is the Guadalquivir delta in Andalucía, where hundreds of thousands of birds winter, and many more call by during spring and autumn migrations. Other important coastal wetlands include the Albufera in Valencia and the Ebro delta in Catalunya.

Inland, thousands of **ducks** *(pato)* spend the winter in Castil-la-La Mancha and at Laguna de Gallocanta, in Aragón. The Laguna is Spain's biggest natural lake (though it can virtually dry up in summer) and supports a sizeable **crane** *(grulla)* popula-tion. Laguna de Fuente in Andalucía is Europe's main breeding site for the **greater flamingo** *(flamenco)*, with as many as 16,000 pairs rearing chicks in spring and summer. You can see this beautiful pink bird in many other saline wetlands along the Mediterranean and southern Atlantic coasts.

Other Birds

There are two other large, uncommon birds, both famous for their elaborate male courtship displays. The **great bustard** *(avutarda)* lives mainly on the *meseta*, with small pockets in the Basque Pyrenees and Andalucía. An estimated 14,000 survive, severely under pressure from the modernisation of agriculture and illicit hunting. A mature male of what has been called the 'European ostrich' – and what is indisputably Europe's largest bird – can be over a metre tall and weigh in at more than 18kg. The male in flight has been compared to a goose with eagle's wings. The **capercaillie** *(urogallo)* is a giant, black grouse. This shy bird, of which Spain still shelters around 1500, lives in northern mountain woodlands, mainly in the Cordillera Can-tábrica and Catalan Pyrenees. The male doesn't just dance; he sings and trills like Julio Iglesias on Ecstasy.

If you travel in central western Spain, you're certain to see storks. The **white stork** *(cigüeña blanca)* – in fact, black and white, with a red bill and legs – winters in Africa and, like so many tourists, chooses the best time of year to visit. It nests from spring to autumn on chimneys, towers, electricity pylons, anything nice and high, even right in the middle of towns. The **black stork** *(cigüeña negra)*, much rarer, also migratory and all black, has been reduced to around 200 pairs in Spain because of pollution of its watering and feeding places. Furtive – with good reason – its stronghold is the western part of the southern *meseta*, where it tends to build its nest on cliff edges.

Among the most colourful of Spain's birds are the **golden oriole** *(oropéndola)*, which spends the summers in orchards and deciduous woodlands (the male has an unmistakable bright yellow body); the orange, black and white **hoopoe** *(abubilla)*, with its distinctive crest and long bill, is common in open woodlands, on farmland and golf courses; and the flam-boyant gold, brown and turquoise **bee-eater** *(abejaruco)*, which nests in sandy banks in summer. All are more common in the south. Various **woodpeckers** *(pitos* or *picos)* and **owls** *(búhos)* inhabit mountain woodlands.

Pine Processionary Caterpillar

Even the birds turn up their bills at the pine processionary moth, whose hairy caterpillars devour pine needles, threatening whole forests. Between October and March you can see their large silvery nests on the sunnier side of trees.

Come spring, they're on the march in single file, as fat as your little finger and 5cm long. Along the branch, down the trunk, into the roots: they bury themselves underground and enter the chrysalis stage. In July, the cycle begins again as the female moths fight their way loose and lay their eggs in another tree victim. Bristling with irritating hairs, the cater-pillars can provoke a nasty al-lergic reaction if you touch them. Applying vinegar is said to provide relief.

Green woodpecker

[Continued from page 26]

NATIONAL PARKS & RESERVES

Spain's most ecologically important and spectacular walking areas – about 40,000 sq km if you include national hunting reserves – are almost all under some kind of official protection, with varying degrees of conservation and access. A *parque natural* (nature park), for instance, the most frequent category of protected area, may include villages, hotels and camping grounds. In others, access may be limited to a few walking trails, while a few reserves allow no public access. Controlled hunting is often still permitted – indeed in some parks, such as the Parque Nacional de Cazorla, a combination of restocking and vigilance has actually led to an increase in the variety and quantity of larger species of wildlife. The most popular parks often have a visitors centre. Even though information is usually provided only in Spanish, illustrative panels and video transcend language, and you can frequently pick up useful suggestions for walking routes. See also Information Sources within the individual walks chapters.

National Parks

A *parque nacional* (national park) is an area of exceptional importance for its plants, animals, geomorphology or landscape.

Spain currently has 13 *parques nacionales*, seven on the mainland and six offshore. Collectively they occupy over 3000 sq km, representing around 0.6% of the total landmass. Embracing some of Spain's most spectacular areas for walking, they enjoy the greatest degree of environmental protection – no mining, logging or other exploitation of natural resources, no hunting and a very strict control over construction.

The general pattern is for each to be governed by a committee with representation from both the central Ministerio del Ambiente (Ministry of the Environment) and, in an increasingly decentralised Spain, the appropriate regional government.

The 1916 Ley General de Parques Nacionales (General Law for National Parks) stimulated a modest beginning. First to be designated was the small Parque Nacional de la Montaña de Covadonga, nowadays incorporated into the much larger Parque Nacional de los Picos de Europa (see p201), then the kernel 20 sq km of the Valle de Ordesa was approved for national-park status. It too has been expanded over the years, these days forming part of the Parque Nacional de Ordesa y Monte Perdido, which embraces more than 150 sq km of rugged terrain.

Nearly 40 years passed before another outstanding natural area was accorded similar status. In 1954, the spectacularly barren volcanic area around Teide, at 3718m Spain's highest peak, was established on Tenerife in the Canary Islands. A year later the Parc Nacional d'Aigüestortes i Estany de Sant Maurici was created in the Catalan Pyrenees.

In 1975 the Ley de Espacios Naturales (Natural Areas Law) tightened the rules and regulations for national parks: they now conform to internationally agreed norms for areas meriting such a title.

Three years later came the long-overdue upgrading of Doñana, one of Europe's most important wetlands and a haven for birds, both breeding and migratory.

Spain's largest national park, that of the Sierra Nevada has received maximum protection since 2000. Newest of all is the Parque Nacional Marítimo Terrestre de las Islas Atlánticas de Galicia, a small archipelago off the coast of northwest Spain, declared in 2002. You'll find a couple of enticing walks on its main islets, the Illas Cíes (see p227).

Other Protected Areas

These are administered by Spain's 17 regional governments. There are literally hundreds of such areas, falling into at least 16 classifications with a bewildering variety of terminology: *reservas naturales*, *parques ecológicos*, *áreas naturales*, *zonas protegidas*, just plain *parques* – and just about every other permutation of these names. They range in size from 100-sq-m rocks off the Balearic Islands to the mountainous 2140-sq-km Parque Natural de Cazorla (see p290). The Áreas Naturales de la Serra de

Tramuntana protect the spectacular mountain range in the north of Mallorca.

Reservas Nacionales de Caza

Some 15,000 sq km of wilderness areas around the country are *reservas nacionales de caza* (national hunting reserves), sometimes called *cotos nacionales de caza*. These are usually well conserved for the sake of the wildlife that is to be hunted. Public access is usually unrestricted (some hunting reserves even include villages or towns) and you may well walk across one without even knowing it. In the hunting season (notices or gunfire will alert you to when that may be), brightly coloured clothing can reduce the risk of your being mistaken for a hapless chamois.

POPULATION & PEOPLE

One of Spain's greatest riches is the regional, linguistic and cultural diversity of its 40 million people. Though most take pride in being Spanish when the national football team is on a winning streak or when the Olympic Games come around, in other contexts regional loyalties often take precedence. It's quite possible, for example, for a Valenciano to refer to someone from the *meseta* as an *extranjero* – literally a 'foreigner', but in this context more accurately translated as 'stranger' or 'outsider'.

Spain is one of Europe's least densely populated countries, with only about 80 people per square kilometre. The spaces beckoning to walkers are, in fact, even wider and more open than this round figure suggests. More than half of Span's population lives in cities and most of the rest are in towns of 10,000 or more inhabitants. In this century, the least fruitful soils of Andalucía, the *meseta* and Galicia have been abandoned in favour of the industrialised regions of Catalunya, the Basque Country (País Vasco, known as Euskadi or Euskal Herri to the Basque people) and other areas with greater opportunity for employment.

To maximise the cultivable land, people in rural areas have for centuries concentrated in *pueblos* (villages), from where farmers travel out to their fields in the morning and back at night. (The Basque Country is the exception; only here are you likely to see the land dotted with single farmsteads, as in much of the rest of rural Europe.) This, in a land of over 505,000 sq km, leaves an awful lot of space. Aragón, for example, has only around 20 people per square kilometre (if you exclude its capital, Zaragoza), and if you walk the Aragonese Pyrenees you'll wonder where even this small number got to.

Regional Differences

The peoples with the strongest sense of local identity, reinforced by the fact that each has its own language, are the Catalans, Basques and, to a lesser extent, Galicians. Each lives on the fringes of the country whose heartland, geographically speaking, is Castilla.

The Catalans are great walkers: their network of refuges and trails is the most developed in the nation and there's a considerable body of walking and mountaineering literature in Catalan. But even mountaineering isn't free from regional politics; when the first team from Catalunya to conquer Everest hauled themselves to the summit, they planted only the Catalan flag.

The Andalucians, or Andaluz, live in Andalucía, Spain's largest autonomous region and home to sherry, flamenco, gazpacho, flamboyant fiestas and intense summer heat.

The Basques claim to be the original inhabitants of the Iberian Peninsula and there's some evidence – from Basque place names in the Catalan Pyrenees and Andorra to the results of recent blood-group studies – to support this argument. Their unique language, known to be non-Indo-European and perhaps the oldest in Europe, is all but impenetrable to outsiders. Their rich cuisine alone is a powerful reason to visit the Basque Country.

Galicia, together with Andalucía in the south and Extremadura in the west, is one of Spain's poorest areas. Over the centuries many Galicians have emigrated to other regions of Spain, Europe or the New World. Living amid mists and greenness, and surrounded by what is an often forbidding sea, Galicians frequently identify with other Celtic peoples living on Europe's western fringes, such as the Bretons, Irish and Scots; you'll even hear the bagpipes, a popular local instrument.

A more recent movement of peoples is the southward push of northern Europeans, a high proportion of them retired and seeking sunshine. Concentrated in the main on the Costa del Sol and Costa Blanca are more than 200,000 permanent residents from other EU countries, particularly Britain, Germany, the Netherlands and Scandinavia, and an equivalent number of winter migrants.

SOCIETY & CONDUCT

There's little in local customs and behaviour that's likely to throw you. On the trail, you are likely to be greeted with a hearty *hola* at any time of day, *buenos días* up to 2pm and *buenas tardes* from then on. To these, you can bounce back the same reply. When entering a shop, bar or restaurant many people will give such a greeting, whether murmured discreetly or robustly sung out to all present. Similarly, when leaving, it's polite to throw out a generalised *adiós*. When in a restaurant many Spaniards will say *!Que aproveche!*, the equivalent of *bon appétit* (enjoy your meal).

Anglo-Saxons are often struck by the more economical use by the Spanish of *por favor* (please) and *gracias* (thank you), and it's true that they occur less in Spanish than in many English social interactions. However, this doesn't mean that Spaniards are less polite. They often convey a sense of courtesy through other means: by intonation, gesture or facial expression. In some contexts, it's just not deemed necessary. Why, they will argue, should you say 'thank you' to a shopkeeper for handing over goods at the end of a straight commercial transaction from which both parties have benefited?

For walking – and, indeed, throughout contemporary Spanish life – the dress code is as informal as you care to make it. Whenever the weather allows, shorts are the walking norm for both women and men. Some people may look askance at you if you visit a church with knees or shoulders bared, but they are a dwindling minority.

When staying in *refugios* (mountain huts or refuges) etiquette usually observes lights out and silence from 10pm or even earlier, and you're unlikely to be left sleeping much after 6.30am.

Facts for the Walker

SUGGESTED ITINERARIES

Spain is a big country and public transport, although usually reliable, may not be frequent. You don't want to lose too much time travelling so, if in doubt, limit yourself to one walking area and plan to come back. See the Table of Walks (pp4–7) for more information on the walks mentioned below.

One Week

You might want to base yourself in one place and do a number of day walks. For suggestions, see What Kind of Walk? (p37). To vary the flavours, consider:

Sistema Central Take two days to limber up in the Sierra de Candelario, then take on the more challenging Alta Ruta de Gredos.

Valencia Try the dramatic Els Ports Loop plus two or three days of gentler walking on Ruta La Marina Alta.

Two Regions Loop around Els Ports then head for Madrid to sample some of the shorter walks in the Sistema Central.

Pyrenean Traverse Base yourself in Canillo (Andorra), Espot, Benasque or Torla, mixing day walks and overnighters.

Two Weeks

Mountain & Coast Sample the Picos de Europa Circuit, then have a couple of days by the ocean on the Spindrift Walk in Galicia.

Andalucía Do day walks in the Parque Natural de Cazorla (Sierra de Cazorla Loop, Barranco del Guadalentín, Río Borosa), dividing the remaining time between the valleys of Alpujarras and the Sierra Nevada.

Highlights

Some like it hot, others prefer winter's chill. Some go for long, testing walks; others enjoy a hands-in-pockets, easy-breathing stroll. We've selected a few of our favourites. See the Table of Walks (pp4–7) for more information.

Beside the Seaside

Explore the beaches, dunes, cliff-top lookouts and lighthouses of the Illas Cies, Spain's newest national park, on the Illa do Faro or Illa Monte Agudo walks.

Snake along 52km of southern Spain's most spectacular seaboard on the Cabo de Gata Coast walk.

Go from city streets to isolated cliffs in 15 minutes on the San Sebastián to Hondarribia walk.

Tread a Little History

Join the flow along the Camino de Santiago (Way of St James), Europe's premier cultural walking highway.

Take the Alpujarras Tour, weaving your way between fascinating white villages founded by Muslims.

Wildlife

Gaze at the seabirds and raptors occupying the airspace above the Monestir de Sa Trapa walk.

Keep your eyes peeled for ibex, wild boar, deer and mouflon along the Barranco del Guadalentín walk.

Whistle with the marmots among the boulder fields of the Pyrenean Traverse.

Breathtaking Ridges

Walk, scramble and climb along the rough Serra de Bérnia ridge overlooking the Mediterranean on the Serra de Bérnia Traverse.

Edge yourself along the Anboto Ridge to the summit of a sacred peak on the Urkiola: Anboto Ridge walk.

Pick your way along the Cresta de l'Estanyó with all of Andorra at your feet, on the Pic de L'Estanyó walk.

Stretch Yourself

Trek from the tiny principality of Andorra through the Catalan Pyrenees to their taller Aragonese brothers on the 23-day Pyrenean Traverse.

Walk the nine-day Picos de Europa Circuit for alpine lakes, lunar landscapes and dense beech woods.

Haul yourself to the top of mainland Spain's highest and third-highest peaks on the three-day Sierra Nevada Traverse.

Island & Mainland Enjoy a week's walking on Mallorca, then catch a ferry to Denia on the mainland to attack Valencia's Serra de Bérnia Traverse and the mountains of the Ruta La Marina Alta.

More than Two Weeks

Camino de Santiago Walk a section of this popular pilgrim trail.

Pyrenean Traverse Walk Andorra to Espot (Days 1 to 6), then do walks within the Parc Nacional d'Aigüestortes i Estany de Sant Maurici (Estany Llong, Refugi de Colomina, Port de Ratera d'Espot). Alternatively, walk Days 12 to 19, from Benasque to Torla, a good base for walks in the Parque Nacional de Ordesa y Monte Perdido.

WHEN TO WALK

Whenever you plan to walk, there'll be a region of Spain that will be at its best. If the climate of the moment on the mainland is too extreme, consider the Balearic Islands (Islas Baleares). Mallorca's snow-free Serra de Tramuntana offers bracing walking during and on either side of winter. Similarly, the Camino de Santiago, at its best from June to October, can be walked at any time, though you may want to avoid the hottest and most popular months of July and August. Galician coastal routes are also accessible throughout the year, though heavy winter rains from the end of November until well into March can dampen enthusiasm.

The mild-season window for some of the high-level walks is open only briefly. In Andalucía's Sierra Nevada, the Picos de Europa in the Cordillera Cantábrica and on the higher walks in the Pyrenees, snow can block passes until the second half of June and begins to fall again in early September. Galician sierra routes are also primarily summer walks, though they are passable at any time between June and October. Snow dusting outside these months can make trail finding difficult. Above 2500m in the Pyrenees, manageable snow can linger in the dips until well into July. Pyrenean *refugios* (mountain huts or refuges) are mostly open from mid-June to mid-September, though a minority of more accessible ones stay open year-round.

Andalucía in general has a justified reputation for uncomfortably hot summers. Most of the walks we describe are at their best between April and October, though some of the lower ones are better avoided in July and August. This said, they can be walked at any time, with one important exception: the Sierra Nevada, best left to skiers in winter.

In the Balearic Islands and inland from Valencia's Costa Blanca, July and August can be uncomfortably hot. March to May, when the wildflowers are at their best, is the optimum time. For this same reason, the Els Ports region in the north of Valencia is best walked from late April to June.

Given their proximity to Madrid, parts of the Gredos and Guadarrama sierras can become quite crowded, especially at weekends. They're best walked in early or late summer when the climate's relatively benign and the trails emptier.

Most residents of Spain and a fair percentage of those in Western Europe holiday in the Iberian peninsula from mid-July until the end of August, stretching facilities to the limit (Spain and its offshore islands receive more than 50 million visitors a year). At these times, as well as during Semana Santa (Easter Week), it's essential to reserve accommodation in *refugios* in the Pyrenees and most other areas. Hotels in popular walking areas then tend to jack up their prices and are almost invariably full.

Walkers and ski tourers do attempt the high mountain routes in winter but we confine our recommendations to walking at less forbidding times of the year.

Overall, June and September are the optimum months for walking. Days are still relatively long, temperatures are milder, camping grounds, *refugios* and hotels are less overwhelmed and the trails are less crowded.

WHAT KIND OF WALK?

In popular tourist areas, such as Mallorca, we concentrate on day walks, accessible by public transport. On the mainland, you can radiate out each day from, for example, Oviedo and Santiago de Compostela in the north of Spain or Cazorla and Ronda in Andalucía, with each venue offering a week's worth of walking. All chapters except

GR & PR Routes

Spain is crisscrossed by numerous marked trails, some of which overlap in part with our own routes.

A **Sendero de Gran Recorrido** (GR), or long-distance trail, is signalled by red-and-white striped trail markers. Spain has more than 50 GRs, each with a minimum length of 50km. The GR11 runs the length of the Pyrenees and is mirrored by the French GR10, which snakes its way along the mountain chain's northern slopes. Several GRs link with trans-European trails. The GR65, for example, which follows the Camino de Santiago fairly closely through Navarra, begins in the woods of Bohemia in the Czech Republic, while the GR10 runs from Puçol, north of Valencia, to Lisbon on Portugal's Atlantic coast. If you walk the Els Ports routes in the north of the Valencia region, you'll be following part of the GR7. Also known as the E3, it begins in Crete, enters Spain via Andorra and runs through Murcia and on to Gibraltar.

Shorter **Senderos de Pequeño Recorrido** (PRs) pop up everywhere. Normally indicated by yellow-and-white trail markers, they're administered locally. Usually selected because they're scenic, they sometimes have an accompanying booklet or explanatory panel at the beginning or end of the walk.

❋ ❋ ❋ ❋ ❋ ❋ ❋ ❋ ❋ ❋ ❋ ❋

Mallorca also describe linear or circular walks of much longer duration.

ORGANISED WALKS
Organised Walks Within Spain
Most Spaniards tend to walk independently in small groups of friends or in larger packs from outdoor clubs or scout groups. Organised tours do exist, such as the guided day walks led by national park staff. In popular tourist areas such as Mallorca, outings are organised by private companies but unless your Spanish is good you'll miss out on a lot.

Terra Ferma (☎/fax 96 589 03 92; W *www .terraferma.net; Calle Lepanto 13, Villajoyosa 03570, Alicante)* is a warmly recommended,

environmentally committed walking and climbing outfit on the Costa Blanca whose staff speak excellent English. It can organise customised tours from one day to a week or more of trekking.

Spain Step by Step (☎/fax 93 302 76 29; e *nicholas.law@wanadoo.es)* is a small, up-market Barcelona-based, English-run operation that prepares tailor-made walking tours for groups of two to eight people.

Walk Operators Abroad
Alto Aragon (☎/fax 01869-337339; W *alto aragon.co.uk; 31 Heathside, Esher, Surrey, KT10 9TD, UK)*, a small company warmly recommended by more than one reader, has a base in both the UK and Spain. It organises walking holidays in the Pyrenees plus horseriding and cross-country skiing breaks.

Most of the big British-based walking tour operators include Spain within their international programmes. Favourite destinations include the Picos de Europa, Andalucía, Mallorca, the Islas Canarias and the Aragonese Pyrenees. The operators include:

ATG Oxford (☎ 01865-315678, fax 315697, W www.atg-oxford.co.uk) 69–71 Banbury Rd, Oxford OX2 6PJ
Explore Worldwide (☎ 01252-760000, fax 760001, W www.explore.co.uk) 1 Frederick St, Aldershot, Hants GU11 1LQ. It is ecosensitive and has been recommended.
Exodus (☎ 020-8675 5550, fax 8673 0779, W www.exodus.co.uk) 9 Weir Rd, London SW12 0LT
Headwater (☎ 01606-720033, fax 720034, W www.headwater.com) The Old School House, Chester Rd, Northwich, Cheshire CW8 1 LE
HF Holidays (☎ 020-8905 9558, fax 8205 0506, W www.classicwalking.co.uk) Imperial House, Edgware Rd, London NW9 5AL
Ramblers Holidays (☎ 01707-331133, fax 333276, W www.ramblersholidays.co.uk) Box 43 Welwyn Garden City AL8 6PQ. The big daddy of them all, Ramblers is an offshoot of the Ramblers Association and has been in business for more than 50 years.
Sherpa Expeditions (☎ 020-8577 2717, fax 8572 9788, W www.sherpaexpeditions.com) 131A Heston Rd, Hounslow TW5 0RF
Waymark Holidays (☎ 01753-516477, fax 517016, W www.waymarkholidays.com) 44 Windsor Rd, Slough, SL1 2EJ

Responsible Walking

Rubbish

- If you've carried it in, you can carry it out – everything, including wrappers, citrus peel, cigarette butts and empty packaging. Make an effort to pick up rubbish left by others.
- Sanitary napkins, tampons and condoms don't burn or decompose readily, so carry them out, whatever the inconvenience.
- Don't bury rubbish as this disturbs soil and ground cover and encourages erosion and weed growth. Buried rubbish takes years to decompose and will probably be dug up by wild animals that maybe injured or poisoned by it.
- If you're camping, remove all surplus food packaging before you go on your walk and put small-portion packages in a single container to minimise waste.

Human Waste Disposal

Contamination of water sources by human faeces can lead to the transmission of giardia, a human bacterial parasite; gastroenteritis is probably caused by exposed human faecal waste.

- If there's a toilet at a camp site, use it.
- Where there isn't one, bury your waste. Dig a small hole 15cm deep and at least 30m from any watercourse, 50m from paths and 200m from any buildings. Take a lightweight trowel or large tent peg for the purpose. Cover the waste with a good layer of soil and leaf mould. Toilet paper should be carried out. As a last resort burn it, but this is not recommended in a forest, above the tree line or in dry grassland. Ideally, use biodegradable paper.

Camping

- If camping near a farm or house, seek permission first.
- In remote areas, use a recognised site rather than creating a new one. Keep at least 30m from watercourses and paths. Move on after a night or two.
- Pitch your tent carefully, away from hollows where water is likely to accumulate, so you won't need to dig damaging trenches if it rains heavily.

- Leave your site as you found it – with no trace that you've passed by.

Washing

- Don't use detergents or toothpaste in or near streams or lakes; even it they are biodegradable they can harm fish and wildlife.
- To wash yourself, use biodegradable soap and a water container at least 50m from the watercourse. Disperse the wastewater widely so it filters through the soil before returning to the stream.
- Wash cooking utensils at least 50m from watercourses using a scourer or gritty sand instead of detergent.

Fires

Every summer, forest fires ravage large areas of Spain.

- Use a safe existing fireplace rather than making a new one. Don't surround it with rocks – they're just another visual scar – but clear all flammable material for at least 2m. Keep the fire small and use the minimum of dead wood.
- Be absolutely certain the fire is extinguished. Spread the embers and drown them with water. Turn the embers over to check the fire is extinguished throughout. Scatter the charcoal and cover the fire site with soil and leaves.

Access

Some walks in this book pass through private property, though it may not be obvious at the time, along recognised routes where access is freely permitted. If there's any doubt, ask if it's OK to walk through – you'll rarely have any problems.

Tread Lightly

In high mountain areas such as the Sierra Nevada, Picos de Europa and Pyrenees, the growing season is short and the vegetation hardy yet fragile. Where possible, tread on rock or stone rather than grass, plants or soil. Similarly, tree roots on popular paths, while a lot more resistant, can only take so much battering from boots.

ACCOMMODATION

Many accommodation places have separate price structures for the *temporada baja* (low season); *temporada media* (mid-season); and *temporada alta* (high season), when prices in tourist areas are often jacked up significantly.

The *temporada alta* can vary from region to region, but anticipate premium prices during August and probably July, from Christmas to 6 January and during Semana Santa (Easter Week). At such times it's wise – and in some regions essential – to reserve in advance.

Impuesto sobre el Valor Añadido (IVA; value-added tax) is levied on accommodation at the rate of 7%. In more modest places it's nearly always included within the room price and you won't even be aware of it. However, hotels vary in their way of quoting prices. To ask 'Is IVA included?' say *¿Esta incluido el IVA?* (IVA is pronounced **ee**-ba).

The annual *Guía Oficial de Hoteles* (€8), available from most bookshops, lists all but the cheapest categories of accommodation and details their facilities and prices.

Unless otherwise stated this book quotes the high-season tariff, so outside peak periods you might be in for a pleasant surprise.

In Cities, Towns & Villages

Camping We call an area with facilities, where a fee is normally demanded, a camping ground, reserving the term camp site for more informal places where it's possible to pitch your tent.

Spain has around 1000 official camping grounds, known as *campings*, which are graded into three classes according to their facilities. Their quality ranges from reasonable to very good. In July and August in popular tourist areas, tents and vehicles are packed cheek by jowl. This said, a camping ground will almost invariably find space for a walker with a lightweight tent.

Even 3rd-class camping grounds often have hot showers and probably a small store and bar. A typical nightly fee for a 2nd- or 3rd-class operation is €3 to €4 for a small tent and the same again per person.

Now and again you may come across a *zona de acampada* or *área de acampada*, an area where camping is permitted but there's no charge. There are rarely any facilities, however, so these can be decidedly unhygienic.

It's worth investing €6 in the annually updated *Guía Oficial de Campings*. Available in most bookshops in Spain, it lists most of the country's camping grounds, together with their facilities and prices.

Hostels Spain's 180 or so *albergues juveniles* (youth hostels), not to be confused with *hostales* (budget hotels), are often the cheapest places for lone travellers but two people can usually get a double room elsewhere for a similar price. Prices often depend on the season and vary between €4 and €13 for under-26s and between €5 and €18 for 26-and-overs. In some hostels the price includes breakfast. A few hostels require you to rent sheets (around €2 for your stay) if you don't have your own or a sleeping bag.

Most youth hostels are members of the **Red Española de Albergues Juveniles** *(REAJ or Spanish Youth Hostel Network;* **W** *www .reaj.com)*, the Spanish affiliate of Hostelling International (HI).

However, most hostels are managed by regional governments. Each region usually sets its own price structure. Some have central booking services. These include:

Andalucía (☎ 902 51 00 00, **W** www.inturjoven .com)
Catalunya (☎ 93 483 83 10, fax 93 483 83 50, **W** www.tujuca.com)
Madrid (☎ 91 543 74 12, fax 91 544 00 62)
Valencia (☎ 96 386 99 52, **W** www.ivaj.es)

Quite a few hostels require a HI card or membership card from your home country's youth hostel association; others don't (even though they may be HI hostels). But nonmembers will never be shown the door, merely charged more, with the additional charges eventually accumulating into a membership.

Pensiones, Fondas & Casas de Huéspedes At the cheaper end of the standard accommodation pyramid is the *pensión* (signed 'P' on a rectangular blue sign), which is basically a small private hotel. Many are being upgraded and offer a choice between cheaper rooms without a bathroom and others with full bathroom facilities. Prices for a single room generally vary between €10 and €20 and, for doubles, from €15 to €25 or so.

Cheaper, though much less common (officially, the categories don't exist any more but they'll be around on the ground for some years to come), is the *fonda* (indicated by a white 'F') and *casa de huéspedes* (signed 'CH'). The latter translates literally as 'guesthouse', though nothing could be further from the image of genteel languor that such a term in English conjures up. Usually clean enough, though the plumbing may be eccentric, very few rooms have a bathroom attached.

Hostales Next up the scale is the *hostal*, graded according to a three-star system. Some are little different from *pensiones*, while a three-star *hostal* may be considerably more comfortable and most or all rooms will have bathrooms. Room prices range from around €12/18 for the cheapest singles/doubles with shared bathroom to as much as €40/50 at the best *hostales*. A *hostal-residencia* doesn't provide meals.

Casas Rurales In recent years there has been heavy investment in developing and promoting rural tourism to bring income to what are often economically deprived areas. *Casas rurales* are usually comfortably renovated village dwellings or farmhouses with a room or two for guests. Some offer only accommodation while others provide meals or self-catering facilities. Prices vary enormously: a double room can cost anywhere between €15 and €50. Tourist offices usually provide details of local *casas rurales* and of any reservation agencies.

Hotels There is a grading system of one to five stars for *hoteles* (hotels). The stars, as in the grading of *pensiones* and *hostales*, reflect facilities and not necessarily price or quality. There'll probably be a restaurant and even the cheapest room normally has a bathroom. Prices cover the whole gamut from €25 to over €300. Packing at least the relevant pages of the *Guia Oficial de Hoteles* can save you a detour to a place that may turn out to be beyond your price ceiling.

Paradores is a state-run chain of more than 80 luxury hotels, many in converted castles, palaces, mansions and monasteries. Room-only prices start at €60.45/75.55 for singles/doubles in the low season, while you're looking at €100 or more for a double in most paradores in the high season. You can book a room at any parador via the **central reservation system** (☎ 91 516 66 66,

fax 91 516 66 57; ⓦ *www.parador.es)*. A parador is also a great place for a drink after a day's walking. Their restaurants usually offer regional specialities and, while not cheap, are normally excellent value for money.

On the Walk
Day walks and some stages of longer walks begin and end within a bus ride of a population centre, where you'll normally find accommodation and sometimes a camping ground. Two other options on many longer walks are camping wild or staying in *refugios*.

Camping A lightweight tent confers liberty and independence. If you have one, you can still opt for something cosier, should the mood take you. If you're without one, you're obliged to head for the nearest *refugio* or village – where you may arrive to find all options full. Those three or four extra kilos will more than justify themselves every time you pitch your tent.

However, you can't expect untrammelled freedom. *Parques nacionales* (national parks) and many *parques naturales* (nature parks) and other protected areas prohibit or limit camping within their boundaries. There's also a regulation that says you're not allowed to camp wild within 1km of a camping ground.

Apart from such legitimate restrictions, and others of more localised ambit, the opportunity for wild camping in Spain's open spaces is almost limitless. Within each walk, we indicate particularly attractive or convenient sites – but there are many more waiting to be discovered.

Refugios The larger *refugios* (mountain huts or refuges) are staffed and usually open from mid-June until mid-September though a minority of more accessible ones stay open year-round. During July and August in popular regions such as the Pyrenees it's highly advisable to reserve in advance (you'll find contact details within the relevant walk descriptions). *Refugios* in the Sierra de Gredos and the Sierra de Guadarrama, both easy bus rides from Madrid, are usually packed solid every weekend.

Prices are typically between €10 and €12 for a bunk and around €10 for dinner; if you think the latter's expensive, reflect upon the effort expended to get supplies in. There's rarely equipment for doing your own cooking though many bigger *refugios* set aside an area for this. Sleeping is normally in *literas*, long benches, sometimes double-decker, with mattresses running the length of the dormitory. Blankets are usually provided but not sheets.

Refugios are OK for a night or two – but check carefully how many sleepers there are to a room. Many are fine, like a high-altitude youth hostel; others, where you're in a dormitory among 35 or more sweating, snoring, farting others, are less fun. Their strong point is that the guardians are almost invariably friendly and well informed. Most come back season after season and are invaluable sources of information about walks in the area.

In some regions, there are unstaffed *refugios*, the best of which can be surprisingly cosy. However, at the end of the day, they're only as clean as the last group passing through – and that can be anything from the most fastidious of fellow walkers to a herd of swine. Most unstaffed *refugios* remain open year-round and many others will allow access to one wing outside summer.

FOOD
Local Food
Throughout Spain you'll find plenty of restaurants serving good, simple food at affordable prices and featuring regional specialities. There are also a minority of fairly dire dumps, particularly in tourist haunts. A *mesón* is a simple eatery with home-style cooking, commonly attached to a bar. A *venta* was probably once an inn, and is usually off the beaten track, while a *marisquería* is a seafood restaurant.

Even the tiniest village will usually have a café or bar. Bars come in various guises, including bodegas (old-style wine bars), *cervecerías* (beer bars), *tascas* (bars that specialise in tapas, or bar snacks), *tabernas* (taverns) and even pubs. Many serve tapas and often have more substantial fare too.

Typical Spanish bar and restaurant food is hearty and plentiful rather than gourmet – just what you need after a day in the mountains. It's also healthy because it's based upon typically Mediterranean ingredients such as olive oil (Spain produces one third of the world's olive oil), garlic, onions, tomatoes and peppers (capsicum).

For variety, you can munch your way through a selection of tapas (bar snacks) or *raciones* (larger portions of the same), though this can work out to be expensive. The price, range and quality of à-la-carte items varies enormously from place to place. However, there's almost always a *menú del día* (menu of the day) or *menú de la casa* (house menu) available. Often simply called a *menú*, it has a set price and allows you a choice of items. It typically consists of a starter, main course, a *postre* (dessert) and bread. A *bebida* (beverage), usually a choice of wine, beer or water, may be included.

Some establishments, especially in areas popular with tourists, offer *platos combinados* (literally 'combination dishes'). These may be something like steak, sausage, a piece of fish or bacon and eggs, garnished with a salad, with a supporting cast of some kind of potato dish. There's often a fading, labelled photograph of each variation on the wall, so you know exactly what you're getting. While hardly sophisticated they're wholesome and usually good value for money.

Just about every region in Spain has its specialities; the Basque Country and Catalunya have particularly rich local cuisines. Originating in Valencia, paella is a delicious saffron-coloured rice dish, simmered in richly flavoured stock, that crops up on menus throughout Spain. There are two versions: one with chicken, rabbit, green beans, butter beans and sometimes a snail or two; and *paella de mariscos*, a fancier version scattered with seafood.

Fabada asturiana is an Asturian speciality, a rich stew guaranteed to dispel the chill of winter. It combines white beans, black pudding (blood sausage), hunks of chorizo (a spicy red sausage), cubes of pork fat and stewing beef, diced smoked ham and, optionally, a pig's ear. Subtle it ain't but this heartwarming dish has been known to bring tears to the eyes of a hungry walker.

For the vocabulary to help you navigate a restaurant menu or a trip to the green-grocers, consult Lonely Planet's *Spain* guide, or its *Spanish phrasebook*, which gives an even more comprehensive listing. For a behind-the-kitchen-door lowdown, pack its *World Food Spain*.

When to Eat Spaniards normally eat late and this is reflected in restaurant hours. Lunch will typically be served from around 2pm and people won't look askance if you arrive as late as 4.30pm, expecting to be served. Dinner is rarely offered before 9pm, so if you're ravenous after a long day of walking, make sure you have some snacks in your backpack to tide you over. However, outside normal opening hours many burger

Camping Food

Here's a list of Spanish food terms that may come in handy when shopping for camping supplies. Take only enough food to see you through the walk – then add a little extra, just in case the walk takes longer than planned.

Dehydrated & Powdered Foods
These are ideal for walks of several days' duration, where every gram counts.

azúcar – sugar, sold almost always by the kilogram and very difficult to find in smaller units
cacao – cocoa
café – coffee (instant)
leche en polvo – powdered milk
puré de patatas – instant mashed potatoes
sopa en sobres – dehydrated soup in sachets
té or té de infusion – tea or herbal tea

Staple Foods
These make an excellent, high-carbohydrate base for a meal.

alubias – white beans
arroz – rice
copos de avena – oat flakes
garbanzos – chickpeas; until recently, the staple carbohydrate of the poor. Buy them pre-cooked in jars and decant them into a lightweight receptacle.
lentejas – lentils
muesli – muesli; not easily found but available at health stores and some groceries
pasta – pasta

Semi-Perishable Foods
Choose foods such as cheese and salami, which will last for several days in the heat.

chorizo – the farmer's and hunter's favourite; a spicy red sausage
embutido – cured sausage

jamón de York – sliced boiled ham
jamón serrano – cured ham, full of flavour and similar to prosciutto
lomo – pork loin
longaniza – pork sausage
pan integral – wholemeal bread; not available at all bakeries
queso – cheese
salchichón – salami; tends to be greasy

Tinned Foods
Cans are heavy but carried in small quantities their contents can make a tasty addition to an otherwise bland meal.

atún – tuna
calamares – squid
guisantes – peas
mejillones – mussels
pimientos – peppers
pulpo en salsa – octopus in sauce
sardinas – sardines

Dried Fruit
Frutos secos is the generic term for nuts and dried fruit. As a lightweight energy source they're among the most efficient foods to carry.

albaricoques – apricots
almendras – almonds
avellanas – hazelnuts
cacahuetes – peanuts
dátiles – dates
higos – figs
pan de higo – compressed figs and almonds
pasas – raisins
turrón – a delicious honey and almond nougat

joints and places offer *platos combinados*, a largish serving of meat, seafood or omelette with trimmings.

Those *refugios* (mountain huts or refuges) which are staffed usually have different eating hours, serving dinner earlier, often in two sittings if it's a large place and is full to capacity.

On the Walk

Refugios Most staffed *refugios* serve breakfast and dinner. Some of the larger ones stay open all day and sell drinks, snacks and occasionally lunch. It's advisable to reserve dinner at the same time as your bunk, though they'll never turn a hungry traveller away. You don't have to be staying at a *refugio* to order food so it's quite possible to enjoy an evening meal and then head away to camp somewhere more tranquil.

Buying Food There's usually at least one shop at the beginning and end of each walk we describe. For walks longer than one day we indicate places en route where you can pick up supplies.

For wild camping, most of the major equipment shops in Madrid (see pp66–7) and Barcelona (see pp96–7) sell dehydrated foods. If you have particular favourites, play safe and buy them before leaving home. You shouldn't have trouble picking up some form of high-energy food in even the smallest one-shop village. For a glossary of camping food terms, see the boxed text 'Camping Food' (p43).

Cooking If you eat one meal a day or every other day in a *refugio*, you can dispense with a stove and fuel. However, a stove does confer extra flexibility, and nothing in the world rivals a post-dawn mug of steaming tea or coffee.

DRINKS
Nonalcoholic Drinks

Agua mineral (bottled spring water) is widely available. You can buy it *sin gas* (still) and *con gas* (sparkling). Soft drinks, called *refrescos*, are also sold everywhere. Freshly squeezed fruit juices *(zumos)* are delicious and alto-gether healthier. If fresh fruit is out of season, you can buy juices cheaply in waxed cartons.

It's difficult to get a really bad coffee in Spain, where all but the humblest bar will have an espresso machine hissing away. You can order *café* (coffee) several ways: *solo*, small, black and pungently strong; *cortado*, a *solo* cut with a splash of milk; *café con leche*, coffee with milk; or *descafeinado* (decaffeinated). There's also *café americano*, black and weaker; ask for one in the villages and all you'll get in return is a quizzical stare. If you request tea, you'll probably be served a cup of hot water with a tea bag dangling in it.

Alcoholic Drinks

Just to take a look at the array of bottles behind even the most modest bar is enough to make your liver protest. Most drinkers in a bar will be sipping *vino* (wine), either *tinto* (red), *rosado* (rosé) or *blanco* (white). In Andalucía, and in fancier joints elsewhere, sherry – usually asked for as *un fino* – or its local equivalent is popular. In restaurants, the *vino de la casa* (house wine) can vary from the very palatable to toxic paint stripper. For draught beer, ask for *cerveza de barril* or *cerveza de presión*. If you just ask for *una cerveza*, you'll normally get one in a bottle.

On the Walk

Water is by far the best thirst-quencher when you're walking. It's also the most readily available way to rehydrate. Village *fuentes* (fountains or springs) are often reliable. Walk on if one is signed *agua no potable* (nondrinking water) but don't be too suspicious if it simply says *agua no tratada* (untreated water). In some mountain regions, above the cultivation line and away from areas where livestock graze, it's safe to drink straight from flowing streams. Take advice from locals and *refugio* wardens and carry water purifying tablets. For information on how to treat water that seems suspect, see Staying Healthy (p57).

WOMEN WALKERS

You'll be very unlucky if you have any problems on the trails that are related specifically to your sex. Like walkers everywhere, Spanish hikers tend to be fairly socially enlightened. Younger ones are relaxed in their dealings with the opposite sex, and older walkers are usually free of the prurient interest in foreign women that some dinosaurs still carry over from the repressive social climate of the Franco era.

In towns, you may get the occasional unwelcome stare, catcall or unnecessary comment, to which the best – and most galling – response is indifference. And don't get too paranoid about what's being called; the *piropo* – a harmless, mildly flirty compliment – is deeply ingrained in Spanish society and, if well delivered, is even considered gallant. Serious harassment is much less frequent than you might expect and Spain has one of the developed world's lowest incidences of reported rape.

Sleeping arrangements in many *refugios* often involve a single- or double-decker bench running from one side of the dormitory to the other where male and female, young and old, snore side by side. If this worries you, pack a tent and retain your independence.

In general, as anywhere, it might be risky for a woman to hitch alone.

For general advice consult *Handbook for Women Travellers,* by M & G Moss.

On Spanish Trails

In general, Spain is a very safe country for a woman alone, especially in rural walking areas. Before going to Spain for the first time, I was warned about the attention I might receive from the stereotyped *macho ibérico* (a man unashamed to express his virility and strength). Once there I discovered that the *macho ibérico* was, in fact, becoming an endangered species and that in the rare instance when unwanted advances were directed my way, a firm *'Dejame'* (**Deh**-ha-may; meaning 'Leave me alone!') was sufficient to keep them at bay.

What did bother me at first were the long looks from both sexes. However, rather than an invasion of individual privacy, I found they are part of a Spanish cultural code in which people watching is the norm. Stares don't necessarily have a secondary intent.

You don't see women walking alone in the mountains very often, and this does attract attention. Women on their own (mostly foreigners) provoke reactions among locals of surprise, admiration and concern. It's common to be warned not to go into the hills alone by both men and women repeating advice learned in childhood.

Nancy Frey

WALKING WITH CHILDREN

A quick and statistically quite invalid straw poll of authors of this book and their spouses evoked, 'Don't! Wait until they're at least 16' and 'You'd never drag our kids up a mountain.'

Joking – which they were – apart, there's no need to hang up your boots once the kids come along; walking with children in Spain is no more difficult than elsewhere in Europe.

In some respects, it's easier. The Spanish in general are fond of children. There are no puritanical laws banishing them from places where alcohol is served and, since most cafés are open from breakfast until way after their bedtime, you can always pick up a soft drink or snack. (Bear in mind, however, the late hour at which restaurants serve lunch and dinner, and ensure that you always have a cache of emergency provisions in your backpack.)

Baby food, nappies (diapers), creams and potions and all the other paraphernalia of travelling with the very young are readily available in Spanish towns, though you may not find your favourite brand. If you're planning to walk in less populated areas, stock up in advance.

Before undertaking a route of several days, it might be wise to first establish a base camp and do a number of day or half-day walks to break yourselves in.

Think also of combining walking with other activities such as beach fun. You could, for example, stay at Port de Sóller on Mallorca or on the Costa Blanca in Valencia.

Car-hire rates in Spain are much cheaper than in many parts of Europe and worth considering in preference to waiting for infrequent or nonexistent bus services.

There's a simple rule of thumb for calculating what kids can carry on a walk: most can comfortably walk their age and carry half of it. A 12-year-old, for example, should be able to walk about 12km per day in moderate terrain, carrying a backpack weighing around 6kg.

Lonely Planet's *Travel with Children* has lots of practical advice on the subject, along with first-hand travel stories from a host of Lonely Planet authors and others.

Walks suitable for families with children include the Sóller to Deià (see p273) and Barranc de Biniaraix & Embassament de Cúber (see p275) walks on Mallorca. Other possibilities are the Benamahoma to Zahara de la Sierra walk (see p325) in Andalucía's Sierra de Grazalema and a section of the Ruta de los Lagos walk (see p194) in the Cordillera Cantábrica.

The Pyrenees aren't all that suitable for younger children. This said, Canillo in Andorra makes a great base for a few undemanding half-day walks such as the Basses de les Salamandres walk (see p146). Side trips listed at the end of a walk description and Other Walks, which feature at the end of most chapters, can also be a source of ideas.

DANGERS & ANNOYANCES

You're unlikely to have any trouble on the trails. Should you pass through Madrid or Barcelona, keep a weather eye on your backpack and its pockets, particularly around the stations and in the metro, where petty theft is a thriving business.

MAPS

For major Spanish map stockists, see the Information sections of individual walks chapters. Generally, it's safer to buy all your maps in advance. In the UK, **Stanfords** (☎ 020-7836 1321, fax 7836 0189; ⓦ *www.stanfords .co.uk; 12-14 Long Acre, London WC2E 9LP)*, the world's largest map and guidebook store, operates an efficient mail- and web-order service.

Small-Scale Maps

Michelin produces a 1:1,000,000 *España Portugal* map and six regional 1:400,000 maps covering the whole of Spain. If you're driving, the Ministerio de Fomento 1:300,000 *Mapa Oficial de Carreteras* (€16.25), in a ring-bound book makes a good travelling companion.

Large-Scale Maps

Two public sector bodies, the Instituto Geográfico Nacional (IGN) and the Servicio Geográfico del Ejército (SGE) of the Spanish army, produce maps at walker-friendly scales. Between them, they cover the whole country at 1:50,000 (with the contours 20m apart) and 1:25,000 (with contours 10m apart). IGN produces new and updated maps at 1:25,000 while both bodies maintain their 1:50,000 series. IGN maps cost €3 and SGE sheets, €2.50.

Both series are produced strictly according to a grid, so depending how the grid boundaries fall your coastal map could be 75% sea, and a popular day walk might require two or more sheets. When buying maps, check carefully when a map was *actualizada* (updated) rather than when it was printed; the difference can be considerable.

Two private map companies stand out for reliability and walker-friendliness. Prames produces excellent maps (€4.50) specifically for walkers in the Aragón region (see Maps, p99). Also regional and reliable are the maps (€5) produced by Adrados Ediciones (ⓦ *www.srg-gab.com/adrados)*. You'll find them in major northern cities such as Oviedo and Santander in Cantabria, as well as in even the smallest villages around the Picos de Europa in the Cordillera Cantábrica.

UK-based **Discovery Walking Guides** (ⓦ *www.walking.demon.co.uk)*, who also call themselves Warm Island Walking Guides and the Indestructible Map Company, publish excellent maps (£5) based on IGN 1:25,000 originals for the Balearic Islands and the Alpujarras region in Andalucía, among other Spanish destinations. Each comes in a handy pack with a detailed route description in English and new editions are being produced in an unrippable, unstainable, GPS-compatible format.

Editorial Alpina (W *www.editorialalpina*
.com) produces more than 70 topographical maps (€7) with small accompanying guidebooks in Spanish or Catalan, targeted particularly at walkers and climbers. They cover the Pyrenees and Catalunya fairly comprehensively and also cover parts of the Picos de Europa, Sierra de Cazorla and Sierra de Gredos. Most are at 1:25,000 with contours at 20m intervals. With their five to seven shades of colour, elevation shading stands out clearly. Newer editions, with green covers, are generally more accurate than their red-covered predecessors. Even so, while contours are accurate, some maps have the occasional blinding, disorienting error.

PLACE NAMES

Where a regional language is spoken, we reflect predominant local usage; for example, in the Catalan Pyrenees we call a village, mountain or pass by its Catalan name, while in Galicia we use the Galician form. It's no big deal since the majority of names aren't significantly different from their equivalent in Spanish; for example, Mulleres for Molières, Urdiceta for Ordiceta and Astós for Estós.

USEFUL ORGANISATIONS
Walking Clubs & Associations

The **Federación Española de Deportes de Montaña y Escalada** (*Fedme;* ☎ *93 426 42 67, fax 93 426 33 87;* W *www.fedme.es; Carrer Floridablanca 75, 2nd floor, Barcelona)* is the umbrella organisation at the head of 17 regional federations and more than a thousand clubs. It represents walking and walkers' interests at the national level in Spain.

Nowadays, almost every autonomous region has its own federation. In Madrid, contact the **Federació Madrileña de Montañismo** (☎ *91 527 38 01, fax 91 528 09 31;* W *www .fmm.es; Calle Ferrocarril 22, 1st floor)*. In Barcelona, the **Federació d'Entitats Excursionistes de Catalunya** (☎ *93 412 07 77, fax 93 412 63 53;* W *www.feec.es; Rambla 41)* is a grouping of Catalan clubs and federations.

In areas where there are large expatriate communities there are active walking groups

usually composed of wiry pensioners who are happy to include visiting hikers. For details, check the ads in the local English-language press. One active group is the Costa Blanca Mountain Walkers, based near Benidorm. For further details, see Guided Walks (p256).

Other Organisations

TIVE, the Spanish youth and student travel organisation, is good for reduced-price student and youth travel tickets if you're aged under 26. It also issues various useful documents such as the International Student Identity Card (ISIC), International Teacher Identity Card (ITIC) as well as the Hostelling International (HI) and Federation of International Youth Travel Organisations (FIYTO) cards, all of which offer a range of discounts. There's an office or equivalent (the names sometimes differ) in most major cities, such as in Madrid, **TIVE** (☎ *91 543 74 12; Calle Fernando el Católico 88)* or in Barcelona, **Turisme Juvenil de Catalunya** (☎ *93 483 83 63; Carrer Rocafort 116)*.

Keen bird-watchers might like to contact the **Sociedad Española de Ornitología** (*SEO;* ☎ *914 34 09 10, fax 914 34 09 11;* W *www .seo.org; Calle Melquiades Biencinto 34, Madrid)*, the Spanish Ornithological Society.

DIGITAL RESOURCES

For an excellent website in English, click on W www.wild-spain.com. Covering outdoor activities, nature and ecological concerns, it also has some good links. For more general information about Spain, you might want to call up either W www.okspain.org or W www.tourspain.es, both of which are run by Turespaña, the official Spanish tourist authority.

BOOKS

For walking guidebooks and natural history titles specific to a region, see Books in the Information sections of individual walks chapters.

Lonely Planet

Lonely Planet's fact-packed *Spain* guide makes an ideal supplement to the general information in this book. If you're planning to pass through one of the northern Gateways, travel with the *Barcelona, Barcelona Condensed, Madrid* or *Valencia & the Costa Blanca* guide. Should you be lingering in the Catalan Pyrenees, you'll find *Catalunya & the Costa Brava* useful. If you're planning to walk down south, stow *Andalucía* in your backpack. *Travel with Children* has plenty of practical tips for parents. Lonely Planet's slim-fit *Spanish phrasebook* has a range of terms for most situations you're likely to encounter and is compact enough to slip into a pocket for instant access. Gourmets might like to pack the equally slim but far from slimming *World Food Spain*.

Travel & Exploration

To set your own walking endeavours in perspective, pack *As I Walked Out One Midsummer Morning,* by Laurie Lee, an evocative account of Laurie's adventures walking from Vigo, in Galicia, to Málaga, down south on the Costa del Sol, during turbulent times just prior to the Spanish Civil War.

For an even more impressive – and contemporary – walking endeavour, read *Clear Waters Rising*, an unputdownable account by Nick Crane of his epic trek from Finisterre, Galicia's most westerly tip, to Istanbul. The first third of the book describes his progress through Galicia, segments of the Camino Francés, the Picos de Europa and the Pyrenees.

The Camino de Santiago, in particular, has captured the imagination of writers in English and spawned a shelf or two of writing. For details of recommended titles, see Books (p331).

Natural History

Wildlife Travelling Companion: Spain, by John Measures, is a good traveller's guide, focusing on 150 of the best sites for viewing plants and animals, with details of how to reach them and what you can hope to see.

Spain's Wildlife, by Eric Robins, covers the country's most interesting animals and birds – and their prospects for survival – in an informative way, spiced up with good photos and plenty of personal experience.

If you like to combine your walking with bird-watching, consider packing either *The Birds of Britain and Europe with North Africa and the Middle East,* by Herman Heinzel et al, or *A Field Guide to the Birds of Britain and Europe,* by Roger Peterson et al. *Where to Watch Birds in Southern Spain,* by Andrew Paterson and Ernest Garcia, is also relevant north of Andalucía.

The single best guide to Spain's flowers and shrubs is *Flowers of South-West Europe: A Field Guide,* by Oleg Polunin & BE Smythies. For serious botanists, the classic work remains the three volumes of *Wild Flowers of Spain,* by Clive Innes.

Buying Books

For ideas on where to buy books and maps, see the Information section of walking chapters. Check too in Madrid (see pp66–7) and Barcelona (see pp96–7), both of which have excellent travel bookshops.

NEWSPAPERS & MAGAZINES

Spain's best specialist magazine for walkers and climbers is *Desnivel*, which appears monthly. *Aire Libre* and *Grandes Espacios* are also directed primarily at outdoor activities enthusiasts.

WEATHER INFORMATION

Daily at around 9.30pm, both TVE1 and Antenna 3, a private channel, show the weather forecast for the next 24 hours and beyond. Local papers usually have the weather prognosis in both visual and textual form.

If you speak Spanish well, you can call Teletiempo (€0.45 per minute 8am to 8pm, €0.35 8pm to 8am), the phone information service of the Instituto Nacional de Meteorología. The system is touch-tone interactive and speakers tend to gabble. To access it, dial ☎ 906 36 53, followed by the first two numbers of the postal code of the province you're interested in. For mountain areas, dial ☎ 906 36 53 80 for the Pyrenees, substituting a final ☎ 81 for the Picos de Europa, ☎ 82 for the Sierra de Guadarrama, ☎ 83 for the Sistema Iberico and ☎ 84 for the Sierra Nevada.

PHOTOGRAPHY

Most major brands of film are widely available in Spain and local processing is fast and generally efficient. A roll of print film (36 exposures, ISO 100) costs around €3 to €4 and can be processed for around €8. You sometimes get a better deal if you have two or three rolls developed together. *Diapositiva* (slide film) costs around €5 to €7 and processing, another €3.

Your camera and film will be routinely passed through airport x-ray machines. These shouldn't damage film but you can ask for hand inspection if you're worried.

Taking Photos Outdoors

For walkers, photography can be a vexed issue – all that magnificent scenery but such weight and space restrictions on what photographic equipment you can carry. With a little care and planning it is possible to maximise your chance of taking great photos on the trail.

- **Light & Filters** In fine weather, the best light is early and late in the day. In strong sunlight and in mountain and coastal areas where the light is intense, a polarising filter will improve colour saturation and reduce haze. On overcast days the soft light can be great for shooting wildflowers and running water and an 81A warming filter can be useful. If you use slide film, a graduated filter will help balance unevenly lit landscapes.

- **Equipment** If you need to travel light carry a zoom in the 28–70mm range, and if your sole purpose is landscapes consider carrying just a single wide-angle lens (24mm). A tripod is essential for really good images and there are some excellent lightweight models available. Otherwise a trekking pole, pack or even a pile of rocks can be used to improvise.

- **Camera Care** Keep your gear dry – a few zip-lock freezer bags can be used to double wrap camera gear and silica-gel sachets (a drying agent) can be used to suck moisture out of equipment. Sturdy cameras will normally work fine in freezing conditions. Take care when bringing a camera from one temperature extreme to another; if moisture condenses on the camera parts make sure it dries thoroughly before going back into the cold, or mechanisms can freeze up. Standard camera batteries fail very quickly in the cold. Remove them from the camera when it's not in use and keep them under your clothing.

For a thorough grounding in photography on the road, read Lonely Planet's *Travel Photography*, by Richard I'Anson, a full-colour guide for happy-snappers and professional photographers alike.

Gareth McCormack

Clothing & Equipment

You don't need to spend a fortune on gear to enjoy the outdoors, but you do need to think carefully about what you pack to make sure you're comfortable and prepared for an emergency. Taking the right clothing and equipment on a walk can make the difference between an enjoyable day out or a cold and miserable one; in extreme situations, it can even mean the difference between life and death.

GEARING UP TO WALK

The gear you need for your walking holiday will depend on the type of walking you plan to do. For day walks, clothing, footwear and a backpack are the major items; you might get away with sandshoes, a hat, shorts, shirt and a warm pullover. For longer walks, or those in alpine regions, especially if you're camping, the list becomes longer.

We recommend spending as much as you can afford on quality walking boots and a jacket that's both windproof and waterproof. Splash out to your limit as well on a synthetic pile jacket, if it's likely to be cold, and a tent, if you intend to camp. These are likely to be your most expensive items but are a sound investment, as they should last for years.

The following section is not exhaustive; for more advice, visit outdoor stores, talk to fellow walkers and read product reviews in outdoor magazines.

Clothing

The majority of the walks in this book can be done simply in shorts/skirt and shirt. Invest in a lightweight shirt of a 'wicking' fabric such as polyester, Capilene or polypropylene, all of which move the sweat away from your body.

If it's likely to be cold, better to wear several thin layers of clothing than one or two thicker items. This allows you to add or remove layers as you get colder or hotter depending on your exertion or the weather. Except in hot weather, begin with a wicking underlayer. Your lightweight shorts/trousers and shirt make up the middle layer. Outer layers can consist of sweaters (jumpers), fleece jackets or down-filled jackets. Finally, there is the 'shell' layer, or wind- and waterproof jacket and pants. In Spain, you're unlikely to need all of these unless you go in for high-level winter walking.

Look for clothes that offer warmth, but still breathe and wick moisture away from your skin. Avoid wearing heavy cotton or denim, as these fabrics dry slowly and are very cold when wet. When you are choosing clothes prepare for the worst weather that a particular region might throw at you. The body loses most of its heat through its extremities, particularly the head. Wearing a wool or fleece hat and gloves can prevent this warmth being lost.

When deciding between long sleeves and trouser legs, weigh up the advantages of sun and insect protection against discomfort in the heat.

Waterproof Jacket The ideal specifications are a breathable, waterproof fabric, a hood that is roomy enough to cover headwear but still affords peripheral vision, a capacious map pocket, and a good-quality heavy-gauge zip protected by a storm flap. Make sure the sleeves are long enough to cover warm clothes underneath and that the overall length of the garment allows you to sit down on it.

Overtrousers Although restrictive, these are essential if you're walking in wet and cold conditions. As the name suggests, they are worn over your trousers. Choose a model with slits for pocket access and long leg zips so that you can pull them on and off over your boots.

Footwear

Your footwear will be your friend or your enemy, so choose carefully. The first decision to make is boots or shoes. Runners (trainers) are fine over easy terrain but, for more difficult trails and across rocks and scree, most walkers agree that the ankle support offered by boots is invaluable. If you'll be using crampons or walking in snow you need the rigid sole of a walking boot. Leather boots are heavier and less water resistant than fabric boots lined with a breathable membrane such as Gore-Tex, but pierce a hole in Gore-Tex-lined fabric boots – a more likely occurrence than with a leather boot – and their water resistance will go from hero to zero in an instant.

Buy boots in warm conditions or go for a walk before trying them on, so that your feet can expand slightly, as they would on a walk.

Most walkers carry a pair of 'camp shoes', thongs (flip flops) or sandals. These will relieve your feet from the heavy boots at night or during rest stops and sandals are useful when fording waterways. Spare socks are equally valuable, especially in wet conditions.

[Continued on page 54]

Check List

This list is a general guide to the things you might take on a walk. Your list will vary depending on the kind of walking you want to do, whether you're camping or planning on staying in hostels or *pensiones* (guesthouses), and on the terrain, weather conditions and time of year.

Equipment

- ☐ **backpack** with **waterproof liner**
- ☐ **first-aid kit***
- ☐ **food** or **snacks** (high-energy) and one day's **emergency supplies**
- ☐ **insect repellent**
- ☐ **map**, **compass** and **guidebook**
- ☐ **map case** or **clip-seal plastic bags**
- ☐ **toiletries**
- ☐ **pocket knife** (with corkscrew)
- ☐ **sunglasses** and **sunscreen**
- ☐ **survival bag** or **blanket**
- ☐ **toilet paper** and **toilet trowel**
- ☐ **torch** (flashlight) or **headlamp**, **spare batteries** and **globe**
- ☐ **water container**
- ☐ **whistle** (for emergencies)

Clothing

- ☐ **boots** and **spare laces**
- ☐ **gaiters**
- ☐ **hat** (warm), **scarf** and **gloves**
- ☐ **jacket** (waterproof and windproof)
- ☐ **overtrousers** (waterproof)
- ☐ **runners** (trainers), **sandals** or **thongs** (flip flops)
- ☐ **shorts** and **trousers** or **skirt**
- ☐ **socks** and **underwear**
- ☐ **sunhat**
- ☐ **sweater** or **fleece jacket**
- ☐ **thermal underwear**
- ☐ **T-shirt** and **shirt** (long-sleeved with collar)

Overnight Walks

- ☐ **dishwashing items**
- ☐ **insulating mat**
- ☐ **matches**, **lighter** and **candle**
- ☐ **portable stove** and **fuel**
- ☐ **sewing/repair kit**
- ☐ **sleeping bag** and **liner/inner sheet**
- ☐ **spare cord**
- ☐ **tent**, **pegs**, **poles** and **guy ropes**
- ☐ **towel** (small)
- ☐ **utensils** for cooking, eating and drinking
- ☐ **water purification tablets**, **iodine** or **filter**

Optional Items

- ☐ **altimeter**
- ☐ **backpack cover** (waterproof, slip-on)
- ☐ **binoculars**
- ☐ **camera**, **film** and **batteries**
- ☐ **day-pack**
- ☐ **emergency distress beacon****
- ☐ **GPS receiver*****
- ☐ **groundsheet** (lightweight)
- ☐ **mobile phone****
- ☐ **mosquito net**
- ☐ **notebook** and **pen/pencil**
- ☐ **swimming costume**
- ☐ **walking poles**
- ☐ **watch**

*See the boxed text 'First-Aid Check List' (p56)
**See Safety on the Walk (p61)
***See Navigation Equipment (p52)

NAVIGATION EQUIPMENT

Maps & Compass

You should always carry a good map of the area you are walking in (see Maps, pp46–7), and know how to read it. Before setting off on your walk, ensure that you understand the contours and the map symbols, plus the main ridge and river systems in the area. Also familiarise yourself with the true north-south directions and the general direction in which you are heading. On the trail, try to identify major landforms such as mountain ranges and gorges, and locate them on your map. This will give you a better understanding of the region's geography.

Buy a compass and learn how to use it. The attraction of magnetic north varies in different parts of the world, so compasses need to be balanced accordingly. Compass manufacturers have divided the world into five zones. Make sure your compass is balanced for your destination. There are also 'universal' compasses that can be used anywhere in the world.

How to Use a Compass

This is a very basic introduction to using a compass and will only be of assistance if you are proficient in map reading. For simplicity, it doesn't take magnetic variation into account. Before using a compass we recommend you obtain further instruction.

1. Reading a Compass

Hold the compass flat in the palm of your hand. Rotate the **bezel** so the **red end** of the needle points to the **N** on the bezel. The bearing is read from the **dash** under the bezel.

2. Orientating the Map

To orientate the map so that it aligns with the ground, place the compass flat on the map. Rotate the map until the **needle** is parallel with the map's north/south grid lines and the **red end** is pointing to north on the map. You can now identify features around you by aligning them with labelled features on the map.

3. Taking a Bearing from the Map

Draw a line on the map between your starting point and your destination. Place the edge of the compass on this line with the **direction of travel arrow** pointing towards your destination. Rotate the **bezel** until the **meridian lines** are parallel with the north/south grid lines on the map and the **N** points to north on the map. Read the bearing from the **dash**.

4. Following a Bearing

Rotate the **bezel** so that the intended bearing is in line with the **dash**. Place the compass flat in the palm of your hand and rotate the **base plate** until the **red end** points to **N** on the **bezel**. The **direction of travel arrow** will now point in the direction you need to walk.

5. Determining Your Bearing

Rotate the **bezel** so the **red end** points to the **N**. Place the compass flat in the palm of your hand and rotate the **base plate** until the **direction of travel arrow** points in the direction in which you have been tramping. Read your bearing from the **dash**.

1	Base plate
2	Direction of travel arrow
3	Dash
4	Bezel
5	Meridian lines
6	Needle
7	Red end
8	N (north point)

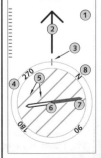

GPS

Originally developed by the US Department of Defence, the Global Positioning System (GPS) is a network of more than 20 earth-orbiting satellites that continually beam encoded signals back to earth. Small computer driven devices (GPS receivers) can decode these signals to give users an extremely accurate reading of their location – to within 30m anywhere on the planet, at any time of day, in almost any weather. The theoretical accuracy of the system increased at least tenfold in 2000, when a deliberate in-built error, intended to fudge the reading for all but US military users, was removed. The cheapest hand-held GPS receivers now cost less than US$100 (although they may have an in-built averaging system that minimises signal errors). Other important factors to consider are weight and battery life.

It should be understood that a GPS receiver is of little use to hikers unless used with an accurate topographical map – the GPS receiver simply gives your position, which you must locate on the local map. GPS receivers only work properly in the open. Directly below high cliffs, near large bodies of water or in dense tree-cover, for example, the signals from a crucial satellite may be blocked (or bounce off the rock or water) and give inaccurate readings. GPS receivers are more vulnerable to breakdowns (including dead batteries) than the humble magnetic compass – a low-tech device that has served navigators faithfully for centuries – so don't rely on them entirely.

Altimeter

Altimeters determine altitude by measuring air pressure. Because pressure is affected by temperature, altimeters are calibrated to take lower temperatures at higher altitudes into account. However, discrepancies can still occur, especially in unsettled weather, so it's wise to take a few precautions when using your altimeter.

1. Reset your altimeter regularly at known elevations such as spot heights and passes. Do not take spot heights from villages where there may be a large difference in elevation from one end of the settlement to another.

2. Use your altimeter in conjunction with other navigation techniques to fix your position. For instance, taking a back bearing to a known peak or river confluence, determining the general direction of the track and obtaining your elevation will usually give you a pretty good fix on your position.

Altimeters are also barometers and are useful for indicating changing weather conditions. If the altimeter shows increasing elevation while you are not climbing, it means the air pressure is dropping and a low-pressure weather system may be approaching.

[Continued from page 51]

Gaiters If you will be walking through snow, deep mud or scratchy scrub, consider using gaiters to protect your legs and keep your socks dry. The best are made of a strong fabric, with a robust zip protected by a flap, and with an easy-to-undo method of securing around the foot.

Socks The best walkers' socks are made of a hard-wearing mix of wool (70–80%) and synthetic (30–20%), free of ridged seams in the wrong places (heels and toes). Socks with a high proportion of wool are more comfortable when worn for several successive days without washing.

Sun Protection
Be sure to take a sun hat (preferably wide brimmed, with a chin strap) and sunglasses, especially when walking near snow, water or sand, where reflected light can cause unexpected sunburn, even on cloudy days.

Backpack
For day walks, a day-pack will usually suffice, but for multi-day walks you will need a backpack between 45L and 90L in capacity. It can be tough deciding whether to go for a smaller or bigger pack. This can depend on your destination and whether you plan to camp or stay in *refugios* (mountain huts or refuges). Your pack should be large enough so that you don't need to strap bits and pieces to the outside. However, if you buy a bigger pack than you really need there's the temptation to fill it. Its weight will increase and your enjoyment will decrease. Assemble the gear you intend to take and try loading it into a pack to see if it's big enough.

A good backpack should:

- be made of strong fabric such as canvas, Cordura or similar heavy-duty woven synthetic, with high-quality stitching, straps and buckles, a lightweight internal or external frame and resilient, smoothly sliding zips
- have an adjustable, well-padded harness that evenly distributes weight
- be water-resistant, with a minimum of external nooks and crannies for water to pool or seep

into; stitched seams can be treated with a sealant such as beeswax
- have a small number of internal and external pockets for easy access to frequently used items such as snacks and maps.

Even if the manufacturer claims your pack is waterproof, use heavy-duty liners (garden refuse bags are ideal; custom-made sacks are available).

Tent
A three-season tent will fulfil the requirements of most walkers. The floor and the outer shell, or fly, should have taped or sealed seams and covered zips to stop water leaking inside. Weight will be a major issue if you're carrying your own tent so a roomy tent may not be an option; most walkers find tents of around 2kg to 3kg (that will sleep two or three people) a comfortable carrying weight. Popular shapes include dome and tunnel, which are better able to handle windy conditions than are flat-sided tents.

Make sure you know how to pitch your tent before taking it away, and always check your poles and pegs are packed.

Sleeping Bag & Mat
Choose between down and synthetic fillings, and mummy and rectangular shapes according to your needs. Down is warmer than synthetic for the same weight and bulk but, unlike synthetic fillings, doesn't retain warmth when wet. Mummy bags are best for weight and warmth, but can be claustrophobic. Sleeping bags are rated by temperature. The given figure (-5°C, for instance) is the coldest temperature at which a person should feel comfortable in the bag. However, the ratings are notoriously unreliable. Work out the coldest temperature at which you anticipate sleeping, assess whether you're a warm or a cold sleeper, then choose a bag accordingly.

An inner sheet will help to keep your sleeping bag clean, as well as adding an insulating layer. These are usually compulsory in youth hostels. Silk 'inners' are the lightest, but they also come in cotton or polypropylene.

For camping, self-inflating sleeping mats are popular and work like a thin air cushion between you and the ground; they also insulate from the cold and are essential if sleeping on snow. Foam mats are a low-cost, but less comfortable, alternative.

Stove

Fuel stoves fall roughly into three categories: multifuel, methylated spirits (ethyl alcohol) or Shellite (white spirits), and butane gas.

Multifuel stoves are small, efficient and ideal for places where a reliable fuel supply can be hard to find. However, they tend to be noisy and sooty and require frequent maintenance.

Stoves running on methylated spirits are slower and less efficient, but safe, clean and easy to use.

Butane gas stoves are commonly sold in camping shops around the world. Although clean and reliable, they can be slow, and the gas canisters can be awkward to carry and a potential litter problem. They are also more wasteful of resources than liquid fuel.

Note that fuel cannot be carried on board aeroplanes.

In Spain, the most reliable option is to carry a butane/propane stove since their *cartuchos* (cartridges) are the only widely available fuel source. Some *droguerias* (shops selling household products) stock *alcohol de quemar* (methylated spirits).

Walking Poles

Think about packing a pair of lightweight telescopic poles. They help you balance and ease the jarring on your knees during steep descents.

Buying Gear

The best advice is to bring your gear with you. This said, Spain is a good place to pick up new items at reasonable prices – and if you're hiking through tax-free Andorra, bargains are even keener (see the Supplies & Equipment section under Andorra la Vella, p145). See also the Supplies & Equipment sections for Madrid (pp66–7) and Barcelona (pp96–7). If you need to top up en route, look for a *tienda de deportes* (sporting goods shop).

Health & Safety

Keeping healthy on the trail depends on your predeparture preparations, your daily health care while travelling and how you handle any medical problem that does develop. While the potential problems can seem quite frightening, in reality few travellers experience anything more than an upset stomach. The sections that follow aren't intended to alarm, but they are worth reading before you go.

PREDEPARTURE PLANNING
Medical Cover

Citizens of EU countries are covered for emergency medical care upon presentation of an E111 form, which you need to get before you travel. In Britain, you can pick one up free at a post office. In other EU countries, obtain information from your doctor or local health service.

Though the form will entitle you to free treatment in government clinics and hospitals, you will have to pay for dental treatment; any medicines bought from pharmacies, even if a doctor has prescribed them; and also possibly for tests. Once home, you may be able to recover some or all of these costs from your national health service.

Health Insurance

Make sure you have adequate health insurance. See Travel Insurance (p365) for details.

Physical Preparation

Some of the walks in this book are physically demanding and most require a reasonable level of fitness. Even if you're tackling the easy or easy–moderate walks, it pays to be relatively fit at the start of your trip, rather than launch straight into them after months of fairly sedentary living. If you're aiming for the demanding walks, fitness is essential.

Unless you're a regular walker, start your get-fit campaign about a month before your visit. Take a vigorous walk of about an hour two or three times per week and gradually extend the duration of your outings as the departure date nears. If you plan to carry a full backpack on any walk, carry a loaded pack on some of your training jaunts.

Immunisations

No immunisations are mandatory for Spain but before any trip it's a good idea to make sure you are up-to-date with routine vaccinations such as diphtheria, polio and tetanus.

First Aid

Detailed first-aid advice is outside the scope of this book but we've listed some basic points under Traumatic Injuries (p59). Read Safety on the Walk (p61) for suggestions

---

First-Aid Check List

Here is a list of items you should consider including in your first-aid kit – consult your pharmacist for brands available in your country.

- [ ] **adhesive tape**
- [ ] **bandages** and **safety pins**
- [ ] **elasticised support bandage** – for knees, ankles etc
- [ ] **small pair of scissors**
- [ ] **sticking plasters** (Band-Aids, blister plasters)

Medications

- [ ] **anti-diarrhoea** and **anti-nausea drugs antihistamines** – for allergies, eg, hay fever; to ease the itch from insect bites or stings; and to prevent motion sickness
- [ ] **antiseptic** (such as povidone-iodine) – for cuts and grazes
- [ ] **cold and flu tablets, throat lozenges** and **nasal decongestant**
- [ ] **painkillers** (eg, aspirin or paracetamol – acetaminophen in the USA) – for easing pain and fever

Miscellaneous

- [ ] **calamine lotion, sting relief spray** or **aloe vera** – to ease irritation from sunburn and insect bites or stings
- [ ] **insect repellent**
- [ ] **sunscreen** and **lip balm**
- [ ] **eye drops** – for washing out dust
- [ ] **water purification tablets** or **iodine**

about preventing accidents and illness. Rescue & Evacuation (see p62) tells you how to summon help if there's a major accident.

Other Preparations

If you have any known medical problems or are concerned about your health in any way, it's a good idea to have a full check up before you travel. If you wear glasses, take a spare pair and your prescription.

If you need a particular medicine, take enough with you to last the trip. Take part of the packaging showing the generic name, rather than the brand, as this will make getting replacements easier. It's also a good idea to have a legible prescription or letter from your doctor to prove that you legally use the medication to avoid any problems as you pass through customs.

Travel Health Guides

If you are planning to be walking in remote areas for some time, you might consider taking a more detailed health guide such as:

Medicine for Mountaineering, by James A Wilkerson, is an outstanding reference book for the layperson. It describes many of the medical problems typically encountered while walking.
The Mountain Traveller's Handbook, by Paul Deegan, includes chapters giving medical and safety advice as well as valuable information on all aspects of travelling in mountainous regions.

Digital Resources

You can find a number of excellent travel health sites on the Internet. From the Lonely Planet home page there are links at ⓦ www .lonelyplanet.com/health/ to the World Health Organization and many other sites.

STAYING HEALTHY
Hygiene

To reduce the chances of contracting an illness, you should wash your hands frequently, particularly before handling or eating food.

Water

Tap water in Spain is almost invariably safe and bottled water or soft drinks are fine.

Water Purification The simplest way of purifying water is to boil it thoroughly. Vigorous boiling should be satisfactory; however, at high altitude water boils at a lower temperature, so germs are less likely to be killed. Boil it for longer up high.

You can also use a chemical agent to purify water. Chlorine and iodine are reliable, whether in powder, tablet or liquid form, and are available from outdoor equipment suppliers and pharmacies. Allow the water to stand for the recommended time. Iodine is more effective but too much can be harmful.

Consider purchasing a water filter. There are two main kinds. Total filters take out all parasites, bacteria and viruses and make water safe to drink. They are expensive but over the years they're more cost effective than buying bottled water. Simple filters (which can be a nylon mesh bag) take out dirt and larger foreign bodies so that chemical solutions work much more effectively; if water is dirty, chemical solutions may not work at all. When buying a filter, read the specifications to find out exactly what it removes from the water and what it doesn't.

Food

Nutrition If your food is poor you can soon start to lose weight and place your health at risk.

Make sure your diet is well balanced. Cooked eggs, meat, tofu, beans, lentils and nuts are all reliable ways to get protein. Fruit is a good source of vitamins. Eat plenty of grains, such as rice, and bread. For longer treks, consider taking vitamin and iron pills.

Common Ailments

Blisters You don't have to limp. Make sure your boots are well worn in before you travel. Wear them on a few short walks before tackling longer outings. They should fit comfortably with enough room to move your toes; ones that are too big or too small will cause blisters. Be sure your socks fit snugly and are specifically made for walkers; even then, check to make sure that there are no seams across the widest part of your foot. Wet and muddy socks induce blisters so even on a day walk pack a spare pair. Keep your toenails clipped but not too short. If you do feel a blister coming on, treat it sooner rather than later. Apply a simple sticking plaster, or preferably one of the special blister plasters that act as a second skin.

Fatigue A simple statistic: most injuries happen towards the end of the day, when you're tired. Although tiredness can simply be a nuisance on an easy walk, it can be life-threatening on narrow exposed ridges or in bad weather. Don't set out on a walk that's beyond your capabilities. If you feel below par, have a day off or take a bus. Don't push yourself; it's sensible to take rests every hour or two – and build in a good half hour's lunch break. Towards the end of the day, take down the pace and increase your concentration. Nibble throughout the day to replace the energy used up; nuts, dried fruit, chocolate and the Spanish favourite, *turrón* (honey and almond nougat) are all good energy snacks.

Knee Pain Many walkers feel the judder on long steep descents. When dropping steeply, to reduce the strain on the knee joint (you can't eliminate it), try taking shorter steps that leave your legs slightly bent and ensure that your heel hits the ground before the rest of your foot. Some walkers find that tubular bandages help, while others use hi-tech, strap-on supports. Walking poles are very effective in taking some of the weight off the knees.

MEDICAL PROBLEMS & TREATMENT

We use generic rather than brand names for drugs throughout this section – check with a pharmacist for locally available brands. Although we do give drug advice in this section, it is for emergency use only. Correct diagnosis is vital.

Environmental Hazards

Altitude Lack of oxygen at high altitudes (over 2500m) affects most people to some extent. The effect may be mild or severe and occurs because less oxygen reaches the muscles and the brain at high altitude, requiring the heart and lungs to compensate

---

Everyday Health

Normal body temperature is up to 37°C (98.6°F); more than 2°C (4°F) higher indicates a high fever. The normal adult pulse rate is 60 to 100 per minute. As a general rule the pulse increases about 20 beats per minute for each 1°C (2°F) rise in fever.

Breathing rate is also an indicator of illness. Count the number of breaths per minute: between 12 and 20 is normal for adults and older children. People with a high fever or serious respiratory illness breathe more quickly than normal. More than 40 shallow breaths a minute may indicate pneumonia.

---

by working harder. Mild symptoms include headache, lethargy, dizziness, difficulty sleeping and loss of appetite. Treat them by resting at the same altitude until recovery, usually only a day or two.

Sun Always protect yourself against the sun. In the rarefied air and deceptive coolness of the mountains, sunburn occurs rapidly. Slap on the sunscreen and a barrier cream for your nose and lips, wear a broad-brimmed hat and protect your eyes with good-quality sunglasses with lenses that filter out UV rays, particularly when walking near water, sand or snow. If you get burnt, calamine lotion, aloe vera or other commercial sunburn-relief preparations will soothe.

Heat Take time to acclimatise to high temperatures, drink sufficient liquids and don't do anything too physically demanding until you are acclimatised.

Prickly Heat This is a nasty itchy rash caused by excessive perspiration trapped under the skin. Keeping cool, bathing often, drying the skin and using a mild talcum or prickly heat powder may help.

Dehydration & Heat Exhaustion Dehydration is usually caused by sweating combined with inadequate fluid intake. Other important causes are diarrhoea, vomiting, and high fever. See Diarrhoea (p59) for more details about appropriate treatment. Symtoms are weakness, thirst and passing small amounts of very concentrated urine.

It's easy to forget how much fluid you sweat out, particularly if a strong breeze is drying your skin. Keep up a good fluid intake – as much as 3L per day.

Dehydration and salt deficiency can cause heat exhaustion. Signs of salt deficiency are fatigue, lethargy, headaches, giddiness and muscle cramps. Taking salt tablets is overkill; just adding extra salt to your food is probably sufficient.

Cold Too much cold can be just as dangerous as too much heat.

Hypothermia This occurs when the body loses heat faster than it can produce it and the core temperature of the body falls.

It is frighteningly easy to progress from very cold to dangerously cold because of a combination of wind, wet clothing, fatigue and hunger, even if the air temperature is above freezing. If the weather deteriorates, put on extra layers of warm clothing: a wind-and/or waterproof jacket, plus wool or fleece hat and gloves are essential. Have something energy-giving to eat and ensure that everyone in your group is fit, feeling well and alert.

Symptoms of hypothermia are exhaustion, numb skin (particularly fingers and toes), shivering, slurred speech, irrational or violent behaviour, lethargy, stumbling, dizzy spells, muscle cramps and violent bursts of energy. Even so, sufferers may claim they are warm and try to rip off their clothes.

To treat mild hypothermia, get the person out of the wind and/or rain, remove clothing if it's wet and replace it with something dry and warm. Give them hot liquids – not alcohol – and some high-energy, easily digestible food. Don't rub victims: instead, allow them to slowly warm themselves.

Infectious Diseases
Diarrhoea Simple things like a change of water, food or climate can cause a mild bout of diarrhoea, but a rushed toilet trip or two is no big deal. If you pay attention to personal hygiene, drink purified water and watch what you eat, your trekking will probably be trouble-free, intestinally speaking.

Should you get the runs, *fluid replacement* (at least equal to the volume being lost) is important. Weak black tea with a little sugar, soda water, or soft drinks allowed to go flat and diluted 50% with water are all good. For severe diarrhoea, oral rehydration salts (ORS) are very useful. In an emergency you can make up a solution of six teaspoons of sugar and half a teaspoon of salt to a litre of boiled or bottled water. Urine is the best guide to the adequacy of replacement – if you have small amounts of concentrated urine, drink more. Keep drinking small amounts often and stick to a bland diet as you recover.

Gut-paralysing drugs such as diphenoxylate or loperamide can bring relief from the symptoms although they don't cure the problem. Only use these drugs if you do not have access to toilets, eg, if you *must* travel. These drugs are not recommended for children under 12 years, or if you have a high fever or are severely dehydrated.

Fungal Infections Sweating liberally, probably washing less than usual and going longer without a change of clothes mean that long-distance walkers risk picking up a fungal infection, which, while an unpleasant irritant, presents no danger.

Fungal infections are encouraged by moisture. So wear loose, comfortable clothes, wash when you can and dry yourself thoroughly. Try to expose the infected area to air or sunlight as much as possible and apply an antifungal cream or powder like tolnaftate.

Traumatic Injuries
Sprains Ankle and knee sprains are common injuries among walkers, particularly on rugged terrain. To prevent ankle sprains, wear boots with adequate support. If you do suffer a sprain, immobilise the joint with a firm bandage, and immerse the foot in cold water. Once the walk is over, keep it elevated for the first 24 hours and, if you can, put ice on the swollen joint. Take painkillers to ease the discomfort. For severe sprains, seek medical attention as an X-ray may be needed to find out whether a bone has been broken.

How to Prevent Mosquito & Midge Bites

- wear light-coloured clothing
- wear long trousers and long-sleeved shirts
- use mosquito repellents containing the compound DEET on exposed areas
- avoid perfumes or aftershave
- impregnate clothes with permethrin as this deters mosquitoes and other insects

Major Accident Falling or having something fall on you, resulting in head injuries or fractures, is always possible when walking, especially if you are crossing steep slopes or unstable terrain. Following is some basic advice on what to do if a major accident does occur. If a person suffers a major fall:

1. make sure you and other people with you are not in danger
2. assess the injured person's condition
3. stabilise any injuries, such as bleeding wounds or broken bones
4. seek medical attention – see Rescue & Evacuation (p62), for details

If the victim is unconscious, immediately check whether they are breathing – clear their airway if it is blocked – and whether they have a pulse – feel the side of the neck rather than the wrist. If they are not breathing but have a pulse, start mouth-to-mouth resuscitation immediately. It's best to move the person as little as possible in case their neck or back is broken. Keep them warm with a blanket or other dry clothing and insulate them from the ground.

Check for wounds and broken bones – ask where the pain is if the victim is conscious. Otherwise gently inspect them all over (including their back and the back of the head), moving them as little as possible. Control any bleeding by applying firm pressure to the wound. Bleeding from the nose or ear may indicate a fractured skull. Don't give the person anything by mouth, especially if they are unconscious.

Indications of a broken bone are pain, swelling and discoloration, loss of function or deformity of a limb. Don't try to straighten an obviously displaced broken bone. To protect from further injury, immobilise a fracture by splinting it; for fractures of the thigh bone, try to straighten the leg gently, then tie it to the good leg to hold it in place. Fractures accompanied by open wounds need more urgent treatment since there's a risk of infection. Dislocations, where the bone has come out of the joint, are very painful, and should be set as soon as possible.

Broken ribs are painful but usually heal by themselves and do not need splinting. If breathing difficulties occur, or the person coughs up blood, seek medical attention urgently as this may indicate a punctured lung.

Internal injuries are more difficult to detect. Watch for shock; signs include a rapid pulse and cold, clammy extremities. A person in shock requires urgent medical attention.

Here are some general points worth bearing in mind:

- Simple fractures don't need fixing straight away but they should be immobilised to protect them from further injury. Compound fractures need much more urgent treatment.
- If you do have to splint a broken bone, check regularly that the splint doesn't cut off circulation to the hand or foot.
- Brief unconsciousness rarely implies serious injury to the brain. All the same, anyone knocked unconscious should be watched for deterioration.

Cuts & Scratches

Wash and treat with antiseptic even small cuts and grazes. Dry wounds heal more quickly so avoid bandages and plasters that keep wounds wet. A sign of infection is the skin margins of the wound becoming red, painful and swollen. More serious infection can cause swelling of the whole limb and of the lymph glands. The patient may develop a fever, and will need medical attention.

Bites & Stings

Bedbugs These critters live particularly in dirty mattresses and bedding, evidenced by spots of blood on bedclothes or on the wall. Bedbugs leave itchy bites in neat rows. Calamine lotion or a sting relief spray may help.

Bees & Wasps These are usually painful rather than dangerous. Calamine lotion or a commercial sting relief spray will ease discomfort and ice packs will reduce the pain and swelling.

Lice All lice cause itching and discomfort. They make themselves at home in your hair (head lice), your clothing (body lice) or in your pubic hair (crabs). You catch lice through direct contact with infected people or by sharing combs, clothing and the like. Powder or shampoo treatment will kill the lice and infected clothing should then be washed in very hot, soapy water and left in the sun to dry.

Snakes To minimise your chances of being bitten always wear boots, socks and long trousers when walking through undergrowth where snakes may be present.

Snake bites do not cause instantaneous death and antivenins are usually available. Immediately wrap the bitten limb tightly, and attach a splint to immobilise it. Keep the victim still and seek medical help, if possible with the dead snake for identification. Tourniquets and sucking out the poison are now comprehensively discredited.

Ticks Most active from spring to autumn, especially where there are plenty of sheep, ticks can cause skin infections and other more serious diseases. They usually lurk in overhanging vegetation, so try to avoid pushing through tall bushes and stay clear of sheep and their haunts.

If you have a tick, suffocate the bastard in cooking oil and watch it drop off, limp and dead. Another approach is to press down around the tick's head with tweezers, grab the head and gently pull upwards. Avoid pulling the rear of the body as this may squeeze the gut contents through its mouth into your skin, increasing the risk of infection.

Women's Health
Walking is not particularly hazardous to your health. However, women's health issues can be a bit trickier to cope with when you are on the trail.

Menstruation A change in diet, routine and environment, as well as intensive exercise,

may lead to irregularities in your menstrual cycle. It's particularly important during the menstrual cycle to maintain good personal hygiene. Anti-bacterial hand gel or pre-moistened wipes can be useful if you don't have access to soap and water. Because of hygiene concerns and for ease while on an extended trip, some women prefer to temporarily stop menstruation; discuss your options with a doctor before you go.

Thrush (Vaginal Candidiasis) Antibiotic use, synthetic underwear, tight trousers, sweating, contraceptive pills and unprotected sex can lead to fungal vaginal infections. The most common is thrush (vaginal candidiasis). Symptoms include itching and discomfort in the genital area, often in association with a thick white discharge. The best prevention is to keep the vaginal area cool and dry and to wear cotton, rather than synthetic, underwear and loose clothes. Treat thrush with clotrimazole pessaries, or a vaginal cream or, if these are not available, a vinegar or lemon-juice douche or yoghurt. To prevent thrush, eat fresh yoghurt regularly or consider taking acidophilus tablets.

Urinary Tract Infection Dehydration and 'hanging on' can result in urinary tract infection and cystitis. Symptoms include burning when urinating and having to go frequently and urgently. Sometimes there's blood in the urine. Drink plenty of fluids and urinate regularly. If symptoms persist, seek medical attention because a simple infection can spread to the kidneys, causing a more severe illness.

SAFETY ON THE WALK
You can significantly reduce the chance of getting into difficulties with a few simple precautions. See the boxed text 'Walk Safety – Basic Rules', (p62). For suggestions on recommended clothing and equipment see the boxed text 'Check List' (p51).

Crossing Rivers
Sudden downpours are common in the mountains and can speedily turn a gentle stream into a raging torrent. If you're in any doubt about the safety of a crossing, look for a safer

Walk Safety – Basic Rules

- Allow plenty of time to accomplish a walk before dark, particularly when daylight hours are shorter.
- Study the route carefully before setting out, noting the possible escape routes and the point of no return (where it's quicker to continue than to turn back). Monitor your progress during the day against the time estimated for the walk, and keep an eye on the weather.
- It's wise not to walk alone. Leave details of your intended route, the number of people in your group, and expected return time with someone responsible before you set off; let that person know when you return.
- Before setting off, make sure you have a relevant map, compass and whistle, and that you know the weather forecast for the next 24 hours. A GPS receiver can also be useful.

passage upstream or wait. If the rain is short-lived the waters should subside quickly.

If you have to cross, look for a wide, relatively shallow stretch of the stream rather than a bend. Take off your trousers and socks, but keep your boots on to prevent injury. Put dry, warm clothes and a towel in a plastic bag near the top of your pack. Before stepping out from the bank, unclip your chest strap and belt buckle. This makes it easier to slip out of your backpack and swim to safety if you lose your balance and are swept downstream. Use a walking pole, grasped in both hands, on the upstream side as a third leg, or go arm in arm with a companion, clasping at the wrist, and cross side-on to the flow, taking short steps.

Dogs

Regard any dog as a potential attacker and be prepared to take evasive action: even just crossing the road can take you out of its territory and into safety. A judiciously applied walking pole can work wonders...

Lightning

If a storm brews, avoid exposed areas. Lightning seeks out crests, lone trees, small depressions, gullies, caves and cabin entrances, as well as wet ground. If you're caught in the open, curl up in a ball and keep a layer of insulation between you and the ground. Place metal objects such as metal-frame backpacks and walking poles well away from you.

Rescue & Evacuation

If a member of your group is injured or falls ill and can't move, leave somebody with them while others go for help. They should take clear written details of the location and condition of the victim, and of helicopter landing conditions. If there are only two of you, leave the injured person with warm clothing, food and water, plus a whistle and torch (flashlight). Mark the position with something conspicuous – say, an orange bivvy bag or a large stone cross on the ground.

Emergency Communications Whatever the crisis, a call to ☎ 112 will alert the emergency services. However, don't expect your mobile phone to elicit action up high in the mountains; often as not, there's no coverage. Some walkers carry an emergency distress beacon, which transmits an internationally recognised distress signal when activated.

Distress Signals If you need to call for help, use these internationally recognised emergency signals. Give six short signals, such as a whistle, a yell or flash of a light, at 10-second intervals, followed by a minute of rest. Repeat the sequence until you get a response. If the responder knows the signals, this will be three signals at 20-second intervals, a minute's pause and a repeat of the sequence.

Helicopter Rescue & Evacuation If a helicopter arrives on the scene, there are a couple of conventions you should be familiar with. Standing face on to the chopper:

- Arms up in the shape of a letter 'V' means 'I/We need help'
- Arms in a straight diagonal line (like one line of a letter X) means 'All OK'

For the helicopter to land, there must be a cleared space of 25m x 25m, with a flat landing pad area of 6m x 6m. The helicopter will fly into the wind when landing. In cases of extreme emergency, where no landing area is available, a harness might be lowered.

Sistema Central

There's more to central Spain than Don Quixote, windmills and vast wheat fields. A spine of 2200m-plus mountains called the Sistema Central rises rather unexpectedly from the *meseta* (high tableland) of Castilla y León and Castilla-La Mancha, providing an oasis of delightful alpine wilderness among the sometimes-bleak expanse of Spain's heartland. A short drive from Madrid the well-watered valleys and rugged peaks are extremely popular with *madrileños* (people living in Madrid), but these attractions are little known by foreign tourists.

The Sierra de Gredos forms the western and most dramatic section of the Sistema Central and is the target for mountaineers and climbers as well as walkers in search of dramatic ridge traverses. The Sierra de Guadarrama, while less grand than its western neighbour, is a very popular weekend getaway and winter ski destination, but La Pedriza and the GR10 offer some rewarding challenges for walkers.

This chapter describes many of the most spectacular walks in the Sistema Central. Some walks include popular tourist routes, but rest assured there's fantastic scope for getting well off the beaten track. Walk times given include actual walking time only, not rest, eating or sightseeing stops.

HISTORY

Evidence of Neolithic and Celtic peoples has been found on the southern slopes of the range. Generally speaking, the history of the Sistema Central reflects events unfolding in the *meseta* and rest of Spain, with the region resisting and succumbing to numerous invasions over the centuries, and repeatedly changing hands. The mountain terrain made an ideal base for guerrilla activity against the forces of Napoleon and Franco.

In 1978 Spain became a constitutional monarchy and a process of decentralisation began. Now the Sistema Central is governed by four regions: Castilla-La Mancha, Castilla y León (which has authority over most of

Highlights

MATT FLETCHER

Balancing rock formations in the spectacular terrain of La Pedriza

- Looking over the Circo de Gredos, the savage cliffs of Los Tres Hermanitos and Almanzor from the El Morezón ridge, on the Alta Ruta de Gredos walk (p70)

- Walking across the ridge from Covacha and exploring the western Gredos on the Covacha Walk (p76)

- Wondering through Hoyo Moros, a beautiful glacial corrie below Calvitero, on the Sierra de Candelario walk (p80)

- Exploring the eroded rock formations, fallen boulders, tall spires and narrow gullies of La Pedriza on the Cuerda Larga walk (p88)

the Sierra de Gredos), Extremadura and the Comunidad de Madrid (which governs the Sierra de Guadarrama). Recently these new authorities began promoting rural tourism in an effort to bring money and employment into the mountains.

SISTEMA CENTRAL

Sistema Central

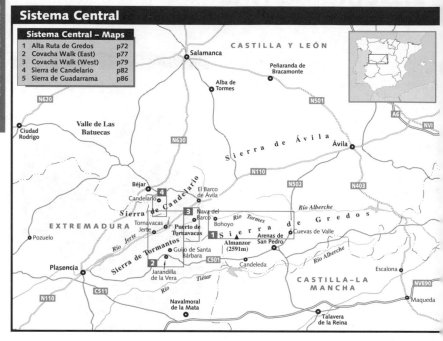

NATURAL HISTORY

Formed more than 300 million years ago in the late Palaeozoic period, then resculpted 275 million years later, the Sistema Central is divided by the Río Alberche into the western Sierra de Gredos and eastern Sierra de Guadarrama. The geology of the range (predominantly granite plus some gneiss and the odd seam of quartz) means springs well up close to the summits. These water sources and snowmelt from the highest peaks keep the valleys well watered year-round.

Massive glaciers carved many of the valleys in the range during the last Ice Age 10,000 years ago (glaciation is obvious in the central Gredos, far less so in the Guadarrama), then the landscape remained unchanged until the Middle Ages when humans began to make a significant impact on the environment. Until then the Sistema Central had a thick cover of deciduous trees such as holm, Pyrenean and cork oaks, with indigenous Scots pine appearing on the higher slopes. Only remnants of these forests survive today, mostly in river valleys and inaccessible areas. In places ancient forests have been replaced with black or Corsican pine plantations, but a wide range of animals and plants is still found.

CLIMATE

The Sistema Central has a climate of extremes: fiercely hot summers and bitterly cold winters with icy northerly winds. However, unlike the surrounding *meseta* (that often receives less than 400mm of rain each year) the mountains are well watered, with between 1000mm and 1500mm of precipitation annually, a good third of it falling as snow in winter and the rest as heavy showers in autumn and spring.

Winter walkers should be prepared for blizzard conditions, while in autumn and spring the weather can change quickly, with low cloud bringing plummeting temperatures, fierce winds and almost horizontal

freezing rain. These occasional storms can occur until mid-June when the last of the snow should have melted from the highest peaks and gullies. Indeed, many *madrileños* believe that the weather only becomes predictable after 1 June, which *should* bring three months of cloudless skies.

The Sierra de Guadarrama is usually snow-free earlier than the Gredos, its higher and grander neighbour, whose high passes and north-facing gullies can be affected by snow until July.

INFORMATION
Maps
The IGN Mapas Provinciales 1:200,000 *Ávila*, *Cáceres* and *Madrid* cover the Sistema Central, but for general planning check out Michelin's 1:400,000 map No 444 *Central Spain*.

Buying Maps Some maps may be available in Access or Nearest Towns (shops are listed), but Madrid is *the* place for map shopping.

La Tienda Verde (☎ 91 533 07 91, fax 91 533 64 54; W *www.tiendaverde.org; Calle Maudes 38; metro Cuatro Caminos*) is probably the best-stocked walking and mountaineering map shop in Madrid. The staff are knowledgeable and the company publishes an expanding range of own-brand walking maps and guides.

Librería Desnivel (☎ 902 24 88 48; W *www .libreriadesnivel.com; Plaza Matute 6; metro Antón Martín*) is also excellent (and possibly better for books).

Books
Mountains of Central Spain, by Jacqueline Oglesby, provides in-depth coverage of day walks in the Sistema Central.

Information Sources
For information about walking in the Sistema Central contact the national or local mountaineering federations. For details on the former see Useful Organisations (p47). Organisations in Madrid include:

Federación Madrileña de Montañismo (☎ 91 527 38 01, fax 91 528 09 31, W www.fmm.es) Calle Ferrocaril 22. It includes the Escuela Madrileña de Alta Montaña.
Grupo de Montaña del CSIC (☎ 91 547 77 06, fax 91 541 81 95, W www.gmcsic.csic.es) Calle Hileras 4
Montañeros Madrileños CAM (☎/fax 91 518 70 72, W www.montmadrid.org) Carretera Boadilla del Monte 21
RSEA Peñalara (☎ 91 522 87 43, fax 91 522 52 59, W www.penalara.org) Calle Aduana 17

The websites of these organisations contain much useful information about weather, *refugios* (mountain huts or refuges) and events; many offices are open weekday evenings.

Guided Walks
Several groups run trips in Sistema Central:

Espacioaccion (☎ 91 578 00 33, e espacio accion@infornet.es) Calle Marcelino Álvarez 6, Madrid. The speciality here is climbing (including ice) and mountaineering. The company has an indoor climbing wall in Madrid.

Tierra de Fuego (☎ 91 521 52 40, e tierrafuego@ inicia.es) Calle Pizarro 20, Madrid. This company has a solid reputation and operates a good **map and bookshop** (☎ 91 521 39 62, Calle Pez 21; metro Tribunal).

Trancos (☎/fax 91 521 72 79, w www.trancos rutas.com) Calle Montera 9, Madrid. This company organises day walks in the Guadarrama, plus occasional longer walks elsewhere in Spain.

Turismo Activo (☎/fax 920 34 83 85, w www .turactiv.com, La Fragua, Barajas, Navarredonda de Gredos, Ávila). This operator runs all kinds of adventure and nature activities in the Gredos, from cross-country skiing to mushroom gathering.

GATEWAY
Madrid

The major walking areas of the Sistema Central are within easy reach of Spain's capital, which has some good outdoor shops and information sources. Packed with bars and restaurants, Madrid is a great place to spend a few days; few people have rest and recuperation on their minds at the weekend, when the city doesn't sleep much before dawn.

Madrid also has a host of good parks and open spaces, famous art galleries and numerous open-air swimming pools.

Information For city information head to the **tourist information office** (general inquiries ☎ 902 10 00 07, this office ☎ 91 588 16 36; w www.comadrid.es/turismo; Plaza Mayor; metro Sol). Other branches are found at Chamartín and Atocha train stations, and Aeropuerto de Barajas. For information about getting around the city and surrounding area check out w www.ctm-madrid.es or call ☎ 012.

Supplies & Equipment There's a cluster of walking and mountaineering shops at the top of Calle Ribera de Curtidores (metro Tirso de Molina). At No 1 is the excellent **Casa de la Montaña** (☎ 91 506 10 14); other good bets are **Base: Alcazar Sports** (☎ 91 467 35 11) at No 6 and **Lepazpi** (☎ 91 527 04 37) at No 8. **Gonza Sport** (☎ 91 527 57 48), at Nos 10 and 15, caters for winter and water sports.

Places to Stay & Eat Although Madrid has hundreds of *pensiones* (guesthouses), hostels and hotels, finding accommodation can be a problem between July and September.

Camping Osuna (☎ 91 741 05 10, fax 91 320 63 65; Avenida de Logroño; camping per person/tent/car €4.40/4.40/4.40), near the airport, is about 500m from metro Canillejas; walk north across Avenida de América and then follow Avenida de Logroño. If coming from the airport, bus No 101 sails right past.

Los Amigos (☎/fax 91 547 17 07; w www .losamigoshostel.com; Calle Campomanes 6; metro Opera; dorm beds €15) is one of Madrid's only 'backpacker-style' places. Rates include a light breakfast. Left luggage costs €3 per day.

Hostal Delvi (☎ 91 522 59 98; 3rd floor, Plaza de Santa Ana 15; metro Antón Martín; singles/doubles €18/30) is close to one of the liveliest districts in Madrid. There are dozens of other similar places in this area, which is a 20-minute walk from Atocha station.

Hotel Mónaco (☎ 91 522 46 30, fax 91 521 16 01; Calle de Barbieri 5; metro Chueca; singles/doubles €51.50/71) has a famously salubrious past and quite a gaudy present. Rooms are nice, and quirky.

Hotel Arosa (☎ 91 532 16 00; e arosa@ hotelarosa.com; Calle Salud 21; metro Gran Vía; singles/doubles €113/174), just off the Gran Vía, is upmarket and in a great location. Ask about cheap weekend deals.

Madrid is absolutely packed with places to eat and drink and it's relatively easy to find a restaurant offering a three-course *menú del día* (fixed-price meal) for less than €8.

La Finca de Susana (Calle Arlabán 4; metro Sol) has a varied *menú* of stylish Spanish dishes (including some vegetarian options) and you can eat really well for €15. Reservations are not possible so get there before 9pm.

Expensive, but good fun, are a clutch of bars/tapas places off Plaza de Santa Ana. Try **Viva Madrid** (Calle de Manuel Fernández y González 7), **Los Gabrieles** (Calle de Echegaray 7) and **España Cañí** (Plaza del Ángel 14). They're ideal places to kick off an evening.

Getting There & Away Hundreds of international flights arrive daily at Madrid's

Aeropuerto de Barajas, 13km northeast of the city and, as you might expect, there are bus and train connections to a huge number of destinations across Spain, including most of the Gateways mentioned in this book.

Madrid has two main train stations: **Atocha** (☎ *91 506 68 46*), south of the city centre, which serves areas south of Madrid; and **Chamartín** (☎ *91 300 69 69*), in the north, which handles destinations north of Madrid (and international departures). *Cercanía* (short-range suburban trains) and *trens regionales* (regional trains) services to the Sistema Central usually leave from Chamartín.

Madrid's main bus station is **Estación Sur de Autobuses** (☎ *91 468 42 00; metro Méndez Álvaro*), although other buses leave from **Estación de Conde de Casal** (☎ *91 551 56 01; metro Conde de Casal)* and **Intercambiador de Ave de América** (☎ *91 745 63 00; metro Ave de América).*

For information on travelling between Madrid and destinations inside and outside Spain see Getting Around (p372), and Getting There & Away (p370).

Sierra de Gredos

This majestic and dramatic range consists of three overlapping ridges beginning in Extremadura and stretching northeast towards the Sierra de Guadarrama in the Comunidad de Madrid. The central section of the Gredos, stretching for 55km from Puerto del Pico (1391m) in the east to Puerto de Tornavacas (1274m) in the west, is the highest and most rugged of the lot; at its heart lies the Reserva Nacional del Macizo Central de Gredos, a 230-sq-km hunting reserve.

The two sides of the range differ greatly. On the northern side are stunning glacial valleys with clear turquoise lakes and rich *cervunales* (summer pastures) that lead through rolling *paramera* (moorland) down to the Río Tormes valley (running east to west) at 1500m to 1000m above sea level.

To the south, the terrain drops rapidly past the formidable barrier of dark, jagged pinnacles and fantastic granite cliffs to the villages of the Río Tiétar valley, 500m above sea level.

Bus services operate along both sides of the range and there's plenty of accommodation in the villages plus a network of *refugios* in the mountains. Great camp sites abound.

While the Gredos might be dismissed as minor league by aficionados of the Pyrenees and Picos de Europa, the area has undeniable attraction – principally the accessibility of a beautiful and rugged alpine landscape and the variety of challenges presented by this small and relatively underpopulated area. Long ridge walks, peak bagging, leisurely strolls and serious mountaineering can all be undertaken here, just a short journey from Madrid. The popular areas receive hundreds of visitors, but a short walk up to a high ridge will leave the crowds behind.

HISTORY

The southern slopes of the Sierra de Gredos have been settled since the Iron Age. While Roman settlement in the area was limited, the road over Puerto del Pico remains as testament to their presence. It wasn't until after the Reconquista that permanent colonisation of the northern slopes began and the native oak forests were cleared cultivating vegetables, cereals, olives and vines on the southern slopes and rearing sheep on the northern side, a pattern of land use that continued until relatively recently.

The high mountains were exclusively the domain of shepherds and hunters until 1834 when the first recorded exploration of the mountains took place. However, it was not until 1899 that Almanzor was climbed.

More general interest in the Gredos began with Alfonso XIII, who liked to hunt in the region. He worked to protect dwindling stocks of Gredos ibex (see the boxed text 'The Gredos Ibex', p68) and in 1926 actively encouraged the building of Spain's first parador (luxury state hotel) in Navarredonda, though mountaineering *refugios* had been established in the area 10 years before (sadly, many are now in ruins).

In the 1970s the region was 'discovered' by tourists and today tourism is highly concentrated around the Plataforma trailhead and Laguna Grande; this has had a negative impact on these environments.

NATURAL HISTORY

From late spring the slopes of the Gredos are ablaze with flowers including region-specific crocuses such as St Bernard's and martagon lilies, and scented thickets of rock roses. Two regional endemics are *Reseda gredensis*, which has slender, white flower spikes, and the pale yellow-flowered snapdragon.

The granite uplands supports a wide variety of heather and shrubs including two species of broom: one with white, pea-like flowers and the other with more characteristic yellow flowers (the latter forms dense waist-high cover and is the bane of walkers).

Several species of eagle are found in the Gredos: Spanish imperial (with a white crown and mantle); Bonelli's (quite rare); golden; booted; and short-toed. Griffons and black vultures soar above the peaks, while the mountains are one of the few havens for azure-winged magpies. Rock buntings (with striped heads) are seen at higher altitudes and occasionally red-legged partridges appear.

The Reserva Nacional del Macizo Central de Gredos helps protect a subspecies of Spanish ibex (see the boxed text 'The Gredos Ibex'), as well as the rare pardel lynx, civets, wild boars, fallow and red deer.

The venomous scowling viper is found locally. Other reptiles include the Iberian rock lizard, the striking turquoise-and-black mottled *verdinegro* lizard (found above 2000m) and the eyed or jewelled lizard (up to 80cm long, with beautifully blue spots on a green-and-brown back).

PLANNING
When to Walk

Facilities and bus schedules are geared towards July and August visitors, when the shore of Laguna Grande becomes a sea of campers and intense heat plagues ascents from the south. Snow permitting, the best time to walk is late June or September, when the crowds aren't around (Elola and Reguero Llano *refugios* are open daily from the beginning of June to the end of September). Avoid the busy summer weekends.

What to Bring

Bring all equipment and supplies from Madrid and wear a strong pair of boots. Few people bother to pitch a tent in summer – a three-season sleeping bag and mat will usually suffice, but check the weather forecast!

Maps & Books

For planning, Adrados Ediciones' 1:135,000 *Parque Regional de la Sierra de Gredos* map is best – the 1:25,000 enlargement of

The Gredos Ibex

You are almost guaranteed to see the Gredos ibex while walking in the Sierra de Gredos. Large numbers of animals graze the remote high pastures at dawn and dusk. Males and females live in separate herds, except during the rut between November and January. Herds of females and young can number up to 30; male mixed-age groups are smaller, while old males are solitary and can often be seen perched on seemingly inaccessible peaks, silhouetted against the sky

An endemic subspecies of the Spanish ibex, the Gredos ibex is a small, agile mountain goat with large eyes, a medium-brown coat, black markings and lighter areas on the neck and thighs. You'll often hear the animals' warning signal (a short, piercing whistle) before you see them.

At the beginning of the 20th century the Gredos ibex was hunted almost to extinction. The species was saved by King Alfonso XIII, who liked hunting the beautiful animals so much that in 1905 he declared the heart of the Gredos a *coto real* (royal hunting reserve, now known as Reserva Nacional del Macizo Central de Gredos) to protect the last stock. For the ibex it was a perverse kind of salvation, but since then the population has increased from a low point of fewer than 10 to around 5000.

No longer constantly threatened by people, the ibex are tame to the point of being cheeky. In fact, there are now so many of these animals that disease and overgrazing have become problems. Hunting – still practised in the area – helps a little with population management.

the central Gredos is also very useful. The IGN 1:25,000 series is geographically accurate, but shows few paths. Numerous tourist maps cover the Gredos, but no single sheet displays all the paths, dirt roads and *refugios*.

Spanish-speaking readers have a wealth of detailed route guides to choose from (although many concentrate on day walks), including the excellent *Gredos: Turismo-Desporteo-Aventura*, published by Desnivel, and *Gredos: Guía de Ascensiones y Excursiones*, by Carlos Frías.

Information Sources

In Madrid the **Castilla y León tourist office** *(Oficina de Promoción Turística de Castilla y León;* ☎ *91 554 37 69;* W *www.jcyl.es/turismo; Calle Alcalá 79; metro Retiro)* is good for background information, not walking queries.

Tourist offices are found throughout the Gredos and mentioned under the relevant town headings. In addition to national and local mountaineering organisations try contacting:

Centro de Interpretación (☎ 927 17 70 18) Calle Real de Arriba 3, off Plaza de la Iglesia, Tornavacas. This good information centre concentrates on walking through the Reserva Natural de Garganta de los Infiernos and western Gredos.

Grupo Gredos de Montaña (☎/fax 920 37 26 45, W www.guiatietar.com) Plaza Federico Fernández 5, Arenas de San Pedro. In theory this small, information-packed office is open Monday to Saturday from 7pm to 10pm, but call in advance.

Oficina de Turismo del Valle del Jerte (☎/fax 927 47 25 58, W www.interbook.net/personal/jerte/) Cabezuela del Valle. There is more than your average amount of walking information here, including route guides for the western Gredos and Valle del Jerte.

Hundreds of *casas rurales* (rural houses or farmsteads) in the Gredos are available for rent. See Casas Rurales (p41) for more information, or contact:

Ávila La Casa (☎ 902 20 01 90, W www.avilalacasa.com). It also promotes various hotels and rural businesses.

Casas de Gredos (in Ávila ☎ 920 20 62 18, countrywide ☎ 902 42 41 41, W www.casasgredos.com)

ACCESS TOWNS
El Barco de Ávila

This picturesque little town is something of a hub for transport around the north side of the Gredos and is a nice spot to rest up or prepare for a walk.

Reflo Papelería *(Calle Mayor 24)* has a fair selection of 1:25,000 topographical maps, plus other tourist maps and walking guides.

Information Make general inquiries at the **tourist information office** *(☎ 920 34 08 44; Plaza de España; open Wed-Mon July-Sept, Sat & Sun Oct-June).*

Places to Stay & Eat The best-value place in town, **Hostal Rosi** *(☎ 920 34 00 55; Campillo 22; singles/doubles with bathroom €18/36)* has plenty of space.

Hotel Bellavista *(☎ 920 34 07 53, fax 920 34 08 74; Carretera de Ávila 15; singles/doubles €50/60)* provides good post-walk luxury.

Hotel Manila *(☎ 920 34 08 44, fax 920 34 12 91; Km 337 on the N110; singles €35-50, doubles €47-68)*, on the way to Plasencia, is El Barco's most upmarket choice. Sharply reduced weekday rates are often available.

There are also at least eight **casas rurales** in and around town.

Local **food shops** and **delicatessens** line Calle Mayor. The best **supermarket** is on Carretera de Ávila.

The **bars** and **restaurants** around Plaza de España are the town's best. **Restaurante El Casino** *(☎ 920 34 10 86; full meals €25-35)* is a cut above the rest.

Getting There & Away Buses run by **Ávila-Piedrahita-Barco Automotives** *(APBA;* ☎ *91 530 30 92)* and **Cevesa** *(☎ 91 539 31 32)* have very similar departure times from Madrid's Estación Sur de Autobuses (€9.80, 2½ hours, two daily). Two of Cevesa's services continue through Puerto de Tornavacas to Plasencia.

Between Monday and Saturday **Muñoz Travel** *(☎ 920 25 17 30)* has one bus from **Ávila bus station** *(☎ 920 22 01 54)* to El Barco de Ávila via the villages of Valle de Tormes (€5.35, two hours, one daily).

Arenas de San Pedro

Arenas is a beautiful little town with a rather tumultuous history, having been much besieged. The town's motto roughly translates as 'Always burning and always faithful'.

Information The **tourist information office** (☎ 920 37 23 68; W www.ayto-arenas.com; Plaza San Pedro) is in the centre of town. The Grupo Gredos de Montaña (see Information Sources, p69) is based here.

Supplies & Equipment On and just off Calle Triste Condesa (the main street) are a selection of local **food shops**, small **supermarkets** and **Mercado de Abastos** (Calle Maria Sanabria).

Librería la Nava (Calle del Dr Lorenzo-Velazquez) has a fair selection of Gredos guides and maps, including some IGN 1:25,000 maps.

Places to Stay & Eat In a pleasant location beside the Río del Arenal, 1.9km out of town, is **Camping Riocantos** (☎ 920 37 25 47; open July-Sept).

Hostel Lumi (☎ 920 37 16 35; Ave Pintor Martínez Vázquez; rooms with toilet/bathroom €25/29) is close to the bus station.

Hostal El Castillo (☎ 920 37 00 91; Carretera de Candeleda 2; singles/doubles/triples with washbasin €18/24/31, singles/doubles/triples with bathroom €23/30/39), beside the 14th-century Castillo de Don Álvaro de Luna Triste, is very pleasant.

Hostería Los Galayos (☎ 920 37 13 79, fax 920 37 18 20; Plaza de Condestable Dávalos; singles/doubles €40/46), a short distance away, has smart rooms but isn't stunning value. However, the restaurant is pretty good; the menú del degustación (menu of local dishes) costs €17.

Cheaper **places to eat** are found along Calle Triste Condesa.

Getting There & Away Bus services run by **Doaldi** (☎ 91 530 48 00) travel between Madrid's Estación Sur de Autobuses and Arenas (€7.90, two hours, five daily). Two services continue to Cuevas del Valle and one to Jarandilla de la Vera.

Alternatively catch a regionales train from Chamartín to Ávila (€5.35, 1½ to two hours, 20 daily), then the **Muñoz Travel** (☎ 920 25 17 30) bus for Candeleda via Cuevas del Valle and Arenas (€4.50, 1½ hours; one daily Monday to Friday, plus an extra service on Friday between October and July).

Alta Ruta de Gredos

Duration	5 days
Distance	57km
Difficulty	moderate–demanding
Start	Cuevas del Valle (p71)
Finish	Bohoyo (p71)
Transport	bus

Summary A challenging traverse of the central Sierra de Gredos, with a side trip that includes the Cinco Lagunas and an ascent of Almanzor

This fine, undulating ridge walk traverses the best of the central Gredos without relying on popular paths, conventional routes or complicated transport connections. It offers an opportunity to ascend Almanzor (2591m; the highest peak in the range) as part of a side trip that adds a day to the walk. The route is possible in three long, hard days, but allow for at least two nights at Refugio José Antonio Elola (Refugio Elola) if you want to explore the Circo de Gredos area at the heart of the range. Climbers have no problem finding challenging routes here, or at Los Galayos southeast of La Mira.

Refugios are scattered across the Gredos. Some are simple shepherds' huts; others offer a restaurant service. However, carrying camping equipment gives you more flexibility and there are some great camp sites – when climbing Almanzor we found a group camped on ledges just 2m below the summit!

Simple exits to the south and north of the range are possible at regular intervals along the ridge and daily buses connect Madrid with villages on both sides. Adventurous souls prepared to do some scrambling can extend the route along the length of the main ridge past Covacha to Puerto de Tornavacas, although it doesn't stop there. A couple of difficult routes lead to the Sierra de Candelario, enabling determined walkers to link all three Gredos walks described in this chapter.

PLANNING
Maps

It's possible to use IGN's 1:50,000 *Macizo Central de Gredos* map for the entire walk (there's a 1:25,000 section of the Circo de Gredos). However, for more topographical detail (but without many paths marked) use IGN's 1:25,000 map Nos 578-II *Mombeltrán*, 578-I *El Arenal*, 577-IV *El Raso*, 577-II *Laguna Grande* and 577-I *Bohoyo*.

Editorial Alpina's 1:40,000 *Sierra de Gredos* map shows more footpaths, but is a little inaccurate in positioning them.

NEAREST TOWNS
Cuevas del Valle

Starting early from Madrid, you could reach this pretty little village and start the walk on the same day.

Places to Stay & Eat The only drop-in accommodation is **Pensión Moli** (☎ 920 38 30 48; *singles/doubles with bathroom* €18/30); it includes breakfast and has a reasonable restaurant. You could try **Casa Rural Morrera** (☎ 920 38 32 26; *doubles* €42); it has cheaper weekday rates and also includes breakfast.

There are a number of **bars** and **grocery shops** in the Plaza de Constitución, but you're best to bring supplies from Madrid.

Getting There & Away Direct services are run by **Doaldi** (☎ 91 530 48 00) to Cuevas del Valle from Madrid (€8.85, three hours, two daily). Two extra services run on Friday evening.

Alternatively catch a **Muñoz Travel** (☎ 920 25 17 30) bus from Ávila or Arenas (€2, 25 minutes). For more details see Getting There & Away for Arenas de San Pedro (p70).

Bohoyo

At the end of the walk, this town has a pleasant centre with several **bars** and **restaurants** clustered around the church. There are a few **casas rurales** (see Information Sources, p69), but no hotel accommodation.

Getting There & Away Bohoyo's bus stop is 2.2km from the village (down) on the C500.

The daily **Cevesa** (☎ 91 539 31 32) bus from Bohoyo to Madrid (€10.45, 3½ hours) starts in El Barco de Ávila and passes through Bohoyo at around 3.40pm. Coming from Madrid there is an additional bus on Saturday and Sunday from July to mid-September.

The **Muñoz Travel** (☎ 920 25 17 30) bus between Ávila and El Barco de Ávila (see Getting There & Away for El Barco de Ávila, p69) passes through Bohoyo at around 6.35pm, returning towards Ávila at 6.50am the following day.

Alternatively call El Barco de Ávila's only **taxi** (☎ 608 92 53 82) to collect you (€10), and then catch a bus from there. A Bohoyo taxi may also be available between July and September (ask in any of the bars).

GETTING TO/FROM THE WALK

If you're not going to make it to Cuevas del Valle the night before starting the walk don't fret. The Muñoz Travel bus from Arenas arrives at the trailhead before 8am and can drop you at Puerto del Pico 15 minutes later (removing the 1½ hour walk up the valley).

You could also catch a later bus to Cuevas del Valle from Arenas and cut the first day quite short (there are plenty of places to camp en route).

Another option is to catch the evening Muñoz Travel bus from Ávila to El Barco de Ávila and disembark at **Hostal Venta Rasquilla** (☎ 920 20 75 71; *junction of the N502 & C500; singles/doubles* €12/24) 6km north of Puerto del Pico. Walk to Puerto del Pico to pick up the walk the next morning.

THE WALK (see map p72)
Day 1: Cuevas del Valle to Los Cervunales

5½–6½ hours, 12.5km

The day starts with a 547m climb (1½ hours or take the bus) north along the **Roman road** that leads from Cuevas del Valle to the pass of **Puerto del Pico**.

From the pass, head west past the war memorial to a cairn-marked, well-worn path

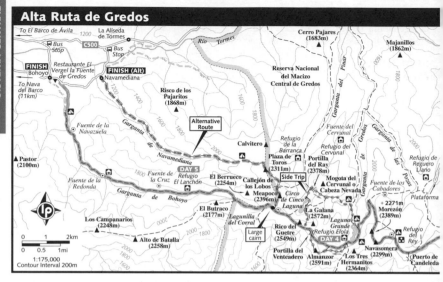

Alta Ruta de Gredos

that climbs away across the southern slopes of La Casa (1847m), then settles into a 45-minute traverse southwest to the spur of Risco del Cuervo. Ignore paths heading south and head west through a jumble of rounded boulders and then towards four tall pines and a *fuente* (spring; also fountain or water source). The area is a fine, shaded **camp site**.

From here the trail steadily traverses southwest for just over an hour, passing over one spur before cairns lead south down a second spur to the end of a dirt road where a simple **hut** (with fireplace) and animal enclosure are found. Turn right (north) beside the hut and head up a well-made ancient trail that loops west past a *fuente* before climbing north, reaching Puerto del Arenal (1818m) in 1¼ hours.

Turn left at the pass (unless the rocky, rugged peak of La Fría (1983m) appeals to the scrambler in you) and work your way west around a small boulder-strewn peak (1891m) to a saddle where the path splits. Avoid the faint track that keeps close to the ridge and traverse northwest through the broom to Fuente del Cervunal and a beautiful area of **high pasture** (marked as Los

Cervunales) that attracts ibex and wild boar at dawn and dusk. It's a great **camp site** and a private (locked) hut overlooks this beautiful spot.

Day 2: Los Cervunales to La Mira

4½–5 hours, 11km

Head southwest across the meadow to a pronounced gully, the source of Garganta de Cabrilla. Head south up to Puerto de la Cabrilla on the true right bank of the gully. This is the beginning of 1½ hours without an obvious path, during which there's much broom to bash through. Then turn right (west) along the ridge, passing into **Reserva Nacional del Macizo Central de Gredos** and by a large white quartz cairn before cutting around the 2024m peak, over Mojón de las Tres Cruces and southwest to the trig point on **Mediodía** (2219m).

Head west from the peak to a granite post then southwest down to Puerto del Peón (2028m), where a well-marked trail heads southwest along the high ridge of the central Gredos. After an hour or so the track begins a gruelling, rocky climb to a stony and desolate area of flatter land northeast of

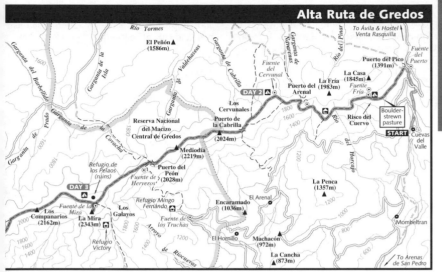

Alta Ruta de Gredos

La Mira before heading southwest to the ruins of **Refugio de los Pelaos** (2259m). The ruins provide a sheltered **camp site**, while **La Mira** (2343m) itself is 15 minutes due south across the well-watered meadows (a popular ibex grazing area). On the summit is the ruined tower of an former optical telegraph station.

The steep, rocky route down (274m) to **Refugio Victory** (☎ 91 739 96 58; accommodation per person €4; open daily July-Sept & many weekends throughout the year) lies to the southeast, diagonally across the meadow, should a night on the tops not appeal. The refugio is a simple affair with a large communal area downstairs and sleeping space for 16 people upstairs. The hut is popular with climbers drawn to the granite cliffs and vicious, teeth-like ridges of Los Galayos (there's some good climbing information at ⓦ www.summitpost.com).

Day 3: La Mira to Refugio Elola
4½–6 hours, 12.5km
Head west from the ruined Refugio de los Pelaos and pick up a well-worn path that turns southwest along a ridge of small, rocky summits. After crossing a very rocky

section below Los Campanarios (2162m), about 1¼ hours from La Mira, the trail splits. To the northwest a wide valley leads to the meadows surrounding **Refugio de Reguero Llano** (Refugio Llano; ☎ 689 41 26 39; accommodation per person €10; open year-round but phone ahead) above Plataforma road head (about an hour away). Food is available if ordered in advance.

However, don't fork right: our route turns left onto a path heading southwest to Puerto de Candeleda (a popular route onto the ridge) where a faint trail cuts west through a meadow and up to the ruins of **Refugio del Rey** (the thick walls provide some shelter). There's a good fuente northwest of the refugio.

From the ruins an alternative route heads north skirting Morezón, but head west, picking up the trail leading across the northern flank of Navasomera (2299m) to an isolated meadow. Continue west up one of a host of paths climbing onto the rocky ridge of **Morezón** (2389m) that forms part of the **Circo de Gredos**, the horseshoe of cliffs encircling Laguna Grande. The views across to Almanzor (2591m) are fantastic.

There is considerable confusion as to the precise names and locations of many of the peaks found on this section of ridge, but we have followed the height and position of Morezón as marked on the IGN 1:25,000 series (and marked by a cross on the ground). Numerous mountaineering possibilities lead across the jagged peaks of Los Tres Hermanitos and you could descend steeply to Laguna Grande in several places.

From Morezón head north to the flat, barren 2366m peak at the northern end of the ridge and then head northeast (directly towards Refugio Llano). Descend gently off the summit through a narrow, shallow channel for about eight minutes to a small col that offers a steep route down (northwest) to the Laguna Grande. If this short cut is too much with a heavy pack simply descend a little further onto a major ridge and trail. Turn left and continue along the ridge for five minutes before bearing left and heading gently down to the Trocha Real (King's Way), a path linking Refugio Llano and **Refugio Elola** (☎ 920 20 75 76, in Madrid ☎ 91 347 61 53; W galeon.com/refugioelola; accommodation per person €4.05; open June-Oct & weekends year-round). Turn left and you'll reach the *refugio* 50 minutes later, after walking around **Laguna Grande**. There is a permanently open winter annexe,

---

Ice Climbing in the Gredos

While the Gredos is primarily a summer walking destination, Refugio Elola is open on weekends throughout winter to cater for hardy walkers, mountaineers, adventurous skiers and ice climbers. The north-facing cliffs of Circo de Gredos are particularly suited to ice climbing and provide some excellent, challenging routes, most up frozen waterfalls. January to March is the best time for winter sports.

Several climbing and mountaineering companies operate from the *refugio* and some, including **Espacioaccion** (☎ 91 578 00 33; e espacioaccion@infornet.es), run ice-climbing classes for beginners. Alternatively, approach the mountaineering organisations in Madrid: see Information Sources (p65) for details.

---

restaurant (three-course evening meal €9.95) and **shop** selling emergency rations such as beer and chocolate. Some English is spoken.

Side Trip: Almanzor & the Cinco Lagunas
6½–8 hours, 10km, 841m ascent/descent
This excellent side trip joins two attractions with one simple traverse, saving time and unnecessary climbing.

From Refugio Elola follow the cairned path that climbs behind the *refugio* and then heads southwest up the valley. After 25 minutes you will pass the end of a bold spur leading down from Ameal de Pablo (2509m). A couple of minutes from the *refugio* you pass the turn off to Portilla del Venteadero (see Day 4). Continue west across a dry river bed and then turn southwest up a rocky gully towards Portilla Bermeja (2416m). After a 20-minute climb bear right as the trail leads west up a narrow, steep, boulder-filled gully. After 45 minutes you'll reach a small col (2550m) just southwest of Almanzor. However, be warned that the last section involves climbing a passage of gully that's very worn by the feet of thousands of tourists who pass through. Many of the rocks are loose and there's a landslide waiting to happen.

From the col scramble/climb/traverse right (north) for about 20m. To your right (east) should be two corridors up the western face of the peak. Take the one on the left to arrive at **Almanzor** (2591m) after a 10-minute climb. Technically it's a simple ascent, but it's a little taxing and the summit is exposed. However, the views across the whole of the Gredos make it well worth the effort.

After descending from the summit don't return to the narrow gully, but turn right (north), passing through a small col onto the eastern side of the ridge. From here a steady 40-minute traverse to Portilla del Venteadero (Cerro del Venteadero; 2484m) *is* possible (although it seems out of the question when viewed from the *refugio*!). The summit of La Galana (2572m), due north of here, is not for non-climbers – a crevasse must be crossed and a narrow cliff-top traverse is required.

From south of La Galana an obvious path leads northwest to a small pass overlooking

Laguna de Güetre, which is reached via a scree slope. Turn left (west) to pick your way down a boulder field to the **Cinco Lagunas**.

You have two ways to complete the loop. Either follow the cairn-lined path on the eastern side of the largest lake east up a 300m scree slope to a 2378m pass (sometimes marked as Portilla del Rey). Otherwise take the path that leads from the northernmost lake to Portilla del Rey (2378m) before leading east into the Gargantón valley, across Risco Negro and back to Refugio Elola (about 2½ hours). Numerous other exits/entrances to/from the Cinco Lagunas are possible.

Day 4: Refugio Elola to Refugio El Lanchón

5½–6½ hours, 9km

Head west up behind the *refugio* on the trail to Almanzor, but after a couple of minutes bear off right onto a cairn-lined path that climbs west along the northern side of a spur emanating from Ameal de Pablo. After about an hour you'll reach a rocky pass around the southern side of the crooked-looking summit. Continue west across a small meadow and up a rocky slope to Portilla del Venteadero (Cerro del Venteadero; 2484m).

From the pass follow the rough path northwest, dipping down beneath the cliffs encircling the Cinco Lagunas and on past Portilla de las Cinco Lagunas (2358m) to flatter ground and a *fuente*. About 200m further north a wall running east-west marks the boundary of the Reserva Nacional del Macizo Central de Gredos and the beginning of the watershed that forms the Garganta de Bohoyo.

From here you could pick up the trail for the alternative finish. However, the main route heads northwest down to Bohoyo along the simple trail beside Garganta de Bohoyo. Break the journey at **Refugio El Lanchón** after about 1½ hours of beautiful valley walking (stick to the true right bank after about an hour when the valley becomes more vegetated). This overnight stop means you don't have to rush to catch a bus

from Bohoyo and gives you time to appreciate the **valley** with its stark but beautiful landscape of streams, slabs of pink, weathered granite and bright green grass.

Refugio El Lanchón is very simple, much more a shepherds' hut than walkers' *refugio*. You could get about four people on the rickety sleeping platform and a couple on the floor.

Alternative Finish: Navamediana

4–5 hours, 13km

A shorter alternative finish continues north across the western flanks of Meapoco (2396m) and Plaza de Toros (2311m) to the Garganta de Navamediana, which can be followed down a narrow, intimate valley to **Navamediana** in about 3½ hours (from Plaza de Toros). From this traditional Gredos village (which doesn't have so much as a public phone) it's less than 2km to a bus stop on the C500 (which is served by the same buses as Bohoyo).

Day 5: Refugio El Lanchón to Bohoyo

3–3½ hours, 12km

Downstream from the *refugio* the valley becomes increasingly vegetated and the trail becomes more obvious, cutting down through a meadow and arriving at Fuente de la Redonda and a very simple hut. After a further 20 minutes the trail forks. Go right here then, a few minutes later, join a 4WD track that leads down the valley and into a wide, flat area of agricultural land.

Roughly 30 minutes after joining the 4WD track turn left beside a ruined farmhouse as the track climbs northeast through oak woodland. This trail soon leads across a cattle grid. Head north down the dirt road, but then bear left (northwest) across open country to a sealed road east of Bohoyo. Turn left then cross the now-wide Garganta de Bohoyo to **Restaurante El Vergel la Fuente de Gredos**, an ideal place to soak sore feet in the beautiful river, sink a few drinks and arrange a taxi.

The centre of Bohoyo is about 800m west and the bus stop is on the C500 a further 2.2km away.

Covacha Walk

Duration	3 days
Distance	54.5km
Difficulty	moderate–demanding
Start	Nava del Barco (p76)
Finish	Tornavacas (p76)
Nearest Town	El Barco de Ávila (p69)
Transport	bus, taxi

Summary An exploration of western Gredos offering a climb up a glacial valley, tricky ridge walking around Covacha and a delightful traverse through a nature reserve along Ruta de Carlos V

This walk is centred around an ascent of Covacha (2395m; highest peak in the western Gredos) after a beautiful walk up the glacial Valle de Garganta de Galin Gómez. You could easily leave it there, a peak-bagging exercise completed in one long or two short days. However, from the peak and ridge walk high above Laguna del Barco there's a great descent to Jarandilla de la Vera, from where there's a long but relatively easy walk into the Valle del Jerte and Tornavacas.

This would be an ideal continuation of the Alta Ruta de Gredos traverse (see Alta Ruta de Gredos Extension, p91, under Other Walks) and there are loads of options for extensions and alternative routes from this popular peak (Editorial Alpina's 1:50,000 Valle del Jerte map has dozens of options). From Puerto de Tornavacas it's possible to scramble up onto the Sierra de Candelario (see the boxed text 'Tornavacas to Calvitero Link', p81). This route could be cut short in Jarandilla de la Vera. However, this would be a shame as the third day is a wonderful, relatively easy romp along the Ruta de Carlos V, or Camino Real (royal route), which passes through Reserva Natural de Garganta de los Infiernos, one of the last places in central Spain where you have a chance to see the rare black stork and other protected species.

PLANNING
What to Bring

You'll need to camp for at least one night en route, but a few shepherds' huts and one refugio are found along the way.

Maps

Editorial Alpina's 1:50,000 Valle del Jerte map is very useful for trails and options, but is rather inaccurate: the path shown snaking up the true right bank of the Garganta de Galin Gómez is a non-starter; Refugio Palomo near Puerto de Tornavacas has long-since closed; and the paths around Capilla-Refugio de las Nieves are marked incorrectly.

For accurate topographical detail (but without many paths marked) use IGN's 1:25,000 map Nos 576-I Tornavacas, 576-II Solana de Ávila, 576-III Cabezuela del Valle, 576-IV Laguna del Barco, 599-I Aldeanueva de la Vera and 599-II Jarandilla de la Vera.

NEAREST TOWNS

See El Barco de Ávila (p69).

Nava del Barco

There are a couple of **casas rurales** in Nava del Barco (for contact information see Information Sources, p69) and some inviting overnight **camp sites** just southwest of the village, which has a couple of **grocery shops** and a few **bars**.

Tornavacas

Surrounded by cherry orchards that typify the Valle del Jerte, this village at the end of the walk is very pleasant indeed.

Tornavacas has an ATM and other services including **grocery stores**, **delicatessens** and the **Centro de Interpretación** (see Information Sources, p69).

Places to Stay & Eat At the beautiful **Casa Rural Antigua Posada** (☎ 927 17 70 89, fax 927 17 73 84; Ave de la Constitución 37; doubles €54-72, mid-week & off-peak €30.50-36.60; often closed Mon) prices include breakfast.

About 1.5km northeast of Tornavacas is **Hostal Puerto de Tornavacas** (☎/fax 927 19 40 97; Km 357 on N110; singles/doubles with bathroom €19/31), which has a reasonably good restaurant.

Getting There & Away The Plasencia-Madrid service (via El Barco de Ávila) run by **Cevesa** (☎ 91 539 31 32) passes through Tornavacas (€11, two daily). You can also flag the bus down at Puerto de Tornavacas.

GETTING TO/FROM THE WALK

The easiest way to reach the trailhead is to take a taxi from El Barco de Ávila (€8). Alternatively, it's a 6km road walk from the Umbrías turn on the N110 where Cevesa's Madrid-Plasencia bus can drop you. This service returns through Tornavacas at the end of the walk: see Getting There & Away (p76–7).

If you're cutting the walk short a **Doaldi** (☎ 91 530 48 00) service goes from Jarandilla de la Vera to Madrid (€12.30, 3½ hours, one daily) via Arenas de San Pedro.

THE WALK (see maps p77 & 79)
Day 1: Nava del Barco to Laguna de los Caballeros
4½–5 hours, 11km, 980m ascent

From Nava del Barco's central square beside Arroyo de la Garganta de Galin Gómez, walk south down Calle del Puente, past bars El Puente and La Fuente and onto a dirt road, which soon forks. Take the left fork, following the track to a small stream and a huge balancing rock. Head southwest over rocky, open ground (some good **camp sites** lie down to the left) then down a boggy walled lane leading to a dirt road. Turn right (away from the river) then left at a T-junction to arrive at a bridge (and small car park) five minutes later.

Cross the bridge and follow the major dirt road around Cerro del Camocho then head southwest for 25 minutes to a set of green gates. For the next 15 minutes follow the faint track south up to a well-built **shepherds' shelter**. Cairned trails lead to a second hut in about 30 minutes and then, shortly afterwards, across the rocky riverbed to a small **shrine**.

The trail now changes into a beautiful, well-constructed path that zigzags up the now rugged, rocky valley, around a series of waterfalls and up to **Laguna de la Nava**, about an hour from the shrine. Surrounded by towering peaks and scree slopes, the turquoise lake is a classic glacial creation and the dam wall makes a beautiful flat **camp site**.

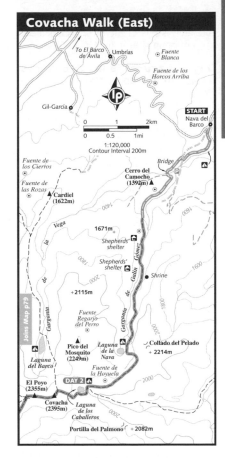

From the eastern end of the dam head southeast, passing to the right of a ruin and then climbing to a saddle. Bear right and walk roughly southwest beside the humble beginnings of Garganta de Galin Gómez, crossing the stream and climbing to the crest of a ridge on the stream's true right bank where the watercourse bends right. Head roughly west and bear right until **Laguna de los Caballeros** becomes visible as the ground falls away. From here bushwhack west to a gully (and Fuente de la Hoyuela) before cutting down to the valley floor. It's not an easy (or quick) descent so pick the

SISTEMA CENTRAL

route that's most comfortable for you. The lake area is one of the most secluded and tranquil **camp sites** in the Gredos.

Day 2: Laguna de los Caballeros to Jarandilla de la Vera
5½–6 hours, 15.5km, 375 ascent, 1787m descent

Visible from afar, the path to **Covacha** (2395m) zigzags up to a col from the southern side of the lake. From the col turn right (west) and follow red arrows up and over a series of rocky slabs and into a narrow pass, before turning left (southwest) on the final push to the summit.

From the summit scramble west, following cairns over the rocky, often-exposed peaks and ridges of El Poyo (2355m) and La Azagaya (2367m) to a saddle. Here the ridge climbs again before turning northwest towards Alto de Castifrío (2308m) and an easy four-hour alternative route to Puerto de Tornavacas. However, from the saddle cut down southwest and up onto the Cuerda Mala, a ridge emanating from Cerro del Estecillo (2259m). Here you can either scramble along the ridge or traverse through the broom to a pass, Portilla de Jaranda (2036m). Both routes suffer from dense scrub cover.

From the large cairn at the pass a well-worn path snakes down the western side of the valley, passing a number of traditional, thatched **goatherds' huts** (that provide good shelter) after about 1¼ hours. After another 35 minutes the path cuts down and crosses **Garganta de Jaranda**, by a set of falls and a series of great, welcoming pools. An alternative route (see Alternative Route: Guijo via Capilla-Refugio de las Nieves) leads off soon after the crossing.

Meanwhile, the main route moves easily down the valley (increasingly blessed with pools and waterfalls), recrossing the stream, travelling over a section of dry riverbed and past some farm buildings to a bridge. Cross to the true left bank and follow the track into a gully where a right fork onto the lower of two paths leads up to **Restaurante El Trabuquete** in **Guijo de Santa Barbara**.

This picturesque village is a nice place to stay and eat. The cheapest *casa rural* is

Santa Bárbara (☎ 927 56 04 24; *off Calle Nueva beside Bar Olúge; doubles €36*) and the most expensive is **Camino Real** (*☎/fax 927 56 11 19; Calle Monje 27; half-board doubles €65*).

From Plaza de la Fuente walk to the end of Calle Nueva. Turn right and after 20m turn left down Camino Real, which reaches the outskirts of **Jarandilla de la Vera** in about 30 minutes.

Alternative Route: Guijo via Capilla-Refugio de las Nieves
2 hours, 7km

A simple alternative for the budget-minded walker looking to avoid pricier accommodation in Guijo and Jarandilla leads to the left a couple of minutes after crossing the Garganta de Jaranda. Take a well-worn path up to **Capilla-Refugio de las Nieves** (1508m; reached in 45 minutes). This chapel and *refugio* has two bare rooms (one with a fireplace) and makes a reasonable overnight stop. The next day cut down to a well-made trail due west of the *refugio*, turn left and follow it south to Guijo in 1¼ hours, where it rejoins the Day 2 route to reach Jarandilla de la Vera in 30 minutes. Note this alternative makes for a long Day 3.

Jarandilla de la Vera
This is a pleasant little town, well-used to (mainly Spanish) tourists and weekenders.

Northwest of town, **Camping Jaranda** (☎ 927 56 04 54; *Km 47 on the C501; tent sites per person €3.20, bungalows €47-51*) has a restaurant. Its bungalows sleep four.

In town there is **Hostal Marbella** (☎ 927 56 02 18; *on the C501; doubles €42*). At **Hotel Jaranda** (☎ 927 56 02 06; e hotel@ hoteljaranda.com; *Ave Soledad Vega Ortiz 101; singles/doubles €30/52*) rates include breakfast. **Hostería Gante** (☎ 927 56 12 00; *Plaza Soledad Vega; singles/doubles €28/ 48*) has slightly better rooms, but top of the heap is **Parador de Jarandilla de la Vera** (☎ 927 56 01 17; e jarandilla@parador.es; *doubles €107*).

If you want to finish the walk here, there is a bus to Madrid, see Getting to/from the Walk (p77).

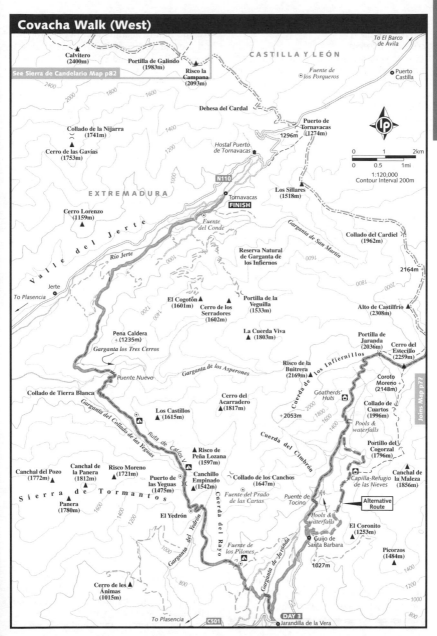

Covacha Walk (West)

See Sierra de Candelario Map p82

Calvitero (2400m)

Portilla de Galindo (1983m)

Risco la Campana (2093m)

CASTILLA Y LEÓN

To El Barco de Ávila

Puerto Castilla

Fuente de los Porqueros

Dehesa del Cardal

Collado de la Nijarra (1741m)

Cerro de las Gavías (1753m)

Hostal Puerto de Tornavacas

Puerto de Tornavacas (1274m)

1296m

EXTREMADURA

Cerro Lorenzo (1159m)

N110

Tornavacas FINISH

Los Sillares (1518m)

Valle del Jerte

Fuente del Conde

Garganta de San Martín

Collado del Cardiel (1962m)

Río Jerte

Reserva Natural de Garganta de los Infiernos

2164m

To Plasencia

Jerte

El Cogotón (1601m)

Cerro de los Serradores (1602m)

Portilla de la Veguilla (1533m)

Alto de Castilfrío (2308m)

La Cuerda Viva (1803m)

Pena Caldera (+1235m)

Garganta los Tres Cerros

Portilla de Jaranda (2036m)

Cerro del Estecillo (2259m)

Risco de la Buitrera (2169m)

Cuerda de los Infiernillos

Coroto Moreno (2148m)

Puente Nuevo

Garganta de los Asperones

Cerro del Acarradero (1817m)

Goatherds' Huts

Collado de Cuartos (1996m)

Collado de Tierra Blanca

Garganta del Collado de las Yeguas

Ruta de Caños V.

Los Castillos (1615m)

+2053m

Cuerda del Cimbrón

Pools & waterfalls

Portillo del Cogorzal (1796m)

Canchal del Pozo (1772m)

Canchal de la Panera (1812m)

Risco Moreno (1721m)

Risco de Peña Lozana (1597m)

Capilla-Refugio de las Nieves

Canchal de la Maleza (1856m)

Sierra de Tormantos

Puerto de las Yeguas (1475m)

Canchillo Empinado (1542m)

Collado de los Canchos (1647m)

Puente de Tocino

Alternative Route

Panera (1780m)

Cuerda del Rayo

Fuente del Prado de las Cartas

Pools & waterfalls

El Coronito (1253m)

El Yedrón

Garganta del Yedrón

Fuente de los Pilones

Garganta de Jaranda

Guijo de Santa Barbara

Picorzos (1484m)

1027m

Cerro de les Ánimas (1015m)

To Plasencia

C501

DAY 3

Jarandilla de la Vera

0 1 2km
0 0.5 1mi
1:120,000
Contour Interval 200m

Day 3: Jarandilla de la Vera to Tornavacas

7–9 hours, 28km

Retrace your steps towards Guijo then, two minutes after turning right off the C501 onto a concrete track, fork left onto Ruta de Carlos V. Follow the red-and-white markers (these mark the whole route, but are most easily seen when walking from Tornavacas to Jarandilla) to Puente de Palo, a footbridge. Cross the Garganta de Jaranda, head west to the dirt road, turn left then quickly cut back right to start a 10-minute climb northwest along a well-used dirt road to a tarmac road. Walk left for 60m, then turn right (west) onto a narrow trail leading up to a wide track. Turn right; then after 10m bear left (northwest) onto a narrow trail that zigzags up the slope before bearing northwest across more open ground to Fuente de los Pilones and two large oak trees (a possible **camp site**). Continue northwest for 15 minutes, passing a large boulder before forking right (west) to a rocky promontory. A couple of minutes later, just past some farm buildings, fork right (north) and head up through the broom into the **Valle de Garganta de Yedrón**. You'll reach the stream after 35 minutes.

Cross the stream and follow the trail as it zigzags northwest up past a *fuente* onto the ridge of Canchillo Empinado (1542m). Traverse north to Puerto de la Yeguas then drop down and cross Garganta del Collado de las Yeguas before heading northwest through a meadow at the beginning of a beautiful, 1¼-hour walk down the stunning, steep-sided valley towards Garganta los Tres Cerros.

Upon reaching a ridge marking the point two valleys meet high above Garganta los Tres Cerros, there's a tight zigzagging trail down to a junction of walking trails. Turn right and then right again at the next junction to head northeast up the valley to **Puente Nuevo** (a wonderful stone bridge), which you reach in 20 minutes. Cross and follow the trail west up to a 4WD track. Turn left, pootle along for about 10 minutes (avoiding switchbacks left) to a T-junction, then turn right before quickly cutting back left (north) down a narrow gully.

You'll soon join a 4WD track and the route northeast becomes fairly straight and simple. About 15 minutes after crossing a five-way junction (at which you should go straight ahead) turn left down a narrow track to another 4WD track that's soon joined by the GR10. You'll reach a tarmac road 50 minutes later. Turn left, left again across the Río Jerte and then right onto a concrete road. Upon reaching a dead end turn left into **Tornavacas**.

Carlos' Way

The third day of the Covacha Walk follows the route taken by the Holy Roman Emperor Carlos V in October 1556.

Son of the seemingly unlikely pairing of Juana the Crazy and Felipe the Handsome, Carlos inherited huge swathes of Spain, France, Germany and Italy at the tender age of 16. He later became the Holy Roman Emperor, but after 40 years of rule he abdicated and retired to Yuste monastery. He described his mountain crossing from Tornavacas to Jarandilla as the 'last pass of his life', but suffered little hardship – he was carried the whole way in a sedan chair.

Sierra de Candelario

Duration	2 days
Distance	23.5km
Difficulty	moderate
Start/Finish	Candelario (p81)
Transport	bus

Summary A leisurely two-day walk up a beautiful valley to one of the most stunning corries in the Gredos, with loads of scope for further exploration

The Sierra de Candelario is divided from the western end of the Sierra de Gredos by the Valle de Aravalle, through which the N110 linking Plasencia and El Barco de Ávila passes. It's a small range and does not provide the scale and variety of landscapes found elsewhere in the Gredos. However,

Tornavacas to Calvitero Link

An interesting and challenging route joins the Covacha Walk (see p76) and the Sierra de Candelario walk. The 12.5km route takes 5½ hours, involves 1124m of descent and isn't recommended for those with heavy packs or a fear of heights, as some climbing and considerable exposure are involved. The best maps to use are IGN 1:25,000 map Nos 576-1 *Tornavacas* and 576-II *Solana de Ávila*.

From Tornavacas head north out of Plaza de la Iglesia, bear right across the stream and up Calle Real de Arriba. Fork right upon reaching a *fuente* and follow the red-and-white markers of the GR10 Puerto de Tornavacas in about 1¼ hours. Turn left, cross the N110 and head northwest up the dirt road opposite, climbing for about 25 minutes until the dirt road meets a stone wall and cuts back west. Bear right and climb northwest through the broom beside the wall. After an hour you'll reach a faint trail below the summit ridge of Risco la Campana (2093m); the trail leads around the peak to Portilla de Galindo (1983m).

From the pass you have two options. The main route heads west through the broom and along a rocky, tricky ridge to Cumbre de Talamanca (2394m), but after Portilla de Talamanca the route (marked with cairns) is very exposed – some sections are a nerve-wracking scramble/climb. The other route is slightly longer, although the terrain is easier. It cuts across Hoyo Malillo (an area of high pasture with an excellent camp site) then heads upstream along the Arroyo Malillo, around a waterfall – some straightforward but exposed climbing is required – and into an area of seasonal lakes and high pasture. To the west of this stunning glacial bowl a steep scree slope leads to Tranco del Diablo, 40 minutes northeast of Calvitero. To pick up Day 2 of the Sierra de Candelario walk, see Side Trip: Ascent of Calvitero (p83).

Hoya Moros, the tranquil, boulder-strewn corrie ringed by the stunning cliffs of Los Hermanitos and Calvitero (2400m; the highest peak in the range) at the head of the Cuerpo de Hombre valley, is simply stunning and there are enough challenges in the area to occupy a number of days.

In theory this lengthy and enjoyable walk could be done in one very long day, but the climb from the picturesque (and touristy) village of Candelario is taxing. Camping in Hoya Moros is highly recommended and there are plenty of possible distractions and side trips. These include a loop around Los Hermanitos from Hoya Moros, a trip down to Lagunas El Trampal, an ascent of Canchal Negro (2364m) or an exploration of the ridges to the southeast and southwest into the Valle del Jerte (see the boxed text 'Tornavacas to Calvitero Link').

PLANNING
Maps
Editorial Alpina's 1:50,000 *Valle del Jerte* map covers the walk, but is plagued by inaccuracies (Calvitero is incorrectly identified as El Torreón). IGN 1:25,000 map Nos 553-III *Béjar* and 576-1 *Tornavacas* accurately cover the walk.

NEAREST TOWN
Candelario
The walk begins and ends in this beautiful, tourist-oriented mountain village 5km above Béjar, which has a useful **tourist information office** (☎ 923 40 30 05; [e] *turismobe jar@hotmail.com*) opposite the bus station.

Candelario has a couple of ATMs, shops specialising in local delicacies and numerous **bars**, **restaurants** and **hostels** (although many only open between July and September or at weekends).

Places to Stay & Eat Although the rooms are not great **Hostal El Pasaje** (☎ 923 41 32 10; *Calle Eras; singles/doubles/triples €21/ 33/55*) is open year-round. At weekends and during the high season a good bet is **Hostal La Sierra** (☎ 923 41 33 15; *Calle Mayor 69; doubles €31*). Both places have reasonable restaurants.

Hotel Cinco Castaños (☎/fax 923 41 32 04; *Carretera de la Sierra; camping per person/tent*

€3/3, singles/doubles €43/55) has some well-equipped rooms. The camping ground here is open June 30 to October 1 and has a pool and small shop.

Numerous **cheap eateries** are found on Ave del Humilladero and around Plaza de Solano, while **Bodega la Regadera** (top of Calle de Pedro Muñoz Rico) is an excellent little bar specialising in beef snacks and cheap red wine.

Mesón la Romana (☎ 923 41 32 72; Nuñez Losada 4; full meals €20-30; open July-Sept & weekends), off the top of Calle Mayor, is probably Candelario's best – and most expensive – restaurant.

Getting There & Away Between Madrid's Estación Sur de Autobuses and Béjar **APBA** (☎ 91 530 30 92) and **Cevesa** (☎ 91 539 31 32) both offer very similar services (€11.30, three hours, two daily). Cevesa's services go via El Barco de Ávila, while APBA has an express service.

Alternatively, go via Salamanca (from Madrid numerous **Auto-Res** (☎ 902 02 09 99) buses and frequent trains go here), from where **La Serrana** (☎ 923 22 01 87) has services to Béjar (€4, 2¼ hours, five daily).

La Serrana also runs buses between Béjar and Candelario (€0.80, 4.5km, at least five daily) or you could take a taxi from the bus station (€6).

THE WALK
Day 1: Candelario to Refugio Cueva de Hoya Moros
5–5½ hours, 11.5km, 959m ascent

From the centre of Candelario walk up Calle Mayor, turn right (west) at El Canton (a building), fork left then turn left onto the road to La Plataforma El Travieso. Bear right towards **Hotel Cinco Castaños** then continue down Camino del Calvario. Fork right after 10 minutes and continue steadily southwest to a sealed road east of Embalse de Fuente Santa (or Embalse de las Angosturas). Turn left then 10 minutes later fork left (south) down a forestry road through green metal gates. Bear right through a second set of gates and head into open oak woodland. Upon reaching a T-junction

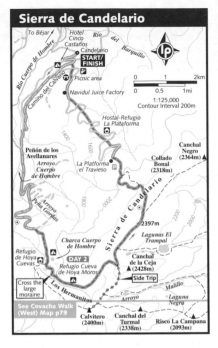

around 30 minutes later turn right (west) then bear right (south) at the next junction. After fording Arroyo Peña Gordas climb steadily through two more hairpins and pass a *fuente* (on the right) before reaching a third (left) bend. At the apex of this bend pick up the well-marked path that runs southeast along a ridge parallel to the stunning, glacial **Cuerpo de Hombre valley**.

After 30 minutes, with Los Hermanitos in full view and a small meadow on the left, the track bears right (south) through chest-high broom and across rock slabs to a set of falls. Head upstream into a wide meadow. To the southwest lies the rather decrepit **Refugio de Hoya Cuevas** (the windows are gone, but the door and roof are relatively sound), which is mainly used by climbers drawn to the sheer granite cliffs of Los Hermanitos.

Head southeast across the meadow, picking out a suitable route for the steep, rocky climb up to a second narrow meadow. Walk south beside the meandering river before crossing to the western side of the valley to climb around another waterfall to another section of beautiful pasture. Head along the true left bank of the river then climb under, over and through the moraine. This scramble will bring you out into the most stunning glacial corrie, **Hoya Moros**. Ford the river and make your way southeast through the soft pasture to a large cairn-topped boulder. One hundred metres east is **Refugio Cueva de Hoya Moros**, a shallow-walled cave. It may be damp in winter, but this place is one of the most stunning camping spots in the Sistema Central.

Day 2: Refugio Cueva de Hoya Moros to Candelario
4–4½ hours, 12km
From the *refugio* head northeast across the meadow, then bear left to a grassy strip that leads northeast up between difficult rocky slopes and patches of broom. Climb steeply for 30 minutes to a flatter, barren landscape, then pick out the remains of a fence and line of large cairns and follow them east up to a path below a jumble of large, rounded rocks. Southeast of here is the level summit of **Canchal La Ceja** (2428m), marked with a small metal rocket. Head off along the right (south) trail here for the Ascent of Calvitero side trip.

The main route turns left here. Follow the trail northeast along the Cuerda del Calvitero passing to the east of a **peak** marked 2397m (wrongly labelled as El Calvitero, 2405m, on the Editorial Alpina map, but offering good views) before the trail forks. Go left, following the trail in a more northerly direction as it descends through broom, past a giant cairn to a *fuente*. With La Plataforma El Travieso in full view the path splits. Turn left and pick your route down to the trailhead. Turn right along the road, then after a left bend bear right through a gap in the crash barrier and down a steep shortcut to **Hostal-Refugio La Plataforma** (☎/fax 923 40 18 00; singles €18, doubles €32-36; open July-Sept), 8km south of Candelario. The hostel has a restaurant, good views and a gentle breeze.

By walking underneath the electricity pylons that lead down from the hostel, you'll reach Candelario after about 1½ hrs. The path is steep in places and crosses the road a couple of times before emerging onto flatter land beside the Navidul juice factory. Turn right and head down the road to a right bend, where a vague track leads left into pine woodland. Follow it, but then head north to a dirt road. This leads northwest to a picnic area with a dry *fuente*. Turn right and walk past a fire lookout, forking left shortly afterwards down past a viewpoint and three stone crosses. Continue east for 50m before looping around a jumble of rocks and cutting down north to a road. Turn left then quickly bear right down through more woods and return to the road 200m east of Hotel Cinco Castaños. Turn left and head into Candelario.

Side Trip: Ascent of Calvitero
1½ hours, 4km
From the jumble of boulders and the main trail northwest of Canchal de la Ceja a cairn-marked trail heads south before turning southwest and crossing a saddle to **Calvitero** (2400m). You reach Calvitero after negotiating the **Devil's Step** – a steep channel in the rock (a fixed steel rope helps you do the simple climb).

The views are stunning, especially of Los Hermanitos, but on a good day the whole Sierra de Gredos is visible, as are the plains out to Salamanca.

Retrace your steps to rejoin the main route.

Sierra de Guadarrama

Slightly overshadowed by its grander neighbour on the Sistema Central, the Sierra de Guadarrama offers some great, easily accessible walking. The ski resorts and large number of day-trippers from Madrid may have taken their toll on some regions, but the high ridges and remote peaks are remarkably undisturbed. Certain areas demand attention despite being tourist targets – we highly recommend climbing Peñalara and Siete Picos and exploring La Pedriza – while the GR10 and Cuerda Larga long-distance paths cross the bulk of the mountain chain.

Only 50km north of Madrid at the closest point, these mountains are well within day-trip range of the capital and efficient train and bus services bring the urban hordes into the mountains each weekend.

HISTORY

The history of the Guadarrama is similar to that of the Gredos, although the range has frequently played a role in defending Madrid (the mountains have long been known as Mons Carpetani, or protector of Madrid). During the Spanish Civil War Republicans defending Madrid (including the International Brigades) fought along the ridges around the watershed of the range – evidence of trenches and other fortifications can still be seen.

In 1923 a narrow-gauge railway from Cercedilla to the 1830m-high pass of Puerto de Cotos was opened. The subsequent influx of *madrileños* may have upset the Los Doce Amigos mountaineering society, which had established *refugios* in the range 10 years earlier, but a tourist industry was born. Increased car ownership and society's greater affluence in the 1970s led to the limited, north-facing ski fields of the central Guadarrama being developed, while a large number of second homes and chalet housing developments sprouted below the southern slopes.

NATURAL HISTORY

The Sierra de Guadarrama has a similar natural history to the Gredos (see Natural History, p68) and it also shares some of the differences between the southern and northern slopes (see History, p67), although differences are often not as pronounced and there is certainly less glaciation.

The area of La Pedriza is an exception to the general terrain of the Sistema Central. Here, numerous faults and extensive erosion of the softer, warmer-coloured rock have produced a strange landscape of towering rounded pinnacles, narrow passes, smooth domes and balancing rock sculptures.

The northern side of the range is almost completely covered by Scots pine plantation

forest. Spanish bluebells and toad flax, which has large, snapdragon-like flowers, are found in the pine forests.

White storks, considered a good omen, are found in most villages in the mountains and foothills. Colonies of seven or eight nests can be seen at Manzanares El Real. You'll be very lucky to see Spanish ibex, wildcats or wild boars, but be wary of the hairy brown-and-black caterpillars of the pine processionary moth (see the boxed text 'The Pine Processionary Caterpillar', p32) and their large nests (like a dense spiderweb) in pine trees.

PLANNING
When to Walk

The area is busy all year and is often swamped at weekends between June and September. Some *refugios*, hostels, restaurants and tourist-oriented shops only open during the ski season, high summer or on weekends. Unlike areas of the Gredos, the snow cover has largely disappeared by mid-May, although freezing temperatures and driving rain and sleet can occur until June. Visit in May, June or September if you can.

Maps & Books

La Tienda Verde's 1:50,000 *Sierra de Guadarrama* map covers the whole of the range and can be used for most walks in the area. Editorial Alpina's 1:25,000 *La Pedriza* map covers the eastern half of the Cuerda Larga walk, while the 1:25,000 *Guadarrama* map covers the western half, and the whole of the Valle de la Fuenfría walk.

Domingo Pliego's *100 Excursiones Por La Sierra de Madri* is a comprehensive Spanish-language guide to the area. The author has written dozens of guides to the Sistema Central,

Information Sources

Comunidad de Madrid's main **tourist office** (☎ 91 429 49 51; W *www.comadrid.es/turismo; Calle Duque de Medinaceli 2, Madrid; metro Sevilla)* can supply *some* information about the Sierra de Guadarrama, but don't get your hopes up. A better bet are the many mountaineering federations in Madrid (see Information Sources, p65).

For good local walking information head to the **Centro de Información Valle de la Fuenfría** *(☎ 91 852 22 13; 2km north of Cercedilla)*. It has information on guided walks incorporating special mountain trains. **Casa del Parque de los Cotos** *(☎ 91 852 08 57; Puerto de Cotos)* covers the trails and wildlife surrounding Peñalara.

Useful websites include:

Deportal Madrid has a list of local mountaineering organisations and *refugios* **W** www.deportal madrid.com/montana.htm

Sierra Norte has a full list of *refugios* in the region **W** www.sierranorte.com

ACCESS TOWN
Cercedilla

Cercedilla is geared to summer-season visitors, corporate training centres and second homes for *madrileños*. However, enough grocery shops, restaurants and bars open year-round to make it worth spending a night or two, even though the excellent transport links to Madrid mean you don't have to.

Places to Stay & Eat A good option is the large and friendly **Hostal Longinas-El Aribel** *(☎ 91 852 15 11;* **e** *elaribel@yahoo.es; singles/doubles with bathroom €25/40, singles/doubles without bathroom €18/30)*, 30m north of the train station, which has a good-value bar and restaurant.

Alternatively, **La Maya** *(☎ 91 852 22 52; Carrera del Señor 2; doubles with bathroom €40)* has OK food, but the food at **La Muñoza** *(Plaza Mayor)* and **El Frontón** *(opposite train station)* is much better.

Getting There & Away From Madrid's **Atocha station** *(☎ 91 506 68 46) cercanía* and *regionales* rail services go to Cercedilla (€3.35, 1¼ hours, 20 or more daily) via Chamartín. Connections to/from Ávila are also possible.

Larrea's *(☎ 91 530 48 00)* No 684 buses run between Madrid's Montcloa bus station and Cercedilla (€2.75, 1½ hours, almost hourly).

If you need a taxi call ☎ 619 22 62 72 or ☎ 619 80 64 52.

Valle de la Fuenfría

Duration	6½–7½ hours
Distance	23km
Difficulty	easy–moderate
Start/Finish	Cercedilla (p85)
Transport	train, bus

Summary An accessible and rewarding walk that includes an ascent of Siete Picos and a ridge walk across Cerro Peña Águila

Thanks to good early-morning and evening rail and bus connections to Cercedilla this relaxed loop around Valle de la Fuenfría is achievable as a day trip from Madrid. The trail is well marked and, although the valley is popular with *madrileños* during the year (ski-mountaineering takes over from walking once winter arrives), the route avoids crowds until Puerto de Fuenfría.

The section from Siete Picos to Cercedilla forms part of Day 3 of the Cuerda Larga walk (see p90) so walkers planning to tackle that could cut this walk short at Puerto de Fuenfría and take the Roman road back down to Cercedilla. Alternatively from the pass the GR10.1 to Puerto de Cotos could be picked up, combining the two routes described here into a four-day walk. Another possible extension would be along the GR10 southwest to El Escorial (see Western Guadarrama, p91, under Other Walks).

THE WALK (see map p86)

Turn left out of the Cercedilla train station, pass left under the railway and cross a bridge over the Río de la Venta. Cross to the western side of the road and walk past Fuente de Marino before bearing right up Paso de Canalejas. Fork right at the next junction and right again at a T-junction onto Camino de los Campamentos. This well-used dirt road climbs steadily for the next 25 minutes to a green barrier just past Campamento La Peñota. Cut up left (west) across a large clearing, past a *fuente* and onto a trail marked with red dots that in 45 minutes leads northwest through the woods to a forestry track.

Go right (north) across the track onto a path going northwest up the mountain to a ridge, a dry-stone wall and the GR10 (with red-and-white markers). Turn right and follow the GR10 north past a lesser peak (with a ruin at its base) to the summit of **Cerro Peña Águila** (2009m; Peña del Águila on the Editorial Alpina *Guadarrama* map). The views across the north side of the Gredos, look out over the *meseta* of Castilla y León and east to Siete Picos (2138m), Peñalara (2430m).

Descend northeast on the western side of the wall to a dirt road. Turn left and walk past a *fuente* to arrive in Puerto de Fuenfría (1796m) in about 40 minutes. There's another *fuente* just north of the pass.

Head south of the pass then left after 150m onto a wide track that climbs southeast to a **viewpoint** overlooking the whole of Valle de la Fuenfría. From this vantage point climb east to Collado Ventoso, a grassy saddle with a *fuente* to the southwest. A number of paths diverge from this point. To skip climbing Siete Picos pick up the trail (with yellow markers) heading southwest from the western side of the saddle to Pico de Majalasna.

To go to the peak follow cairns south from the col up to Umbría de Siete Picos ridge, which you reach in 30 minutes. Once on the ridge, traverse east (follow the red target

Sierra de Guadarrama

symbols) through a jumble of minor peaks to **Siete Picos** (2138m), marked with a triangulation point. A mass of eroded rock forms the summit. It's best climbed from the northeast.

Retrace your steps to a small col before the westernmost peak of the summit ridge and pick up a path, marked with red-and-yellow targets, that descends southwest through a stretch of open pine woodland to Pico de Majalasna (1933m).

Head south through the meadow beside the peak, pass a *fuente*, then follow round, yellow trail markers down a winding track to a dirt road. Turn left (south) and walk along this flat

spur to a left bend and the Los Miradores viewpoints. Bear left off the road and head to the southernmost viewpoint before swinging right and following yellow trail markers on a 30-minute descent to a wide, open saddle. Here the route cuts back northwest (although routes to the east and southwest lead down to the outskirts of Cercedilla) and in 30 minutes crosses a footbridge before cutting up to a sealed road 200m south of bar-restaurant **Las Dehesas Casa Cirilo** (☎ *91 852 02 41*), a very welcome stop after a long day in the mountains. Cercedilla is a 40-minute walk or a €6 taxi ride south.

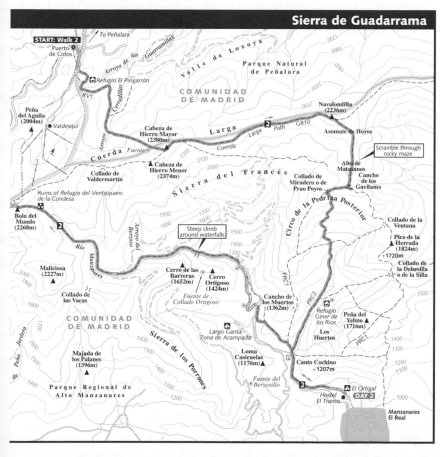

Sierra de Guadarrama

Cuerda Larga

Duration	3 days
Distance	54km
Difficulty	moderate
Start	Puerto de Cotos (p88)
Finish	Cercedilla (p85)
Transport	train

Summary An enjoyable introduction to the Sierra de Guadarrama's peaceful valleys, high ridges and summits

This is a simple walk through Parque Natural de Peñalara, along a short section of the Cuerda Larga long-distance path, and the dramatic Parque Regional del Alto Manzanares (an area more commonly known as La Pedriza). The final leg simply heads along the tranquil valleys of the Río Manzanares to Puerto de Navacerrada before crossing Siete Picos en route to Cercedilla.

This route offers a taste of the great walking available once you leave the crowds behind. There are a number of possible extensions, side trips and deviations. The complete Cuerda Larga, a classic 18km walk, stretches across a section of high ridge running northeast from Puerto de Navacerrada to Puerto de la Morcuera. It would be a worthy extension to this route.

Highly recommended as a warm up for this walk is an ascent of Peñalara (2429m; see Peñalara Ascent, p91, under Other Walks) from Puerto de Cotos, possibly including a loop through the Lagunas de Peñalara. It's also easy to spend at least two days in La Pedriza scrambling around the eroded peaks.

NEAREST TOWNS & FACILITIES
See Cercedilla (p85).

Puerto de Cotos (Puerto del Paular o de los Cotos)
With good bus and train connections to Madrid you don't *have* to stay at the trailhead the night before, but it's a nice option. There's an information office for the Peñalara area, see Information Sources (pp84–5).

Club Alpino Español's **Albergue Refugio Coppel** (☎ 615 16 80 81/83, in Madrid

☎ 91 522 79 51; [e] *club alpe@teleline.es; half-board per person €16-20*) is above the pass and has a range of varied and very reasonable accommodation.

Just off the road to Valdesquí is **Refugio El Pingarrón** (☎ 91 580 42 16; *accommodation per person €2.15; open Sat & Sun, annexe always open*). Perched high above Arroyo de las Guarramillas, its annexe sleeps about six; an IYHA membership card is required. Ski lifts blight the view south, northeast the beautiful Valle de Lozoya is fair compensation.

At the top of the pass is **Venta Marcelivo** (☎ 91 852 19 24; *menú del día €10*), a reasonable bar-restaurant. There's also a small **bar** at the train station. Both often close after the last train to Cercedilla.

GETTING TO/FROM THE WALK
From Cercedilla **mountain trains** (☎ 91 506 61 95) head up to Puerto de Cotos (€3.35, 45 minutes, four daily) via Puerto de Navacerrada. The fare is the same ex-Madrid. Twice as many services run on Saturday.

A taxi from Cercedilla costs about €18.

Larrea's (☎ 91 530 48 00) No 691 bus to Puerto de Cotos (€3.20, 70 minutes, one daily, two daily on weekends) leaves from Moncloa bus station in Madrid.

If you just feel like exploring La Pedriza (a great two-day option) or cutting the route short then Larrea's No 724 buses for Manzanares El Real leave from Plaza de Castilla in Madrid (€2.10, 50 minutes, every half hour).

THE WALK (see map p86)
Day 1: Puerto de Cotos to Manzanares El Real
6–7 hours, 21km

From Venta Marcelivo in Cercedilla walk southeast down a wide sealed road towards the Valdesquí ski area. After 10 minutes turn left onto a track which leads southeast to **Refugio El Pingarrón**.

From the *refugio* a path (marked RV1) descends south across Arroyo de las Guarramillas then loops around a spur through pine woodland down to a junction. Fork right off the RV1 and traverse south above the Arroyo Cerradillas to a small clearing where the trail bends left down to the arroyo. Cross it and follow the meandering trail in a south-southeasterly direction across two more streams and up to the true left (west) bank of a third. Head upstream along a cairn-lined path, bearing left (southeast) after about 25 minutes, to reach the ridge of a spur 20 minutes later. There's a *fuente* 50m southwest.

Proceed southeast, climbing to meet the Cuerda Larga (and GR10) at a saddle between Cabeza de Hierro Menor (2374m) and **Cabeza de Hierro Mayor** (2380m). Turn left and follow the red-and-white markers to the higher peak. The views are magic. Much of the Cuerda Larga can be seen and the cliffs of Circo de la Pedriza Posterior look as dramatic as anything in the Sistema Central.

Red-and-white markers now lead east along the undulating ridge for just over an hour to Navalondilla (2236m), where the Cuerda Larga bears left (northeast) to La Najarra (2106m). However, bear right (southeast) to a lower, rocky peak, Asomate de Hoyos, and pick up a cairn-lined path leading south into the broom. It travels through a rocky maze around Alto de Matasanos (2106m) to Cancho de los Gavilanes, a col just north of the stunning eroded cliffs that form the boundary of **La Pedriza**. Head southeast to **Collado del Miradero o de Prao Poyos** (1878m), a wider col, where there's a meeting of trails. The PRC1 forms a circuit around La Pedriza (see the boxed text 'La Pedriza Circuit' – an excellent day out from the described route); continue south on the PRC2 through the heart of the park to the car park at Canto Cochino. Both trails are signed with yellow-and-white markers.

The well-equipped **Refugio Giner de los Ríos** (☎ 91 522 87 43; *accommodation per person €4, half-board €15; open daily July–mid-Sept, open Sat & Sun year-round*) is reached after descending for 1½ hours; always phone in advance.

In **Canto Cochino**, which you reach 30 minutes later, there are two bar-restaurants. **Largo Ganta Zona de Acampada** (a camping ground with some facilities, but no drinking water) is 1.5km west past the medical centre.

A beautiful 40-minute walk southeast beside the Río Manzanares brings you to a clutch of **restaurants** (like those at Canto Cochino, out of high season many open at weekends only) and a car park on the outskirts of **Manzanares El Real**. Close by is the smart camping ground **El Ortigal** (☎ 91 853 01 20; *camping per person €6*), while a little further downstream is the simple **Hostal El Tranco** (☎ 91 853 00 63, *Calle del Tranco 4; singles/doubles with shared bathrooms €21/34*). The centre of Manzanares El Real is a 25-minute walk away.

La Pedriza Circuit

At the end of Day 1 of the Cuerda Larga walk (p88) the route drops through Circo de la Pedriza Prosterior, a near-perfect horseshoe of tall, rounded cliffs surrounding a rocky labyrinth and 'adventure playground' for climbers, scramblers and walkers.

With yellow-and-white trail markers the PRC1 makes a complete circuit of La Pedriza and requires you to occasionally crawl under huge balancing boulders, scramble up tall boulder stacks or squeeze through high, narrow passes. It's great fun, but can take 10 to 12 hours (with 1000m of ascent and descent) and there are no *fuentes* close to the ridges, so carry plenty of water. It's a good idea to spend two days in the park or shorten the circuit by cutting down west to Refugio Giner de los Ríos, where the GR10 crosses the route at the Collada de la Dehesilla o de la Silla. There are also dozens of alternative routes and the ascent of Peña del Yelmo (1716m) to consider. This ascent requires a couple of basic climbing moves and is best approached from the northeast.

La Tienda Verde's 1:15,000 *La Pedriza del Manzanares* map is essential. The circuit begins at Canto Cochino, around 2.5km from Hostal El Tranco and the El Ortigal camping ground, and about 4.5km from the centre of Manzanares El Real.

Cross the bridge and head northwest up the slope, following the trail markers to a junction. Turn right and follow the PRC1 (often marked as the PR1) across Cancho de los Muertos. The fun is just beginning.

Day 2: Manzanares El Real to Puerto de Navacerrada

5–6 hours, 18km

For almost all of its length this route follows the Río Manzanares to the Bola del Mundo, from where it's a simple descent to Puerto de Navacerrada.

Retrace your steps to Canto Cochino then walk upstream along the true left bank of Río Manzanares. After 15 minutes a footbridge allows you to cross the river to the left and climb up to a road.

Turn right and follow the steadily climbing road for 30 minutes to a road bridge across the Río Manzanares. Use the steps on the left to climb up to a path that quickly leads past a reliable *fuente* to a simple footbridge. Cross; then zigzag up the cairn-lined path that heads west up through a gorge around a series of waterfalls to arrive at Arroyo del Berzoso in 40 minutes. Bear left (south) here, sticking close to the river initially, and continue to a dirt road east of **Maliciosa** (2227m). Walk left along the road to a bridge, where a path on the true left bank follows the river northwest through a tranquil, grassy valley to the ruins of **Refugio del Ventisquero de la Condesa**, 200m below the TV transmitters on **Bola del Mundo** (2268m). It's a steep climb (due west) to the peak. There are expansive views from the triangulation point on the top. The evening light beautifully illuminates the flat, arid plains of Castilla-La Mancha to the south and the outline of the Sierra de Gredos to the southwest. Madrid looks like a desert mirage. From the TV transmission station a concrete road descends through ski infrastructure to Puerto de Navacerrada.

Puerto de Navacerrada

This place is geared towards a short, money-spinning, ski season and can feel like a ghost town in summer.

Albergue Álvaro Iglesias (☎ 91 852 38 87; [e] tive.juventud@comadrid.es; dorm beds for those 26 yrs & over €7.80/10.80; open 15 Sept-15 Aug) is a huge 92-bed place just down from the pass. Rates include breakfast; IYHA cards are mandatory.

Albergue Puerto Navacerrada (☎ 91 852 14 13, fax 91 852 33 46; half-board per person

€17-20; open Sept–mid-June), west from the pass, is a good best out of summer.

Hotel Pasadoiro (☎ 91 852 14 27, fax 91 852 35 29; singles/doubles €36.50/51.50), 50m south of the pass, has a restaurant, although **Restaurante Venta Arias** (menú del día €11), across the road, is better value.

Day 3: Puerto de Navacerrada to Cercedilla

3–4 hours, 15km

From the top of the pass head west straight up a small ski slope to a ridge. Turn left and follow a wide track just north of the ridge (a left fork offers a direct route across a series of rocky peaks) to a saddle with a large boulder and a junction of trails. Head west along a wide track then, after 30m, fork left onto a cairn-marked trail that leads straight up the mountain to **Siete Picos** (2138m). The rest of the walk follows the last section of the Valle de la Fuenfría walk (see p85); it takes two to 2½ hours to reach Cercedilla.

Other Walks

SIERRA DE GREDOS
Gredos Crossing

One popular three- to four-day north-south crossing of the Gredos leads from Navalperal de Tormes (catch the Gredos bus from Madrid's Estación Sur de Autobuses) up Garganta del Pinar or across the Cuerda de los Barquillos (a long ridge) to the Cinco Lagunas and on to Refugio Elola. You then have the option of descending southwest along Garganta Tejéa from Lagunilla del Corral (which is west of Almanzor) to El Raso or heading east to Morezón and then south through Puerto de Candeleda down to Candeleda itself. Buses to Madrid run daily along the C501 south of the range. You'll need the IGN 1:50,000 Macizo Central de Gredos map.

Eastern Gredos

By basing yourself at Cuevas del Valle (see p71) and using the weekday Muñoz Travel buses to/from Ávila, you can do day walks up La Fría (1983m; west of Puerto del Pico) and Torozo (2021m; east of the pass). Both walks could also be turned into circular routes. The former goes straight up to the peak before descending via Puerto del Arenal and traversing back to the pass (or dropping down to El Arenal, which is also served by occasional buses). The latter peak could form part of a loop through San Esteban del Valle. IGN 1:25,000 map Nos 578-II Mombeltrán and 578-I El Arenal cover these walks.

Alta Ruta de Gredos Extension

It's possible to extend the Alta Ruta de Gredos to Puerto de Tornavacas. However, there's no set path from Portilla del Venteadero to Covacha, and broom and rugged, rocky peaks can make life difficult. El Butraco (2177m) is the most difficult (and rocky) section, but some of the ridge leading to it can be bypassed with a 30-minute detour along Garganta de Bohoyo. Around Cancho (2271m) is also tricky and it's essential to leave the ridge at Portilla del Palomo, thus avoiding the jagged cliffs of Riscos Morenos above Laguna de los Caballeros.

Four days allows for a comfortable traverse between Refugio Elola (see Day 3 of the Alta Ruta de Gredos walk, pp73–4) and Puerto de Tornavacas, camping at the top of Garganta de Bohoyo on the first night, near Alto de las Becedillas Los Peones on the second and Laguna de los Caballeros on the third.

A good planning map for exploring the Gredos is Adrados Ediciones 1:135,000 Parque Regional de la Sierra de Gredos. Numerous IGN 1:25,000 maps cover the route.

SIERRA DE GUADARRAMA
Northeast Guadarrama

A number of good routes tag onto the Cuerda Larga walk (see p88). A two-day option starts at Garganta de los Montes (which has a train station and bus links to Madrid), from where a pleasant trail runs the 10km to Cancencia and up to Puerto de Cancencia. From here the GR10.1 takes a fairly steady route to **Refugio Puerto de la Morcuera** (☎ *91 580 42 16*), which lies 1km north of Puerto de la Morcuera (1796m). From the pass the Cuerda Larga walk can be reached via Najarra (2106m). The best map to use is the La Tienda Verde 1:50,000 Sierra de Guadarrama.

Western Guadarrama

The route between Cercedilla and San Lorenzo de El Escorial (a town that has drawn royals and *madrileños* for centuries) follows the GR10 across the ridges on the border with Castilla y León and the Comunidad de Madrid. En route is Valle de los Caídos (The Valley of the Fallen), which contains Franco's remarkable, perversely self-indulgent tomb. This walk would take at least three days and a number of simple *refugios* and huts lie en route. La Tienda Verde's 1:50,000 *Sierra de Guadarrama* map covers the walk.

Peñalara Ascent

The simple ascent of Peñalara (2430m; the highest peak in the Guadarrama) is excellent preparation for the Cuerda Larga walk (see p88); you can overnight at the hostel in Puerto de Cotos and be bright eyed and bushy tailed for the Cuerda Larga walk in the morning. Taking around three hours, the route has 600m of ascent and descent. To avoid retracing your steps from the summit it is possible to return to Puerto de Cotos via Laguna de los Pájaros or via Laguna Grande de Peñalara. The best map is the La Tienda Verde 1:50,000 *Sierra de Guadarrama*, plus the leaflet from the information office in Puerto de Cotos: see Information Sources (p84–5).

The Pyrenees

The core of this chapter is a 23-day traverse from the principality of Andorra, in the east, to Sallent de Gállego, in the west of Aragón.

But three weeks or so is more time than many walkers can spare. For those who prefer to radiate out from a base or linger in a particularly scenic area, we include three separate sections. Each has suggestions for walks that when used in conjunction with the relevant day walks from the Traverse give a whole week of trekking.

In the Andorra section three one-day walks radiate from Canillo and Soldeu. Of deliberately varying standards of difficulty, they can be savoured for their own sake or used as a warm-up for the traverse. The Parc Nacional d'Aigüestortes i Estany de Sant Maurici section has three extra walks amid some of the most spectacular scenery in the Pyrenees, while within the Aragonese Pyrenees section are suggestions for further day walks based upon the village of Benasque.

HISTORY

The distressing news for walkers is that the Pyrenees no longer exist. Physically, of course, they're as impressive as ever. However, many Spanish use the metaphor of the Pyrenees' disappearance to describe Spain's coming in from the cold after centuries of relative isolation from the rest of Europe – a process that began soon after the death of General Franco in 1975 and culminated in Spain's entry into the EU in 1986.

Hydro schemes in the Pyrenees contributed to Spain's economic recovery from the ravages of the Spanish Civil War. In the 1950s and 1960s Spain invested massively in developing small-scale hydroelectric plants, mainly to service the towns and villages of the Pyrenean valleys. Most of the reservoirs are natural, though dams at their heads have often augmented their depths.

Traditionally the mountains have maintained an agricultural economy based on sheep and cows. Summer pastures were used not only by local villagers but also by

THE PYRENEES

Highlights

DAMIEN SIMONIS

The national park namesake lake – Estany de Sant Maurici

- Picking your way along the Faja de Pelay trail, clutching the contours high above Valle de Ordesa on the Pyrenean Traverse, Day 19 (p133)

- Camping wild and free west of Collado de Piedrafita on the Pyrenean Traverse, Day 22 (p141)

- Looking over all Andorra from the spine of Cresta de l'Estanyó on the Pic de l'Estanyó walk (p148)

- Walking just about anywhere in Parc Nacional d'Aigüestortes i Estany de Sant Maurici (p150)

shepherds and cowherds who transmigrated from much further afield (see the boxed text 'La Trashumancia', p144). Many of the trails described in this chapter were created to provide access to these lush, upland grasses. And many of the fanciful tracks still indicated on maps were once shepherds' routes and are now overgrown and under-used except by occasional trekkers hacking their own way with compass and map.

NATURAL HISTORY

The natural history of the Pyrenees is long and turbulent. Some 350 million years ago they were already a formidable mountain chain of igneous rock formed by solidified magma from the earth's molten heart, their summits capable of dwarfing today's 3000m giants.

Over tens of millions of years of slow erosion the mountains were ground down to a vast plain which was then invaded by the sea. Grain by grain, shell by shell, sediments accumulated in layers on the ocean bed. (In places such as the Parque Nacional de Ordesa y Monte Perdido you can still see sandstone bands, sometimes straight as a layer cake, often in convoluted whorls.)

About 25 million years ago the Iberian tectonic plate slammed into the European one with a force sufficient to compress and fold upwards slabs as big as today's peaks, from which the seas streamed and departed.

From this moment on, erosion has been the principal force shaping the range we see today. During the successive ice ages of the last million years ice covered all but the highest peaks and has left a distinctive imprint on the landscape (see the boxed text 'Signs of a Glacial Past', p23).

Mountain, or black, pine, squat with grey-black bark and hardiest of the conifers, occupies the reaches just below the tree line. Fir and Scots pine thrives at lower altitudes. Deciduous trees include rowan, hazel – a rich source of nutritious nuts in autumn – silver birch, elm, mountain oak, elder and, particularly in Aragón, forests of beech trees. Down in the damp lower valleys, goat willow, common ash and aspen abound.

In all but alpine environments, low banks of azaleas brush against your knees. Around them grow juniper bushes with their characteristic greyish berries, broom with bright yellow flowers, bilberries and wild raspberries (ready to pick in late summer), heather, dog roses and, at lower altitudes, clumps and stands of boxwood.

In general, June is the best time for viewing wildflowers. Common at subalpine level are white and leafless crocuses, the carline thistle (see the boxed text 'Charlemagne & the Thistle') and various varieties of gentian including great yellow and – found everywhere when in season – bright blue trumpet gentians. Most flourish in meadows along with the pink stars of moss campions, alpine pasques, wild daffodils in abundance and mountain iris.

For more on the Pyrenees' typical alpine, subalpine and mountain vegetation, see Watching Wildlife (p27).

You stand a reasonable chance of seeing chamois (*rebeco* in Spanish, *sarrio* in Aragonese and *isard* in Catalan), albeit at a distance. Roe and red deer are less timid but less widely distributed. Only a few brown bears survive in the Pyrenees and a positive but contentious programme is under way to reintroduce them. Listen for the characteristic warning whistle of marmots, shaggy clowns of the high boulder fields. Strangest of all is the shy, rare *desman*, an aquatic, mole-like creature peculiar to the Pyrenees, whose closest relatives live in the Caucasus mountains of Georgia.

As your chances of spotting one of the six brown bears reputedly surviving in the Pyrenees are near nil, the only potentially harmful beastie on your path is the Pyrenean viper, a snake that, given a chance, will scuttle away before you're even aware of it.

Charlemagne & the Thistle

As Emperor Charlemagne's army was passing through the Pyrenees, on its way to do battle with the Arab occupiers of Spain, the plague struck. When the emperor prayed to God for help, says the legend, an angel appeared to him and instructed him to fire an arrow into the air and whichever plant it pierced on its descent would prove to be an effective remedy. The arrow fell upon a kind of ground-hugging thistle, still common in the Pyrenees and still used as a natural remedy. It's called *carlina*, in both Catalan and Spanish, after Carlomagno – Charlemagne.

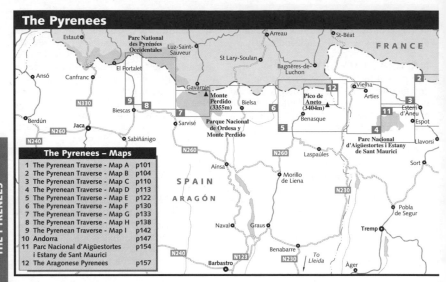

The Pyrenees

Wheeling above the upland valleys and peaks are a variety of birds of prey, including golden, booted and Bonnelli's eagles. You'll probably spot griffon and Egyptian vultures. Rarer is the bearded vulture or lammergeier, in Spanish *el quebrantahuesos*, the bone-smasher, from its habit of flying high and dropping bones onto the rocks so that it can peck at the marrow.

CLIMATE

The weather can change in the twinkling of an eye. Summer mountain storms build up during the afternoon and break in the early evening. So aim for an early start each day – then you can dawdle or take evasive action, should the clouds build up. While such storms usually pass quickly, they can be intense: hailstones the size of marbles pelt down even in midsummer.

INFORMATION
When to Walk

The walking season, unless you're an experienced mountain trekker comfortable with both snow and ice, is the window between mid-June and early September. Come any earlier and you'll be facing intimidating snowbanks; come later and the weather is increasingly unreliable.

Maps

The Pyrenees are well endowed with maps for walkers.

Small-Scale Maps Firestone produces a good overview map of the Pyrenees at 1:200,000, covering both the French and Spanish sides of the frontier. Editorial Everest does a worthy alternative, available in either book or folding format at 1:230,000.

Large-Scale Maps The most readily available maps are produced by **Editorial Alpina** (Ⓦ *www.editorialalpina.com)*; they come in a variety of scales. Be sure to buy the latest edition (the cover of recent issues is green rather than their traditional red). For the lowdown on other worthwhile series and more detailed consideration of maps see the Planning sections of the regions and individual walks.

Buying Maps To be sure of getting the ones you need, buy all your maps in advance. Shops in popular tourist towns and villages such as Andorra la Vella, Espot, Benasque,

Bielsa and Torla often sell the Alpina map for their area but few, if any, alternatives.

Books

Douglas Streatfield-James' *Trekking in the Pyrenees* is excellent, offering a wide range of walks, from half-dayers to demanding treks of a week or more. Be sure to pick up the 2nd edition (2001) or a later one since this has much more detailed coverage of Spanish slopes, including a traverse from the eastern Basque Country almost as far as Andorra, described from west to east.

Walks & Climbs in the Pyrenees, by Kev Reynolds, also well written, concentrates much more upon the French side than the Spanish.

Quite stimulating is *Pyrenees High Level Route,* an abridged and fairly pedestrian – forgive us but it's true! – translation of *La Haute Route des Pyrénées,* the classic French work by the granddad of all Pyrenees walkers, Georges Veron. However, he's not for beginners or even intermediate walkers. Master of navigation with an unparalleled knowledge of the mountains, he gives route descriptions that are often minimal and frequently just strikes out where no path exists.

Through the Spanish Pyrenees GR11: A Long Distance Footpath, by Paul Lucia, follows this long-distance Pyrenean trail.

For flowers, *Wild Flowers of the Pyrenees,* by AW Taylor, is worth picking up. For detail, check Lance Chilton's *Plant List for the Pyrenees.* Amateurs who just enjoy identifying flowers from a clear photo will find the *Guía de Flors d'Andorra,* with photos and minimalist text by Doreen Lindley, excellent. Ironically, it's only available in Catalan but each photo is accompanied by the flower's Spanish, French, English and Latin names – and most entries are valid for the Pyrenees in general.

Bird-watchers will find *A Birdwatching Guide to the Pyrenees,* by Jacquie Crozier, an informative companion.

Information Sources

The two principal walking organisations in Catalunya are the **Federació d'Entitats Excursionistes de Catalunya** (☎ 93 412 07 77; W *www.feec.es*) and one of its constituent groups, the **Centre Excursionista de Catalunya** (*CEC;* ☎ 93 315 23 11). Their equivalent in Aragón is the **Federación Aragonesa de Montañismo** (*FAM;* ☎ 976 22 79 71).

Place Names

We use the form the locals use, opting for the Catalan name in Andorra and the Catalan Pyrenees and the Spanish form elsewhere. You'll often find a variety of spellings from one map to another and even within the same text. One pass in the Catalan Pyrenees, for instance, is labelled variously as Port d'Onhla Crestada (Aragonese), Port de Collcrestada (Catalan) and Güellicrestada (Spanish). Farther west in Aragón, a pass can be the Puerto Chisten, Puerto de Chistau or Puerto de Gistaín, depending on which book or map you consult. This isn't necessarily cartographic carelessness; it reflects a shift in language or dialect from one valley to another – or the fact that, until quite recently, some place names had never been written down.

Other Information

If you're walking in late summer you may find that what we or your map present as a small tarn is nothing more than cracked mud or a circle of more luxuriant grass. Such pools come and soon go after heavy rain or the early summer snow thaw.

By contrast, what may be a clearly identifiable track in late summer may be nothing more than a red line on the map after the snows have melted and the fresh spring grass begins to grow. Those same snows will also probably have demolished any small stone cairns last year's walkers may have laid.

When planning your walks, bear in mind that the times we quote cover only the *actual walking time*, not including stops for rest or food.

GETTING AROUND

Public transport, rarely frequent and being chopped back year by year, runs rather more regularly in summer. Since most services are few and far between, check times with the local tourist office.

For walks in Andorra the nearest town accessible by bus is Andorra la Vella (where there's also a good local bus service up the valley) from Barcelona, Madrid or Latour de Carol (France; also accessible by train).

For Vall Ferrera and Vall de Cardós, the nearest accessible town is Llavorsí from Lleida, Barcelona and Pobla de Segur (from where trains run to Lleida).

For Parc Nacional d'Aigüestortes i Estany de Sant Maurici, go to La Guingeta from Lleida, Barcelona and Pobla de Segur.

For Vall d'Aran, buses go to Vielha (which also has a good local bus service) from Lleida and Barcelona.

For La Ribagorça and Posets massif buses reach Benasque from Lleida and Barcelona via Barbastro.

For Parque Nacional de Ordesa y Monte Perdido buses reach Torla from Jaca, Huesca and beyond via Sabiñánigo.

Buses from Sabiñánigo serve both Panticosa and Sallent de Gállego.

Where buses no longer ply most villages have a taxi service, whether formally established or just someone who's prepared to do a run when asked. Inquire at the tourist office – in summer, there's a small office in most villages with tourism aspirations – or, for the real lowdown, in the local bar. A small investment can save you an hour or more of unexciting road walking.

A key train access point for the Catalan Pyrenees is Pobla de Segur, which is connected by train with Lleida (see p97).

GATEWAYS
Barcelona

Barcelona, one of Europe's most vibrant cities, has superb air connections to the rest of Europe and direct flights to/from North America. There are reasonable bus and train links to Andorra and the Catalan Pyrenees.

Information The Oficina d'Informació de Turisme de Barcelona (*in Spain ☎ 906 30 12 82, from abroad ☎ 93 368 97 30; Plaça de Catalunya 17-S; open 9am-9pm daily*) gives city information and can book accommodation.

Supplies & Equipment A first-class travel bookshop that also carries a wide range of maps is **Llibreria Altaïr** (*☎ 93 342 71 71, fax 93 342 71 78; w www.altair.es; Gran Via de les Corts Catalanes 616*).

Two well-stocked shops selling walking equipment are **Edelweiss** (*☎ 93 454 83 09; Carrer Comte de Urgell 72; metro Urgell*) and the nearby **Campama Esport** (*☎ 93 453 50 01; Carrer Comte de Urgell 95; metro Urgell*).

Places to Stay & Eat Whatever the season, it's essential to book in advance. For online reservations consult w www.barcelona-on-line.es.

Hostal Campi (*☎ 93 301 35 45, fax 93 301 41 33; e hcampi@terra.es; Carrer Canuda 4; singles €19, doubles with/without bathroom €44/37*) is an excellent deal.

Hostal Levante (*☎ 93 317 95 65; Baixada Sant Miquel 2; basic singles from €27, doubles with/without bathroom €52/46*) is large and bright.

Hotel Jardi (*☎ 93 301 59 00; Plaça de Sant Josep Oriol 1; singles/doubles €60/75*), recently refurbished, is a gem.

All three are in the **Barri Gòtic**, the heart of the old town, which is rich in places to eat for all budgets.

Left: In late spring the slopes of the Sierra de Gredos light up with wildflowers. **Top Right**: The crumbling ruins of Refugio de los Pelaos (2259m) provide walkers on the Alta Ruta de Gredos with a sheltered camp site near La Mira. **Bottom Right**: Hunted almost to extinction in the early 20th century, the Spanish ibex is now a reasonably common sight in the remote pastures around the Cinco Lagunas.

INGRID RODDIS

DAMIEN SIMONIS

Top: Circo de Soaso, in the Parque Nacional de Ordesa y Monte Perdido. **Bottom**: Expansive views from the Port de Ratera d'Espot in the Parc Nacional d'Aigüestortes i Estany de Sant Maurici, en route to Refugi de Colomers.

Getting There & Away For airlines serving Barcelona's **El Prat airport** (☎ 93 298 38 38) see Air under Getting There & Away (pp370–2).The airport has plenty of car-rental outfits if you want to bypass the city and head straight for the hills. **Novatel Autocars** (in Barcelona ☎ 93 436 61 70, in Andorra ☎ 803 789; Ⓦ www.andorrabybus .com) does four runs daily (€24) between the airport and Andorra la Vella's bus station.

Buses run to most large cities in Spain. A plethora of companies operates to different parts of the country, although many come under the umbrella of **Alsa-Enatcar** (☎ 902-42 22 42; Ⓦ www.alsa.es). The main inter-city bus station is the modern **Estació del Nord** (☎ 93 265 65 08; Carrer d'Alí Bei 80).

Barcelona has good train connections to most major Spanish cities. Most services depart from **Estació Sants** (Plaça dels Països Catalans).

Lleida

Lleida is a likeable place with a long and varied history. Turisme Lleida's **Centre d'Informació i Reserves** (☎ 902 25 00 50; Carrer Major 31 bis; open 11am-8pm Mon-Sat, 11am-1.30pm Sun) is the best place for city information. **Caselles** (Carrer Major 46) has material on the Pyrenees.

Places to Stay & Eat Handy for the train station is **Hotel Ramon Berenguer IV** (☎ 973 23 73 45, fax 973 23 95 41; Plaça Ramon Berenguer IV 2; singles/doubles with bathroom €29.50/37).

Hostal Mundial (☎ 973 24 27 00, fax 973 24 26 02; Plaça de Sant Joan 4; singles €20, doubles with bathroom €26), with an entrance on Carrer Major, is a friendly place with worthy rooms and offers cheap meals.

Getting There & Away Daily bus services by **Alsina Graells** (☎ 973 27 14 70) include up to 13 buses (three on Sunday) to Barcelona (€14.05, 2¼ to 2¾ hours).

Lleida is on the Barcelona–Zaragoza–Madrid train line. Around 15 to 20 trains daily run to Barcelona (€7.90 to €18.50, two hours). Up to five daily trains head to Madrid.

Trains leave Lleida for Pobla de Segur (€4.15, 1½ hours, three daily), a key access point for the Catalan Pyrenees. The Alsina Graells bus stop in Pobla de Segur is on Calle Font, a 10-minute walk from the train station.

The Pyrenean Traverse

Duration	23 days
Distance	305.7km
Difficulty	moderate–demanding
Start	Canillo (Andorra; p98)
Finish	Sallent de Gállego (p99)
Transport	bus
Summary	An exhilarating east-to-west trek through the most spectacular part of the Spanish Pyrenees, including a pair of national parks

This challenging traverse starts in the tiny Principality of Andorra and ends in the otherwise inconsequential village of Sallent de Gállego, deep in the Aragonese Pyrenees. Spectacular throughout, its major highlights are the two national parks that lie on the Spanish side of the border – the Parc Nacional d'Aigüestortes i Estany de Sant Maurici and the Parque Nacional de Ordesa y Monte Perdido – plus Parque Posets-Maladeta, which is rugged and encompasses several of the Pyrenees' highest peaks.

We've set out a flexible itinerary to allow for varying amounts of time and fitness levels. Within most stages you'll find a camp site or unstaffed *refugio* (mountain hut or refuge) so you can knock off early or push on beyond the day's official end. The stages are, of course, an artificial division; on many days you can plan your own route, especially if you have the flexibility of a tent. We highlight some choice wild camping spots but practically any flat five square metres – provided you're not contravening *parque nacional* (national park) or *parque natural* (nature park) regulations – can be your bed for the night.

In the two national parks areas within strolling distance of the shuttle-bus terminals can be thronged with walkers in high summer. Apart from these two tourist magnets, trails are lightly trodden and it can be quite an event to meet other trekkers. If you like to walk alone, you'll scarcely see another soul between Canillo in Andorra and Espot in the Catalan Pyrenees (Days 1 to 6 of the traverse). You're also guaranteed solitude on the long and quite tough route between the Hospital de Vielha (Day 10) and Benasque (Day 12).

This table lists the days of the traverse as we describe it (not including Alternative Days, of which there are four):

day	from	to	km
1	Canillo	Arinsal	17.5
2	Arinsal	Refugi de Vall Ferrera	15
3	Refugi de Vall Ferrera	Refugi de Baborte	6.5
4	Refugi de Baborte	Lleret	18.8
5	Lleret	La Guingeta	14
6	La Guingeta	Espot	10.8
7	Espot	Refugi de Colomers	18.5
8	Refugi de Colomers	Refugi Ventosa i Calvell	8
9	Refugi Ventosa i Calvell	Refugi de la Restanca	6
10	Refugi de la Restanca	Hospital de Vielha	9.5
11	Hospital de Vielha	Meadows below Collado del Toro	8.5
12	Meadows below Collado del Toro	Benasque	20.5
13	Benasque	Refugio Ángel Orus	10.5
14	Refugio Ángel Orus	Refugio de Estós	14.5
15	Refugio de Estós	Refugio de Viadós	10
16	Refugio de Viadós	Parzán	20
17	Parzán	Valle de Pineta	16
18	Valle de Pineta	Valle de Añisclo	7.5
19	Valle de Añisclo	Torla	23
20	Torla	Bujaruelo	10
21	Bujaruelo	Balneario de Panticosa	18
22	Balneario de Panticosa	Refugio de Respomuso	12.3
23	Refugio de Respomuso	Sallent de Gállego	10.3

The Fast Lane

Here are some possible short cuts and bypasses if your time in the mountains is limited. But don't bust a gut. Unless you're a human tornado, consider building in a rest day or two in, for example, Espot at the end of Day 6 or Benasque, at the end of Day 12, the halfway point. Another option, of course, is to do the traverse over a couple, or even three, holidays.

- Omit Day 1 and join the route at Arinsal
- Take a taxi (€50) from Refugi de Vall Ferrera (end Day 2) to Espot, skipping Days 3 to 6
- Extend Day 5 and omit Day 6 by taking a taxi (€9) between La Guingeta and Espot
- Omit Days 8 and 9, walking directly from Refugi de Colomers to Refugi de la Restanca. Push on to the Hospital de Vielha (end Day 10) and save yet another day
- Take the easy valley route between Benasque and Refugio de Estós (Alternative Day 13) and omit Days 13 and 14. Continue to Refugio de Viadós (end Day 15)
- Get an early start to Day 19, walk or take the shuttle bus from Pradera de Ordesa to Puente de los Navarros and continue to Bujaruelo (end Day 20)

NEAREST TOWNS
Canillo

The Andorran village of Canillo tends to be much more subdued than Soldeu 7km to its east. You'll find a helpful **tourist office** (☎ 851 002) that's particularly helpful with assisting on hiking information. It runs daily guided walks throughout summer. You can relax after a day in the mountains here at the sauna or swimming pool of the **Palau de Gel**, Canillo's local sports complex and ice rink.

Camping Santa Creu (☎ 851 462; camping per person/tent/car €2.85/2.85/2.85) is the greenest of Canillo's five camping grounds and, since it's the farthest from the highway, the quietest.

Hotel Comerç (☎ 851 020; rooms with washbasin €23) is a long-established favourite, to which regulars return year after year.

Hotel Canigó (☎ 851 024, fax 851 824; singles/doubles/triples/quads with bathroom €21/36.50/46/55) offers good value accommodation.

Cal Lulu (☎ 851 427; menú €11.50, mains €10-13, pizzas €7-8.75) serves great Catalan and French dishes which come in generous quantities.

The restaurant located at the **Palau de Gel** sports complex has an excellent-value weekday menú (fixed-price meal; €7.30) and its weekend menú festiu (€15.30) is truly gourmet. Its bar is a good spot for a snack.

Buses run from Andorra la Vella to Canillo (€1.65, hourly) between 8am and 8pm and continue to Soldeu on the half-hour. To return from Soldeu, they leave hourly, on the hour, until 8pm.

Sallent de Gállego

The small **tourist office** (☎ 974 48 80 12; open 10am-1pm & 5pm-8pm daily) functions from July to mid-September.

There's a basic **zona de acampada** (camping per person/tent €1.50/1.50; open June-Sept), a simple camping ground run by the municipality, just northeast of the village.

Hostal Centro (☎ 974 48 80 19, fax 974 48 81 25; singles/doubles/triples/quads with bathroom €27/42/56/72), a small, family-run place, has a tasty menú (€11) on offer.

Hotel Balaitus (☎/fax 974 48 80 59; e balaitus@ctv.es; singles/doubles/triples/quads with bathroom from €24.65/38.35/47.20/58.30) is a charming place, crammed with antique furniture and family mementoes. Prices rise by about 40% in July and August.

From Monday to Saturday **Alosa/La Oscense** (☎ 974 48 00 45) buses go to Jaca via Sabiñánigo (two daily). From Jaca there is onward transport available to Zaragoza and Pamplona. From Sabiñánigo buses travel to/from Huesca (€4.05, 45 minutes, four daily), where there are links to Lleida and Barcelona. **Jose Domec** (☎ 974 48 82 68, 619 75 75 50) runs the local village taxi service.

PLANNING
Maps

Prames (W www.prames.com) publishes a pack of 47 1:40,000 maps (€21.25) plus an accompanying booklet (in Spanish) that covers the whole of the GR11 trail from the Atlantic to the Mediterranean. It also produces excellent 1:25,000 maps (€4.50) for most of the Aragonese Pyrenees.

In a fruitful example of trans-frontier collaboration, Rando Éditions and the Institut Cartogràfic de Catalunya (ICC) have jointly published a series of seven 1:50,000 maps covering Andorra and sectors of the Catalan and Aragonese Pyrenees. Contours are at 20m intervals and areas of steep terrain have clear elevation shading. However, not all paths, confidently indicated in red, exist on the ground.

You can cover all 23 days of the Pyrenean Traverse with only four sheets from this series, each of which contains considerable overlap:

map title	map number	days
Andorra Cadí	21	1 & 2
Pica d'Estats Aneto	22	2–11
Aneto Posets	23	11–17
Gavarnie Ordesa	24	16–23

At €8.75, they're a bargain. But they're huge and will wrap you like an Egyptian mummy in high wind. Consider chopping them up into more manageable segments and maybe laminating them before setting out on the walk.

Editorial Alpina (W www.editorialalpina .com) maps are the most readily available; come with scales of 1:25,000, 1:40,000 and an eccentric 1:30,000; and sell for €5.45 to €7. They're very reliable for topography as they have particularly clear elevation shading. However, the location of superimposed features such as the refugios, camping grounds and even some footpaths should sometimes be treated with scepticism. Be sure to buy the latest edition (the cover of recent issues is green rather than their traditional red), which tends to be more accurate.

For the full traverse, you'll need:

map title	days
Andorra	1 (Canillo to Arinsal)
Pica d'Estats	2–4 (Arinsal to Lleret)
Sant Maurici	5–7 (Lleret to Refugi de Colomers)
Vall de Boí	8 & 9 (Refugi de Colomers to Refugi de la Restanca)
Val d'Aran	10 & 11 (Refugi de la Restanca to Coll de Mulleres)
La Ribagorça	10 & Alt 11 (Refugi de la Restanca to Collada de Ballibierna)
Maladeta Aneto	12 (La Besurta & Benasque)
Posets Perdiguero	13–15 (Benasque to Refugio de Viadós)
Bachimala	16 (Refugio de Viadós to Parzán)
Ordesa Monte Perdido	17–20 (Parzán to Bujaruelo)
Vignemale Bujaruelo	21 (Bujaruelo to Panticosa or Balneario de Panticosa)
Panticosa Formigal	22 & 23 (Balneario de Panticosa to Sallent de Gállego)

THE WALK
Day 1: Canillo to Arinsal
6¼–7¾ hours, 17.5km

You can do Day 1 simply as a day walk, returning to Canillo from Arinsal by bus via Andorra la Vella. Similarly, the first part of the day (as far as Ordino) makes a pleasant half-day excursion, leaving you time to explore the village before returning by bus via Andorra la Vella.

Walk 1.4km from Canillo down the Andorra la Vella road to the Mobil petrol station. Take a track to the right, signed 'Coll d'Ordino'. Where the track ends at a lone building, take a steep path right. Intermittently signed with yellow blobs and red arrows, this soon begins to climb steeply southwestwards up the flank of a valley. About 30 minutes from the main road, follow two sides of a rectangular boundary wall around a meadow. Pass well to the left of the ruined Borda de N'Andrieta, reached after around 1¼ hours' walking, and hug its

boundary wall to cross the head of the valley and re-enter pine forest.

Five minutes later, as you leave the forest and enter the Planell de les Basses, an open meadow, aim for a broad, double-trunked pine directly ahead. Around 30m beyond, pick up the first of the red-and-white GR11 stripes that you'll be following for the rest of the day. Turn right along this intersecting path to reach the **Coll d'Ordino** (1979m) after a total walking time of 1½ to 1¾ hours.

From the col, a well-defined track drops westwards towards the tight valley of the Riu de Segudet. After a little under 15 minutes turn sharp right beside a metal fence to pass a *merendero* (picnic spot) and the Font de la Navina spring. Twenty minutes or so later turn right at a T-junction with a chain barrier to describe a hairpin around another *merendero* and a small pool. The route, which frequently hops from bank to bank, follows a stream that drops from the pool, passing beside the Casa Redort farm.

Thirty minutes from the T-junction turn right to leave the stream. Follow the twists and turns of the track as it climbs the west flank of the Vall de Casamanya. Around 20 minutes from the last turn there's an easily missed sharp left turn beside a wooden fence. The narrow path crosses several small lateral *barrancos* (gullies or ravines) and is steep but mercifully brief.

Once at valley level with 4¼ to 4¾ hours of walking under your belt, **La Cortinada**, with its 17th-century church and restored water-powered flour mill and sawmill, merits a short stop. To avoid the sealed road to Arans, take the cart track on the true left (east) bank of the river. Both La Cortinada and Arans are attractive villages, now almost entirely given over to rural tourism.

Should you wish to postpone the tough ascent to the Coll de les Cases until the next day, there are two possibilities right beside the route: **Hotel Sucará** (☎ 850 151, fax 849 151; e hotelsucara@andorra.ad; singles/doubles with bathroom from €28/38) – whose restaurant does excellent Andorran cuisine – in La Cortinada; and **Hotel Arans** (☎ 850 111, fax 850 380; doubles €35) in Arans.

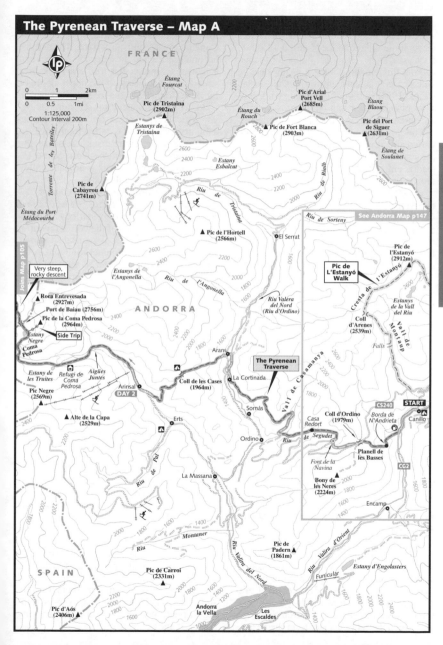

The Pyrenean Traverse – Map A

FRANCE

1:125,000
Contour Interval 200m

0   1   2km
0 0.5   1mi

Étang Fourcat

Pic de Tristaina
(2902m)

Pic d'Arial
Port Vell
(2685m)

Étang Blaou

Étang du Rouch

Pic de Fort Blanca
(2903m)

Pic del Port
de Siguer
(2631m)

Estanys de
Tristaina

Étang de
Soulanet

Pic de
Cabayrou
(2741m)

Torrente de les Bateies

Étang du Port
Médocourbe

Riu de Tristaina

Estany Esbalcat

Riu de Rialb

See Andorra Map p147

Pic de l'Hortell
(2566m)

El Serrat

Riu de Sorteny

Pic de
l'Estanyó
(2912m)

Joins Map p105

Very steep,
rocky descent

Roca Entrevesada
(2927m)
Port de Baiau (2756m)
Pic de la Coma Pedrosa
(2964m)

Estany
Negre
Coma
Pedrosa

Side Trip

Estanys de
l'Angonella

ANDORRA

Riu de l'Angonella

Riu Valéra
del Nord
(Riu d'Ordino)

Pic de
L'Estanyó
Walk

Cresta de l'Estanyó

Estanys de
la Vall
del Riu

Coll
d'Arenes
(2539m)

Vall de
Montaup

Falls

Estany de
les Truites

Refugi de
Coma
Pedrosa

Aigües
Juntès

Arinsal

DAY 2

Arans

Coll de les Cases
(1964m)

La Cortinada

The Pyrenean
Traverse

Vall de Casamanya

START

Pic Negre
(2569m)

Alte de la Capa
(2529m)

Erts

Sornás

Casa
Redort

Coll d'Ordino
(1979m)

CS240

Borda de
N'Andrieta

Canillo

Ordino

Riu de Segudet

Planell de
les Basses

CG2

Font de la
Navina

Riu de Pal

La Massana

Bony de
les Neres
(2224m)

Encamp

Montaner

Riu

Pic de
Padern
(1861m)

Riu Valira del Nord

Riu Valira del Orient

Estany d'Englosters

Pic de Carroí
(2331m)

Funicular

SPAIN

Pic d'Aós
(2406m)

Andorra
la Vella

Les
Escaldes

In **Arans** (1385m), the route crosses the sealed road beside Hotel Arans, meanders through the village to the 'Camí del Coll de les Cases' sign. Allow 1¼ hours for the ascent as this narrow footpath heads steeply, with scarcely a kink, up to the **Coll de les Cases** (1964m). If you're camping wild, consider pitching your tent on the grass, saving the descent to Arinsal until next morning.

The descent to Arinsal (1465m) is more varied and altogether more pleasant, though the stark buildings of this nouveau riche ski resort, entered along Carretera les Feixes, represent a brutal return to civilisation.

Arinsal

Camping Xixerella (☎ 836 613, fax 839 113; camping per person/tent €4.50/4.50; open Nov-Sept) is the nearest camping ground. Large, well equipped and with an outdoor pool, it's about 4km south on the road to Andorra la Vella. The last bus down from Arinsal departs at 7.45pm and the first up passes the camping ground about 8.15am.

Hostal Pobladó (☎ 835 122, fax 836 879; e hospoblado@andornet.ad; basic singles/doubles €15/29, singles/doubles with shower €20/39, singles/doubles with bathroom €27.50/42; open July–mid-June), beside the cabin lift, is friendliness itself, with a lively bar offering Internet access on the side. All prices include breakfast.

Hotel Aymá (☎ 83 52 95, fax 83 60 32; doubles/triples with bathroom €37/55.50) is a small, long-established family hotel where you'll eat like royalty.

Hotel Coma Pedrosa (☎ 737 950, fax 737 951; doubles with bathroom €44) is welcoming and popular with skiers and summer walkers.

Day 2: Arinsal to Refugi de Vall Ferrera

6–6½ hours, 15km

A constant and at times steep climb to the Port de Baiau is followed by a long, fairly gentle descent of the upper reaches of Vall Ferrera. A pair of telescopic poles are useful for negotiating the snow you may find above the Estany Negre and to ease you down the very steep descent on shale from the pass.

At Arinsal's upper limit go through the road tunnel beside a notice, signed 'Vall de Comapedrosa', and turn right. The tarmac becomes shale and the track zigzags beyond a barrier to mount the true left bank of a stream that originates on the upper slopes of Pic de la Coma Pedrosa (see Side Trip, p103).

At Aigües Juntes, about 15 minutes beyond the barrier, cross the stream and its tributary by a pair of wooden footbridges to begin the slow, switchback ascent of the valley coming in from the west. Some 1½ to 1¾ hours from Arinsal a broader valley opens up beyond a false col.

Refugi de Coma Pedrosa (2260m; ☎ 327 955; dorm beds €7, meals €11.50; open June-Sept), Andorra's only staffed refugio, is just to the left (south) of the col. A favourite day-trip destination from Arinsal, it serves food and drinks to all-comers and makes for a good staging post if you're undertaking a side trip to Pic de la Coma Pedrosa.

Take a moment or two to enjoy the Estany de les Truites, a small lake just beyond the refugio, before continuing westward up the main valley. Thirty to 40 minutes beyond the refugio the path zigzags steeply northeast up the cirque of the Coma Pedrosa (Rocky Bowl) to a small tarn. The much larger **Estany Negre** (aptly if unimaginatively named Black Pool) broods no more than 10 minutes beyond.

From here to the pass at **Port de Baiau** (2756m) thick but manageable snow can linger well into July. At the col, a good half-hour beyond the second pool, savour the view back to the Estany Negre and northeast to the cairned summit of Pic de la Coma Pedrosa. Here the trail leaves Andorra to drop into the Spanish province of Lleida.

The descent to the Estany de Baiau is steep and decidedly hairy, requiring all your attention, particularly if you're carrying a full backpack. Scree and loose stones are followed by what seems an interminable clamber over boulders. Be guided by the mini-cairns, which are more plentiful and visible than the GR11 trail markers. In early summer, you can avoid some of the scramble by picking your way along the lingering banks of snow.

After negotiating a final tumble of rocks at the northeast shore of the tarn you reach **Refugi Josep Montfort** (2517m), 3¾ to 4¼ hours from Arinsal. It's the first of several *refugios* you'll come across in Catalunya run by the excellent Federació d'Entitats Excursionistes de Catalunya (FEEC). Unstaffed, it only has 12 bunks.

From the *refugio* head initially west (don't drop too much towards the lower, smaller pool) and continue down into the valley of the Torrent de Baiau. Once beyond the Estanys d'Escorbes there are plenty of potential **camp sites** in the meadows to the north of the track.

After splashing across several tributaries of the main stream that tumble in from the southwest you see a lone cabin in the meadows of the **Pla de Boet**, near the banks of the torrent (now elevated in name and status to Riu Noguera de Vall Ferrera).

Once a popular summer grazing area for livestock, the meadows make an idyllic **camp site**. For a roof over your head continue to join a broad 4WD track and, just over five minutes later, take a wooden bridge right to the **Refugi de Vall Ferrera** (1940m; ☎ 973 62 43 78; dorm beds €10.75; meals €12; open June-Sept). A friendly, popular place, run by the FEEC, it has capacity for 20 and you'll need to reserve (ring between noon and 5pm since their phone operates on solar power). If you're entering or leaving the traverse at this point you stand a reasonable chance of hitching a lift to Llavorsí, which has limited bus links to Barcelona and Lleida (for information on these buses see Vielha, p117, and Espot, pp151–2). Try hitching from the parking area near the Refugi de Vall Ferrera – the upper limit for vehicles, where many day-walkers leave their cars. For a taxi, call **Josep Maria Llor** (☎ 973 62 43 53, 609 35 79 26) or **Josep Maria Lladós** (☎ 973 62 44 11).

Side Trip: Pic de la Coma Pedrosa
2–2½ hours, 1.8km
This is a demanding ridge walk to Andorra's highest point, Pic de la Coma Pedrosa (2964m), which offers spectacular views. From the southeast shore of Estany Negre head northeast, following yellow dots and occasional small cairns.

Day 3: Refugi de Vall Ferrera to Refugi de Baborte
3¾–4¼ hours, 6.5km
Vall Ferrera and Vall de Cardós, the next major valley to the west, are sandwiched between the more popular tourist areas of Andorra and the Parc Nacional d'Aigüestortes i Estany de Sant Maurici and remain relatively isolated and unspoilt.

This is a fairly short stage after the exertions of the previous two. If you're tenting and want to extend the day, the upper Ribera de Sellente valley (see Day 4, p104), about 1¼ hours beyond Refugio de Baborte, has some splendid **camp sites**.

As far as Estany de Sotllo (**so**-yo), on the much-trodden main route to Pica d'Estats, you won't be short of company. Further west you're unlikely to see anyone all day.

Fifteen to 20 minutes above Refugi de Vall Ferrera turn left at a fork where a sign points west to Pica d'Estats. The track crosses several rocky spurs – one of which requires special concentration – then drops to meet the Barranc de Sotllo about an hour beyond the *refugio*. Cross over a wooden bridge to the true right bank of the torrent.

The path climbs over three lateral moraines straddling the valley. Tackle each on its west side. The route, in places more stream than path, is well cairned – grooved, even – by the thousands of walkers who have passed on their way to bag Pica d'Estats.

As you cross the third ridge, two hours from the *refugio*, **Estany de Sotllo** shimmers ahead, probably with a tent or two adding colour to its north shore. This is a popular base for a morning attack on Pica d'Estats (see Pica d'Estats, p105, under Other Walks).

On the small plain beside the north shore, leave the main track and head west-north-west, initially beside a waterfall, following the lake's main feeder stream. It makes a great trail marker – fortunately, since there's no path and only sporadic cairns – drawn like a length of string between the Estany de Sotllo and your intermediate goal, an unnamed pool, 30 to 40 minutes away.

THE PYRENEES

The Pyrenean Traverse – Map B

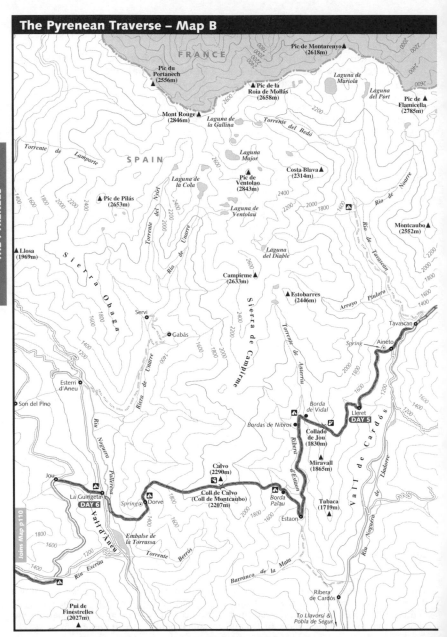

FRANCE

Pic de Montarenyo▲
(2618m)

Pic du
Portanech
▲(2556m)

Pic de la
Roia de Mollás▲
(2658m)

Laguna de
Mariola

Laguna
del Port

Pic de
Flamicella▲
(2785m)

Mont Rouge▲
(2846m)

Laguna de
la Gallina

Torrente del Bedó

Torrente de Lamparte

S P A I N

Laguna
Major

Laguna de
la Cola

Pic de
Ventolao▲
(2843m)

Costa Blava▲
(2314m)

Río de Noarre

▲ Pic de Pilás
(2653m)

Laguna de
Ventolau

Montcaubo▲
(2552m)

Río de Tavascan

Torrente del Nyiri

Río de Unarre

▲ Llosa
(1969m)

Laguna
del Diable

Sierra Obaga

Campirme▲
(2633m)

▲ Estobarres
(2446m)

Arroyo Piulora

Tavascan

Servi

Sierra de Campirme

Spring Aineto

Gabás

Torrente de Aurrru

Riera de Unarre

Estobarres
d'Aneu

Son del Pino

Borda
de Vidal

Bordas de Nibros

Lleret
DAY 5

Riu Noguera Vallferena

Ribera d'Estaon

Collado
de Jou
(1830m)

Vall de Cardós

Calvo
(2290m)

Miravall
(1865m)

Jou

La Guingeta
DAY 6

Spring Dorve

Vall d'Aneu

Coll de Calvo
(Coll de Montcaubo)
(2207m)

Borda
Palau

Estaon

Tabaca
(1719m)

Riu Noguera de Lladorre

Embalse de
la Torrassa

Torrente Berros

Riu Escrita

Barranco de la Mata

Ribera
de Cardós

Pui de
Finéstrelles
(2027m)▲

To Llavorsí &
Pobla de Segur

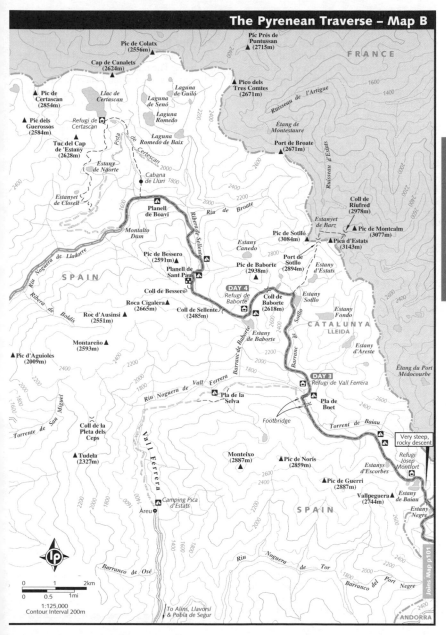

The Pyrenean Traverse – Map B

FRANCE

Píc Prés de Puntussan (2715m)

Pic de Colatx (2556m)

Cap de Canalets (2624m)

Pico dels Tres Comtes (2671m)

Ruisseau de l'Artigue

Laguna de Guiló

Laguna de Senó

Pic de Certascan (2854m)

Llac de Certascan

Étang de Montestaure

Laguna Romedo

Pic dels Guerossos (2584m)

Refugi de Certascan

Port de Broate (2671m)

Ruisseau d'Estats

Laguna Romedo de Baix

Tuc del Cap de 'Estany (2628m)

Pista de Certascan

Estany de Naorte

Cabana de Lluri

Coll de Riufred (2978m)

Estanyet de Closell

Riu de Broate

Estanyet de Barz

Pic de Montcalm (3077m)

Montalto Dam

Planell de Boavi

Pic de Sotlló (3084m)

Pica d'Estats (3143m)

Ribera de Sellente

Estany Canedo

Pic de Bessero (2591m)

Port de Sotlló (2894m)

Estany d'Estats

SPAIN

Planell de Sant Pau

Pic de Baborte (2938m)

Riu Noguera de Lladorre

Coll de Bessero

DAY 4 Refugi de Baborte

Coll de Baborte (2618m)

Estany Sotlló

Roca Cigalera (2665m)

Coll de Sellente (2485m)

Estany Fondo

Roc d'Ausinsi (2551m)

CATALUNYA LLEIDA

Ribera de Boldis

Estany de Baborte

Barranc de Sotlló

Montareño (2593m)

Estany d'Areste

Barranc de Baborte

Étang du Port Médocourbe

Pic d'Aguioles (2009m)

Riu Noguera de Vall Ferrera

DAY 3 Refugi de Vall Ferrera

Torrente de San Miguel

Pla de la Selva

Pla de Boet

Footbridge

Torrent de Baiau

Very steep, rocky descent

Coll de la Pleta dels Ceps

Vall Ferrera

Refugi Josep Montfort

Tudela (2327m)

Monteixo (2887m)

Pic de Norís (2859m)

Estanys d'Escorbes

Estany de Baiau

Camping Pica d'Estats

Pic de Guerri (2887m)

Vallpeguera (2744m)

Estany Negre

Àreu

SPAIN

0 1 2km
0 1mi

1:125,000
Contour Interval 200m

Barranco de Osé

Riu Noguera de Tor

Barranco del Port

Negre

To Alins, Llavorsí & Pobla de Segur

ANDORRA

Joins Map p101

THE PYRENEES

From the near end of this pool head steeply upwards, aiming for **Coll de Baborte** (2618m) to the southwest, just south of Pic de Baborte. At the pass, reached after 30 to 45 minutes of scree scrambling following a scarcely discernible trail, a metal sign directs you towards Refugi de Baborte, a further 35 to 45 minutes away. As you descend into the valley look for cairns rather than traces of the path, which loses itself among the boulders.

Keeping a couple of small tarns to your right, aim for a small nick southwest and dead ahead. Once you're beyond a pair of more substantial tarns, also on your right, **Refugi de Baborte** (2438m; unstaffed; free) and, below, the heart-shaped lake come into view. Resembling a giant freight container from outside, it can accommodate eight and, with its well-insulated, wood-panelled walls, is cosy inside. Campers will find plenty of **camp sites** on the springy grass near the lake.

Day 4: Refugi de Baborte to Lleret

5¼–5¾ hours, 18.8km

Starting with a short, sharp climb and ending in a longish but gentle ascent, the day is, in the main, delightfully downhill.

From the *refugio*, head west and up towards a bank of distinctly red rock and scree. If you're lucky you might hit one of the vague trails that zigzags through the boulder field and up to **Coll de Sellente** (2485m). If not, it doesn't matter since no path is better than another. Once over the col, reached in a little more than 30 minutes and indicated by a couple of poles and a Refugi de Baborte sign, keep heading rigorously northwest. The navigation is easy but if in doubt look for the cairn topping a giant erratic. Hereabouts, where the grass is plentiful and humans few, there's a good chance of seeing chamois.

After Coll de Bessero, a hump across the valley, the route turns right (north) and descends to **Planell de Sant Pau** (2240m), with a striped pole at its heart, and the ruins of the Sellente *refugio*. Cross the brow of another minor col and drop into lush **Ribera de Sellente** valley, hopping over several rivulets to get to the stream's true right bank. There's a cricket pitch and more **camp sites**.

A little over half an hour beyond Planell de Sant Pau look for the indistinct point where the trail crosses back to the true left bank. A clue is the twisted dead tree on the right bank. The path is evident, except where cows have trashed it, and stays level as the stream falls away. Where they rejoin, about 30 minutes later, cross to the true right bank over giant stepping stones of metamorphic rock (after rain the first two or three minutes of path after you've crossed are stream).

After crossing the torrent for one last time, tottering over a log, you enter woodland and the path becomes a well-maintained track. This drops gently in switchbacks through fir and pine to a log bridge over Riu de Broate and into the fertile meadows of **Planell de Boavi**, with several gorgeous **camp sites**.

A 20- to 30-minute walk from the log bridge to the barrier marks the limit for vehicles, then it's 6km to the village of **Tavascan** (1167m). More than five minutes beyond the barrier is a dam and the small hydroelectric plant of Montalto, driven by the Noguera de Lladorre – and also by water from Vall Ferrera, whose passage by subterranean pipe was much easier than your two-day trek.

Detrashing the Planell de Boavi

By midsummer the riverside meadows of the Planell de Boavi would be strewn with rubbish, cast by day visitors and campers, many of whom stayed for days, taking advantage of this free, accessible space. The place was also a health hazard, the faeces count rising as the peak holiday month of August progressed.

The solution was simple; the area was declared a protected zone for hunting and fishing – and a barrier was slung across the access track, a half-hour's walk downstream.

That half-hour is crucial. There's still open access for those who make the effort and the Planell de Boavi these days is almost as pure as the more lightly trodden meadows above.

Officially, all camping is forbidden. In practice, if you pitch your tent at dusk and move on early next morning – leaving no trace of your presence – no-one will object.

In Tavascan the cheapest accommodation option is **Pensió Casa Feliu** *(☎/fax 973 62 31 63; per person B&B €24, half-board €32.15)*. **Hotel Llacs de Cardós** *(☎ 973 62 31 78, fax 973 62 31 26; W www.llacscardos.com; per person B&B €25.30, half-board €37.70)*, next up, is an attractive, welcoming family-owned place. Stock up at the small **grocery store** in town since there's no shop between here and La Guingeta at the end of Day 5. If it seems to be closed ring the bell. There's also a small seasonal **tourist office** *(☎ 973 62 30 79; open 9am-2pm & 3.30pm-6pm daily June-Sept)*.

Once across Tavascan's fine, steeply arched stone bridge, turn almost immediately right to pass by the village water trough. Walk under an arch to join the ancient and occasionally overgrown path connecting Tavascan and Lleret. It's still banked and paved in places with large, rectangular slabs of rock.

The partly ruined, partly inhabited hamlet of **Aineto**, about 20 minutes beyond Tavascan, also has a flowing water trough. From here and well into Day 5, notice the abandoned *bordas* (mountain huts used in summer by shepherds and cowherds), their stones falling gale by gale back into the hillside from which they came. Bear right at a sign reading 'Lleret' and after 100m turn sharp left up a path. This enters a wood of hazel, ash and oak, climbing steeply along and beside a rocky streambed. After about half an hour the route turns south to maintain a fairly constant level, high on the flanks of the Vall de Cardós. After it levels out there's a basic stone shelter that can squeeze in a solo walker.

About 1½ hours beyond Tavascan the path comes out of the woods at a sharp bend in the sealed road. Turn right for the hamlet of **Lleret** (1380m), only a couple of minutes away.

Casa Rabasso *(☎ 973 62 32 12; e rabasso@terra.es; per person with/without bathroom €18.10/12.65, half-board with/without bathroom €31.85/26.40)*, just below the church, does lip-smacking home cooking based on fresh ingredients from the friendly owners' farm. It's the only accommodation choice in this tiny pueblo but they will ensure somehow that you have a roof over your head, should you find it full. Half-board is obligatory in July and August.

Day 5: Lleret to La Guingeta

6½–7½ hours, 14km

This is a longish roller coaster of a day as you pass over Collado de Jou to leave Vall de Cardós, drop gently down the Ribera d'Estaon valley and cross to Vall d'Àneu via Coll de Calvo.

Where the tarmac ends above Lleret take a wide, grassy cart track that heads uphill at right angles. There are no GR flashes for a kilometre or so but don't let this faze you. Stick with the track as it heads south then wriggles northwest before petering out at a drinking trough for livestock.

From here it's 15 or so minutes of hard work through chest-high broom to **Collado de Jou** (1830m). The pass, reached after 1¼ to 1½ hours of walking, has impressive views in all directions and makes a great snack stop.

If you lose the path down to the valley of the **Ribera d'Estaon** amid the thick broom, no matter; just head in a northwesterly direction for the evident ruined Borda de Vidal, less than 1km away. Once you reach the small river turn left and continue south, downstream, along an ancient track, hacked from the hillside and cobbled in places to give access to the upstream *bordas* – such as the Bordas de Nibros, yet another uninhabited cluster of farm buildings, which you can roam around. Hereabouts too are several grassy spots that make ideal **camp sites**.

Beside a rocky outcrop, about 30 minutes after reaching the valley floor, there's an abrupt change from tangled path to a wide, though long-abandoned, cart track. It's pleasant, undemanding walking – just you, the trail and the churning river – for a further 45 minutes to one hour until you turn right down a steep dirt path to meet a sealed road heading away from the river. Turn right again for **Estaon**, already visible and scarcely five minutes away.

Leave Estaon (1240m) by the slate steps next to the higher of its two *fuentes* (water troughs). Ensure your bottles are full since there's no other reliable source of water until Dorve, way over the other side of Coll de Calvo.

Take a vague switchback path northwards up a rocky crag. The path soon improves and climbs high above the Ribera d'Estaon. Just over 20 minutes from Estaon it turns left to pass near the Borda Palau, whose meadows make a reasonable **camp site**. As you emerge from the trees the trail veers west and you begin to push your way through thigh-high broom, dog rose bushes and, in the higher reaches, juniper.

Thirty to 40 minutes above the *borda* aim for a long-defunct telegraph pole on which is attached a sign, 'Dorve'. Five minutes later be vigilant as the indistinct path veers northwest beside the just-discernible ruins of an old *borda*. After about half an hour it enters a sparse pine wood, where it becomes more evident. The wood, interspersed with the occasional clearing, continues until **Coll de Calvo** (also called Coll de Montcaubo; 2207m), two to 2¼ hours from Estaon. From here you get your first views of the higher peaks within the Parc Nacional d'Aigüestortes i Estany de Sant Maurici.

At first the slope on the western side of the pass is less steep, the track's easier to distinguish and you can maintain a steady clip. Around 10 minutes below the pass there's an easily missed turn as a GR flash on a dead log directs you right (northwest) to begin the long descent to the Vall d'Àneu.

As you emerge from a wood, a little less than an hour from the col, you can see the abandoned hamlet of Dorve and, beyond it, the slender, emerald Embalse de la Torrassa dam. From here to Dorve the GR signing is lamentable. In the upper reaches you're fighting your way unsupported through broom while, lower down, deceptive cattle paths crisscross the meadows.

If, like most walkers, you temporarily lose the thread, simply aim for the valley's western flank where a clear track of much greater antiquity than the unkempt GR11 will lead you down to **Dorve**, a forlorn cluster of buildings. It does, however, preserve its flowing *fuente*, which offers the first reliable water since Estaon – and you can find a decent **camp site** in the surrounding meadows.

From Dorve a clear track (excessively signed, here where there's zero chance of going astray!) leads you in about 45 minutes to the lake and **La Guingeta** (945m).

La Guingeta

A staging post on an important highway, La Guingeta makes a good, if unexciting overnight stop.

Camping Vall d'Àneu (☎ 973 62 63 90; *camping per person/tent €3.75/3.75; open Easter-Sept)*, about 500m south on the other side of the highway, belongs to the same family as Hostal Cases.

Nou Camping (☎/fax 973 62 60 85; W *www .noucamping.com; camping per person/tent €4.10/4.10; open Easter–mid-Sept)* is a trimmer and more luxurious camping option.

Hostal Cases (☎ 973 62 60 83, fax 973 62 65 53; e *hostalcases@eresmas.com; rooms per person with/without bathroom €12.65/ 9.35, half-board €25.85)* is a friendly place that's excellent value for money.

La Guingeta is the nearest point to the Parc Nacional d'Aigüestortes i Estany de Sant Maurici with public transport access. **Alsina Graells** (*in Lleida* ☎ 973 26 85 00) runs buses from Lleida to La Guingeta via Pobla de Segur (one daily Monday to Saturday). The return bus to Lleida passes La Guingeta at the awful hour of 5.30am; and, Pobla de Segur (where it links with a connection for Barcelona) at 6.30am.

Alsina Graells (*in Barcelona* ☎ 93 265 68 66) also runs buses between Barcelona and the Pyrenees (two daily). One bus goes to La Guingeta. The other terminates in Pobla de Segur and connects with the bus from Lleida to La Guingeta.

Day 6: La Guingeta to Espot
2–2½ hours, 10.8km

This is an easy, rather uneventful transitional day. One option is to whistle up a **4WD taxi** (☎ 973 62 41 05) from Espot for €9 per vehicle and omit it altogether.

The first part's fun enough. Leave La Guingeta along the lane opposite Hotel Poldo and turn right at a T-junction. Brief tarmac gives way to an old cart track. This soon narrows to a cobbled, stepped path that leads to **Jou** (1305m) after 45 minutes to an hour of steady uphill climbing. Once you meet the electricity pylons that run up the valley to supply the cluster of houses that is Jou you know you're only 10 minutes or so away.

From Jou it's 5km along a sealed, virtually traffic-free minor road to the highway linking Espot and the Vall d'Àneu. At the junction you can head straight up the main road to **Espot** (1320m) or, for an altogether more pleasant alternative, cross the Riu Escrita at the array of flags beside Camping La Mola to take a wooded track above the river's true right bank.

Espot

Many walkers spend a night or two in Espot with its four camping grounds, hotels for all budgets, restaurants, good park information office and plentiful opportunities for side trips. For details see Espot (pp151–2).

Day 7: Espot to Refugi de Colomers

6½–7 hours, 18.5km

This is a truly five-star day, passing Estany de Ratera, one of the national park's major jewels, crossing Port de Ratera de Colomers and finishing with a magnificent stepped, lake-stippled descent.

Exactly 2km along the pocked road from Espot turn right at a sign for Estany de Sant Maurici and Refugi Ernest Mallafré. Cross the Riu Escrita and follow its true left bank through a mixture of broadleaf woodland, pine trees and meadow.

About halfway to the lake, after a pleasant hour's walking with few others for company, you meet the throng. Day visitors by the hundred stream in from the car park at **Prat de Pierró**, where an information cabin marks the entrance to the park and the limit for private vehicles. The riverside path from here to the lake is a conduit for around 95% of those park visitors who walk in.

You can take water on board roughly 45 minutes beyond Prat de Pierró at the Font de l'Ermita, beside a small chapel, or a little further along from the Font de Sant Maurici (1910m), beside the northeast shore of the **lake**.

From the spring follow the lakeside track, signed 'La Cascada' (waterfall). Turn right (north) at a similar sign to refresh yourself in the rainbow spray of the **Cascada de Ratera**.

Bear left at a sign, 'Estany de Ratera' and turn left again onto a 4WD track some five minutes later at a T-junction to rejoin the GR11 trail markers. Views south to the Pic dels Feixans de Monestero and the Gran and Petit Encantats – both official symbols of the park – are unsurpassed.

At a fork soon after the splendid tarn **Estany de Ratera** (2150m), about an hour from Estany de Sant Maurici, choose the left option then turn sharp right (northwest) to leave the jeep track and take a well-trodden path. This soon crosses to the true left bank of the stream that you'll be following to its source at the lake just below Port de Ratera. About 15 minutes later ignore a side path for Refugi d'Amitges that turns away to the right. Keep looking for the poles that mark the trail from here until shortly before the col.

Once beyond Estany d'Obagues de Ratera (also known as Estany de la Munyidera) the path briefly crosses to the true right bank to avoid the worst of the first of a pair of boulder fields. It threads its way through the second, reducing, but not eliminating, the amount of scrambling required.

The grade stiffens briefly as you approach Estanyet del Port de Ratera, a tiny lake at the valley's head. Having curled around a bulge above its northeastern shore you reach **Port de Ratera d'Espot** (2580m), a mere 50m above the tarn and 2¼ to 2½ hours from Estany de Sant Maurici.

Stroll northwest along the flat, grassy saddle, passing Port de Ratera de Colomers, to begin the stepped descent. Take the left

---

Scared? We Were Petrified

Two chamois hunters, so the story goes, were rash enough to mock a group of pilgrims toiling by on their way to the tiny chapel below the lake of Sant Maurici. But God swiftly intervened on the side of His faithful. To this day, if you look back from the road leading to Estany de Ratera and apply an ample pinch of salt, you can see the hunters' forms, petrified for all eternity, nestling between the two Pics Encantats, the enchanted peaks.

The Pyrenean Traverse – Map C

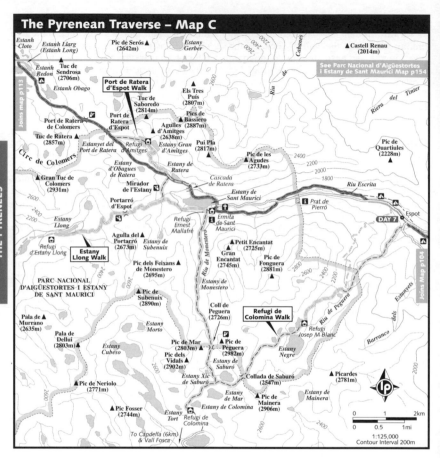

fork at a signed junction where the routes to the *refugios* of Colomers and Saboredo diverge. From here on there are infinite tempting **camp sites** beside the lakes, big, small, named and nameless, which stipple the valley: the extensive **Estanh Obago** (2242m), whose tip soon comes into view; **Estanh Redon** (Round Pond); and **Estanh Llarg**, also known as Estanh Long (Large and Long Pond). Full marks to the locals for accuracy, even if they fall short on originality. The route skirts to the southwest of each of the lakes, linked one to another by a stream, like beads on a necklace.

After the merest glimpse of Estanh Cloto and the low ranges behind the Vall d'Aran a wooden sign directs you left (west) over a small hill and down to Estanh Major de Colomers. Cross the dam to **Refugi de Colomers** *(2130m; ☎ 973 25 30 08)*, some two hours after crossing Port de Ratera d'Espot, at the end of one of the most spectacular days of walking that the Pyrenees can offer.

The *refugio* accommodates 40, does meals and has an area for self-caterers. The downside is that there's just one outside tap and a single squat toilet, perched over the dam (no swimming in *this* lake!).

There's just enough space to mount a tent on the lake's west bank, beside a stone hut, which, as it occupies the site for the proposed new *refugio*, may no longer be around when you pass by.

Side Trip: Salardú
6–6½ hours, 24km
If you're camping or self-catering consider visiting Salardú, down the beautiful valley of the Riu d'Aiguamòg, or Arties from Refugi de la Restanca (see Side Trip: Arties, p115) stock up on food, as there are no shops until Benasque at the end of Day 12. This is also a convenient entry or exit point from the walk.

After half an hour of descent you can clip 3km or so from the walk by taking a 4WD shuttle taxi (€3) that runs between July and September. At the taxi's lower point you stand a reasonable chance of hitching a lift to Salardú from one of the cars parked here at the limit for private traffic. A **taxi** (☎ 610 29 45 56) to Salardú from here will set you back a fat €36.

Here too are the hot springs, Banys de Tredòs. The **Hotel Baños de Tredòs** (☎ 973 25 30 03; *singles/doubles €90/120*) may not be your automatic overnight choice, but after a few days of minimal hygiene a half-hour hydromassage for €10 (€16 for a couple) is a sensual delight.

Retrace your steps to return to the route.

Salardú
The village of Salardú (1268m), 'capital' of the Naut Aran (Upper Aran) region, offers groceries, accommodation (but no camping ground) and transport to the wider world.

The **tourist office** (☎ 699 96 90 44; *open 10am-1.30pm & 4.30pm-8pm daily July-Sept*) occupies a kiosk just off the main road. The village has an ATM.

Auberja Era Garona (☎ 973 64 52 71, fax 973 64 41 36; [e] eragarona@aran.org; *B&B under 25/other €15.05/19.25*) is a Hostelling International-affiliated youth hostel with capacity for 190. Rooms are for four or six people and it's advisable to reserve ahead.

Xalet-Refugi Juli Soler Santaló (☎/fax 973 64 50 16; *dorm beds €9, 4-person room with shower per person €14.40, dinner €10.20 &*

half-board €26.45; open Dec-May & mid-June–mid-Oct), run by the admirable CEC, also has more than 100 beds – and a particularly cosy bar.

Pensió Montanha (☎ 973 64 41 08; *basic singles/doubles €18/25, singles/doubles with bathroom €25/31*) is a quiet enough place, despite being above the bar of the same name.

Hotel deth Païs (☎ 973 64 58 36, fax 973 64 45 00; *Plaça dera Pica; singles/doubles/ triples/quads with bathroom €46.05/63/ 82/99; open Dec-Mar & July–mid-Sept*) is an excellent top-end choice.

Salardú has a **grocery shop** and **supermarket**. For something more subtle than hostel fare, you can dine agreeably at **Eth Cabilac** (☎ 973 64 42 82; *Carrer Major 12; menú €15, mains €9.50-12.50*), whose adjacent bar does good tapas and snacks.

From mid-June to September a daily bus from Vielha to Barcelona calls by at 11.25am, reaching Barcelona at 6.20pm. Alternatively, take a local bus to Vielha (see p117), from where the choice is a little wider.

Day 8: Refugi de Colomers to Refugi Ventosa i Calvell
3¾–4¼ hours, 8km
This is a short, fairly easy day that diverges from the main GR11. After a steady ascent to the Port de Colomers it's downhill all the way past lakes and tarns to the dark Estany Negre and the night's *refugio*, perched above it.

Taking a Short Cut

If you're intent upon progressing westwards from Refugi de Colomers, you can omit much of Days 8 and 9 and walk directly along the blazed GR11 to Refugi de la Restanca (see the end of Day 9). Quite a few GR11 walkers push themselves beyond Refugi de la Restanca as far as the Hospital de Vielha in one long stage, continuing along the Day 10 route and so saving themselves yet another day. You'll miss the awesome bowl of the Circ de Colomers and a spangle of lakes and tarns but, if time is at a premium…

It's a colour-coded start to the day. Set out northwestwards from the Refugi de Colomers, initially following the GR11's red-and-white bars upstream along La Gargantera brook. After about five minutes turn left (southwest) to follow the red-and-yellow blazes of a pair of day walks, devised and maintained by Josep Baques i Sole, warden at Refugi de Colomers, and his team. Five minutes later, pass by a small stone building, site of the proposed new *refugio*. Ascend southeastwards to cross the outlet of Estany Mort (literally, 'dead pool'), seething with frogs despite its name.

Where the red-and-yellow trail markers diverge stay on red, aiming for a multicoloured pole. Continue southwards up the true right bank of a stream that cascades from lake to lake. The path improves and cairns become more frequent as you pass to the east of Estany de Cabirdonats.

Tarns, some no bigger than puddles with attitude, others slowly evaporating under the summer sun, multiply as you push further into the grey moraine at the base of the awesome bowl of Circ de Colomers.

The trail becomes less evident as you skirt the first two of a group of tarns scattered across the cirque and known collectively as the Estanyets del Port. As the red flashes trail away eastwards after about 1¼ hours of walking, the cairns give out – or rather the base of the bowl is spattered with natural cairns – and the path is sometimes difficult to discern as you continue heading straight (south).

At an unnamed lake shaped like a pulled tooth bear southwest towards **Port de Colomers** (2591m), a distinctive notch against the skyline, which retains a white bib of snow until well into July. Keep heading resolutely up and southwest, hugging the east side of the narrow valley that descends from the pass, to reach the col 2¼ to 2½ hours into the day.

From the pass you're rewarded for the hard slog of the last 100m of altitude change by heart-stopping views westwards to the severe Besiberri ridge on the horizon and a scattering of lakes in the valley at your feet.

After a little less than 15 minutes of steepish descent be sure to cross to and veer away from the true left bank of a small stream, following the main path and disregarding the cairns that entice you farther down the valley. Dropping along a cairned trail, pass well above the marshy flats of Tallada Llarga to reach the first of the **Estanyets de Colieto**.

Now begins a joyous descent, hopping from lake to tarn, always with the snow-flecked Besiberri ridge as a backdrop. Less rhapsodic is the unavoidable boulder scrambling as you pick your way along the north shore of the tiny La Bassa tarn, just before the brief but lung-challenging ascent to **Refugi Ventosa i Calvell** (☎ 973 29 70 90), reached after 1½ to 1¾ hours' walking from the pass. At 2222m and overlooking **Estany Negre**, the *refugio* is often full despite its capacity for 80, so it's particularly important to reserve.

Side Trip: Caldes de Boí
4½–5 hours, 17km
You can end or join the Pyrenean Traverse quite easily by following this entry and exit route, popular with weekend walkers. A good path descends in 1½ hours from Refugi Ventosa i Calvell to the roadhead at the southern end of the Embassament de Cavallers dam (1725m), where you have a reasonable chance of hitching down. Around 4.5km of road walking brings you to Caldes de Boí, a spa with luxury hotels. For a wider choice of accommodation at more reasonable rates it's worth pushing on to Boí.

Boí
If making Boí your base for any time visit **Casa del Parc** (☎/fax 973 69 61 89; open 9am-1pm & 3.30pm-6.45pm daily), the Parc Nacional d'Aigüestortes i Estany de Sant Maurici information office, for more walk suggestions. This office and the one in Espot run a 15-minute audiovisual introduction to the park, with an optional English version, and sell walking maps.

Boí has several *cases de pagès* (the Catalan name for *casas rurales*, or houses with rooms to let), including the **Casa Guasch**

The Pyrenean Traverse – Map D

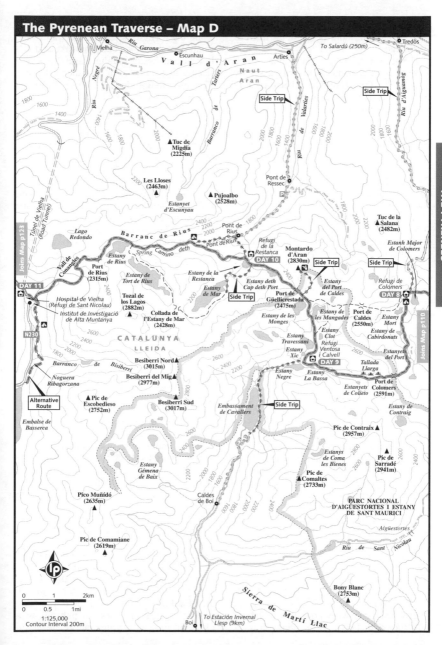

THE PYRENEES

(☎ 973 69 60 42; Carrer Major 3; doubles €24), a charming stone house in the heart of the village.

The bus (originating in Barcelona) which leaves Lleida at 9am for Vielha passes by Pont de Suert at 11am. Here, between July and mid-September, it connects with a local bus which leaves at 11.15am for Caldes de Boí. In the opposite direction the bus departs from Caldes de Boí at 2pm, connecting with the return service for Lleida and Barcelona in Pont de Suert at 2.30pm.

Day 9: Refugi Ventosa i Calvell to Refugi de la Restanca
2¾–3¼ hours, 6km

This is a brief stage, allowing time for one of two strongly recommended side trips: the ascent of Montardo d'Aran or a visit to the magnificent Estany de Mar.

Head north from the *refugio*, following cairns to pass by a chain of lakes. First comes tiny Xic and beside it, a sign 'Coret Oelhacrestada' (the Catalan form of Port de Güellicrestada), then Travessani, followed by Clot, les Mangades and les Monges.

Around half an hour into the day the path leaves the shore of Estany Travessani to climb above a large slab of granite on its south side. As you rejoin the lake look out for a far-from-evident but important junction that cries out for a sign. Here, the more lightly trodden path to the Port de Güellicrestada (Port d'Onhla Crestada in Aragonese) and Refugi de la Restanca – the option you take – continues due north, splitting from the main and more evident trail, which bears northeast to Port de Caldes.

As you approach the lip of Estany de les Mangades after about an hour of walking aim for a multicoloured pole, cross the stream which drains from the lake, and head northwest towards **Port de Güellicrestada** (2475m). This must be one of the gentlest approaches to a pass in all of the Catalan mountains.

At the pass, 1½ to 1¾ hours from your starting point, you again pick up the red-and-white markers of the GR11. There's a sharp, 30-minute drop down a stony trail to **Estany deth Cap deth Port** that negotiates a mas-

sive, clearly signed and cairned boulder field along the way. Walk around the wall of the small dam that holds back this lake and follow the path beside the sluice as it drops very steeply to Estany de la Restanca (2010m). The smart **Refugi de la Restanca** *(☎ 908 03 65 59)* is at the near end of the dam. Allow 1¼ to 1½ hours from pass to lake.

Albert Betrán, the warden, who has been looking after walkers for more than 20 years, and his team run a tight ship. With 80 places, the *refugio* does meals, snacks and drinks, accepts Visa and – a rarity among high mountain *refugios* – has a public telephone.

Although the rocky area around the dam isn't conducive to camping, you can just find yourself a couple of handkerchiefs' worth of flat, stone-free ground for a **camp site**. Alternatively, if you continue a further 45 minutes along the Day 10 route, you'll meet a delightful meadow, ideal for camping, where the track from the *refugio* meets the Camino deth Pont de Rius.

Side Trip: Montardo d'Aran
2–2½ hours, 6.5km

The superb views from the summit of Montardo d'Aran repay in full the energy you'll burn in undertaking this popular detour. About 300m before reaching the Port de Güellicrestada break off to the right and head cross-country over the small plain to join a clear path which rises northeast quite gently before zigzagging more severely northwards.

After mounting a rocky couloir the path reaches a relatively flat area leading to the base of a false summit (2781m). From here, cross a pronounced saddle and continue to the true **summit** (2830m), from where the panorama is superb.

Side Trip: Estany de Mar
2–2½ hours, 6km

From the *refugio*, head south along the east shore of Estany de la Restanca. A good path, with one tight spot of boulder clambering, scales the first bluff to a flat, grassy area flanking the outfall of the upper lake. It then zigzags up a second palisade to a chute from where you emerge, after no more than an hour, to a view over Estany de Mar (2230m).

The forbidding Besiberri Nord peak (3015m) to the south provides a suitable backdrop to the expanse of water that merits the name 'Mar' (sea). Having come this far, it's worth continuing at least a little further along the southeast bank of the lake on a vague, narrow trail marked by sporadic cairns.

If you can spare an entire day, consider taking in the lakes of Tort de Rius and Rius to do a popular loop walk that links with the GR11 to return to the *refugio*. To complete the full-day circuit of the three lakes continue along this trail as far as the Collada de l'Estany de Mar (2428m), then descend to approach the lakes of Estany de Tort de Rius and Estany de Rius from the southeast.

Return to the Restanca *refugio* from the latter by following in reverse the first section of Day 10 along Barranc de Rius.

Side Trip: Arties
4½–5 hours, 18km
This is the second access route between the Pyrenean Traverse and Vall de Aran (the other drops from Refugi de Colomers to Salardú – see Side Trip: Salardú, p111). If you've been staying in *refugios* or camping wild for several days, you may welcome a break for rest and reprovisioning. Bear in mind that the next opportunity for stocking up is in Benasque, three days away.

From the Restanca lake it's about 45 minutes of pleasant descent through pine forest to the pretty Riu de Valarties valley. The path meets a river at a place still called Pont de Rius (Rius Bridge; 1700m), even though there hasn't been a bridge for decades. Between July and September a **4WD shuttle service** runs from here to Pont de Ressec, saving you, for the modest outlay of €3, around 3km of walking. From the car park at the limit for private vehicles you've a good chance of a lift along the sealed road that descends to Arties (1144m). Otherwise, you can slog it on foot (allow 1¼ hours at a brisk pace) or ring for a **taxi** (☎ 610 29 45 56; €25-30).

Arties
Arties has a small **tourist office** (☎ 669 34 97 27; open 10am-1.30pm & 4.30pm-8pm daily July–mid-Sept) and an ATM.

Camping Era Yerla d'Arties (☎ 973 64 16 02; e yerla@coac.net; camping per person/ tent €4.10/4.10) is the only camping ground in the upper Aran valley. Riverside and well maintained, it has a bar that serves a wide range of *bocadillos* (sandwiches).

Pensió Montarto (☎/fax 973 64 08 03; singles/doubles/triples with bathroom €24/ 40/47), on the main road, is a good choice if you prefer a roof over your head.

La Sal Gorda (☎ 973 64 45 31; menú €12, mains €12.50-17), on the main road, is a good choice for a meal.

Restaurante Urtau (☎ 973 64 09 26; Plaça Urtau; mains €9.30-15.50) is stylish and the perfect antidote to an excess of *refugio* cuisine.

Iñaki Sidreria (☎ 973 64 42 07), also on the main drag, is the place to slake a mountainous thirst with their cider from barrel or bottle. They also serve ample meat dishes (€7 to €11.50) and have a decent wine selection.

The village includes a **supermarket** and **Gourmet Juantxo**, which is a well-stocked delicatessen.

Day 10: Refugi de la Restanca to Hospital de Vielha
4–4½ hours, 9.5km
This is a day for striding out. From Refugi de la Restanca the altitude difference to the Port de Rius is 400m. Many walkers will start from Pont de Rius in the Riu de Valarties valley after visiting Arties and from here it's 650m. Either way, the ascent's fairly gradual along a clear, good-quality trail that scarcely makes you pant, except for the steeper final push of 30 to 40 minutes to the shore of Estany de Rius.

If you've left the mountains to visit Arties and Naut Aran, rejoin the Pyrenean Traverse at Pont de Rius. Here, where the woodland trail that climbs to the Refugi de la Restanca takes off left, go straight ahead in defiance of a GR 'X' sign indicating no entry. (This unsigned route features incorrectly as the main GR11 tracing on the

Mapa de la Travessa dels Refugis del Parc Nacional d'Aigüestortes i Estany de Sant Maurici, the national park map). Cross the river to pick up a cairned – though, early in the season, very overgrown – path running above the true left bank. You're walking the **Camino deth Pont de Rius** (Camino del Pont de Rius) which, until the construction of the Túnel de Vielha, was a well-travelled access route to the upper Aran valley.

After about an hour and 250m of vertical ascent, you rejoin the GR11 about 2km west of Refugi de la Restanca. Just below the junction of the two trails is a glorious meadow, where marmots wolf-whistle you from the scree, ideal for a **camp site** if you've made an afternoon departure from Arties. A night here leaves you well poised to continue to Refugi de Mulleres (Molieres) on Day 11 and reach Benasque on the following day. For this reason, you might

consider pushing on and forgoing the considerable delights of the Hospital de Vielha.

If beginning the day from Refugi de la Restanca, you have two choices. The easier and more travelled alternative is to stick to the GR11, which crosses the dam to curl away northwestwards. Once over a hillock the path drops steeply, running parallel to the electricity pylons leading from the dam into the main valley, and joins the Camino deth Pont de Rius.

The even more scenic but considerably more arduous choice is to take in Estany de Mar and the equally large Estany de Tort de Rius (see the Side Trip: Estany de Mar, pp114–15) and rejoin the main route at the eastern end of Estany de Rius. This will add about two hours' walking to what isn't a very tough day.

As you progress up the Riu de Valarties valley ignore all cobbled paths engineered by the power company, enticing you to go up and left; each leads to a dead end at various waterworks. One to 1¼ hours after the junction of the GR11 and the path from the Riu de Valarties valley, you'll pass the remains of the dam construction buildings and a trash-strewn *fuente* beneath a small tower. Around five minutes later you draw level with the outlet of **Estany de Rius**.

From here it's well worth making a brief detour to visit the more appealing **Estany Tort de Rius**, 10 minutes to the southeast. There's many a tarn and pool ahead but these are the last substantial lakes you'll see for the next several days of the traverse.

It takes about 40 minutes to circumnavigate all the arms and crannies of Estany de Rius to reach **Port de Rius** (2315m). From this pass you see for the first time the mountains of the Aragonese Pyrenees against the skyline, with Pico de Aneto, the highest summit of the whole chain, the northernmost pinnacle. Way below, traffic speeds along the road towards the tunnel to Vielha. The large building beside the highway is the University of Barcelona's high mountain research institute (Institut de Investigació de Alta Muntanya). Both appear deceptively near since the trail drops sharply in switchbacks then curls into the **Vall de Conangles**, away from

---

El Túnel de Vielha

It was 22 years after the first cut that the strategic road tunnel linking the Vall d'Aran with Spain was completed. Until it opened, the only communication between the valley and the outside world was northwards, to France, once the first snows of winter blocked the pass in September and until the spring snowmelt as late as June.

The Vall d'Aran had been politically affiliated to Spain since the 14th century. The purpose of the tunnel was to reinforce economic and cultural links with Spain and diminish the Gallic influence. Plagued by accidents and financial difficulties, the boring proceeded in fits and starts.

With the outbreak of the Spanish Civil War, work stopped completely. It resumed in 1941, with the forced labour of Republican prisoners. If you look around and above the tunnel entrance, you can still see traces of the bunkers that protected the project from the raids of their guerrilla comrades, fighting from their bases in the mountains.

Finally opened in 1948, at 5.3km it's the longest road tunnel in the Pyrenees.

El Hospital

You don't have to be sick to spend the night in an *hospital*. The history of these places, built at the base of important passes, goes back to medieval times and recalls the original meaning of the word: a place where hospitality is offered, a haven for rest and refuge. Often established and maintained by charitable foundations such as the Knights Templar, the Knights of St John of Jerusalem and the Orden (Order) de los Hospitalarios, they offered modest, safe lodging to foot travellers at a time when walking was more hazardous than it is today.

Some still serve as *refugios* for walkers. Two are possible overnight stops on the Pyrenean Traverse. The Hospital de Vielha was founded in 1192 at the base of an old *camino* which crosses the Coll de Toro into the Vall d'Aran. The Hospital de Benasque sits beside a camino leading to the Portillón de Benasque, once a popular smugglers' route into France.

❁❁❁❁❁❁❁❁❁❁❁❁❁❁

your destination, reaching the valley bottom about an hour from the col. From here you descend gently through pines, which yield to beech and birch.

The final 20 minutes of the day are an easy stroll down a wide cart track, from which you take a clear path left to descend to the **Hospital de Vielha** (Espitau de Vielha in Aragonese), also known as the **Refugi Sant Nicolau** (*☎/fax 973 69 70 52; dorm beds €8.50, half-board €21*), poised beside the southern entrance to the Túnel de Vielha. Modified over the centuries, its stone architecture is more distinctive than that of many alpine huts. In view of the difficult days to follow, you won't regret cosseting yourself here for a night. Run by the *ajuntament* (local authority) of Vielha and with space for 50, it has a restaurant and genuine bar that gives it the atmosphere of a Spanish roadside inn.

If you're tenting, you'll find decent **camp sites** 45 minutes beyond the Hospital de Vielha on the route to the Coll de Mulleres

(see Day 11) or at a popular picnic spot 20 minutes into Alternative Day 11.

Vielha

Vielha is the main town in the Vall d'Aran. Its **tourist office** (*☎ 973 64 01 10; w www .aran.org; Carrer Sarriulèra 10; open 9am-9pm daily*) carries information about the whole valley.

From mid-June to the end of September **Alsina Graells** (*☎ 93 265 68 66*) runs buses from Barcelona to Vielha (€27.70, seven hours, one daily) via Pobla de Segur, Llavorsí and La Guingeta. During the same period one bus daily leaves Vielha for Barcelona.

A year-round bus route (€14.05, 5¼ hours, two daily) connects Barcelona with Vielha via Lleida and the Túnel de Vielha.

From late June to mid-September 10 buses a day (six on Sunday) connect Vielha with villages such as Salardú and Arties (see Side Trip: Salardú, p111, and Side Trip: Arties, p115). Off the main valley road you're dependent on taxis.

Day 11: Hospital de Vielha to Meadows below Collado del Toro
6–7½ hours, 8.5km

If you're in good shape it's possible to reach La Besurta and the shuttle-bus service to the Hospital de Benasque in one long day from the Hospital de Vielha. It's better, however, to either stretch Day 10 and overnight at Refugio de Mulleres or camp en route and take this tough walk at a less demanding pace. You'll find a pair of telescopic poles useful on both sides of the col. A further alternative, longer but less demanding, is to walk to Benasque via Collada di Ballibierna (see Alternative Days 11 & 12, pp119–20).

This is the most challenging but also one of the most satisfying stages of the whole traverse. Up Barranco de Mulleres (Molières), over the col of the same name and down into Valleta de la Escaleta; it's easy enough to summarise but it's a tough one, with altitude changes totalling 2400m, of which 1300m is ascent. But the rewards match the considerable effort invested and, while it would be unwise to attempt the pass alone, this stage is nothing to shy away from. It's demanding because of the difficulty in following the trail during the last 45 minutes to Coll de Mulleres and because the last 10m to the col are steep enough to require a four-limbed clamber.

The route as far as the Estanyets de Mulleres tarns is uncomplicated and well marked. From the Hospital de Vielha (1630m) pick your way over the rubble around the mouth of the road tunnel to a clear cart track. Leave it after about 15 minutes to take a path that rises through beech wood beside the stream's true left bank. A further 15 minutes later pass the magnificent **Cascada de Mulleres** waterfall and, soon after a small, grassy flood plain that makes an ideal **camp site**.

About two hours out, clamber up the wall of a cirque, briefly using all four limbs. Around an hour later, a just-visible arrow on a granite boulder points towards **Refugio de Mulleres** (or Molières; 2360m), a bright-orange, 12-person, unstaffed *refugio* only five minutes away above an icy lake. This is the first of four tarns that you'll pass as you work your way up Barranco de Mulleres, though some may be masked under snowpack. The patch of grass beside the *refugio* and the shores of the first two of the four tarns are all possible **camp sites** – the last until you're well over the col.

From the *refugio* turn-off to Coll de Mulleres it's a two- to 2½-hour ascent entirely over rock, varying from huge slabs to slippery scree, probably with some snow cover. Beyond the lakes, the track, now much less trodden, becomes more spindly and you're reliant upon cairns and the occasional ultra-discreet vermilion trail marker.

Coll de Mulleres (2928m), the highest pass on the Pyrenean traverse, isn't easy to distinguish against the skyline, even when it's almost on top of you. Just below the serrated rocks that mark the pass lock into the tracks of those who have gone before and head west across a narrow snowfield. The last 10m are a true climb and a real pig, especially if you're lugging a full pack.

The quite stupendous views of Pico de Aneto – the highest summit in the Pyrenees – and the Glaciar de la Maladeta to the west; the upper slopes of the Valleta de la Escaleta before you; and the peaks parting Aragón from Catalunya to your right more than justify every bead of sweat expended.

To avoid the **Glaciar de Mulleres** directly below you follow the ridge along its less steep, western side towards Pic (Tuc) de Mulleres (3010m), identified by the iron cross at its summit. Just west of the peak follow the intermittent line of cairns that drops northwards to join a feeder stream of the highest tarn of the Valleta de la Escaleta. More simply, just dig in your heels and poles to yomp straight down the snow-covered glacier to the tarn, 35 to 45 minutes away. There's just enough flat space here for a **camp site**, but camping options increase in quantity and quality as you descend the valley.

Skirt around the tarn to its right. Once the glacier and snow give out you stride for a time over huge, smooth slabs of mottled granite, comfortable as the living room carpet after what you've recently experienced.

Shortly before drawing level with the evident Collado dels Aranesos (2455m), which leads back to Catalunya, pass a small tarn on its left (west) side then switch to the true right bank of the stream flowing from it. Beyond the tarn it's greenness once more, the gradient becomes less steep and there's even a hint of path again.

After passing over a rocky bluff above the west bank of a larger tarn you emerge into meadows just below the Collado del Toro, a clearly visible nick to the east (see Side Trip: Estany del Collado de Toro). Interlaced with streams, the meadows are a paradise for campers.

Side Trip: Estany del Collado de Toro

45 minutes–1 hour, 1km

Leave your backpack behind a boulder in the meadows below Collado del Toro and take an easy side trail to a minor pass, Collado de Toro (2235m). Just beyond it is the pretty **Estany del Collado de Toro**, shaped like a figure of eight and hemmed in by Pomer to the east and Peña Nere on the north. If you want to walk further you can skirt the lake along its northwest shore, following cairns but no path, to a possible **camp site** overlooking the Vall d'Aran watershed.

Alternative Days 11 & 12: Via Collada de Ballibierna
10½–12 hours, 36km

This variant follows the GR11, which passes to the south of the Maladeta massif. With its familiar red-and-white blazes, it's a much longer, less demanding but still challenging route into Aragón. If you wish and if you get your timing right you can take a 4WD taxi from the *refugio* beyond Pleta de Llosás to Benasque and omit the final 10km of walking.

From the Hospital de Vielha follow the main N230 road south for 200m and turn left onto a path. After 20 minutes or so you pass beside a popular picnic spot that offers some tempting shaded **camp sites** (bona fide trekkers, putting up their tent at dusk and moving on next day, are allowed to overnight here).

A few minutes later, fork right, go through a meadow and cross the Barranco de Besiberri, a tributary of the Noguera Ribagorçana. About an hour beyond the Hospital, cross to the true right bank of this more substantial river at a concrete footbridge and follow the main road for 200m.

At the far side of the road bridge where the Río Salenques flows into the Embalse de Basserca (Senet) dam turn right onto a trail that mounts the true right bank of the stream. You ascend fairly gently, walking a springy carpet of beech leaves, until, around 45 minutes beyond the bridge, you reach a flattish patch of terrain where Barranc de Salenques meets Vall d'Anglíos.

Continue west up the Vall d'Anglíos. The path, at first overgrown and difficult to distinguish early in the season, ascends very steeply with scarcely a zig or a zag through beech wood, which yields to silver birch, then fir and mountain ash. Wild strawberries and bilberries offer occasional and welcome refreshment. Once thickets of pine take over the gradient, though still enough to make you puff, slackens a little, then levels out for the final kilometre to the first of the **Estanys d'Anglíos** lakes (2220m), reached after 3¼ to 3½ hours of walking.

Contour around the lake to the south, passing by a doll's house of a **refugio** which

can just squeeze in four people (get there early if you want to bag a square metre or two). Just beyond, the GR11 splits. Take the westerly option to sneak between the second and third tarns, then head up a grassy bank to follow the small Riu Güeno upstream. You'll find this option frustratingly boulderstrewn but it's smooth as a helter-skelter compared with the alternative route.

Beyond the last of three small, inky tarns, reached some 35 to 45 minutes beyond the *refugio*, the route climbs steeply over boulders to the evident dip of **Colladeta de Riu Güeno** (2325m), after an altitude gain of 300m. The GR11 is well signed but you're just as well off picking your own way up and around the hefty granite slabs.

Drop steeply to curl around the western shore of the **Ibón Cap de Llauset** (*ibón* is Aragonese for lake). If you prefer to postpone the ascent to Collada de Ballibierna until the morrow (you're now about five hours into the walking day), the northwest corner of the lake makes a comfortable **camp site**.

To continue, follow the lake's outflow stream to rejoin the alternative GR11 route at a green sign. From this junction it's a further 300m of height gain over granite boulders to **Collada de Ballibierna** (or Vallibierna or Vallivierna or even Vallhiverna – all four variants are current!) at 2720m, with the possibility of snowfields on either side of the pass.

Drop westwards steeply from the pass. For the first 10 minutes you're better off picking your own route through the boulders rather than slithering down the skiddy, overtramped GR11 tracing. Once at the upper of the two **Ibóns de Ballibierna** you'll find that its grassy southeast shore makes a good **camp site**, after a total of 6½ to seven hours of walking.

To avoid unnecessary boulder hopping, keep high on the north side of the tight barranco connecting the two lakes, then wend your way around the north shore of the downstream one, reached one to 1¼ hours after leaving the col.

The descent beyond the lower lake is gentle, grassy and glorious. At valley level, the meadows of **Pleta de Llosás** (2200m) make a pleasant place to rest or **camp**. After entering sparse pine forest you reach, some 30 minutes beyond the meadows and eight to nine hours' walking from the Hospital de Vielha, Puente de Coronas (1950m) and an unstaffed **refugio** with room for 12 or so. The area around the hut has some inviting **camp sites**.

From July to mid-September a **4WD taxi** (€8) descends from Puente de Coronas to Plan de Senarta at 1pm, 4pm and 6pm, allowing you to clip a good 10km off this stage (the 1pm and 6pm services continue as far as Benasque). Otherwise, it's an easy and uneventful stroll down a forested track that follows the northern flank of Barranco de Ballibierna.

Some 35 to 45 minutes beyond the first *refugio* is another. Domed, smaller and less inviting, it's fine if you fancy postponing the final haul into Benasque.

About an hour later, limbo dance under a barrier that prevents vehicle access from below and turn left (west) at a T-junction to follow a sign 'Benasque, Estós, GR11'. (A right turn brings you, in about 300m, to the **Plan de Senarta** and **Camping Municipal Senarta** *(☎ 974 55 10 01; camping per person/ tent €2/1.70; open July-Sept)*, on a grassy plain.

Follow the east shore of the **Embalse de Paso Nuevo** reservoir. Some 15 to 20 minutes from the junction you can avoid a long hairpin in the 4WD track by taking an easily overlooked path to the right. After 50m bear left to descend through a thicket of box-wood, then turn right as you rejoin the track.

Less than half an hour later you pass the entrance of **Camping Ixeia** *(☎ 974 55 21 29; e ixea@ctv.es; camping per person/tent €3/ 3; open June-Sept)*. This unkempt, informal, walker-friendly camping ground, run by a qualified mountain guide, has an excellent walking library and sells relevant maps. It also has a cosy **refugio** *(dorm beds €9)* with free access to showers and bathroom.

Barely three minutes later the route bears right to pass under the Puente San Jaime and the highway and almost goes through **Camping Aneto** *(☎/fax 974 55 11 41; camping per person/tent €3.60/3.60)*. Set in large, attrac-

tive riverside grounds, it sells a good range of walking maps and guidebooks in Spanish and has a washing machine.

From the bridge it's a 3.8km walk south to Benasque (1140m).

Day 12: Meadows below Collado del Toro to Benasque
5–6 hours, 20.5km

In a little under an hour of easy walking (look for the caves in the hillside, rated highly by speleologists), you emerge into the wide **Plan de Aiguallut**. Here, cows browse, picnickers paddle and all is satisfyingly green and fertile.

A green metal *refugio* – even the huts are green around here – offering spartan space for eight, perches above the downstream end of the meadow. Just below it is **Cascada de Aiguallut**, down which the river hurtles before disappearing into **Forau de Aiguallut**.

At **La Besurta**, about 30 minutes walk from Plan d'Aiguallut (or 1½ hours via Refugio de la Renclusa – see Alternative Route, p123), there's a small stall serving cold beer and soft drinks, *bocadillos* (€3) and *platos combinados* (€6) – a small gastronomic delight after a few days on the trail.

A **shuttle bus** (€2 one way) travels the 5.5km from La Besurta to the Hospital de Benasque. In principle it runs at least every 30 minutes in each direction, though the driver tends to adjust the schedule to suit his personal life. Buses departing from La

Forau de Aiguallut

The Forau (meaning cave or pothole in Aragonese) de Aiguallut is a cauldron into which swirl all the waters flowing from the surrounding mountains – from Glaciar de Mulleres to the Maladeta massif. Once underground the run-off forms a subterranean river on a bed of limestone. It loses some 600m in height over only 4km before re-emerging at Artiga de Lin in Vall d'Aran. From here the river joins the Riu Garona, called La Garonne once it crosses the French border, and flows into the Atlantic Ocean near Bordeaux.

Besurta (three daily) continue to Benasque, stopping by request at Puente de San Jaime (for Camping Ixeia and Camping Aneto – see the end of Alternative Days 11 & 12, pp119–20). At other times you shouldn't have too much trouble finding a lift down to town from the car park beside the lower bus terminal near the Hospital de Benasque.

While most walkers prefer to catch the bus to Benasque, it's possible to walk from La Besurta, for the most part off-road, via the old **Hospital de Benasque** (☎ 974 55 20 12, fax 974 55 10 52; ⓦ www.llanosdelhospital .com; beds €16, singles/doubles with bathroom €52/57) – see the boxed text 'El Hospital' (p117). Around 500m east of the lower terminus of the shuttle bus running down from La Besurta, it offers the choice of refugio-style beds in rooms for four or seven in its **Albergue** or hotel-style accommodation in its **Hostal**. Both are excellent value for money and the **restaurant** does a great-value menú at €13.

Alternative Route: Via Refugio de la Renclusa

1½–1¾ hours, 3km

Refugio de la Renclusa (☎ 974 55 21 06), with capacity for 96, is staffed from June to mid-October and keeps a small annexe open year-round. Until its expansion programme is completed it's as much building site as mountain hut. All the same, it's a friendly place, offering meals, drinks and snacks, and has a self-catering area. It's a very popular base camp for climbers and those planning an ascent of Pico de Aneto. As it's also near vehicle access (whole coachloads of walkers are decanted daily), advance booking is essential. Just near the refugio is another impressive forau beside a small chapel.

From Plan de Aiguallut take a faint trail leading initially westwards from near the green metal shelter. The first part of the ascent to Coll de la Renclusa (2270m) is steep. Navigation isn't always easy as far as the pass but the trail is well cairned in its latter stages. To the refugio from Plan de Aiguallut takes about an hour, and La Besurta lies 30 to 40 minutes beyond, down the eastern flank of Barranco de la Renclusa.

Parque Posets-Maladeta

The park was declared a protected area in 1994. It covers 332 sq km and encompasses the two highest massifs in the Pyrenees and 13 of the range's major glaciers. Nearly all the park lies above 1800m, including the Pico de Aneto (3404m), the highest mountain in the Pyrenees.

It owes its shape, like so many other areas of the chain, to the ice ages, which created the characteristic U-shaped valleys, giant cirques at their head, hanging valleys high on their flanks and scooped depressions, today filled by more than 100 ibóns, or mountain tarns.

Following the region's upgrade to park status vehicle access is now restricted.

Refugio de la Renclusa can be visited from La Besurta as an undemanding 3km return trip. From La Besurta, head back towards Plan de Aiguallut and fork right (south) after about 10 minutes.

Benasque

With its cobbled streets, 13th-century church and old greystone houses, roofed in slates the shape of fish scales, Benasque's roots are deep. Nowadays, it's a small, bustling holiday centre where most of the new blends sensitively and harmoniously with the old.

The **tourist office** (☎/fax 974 55 12 89; ⓦ www.benasque.com; open 10am-2pm & 5pm-9pm daily) is on Calle Sebastián.

The small Parque Posets-Maladeta **visitors centre** (☎ 974 55 20 66; open 10am-2pm & 4pm-8pm daily late June–mid-Sept, 10am-2pm & 3pm-6pm Sat & Sun mid-Sept–Easter, 10am-2pm & 4pm-8pm Sat & Sun Easter–late June), 1km from Benasque just off the road to Anciles (see Day 13, pp124–5), has display panels and a good 15-minute video in Spanish about the park.

There are at least three ATMs in town. Perhaps worth a visit, 12 sweaty days into the traverse, is **Lavandería Ecológica Ardilla** (Carretera de Francia; open 9am-2pm & 5pm-9pm daily), a laundrette that will wash and dry a load, with same-day service, for €10.

THE PYRENEES

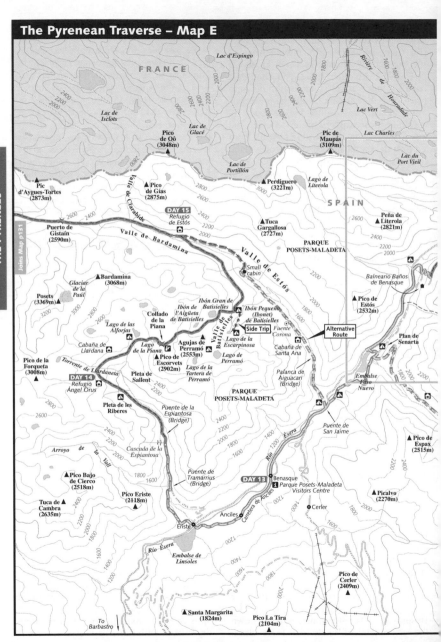

The Pyrenean Traverse – Map E

FRANCE

Lac d'Espingo

Rivière de Houmédiade

Lac Vert

Lac de Isclots

Lac de Glacé

Pico de Oô (3048m)

Lac de Portillón

Pic de Maupás (3109m)

Lac Charles

Lac du Port Vieil

Pic d'Aygues-Tortes (2873m)

Pico de Gías (2875m)

Perdiguero (3221m)

Lago de Literola

SPAIN

Peña de Literola (2821m)

Puerto de Gistaín (2590m)

DAY 15
Refugio de Estós

Valle de Clarabide

Valle de Bardamina

Tuca Gargallosa (2727m)

PARQUE POSETS-MALADETA

Balneario Baños de Benasque

Bardamina (3068m)

Small cabin

Valle de Estós

Pico de Estós (2532m)

Posets (3369m)

Glaciar de la Paül

Ibón Gran de Batisielles

Ibón de l'Aigüeta de Batisielles

Ibón Pequeño (Ibonet) de Batisielles

Fuente Corona

Plan de Senarta

Collado de la Piana

Lago de las Alforjas

Lago de la Piana

Side Trip

Lago de la Escarpinosa

Alternative Route

Cabaña de Llardana

Pico de Escorvets (2902m)

Agujas de Perramó (2553m)

Valle de Batisielles

Lago de Perramó

Cabaña de Santa Ana

Pico de la Forqueta (3008m)

Torrente de Llardaneta

Lago de la Tartera de Perramó

Palanca de Aiguacari (Bridge)

Embalse Paso Nuevo

DAY 14
Refugio Angel Orús

Pleta de Sallent

PARQUE POSETS-MALADETA

Pico de Espax (2515m)

Pleta de les Riberes

Puente de la Espiantosa (Bridge)

Río Ésera

Puente de San Jaime

Arroyo de la Vall

Cascada de la Espiantosa

Pico Bajo de Cierco (2518m)

Puente de Tramarrius (Bridge)

Picalvo (2270m)

Pico Eriste (2118m)

DAY 13
Benasque
Parque Posets-Maladeta Visitors Centre

Tuca de Cambra (2635m)

Ancíles

Carretera de Ancíles

Cerler

Eriste

Pico de Cerler (2409m)

Río Ésera

Embalse de Linsoles

To Barbastro

Santa Margarita (1824m)

Pico La Tira (2104m)

Joins Map p131

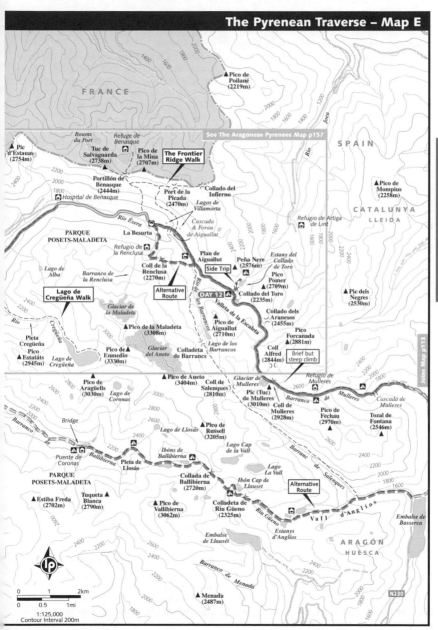

Barrabés Esquí y Montaña (☎ 974 55 13 51; W www.barrabes.com; Carretera de Francia) has two megashops selling a huge range of walking and outdoor equipment. It also stocks Benasque's best selection of maps and guidebooks.

Deportes Aigualluts (☎ 974 55 12 15; Avenida de los Tilos) carries a decent but smaller range of walking gear.

Rodolfoto bookshop (☎/fax 974 55 16 50; Avenida de los Tilos 2), down a passageway nearly opposite the tourist office, also carries a good stock of maps.

If you want to tell your folks back home what a lovely time you're having, **Pub Cybercafé Surcos** (Calle San Pedro; open 5pm-3am daily) charges €3.20 per hour for online access.

Places to Stay & Eat For information on **camping grounds** near Benasque, see the end of Alternative Days 11 & 12 (pp119–20).

Accommodation in Benasque itself is abundant, for any budget – though unless you've reserved you'll have difficulty finding a bed in this up-and-coming resort that caters to summer hikers and winter skiers.

Hostal Solana (☎/fax 974 55 10 19; Plaza Mayor 5; basic singles/doubles €16/22.55, singles/doubles with bathroom from €29/45) is an economical place with clean, bright rooms.

La Fonda de Vescelia (☎ 974 55 16 54, fax 974 55 28 02; e vescelia@terra.es; Calle Mayor 5; dorm beds €7.25, basic rooms per person €19.85, half-board €30.65), next door, has an agreeably hippy air about it (they also run the adjacent esoteric goods shop). Its café has plenty of vegetarian options and Internet access too (€3 per hour).

Hotel Ciria (☎ 974 55 16 12, fax 974 55 16 86; W www.hotelciria.com; Avenida de los Tilos; singles/doubles with bathroom from €40.60/63.15) is a welcoming, family-run mid-range choice. Rates include breakfast. The menú (€14.50) at its restaurant, **El Fogaril**, includes a range of local specialities and is exceptional value.

La Pizzeria (☎ 974 55 15 76; Calle Los Huertos; mains €4.75-9.25) does pizzas, pasta and salads to eat in or take away.

For a meal the best pickings are along Avenida de los Tilos and its continuation, Calle Mayor.

Bar La Compañía (Avenida Luchon 19) is a convivial cafe with shelves of reading matter relating to walking and the mountains.

Restaurante Sayo (☎ 974 55 16 97; Calle Mayor 13) opens daily and serves a filling menú for €11.

Capricho Charro (☎ 974 55 15 05; Calle Mayor) is a stylish place specialising in quality tapas (around €1.50) and raciones (€5 to €7); it has good jazz background music.

El Pesebre (☎ 974 55 15 07; Calle Mayor 45; mains €11-13; open mid-June–Sept & Dec-Easter) is an intimate restaurant that serves an imaginative range of dishes.

Getting There & Around Regular **Altoaragonesa** (in Barbastro ☎ 974 31 12 93) buses run between Benasque and Barbastro (€5.70, two hours). There are two services daily except Sunday (one service). From Barbastro buses run to Barcelona (€10.55, 3½ hours, four daily), Lleida (€4.30, 1½ hours, four daily) and Huesca (€3.20, 50 minutes, up to seven daily). There are also six services a day from Barbastro to Monzón (€1.05, 20 minutes), from where there are frequent trains for Zaragoza, Lleida and Barcelona.

From July to mid-September a bus leaves Benasque for La Besurta (€5 single, €8 return) at 4.30am (a redeye run for walkers wanting to attack Aneto – see Pico de Aneto, pp158–9, under Other Walks) plus 9am and 1.30pm. For details of the reverse run and of the shuttle service between Hospital de Benasque and La Besurta see the Day 12 description (p120). During these months cars can travel beyond Hospital de Benasque and up to La Besurta only between 8pm and 8am; for the rest of the year access is unrestricted.

For a taxi call **Daniel Villegas** (☎ 609 44 88 94) or **Pedro Erusue** (☎ 974 55 11 91).

Day 13: Benasque to Refugio Ángel Orus
4–4½ hours, 10.5km

From Benasque cross the ring road beside Barrabes Ski Montaña and take the Carretera de Anciles. This quiet, leafy lane brings you to **Anciles** (1100m) after 1.5km. Even though you've scarcely had time to warm up, it's worth taking an early break to wander its lanes, bordered by 17th- and 18th-century *señorial* (stately) houses, roofed in the local slate. On the west side of this charming hamlet follow the dusty track, a continuation of the main street, that leaves the village, passing by a couple of flowing *fuentes*. Pick up yellow-and-white trail markers and take a right turn, signed 'Eriste', to follow a shady lane through hayfields as far as a bridge over the Río Ésera, opposite a power plant.

You should be in **Eriste** (1118m) within an hour. Go through the central square, to the left of the church and up to the top of the village. The trail that you follow into the ravine is signed 'Puente de Tramarrius, Refugio Ángel Orus'.

Eriste shows its most photogenic side as you climb above it – rooflines, hayfields and the head of the Linsoles reservoir with its canoes and sailing boats divert attention from the valley's industrial scars. Just under an hour later cross the old **Puente de Tramarrius** (1245m) to mount the east (true left) bank of the river and meet a 4WD track. Continue upstream along this wider trail.

Count on a bit more than another hour, or a total of two hours from Eriste, passing by an abandoned pyrite mine to reach the **Cascada de la Espiantosa** (1505m), an impressive waterfall. The area around the falls makes an excellent lunch stop. Cross the nearby Puente de la Espiantosa – a mundane concrete bridge that can't compare with the magnificent arch of the Puente de Tramarrius earlier. A sign above the car park gives an accurate duration of 1½ hours to the Ángel Orus *refugio*.

After 20 to 25 minutes the path levels out briefly before resuming its upward progression, moving away from but always heading back to the Aigüeta de Eriste, the splendid stream that cuts through the valley. You're following yellow-and-white blazes and also red plastic markers hanging from the trees – trail markers for winter walkers and skiers. From **Pleta de les Riberes** (1815m), a small grassy area, the path zigzags steeply northwest up to **Refugio Ángel Orus** *(2150m;*

☎ 974 34 40 44; dorm beds €9.70). You normally need to reserve ahead (essential at weekends), despite its capacity for 100, as it's the most popular base camp for an assault on Posets mountain. It's also the only choice other than the stark Cabaña de Llardana (see Day 14, pp126–7) for noncampers walking this side of the massif.

Alternative Day 13: Benasque to Refugio de Estós
3½–4 hours, 12km

If you take this easy walk – the main GR tracing – up Valle de Estós to the *refugio* of the same name, you can save a day by omitting Days 13 and 14. However, if you do, you'll be depriving yourself of some spectacular mountain walking in the shadow of Posets.

The valley route is a well-trodden one, a 4WD track for the most part and popular with day-trippers from Benasque. You can either savour a short stage and overnight at Refugio de Estós or continue to Refugio de Viadós (see Day 15, pp127–8) – thus saving yourself yet another day. It makes for a long haul but many walkers undertake it.

Leave Benasque by the sealed road that heads north to La Besurta (if you'd prefer to avoid this stretch of road take the La Besurta bus as far as Puente de San Jaime (€1); for times, see Getting There & Around, p124).

Valle de Estós takes off northwest from the Río Ésera. At **Puente de San Jaime**, 3.8km north of town, turn right then left to go under the road bridge, beside Camping Aneto and over an older arched bridge. After passing a small dam cross the Palanca de Aiguacari (*palanca* in Aragonese means bridge) onto the true right bank. Shortly beyond a pair of green metal gates, **Cabaña de Santa Ana**, once a chapel, can accommodate 12 for a spartan overnight stay. Soon the steepness abates and the valley broadens into fine meadow interspersed with hazel, ash and beech trees.

Forty-five minutes or so from Puente de San Jaime pause to refill your water bottles – and if the season's right, munch a few wild strawberries – at Fuente Corona. At a junction 10 minutes later take a right fork signed 'Refugio de Estós'. After a further hour the

4WD track dwindles to a broad footpath, sunken from the tramping of so many boots, just beyond a small, locked cabin, the upstream limit for motor vehicles.

Forty-five minutes later, after a final 10 to 15 minutes of steep climb, you reach **Refugio de Estós** with its welcome terrace and icy-cold drinks. For more about the *refugio*, see the end of Day 14.

Day 14: Refugio Ángel Orus to Refugio de Estós

6–7 hours, 14.5km

This makes for a long day. However, if the mood takes you there are several spectacular places en route where you can break off to camp.

From the *refugio* pick up the red-and-white flashes of the GR11.2 variant and head northwest (the northeasterly tracing on the Alpina map is no longer practicable), continuing beyond a sign, 'Posets, Llardaneta'.

After 35 to 45 minutes turn right where the trail splits, to follow a sign 'Collado de la Piana,' and cross the Torrente de Llardaneta. You have to rely on the low cairns but navigation is no problem as far as the **Cabaña de Llardana**, which is visible from the junction. This spartan hut can accommodate four people plus baggage and has abundant water from nearby seeps. There's also just enough space to pitch a tent.

Keeping the height, bear northeast over turfed-in boulders, forging your own way as the GR signing on this stretch is absurdly stingy. About half an hour beyond the cabin you need to drop steeply to intersect with a path coming up from the main valley. From here on the trail marking improves.

You reach the double **Lago de las Alforjas** (2400m) one to 1¼ hours past the *cabaña*. It's one of a dozen or more lakes tucked around the eastern and southern slopes of the just-visible Posets and Bardamina crests. There are two to three good **camp sites** around its western shores.

Allow one to 1¼ hours to reach the obvious Collado de la Piana, which is just north of Pico de Escorvets (2902m). Leaving the lake, head briefly – and implausibly – south along (oh joy!) a near-level gulley before

ascending northeast. Pick your way above the north bank of the often frozen tarn of La Piana (the southern route indicated on both Prames and Alpina maps is emphatically blocked by landslide) to reach **Collado de la Piana** (2660m). Here there are magnificent panoramas west to the Posets crest (second-highest in the Pyrenees at 3369m), and east to Maladeta and the Ixeia pinnacles.

At the saddle you meet the first of the rare wooden poles that mark the next stretch of this GR11 variant. They're so infrequent as to be all but useless – and totally so if there's the least wisp of mist. (When we asked one of the wardens at the Refugio de Estós if there were plans to improve the deficient signing, he just shrugged and pointed out that the cows would uproot most of the poles anyway!).

Drop eastwards and pass to the left (north) of a pair of tarns, both visible from the col, and two of a spattering of pools on this side of the massif. A steep, rocky descent of about 1½ hours brings you to the **Ibón de l'Aigüeta de Batisielles** and its satellite pools, each of whose banks offer attractive **camping**.

Cross to the true left bank of its outlet stream to drop steeply and curl around the south shore of the larger **Ibón Gran de Batisielles** (2260m), which also offers great **camping**. As you leave the lake be sure to stay well above and to the left of the steep valley that runs away southwards.

Now comes the payoff for all the scrambling since the Collado de la Piana as you lope down an easily identifiable path through sparse pine to emerge into the lush, though in places marshy, pine-ringed meadows that enfold the **Ibón Pequeño de Batisielles** (1950m), a reedy pond.

Here you can choose from various **camp sites**, the best and driest being between the two forks of the Río de Batisielles. The only drawback to otherwise idyllic camping is that it's also a favourite grazing area of local cows and consequently the hunting ground of some particularly predatory horseflies. For the tentless there's a very basic, green metal **shelter**, sleeping three at a squeeze, on a knoll just southeast of the flats and another one beside the pool that can just accommodate four.

From the shelter beside the pool strike northeast along an evident, intermittently blazed trail. After an initial climb of about five minutes there's little net altitude gain as you stride through a mixture of pine forest and grassland. Enjoy the fine vistas across the Valle de Estós to the peaks of Pico de Gías, Pico d'Oô (no typing error here!) and the mighty Perdiguero. The Refugio de Estós, perched well above the riverside meadows, comes into sight long before you cross the Río de Estós by a stout wooden bridge for the final brief climb to its terrace.

Refugio de Estós *(1890m; ☎/fax 974 55 14 83; dorm beds €9.70)* is the largest *refugio* in the Pyrenees, with room for 185. The friendly warden, Juan Antonio Turmo, has run it ever since 1984, when the new building rose from the ashes of a devastating fire. Since it's a popular venue for groups, day visitors and overnighters from Benasque, reservations are essential. It serves drinks, snacks and meals, and has hot showers and its own generator powered by a nearby torrent. Rare among *refugios*, it accepts Visa and MasterCard.

Side Trip: Lago de la Escarpinosa
1¾–2 hours, 4km
From the Ibón Pequeño de Batisielles head southwest through pine forest up an idyllic streamside path to the Lago de la Escarpinosa (2040m). Here, where the grass is limited but luxuriant, is another splendid spot for an overnight **camp**.

Day 15: Refugio de Estós to Refugio de Viadós
4–4½ hours, 10km
Two signs greet you in quick succession as you leave the *refugio*. One posits two hours to the Puerto de Gistaín; the other, 1½ hours. Put your faith in the former, then add some…

The path descends gently on the north (true left) side of the river to meet the valley bottom after about 20 minutes' walking. The Clarabide stream descends southwards down a sheer valley to meet the main Río de Estós watercourse at about 2050m, 45 minutes to an hour above the *refugio*. It's a pretty spot to rest and replenish your water

supplies – the last dependable water for quite some time.

Once you've crossed to the south side of the Río de Estós's first dribblings you face a rather monotonous westward haul over scree and rock up a long, dry tube of a valley. It's not too arduous, however, if you stick to the red-and-white trail markers of the GR11, which snakes smoothly between and around obstacles, avoiding most rock scrambling.

Aim for a notch on the south side of the bowl, then walk around the head of the valley to reach the true pass (2590m), known variously as the **Puerto de Gistaín**, Puerto Chistén and Puerto de Chistau, 2¼ to 2½ hours from the *refugio*.

There's really a double pass here, separated by a narrow moor. Before you move on take a last glance backwards at the Aneto massif, dominating the eastern horizon. Some 10 minutes from the second, minor col, cross to the true left bank of the gully which drops steeply away westwards. From here until the confluence of streams at **Añes Cruces** (2060m), it's a gentle, grassy descent, except for the last 10 minutes or so, which require all your attention as the path crosses steep scree.

At the confluence, reached about an hour beyond the pass, cross both tributaries, as well as an upstart little stream, to join the west (true right) bank of the river, from here on known as the Cinqueta de Añes Cruces. Conspicuous on the hillside are two **cabins**, one low and squat, the other newly constructed. If the shepherds aren't in residence, the latter, especially, makes a good overnight flop.

The path is straightforward. As you gradually round the mountain, walking through wide, floral meadows, there are unsurpassed views of the entire west face of Posets. Allow 1¼ to 1½ hours from the confluence to **Granjas de Viadós** (Biadós), a hamlet of a dozen or so scattered farmhouses.

The privately owned **Refugio de Viadós** *(1760m; ☎ 974 50 61 63; dorm beds €5.20; open July-Sept)* is outstanding and extremely reasonable. With 65 bunks and a cosy bar and dining room, it's a friendly, popular family operation. The filling meals are a bargain at €10.

The owner, Joaquin Cazcarra, also runs **Camping El Forcallo** (☎ 974 50 61 63; *camping per person/tent €2.70/2.70; open July-Aug*), 1.3km down the hill. There's no shop but it has a pleasant bar, where meals cost €9.

Side Trip: Lago de Millares
5–5½ hours, 10.5km
Time permitting, set aside a full day for the challenging yet satisfying return trip from Refugio de Viadós, up and out of the woodland around Barranco de Ribereta to the Lago de Millares (2400m), which sparkles and spreads below the Pico de la Forqueta. The gradient is steep in places but you're on path the entire way.

Side Trip: Señal de Viadós
3½–4 hours, 7km
Stunning 360-degree vistas make the 840m ascent from Viadós to Señal de Viadós (2600m) – a spectacular viewpoint – well worthwhile. Allow a generous half-day for this return trip, north-northeast of the *refugio*.

Day 16: Refugio de Viadós to Parzán
5½–6½ hours, 20km
After the challenge of the Posets rim, you deserve this easy, uncomplicated day of attractive walking, primarily through meadow

---

Camping Wild in Aragón

As everywhere in the Pyrenees, camping is normally forbidden in national parks and designated conservation areas such as Parque Posets-Maladeta.

Outside these areas, regulation 79/1990 of 8 May 1990 decrees that above 1500m you can camp anywhere that's more than two hours' walk from a vehicle access point. Below 1500m you have the right to pitch your tent anywhere more than 5km from a designated camping ground and 1km from an urban centre. It's forbidden to camp within 100m of a river or road. If anyone should challenge you, just quote *decreto 79/1990 del ocho de mayo* back at them!

---

and pine forest, which makes a gentle prelude to the altogether sterner stuff ahead. There's an ascent to 2300m but it's never too strenuous. Steel yourself, however, for the final unexciting 8.5km descent along a 4WD track from below Lago de Urdiceto to Valle de Bielsa. Few 4WDs venture this way so you're unlikely to get a lift.

From Refugio de Viadós the GR11 briefly takes to the trees but you're just as well off following the 4WD track downhill past Camping el Forcallo.

It's about 45 minutes from the *refugio* to the La Sargueta turn-off (1540m), 1km downstream from the camping ground. Take the track to the right, signed 'Urdiceto, Parzan'. After 30 minutes turn right at a cluster of farms, the Bordas de Lizierte, to mount a steep path and briefly enter the welcome shade of a pine wood. You soon bear right to join a wider jeep track and, within 20 to 30 minutes, reach the small pass and meadow of **Las Collás**, or Las Colladas (1846m).

The track dips briefly to Barranco de la Basa as **Cabaña Sallena**, the only structure on the opposite hillside, comes into view. The countryside is an appealing mix of piny ravines and turf. A view to the west of the bare Punta Suelza (2973m) provides a sample of the tougher terrain to come.

The 4WD track peters out at the *cabaña* (capable of sleeping up to six intimate friends) to become a clear footpath. About 30 minutes beyond the cabin there's a deep, inviting pool, ideal for a dunk on a hot day, where you cross to the stream's true right bank. No more than 10 minutes beyond is a tiny, tumbling stone **shelter** that could provide strictly emergency accommodation.

As you angle up the ridge separating the two *barrancos*, Montarruegos and Sallena, the path winds and undulates a little before slipping through **Collada de Urdiceto** (Ordiceto; 2326m), also known as Paso d'es Caballos, 3½ to four hours into the day. If you want to stay up high, try the wonderful **camp sites** in the meadows before the pass.

At the pass there's a recently constructed shepherd's hut that offers simple accommodation. Just beyond it the path meets a dirt access road that leads out left to Lago de

DAVID TOMLINSON

INGRID RODDIS

Top: The pretty Ara valley near Torla, is followed on the Pyrenean Traverse. **Bottom**: A walker's playground, the Parc Nacional d'Aigüestortes i Estany de Sant Maurici offers scenery among the most spectacular in the Pyrenees.

JOSE PLACER

OLIVER STREWE

MATT FLETCHER

Top Left: La Jelguera village seen from El Naranjo de Bulnes (2519m), the signature peak of the Parque Nacional de los Picos de Europa. **Top Right**: Olives are grown in vast quantities throughout southern Spain. **Bottom**: Looking across cloud-shrouded Valle de Guadalest to the Serra de Bérnia's mighty ridges, from Fuente Forata on the Ruta La Marina Alta.

Hydropower & Hydrotrash

Purists deplore the tinkering with nature of the small-scale hydroelectric schemes that dam and distort high mountain tarns. But which is the least environmentally damaging and which takes most from the earth? A coal, oil or gas-fired generating station? A nuclear plant? Or whirring turbines, driven by a source of energy that drops from the sky and continues its downward journey unchanged?

There is something of a downside in the Pyrenees. Though many water pipes linking one lake with another are buried deep underground, there are some monumentally ugly wide-bore tubes that drop water from dam level to turbines further down in the valley. Around the dams you'll often see the abandoned debris of their construction: a twisted stretch of narrow-gauge railway line, the concrete pad of a demolished hut or the rusting pylons of long-abandoned cable lifts.

Then again, there's a special spin-off for walkers. Several Pyrenean mountain *refugios* started life as rest houses for workers on the dams and were given over to walking clubs and societies once construction was over.

Urdiceto (2390m), a stark, monochrome blot amid grimly rocky terrain – not really worth a detour. There are, however, a few turfy flat spots here for a **camp site** if you want to postpone the descent to Parzán.

Otherwise, turn right down the dirt road, then almost immediately left onto a path which cuts off a couple of long zigzags before rejoining the 4WD track 15 to 20 minutes later. After a further 15 minutes on the track turn left onto a path that runs beside a small dam and hydroelectric station and soon rejoins the 4WD track. From here on it's an uneventful descent, albeit with pleasant views, to the main highway, the Carretera de Francia, 1.5km north of the hamlet of Parzán.

Parzán

Parzán has a couple of *casas rurales*, each with four rooms and common bathroom: **Luis**

Zueras (☎ 974 50 11 90; Casa Marion; doubles €19) and **María Jesús Fumanal** (☎ 974 50 11 24; Casa Quilez; singles/doubles €14/18).

La Fuen (☎ 974 50 10 47; w www.mon teperdido.com/lafuen; Carretera de Francia; singles/doubles with bathroom €24/36), on the main road, is a welcoming small hotel with a cosy bar and a restaurant that does an excellent dinner *menú* for €10.50.

Opposite La Fuen are a **café**, a **Spar supermarket** and a **grocery** – an essential call as you won't meet another shop until Torla at the end of Day 19.

Day 17: Parzán to Valle de Pineta
5½–6 hours, 16km

The route follows the GR11 tracing. After 8.5km of 4WD track up the attractive valley of the Río Real it's springy turf or clearly delineated path for the rest of the day with spectacular views of Valle de Pineta and the impressive cirque at its head. A gain of almost exactly 1000m in elevation to Collado de Pietramula is followed by a mostly undemanding walk down to the base of Circo de Pineta.

Just north of Parzán turn left off the Carretera de Francia and follow the narrow sealed road until you reach the small hamlet of **Chisagües** 45 minutes after the junction. Continue along what becomes graded track, originally made to serve the long-abandoned silver and lead mines above Chisagües. It's a steady, uneventful rise up the valley, the views improving at every bend.

At one particularly acute hairpin bend, 6.5km beyond Chisagües, leave the track, cross the Río Real (a mere trickle here) and work your way on turf upwards and westwards through a jumble of rocks at the base of Pietramula, the slab of mountain to the left.

At the **Collado de Pietramula**, or Piedramula (2150m), about 30 minutes' uphill work beyond the river crossing, drink in the first dramatic views of the sheer western flank of the Valle de Pineto, the notch of the Collado de Añisclo, tomorrow's challenge, and the Glaciar de Monte Perdido.

A short, steep drop leads to the **Llanos de Estiva** plains, one vast potential **camp site**,

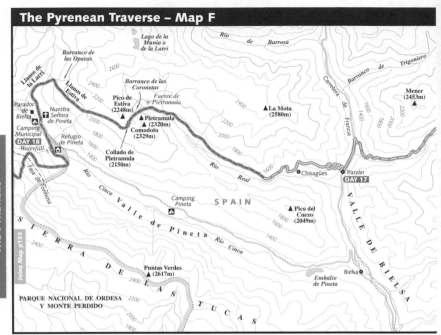

The Pyrenean Traverse – Map F

several football fields long, with a flowing water trough on its northern slope. At its limit, 20 to 30 minutes beyond the col, the grassy semblance of a path leads into a stony 4WD track. A couple of bends beyond a locked shepherd's hut on your right turn sharp right onto a pleasant, grassy path.

Shortly after the trail enters pinewood and begins to descend more steeply look out for an easily missed 90-degree turn southwest. A couple more twists and the route descends emphatically and unambiguously southwestwards, down to the grassy **Llanos de la Larri** (1560m), 1½ to 1¾ hours beyond the col.

Cross over the rim of this wide hanging valley to drop down through a wood of beech, holly and boxwood, each a delight after day upon day of conifers, to the small chapel of Nuestra Señora de Pineta (1250m) and its adjacent *fuente* about half an hour later.

Here, at the head of the valley, you've a binary choice of both accommodation and camping ground.

For a touch of four-star luxury at equivalent prices turn right for the **Parador de Bielsa** (☎ *974 50 10 11, fax 974 50 11 88; singles/ doubles with bathroom from €74/92*). To fortify yourself for the morrow and the toughest ascent of the whole traverse, consider awarding yourself a gourmet dinner (€18 for their excellent set menu) at the restaurant, from where the views of the Circo de Pineta are stunning.

More modest but not necessarily less agreeable, the smart **Refugio de Pineta** (☎/*fax 974 50 12 03; dorm beds €9*), run by the Federación Aragonesa de Montañismo (FAM), is 1.5km down the valley. Even though it keeps about 25% of places for walk-ins, we strongly advise you to reserve. You don't have to be staying to tuck into one of their copious meals (€8.70).

The **Camping Municipal** (*camping per person/tent €1.80/1.50*) is a huge tented area, like the scene before the battle of Agincourt or Gettysburg. You'll have little

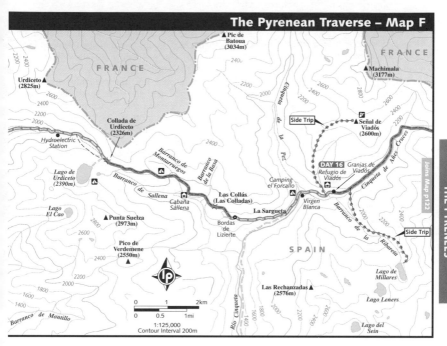

The Pyrenean Traverse – Map F

trouble finding a pitch. The ratio of squatter toilets and cold-water washbasins to campers, however, is lamentable. There's a small bar that serves *bocadillos*.

For comfort under canvas you're much better off walking or hitching a further 3.5km along the road from the *refugio* to the impeccable **Camping Pineta** (*☎/fax 974 50 10 89; camping per person/tent €3.50/3.50; open Easter–mid-Oct*), where the water in the free showers is piping hot and the toilets are the fastest flushing in the west. It also has a small **supermarket** – useful for stocking up on essential provisions for the next stage – and a good **restaurant** (*menú €10*).

Day 18: Valle de Pineta to Valle de Añisclo

4½–5¾ hours, 7.5km

Make no mistake, the major part of today is a tough, strenuous walk which will have you clambering up rocks and over fallen trees and negotiating minor landslides. Statistically

speaking, the climb from the Pineta valley bottom to Collado de Añisclo represents a vertical ascent of just under 1200m in almost exactly 2km of walking and scrambling. Put another way, you're heaving your way up a gradient of just under 60%. The considerable compensation comes from the ever more spectacular views at your back of Valle and Circo de Pineto as you advance.

The GR11 crosses to the true right bank of the river by way of the bridge beside the Camping Municipal, then turns left to follow a well-blazed trail that roughly parallels the stream. (If you're rejoining the route from Refugio de Pineta, take the broad path heading west from the *refugio* and, after some 200m, head upstream along the wide, dry river bed – in early summer it may have to be boots and socks off to ford the watercourse. At its first bend, turn left at a sign pointing back to the *refugio* and pick up the GR11).

The path meanders along the wide riverbed, crosses a water meadow, snakes

The GR11 Backtracks

It's a principle of GR trails in Europe that they should be accessible to all. But from Collado d'Añisclo the original GR11 route followed, and continues to follow, a potentially danger-ous 500m traverse around the usually wet, often snowbound rock of Punta de las Olas.

In response to widespread criticism the GR11 committee approved an alternative, also marked with the red-and-white bars of the official GR trail.

Uniquely, the 'variant' now features in the official handbook as the recommended route, while the original life-threatener has been relegated to an option in italics.

✿ ✿ ✿ ✿ ✿ ✿ ✿ ✿ ✿ ✿ ✿ ✿

along the base of the cliff then, around 15 minutes beyond the *refugio* turning, begins to climb in earnest. Something over 30 min-utes later, cross a wide *barranco* and swift stream. Fill your water bottles here as there's no more water until you're over the Añisclo pass. Until roughly halfway, the obvious trail mounts steeply through a tunnel of silver birch, boxwood, hazel and beech, their deep shade more than compensating for the absence of views.

At about 1900m the path intersects with the enviably flat Faja de Tormosa route, which contours around from Circo de Pineta to the west. As the trees begin to thin out and become more stunted you'll notice a dispro-portionate number lying dead. They aren't victims of disease or insects; the slope is renowned for its springtime avalanches that sweep everything but the most pliable, re-silient vegetation before them.

The steepest stuff is now behind you. Al-though there's plenty of scree ahead that will have you slithering, four-limbed manoeuvres are all but over, except for a short, mean traverse about 15 minutes before the saddle.

Walking times to **Collado de Añisclo** (2470m) vary enormously, from around three hours to well over four. If you're run-ning short of energy, there's an unspoilt spot with water and some level turf for a **camp site** no more than 50m vertical descent on

the south side of the ridge. As you savour the fine views of the head of the Valle de Añisclo canyon, you can see the deep inci-sion of Barranco de Fon Blanc, slicing in from the west.

At the pass, it's time to decide between the high road and the low road: the original GR11 route via the Puntas de las Olas tra-verse and the more trodden variant down the Añisclo canyon. Unless you're an experi-enced mountaineer we strongly recommend that you avoid the former (see the boxed text 'The GR11 Backtracks'). Should you opt for it, take particular care when negotiating the tranche that requires cable support when there's snow around – which is most of the year. This variant takes between two and 2¼ hours as far as Collado Arrablo.

Even though you lose around 750m in al-titude, we equally strongly recommend the GR11 variant via the alluring **Valle de Añisclo** both because it's safer and for its own sake; it will only take you a couple more hours of walking.

To follow it, head briefly west from the pass then begin to drop down the valley, keeping fairly high up its eastern flank. A series of gentle drops, each ending in a waterfall and a pool deep enough to bathe in; green sward; alpine flowers; and a choice of camp sites at each giant step make the upper valley one of the major highlights of the whole Pyrenees crossing.

You'll be happier up higher; the area around Casa de los Cazadores, farther down the valley, tends to fill up with campers as sunset approaches – and one unfortunate con-sequence of so many overnight visitors is that there's far too much crap around for comfort.

Across a metal bridge just below the last of the inviting pools is the squat, dry hut of **Casa de los Cazadores** (Hunters' House), 1¼ to 1½ hours from the col. It can accommodate five snuggled close together. Just beyond it is a rocky overhang that provides **shelter** for a similar number.

Alternative Camp Sites

Should you have any stamina left when you reach Casa de los Cazadores, consider con-tinuing for around a further 1¼ hours as far as the alpine meadows above the bare rock of Barranco de Fon Blanca (see Day 19). This may leave you drained but it will allow you to descend to Pradera de Ordesa comfortably the following day and maybe continue up Valle de Bujaruelo.

Day 19: Valle de Añisclo to Torla
7½–8½ hours, 23km

Steel yourself to rejoin the madding crowd. After an ascent to Collado Arrablo the route drops via the teeming Refugio de Góriz to the floor of Valle de Ordesa. As you draw closer to the shuttle-bus terminal at Pradera de Ordesa throngs of tourists seem to outnumber the trees.

One option is to delay the inevitable, enjoy a short day and spend the night, probably in the company of a hundred others, in or around Refugio de Góriz. From here, the fit can undertake the demanding day trip to the summit of Monte Perdido (3355m; see Monte Perdido, p159, under Other Walks).

Start out with some steep two-steps-up-one-back scree scrabbling just below the spectacular **Cascada de Fon Blanca** waterfall. Though it's abrupt and confronts you before you've time to catch your second wind, it's like a short stroll to the shops compared with yesterday's exertions as scree alternates with rocky outcrop, giving much more purchase.

As you continue to ascend the gaunt, narrow valley of the Barranco Arrablo (also known as the Barranco de Fon Blanca) the steepness eases markedly. After a little under 45 minutes cross to the true right bank of the shallow stream, dipping in your water bottles as you do; Ordesa is strictly limestone and surface water is at a premium away from the valley bottom.

Around 20 minutes later there's a brief, steep, hands-and-feet southwesterly traverse before the route resumes its westward progress below the valley's upper rim. Here, the path leaves behind the uniform

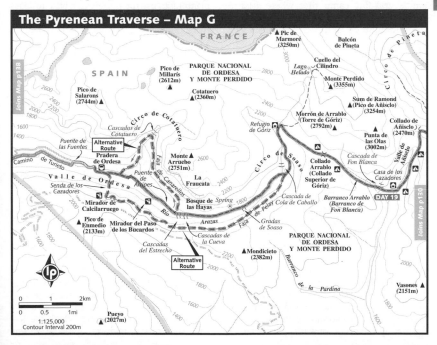

The Pyrenean Traverse – Map G

grey rock of the canyon and emerges into a green alpine meadow – a perfect **camp site** shared only by marmots.

A short while later there's a final, four-limbed climb, no more than five minutes long, up the face of a bluff with plenty of handholds and footholds. Once you heave yourself over the ridge it's pleasant upland striding to **Collado Arrablo** (2343m), also known as Collado Superior de Góriz, reached two to 2¼ hours into the day. From your right (east) the GR11 path from the Punta de las Olas traverse (see the boxed text 'The GR11 Backtracks', p132) trickles in, deceptively innocuous in its final stage.

From the saddle you have good views of the summits to the north: from right to left, Punta de las Olas (3002m), Sum de Ramond (also called Pico de Añisclo; 3254m), Morrón de Arrablo (or Torre de Góriz; 2792m) and, lording it over all, imperious Monte Perdido (3355m).

About 15 minutes beyond the pass there are several fine **camp sites** where a large stream flows through a meadow. Once you reach **Refugio de Góriz** *(2150m; ☎/fax 974 34 12 01; dorm beds €9, dinner €11.80)*, some 20 minutes later, you may well wonder why you've bothered. Multilingual signs inform you with commendable directness, 'those camping can't use any of the *refugio's* services'. Such a proscription, however, doesn't apply to their drinks, snacks or, if you're lucky enough to be able to order one, meals.

The staff are pleasant enough, but the *refugio*, overstressed, overwhelmed and understaffed, sits squarely astride several main routes: up to France via the Brecha de Rolando, through which French trekkers pour in their hundreds; to Pineta via the Cuello del Cilindro; down to the Ordesa canyon; back where you've come from – and, of course, the classic day trip up to Monte Perdido. In summer it's under enormous pressure to accommodate a huge number of walkers. It's wise to reserve both meals and sleeping space as much as a month in advance. The environs of the *refugio* are like an earthquake disaster zone from early afternoon onwards, with tents –

which you can't erect until nightfall – and bodies everywhere.

It makes sense to overnight here if you're planning to use the *refugio* as a base for bagging Monte Perdido (see Monte Perdido, p159, under Other Walks). Otherwise, do yourself, the wardens and the environment a favour and head down the valley to Pradera de Ordesa, still three to 3½ hours away.

About 40 minutes south of the hut, the path divides. The more evident – and more hazardous – route bears right just above the Circo de Soaso. The GR11, on this occasion prudence itself, describes a relatively gentle zigzagging course down the valley's southeastern flank. Some 20 minutes down the switchbacks the trail again divides. Take the right-hand path to reach the valley bottom, a little downstream from **Cascada de Cola de Caballo** (Horse's Tail Waterfall), a pleasant place for a rest break (the Alternative Route – see p135 – takes the path straight ahead).

From here to Pradera de Ordesa you won't lack company for a moment. About 30 minutes below Cola de Caballo the canyon begins to lose some of its characteristic glacial U shape and the woods become denser. Five minutes beyond the **Gradas de Soaso**, a series of natural steps down which the Río Arazas tumbles, there's a most welcome *fuente*. Another 30 minutes or so brings you to the turn-off for Faja de Canarellos and Circo de Cotatuero (see Alternative Route: Via Cascada de Cotatuero, p136).

At a sign for the Cascadas de la Cueva and del Estrecho waterfalls and La Pradera turn left and soon cross to the stream's south bank via Puente de Arripes. A few minutes later a short detour to the Mirador del Paso de los Bucardos lookout gives excellent views towards the cliffs of the Salarons and Cotatuero peaks.

Continue along the south-bank path and, at a junction with the Senda de los Cazadores trail (see Alternative Route: Via Faja de Pelay), you cross back over the river to reach **Pradera de Ordesa**. The total time from Refugio de Góriz is around three hours.

If you've been on dehydrated goo for the past two days, **Bar-Restaurante La Pradera de Ordesa**, with its rich variety of tapas and *bocadillos*, icy-cold draught beer and a *menú* at €12, is a minor gastronomic paradise.

The car park (these days satisfyingly devoid of private cars, at least in high summer) is the terminus for the Torla shuttle bus, the way most walkers enter and leave the park, and a way to save two hours. For service details see Getting There & Away (pp136–7).

If you'd prefer to walk the 6.5km to Torla descend via an ancient track that links the village with the *bordas* of Valle de Ordesa. It makes a pleasant, easy alternative to the shuttle bus.

Cross the small bridge a stone's throw from Pradera de Ordesa to meet the Camino de Turieto and follow downstream the true left bank of the Río Arazas. The *camino* drops gently through a wood of fir trees and open meadow. A pair of short detours to the right leads to small waterfalls.

At the park boundary, reached after about an hour, the *camino* forks south to Torla, already visible, and north (right) along the GR11 towards Valle de Bujaruelo. Take the Torla option, which soon becomes a sizable dirt track. Roughly 30 minutes later, cross the river by Puente de la Glera and go up a cobbled lane that leads to Torla.

If you wanted to bypass Torla and extend Day 19 you could take the shuttle bus down as far as Puente de los Navarros to save a little boot leather and continue on. Another option is to begin Day 20 from Puente de los Navarros and continue to either Balneario de Panticosa (see Day 21) or Panticosa (see Alternative Day 21), but this makes for a very long day's walk.

Alternative Route: Via Faja de Pelay
6½–7½ hours, 17.5km

'Faja', meaning belt or band, accurately describes this contour-hugging path, high above Valle de Ordesa. Beginning just south of Circo de Soaso, it continues as far as Mirador de Calcilarruego, where you launch yourself on the steep descent down the Senda de los Cazadores, the Hunters' Track.

Follow Day 19 as far as the point, well below Refugio de Góriz, where it bears away right and downhill to meet the valley bottom. Instead, continue straight with no loss of height to join the main Faja de Pelay path coming up from the meadows of Circo de Soaso.

After the hard, uphill work of the previous 1½ days, the Faja is an immensely enjoyable stroll, though the final descent down the ultra-steep Senda de los Cazadores may batter your kneecaps a little.

The path twists its way around one incised ravine after another, rarely rising above 1900m. The views are magnificent the whole way, except where obscured by trees. Keep your eyes focused on the middle ground as well as the canyon and mountain scenery. On this less-trodden trail you stand a good chance of spotting *sarrio*, as chamois are known in Aragonese.

From the point at which you leave the Day 19 route allow between 2¼ and 2½ hours to reach **Mirador de Calcilarruego**.

In the next 1¼ hours or so the path drops 600m vertically on the tight switchbacks of the Senda de los Cazadores, as mountain pine and fir trees gradually give way to silent, shaded beech wood. As you emerging from the wood turn left to reach the service area and shuttle-bus terminus of the Pradera de Ordesa, where you rejoin the main route within 10 minutes.

THE PYRENEES

Alternative Route: Via Cascada de Cotatuero

2½–3 hours, 6km

Head right at the turn-off to Faja de Canarellos and Circo de Cotatuero. The path briefly ascends to meet the Faja de Canarellos trail as it works northwest and the beeches become sparser, giving way to box, pine and fir.

The path hugs the 1700m contour around the flank of Monte Arruebo with the looming cliffs of La Fraucata above. Crossing the lips of numerous hanging valleys and narrowing on occasion to clear rock overhangs, it offers tremendous views of the opposite Faja de Pelay flank of the Ordesa canyon.

It will take you around 1½ hours from Bosque de las Hayas to reach the bridge and tiny shelter below **Cascada de Cotatuero**, which tumbles from Circo de Cotatuero. From here allow 40 minutes to rejoin the main north-bank path along Valle de Ordesa at a junction marked by a small shrine to the Virgen de Ordesa, and another 10 to reach Pradera de Ordesa, to rejoin the main route.

Torla

Torla, an attractive stone-built village and gateway to the Parque Nacional de Ordesa y Monte Perdido, gets crowded in high summer. This said, it's well endowed with restaurants and places to stay and makes an attractive rest stop. There are a couple of **supermarkets**, each with an ATM outside.

Information The **tourist office** (☎ 974 48 63 78; open 9.30am-1.30pm & 5.30pm-9pm Mon-Sat, 9.30am-12.30pm Sun July–mid-Sept) is on Calle Fatas. There's also a small and not too informative **national park office** (☎ 974 48 64 72; Avenida de Ordesa; open 8am-3pm daily).

A useful website (in Spanish) for Torla and the national park is W www.ordesa.com.

The small **Museo Etnológico** (folk museum; Calle de la Iglesia; admission €1; open 11am-2pm & 6pm-9pm daily July–mid-Sept) is beside the parish church.

Places to Stay & Eat Of the three camping grounds around Torla, **Camping Río Ara** (☎ 974 48 62 48; camping per person/tent €3.40/3.40) is handiest for Torla. On the downside, it gets full to the gills in high summer – though the owners are sure to find space for a lightweight tent.

Camping San Antón (☎ 974 48 60 63; camping per person/tent €3.40/3.40; open Easter–mid-October) is nearest to the Parque Nacional de Ordesa y Monte Perdido entrance and a better bet on all counts, especially if you intend to bypass Torla.

Torla has a couple of excellent budget accommodation choices, both open year-round and enough in themselves to entice you off the mountains for a night or two.

Albergue L'Atalaya (☎/fax 974 48 60 22; Calle A Ruata; dorm beds €7) is a friendly, French-run mountain *refugio* that just happens to find itself in town. Their welcoming **bar-restaurant** (menús €9 & €13, platos combinados €6.50) is open to all. Half-board costs €19 and full board of a bed, evening meal, breakfast and picnic lunch is a bargain €27.

Refugio Lucien Briet (☎ 974 48 62 21, fax 974 48 64 80; W www.refugiolucienbriet .com; Calle A Ruata; dorm beds €7, doubles with bathroom €30, triples/quads without bathroom €25/32) is more flexible. Half-board costs an extra €12 per person. It also runs **Restaurante La Brecha**, which does an enticing menú for €10.20. Trekker-oriented, the *refugio* has a small library of walking titles.

Torla's hotels, looking over each others' shoulders, all charge more or less the same rates.

Hostal Alto Aragón (☎/fax 974 48 61 72; singles/doubles with bathroom €25/37) is your cheapest option. The same family runs the slightly dearer **Hotel Ballarín** (☎/fax 974 48 61 55; singles/doubles/triples with bathroom €27/46/54) across the street. It also has a good **restaurant** (menú €9) and offers half-board for an extra €12.50 per person.

Restaurante el Rebeco (☎ 974 48 60 68; Calle Fatas; menú €12), popular and with a folksy decor, offers a number of Aragonese specialities and cuisine a cut or two above the usual tourist fare.

Getting There & Away From July to mid-October shuttle buses (€1.80) run at 15 to 20 minute intervals between the car park on the south side of Torla and Pradera de Ordesa. Buses leave Torla between 6am (7am in October) and 7pm (6pm in October). The last bus down from Pradera de Ordesa leaves at 10pm (9pm in September, 8.30pm in October).

Year-round, buses run from Torla to Sabiñánigo (two daily). From Sabiñánigo, five buses a day go to/from Jaca (€1.15, 15 minutes), with onward transport to Zaragoza and Pamplona; and four, to/from Huesca (€4.05, 45 minutes), with links to Lleida and Barcelona. For bus times ask at the tourist office or phone **Hudebus** (☎ 974 212 32 77).

For Torla taxis ring **Taxi Bella Vista** (☎ 974 48 61 53), based in Hotel Bella Vista, or **Jorge Soler** (☎ 974 48 62 43), who operates from Supermercado Torla.

Day 20: Torla to Bujaruelo
3–3¾ hours, 10km

Given the twin attractions of Torla and the national park, where many walkers will want to linger, we've built in a very short day to allow flexibility.

Rather than slogging it up the highway, retrace your final steps at the end of Day 19 until, almost at the entry to the national park and with about half an hour's walking behind you, rejoin the GR11. Take the left fork, which soon brings you to the Puente de los Navarros.

At **Puente de los Navarros** (1045m), the bridge just to the west of the barrier marking the park entrance, the GR briefly takes to the hills, rejoining the Ara valley at Puente de Santa Elena. However, unless you're particularly keen to slip in an extra gradient – and a brief, easily negotiated passage where you traverse while grabbing a chain – you'll save both time and energy by following the 4WD track that runs parallel to the Río Ara. It's a pleasant walk northwards up Valle de Bujaruelo, the attractiveness marred only by the giant electricity pylons that loom over the valley.

After 2.5km, where the track crosses the small Puente de Santa Elena (or Puente Nuevo), stay on the river's true left bank to take a charming footpath that leads through woodland to Bujaruelo.

Precisely 1.2km from Puente de Santa Elena, Puente de los Abetos leads to **Camping Valle de Bujaruelo** (☎ 974 48 63 48; W www.campingvalledebujaruelo.com; camping per person/tent €3.40/3.40; open Easter–mid-Oct). Alternatively, you can sleep in their **Refugio el Serbal** (doubles/triples/quads from €17.45/24.50/30.65). There's a bar, **restaurant** (menú €9.80) and a small **shop** (a good place to stock up if you've bypassed Torla).

Your other option is to push on for a further 3km to **Bujaruelo** itself (1340m), a splendid spot where the valley broadens out. **Camping San Nicolás de Bujaruelo** (☎ 974 48 64 28; camping per person/tent €3/3; open Easter–mid-Oct) is more spartan yet more walker-friendly. If there's no-one around, just pitch your tent and someone will turn up next morning to collect the fee.

Beside the camping ground is **Mesón San Nicolás de Bujaruelo** (☎ 974 48 64 12; accommodation per person €10, half-board €22.55) on the site of what was once an hospital catering to pilgrims and travellers crossing into France by Puerto de Bujaruelo, also called Port de Gavarnie. Take time out before moving on to look at the ruins of the Romanesque chapel just behind the mesón. The mesón is an excellent deal, offering accommodation in rooms for four with bathroom, and a hearty menú (€12). Though it's prudent to reserve ahead in July and August, the friendly manager will always squeeze you in (the Mesón record is 130 – in a place with a capacity of around 60 – one night when a Pyrenean storm raged and the adjacent camping ground was awash).

Also worthy of note if you've been high for several days and are beginning to smell the same way: the mesón and both the valley's camping grounds offer free hot showers.

Day 21: Bujaruelo to Balneario de Panticosa
6½–7½ hours, 18km

This route, following the GR11 tracing, is shorter than Alternative Day 21 and arguably more varied. However, with a couple of substantial boulder fields to negotiate, it is, if anything, more difficult.

The Pyrenean Traverse – Map H

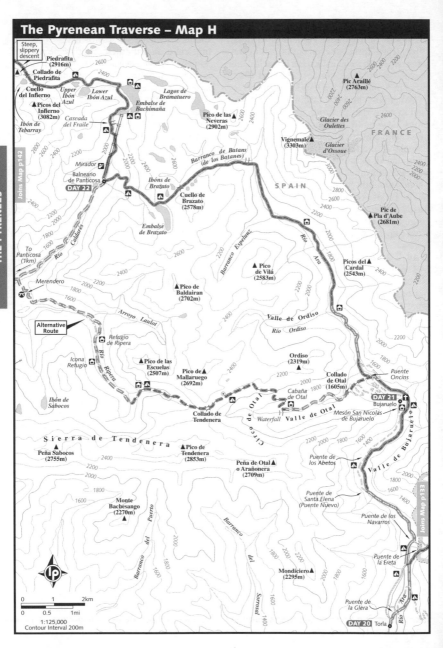

Steep, slippery descent

Piedrafita (2916m)

Collado de Piedrafita

Cuello del Infierno

Picos del Infierno (3082m)

Upper Ibón Azul

Lower Ibón Azul

Ibón de Tebarray

Cascada del Fraile

Lagos de Bramatuero

Embalse de Bachimaña

Pico de las Neveras (2902m)

Pic Araillé (2763m)

Glacier des Oulettes

FRANCE

Vignemale (3303m)

Glacier d'Ossoue

SPAIN

Mirador

Balneario de Panticosa

DAY 22

Barranco de Batans (de los Batanes)

Ibóns de Brazato

Cuello de Brazato (2578m)

Pico de Pla d'Aube (2681m)

Río Ara

Picos del Cardal (2543m)

Joins Map p142

Río Caldarés

Embalse de Brazato

To Panticosa (1km)

Merendero

Barranco Espelunz

Pico de Vilá (2583m)

Pico de Baldairan (2702m)

Valle de Ordiso

Río Ordiso

Alternative Route

Arroyo Laulot

Refugio de Ripera

Icona Refugio

Río Ripera

Pico de las Escuelas (2507m)

Pico de Mallaruego (2692m)

Ordiso (2319m)

Collado de Otal (1605m)

Puente Oncins

Ibón de Sabocos

Collado de Tendenera

Circo de Otal

Cabaña de Otal

Waterfall Valle de Otal

DAY 21

Bujaruelo

Mesón San Nicolás de Bujaruelo

Sierra de Tendenera

Peña Sabocos (2755m)

Pico de Tendenera (2853m)

Peña de Otal o Arañonera (2709m)

Valle de Bujaruelo

Puente de los Abetos

Monte Bachesango (2270m)

Barranco del Puerto

Puente de Santa Elena (Puente Nuevo)

Puente de los Navarros

Barranco del Sorrosal

Puente de la Ereta

Mondiciero (2295m)

Joins Map p133

Puente de la Glera

DAY 20 Torla

Río Ara

0   1   2km
0   0.5   1mi

1:125,000
Contour Interval 200m

THE PYRENEES

From Bujaruelo, the clearly marked GR11 route forms a sickle shape: straight up the Río Ara valley, then curving left to mount Barranco de Batans (de los Batanes). It then crosses the watershed at Cuello de Brazato and curls down to the spa resort of Balneario de Panticosa.

Cross Bujaruelo's fine single-arched stone bridge to follow the Río Ara's true left bank upstream – if, that is, you can resist taking a dip in the limpid blue pools.

At a T-junction, reached after about 20 minutes' walking, go right to take a 4WD track and follow it for 7.5km of gradual, effortless ascent of the Río Ara valley as far as the mouth of Barranco de Batáns at 2050m. The gorge narrows as you gain height. Just over the hour mark, there's a small cowherds' **refugio** (1640m) where the imposing Valle de Ordiso tumbles in from the west.

No more than 10 minutes later, cross a small col for the first breathtaking view of the imposing, unscaleable southwest face of Vignemale (3303m). From here on the landscape becomes altogether more rugged and alpine.

After a further hour, just beyond a second, spartan, cowherd's **refugio** and over a lateral moraine, the whole wide plain where Barranco Espelunz meets the main valley is a potential **camp site**.

Shortly after passing a solitary rain gauge about three hours from Bujaruelo, and with the cirque at the head of the valley already in view, stick to the river as the more distinct path heads away north to the frontier with France. Turn west just before a waterfall (it's the stream that you'll follow to its source going out with a splash as it tumbles into the beginnings of the Río Ara).

The trail climbs fairly gently, crossing to the stream's true left bank after around 20 minutes. You're again among gritty granite boulders and slabs – hard nonporous rock where the water gurgles at surface level rather than percolating underground. The route soon shifts back to the right bank to avoid the worst of the chaos of boulder fields.

After passing the lowest of three small pools, it's boulder hopping for a good 20 minutes until you reach the top tarn. From here, the going underfoot, though scarcely smooth, eases as the path zigzags – sometimes in defiance of the GR's steeper, more punishing tracing – up to **Cuello de Brazato** (2578m), reached 1½ to 1¾ hours after leaving the Ara valley.

Immediately west of the pass keep well above the Ibóns de Brazato as you manoeuvre your way over more boulders and scree to cross a saddle and enjoy an easy yomp down to the head of **Embalse de Brazato** dam.

Balneario de Panticosa and its lake, though soon in sight, are still a good 1½ hours away. The trail from the dam head is even too easy, descending by long, shallow switchbacks that you'll be tempted to shortcut. There's no camping around the *balneario* so, about 30 minutes from Embalse de Brazato, where a giant wide-bore water pipe drops down the hillside from the north, you might want to detour a little off route to **camp** in a pleasant meadow with running water.

Balneario de Panticosa

There's an excellent FAM-run *refugio*, **Casa de Piedra** (☎ 974 48 75 71, fax 974 48 74 86; dorm beds €9, half-board €21), in town. Accommodation is in rooms for four to 14, with bathroom. Despite its capacity for more than 100, it's wise to reserve ahead in high summer. At such prices, it's the bargain of the *balneario*.

Hotel Continental (☎ 974 48 71 61, fax 974 48 71 37; singles with bathroom €42, doubles with shower/bathroom €40/48; open Easter–mid-Oct) is the cheaper of the two hotels. That number will rise to three once renovations to the five-star Grand Hotel are completed. Guests have free access to the *balneario*'s outdoor heated pool or you can cough up for a variety of soothing water-based options: sauna, bubble bath, a high-pressure hosing down and even, to clear those tubes, a *ducha nasal* (nasal shower)!

Bazar Moderno, which has a few local cakes and specialities among its knick-knacks, is, cafés and restaurants apart, the only place selling food. Pop your nose into the splendidly ornate **Casino** (menú €16.50), in fact a bar and restaurant, even if it's only for a drink.

THE PYRENEES

Alternative Day 21: Bujaruelo to Panticosa via Collado de Tendenera

7½–8 hours, 23km

This alternative, but for a couple of tricky navigation points, is a day of clearly defined dirt paths with scarcely a stone to clamber over. You'll work hard as you ascend from Valle de Otal but, once over Collado de Tendenera, it's downhill all the way to Panticosa.

At the junction where Day 21 goes onto a 4WD track turn left to cross the river by Puente Oncins. Just over the bridge head west across a meadow for no more than 200m to pick up a vague trail marked by equally faint GR11 trail markers (the 'official' GR route now goes further north – see Day 21). As the trail enters evergreen wood and climbs southwestwards navigation isn't easy. Once in open meadow again you'll probably lose the authentic trail, overrun by new grass and competing cattle paths. However, if you keep on a southwest bearing and aim for **Collado de Otal** you shouldn't go wrong. If you do, extricate yourself by heading for the 4WD track (south), which describes a series of hairpin bends up the hillside.

Once over the col drop gently to the broad, grassy valley, through which the Río Otal snakes. Collado de Tendenera is obvious at the far, western end, flanked by its outriders, Pico de Tendenera (2853m) to the south and Mallaruego (2692m) to the north. From here it's easy, level striding on good-quality 4WD track to **Cabaña de Otal** – more cowshed than *refugio* but fine as an emergency shelter – reached after 1¼ to 1½ hours.

Continue due west and to the right of a small waterfall. Keep to the north (true left) bank of the stream that feeds it, passing a large metal rain gauge as you ascend to the head of the valley. Here the path veers north and climbs more steeply out of the bowl. About 50 minutes after the *cabaña*, beyond a metal sheepfold and before a multicoloured pole, follow the path, against all your instincts, as it turns back on itself and heads northeast, away from the col, for what seems an age.

Finally, after a good 25 minutes, the route turns sharply left beside a stream that crosses the main path. Overgrown and marked only by slowly decaying wooden pegs striped with the familiar red-and-white bars, it heads firmly northwest to become once more an evident path.

It's wild stuff up here. The rifts, whorls, bands and squashed contours of the rock become increasingly dramatic as you gain altitude in long arcs and there's not a sign of humanity except for the red-roofed *cabaña* below and the path at your feet. A little under an hour from the turn, at about 2200m, the trail passes over a small spring seeping from the rock just below the saddle. The grass here makes a cosy lunch spot or **camp site** if you've started the day south of Bujaruelo.

Collado de Tendenera (2325m) appears deceptively close but it takes another 20 minutes from the spring to reach the pass, where karst and sandstone meet. Take a last look east to where the border summit of Tallón (Taillon), at 3144m, guards Puerto de Bujaruelo, the nick you've had in view ever since the start of the day.

About 40 minutes below the col, pass a small **refugio** which sleeps four. There's water nearby and **camping** is possible if you beat down the long grass. Ten minutes later the path crosses to the true left bank of the stream it's been following, then veers away around a small bluff. Enjoy the unexpectedness of a magnificent view over the valley, through which the Río Ripera drains the cirque, and the giant wall of the Sierra de Tendenera. To the north juts the pronged peak of Balaitous (3151m) on the Franco-Spanish border.

After 15 minutes the path crosses the Río Ripera to meet a well-maintained 4WD track that mounts the valley. Some 20 minutes from the junction you pass a simple **refugio**, a possible overnight stop. From here on the challenges are over, the walking's simple and there remains only a considerable horizontal rather than vertical distance.

Some 10 minutes beyond the *refugio* the path crosses to the river's true right bank at a ford that may have you paddling when the river's in spate. A couple of minutes later it passes **Refugio de Ripera**, a spartan concrete block with capacity for six. From here on, the red-and-white flashes that, fresh or fading, have been around for most of the day, are supplemented by blue-and-white, then orange-and-white blazes as the path joins other trails coming up from Panticosa. Once it widens to become a track and makes a sharp left turn as the Arroyo Laulot stream comes in from the east it's an hour of fairly unexceptional walking to the *merendero* above Panticosa and a further 30 minutes into the village itself.

Once you hit the main road you have the option of hitching 5.5km up the road to Balneario de Panticosa (with a good *refugio*; for details, see the end of Day 21) so that you're poised for the next day's departure.

Panticosa

The **tourist office** (☎ 974 48 72 48; Calle San Miguel 39; open 10am-1pm & 5pm-8pm daily) delivers an offhand, uninformed service. There's a good website in Spanish, ⓦ www.valledetena.com, listing facilities in the Tena valley, which embraces both Panticosa and the *balneario*.

Hostal Residencia Navarro (☎/fax 974 48 71 81; singles/doubles/triples/quads with bathroom €27/39.25/55.30/69.45), opposite the church, offers the most reasonable food and accommodation. The *menú* is a bargain €8.15 and half-board is €32.15 per person.

Panticosa has a couple of **bakeries** and **supermarkets**, which are useful for picking up provisions as Balneario de Panticosa, starting point for Day 22, has no food shop.

For a taxi between Panticosa and the *balneario* (around €8), call **Jose Domec** (☎ 974 48 82 68, 619 75 75 50), based in Sallent de Gállego (see Day 23, p142). In July and August only, one bus a day runs between them, leaving Panticosa at 11.30am and returning from the *balneario* at 5.20pm – of little use unless you intend to spend a rest day at the spa.

Day 22: Balneario de Panticosa to Refugio de Respomuso

6–6½ hours, 12.3km

The official GR11 handbook recommends a 21.5km marathon with more than 2500m of altitude change from Balneario de Panticosa to Sallent de Gállego, quoting an overly optimistic time of eight hours. We prefer to break the journey into one longish and one

shorter day, overnighting at the excellent Refugio de Respomuso with the possibility of camping nearby or breaking earlier to savour one of the fine **camp sites** en route.

Leave Balneario de Panticosa by the path behind Casa de Piedra and head north up a well-established path, popular with day-walkers going to the Embalse de Bachimaña reservoirs. The progressively more splendid views back to the balneario and its lake compensates for the steepness of the ascent.

From the base of the **Cascada del Fraile** waterfall a series of steep zigzags leads to the head of the lower **Embalse de Bachimaña** (2180m), 1½ to 1¾ hours into the day. On the eastern shore of the reservoir are a pair of simple **shelters** and a potential **camp site**.

Towards the end of the reservoir's west shore, after passing a small island in the lake, there's a fork. Follow the GR11 as it ascends northwestwards and resist the temptation to stay on the evident, enticingly flat, track, which ends in nothingness at the lake's edge.

The first **Ibón Azul**, reached one to 1¼ hours beyond the lower Embalse de Bachimaña, is a fairly scruffy spot with an unpleasant, doorless metal shelter daubed with racist slogans.

Turn your back on it and attack the steep 15- to 20-minute boulder clamber up to the altogether different upper Ibón Azul. Unmarred by human construction and in a stunning setting below the Infierno and Piedrafita, which flank the obvious 'V' of Cuello del Infierno ahead, its lakeside meadows offer the best **camp site** east of the pass.

From the tarn allow an hour to reach **Cuello del Infierno** (Hell's Neck; 2721m), ascending through chaotic, fragmented rock where scarcely a blade of anything green grows. From the pass, nowhere near as hellish as its name implies, there are great views east over the lakes of Bachimaña and Bramatuero and over the often semifrozen Ibón de Tebarray, directly below you to the west.

Hell comes some 15 minutes later as you ease yourself over the rim of **Collado de Piedrafita** (2782m) to descend steeply on a slope of scree and shale where snow may persist until late summer. Negotiate this, curl around a shoulder, and heaven stretches

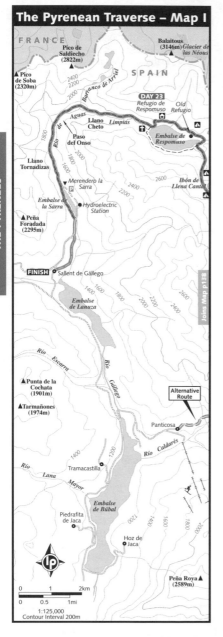

The Pyrenean Traverse – Map I

FRANCE

Pico de Saldiecho (2822m)

Balaitous (3146m) *Glacier de las Néous*

Pico de Soba (2320m)

SPAIN

Barranco de Arriel

2400
2200
2000

DAY 23
Refugio de Respomuso
Old Refugio

Río de Aguas Limpias

Llano Cheto

Embalse de Respomuso

Paso del Onso

1800

Llano Tornadizas

2000

1600

Merendero la Sarra

2600

Ibón de Llena Cantal

2400

2200

Embalse de la Sarra

Hydroelectric Station

Peña Foradada (2295m)

1400

FINISH Sallent de Gállego

1400 1600 1800 2000 2200 2400 2600

Joins Map p138

Embalse de Lanuza

1800

Río Escarra

Río Gállego

Punta de la Cochata (1901m)

Tarmañones (1974m)

Alternative Route

Panticosa

Río Caldarés

Río Lana

Tramacastilla

Mayor

Embalse de Búbal

1200 1400 1600 1800 2000

Piedrafita de Jaca

Hoz de Jaca

Peña Roya (2589m)

0   1   2km
0   0.5   1mi
1:125,000
Contour Interval 200m

LP

before you: the bijou Ibón de Llena Cantal, a series of grassy, stepped meadows, and, glinting in the valley, Embalse de Respomuso.

Depending on conditions below the col (the tough stuff, brief in terms of distance, will take at least 15 minutes), it's around 45 minutes down to **Ibón de Llena Cantal** (2450m). On its east shore next to a striped pole is a **camp site** bordering on perfection.

Some 20 minutes of yomping descent over springy turf raeches a wide meadow and another five-star **camp site**. After a further 20 minutes there's scope for confusion as the GR11 splits both right and left around **Embalse de Respomuso** and a variant, marked in fading paint, goes straight ahead. For the Refugio de Respomuso the easiest way is to turn right on the level track to reach the *refugio* about 30 minutes later. On the other hand, if you want to **camp**, go straight ahead to the water meadows at the base of a small ridge running east–west as tents aren't allowed in the immediate environs of the *refugio*.

Refugio de Respomuso (2200m; ☎/fax 974 49 02 03; dorm beds €9.70, dinner €11.50; open May–mid-Dec), with draught beer, hot showers and Rioja and local Somontano wines, is a palace among mountain huts. The staff are friendliness itself and prices are *refugio* average. It's essential to reserve in July and August and advisable at other times since the place is often booked by groups.

Day 23: Refugio de Respomuso to Sallent de Gállego
3–3½ hours, 10.3km
The dam head, 15 minutes west of the *refugio*, is full of industrial detritus, abandoned after its construction. What's billed on the map as a *refugio* is now dilapidated and the chapel is locked – neither merit a detour. From a sign, 'La Sarra', head straight down the valley of the Río de Aguas Limpias on a good-quality path. It's a popular trail and, with under three hours to go on this, the very last leg of the Pyrenean Traverse, you can have the satisfaction of acknowledging panting, overheated uphill toilers with a superior smile and a cheery, even-breathed greeting.

An hour from the dam the green bowl of **Llano Cheto** spreads out, watered by the twin cascades of the Río de Aguas Limpias and the Barranco de Arriel. At the narrows of **Paso del Onso**, around 1700m, the gorge bends south. The path tunnels through a fine wood of beech trees that offers the first real shade since above Balneario de Panticosa and harbours some attractive lunch spots.

Thirty to 40 minutes from Llano Cheto the track rounds a shoulder to reveal the wide meadows of **Llano Tornadizas** and the first distant glint of **Embalse de la Sarra**. Another 30 minutes brings you to the head of the dam, with a car park, picnic area and **Merendero la Sarra** *(open July-Sept)* which does *bocadillos*, tapas and has a *menú* for €15.

Take the reservoir's west bank, opposite the turbines of the hydroelectric station. At the dam head continue southwards along a sealed road then, about 10 minutes later, turn left and push your way down an overgrown path to the valley floor to meet a cart track that leads into Sallent de Gállego (1320m; see p99).

Bury My Boots at Wounded Knee

There were three days to go to the end of the Pyrenean Traverse and, complaining at so much up and downing, my knees were signalling regularly that they wanted to stop.

Then my boots, which had seen me through *Walking in France* and – so nearly – two editions of *Walking in Spain*, had tramped Alaska, the Yukon and patches of Patagonia, gave up the ghost. Within three hours of each other, like a pair of twins that can't live without one another.

The timing was uncanny but not, I suppose, all that surprising; except when I'd occasionally stubbed my toe and hopped a pace or two, cursing foully, they'd always been walking in tandem.

They and I managed to stagger through those final three days as far as Sallent de Gállego. And there, in some corner of a foreign field just off the GR11, I buried them. Tread lightly as you pass.

Miles Roddis

Andorra

A few days' hiking around Andorra can be a limbering-up exercise in preparation for the Pyrenean Traverse (see p97), specifically for Days 1 and 2, during which you cross into Catalunya. Or it can be a walking experience in its own right. In addition to the three routes that we describe, you'll find a wealth of ideas in the English-language publications listed under Books (see p144).

Slip Andorra into the conversation and people will tell you, with horror or joy, that it's all skiing and shopping. They'll also probably add that it's a one-road, one-town mini-state, its only highway, which links Spain and France, cutting a swathe through its only town, Andorra la Vella – which in turn is little more than a vast traffic jam bordered by cut-price temples to human greed.

They're right to a degree, but also very wrong. Free yourself from Andorra la Vella's tawdry embrace along good-quality secondary roads and you'll find villages as unspoilt as any in the Pyrenees. Despite the fact that Andorra, with a population of no more than 65,000 and an area of only 464 sq km, manages to absorb some eight million visitors a year, there are still areas where you can be completely alone. And Andorra's small, friendly tourist offices offer support that's second to none.

HISTORY

According to legend, Andorra was founded in around 784 AD by Emperor Charlemagne to thank the locals for guiding his troops through the mountains on their way to face the Arabs occupying the Spanish peninsula. Charlemagne's grandson granted the Valls d'Andorra (valleys of Andorra) to the count of Urgell from La Seu, further south in present-day Catalunya. He, in his turn, bequeathed the valleys to the local bishop of La Seu d'Urgell.

Following an obscure 13th-century dispute, a modus vivendi was established to share Andorra between the Catalan bishop and a feudal count over the French border. The contemporary consequence is that a very nominal suzerainty over Andorra – an

La Trashumancia

Winter in the plains; summer in the mountains. As many a ruined *borda* or upland cabin eloquently tells, the annual migration of shepherds or cowherds and their animals is a dying – but far from dead – way of life.

It's estimated that around 150 families still depend upon the twice-yearly *anant de cabanera*, the migration to the mountains of some 100,000 sheep, the larger flocks with more than 4000 head. They follow centuries-old *camins ramaders*, tracks to the Pyrenees, nowadays sliced through by new roads, dams, housing estates and holiday developments.

In Aragón, too, there still exists a network of routes, known as *cabiñeras*. In spring and autumn, twice a year, the flocks are driven some 200km to and from the basin of the river Ebro, down in the plains, to the high alpine meadows of the Pyrenees.

A strange coincidence: the dates of departure, usually 24 June and 29 September, are, almost to the day, the opening and closing dates of mountain *refugios* for walkers. Is this merely obeying the weather or some deeper instinct?

independent state and member of the United Nations – is shared between France and Spain, which only get upset if the smuggling, particularly of tobacco, gets out of hand.

Andorra is at the junction of two GR trails: the GR11, which links the Atlantic Ocean with the Mediterranean on the Spanish side of the Pyrenees; and the GR7, which runs from Lisbon all the way to the Black Sea.

NATURAL HISTORY

Andorra's lines of communication are largely determined by its river valleys, which were created long before the cataclysms of successive ice ages. The principal river, the Riu Gran Valira, flows southwards into Spain. It's formed by the confluence of the Valira del Nord, which collects the headwaters of the catchment area around Soldeu; and the Valira d'Orient, fed by waters funnelled down the Arinsal and Ordino valleys.

PLANNING
Maps

Two good maps cover Andorra and include all the walks in this section. The 1:50,000 *Andorra & Cadi* map is produced by the French Rando Éditions with input from the Institut Cartogràfic de Catalunya. First issued in 2001, it's reliable and walker-friendly though some of the trails, indicated in firm red lines, are much less obvious on the ground.

Editorial Alpina covers the whole of the principality in one 1:40,000 map, *Andorra*. Be sure to pick up the 2002 edition, which is a distinct improvement upon its lackadaisical predecessor.

Another – and cheaper – alternative is the 1:50,000 *Mapa de Refugis i Grans Recorreguts d'Andorra*, which is quite adequate for walking and pinpoints all of Andorra's 26 *refugios* and network of marked trails.

Books

Valls de Canillo 2002 Bienvenus/Welcome, a free booklet produced by the parish of Canillo, has descriptions of eight day or half-day walks within its boundaries. The parishes of Massana and Ordino have also jointly produced an excellent free walking booklet, *Thirty Interesting Itineraries on the Paths of the Parishes of Ordino and La Massana*, available from either parish's tourist office.

The pamphlet *Sport Activities*, produced by the national tourist office, presents as many as 52 walks within the principality, though it needs to be supplemented by a good map.

Information Sources

For the latest weather information, you can call ☎ 848 852 (Spanish), ☎ 848 853 (French) or ☎ 848 851 (Catalan).

GETTING AROUND

Ask at any tourist office for the free leaflet giving current timetables for the eight bus routes radiating from the capital, all run by **Cooperativa Interurbana** (☎ 820 412).

ACCESS TOWNS

See Canillo (pp98–9).

Andorra la Vella

Andorra la Vella, capital of the principality, has little to detain you, apart from some great walking-gear shops. You're better poised for the walks in this section if you stay in Canillo or Soldeu.

Information The friendly **municipal tourist office** (☎ 827 117; Plaça de la Rotonda; open 9am-1pm & 4pm-8pm Mon-Sat, 9am-1pm Sun Sept-June, 9am-9pm daily July-Aug) is well endowed with information about the city and the whole of Andorra.

Andorra has a walking and mountain-eering group, **Club Pirinenc** (☎ 822 847; Carrer Bonaventura; open 5pm-8pm Mon-Fri).

For readers of Spanish, French or Catalan, **Llibreria Jaume Caballé** (☎/fax 829 454; Avinguda Fiter Rossell 31) has a splendid collection of antiquarian and new travel books and carries a comprehensive range of walking and travel maps.

Supplies & Equipment Andorra la Vella is the place to stock up on mountain gear at prices that can't be beaten anywhere in Western Europe. There's no shortage of sports shops. The largest of the three branches of **Viladomat** (☎ 800 805; Avinguda Meritxell 110), one of the best for walkers, also stocks walking maps. But it's not alone; browse around – if you can stand the intrusive traffic.

Places to Stay & Eat Should you find yourself stuck in town, **Hostal del Sol** (☎ 823 701; Plaça Guillemó; singles/doubles/triples with shower €12.20/24.50/36.50) is a friendly place with spruce, excellent-value rooms.

Papanico (☎ 867 333; Avinguda Príncep Benlloch 4) has tasty tapas from €2.10 and serves a range of sandwiches, platos combinados and mains. Self-caterers will enjoy wandering the aisles of the well-stocked supermarket on the 2nd floor of the **Pyrénées department store** (Avinguda Meritxell 21).

Getting There & Away Unless you walk over the mountains the only way into or out of Andorra is by road.

Alsina Graells (in Andorra ☎ 827 379, in Barcelona ☎ 93 265 68 66) has eight buses daily between Barcelona's Estació del Nord and Andorra la Vella (€18, 3½ to four hours).

Four direct buses a day run between Barcelona's El Prat airport and Andorra la Vella (for details see Barcelona, pp96–7).

Samar/Alsa (in Andorra ☎ 826 289, in Spain ☎ 902 42 22 42) runs daily except Sunday between Andorra and Madrid (€33, nine hours) via Lleida (€9).

If coming from France, **Autocars Nadal** (☎ 805 151) has two buses a day (€20, 3½ to four hours) on Monday, Wednesday, Friday and Sunday, linking Toulouse's bus station and Andorra la Vella.

By rail the most convenient option is to take a train from Toulouse to either L'Hospitalet (2¼ to 2¾ hours) or Latour-de-Carol (2½ to 3¼ hours), both in France. From Latour-de-Carol station, daily **Hispano Andorrana** (☎ 821 372) buses leave for Andorra (€8.20, two daily). In the reverse direction, one bus departs from Andorra la Vella at 7.30am, while the second, and last of the day, leaves at 10.30am. The early one allows you to connect with trains to Toulouse – and also to Barcelona in Spain.

Soldeu

Soldeu has a small **tourist office** (☎ 852 492; open 10am-1pm & 3pm-6pm daily Dec-Apr, July & Aug). **Slim Jim's** has three Internet terminals (€6.70 per hour).

There are two camping grounds near town, both basic and neither with a shop.

Camping Font de Ferrosins (☎ 347 119; camping per person/tent/car €2.30/2.30/2.30; open mid-June–Sept), 1km into Vall d'Incles, has showers.

Camping Incles (tent & up to 3 campers €3; open mid-June–Aug), at the head of the valley and as spartan as they come, has a small bar and is a good place to meet other trekkers.

Hotel Roc de Sant Miquel (☎ 851 079, fax 851 196; e hotelroc@andorra.ad; singles/doubles with bathroom €21/30; open May-Nov) is run by a pleasant young Anglo-Andorran couple. Both are ski instructors and experienced walkers and lead guided nature walks and hikes. Room rates include breakfast.

The cheerful restaurant of **Hotel Bruxelles** does well-filled sandwiches, whopping burgers and a tasty *menú*.

Slim Jim's (☎ *852 567*) offers picnics for walkers (€6) that you can order in advance by phone. You can also revive yourself with a megamug of tea or beer at the end of the day.

Hourly buses run from Andorra la Vella to Soldeu (€2.50) via Canillo between 8am and 8pm.

Basses de les Salamandres

Duration	3¾–4¼ hours
Distance	12.5km
Difficulty	moderate
Start/Finish	Pont d'Incles
Nearest Town	Soldeu (p145)
Transport	bus

Summary A steep, semi-wooded climb from Vall d'Incles, a gentler ascent over open ground to four tarns, a lope down the Riu del Manegor valley and back along Vall d'Incles

This walk gives you all the ingredients that make the Andorran experience: forest, mountain tarns, sheer rock formations, tumbling streams – and a gently green valley to bring you home.

GETTING TO/FROM THE WALK
Walk out of Soldeu along the CG2 towards Canillo and Andorra la Vella. After 1km you reach the bus stop (if you're coming from Canillo, hop off here) and tight bend at Pont d'Incles.

THE WALK (see map p147)
From the bus stop beside the CG2 at Pont d'Incles, 1km north of Soldeu, continue northwards along the narrow tarmac road that leads into Vall d'Incles to reach a sign, 'Roca de l'Home Dret', after 600m. Turn left to follow the yellow trail markers that lead you upwards beside a small stream and beyond a ruined *borda*.

After 20 to 25 minutes of fairly arduous uphill work through meadow and sparse forest the track veers southwest and levels out, offering fine views back to the head of Vall d'Incles, one of the prettiest valleys in all the Pyrenees. Follow the path as it curls around the flank of the mountain, maintaining a fairly steady height.

The path passes **Roca de l'Home Dret** (Straight or Upright Man), an isolated rock, after about 45 minutes' walking, then drops a little before entering the welcome shade of a pine forest. Ten minutes beyond the rock turn right to follow a sign, 'Estanys de Querol, de les Salamandres i dels Estanyons'. Fifteen to 20 minutes beyond this junction turn right (northeast) at a second fork, also signed for the lakes.

The trail crosses a broad meadow before the final shortish ascent to **Estany del Querol**, first of the pools, reached after 1½ to 1¾ hours of walking and an attractive spot for a breather.

Still heading northeast, pass another smaller pool that may be merely a peaty mire at the end of summer and push up to the twin **Basses de les Salamandres** (Salamander Pools), no more than 15 minutes beyond the first tarn.

Now comes the only piece of navigation that's in any way tricky: as the yellow blobs give out head straight up a scarcely definable path to the top of the next ridge. Then, keeping a northeast bearing and dropping gently but not too significantly, work your way around the flank of the mountain until you intersect at right angles with a steep and more evident trail coming up from Vall d'Incles. There are several vague tracks to choose from, a few made by boots, most by the hooves of the wild horses that graze the lush summer grass. It really doesn't matter which one you select.

Once more guided by yellow circles, turn left (north) to follow a stream, soon crossing on stepping stones just downstream from a waterfall onto its true left bank to reach **Refugi de Cabana Sorda** (2295m) after a total walking time of 2¼ to 2½ hours. Just above the *refugio* is the pool of the same name, the biggest of the day, where you can

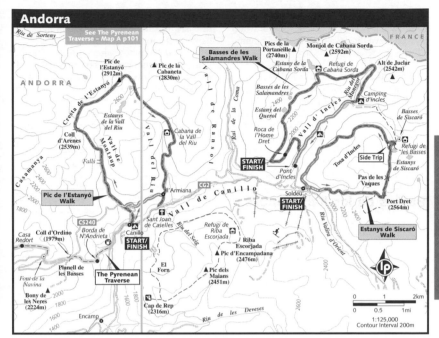

Andorra

See The Pyrenean Traverse – Map A p101

ANDORRA

FRANCE

Riu de Sorteny

Pic de l'Estanyó (2912m)

Pic de la Cabaneta (2830m)

Pics de la Portaneille (2740m)

Monjol de Cabana Sorda (2592m)

Estany de la Cabana Sorda

Refugi de Cabana Sorda

Alt de Juclar (2542m)

Camping d'Incles

Basses de Siscaró

Cresta de l'Estanyó

Estanys de la Vall del Riu

Basses de les Salamandres Walk

Basses de les Salamandres

Vall de la Coma

Estany del Querol

Roca de l'Home Dret

Vall d'Incles

Riu del Manegor

Coll d'Arenes (2539m)

Cabana de la Vall del Riu

Refugi de les Basses

Estanys de Siscaró

Falls

Tosa d'Incles

Side Trip

START/ FINISH

Pont d'Incles

Pas de les Vaques

Casamanya

Pic de l'Estanyó Walk

l'Armiana

CG2

Vall de Canillo

Soldeu

START/ FINISH

Port Dret (2564m)

CS240

Sant Joan de Caselles

Coll d'Ordino (1979m)

Borda de N'Andrieta

Canillo

START/ FINISH

Refugi de Riba Escorjada

Riba Escorjada

Pic d'Encampadana (2476m)

Riu Valira d'Orient

Estanys de Siscaró Walk

Casa Redort

Planell de les Basses

The Pyrenean Traverse

El Forn

Pic dels Maians (2451m)

Font de la Navina

Bony de les Neres (2224m)

Cap de Rep (2316m)

Encamp

Riu de les Deveses

THE PYRENEES

0   1   2km
0   0.5   1mi
1:125,000
Contour Interval 200m

---

replenish your water bottles, cool your feet and drink in the grandeur of the near sheer walls that enclose it.

From the *refugio*, strike east around the flank of Monjol de Cabana Sorda (2592m), now guided by red-and-yellow flashes. It's glorious walking of the kind you need towards day's end as the path descends gently through open meadow, then more abruptly to meet the narrow valley of the Riu del Manegor, some 45 minutes beyond the *refugio*.

Here the route describes a dog's leg, crossing to the true left bank of a gurgling beck. Once you reach Vall d'Incles, after some 20 minutes of easy descent, you can maintain a steady clip along the narrow, lightly trafficked tarmac road. This follows the valley bottom, bringing you to the CG2 and your point of departure after 3km of easy walking. Alternatively, if you're staying in Soldeu, you can exit left along a signed cart track after 500m. This joins the

last stage of the Estanys de Siscaró walk after around 1km.

Estanys de Siscaró

Duration	4–4½ hours
Distance	12km
Difficulty	moderate
Start/Finish	Soldeu (p145)
Transport	bus

Summary A steep ascent to the col of Port Dret, brief level walking, then a short, precipitous drop to the Estanys de Siscaró followed by woodland strolling around the flanks of the Tosa d'Incles

We grade this walk moderate because of the steep ascent at the beginning of the day and the navigating required on the short stretch just before Port Dret.

You'll probably be walking alone for most of the day apart from the short section immediately below the Estanys de Siscaró. These twin lakes are a popular spot for walkers who leave their vehicles beside Camping d'Incles at the end of the tarmac road.

THE WALK (see map p147)

At the head of the small lane beside Esports Calbó, an outdoor equipment shop on the main road near Soldeu's eastern limit, a sign reads 'Coma Bella, Clots de l'Os' and 'Port Dret'. Head eastwards along the lane away from the village, following the clear yellow blazes. At a junction a little beyond a small farm, reached after about 10 minutes, keep left, following the main cart track. Beside a water tank opt for the narrow path that climbs beside the stream's true left bank, zigzagging its way up the mountainside in a generally easterly direction.

At a signpost, some 45 minutes from Soldeu, you have a choice: to go straight ahead, as the sign, 'Estanys de Siscaró', beckons (rejoining the route at Pas de les Vaques) or, to turn right, following the sign 'Port Dret' for a more challenging variant.

Taking the Port Dret option, you enter a more open pine-stippled meadow about 10 minutes from the fork. Walk directly east up the lush turf above the tree line, still following reliable yellow blobs. When these peter out, keep heading consistently up the valley until you reach the pass at **Port Dret** (2564m), about 1½ hours from Soldeu. Once you've had your fill of the plunging vistas to the east, turn sharp left (north) along a clearly defined path to reach a second col, **Pas de les Vaques**, after 10 to 15 minutes of level walking. Identified by its giant cairn, it too offers a magnificent view down upon the twin lakes of the **Estanys de Siscaró**, like a pair of blue eyes gazing back at you.

It takes about 20 minutes of steep descent, guided by red-and-yellow markers, to reach the bank of the right-hand, eastern lake – an ideal spot for a breather or lunch break. The lakes take their name from the Catalan *siscall*, or glasswort, a rush-like plant that grows at their edges and in the flood plain below.

Leave the pool at its northern corner to drop steeply and beside the stream flowing

from it towards the flood plain, Les Basses de Siscaró, and the tiny **refugio** of the same name in its northeast corner.

Around 10 minutes beyond the lake and well before the valley bottom strike left (northwest) to again pick up yellow trail markers. Less than 10 minutes later turn right as the path intersects with a more direct but less scenic variant dropping from the lakes. After intersecting with a path coming up from the *refugio* the trail enters woodland. Every now and again you'll catch glimpses of the Vall d'Incles below, but for the most part it's just you, the trees and their welcome shade. Stick to the yellow trail markers – keep your gaze high since many of them are up on the trees – and you'll soon find yourself on an evident track. Threading its way through woodland, punctuated by clearings and streams, it leads to a crossroads after about another hour of walking, where a sign points right to Incles and left to Soldeu. Turn left along the 4WD track to reach Soldeu around 30 minutes from the junction.

Pic de l'Estanyó

Duration	6½–7½ hours
Distance	15.5km
Difficulty	demanding
Start/Finish	Canillo (p98)
Transport	bus

Summary An ascent to Coll d'Arenes, a scramble and clamber along Cresta de l'Estanyó to Pic de l'Estanyó, followed by a descent of Vall del Riu

Make no mistake, this is a tough one. The difficulty lies in the narrow (at times no more than 2m wide), jagged spine of the Cresta de l'Estanyó and in the length of the walk.

There's nothing we can do about the former but the route can be chopped quite neatly into less daunting sections. You can do the first and last sections of the walk, on either side of the crest, separately. Each is a pleasant up-and-down walk, of moderate difficulty, passing through meadows and beside *bordas*.

The return trip to Coll d'Arenes takes four to 4½ hours, while an out-and-back walk to the lakes at the base of Pic de l'Estanyó needs six to 6¾ hours.

If you have wheels, you can leave your car 4.6km up the CS240 road above Canillo beside a sign for Coll d'Arenes (see the walk description) and head back to the highway from l'Armiana towards the end of the walk, thus saving yourself about 1¼ hours of walking.

PLANNING

Don't attempt the Cresta de l'Estanyó ridge on a wet day, when the slippery rock can be treacherous. If you're planning to do the ridge, keep your day pack light in case the wind throws you off balance.

THE WALK (see map p147)

Walk up Carrer Major, 25m east of the tourist office in Canillo, pass beside Esglesia de Sant Cerni, the parish church, and continue up a track beside a stream. The route, clearly indicated with yellow circles, crosses the CS240 and hugs the stream, which you'll be following almost to its source. After 30 to 35 minutes of steady ascent the route rejoins the road at a sign, 'Coll d'Arenes'.

The path zigzags up the east flank of Vall de Montaup to a stone building, where you turn left along a grassy cart track. Just beyond a second *borda* bear right along a blazed path. This rises gently to reach a series of waterfalls at a point where the valley closes in and becomes decidedly steeper.

About 45 minutes from the road you round a bend to enter a vast green amphitheatre. Just beyond a locked well a faint path climbs parallel to and well to the right (east) of the tumbling stream. Just beyond a steep 10-minute clamber to a false col there's a deep, shady overhang where the path crosses the stream. Refill your bottles here or at the pipe just above – there's no more water until you reach a tarn beyond Pic de l'Estanyó.

Keep to the left (west) side of the valley above this false col and don't worry if you deviate from the yellow blobs; it's easy cross-country work up and over a couple of

shale fields to **Coll d'Arenes**, two to 2¼ hours from Canillo.

From the pass a smudge of a path leads due north around a knoll, then veers right (northeast) towards the ridge. Don't worry if you lose the sparse, low cairns; keep a northerly bearing and you're bound to hit the ridge about 15 minutes from the pass. On the ridge, progress is *very* slow because of the jagged, friable rock but it's worth all the effort for the spectacular, changing views of the length and breadth of the principality and on into Spain and France. After a large cairn and a saddle that drops away to the east you can briefly up the pace by walking parallel to the cliff edge. But after a second small peak you're again gingerly picking your way along the knife-edge crest with the pools of the Estanys de la Vall del Riu now below to the southeast.

At the summit of **Pic de l'Estanyó** (allow up to 1½ hours from Coll d'Arenes) leave a slip of paper with your name in the sturdy metal box tucked into the rocks, as so many before you have done. To the southeast is the pine-clad valley through which you'll pass on the return to Canillo. Your immediate landmark, however, is a small tarn below and almost due east of the peak (at the end of a particularly dry summer this may be no more than a stain of darker grass). Follow the ridge until the first small breach (about 10 minutes from the peak), where you turn right to head down into the bowl in which the tarn nestles.

About five minutes beyond the tarn cross eastwards over a minor ridge to meet a pair of more substantial pools. On the far, southern shore of either, you'll pick up the yellow trail markers of the signed route connecting Canillo with L'Armiana, the largest of the pools that are known collectively as the Estanys de la Vall del Riu. From here on the route is again impeccably signed in yellow, in contrast with the inadequate marking as you descended from the ridge. High on the eastern flank of Vall del Riu the small Cabana de la Vall del Riu (2160m) is visible, still around 45 minutes away.

After the last of the day's boulder fields comes a brief squelch through the marshy

THE PYRENEES

headwaters of the river that tumbles down into the main valley. Follow the east side of the valley to pass by **Cabana de la Vall del Riu**, an unstaffed *refugio*, something over 1½ hours from Pic d'Estanyó.

After a stretch of easy walking across a meadow turn *sharp* right at a sign, 'L'Aldosa Armiana, Canillo' (don't be seduced by the yellow dots bearing away right – they will lead you to the neighbouring Vall de Ransol). Some five minutes later pass to the right of an intact *borda*. The path descends fairly gradually and via a series of zigzags to cross the torrent by a wooden bridge.

The route curls gently westwards around the hill, leaving the stream to plunge away below. Savour the day's first extended stretch of near-level progress (that scramble along the ridge excepted!) until, about 20 minutes beyond the bridge, you meet a dirt road beside the abandoned houses of L'Armiana. If you've left your vehicle beside the CS240, continue along this road for 15 minutes to meet the highway, then turn right to recover it.

Otherwise, take the faint path that drops to the left and passes through the hamlet to make its way down to the CG2, debouching about 30 minutes later opposite the church of Sant Joan de Caselles, from where it's a 15 minute walk back to Canillo.

Parc Nacional d'Aigüestortes i Estany de Sant Maurici

This national park is one of only two in the Pyrenees (the other being Parque Nacional de Ordesa y Monte Perdido). Despite its relatively small area (20km from east to west and a mere 9km from north to south), it sparkles with more than 50 lakes and tarns and includes some of the Pyrenees' most stunning scenery. The national park lies at the core of a wider wilderness area whose

The General's Will

In the early 1950s there was a flurry in the valleys when it was announced that no less a dignitary than General Franco himself would be paying a visit to inaugurate a couple of hydroelectric projects. For the first time in its long history, the track between the Estany de Sant Maurici and Aigüestortes was rolled and graded, while liberal quantities of whitewash were splashed around.

The cortège swept by. The general – a keen fly fisherman when cares of state allowed – was so impressed by the spectacle from the smart new road that he ordered the creation of Parc Nacional d'Aigüestortes i Estany de Sant Maurici, which was duly inaugurated in 1955.

Once the dust from the cavalcade had settled the road scarcely saw another vehicle. Eaten away by ice, sleet and rain, used again but briefly for equestrian outings, it was formally closed to all motorised traffic in 1995. Nowadays, there are still lingering traces of the general's route, but in a decade or two all evidence will be lost and nature will have reclaimed its own.

outer limit is known as the *zona periférica* and includes some magnificent high country to the north and south.

The park offers enough challenge and variety for a week or more of hiking along its numerous trails. We describe three routes, all of which set out from Estany de Sant Maurici, 8km west of Espot.

In addition, Days 6 to 9 of the Pyrenean Traverse (see pp108–15) are spent within the national park.

HISTORY

According to a well-attested story (see the boxed text, 'The General's Will') it was by order of Generalissimo Franco himself that, in 1955, the area was declared a national park. It was expanded in 1996 to incorporate an additional 3890 hectares, so that its total area including the buffer zone is now 408 sq km.

NATURAL HISTORY

The original granite and slate relief, now modified out of all recognition, was laid down some 200 million years ago during the Primary era. But, as elsewhere in the Pyrenees, it was the grinding, chewing, scraping action of glaciers during the successive ice ages of the Quaternary period that lent the landscape its present shape – its cirques and corries, scoured U-shaped glens and hanging valleys.

PLANNING
Maps & Books

The 1:50,000 *Mapa de la Travessa dels Refugis del Parc Nacional d'Aigüestortes i Estany de Sant Maurici* is more compact than its name. Excellent value at €3, it gives the lowdown on each of the park's 12 *refugios*. With the main trails marked, it serves as a more than satisfactory walking guide. However, its contour lines at 100m intervals can lead to some nasty surprises unless you use it in conjunction with another, more detailed map. If it's not available in the bookshops, you'll find it at either of the park information offices or at *refugios*.

The ICC 1:25,000 *Parc Nacional d'Aigüestortes i Estany de Sant Maurici* is a reliable large-scale map. Editorial Alpina also produces a good park map, the 1:25,000 *Parc Nacional d'Aigüestortes*. Be sure that you get the latest, green edition, which is a great improvement upon its red predecessor. If following the Pyrenean Traverse, you'll need Editorial Alpina's 1:25,000 maps *Sant Maurici* and *Vall de Boí*, and can dispense with the general park map. The Rando Éditions/ICC 1:50,000 *Pica d'Estats Aneto* map gives complete and reliable coverage.

Guidebook to the National Park of Aigüestortes i Estany de Sant Maurici, sold at the national park information offices, gives impressively detailed information on the area's plant, animals and ecosystems – and also describes 25 walking trails within its boundaries.

Information Sources

Espot and Boí (see p112) both have park information offices. To reach the website of the park go to **w** www.mma.es/parques/lared/aigues.

Refugios & Camping

There are as many as 12 *refugios* within the park proper and its *zona periférica*, or buffer zone. You can pick up a good map (€3) that gives details of each (see Maps & Books). Most tend to be full by 3pm in July and August and we strongly recommend that you ring in advance to reserve. The overnight fee is €10 to €11 and meals are generally in the region of €11 to €12. Most keep a wing open for walkers and ski trekkers year-round but are only staffed between mid-June and mid-September.

Officially, camping within the boundaries of the park, is not allowed.

ACCESS TOWNS & FACILITIES
Espot

If you intend to make Espot the base for a walking holiday, call by **Casa del Parc** (*☎/fax 973 62 40 36; open 9am-1pm & 3.30pm-6.45pm daily*), the park information office, for more walk suggestions. This office and the one in Boí run a 15-minute audiovisual introduction to the park with an optional English version, and sell walking maps.

There's no shortage of camping grounds, each one beside the river.

Camping la Mola (*☎/fax 973 62 40 24;* **w** *www.campinglamola.com; camping per person/tent €4.10/4.10; open July-Sept*), spacious and green, is the first you pass as you ascend from the Vall d'Aneu.

On the park (northwest) side of town is the small **Camping Solau** (*☎ 973 62 40 68; camping per person/tent €3.75/3.75*).

Restaurante Pensió Palmira (*☎ 973 62 40 72; per person €16.85*) has spick-and-span rooms, each with bathroom. Its **restaurant** does a copious, great-value *menú* for €10.40.

Casa Felip (*☎ 973 62 40 93; singles/doubles with bathroom €18/30; open Apr-Oct*) is cosy and family-run.

Hotel Saurat (*☎ 973 62 41 62, fax 973 62 40 37;* **e** *hsaurat@jazzfree.com; Plaça Sant Martí; per person B&B €40, half-board €55*) is a popular walkers' choice.

The *menú* at **Restaurante Ivan** (☎ 973 62 41 21; open July & Aug) for €10 is imaginative and magnificent value.

Restaurante Juquim (☎ 973 62 40 09; menú €12.85, mains €6.50-10) is a step more upmarket.

Getting There & Away The limited **Alsina Graells** (☎ 973 26 85 00) bus service (coming from Vielha from mid-June to mid-September, but from Esterri d'Aneu at other times) for Barcelona and Lleida passes through Vall d'Aneu, 8km from Espot. It leaves Lleida every day except Sunday, stopping in Pobla de Segur, Llavorsí and La Guingeta. The return bus to Lleida passes by La Guingeta at the awful hour of 5.30am, Llavorsí and Pobla de Segur (where it links with a connection for Barcelona) at 6.30am.

If notified in advance a 4WD from the **Associació de Taxis d'Espot** (☎/fax 973 62 41 05), on the main street, will deliver you to or collect you from the bus stop on the main Vall d'Aneu road, 8km from the village (€9 per vehicle, but €15 to connect with the 5.30am redeye run).

Estany de Sant Maurici

If you'd prefer to avoid the trip to and from Espot, it's possible to stay at the very friendly **Refugi de Ernest Mallafré** (1885m; ☎ 973 25 01 18) just above Estany de Sant Maurici, which accommodates up to 24 people. However, amazingly for so nodal and long established a *refugio*, there's no shower, washbasin, nor even the basic comfort of a squat toilet (see the boxed text 'A Cloacal Calculation').

From Espot, you can undertake an agreeable walk (two hours, 8km) to Estany de Sant Maurici – for a description, see Day 7 of the Pyrenean Traverse (pp109–11). However, many walkers prefer to save their energy for the even more spectacular scenery within the park and invest in a **4WD taxi** ride (€4 one way, €8 return) as far as the lake (last descent 8pm). Taxis usually wait to leave until they're full. You can drive as far as the barrier and parking area at Prat de Pierró (1640m), an hour's pleasant walk below the lake along the route we describe.

A Cloacal Calculation

If the average weight of a morning motion is 250g and if the average high-season *refugio* occupancy is 40, then 10kg a day, or 1 tonne a season, of human nightsoil is being dumped in the immediate vicinity of *refugios* which remain without toilets.

Refugi Ernest Mallafré, for example, doesn't have a single chemical toilet or even a bucket to pee in. Refugi de Colomers, with an official capacity of 40 but often sleeping many more, has one tap for washing and a single-seater shack toilet – from which the effluent flows directly into the lake below. Small wonder that overnighters plod off in the early morning to the nearby rocks and trees. The area around such *refugios* must be among the most polluted in all of Spain. Tread with care...

Estany Llong

Duration	5½–6 hours
Distance	17km
Difficulty	easy–moderate
Start/Finish	Estany de Sant Maurici (p152)
Nearest Town	Espot (p151)
Transport	taxi, bus
Summary	A lake-to-lake traverse of the park along a classic route; magnificent views continue from the intervening pass of Portarró d'Espot

Crossing the park from east to west, this is a classic walk not only because of the spectacular scenery but also for its antiquity. In medieval times the trail was a conduit for goods, people and animals travelling between the lands of the Count of Pallars in the east and those of the fiefdom of Erill to the west. In the first half of this century it became a fashionable leisure route as visitors, marvelling at the splendour of what the locals took for granted, rode on horseback between Espot and the small thermal spa of Caldes de Boí. Nowadays, it's closed to all motor traffic.

Most walkers do this route as a return trip in a day. It's also possible to stay overnight at Refugi d'Estany Llong (advance reservations essential) or continue via Aigüestortes to Boí (see p112), about 9km further along the trail.

THE WALK (see map p154)
From Refugi de Ernest Mallafré follow the track around the south side of Estany de Sant Maurici and through mixed wood of beech, birch and ash plus pine and fir. About 45 minutes out, the track passes a turn-off on the right to the Mirador de l'Estany lookout and then swings west, following and occasionally crossing the stream which tumbles down from the **Portarró d'Espot** pass (2425m).

It's worth pausing at the col to savour the views. To the west is **Estany Llong** (2000m), 3.5km and about one hour's steep descent away. The route here, as throughout the walk, is easy to distinguish.

At the western end of the lake is **Refugi d'Estany Llong** (2000m; ☎ 629 37 46 52), the only *refugio* run by the national park authority. With capacity for only 36, reservations are essential. Serving meals, snacks and drinks, it also makes a pleasant rest stop before the return trip. If you still have energy, consider

The War that Went On

It looks like the ruins of a fine, baroque chapel, up there on the hillside above the Estany de Sant Maurici. In fact, until the 1960s it used to be a military barracks. Why, you may ask, in remote country not far from the frontier with a friendly neighbour and with no major population centre nearer than Lleida, several hours drive away, would anyone want to build barracks?

Their origins relate to the end of both the Spanish Civil War and WWII. In 1939, defeated Republicans and their families streamed across the passes into France. After 1945 Republicans returned and infiltrated the valleys along the frontier to mount a limited guerrilla struggle, which was savagely suppressed by the victorious Nationalist army. For a brief time, the *guerrilleros* (guerrillas) controlled Vall d'Aran and large areas of what is now the national park.

The barracks were constructed to drive out the Republican bands and cow the valleys' residents lest they be tempted to give support to the distant, lost Republican cause.

❀ ❀ ❀ ❀ ❀ ❀ ❀ ❀ ❀ ❀ ❀ ❀ ❀ ❀ ❀

continuing for a further 1½ to two hours as far as the particularly fine scenery at Aigüestortes.

At Aigüestortes, you can pick up a 4WD taxi which will take you as far as Boí, from where you can head out of the valley to Lleida by bus.

Refugi de Colomina

Duration	2 days
Distance	22km
Difficulty	moderate–demanding
Start	Estany de Sant Maurici (p152)
Finish	Espot (p151)
Transport	taxi, bus

Summary Easy walking to Estany de Monestero before the gradient increases, culminating in a steep final clamber to Coll de Peguera, then downhill all the way to Refugi de Colomina; return to the Riu Escrita valley via Collada de Saburó

This walk is graded moderate–demanding because of a very steep ascent to Coll de Peguera.

A return trip of about 2½ hours as far as Estany de Monestero makes an easy, scenic option. Alternatively, you can stretch yourself a little more, add on another 1½ hours to the day's total time and continue to the cirque at the head of the Riu de Monestero valley before turning back.

THE WALK (see map p154)
Day 1: Estany de Sant Maurici to Refugi de Colomina
5½–6 hours, 10km

From the dam at the eastern end of Estany de Sant Maurici pass by Refugi de Ernest Mallafré to follow the Riu de Monestero. Half an hour out a length of boardwalk takes you over a marshy section. Don't worry; the higher you climb, the less tamed the land. In fact, up top a few more clues and signs of humanity would be positively welcome. Beyond a boulder field about an hour from the lake you pass a tiny pool to reach **Estany de Monestero** (2170m) and, beyond it, a glorious, open alpine meadow.

Parc Nacional d'Aigüestortes i Estany de Sant Maurici

See The Pyrenean Traverse – Map C p110

Parc Nacional d'Aigüestortes i Estany de Sant Maurici – Walks

1 Estany Llong
2 Refugi de Colomina
3 Port de Ratera d'Espot

Climbing gently along the true left bank of a stream which flows into Estany de Monestero, thread your way through another jumble of truly huge boulders (the massive square one marks an end to the scrambling), eventually crossing the stream to the true right bank.

Once you reach the cirque at the head of the valley the path climbs south-south-east. Stick to the east side of the bowl, resisting the temptation to head for the middle which – your eyes deceive you – appears less arduous. Over the lip of a false col, reached after two to 2¼ hours, descend to a large, arid basin. Here begins the much steeper ascent to Coll

de Peguera (2726m) between Pic de Peguera (2982m) and Pic de Mar (2803m) to its west.

From the col, follow a sign to Refugi de Colomina and walk southwards to **Estany de Saburó**. Either take the path along the lake's western bank, which is steep yet stepped, or, for a less demanding alternative, pass close to the eastern shore of Estany Xic de Saburó.

Past the west shores of Estany de Mar and Estany de Colomina (2408m), is **Refugi de Colomina** *(2395m; ☎ 973 25 20 00)* less than an hour's walking from Estany Xic de Saburó. This wooden *refugio* has 40 places and serves meals and drinks. If you prefer camping descend to Estany Tort, a short distance to the west, which has plenty of **camp sites**.

An alternative to the next day's walk to Espot is to exit via Capdella and Vall Fosca. Pick your day carefully, however, as transport options from Capdella are limited. On weekdays in the school year a bus departs from Pobla de Segur (5.15pm) and returns from Capdella (8am). During school holidays it runs Monday, Wednesday and Friday. Otherwise, you must depend on a taxi (€31) – ring **Carles Moyes** (☎ 649 44 21 81) in Capdella.

If you leave the park via Capdella, **Refugi Tacita** (☎ 973 66 31 21; W www.tacitahostel .com; dorm beds €15), near the electricity generating station, is a welcoming, recently established private *refugio* with self-catering facilities. It has places for 23 and the rate includes breakfast.

Also near the electricity generating station, 1.8km below the village, is **Hostal Leo** (☎ 973 66 31 57), about which readers have reported very positively.

Day 2: Refugi de Colomina to Espot
5–5½ hours, 12km

You can retrace your steps over Coll de Peguera or vary the journey by crossing back into the main valley via Collada de Saburó.

The latter route is a variant of the GR11 and is well marked with red-and-white bars. Head northeast from the *refugio* to follow the west bank of both Estany de Colomina and Estany de Mar. After ascending a steep gully pass a ruined building and descend to the dam head of **Estany de Saburó**; cross over. Curl around the lake and climb to **Collada de Saburó** (2670m) at the national park border.

Pass by three small lakes before dropping to Estany Negre. Once across the dam head, take a path that leads off north. From it a short detour leads left to **Refugi Josep Blanc** (2350m; ☎ 973 25 01 08), with capacity for 40 and normally full to the gunwales. Here you can get a drink or snack.

Continue until you reach another small lake and a forest *refugio* (not open to the public), from where the path descends in parallel with the Riu de Peguera to emerge on the sealed road on the outskirts of Espot.

Port de Ratera d'Espot

Duration	4½–5 hours
Distance	14.5km
Difficulty	moderate
Start/Finish	Estany de Sant Maurici (p152)
Nearest Town	Espot (p151)
Transport	taxi, bus

Summary Superb views as you leave the crowds behind, taking in Estany de Ratera, the lake and *refugio* of Estany Gran d'Amitges and Port de Ratera de Colomers; return via Mirador de l'Estany

This circular route follows the early part of Day 7 of the Pyrenean Traverse, diverging to take in the three Estanys d'Amitges on the outbound leg and Mirador de l'Estany on the way back.

THE WALK (see map p154)
Follow Day 7 of the Pyrenean Traverse (pp109–11) from Estany de Sant Maurici as far as the instruction 'at a fork soon after…**Estany de Ratera**…choose the left option'.

Here, if you fancy nothing more taxing than an easy 2½-hour stroll, keep left to pass by Mirador de l'Estany and return by the south bank of Estany de Sant Maurici. Otherwise, go right in the direction of the *refugio*. Now climbing more steeply, the track nudges out of a pine forest to enter a rocky world with an occasional copse of trees. Stay with the 4WD track to Estany Gran d'Amitges, the largest of a series of three tarns, behind which rise the spiky Agulles d'Amitges, the twin Pics de Bassiero and Tuc de Saboredo.

No more than 212m of vertical distance separate the shores of lakes Ratera and Amitges but the contrast between the former's pine-clad charm and the latter's harsh, denuded splendour is total.

The **refugio** (2380m; ☎ 973 25 01 09; W www.amitges.com) beside **Estany Gran d'Amitges** (2362m), about 1½ hours from the start, is a popular overnight spot with spaces for 66. It does meals, snacks and drinks and makes a congenial rest stop. A trail leads from it between the two upper lakes and across scree (here lies the only

THE PYRENEES

difficulty in what would otherwise be an easy walk). Continue up to **Port de Ratera d'Espot**, which you reach after a little less than another hour. At this point the trail rejoins Day 7 of the Pyrenean Traverse. It's well worth following it for another 10 minutes or so along the saddle as far as **Port de Ratera de Colomers**, from where there are great views of the necklace of lakes falling away to the southwest.

Returning to Port de Ratera d'Espot, take the Day 7 route in reverse around Estanyet del Port de Ratera and follow it until it rejoins the main track. You've now come full circle. One hundred metres beyond, where the paths meet, turn right to **Mirador de l'Estany** with its vistas of the mountains reflected in Estany de Sant Maurici. Continuing, you soon reach the trans-park route that links Estany Llong with Sant Maurici. Turn left along it and return by the south bank of Estany de Sant Maurici to the point of departure.

The Aragonese Pyrenees

West of Catalunya lies Aragón, the land of the giants, within whose limits are Days 11 to 23 of the Pyrenean Traverse (see pp117–43). Of the 12 tallest peaks in peninsular Spain, 10 rear up from Aragón. Three of these mountains – Pico de Aneto, Pico de Posets and Pico de Monte Perdido – are within easy reach of the Pyrenean Traverse (see Aragón, p158, under Other Walks).

If peak bagging and glacial heights leave you cold, there are also plenty of gentle valley walks to enjoy. This is tough country, however, with challenging passes between each valley and the probability of snow underfoot late into summer.

The rock subtly changes as you progress towards the setting sun. The upper Noguera Ribagorçana valley is a mix of shale and slate. Farther west, the original granite bedrock is seen more frequently, especially around the Maladeta and Posets region. In some areas, such as Parque Nacional de Ordesa y Monte Perdido, bedrock is overlaid or

cut through by limestone, with its characteristic underground rivers, potholes and caves.

But nothing is regular or ordered. The clash of the European and Iberian tectonic plates and later upheavals on a scale difficult to grasp have left the land folded, crumpled and profoundly askew.

To both east and west, Benasque is surrounded by Parque Posets-Maladeta. Established in 1994, the park contains 13 glaciers, the Pyrenees' highest peak (Pico de Aneto) – and about 2000 varieties of plants.

PLANNING
Maps
Prames' 1:40,000 *Ribagorza* map and Editorial Alpina's 1:25,000 *Maladeta-Aneto* map both cover the area.

Books
Twelve signed walks around the Benasque region, ranging in length from 2km to 20km, are summarised in a free, bilingual leaflet, *Valle de Benasque: El Placer de Caminar* (The Pleasure of Walking), available from the town's tourist office.

ACCESS TOWNS
For a pleasant and well-appointed base in the heart of the Aragonese Pyrenees, head for Benasque (see pp121–4). The Parque Posets-Maladeta visitors centre is here.

Frontier Ridge

Duration	3½ hours
Distance	9km
Difficulty	easy–moderate
Start/Finish	La Besurta
Nearest Town	Benasque (p121)
Transport	bus

Summary An ascent to Portillón de Benasque by a *camino*, easy traverse along the base of Pico de la Mina and a descent to La Besurta via the more westerly of the two Lagos de Villamorta

You can make this a modular day. To the basic walk of around 3½ hours you can graft on two side trips, described on p158.

GETTING TO/FROM THE WALK

For transport between Benasque and La Besurta, see Day 12 of the Pyrenean Traverse (pp120–1).

THE WALK

From the bus stop 300m below La Besurta head northwards up the hill along a faint trail. After 15 minutes a better-defined track comes in from the left. This is the old and, in its time, much-travelled historical link between the Ésera valley and that of Aran. These days, it's a *ruta hípica*, or pony trekking trail (signalled by red-tipped posts), that leads to Port de la Picada and on to Vall d'Aran or into France.

Continue up the trail in a series of fairly gentle zigzags for 40 to 50 minutes until you arrive at a junction, indicated by a pair of *ruta hípica* signs. Don't be seduced into following them and taking the path which heads northeast straight towards Port de la Picada. Instead, continue zigzagging towards **Portillón de Benasque** (2444m), now clearly in view and sitting snug between the twin masses of Tuc de Salvaguarda (2738m) and Pico de la Mina (2707m). After skirting a reedy tarn you should reach the pass about 1½ hours after setting out.

Surprisingly, there's little to see beyond the windy gap (for more spectacular views, see the two side trips on p158). You can, however, clearly identify the path threading eastwards from some ruined huts at the base of Portillón de Benasque. Bizarrely marked '23' (it's part of a French trail that sneaks over the border), the path heads in a dead straight line over bare rock and scree to **Port de la Picada** (2470m), your next *port* of call, still some 45 minutes away, where you stand a very good chance of seeing eagles wheeling overhead.

If you're in the mood for a longer walk, 20 minutes down a well-established trail from Port de la Picada brings you to Collado del Infierno.

Turning back towards home from Port de la Picada, bear left (down and south), passing to the east of a small tarn. As you descend look out for the lower (nearer) of the two Lagos de Villamorta. Turn left (southeast) beside a medium-sized cairn onto a secondary trail. After passing a stony section flanked by stunted pine trees skirt the lower Villamorta pond on its south side. Beyond it the path is virtually invisible, but keep due south and within 10 minutes you should meet the stone 'stairs' on the main track

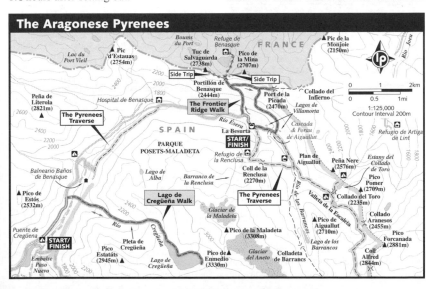

linking the Plan d'Aigüallut and La Besurta, reached about 1¼ hours after leaving Port de la Picada.

Side Trip: Tuc de Salvaguarda
1½ hours, 3km
For spectacular views in all directions, take the evident side trail from Portillón de Benasque to the summit of **Tuc de Salvaguarda** (2738m) to the west. It's much less daunting than the spindly figures of other walkers against what appears to be a razor-edge ridge would have you believe.

Side Trip: Refugio de Benasque
1¼–1½ hours, 2.5km
Less strenuously, it's worth continuing beyond Portillón de Benasque, down into France, for a drink or a snack at the small, staffed **mountain hut** (2249m) run by the Club Alpin Français. It's in a glorious setting at the northeast tip of the first of three lakes called the Boums du Port. It is, however, substantially farther than the 15 minutes claimed by a sign at the col.

Lago de Cregüeña

Duration	5–5½ hours
Distance	11km
Difficulty	moderate
Start/Finish	Puente de Cregüeña
Nearest Town	Benasque (p121)
Transport	bus

Summary As the route ascends woodland briefly becomes plain before the steep climb resumes towards to the stark, rocky bowl in which the Lago de Cregüeña nestles

GETTING TO/FROM THE WALK
Take the shuttle bus that runs between Benasque and La Besurta (see Day 12 of the Pyrenean Traverse, pp120–1) and ask to be dropped off at the Puente de Cregüeña bridge.

THE WALK (see map p157)
The path begins, wide and cairned, near Puente de Cregüeña, just off the main C139 highway between La Besurta and Benasque.

It climbs, almost continuously and with little scope for error, all the way to Lago de Cregüeña. Following closely the course of the Río Cregüeña, it passes through shady woodland that opens out into a small plain, Pleta de Cregüeña, a brief, flattish respite before you attack the steeper and entirely rocky final 550m of altitude gain.

The western fingertip of the lake, which ranks as the third-largest (in terms of volume) in the Pyrenees, is only 3.5km from the Río Ésera as the eagle flies. All the same, the times we give are realistic as the ascent to the lake is steep (1200m over 11km). The setting, a savage cul-de-sac occasionally scaled by technical climbers aiming for the south face of Pico de la Maladeta, is ample compensation for the stiff climb. Return the way you came.

Other Walks

CATALUNYA
Pica d'Estats
Catalunya's highest mountain (3143m), straddling the Franco-Spanish frontier, has a special fascination for Catalan walkers. You can either do it as a 10-hour return trip from Refugi de Vall Ferrera (see Day 2 of the Pyrenean Traverse, pp102–3) or camp overnight at the Estany de Sotllo (see Day 3, p103) and set off next morning for a 2½-hour ascent.

From the pass at Port de Sotllo (2894m), there are two options. The shorter one requires 30 minutes of steep clambering up the ridge. The other, easier choice, despite the near-permanent snow on the northern slopes, descends to the little Estanyet de Barz in France. From here strike right (east) until you're between, though well below, the peaks of Estats and Montcalm (3077m). Make the final push up the gentler north slope via Coll de Riufred (2978m). Pack Alpina's 1:40,000 Pica d'Estats map.

ARAGÓN
Pico de Aneto
Aneto, at 3404m, is the highest summit in the Pyrenees, outstripped on the Spanish mainland only by Mulhacén in the Sierra Nevada. It's a challenge that draws many, both mountaineers and experienced trekkers, and it's not to be underestimated. You'll need crampons and an ice axe – or walking poles at the very least – for the glacier. And don't attempt this strenuous day walk alone.

The classic route, with an altitude difference of 1265m, leads from Refugio de la Renclusa (see Alternative Route, p121). An early morning start is essential. You're well poised if you overnight at the *refugio* or else you can take the 4.30am bus from Benasque to La Besurta (see Getting There & Around for Benasque, pp121–4). The additional distance from La Besurta to the *refugio* and back will add about an hour to the walking day.

Allow 4½ hours for the ascent from the *refugio*. Given the rough terrain, don't count on the descent being all that much shorter. Carry Alpina's 1:25,000 *Maladeta Aneto* map.

Pico de Posets

Views from Posets, at 3375m the second-highest peak in the Pyrenees, are, given its central position among the chain's loftiest peaks, even more staggering than those from Aneto. The ascent, or rather ascents, of Posets will tax you but it's neither as tough nor as dangerous as the haul up to Aneto. Three popular routes thread from the three *refugios* that surround the massif in an equilateral triangle: Estós (see Alternative Day 13 of the Pyrenean Traverse, pp125–6), Ángel Orus (see Day 13, pp124–5) and Viadós (see Day 15, pp127–8). Each, out and back, can be accomplished in a long day. Alpina's 1:25,000 *Posets Perdiguero* map covers all three approaches.

Monte Perdido

Monte Perdido (3355m) defers in height only to Pico de Aneto and Posets, and in popularity, only to Aneto. At any time of the year it's wise to come equipped with ice axe and crampons, or at least walking poles.

The well-cairned main route sets out from the Refugio de Góriz (see Day 19 of the Pyrenean Traverse, pp133–6), the 7km return trip taking six to seven hours. A well-cairned path heads north as far as the tiny tarn of Lago Helado (Frozen Lake; around 3050m), reached some 2½ to three hours out. There you turn sharply right (southeast) for the final ascent up a steep couloir, then follow a rock-strewn snow ridge to the summit. Pack Alpina's 1:40,000 *Ordesa Monte Perdido* map.

THE PYRENEES

Basque Country & Navarran Pyrenees

Like stepping stones in a river, the Basque mountains link the Cordillera Cantábrica and the Pyrenees in a series of dramatic east–west sierras reaching a maximum altitude of 1551m. Parting the area's plentiful waters into those destined to wind up in the Atlantic and those bound for the Mediterranean (via the Río Ebro), these feisty, magnetic limestone ranges shelter unending walking opportunities: misty emerald valleys, enchanted karstic peaks, vivid rural life, beautiful, well-maintained villages and even bustling, attractive cities. Inevitably, legends, curious cultural practices or enticing history enhance the outstanding trails. The chapter features three protected *parques naturales* (Gorbeia, Urkiola and Aizkorri) and a two-day coastal walk connecting San Sebastián to Hondarribia. On the Pyrenees' western end, where the Basque Country (Euskadi in Euskara, the Basque language, or País Vasco in Spanish) borders Navarra, we highlight two days along the spectacular GR11 Pyrenean Traverse (see also the Pyrenees chapter, p92). Be aware that the walk times we give are actual walking time and do not include rest stops.

Euskadi is a small region (7261 sq km) composed of three provinces – Bizkaia (Vizcaya), Gipuzkoa (Guipúzcoa) and Araba (Álava) – poor in agriculture but abundant in raw materials, such as wood, iron and water. Bizkaia and Gipuzkoa border the Atlantic while inland Álava is distinctly Mediterranean. Navarra, a separate autonomous community or region in the Spanish system, shares historical ties with Euskadi (especially the mountain and border areas). The name Euskal Herria refers to the historical Basque Country where Euskara, the mysterious Basque language, was and is, to varying degrees, spoken. The remaining three of Euskal Herria's seven provinces are in France. Euskara bears no relationship to known languages, leading linguists to believe

Highlights

SARA-JANE CLELAND

Rugged cliffs sweep down to long beaches on Spain's Atlantic coast

- Losing yourself in great, enchanted expanses of open beech wood

- Poking your head through Atxular's Eye after traversing the karstic Itxina massif on the Gorbeia Traverse (p165)

- Exploring prehistoric dolmens, medieval roadway and ancient shepherds' pastures on the Around Aizkorri walk (p171)

- Walking in minutes from vibrant San Sebastián to isolated coastal cliffs on the San Sebastián to Hondarribia walk (p176)

it's a Stone Age survivor. Megalithic burial chambers (cromlechs, dolmens and menhirs), perhaps used by ancient Euskara-speakers, are frequently concentrated on mountain passes and high pastures oriented towards the sun.

Basque Country & Navarran Pyrenees

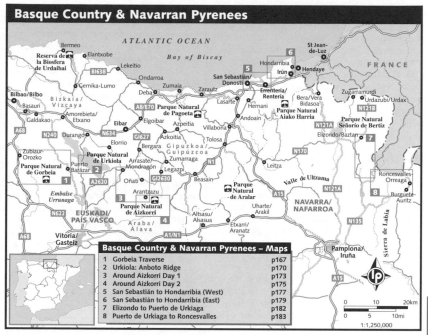

Always with an eye to the exterior and a bold entrepreneurial spirit, coast-dwelling Basques have long enjoyed prosperity through commerce, fishing and emigration. Noncoastal Basques lived in urban areas or dispersed across the rugged countryside in largely self-sufficient farmsteads called *baserria* in Euskara and *caseríos* in Spanish (see the boxed text 'Basque & Navarran Farmsteads'). Shepherding, as practised for thousands of years, is in decline. Stone huts on the high summer pastures and the sound

**BASQUE COUNTRY &
NAVARRAN PYRENEES**

Basque & Navarran Farmsteads

The large, three-storey stone houses often seen isolated in the countryside or high on a hill are *baserria* or farmhouses. They are fundamental to Basque life and a house's roots usually go back several centuries. All *baserria* have unchanging names, and families frequently go by their house's name rather than their own surname. Traditionally, the farmstead was passed on to the child (regardless of sex or birth order) deemed most apt to maintain its integrity.

The *baserri's* bottom level contains the stable for cows, henhouse and workshop. Winter hay and corn are stored on top, and domestic life occupies the 2nd floor, insulated between the other two floors. On average the farmstead occupies about 10 hectares – the majority replanted pine forest (for cash); then a smaller section dedicated to pasture (forage and hay for livestock); and the smallest part, crop land, to cultivate the household garden, corn and potatoes. Fruit (apple, pear, cherry) and nut (walnut and chestnut) trees once surrounded most farmhouses, but many have been replaced with pastures, fewer and less varied gardens, and pines.

of bells in the air are still constants, but shepherds now usually leave their flocks in the mountains and make periodic visits rather than live with them. In the summer, shepherds make delicious cured sheep's-milk cheeses (Idiazabal cheese is a must-try). Cows and horses wandering around many mountain areas are raised for meat – horse meat is sold to France and Italy. Friesian milk cows, often confined to stables, bring in the most euros for farmers.

NATURAL HISTORY

Geologically speaking, the Basque mountains are young when compared with the Cordillera Cantábrica or the Pyrenees. They are composed of limestone and sandstone formed from accumulated ocean-floor sediments, and have been shaped by karstification. This term is used to describe how limestone – calcium carbonate – reacts over time to the eroding properties of water and air. Karstification is the most important erosive process at work producing the dramatic, jagged peaks, rifts, caves and ravines found throughout the region. The area's only granite range, Aiako Harria (Peñas de Aia), is near San Sebastián.

Exploitation of the iron-rich hills is an ancient practice: foundries have produced high-quality iron since the 9th century. By the 14th century many ironworks lined river banks, using water to power their hammers and bellows, and severely damaging the rivers' ecosystems in the process. Beech and oak woods also suffered. To produce 100kg of iron, smiths needed nine sacks of hardwood (oak and beech) charcoal produced by carefully burning huge quantities of wood. Limestone was also painstakingly reduced to lime (to fertilise fields) in enormous ovens built in the woods. Nineteenth-century industrialisation dramatically depleted the ancient forests, leaving many hillsides barren. Monterey pine was planted to reforest and is used in paper mills and furniture, providing supplementary income for farmers. Red spruce, Japanese larch (a deciduous conifer) and Lawson cypress are also commonly planted for commercial harvest. Native mixed forests of ash, hawthorn, birch, hazel and maple are

Beech & Oak: Sacred Trees

Pago in Euskara and haya in Spanish, humidity-loving beech trees are regularly found above 600m on misty, water-soaked northern slopes. Constantly searching for light, the leaves and branches reach out and up producing a darkened forest and nearly plantless, though highly fertile, forest floor. In autumn, the tree's beechnuts provide a vital nutrient source for small mammals.

Communities commonly had a sacred oak (haritz in Euskara and roble in Spanish) where the traditional assemblies (batzarrea), uniting local representatives, were held and local laws (fueros) sworn. The Gernika oak tree, where Bizkaia's representatives would meet, is the most famous; at 300 years, it dried out in 1860. The present tree is its offshoot.

Beech and oak trees are pruned to prolong a tree's survival and productivity for hundreds of years. The main trunk is cut approximately 3m from its base to provoke a proliferation of shoots which grow horizontally and vertically. These are then cut for timber without harming the tree.

more limited in extent. Grand, extensive beech forests still thrive, fortunately.

Other than deer, foxes and several other small mammals, birds are the primary wildlife. Atlantic-facing oak groves shelter woodpeckers, coal tits, woodcocks and the tawny owl. Above 600m, hanging out with the beech, look for black woodpeckers, thrushes and the nuthatch. Griffon and Egyptian vultures and red-billed choughs reign in the limestone heights.

CLIMATE

Euskadi is Iberia's wettest region. Winds and rain arrive from the northwest via the Atlantic Ocean – more precisely the Bay of Biscay (Biscay is Bizkaia anglicised). Rain is frequent and spread evenly throughout the year. Clouds dump primarily on the coast, with a pronounced rain-shadow beyond the highest hills further east and south in Vitoria (Gasteiz) and Navarra. The maritime climate makes for mild winters and cool summers. Moving further inland and in mountain areas, expect greater extremes in temperature. Snow dusts the mountains in winter but rarely sticks, except in the Navarran Pyrenees east of Elizondo.

INFORMATION
Maps
Geo/Estel's 1:250,000 *Euskadi, Navarra, La Rioja* map covers the area described on a single, easy-to-read sheet.

Gobierno Vasco's (GV) 1:25,000 topographic maps are best for walking but can be hard to find. The IGN's 1:25,000 sheets are also reliable. In the series *Cuadernos Pirenaicos*, Sua Ediciones publishes 1:35,000 and 1:50,000 topographic maps and guides; these are good for planning, and highlight walks and climbs in specific areas. Finally, Nondik produces handy, water-resistant 1:40,000 topographic maps to the major Basque mountain areas. Maps can be purchased in major cities and park information centres; don't rely on trailhead towns.

Books
With grave reservations we recommend Mark Kurlansky's engaging *Basque History of the World* as general background reading. Kurlansky's apologist take on ETA, the Basque terrorist group, is in our view morally reprehensible and one-sided journalism.

In Spanish, the best general guide is Anaya Touring Club's *Pirineo Navarro y Montes Vascos*, which has natural and cultural history and route ideas. Iosu Etxaniz's *La Guía de Euskal Herria* is a cultural guide to Euskadi, Navarra and the three French districts. Miguel Angulo is the resident walking and climbing expert. His numerous titles include *Montaña Vasca*, which has 400 itineraries. If you're a sea-lover, Tremoia Kolektiboa's *Rutas y Paseos por Parajes Naturales de Euskal Herria II: La Costa Vasca* describes great walks along Euskadi's 197km coastline.

Information Sources
Regional tourism offices (see Gateways, on this page) and park information centres have the most current information. In Euskadi

tourism offices, ask for the free 1:200,000 *Euskadi* road map, and in Navarra, the 1:400,000 *Navarra: Mapa Guía*. A regional website is W www.basquecountrytourism.net.

Place Names
Euskadi and Navarra have two official languages: Spanish and Euskara. Everybody understands Spanish. The percentage of Euskara-speakers varies regionally. All official signage in both regions, including that on the roads, is bilingual. Many maps may only use the Euskara version of place names. In the text, we either favour the most frequent usage or give both names to avoid confusion.

> ## Warning
>
> Since 1961 the Basque terrorist group, ETA (Euzkadi ta Azkatasuna: Basque Country and freedom), has tried to railroad its goal of creating a totally independent Basque Country onto the Basque people and Spain as a whole through deadly violence. Political figures from opposition parties and members of police and military forces are the primary targets, both within and outside Euskadi, and the usual method is assassination with car bombs or handguns. Political street violence *(kale borroka)*, such as burning of rubbish bins and ATMs, occurs in urban areas.

GATEWAYS
Bilbao (Bilbo) and San Sebastián (Donosti), both in Euskadi, and Pamplona (Iruña; see pp335–6) in Navarra are convenient major cities.

Bilbao
Bilbao, traditionally industrial and grey, has become a showcase of art and culture since the Guggenheim Museum's inauguration in 1997. The **tourist office** (☎ 94 479 57 60; W *www.bilbao.net; Paseo Arenal 1; open 9am-2pm & 4pm-7.30pm Mon-Fri, 9am-2pm Sat & 10am-2pm Sun*) provides local and regional information. The best bookshop for maps and books is **Borda** *(Somera 45)*; it also carries walking equipment and clothing.

Places to Stay & Eat There are no nearby camping grounds. The historical quarter's highlight is **Hostal Iturrienea** (☎ 94 416 15 00; Santa María 14; singles/doubles with bathroom €45/60). More economical is **Pensión Méndez** (☎ 94 416 03 64; Santa María 13, 4th floor; singles/doubles €25/35). Self-caterers can head to the morning public **market** next to the San Antonio church. For *pintxos* (tapas), head to Plaza Nueva; **Victor Montés** is a classic spot. **Restaurante Kaltzo** (Barrenkale Barrena 5) serves excellent mid-day meals for €7.50.

Getting There & Away Bilbao's main bus station, **Termibus** (☎ 94 439 50 77; Gurtubay 1), is the base for most bus companies listed except Ansa. **Alsa** (☎ 902 42 22 42) runs buses between Bilbao and Pamplona (€10, four hours, four daily) and Santiago (€41, 12 hours, three daily). **Unión Alavesa** (☎ 94 427 11 11) also runs to Pamplona. **Ansa** (☎ 94 444 31 00; Autonomía 17) connects Bilbao to Madrid and Barcelona. **Pesa** (☎ 902 10 12 10) regularly links Bilbao and San Sebastián (€7.45, 1½ hours, hourly), as does Alsa (€6, 1½ hours, 10 daily).

Renfe (☎ 902 24 02 02; Abando station, Plaza Circular 2) connects Bilbao to Madrid (€28, 6½ hours, two daily) and Barcelona (€33, nine hours, two daily). **FEVE** (☎ 902 10 08 10; Concordia station, Bailén 2) narrow-gauge rail trains serve the north coast, and **Eusko Tren** (☎ 94 416 13 12; Casco Viejo station, Plaza San Nicolás) goes to destinations within the Basque Country (San Sebastián, Pasaia, Hondarribia).

P&O European Ferries (☎ 94 423 44 77; ⓦ www.poportsmouth.com) links Portsmouth (England) and Bilbao twice weekly.

By car, take the N1 from Madrid to Burgos, the A1 to Vitoria and then the A68 to Bilbao.

San Sebastián (Donosti)

Harmonious integration of urban and natural landscapes reaches its apex in this magnificent coastal city. San Sebastián was once a fashionable getaway for Spanish aristocracy, and its sweeping La Concha beach, art nouveau monumental buildings,

lively historical quarter and out-of-this-world food culture bring visitors in droves.

The **city tourist office** (☎ 943 48 11 66; ⓦ www.sansebastianturismo.com; Reina Regente 3; open 8am-8pm Mon-Sat, 10am-2pm Sun June-Sept, 9am-2pm & 3.30pm-7pm Mon-Sat, 10am-2pm Sun Oct-May) gives local city and provincial information. The **regional tourist office** (☎ 943 02 31 50; Paseo de los Fueros 1) provides information on the Basque Country in general.

Graphos (Mayor 1) stocks English titles and has an excellent selection of walking guides and maps. Another good option is **Librería Bilintx** (Fermín Kalbetón 19). **Deportes Ada** (Mayor 3) has basic last-minute walking supplies. The best overall store for books, equipment and knowledgeable staff is **Idazi** (Usandizaga 18) on the east side of the river.

Places to Stay & Eat It's 30 minutes by bus No 16 from Alameda del Boulevard to **Camping Igueldo** (☎ 943 21 45 02; Padre Orkolaga 69; camping per person/tent/car €3.35/3.35/3.35).

Albergue La Sirena (☎ 943 31 02 68; Paseo de Igueldo 25; under 25/others €13/15) and **Albergue Monte Ulía** (☎ 943 31 02 68; under 25 yrs/others €13/15) are run by the same owner, and rates at both include breakfast. To stay at the Monte Ulía hostel, go first to La Sirena.

In the historical quarter, friendly owners speak English at both **Pensión Aussie** (☎ 943 42 28 74; San Jerónimo 23, 2nd floor; per person in 2- to 4-bed rooms €18) and **Pensión Loinaz** (☎ 943 42 67 14; San Lorenzo 17, 2nd floor; singles/doubles/triples €30/42/60). The latter has in-house laundry and Internet service.

For eating nirvana head to the historical quarter, which is packed with **bar-restaurants** serving delicious *pintxos*.

Getting There & Away The main **bus station** (Plaza Pío XII) hosts **Continental** (☎ 943 46 90 74) buses to Madrid (€24, six hours, six daily) and **Vibasa** (☎ 902 10 13 63) buses to Barcelona (€28, 7½ hours, three daily). Alsa connects to Bilbao, Santander and Santiago de Compostela.

Renfe (☎ *943 42 64 30; Estación Norte, Avenida de Francia*) has trains to Madrid (€30, nine hours, three daily) and Barcelona (€31, eight hours, two daily). **Eusko Tren** (☎ *943 45 01 31; Plaza Easo*) provides coastal and some inland rail services (to Bilbao, Durango, Hondarribia).

By car from Madrid, follow the directions towards Bilbao and take the A8 east to San Sebastián.

Gorbeia Traverse

Duration	7–8 hours
Distance	25.8km
Difficulty	moderate–demanding
Start	Puerto Barázar
Finish	Ibarra
Nearest Towns	Bilbao (p163),
	Puerto Barázar (p166),
	Zubiaur-Orozko (p165)
Transport	bus

Summary Gorbeia, a classic Basque mountain, offers it all: forest, wetland, high pastures and limestone grandeur via the Itxina massif

---

The Parque Natural de Gorbeia, Euskadi's largest with 200 sq km, straddles the provinces of Bizkaia and Álava. Unlike the majority of its jagged, dramatic limestone neighbours, emblematic Gorbeia (1482m), the huge rounded massif at the park's centre, is sedimentary sandstone blanketed thickly with pastures. It's crowned by a 17m cross. The walk also takes in the mesmerising Itxina massif, a craggy limestone labyrinth with vertical walls, slanting plateau and delightful surprises. Some 500 caverns and 100 tortuous kilometres of galleries twist through the range's innards. Mairulegorreta, the most famous of these caves, is 12km long and Neanderthal remains have been discovered inside. The Cascada Gujuli waterfall, another karstic highlight, drops the Río Altube 100m off a sheer cliff. Monterey pine plantations give way to beech woods and mixed oak and hawthorn forests. Reintroduced in 1958, deer are the park's signature mammal.

Come September, the ritual bellowing and brawling of the stags, as they stake claim on the harems, attracts numerous visitors.

The walk can be done from Bilbao using public transport, either in a day, as described, or with an overnight stop in Zubiaur-Orozko or in one of the two *refugios* (mountain huts or refuges) en route. Both the start and finish points are very small, and offer only lodging and meals. For an alternative out-and-back trip of 22km, ascend Gorbeia and return to the trailhead. Carry plenty of water; there is one fountain near mid-route.

PLANNING
When to Walk
Gorbeia receives winter storms, making May to October the best months for walking.

Maps & Books
Nondik's 1:40,000 *Gorbeia* topographical map and guide is recommended.

Not one to slip in your pack, LP Peña Santiago's *Gorbeia: Montaña Vasca* gives sound advice on routes, with topo maps.

Information Sources
Providing basic information in English are two **Parke Etxea interpretive centres**. One is in Álava province in Sarria (☎ *945 43 07 09; open 10am-2.30pm & 3.30pm-6pm Tues-Sun mid-Oct–June, 10am-7pm Tues-Sun June–mid-Oct*) and the other in Bizkaia province in Areatza (☎ *94 673 92 79; open 10am-2pm & 4pm-6pm daily*).

Ask for the publication *Gorbeialdea* (in Spanish) in these centres and regional tourism offices. The centre in Sarria sells books and topographic maps. On the Internet try ⓦ www.gorbeialdea.com.

NEAREST TOWNS & FACILITIES
See Bilbao (p163).

Zubiaur-Orozko
The picturesque Orozko valley and municipality, on Gorbeia's northwestern extreme, is fed by the Río Altube. Zubiaur is Orozko's capital. There are two rural guesthouses in the area: **Agroturismo Exteluzea** (☎ *94 661 01 71; Barrio Donibane; singles/doubles with*

bathroom €24/35) in Zubiaur, and **Agroturismo Garai** (☎ 94 633 05 06; *Barrio Garai 5 in Beraza; singles/doubles with bathroom* €31/39).

Bizkaibus (☎ 902 22 22 65) buses return to Bilbao from Ibarra (via Zubiaur-Orozko) (€2, 1½ hours, five daily Monday to Friday, four Sunday, last departure 7.55pm) and Zubiaur (€1.80, 1¼ hours, hourly Monday to Friday and Sunday). By car from Zubiaur, take the A68 towards Bilbao.

Puerto Barázar

This is essentially a trailhead and car park on the park's east side, with lodging and meals (*menú* – fixed price meal – €8.40) at **Hostal Barázar** (☎ 946 73 95 64; *singles/doubles with bathroom* €17/34; *open Sun-Thur).*

From Bilbao take a La Unión bus to Barázar (€2.60, 50 minutes, one daily Monday to Friday, two Saturday, one Sunday). By car from Bilbao, take the N634 towards San Sebastián and then the N240 south to Vitoria. There's another car park 2.8km along the trail.

GETTING TO/FROM THE WALK

The walk ends in Ibarra, 4.5km from Zubiaur. To connect Ibarra and Zubiaur, walk, hitch, bus (see Zubiaur-Orozko, p166–7) or take a **taxi** (☎ 629 42 57 69) for €6.

THE WALK (see map p167)

From the 'Alto de Barázar (606m)' sign, take a sealed trail, blazed red-and-white and heading right (southwest). Follow the concrete road for 3km without detours, first through conifer forest, then past a recreation area and car park to the **Humedal de Saldropo**, a three-hectare wetland famed for its ancient peat bog. An information hut describes peat extraction and its burning as fuel.

After the hut, at the first fork, head right following the sign indicating Atxurribidea is 45 minutes away. In 100m there's a lime oven on the left; a great oak guards the doorway. After a wooden pedestrian bridge, the concrete ends. Continue 300m along a dirt path to a fork. Turn left and then, nearly 200m later, make another left onto a narrower trail that ascends southwest between wire fences. In 100m cross a dirt road to a footpath that

continues ascending, now without fencing, through forest. Reaching a T-junction, turn left. In less than 10 minutes, where the trail levels and is forested, you'll reach a fork. Head left and cross another trail before beginning a steep 100m ascent to a wider dirt trail on the left. Take this and continue on it for 200m. Make a right-angled turn left onto a footpath that ascends steeply through hawthorn and beech trees. Nearing the top, turn right to walk underneath Atxurri's spectacular overhanging wall. Where the wall ends, turn left at right angles and switchback up to the crown of **Atxurri** (941m).

Turn right (west), following the sign indicating 51 minutes to Aldamiñape along the ridge crest (a wire fence runs along the ridge on your right). In five minutes or so, the trail descends left towards, but does not enter, a cypress grove. After passing a large ash tree and a small beech wood with a cabin on the right, the trail merges into a 4WD road on the right (heading northwest). Reaching a flat saddle, turn hard left and ascend towards several houses visible midway up the slope of Aldamiñape. After the house (with red windows and roof) marked 'Cementos Lemona', you'll reach a fork. Head right and soon the trail reaches a small valley at the base of elongated Aldamín (1376m). Turn left (south) and head cross-country for nearly 1km up to the pass where Aldamín's rocky crest ends. This section is unmarked. Once above, round the ridge's extreme eastern end and rejoin the footpath, now well defined and waymarked. Ascend, keeping the crest on your right and a grassy hill to your left. After 20 minutes, reaching a rain gauge, leave the footpath (which turns left) and continue straight ahead (west) along a grassy saddle for 100m. Take the footpath on the left that ascends directly and steeply to the summit of **Gorbeia** (1481m). Enjoy the grandiose cross and fine views: to the east, Anboto and Aizkorri.

Return to the saddle. Head left, descending around the northwestern edge of Aldamín towards Egiriñao, a valley dotted with beech trees and a house. From the house's right side, take a footpath heading north that is soon signposted to indicate it is 15 minutes to Elorria. Follow the ridge (right) closely and in nearly 15 minutes cross to the slope's other side at Gatzarrieta's (1177m) base. The expansive pastures of Campas de Arraba are ahead. In the base of the valley lies **Refugio Ángel de Sopeña** (☎ 94 633 81 48; *federated walking club members/nonmembers €2.40/ 8; open daily May-Oct, Fri-Sun Nov-Apr*) and, 150m behind it, a fountain. Book ahead to stay here. Federated club members are given preference. Basic mountain fare (eg fried eggs and chorizo sausage) is available from €3.

From the *refugio*, head northwest through pastures for 1.1km to the V-saddle, Kargale-ku pass, between peaks. Reaching the saddle, turn right (north) following yellow-and-white slashes (later red) through limestone outcrops and beech trees into the heart of the **Itxina massif**. Cross the first treeless, lumpy depression along its base, ascending slightly left. At the next grassy pass, head right. After 350m (in another pass) turn right towards a hut; pass it, keeping it on your left. Continue 1.2km to a fork below a rocky outcrop. Left leads to the Cueva de Supelegor in 25 minutes. Instead, go right, and ascend 100m to reach the **Ojo de Atxular** (Atxular's Eye).

Walk through this natural doorway out of the Itxina massif. Zigzag downhill to its base.

To reach **Refugio Hostal Pagomakurre** (☎ 94 633 80 69; *dorm beds €9*) continue straight for 400m (heading north-northeast cross-country and climbing over two stiles) and then right for 2km. Food is available (*menú €14.50*).

From Atxular's base, turn left (northwest) on an unmarked footpath that intermittently disappears. Keep Itxina's vertical walls on your left. After 1km, veering slightly right towards the end, the path meets a wire fence that it follows until the path peters out at a pasture. Head northwest across the pasture; the last spurs of Itxina and Axkorrigan peak (1095m) are visible. Where the pasture ends, join a 4WD road and follow it for 2.8km, without deviations and using three stiles, to Urigoiti village.

Descend straight through Urigoiti, leaving the church on the left and the fountain on the right, to the end of the village. Continue straight through a pasture past two electricity poles on the right. After a small pine grove, cross another field. Following the wooden telephone poles (on your left), pass a hazel grove to another field. Cross it, heading right

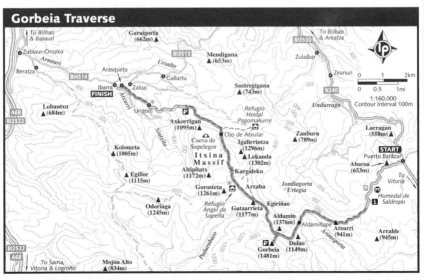

Gorbeia Traverse

Mari, the Basque Goddess

Many Basque hilltops, crowned with crosses or chapels, were once the dominion of Basque divinities. Around the 11th century, Christianity began to make inroads into the Basque Country, primarily via the Puerto de Urkiola. Before (and well after) that time, belief in a myriad of deities was strong. Pre-eminent among them was Mari, or La Dama (the Lady), a beautiful feminine personification of the earth. Taking on diverse forms (tree-woman, horse on the wind, richly dressed or enveloped in flames), Mari dwelled inside the earth connected to the surface via caves or wells frequently filled with glittering gold. Mountain-top caves were her favourite dominions. Weather would improve or worsen whenever she was in residence: fog on Anboto, for example, was a sign of her presence.

Evoking great fear as well as honour and respect, Mari looked after villagers and despised lies, false accusations, vanity, failure to keep one's word and disrespect. Shepherds and other believers would often leave her offerings and explain natural disasters as evidence of her ire.

❀❀❀❀❀❀❀❀❀❀❀❀❀❀

to a cobbled lane, then through another pasture. Descend through Arasqueta along the cement road to the asphalt main road. Turn right along the road, walking parallel to the Río Atxurri for 700m to Ibarra.

Urkiola: Anboto Ridge

Duration	5½–6 hours
Distance	19.5km
Difficulty	demanding
Start/Finish	Puerto de Urkiola (p169)
Nearest Town	Durango (p169)
Transport	bus, taxi

Summary An ascent to a mythic karstic ridge and peak through shepherds' ancient pastures

The 5958-hectare Parque Natural de Urkiola, established in 1989 in southeast Bizkaia, contains one of the Basque Country's most

sacred peaks, Anboto, mythical dwelling of La Dama (see the boxed text 'Mari, the Basque Goddess'). The tortured karstic landscapes of knife-sharp white-grey ridges and dramatic, commanding peaks are definitely the stuff of myths. The limestone massifs of the Sierras de Aramoitz and Anboto part the Mediterranean and Atlantic waters, while the Arangio and Ezkubaratz ranges contain *urkia* (birch in Euskara), which give the park its name. Caves, fissures and curious formations such as the Jentilzubi (Bridge of the Gentiles), an impressive natural archway, and the Damaren Koba (Cave of the Lady), Urkiola's most famous cave, which opens onto Anboto's sheer vertical eastern face, add to the mystique.

The **Santuario de Urkiola**, an odd, unfinished church dedicated to two San Antonios (San Antonio the Abbot, and San Antonio of Padua), dominates the trailhead. The mosaic behind the main altar and the stained-glass windows are particularly fine. San Antonio de Padua's feast day is celebrated on 13 June.

Evidence of human impact extending back thousands of years in the area of the park includes significant Neanderthal remains. Today shepherding and goatherding persist and the high green pastures are crowded with flocks. Forests cover 56% of the park: 30% is reforested Monterey pine, Japanese larch and Lawson cypress, and 26% is native vegetation. Above 600m, on the steep limestone slopes, you'll see holm oak and beech. In thick north-facing woodlands, beeches dominate. The griffon vulture, the park's largest bird, commonly soars in the skies.

The walk tackles the mythical summit of Anboto. It is rated demanding owing to the hair-raising final section to the top, which requires hands and feet (and guts!), but you can easily skip the final ascent, or adapt the walk to a moderate one of 14.5km (four to 4½ hours) by returning from Collado de Pagozelai and eliminating the Anboto section entirely. Two natural springs provide water en route.

PLANNING
When to Walk
The best months are May to October.

Maps & Books

GV's 1:25,000 *Urkiola* topographic map is best. The park's 1:20,000 *Parque Natural de Urkiola* map shows various itineraries but important routes are unmarked. Available from the park's information centre, *Urkiola: Guía del Parque Natural*, in Spanish, is a complete overview of the park's resources.

Information Sources

The **Toki Alai information centre** (*Mon-Fri* ☎ *94 420 68 49, Sat & Sun* ☎ *94 681 41 55; open 10am-2pm & 4pm-6pm daily*), just west and up the hill from Puerto Urkiola, has a permanent park exhibit as well as English-language leaflets, maps and books. Ask in regional and Durango tourist offices for the brochures (in Spanish and Euskara only) *Gorbeialdea* (which has a section on Urkiola), *Durangaldea: Rutas* and *Durangaldea: Cruce de Caminos*.

> ### Warning
>
> Proceed with extreme caution on the last section to the summit of Anboto, which requires scrambling with hands and feet, as well as on the descent from Anboto. Neither should be contemplated in fog, rain or strong winds.

NEAREST TOWNS & FACILITIES
Durango

Durango, in southeast Bizkaia, is an industrial crossroads, commercial centre and capital of the territory from the A8 highway south to the Parque Natural de Urkiola. Numerous factories in the area produce tools and machinery, and smelting is a major industry. Durango's 15th-century Santa María de Uribarri church stands out for its large, 17th-century wooden portico. The **tourist office** (☎ *946 03 00 30; Zabala 2; open 5pm-8pm daily*) has abundant information and walking suggestions. **Iris Sport** (*Barrenkalea 21-34*) has last-minute walking supplies.

Places to Stay & Eat Try out the modern and functional **Albergue-Hostal Errotagaña** (☎ *94 621 60 21; Undagoitia 54, Ikastola Ibaizabal; dorm beds €6.50, singles/doubles*

with bathroom €27/ 36) or ask in Bar Juantxu about rooms in **Hostal Juego Bolos** (☎ *94 681 10 99; San Agustín Alde 2; doubles with/without bathroom €42/34*).

Restaurante Txoko (*Kanpatorrosteta 1*) and **Restaurante Anboto** (*Goienkalea 14*) offer economical eating for €6.

Getting There & Away Durango is connected to Vitoria via the BI623 and to Bilbao and San Sebastián via the N634 highway or A8 toll road. **Bizkaibus** (☎ *902 22 22 65*) runs from both Bilbao and San Sebastián to Durango (€2, 40 minutes, hourly every day). Eusko Tren stops in Durango on the Bilbao–San Sebastián line.

Puerto de Urkiola

Other than the Toki Alai information centre (see Information Sources), two restaurants, **Bizkarra** and **Landajuela** (*menú €8*), and the **Hostal Buenos Aires** (☎ *94 681 20 09; doubles with bathroom €35; closed 15 days in Sept & late Dec*), the pass does not provide any other services.

Getting There & Away The **Continental** (☎ *945 25 89 07*) buses that connect Durango and Vitoria stop at Puerto de Urkiola (€0.85, 15 minutes, six daily). A **taxi** (☎ *94 681 10 01*) from Durango costs €12. By car, take the BI623 south from Durango for 10km to Puerto de Urkiola.

THE WALK (see map p170)

From the church at Puerto de Urkiola, ascend and turn left into the car park's highest tier. (To the right is a gated 4WD road used on the return.) After 50m turn right through birch trees. Use a stile to cross the fence (following red-and-white slashes). Go cross-country (east) straight up the wide grassy slope. Continue ascending towards a fire break and cross it to a false summit. The impressive Aramoitz range (straight ahead) and Anboto (far right) come into view. Ascend, ignoring a trail to the right, and continue to the summit of **Urkiolagirre** (1009m) and an orientation map. Continue east and descend 1km to a dirt road; the peaks loom ahead of you.

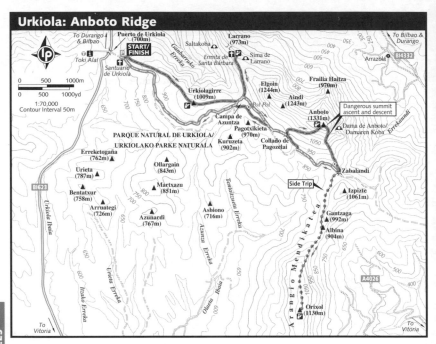

Urkiola: Anboto Ridge

Turn left and in 150m, where the road curves sharp right, take the trail on the left, marked 'PRB202', indicating Larrano is 13 minutes away, and blazed yellow-and-white; you can see it ascending north along the limestone slope to grassy Larrano, the ridge's lowest point. Nearing the ridge-top, take a grassy path on the right to the ridge at the **Ermita de Santa Bárbara** chapel (973m), surrounded by hawthorns and enjoying outstanding views. Return to the dirt road.

Ascend left (southeast) on the dirt road parallel to the mountains past a catchment reservoir, cabin (on the right) and quarry (on the left). Reaching a fork, veer left, gently ascending to **Collado de Pagozelai** (Beech Tree Pass). A wooden sign points left to the top of Anboto (35 minutes). If you'd rather not ascend, continue straight ahead (southeast) along a footpath down to a dirt road. Turn left and in 1km, through a dense beech wood, you'll reach Zabalandi pass (where descending Anboto summiteers rejoin the track).

To ascend Anboto from Collado de Pagozelai turn left and, 100m later, take a trail to the right through beeches. The blazed switchbacks begin. After 25 minutes the beeches disappear and beyond is a false summit. The route now becomes more difficult and dangerous. Turn right and ascend, scrambling, to the visible summit of **Anboto** (1331m). Return the same way to Pagozelai or make an airy and daring descent along Anboto's southeastern face. Continue along the crest for a short way, then veer towards the right, initiating a steep descent on the limestone slope. The way is marked and the goal is in sight: a dirt road next to a cabin in the grassy Zabalandi pass at the base of Izpizte (1061m).

Reaching **Zabalandi** (910m), a sign indicates 'GR12 Orisol' to the south. The side trip described (see p171) leaves from here.

To return, take the dirt road descending west, past a cabin (left) and then a natural spring (above the trail on the right). The road ascends and then levels out for 400m before veering right onto a marked, ascending footpath. In 10 minutes you'll reach Collado de Pagozelai. Return along the familiar road, and 200m before the cabin take a descending trail left through the grassy Campa de Azuntza. Take the footpath that borders, then enters, the woods. From the iron-tasting **Pol Pol** spring, ascend to the dirt road. Turn left and descend 3.5km to the sanctuary.

Side Trip: Orixol Peak
2½ hours, 8.3km
This splendid detour offers superb views and forest walking. From Zabalandi follow the 'Orisol' sign into a beech forest and go 500m to a fork. Head left, briefly ascending and then descending. In 400m the trail reaches a rocky section interspersed with young trees. In 175m, where the trees thin, follow the blazes veering slightly left up the slope (requiring a bit of a scramble). Re-enter the forest for 300m and reach a pasture with a cabin. Take the dirt road on the right past the cabin. Immediately take a footpath on the left for the final ascent (1.2km), initially through a beech wood. Ascend in zigzags. The trail is level for 800m, with Orixol's spur to the right. A few minutes later, after you pass a natural grassy balcony on the right, a group of rocks nearly blocks the path. At the rocks, without descending, turn right and ascend to the small, flat-topped summit of **Orixol** (1130m).

Around Aizkorri

Duration	2 days
Distance	44km
Difficulty	moderate–demanding
Start	Arrasate/Mondragón (p172)
Finish	Arantzazu (p172)
Transport	bus, taxi

Summary From rural valley to extreme mountain heights, enjoy the Basque Country's highest range and most important mountain sanctuary, Arantzazu, on this journey back through time

Starting in the fertile Léniz valley from Arrasate/Mondragón, moderate Day 1 takes an old pilgrimage path through attractive villages and open spaces to fascinating Arantzazu, hanging on the cliffs of a steep-sided ravine enveloped in beech forest. Moderate–demanding Day 2 explores Parque Natural de Aizkorri's lush forests and open meadows. Here flocks of sheep and groups of horses roam freely under the watchful eye of the knife-sharp limestone Aizkorri (literally, 'red rock' or 'naked rock') range, the Basque Country's highest. Topping out at Aitxuri peak (1551m), the range was one of Mari's favourite dwelling places (see the boxed text 'Mari, the Basque Goddess', p168) and contains more than 50 peaks above 1000m. Coming off Aizkorri, the walk briefly joins an ancient cobbled road, some say of Roman origin but more likely medieval, that connected Castile and the north coast via an impressive natural cave, the Túnel de San Adrián. Pilgrims on their way to Santiago de Compostela also used the route to connect to the Camino Francés near Logroño. Prehistoric burial chambers or dolmens also dot the landscape.

PLANNING
When to Walk
The best months are July to September, when fog and rain are less apt to enshroud the crest and make the limestone heights slick.

Maps & Books
Nondik's 1:45,000 *Aizkorri* topographical map and guide is recommended. For some more ideas (in Spanish) on walking around Arantzazu, including wide coverage of cultural and natural history (eg, mushrooming), pick up Urdin Elortza's outstanding book with maps, *Senderos de Oñati*.

Information Sources
Regional tourist offices carry a reasonable range of pamphlets on Arrasate/Mondragón, Oñati, Arantzazu, Aizkorri and the Camino de Santiago in the Basque Country. Oñati, 9km downhill on the only road to/from Arantzazu, is the closest town with a tourist office. It sells descriptions of walks in the area. The Arantzazu monastery's information centre provides specific information on the monastery and of a general nature.

NEAREST TOWNS
Arrasate/Mondragón

Unlike its neighbour, Oñati, which remained under the slavish control of the Guevara counts until the 19th century, Arrasate, a small provincial town, gained independence in 1230. The baroque town hall, **Udala** (*Herriko Plaza Nagusia*), has town maps. **Sportland** (*Garibai Etorbidea 2-6*) has sporting goods and the **Librería Hire** (*Iturriotz 4*) has books on walking but no maps.

Places to Stay & Eat Your top- and low-end options, respectively, are **Hotel Arrasate** (☎ *943 79 73 22; Biteri Etorbidea 1; singles/doubles with bathroom €38/52*) and **Pensión Urizar** (☎ *943 79 12 93; Ferrerias 15; singles/doubles with bathroom €23/33*). For good meals for around €8 head to either **Restaurante Bittori** (*Araba Etorbidea 3*) or **Restaurante Frontón** (*Otalora Lizentziatua*). The latter, on the 3rd floor of the *frontón* (handball court), makes for interesting eating.

Getting There & Away There are **Pesa** (☎ *902 10 12 10*) buses between Bilbao and Arrasate (€4, one hour, three daily). By car, take the GI627 south off the N634 or A8 at Eibar.

Arantzazu

In 1469 shepherd Rodrigo de Balzategi discovered a miraculous statue of the Virgin Mary in a hawthorn tree while tending his flock. Arantzazu (770m), meaning 'place of hawthorns' in Euskara, rapidly became an important pilgrimage destination. Franciscans promptly built a monastery, which celebrated its 500th anniversary in September 2002. Like a phoenix out of the ashes, the church and convent, burnt down and rebuilt in 1533, 1622 and 1834, were reborn in 1950 when the finest avant-garde Basque artists, including Saenz de Oiza and Laorga (the architects), Eduardo Chillida (who made the iron doors), Jorge Oteiza (sculptor of the main facade) and Lucio Muñoz (carver of the 600-sq-metre altarpiece) built the present church. Diamond shapes in limestone cover the exterior and the bell tower, representing the karstic mountains and the hawthorn's thorns.

Places to Stay & Eat Arantzazu has several *hostales*, restaurants and a tourist shop, but nowhere to buy food or supplies. **Hotel Sindika** (☎ *943 78 13 03; singles/doubles with bathroom €29/42*), closest to the trailhead, has a swimming pool and most rooms have gorgeous views. Meals cost €9. Step back in time at **Goiko Benta** (☎ *943 78 13 05; singles/doubles €30/33, doubles with bathroom €36*), a lovely Basque farmhouse. Meals are a pricey €18.

Getting There & Away No buses connect Arantzazu to Oñati; either walk, hitch a ride or take a **taxi** (☎ *658 73 27 09, 606 00 43 40*) for €7. Oñati, nicknamed the Basque Toledo for its wealth of monuments, is a beautiful town worth stopping in before catching a Pesa bus to Bilbao (€4, 1½ hours, two daily Monday to Saturday, one on Sunday).

THE WALK (see map p173)
Day 1: Arrasate to Arantzazu
6–7 hours, 19km

At the beginning and end of today, the various yellow-and-white blazes can be confusing; follow the descriptions carefully. Water is readily available in villages along the way.

The route begins in the centre of Arrasate from Araba Etorbidea street, parallel to the Río Deba (towards Aretxabaleta). Walk the 600m to the roundabout where Arrasate ends, and turn left (towards Bedoña) following the yellow-and-white slashes. Pass under the highway, via a tunnel, to begin a 1.6km ascent along the road to **Bedoña**. At the first fork, head right. Pass the church (left) and continue 10 minutes past several farmhouses to where the asphalt ends. Take a southbound (right) trail that rounds the picturesque rural valley along the slope, through pine forest, and then descends to a crossroads. Continue straight until the trail dies out at an asphalt road. Turn left and in 600m reach the church, fountain and handball court of **Larrino**.

Continue along the asphalt road towards the now visible **Embalse de Urkulu** reservoir (right). In less than five minutes, where the road turns sharply left, take a sealed road right. At the next fork, head right onto a gravel road past a farmhouse to a T-junction. Turn left, rounding the reservoir full of ducks, coots and herons. In 1.5km reach the dam wall. Cross over it and then turn right onto a dirt and stone road. At the first detour left, leave the road and ascend to a pine grove. In 25 minutes you'll reach the **Urruxola Garai** pass. The trail continues past a farmhouse, and straight ahead the Sierra de Aizkorri's first peak, Gorgomendi (1239m), dominates the horizon. This is the halfway point.

Merging left with a descending, wider trail, immediately take a right fork and continue 600m to another fork. Head right to enter Urruxola. Pass two farmhouses (one on the left and the other on the right) and descend along a cobbled path through orchards. Take stairs that lead down to the **Iglesia de Andra Mari**; there's a fountain behind it. Continue down the stairs. In 300m, at an abandoned farmhouse on the left, turn right (without entering the pine grove) onto a trail between stone walls. In 200m reach the houses of Barrenetxe. Turn right, passing between the houses, to a footpath that five minutes later parallels a canal entering the hidden **Río Artixa gorge** beneath Orkatzategi's (874m) steep walls.

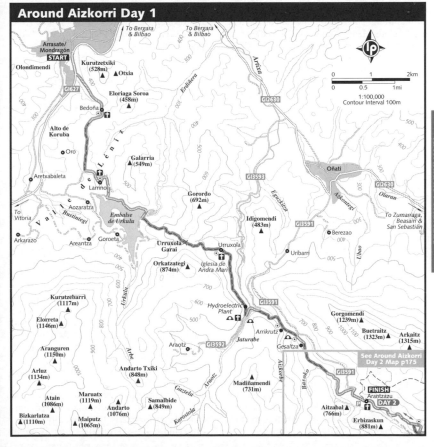

Around Aizkorri Day 1

In 1.1km you'll reach a hydroelectric plant and, soon thereafter, the main road. Head left following the sign 'Arantzazu 4.6km' (really 6km) to a bridge. Ascend 300m and take a trail to the right, the pilgrimage footpath to Arantzazu from Oñati. After a wooded area, make a steep zigzagging ascent through pines. The trail joins a cement road that leads right past the Arrikrutz farmhouse, once a tavern (with a fountain). Cross through an iron gate and switchback up to a wooden gate. Reaching the pass, cross an asphalt road to an oak grove with a fountain. Head right along another asphalt road that descends to the Gesaltza farmhouse. Continue descending briefly along a stone path. At an animal trough, pass through a gate on the left to a pasture. Head straight across to the exit, slightly left of centre midway up the slope. Take a footpath on top of a covered canal for 10 minutes and, after passing through a green iron gate, take a cobbled trail left. At the first fork, head left and in 300m reach a concrete road. Turn left. At the crossroads continue straight past a farmhouse and ascend to the road. Turn right and in 600m reach the unexpected sanctuary. See Arantzazu (p172) for details.

Day 2: Aizkorri & Túnel de San Adrián
7–8 hours, 25km

Collect water for the walk in Arantzazu and Campas de Urbia. The 10.6km return walk from Arantzazu to the Urbia *refugio* is an excellent easy–moderate outing.

Facing the sanctuary, continue straight, first curving right up the road (ignore the road that goes left to Goiko Benta), then left past Hotel Sindika. The road quickly converts to dirt and continues straight without detours for 10 minutes to a car park and trail crossroads. Veer left (east) uphill going around the green gate. Over the next 3.5km the beautiful trail ascends first through conifer and then beech forest without deviations. About 20 minutes from the gate, when the trail curves sharply right, a beech tree on the left harbours a small statue of the Arantzazu Virgin and a natural spring. Over the last kilometre before the top the trail narrows and the ascent steepens.

Reaching the grassy, open top, veer left towards the trees and ignore a trail to the right, leading to Zabalaitz (1264m). The trees lead past a chapel to the **Campas de Urbia**, an enormous karstic depression, which has a fountain and **Refugio Urbiako Fonda** (☎ 943 78 13 16; dorm beds €15, full-board €30); the **bar** serves meals. In the 19th century 30,000 sheep grazed here; now there are around 6000. From here the ascent trail is visible. With the *refugio* to the left, take the descending dirt road that leads to the base of the range. After 150m head cross-country across the grass to again pick up the dirt road, which reaches some shepherds' cabins 20 minutes later. Yellow blazes mark a right-angled left turn through the cabins (sheep's-milk cheese is sold). The eastbound footpath ascends the open slope. Reaching a group of beeches, limestone rocks begin to predominate, as do switchbacks. Soon the impressive crest comes into sight and the ascent alternates between sections of earth and stone passing below Aitxuri (1551m) and Aketegi (1548m). Reaching a grassy pass, bordered by a rocky outcrop giving views of the ridge's other side, the footpath continues through rocks for 10 minutes to the summit of **Aizkorri** (1528m). The Ermita de Santo Cristo (which is always open and at a pinch can be used for shelter) and a simple **refugio** (an empty cabin, almost always closed) watch over the valley below.

Descend southeast along the crest for 200m (past a group of three crosses) to a fork. Veer right and in five minutes, after crossing a bridge-like wall spanning a chasm, turn left (south) – continuing straight leads to Oltza – following yellow blazes and sporadic iron crosses. After 1km the trail enters a young beech wood and the descent stiffens for 25 minutes, finally reaching a clearing in the woods. Turning left, in 300m the medieval pavers lead to the **Túnel de San Adrián**, complete with chapel. Return to the clearing.

Ascend straight (southwest) along the medieval roadway (a Camino de Santiago variant) for 600m and where it turns left uphill, take a path right (west) through the beech wood. Follow the poorly marked red-and-white blazes for nearly 10 minutes to another, better marked trail on the right. Ascend

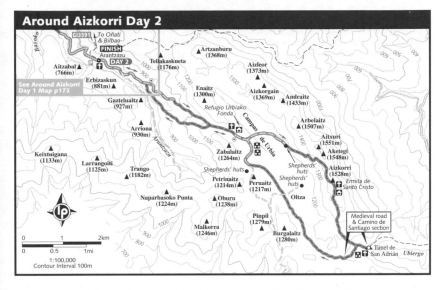

Around Aizkorri Day 2

steeply right and then continue straight, following the blazes. The trail passes through heather, a clearing (head northwest across it) and then re-enters the beech forest. Pass through two depressions and then descend to the first pastures of **Oltza**. Turn left and cross through the middle of the unblazed pasture (the range is to the right) for nearly 1km to a 4WD road. Cross this and continue straight, following stone markers embedded in the earth. Ascend through a beech forest and then descend through open fields, guided by stones, to cabins. Ascend to a wide dirt road. Turn right to reach the Urbia *refugio* in 1km, passing two signposted dolmens on the way.

From the *refugio*, retake the ash-flanked pathway. Where the grassy pass ends, either return along the same path to Arantzazu or take another return route that's 300m longer. To do this, begin descending and after 50m turn left (southwest), fording a narrow muddy zone. Descend through a beech forest following difficult-to-see blue blazes. In 400m the forest converts to pine and soon after, the trail forks. Head right (the left fork descends to Iturigorri), quickly entering a beech wood flanked on the right by a wire fence. Cross a perpendicular trail and continue descending

straight ahead (keep a rocky outcrop on your right) to another footpath; take it right. After crossing a stream bed (usually dry), begin ascending. A wider trail appears; take it left. In 800m the trail continues straight through a clearing in a pine grove offering spectacular views of Gazteluaitz's (927m) vertical faces. The trail eventually gives onto the wide ascent trail. Turn left and descend to Arantzazu.

San Sebastián to Hondarribia

Duration	2 days
Distance	34.1km
Difficulty	moderate
Start	San Sebastián (p164)
Finish	Hondarribia (p176)
Transport	taxi, bus, train

Summary Walk from the city to wild sandstone cliffs in minutes, to an enchanting port and then along the spine of Jaizkibel where the Pyrenees start

This excellent coastal traverse, where the Atlantic laps against the Pyrenees, enjoys outstanding seascapes, cliffs, easy access and historical sea ports as well as solitude, despite its proximity to urban areas. The walk covers the sandstone massifs of Monte Ulía (Ulia Mendia; 201m) on Day 1 and on Day 2, Jaizkibel (545m), lying on the coast between Pasaia and Hondarribia like an enormous beached whale. Replete with watchtowers and castle ruins, Jaizkibel has had a major role in border conflicts. A surprising variety of coastal wildflowers thrive on the trail's borders, and intermittent woods contain examples of Mediterranean (holm oak, laurel, strawberry trees), Atlantic (chestnut, hawthorn, common oak) and exotic (eucalyptus, pine, mimosa) plant communities. From May to August nesting gulls fill the cliffs and cormorants can be seen diving for fish. Brambles can be a nuisance in some sections of the walk.

PLANNING
When to Walk
The coast's temperate climate makes this walk feasible year-round. The driest months are July to September.

Maps
The IGN's 1:25,000 map Nos 40-IV *Jaizkibel*, 64-II *Donostia-San Sebastián* and 41-III *Irún* cover the walk.

NEAREST TOWNS
See San Sebastián (p164).

Hondarribia
Hondarribia, Irún (both in Spain) and Hendaye (France) share the Río Bidasoa and the Bahía Txingudi, which drain into the Bay of Biscay. Hondarribia, meaning 'sandy ford', shelters below Jaizkibel's protective wing and is Gipuzkoa's only walled city. The cobbled, primarily pedestrian, historic quarter enchants with its colourful three-storey, half-timbered homes plastered with geraniums. The **tourist office** (☎ 943 64 54 58; **w** www .bidasoaturismo.com; Javier Ugarte 6; open 9.30am-1.30pm & 4pm-6.30pm Mon-Fri, 10am-2pm Sat) sells a packet of local walks.

Places to Stay & Eat The high point of the village, the **Plaza de Armas y Castillo**

de Carlos V is hosts to the **Hotel San Nikolas** (☎ 943 64 42 78; Plaza de Armas 6; singles/doubles with bathroom €50/57). In the fishing quarter, beyond the city walls, is **Hostal Álvarez Quintero** (☎ 943 64 22 99; Bernat Etxeparre 2; singles/doubles/triples with bathroom from €32/41/48; open Mar-Nov). The **Albergue Juvenil Juan Sebastian Elkano** (☎ 943 64 15 50; Higuer Bidea 7; members €7.20, nonmembers under 30 yrs/ others €8.70/13) is between the lighthouse and the town; breakfast is included.

For well-prepared seafood head to **Restaurante Hermandad de Pescadores** (Zuloaga 12), and for great *pintxos*, **Restaurante Yola Berri** (San Pedro 22). The **Erosle** (Santiago) supermarket has the basics.

Getting There & Away Hondarribia is only 19km from San Sebastián. **Interbus** (☎ 93 64 13 02) connects to San Sebastián (€1.35, 45 minutes, every 20 minutes) departing from San Kristobal Plaza. **Taxi Txingudi** (☎ 609 26 86 66) runs to the airport and San Sebastián from Hondarribia. By car, both the N1 and the A8 toll road link the two towns.

THE WALK (see maps p177 & p179)
Day 1: San Sebastián to Pasai Donibane
2½–3 hours, 11.5km
Collect water before leaving San Sebastián. Lodging options in Pasai Donibane are limited; consider making a day trip and returning the next day to continue.

Starting from the **town hall** overlooking San Sebastián's main beach, Playa de la Concha, take the maritime walkway right (north) towards the **fishing wharf**. Curve left past the aquarium to the Paseo Nuevo seaside walkway. Continue around Monte Urgull until you reach the art nouveau **Puente Zurriola** bridge (to shave off 1.5km, walk east from the town hall down Alameda del Boulevard to the bridge.) Turn left and cross the bridge, passing the **Kursaal** exhibition centre and the popular surfing beach, **Playa de Zurriola**, and continue straight towards Monte Ulía and the buildings ahead.

Two options present themselves. The one described here (1.2km) is more spectacular

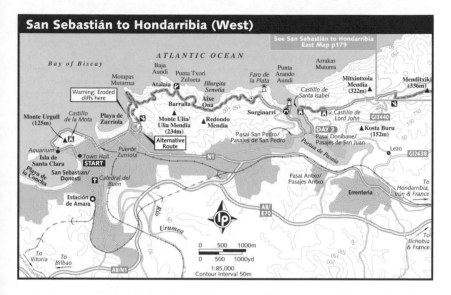

San Sebastián to Hondarribia (West)

but is dangerous at first at the heavily eroded sandstone cliffs. If in doubt, use the safer Alternative Route (see p178). Turn left through the car park to the maritime walkway. On the last lamppost, note the first red-and-white blaze. Where the walkway ends, continue straight along the base of the cliffs. Reaching a small field, the ascent begins of the eroding hillside along a narrow footpath, past a dangerous, steep 20m drop. Briefly descend before ascending along the richly vegetated path to an old military installation. Enter, ascending along the stairs, to rejoin the path above. Reaching a small tower, fork right in ascent and soon enter a forest. Fork left through a thick tunnel of foliage. Where the forest ends, at the cliff top, continue straight.

Continue on the spectacular sandstone cliff-top trail, which soon descends southeast (right) into a pine forest filled with hydrangeas. Reaching a fork, make a hairpin left turn, descending out of the forest and onto a steeply descending cobbled lane towards the ocean. This was used by oxen in the 1890s to haul stone from the quarry below. Josetxu, a retired man, has lovingly toiled for 16 years to clean the forest, recobble the lane, plant and make the trail accessible for others to

enjoy. He may be working. For 20 minutes the obvious trail zigzags down and around a huge, Swiss-cheese outcrop (gulls love the eroded holes) then undulates along the open hillside to a natural **lookout**. The Faro de la Plata comes into sight; 3.4km remain to the lighthouse.

The trail enters a beech, oak and chestnut forest and 10 minutes later reaches a cement road. Descend for 75m along the road and where it curves left, veer right onto a dirt trail through grass, shrubs and then forest. Twenty minutes later the trail ascends inland towards pastures, the brush thickens and the trail reaches a fork. Turn hard left onto a trail flanked with brush. At a T-junction turn left again onto a wider sandstone, then cobbled path. In 20 minutes the lighthouse reappears as well as a curious aqueduct in ruins. The trail winds around a gorge and aqueduct to the base of the romantic **Faro de la Plata**.

Turn right onto the road and continue for 500m. Jaizkibel is to the east. Where the road curves right, turn left onto a wide sandstone path leading to a picnic area. Turn left and cross the picnic area. Look for the marked, zigzagging footpath steeply descending to the lighthouse. Tankers, sailboats and even

Whaling & Shipbuilding

All along the Basque coastline eagle-eyed lookouts in watchtowers kept vigil for the unmistakable approach of the Biscayan whale. Seeing the spout, the lookout sounded the alarm shouting '¡Baliak! ¡Baliak!' (Whale! Whale!) and whalers quickly set out in their small boats. Once the oarsmen neared the huge mammal the harpooner, the elite among fishermen, screwed up his courage and launched his lance, hoping the tail wouldn't send them all into oblivion. Once on land the whale meat was divided (often the choicest piece, the tongue, went to the church as tribute) and the blubber was boiled down for oil. By 1059 fishermen from Bayonne (France) whaled commercially off the coast, and many coastal towns, including Bermeo, Lekeitio and Hondarribia, incorporated the whale into their town seal.

In the 16th century Basque whalers regularly practised their trade in Newfoundland. In 1978 a Basque galleon, the *San Juan,* sunk in 1565 with two whaleboats on board, was discovered in the waters of Red Bay, an important whaling station in Labrador, Canada. *National Geographic* covered the remarkable wreck and its discovery and subsequent investigation in its July 1985 issue (Vol 168, No 1). The boat hailed from Pasai Donibane, where today the art of making wood-framed boats has been revived by a man passionate about preserving a craft nearly lost despite its centuries-long practice. The shipyard in Donibane, **Ontziola** (☎ 943 34 44 78; Donibane Kalea 33; open 11am-2pm & 4pm-7pm July–mid-Sept, 10am-2pm & 3pm-5pm mid-Sept–July) welcomes visitors.

kayaks are often visible in the narrow channel leading to Pasaia, three burghs surrounding Gipuzkoa's largest port and dedicated to scrap transport and shipbuilding: Pasai San Pedro (Pasajes de San Pedro), Pasai Donibane (Pasajes de San Juan) and Pasai Antxo (Pasajes Antxo). Follow the footpath down to the maritime walkway and in 10 minutes reach San Pedro's port. San Pedro has **markets**. Cross in the boat taxi (€0.50; every five minutes all day) to picturesque Pasai Donibane. The boat drops you at Donibane Kalea.

Alternative Route

20 minutes, 750m

From the car park at the east end of Playa de Zurriola, look for the narrow staircase between the school and the bar San Antonio Okindegia. Climb the stairs past a *frontón* (on the left) and continue uphill, veering left onto Zemorilla Kalea. The paved street gives way to uphill steps which merge into a paved trail curving left uphill to a paved road. Ignore stairs to the right near the top (which ascend to the Albergue Monte Ulía). Turn left (past a **mirador** – lookout) to a dirt trail marked with yellow-and-white slashes. Continue through the pine wood, ignoring descending trails, for 10 minutes. When the trail re-enters the forest, look for gardens on the right and a

hidden trail on the left. Turn hard left and ascend through pines towards the coast. After 200m, the trail turns right, joining the main described trail, and opens to cliffs.

Pasai Donibane

The timbered waterfront houses, arcaded streets and moored, colourful boats hemmed in by steep mountains here ooze history and adventure. The people have been shipbuilders and fisherfolk since time immemorial, and author Victor Hugo immortalised the place in *Alps and Pyrenees*. In 1843 he lived in the house that holds the **tourist office** (☎ 943 34 15 56; Donibane Kalea 63; open 11am-2pm & 3.30pm-6.30pm).

Pasai Donibane and San Pedro's only lodging option, whose spartan rooms are usually full in summer, is **Txintxorro** (☎ 943 51 00 83; Lezobidea 2; doubles €36, 3-bed apartment with bathroom & kitchen €64).

Plenty of waterfront dining is available. Try attractive **Restaurante Nicolasa** (Donibane Kalea 9; menú €12) or the most economical, **Restaurante Matxet** (Donibane Kalea 4; menú €6).

A good option is to return to San Sebastián (€0.85, 20 minutes, every 20 minutes) on either **Interbus** (☎ 93 64 13 02) or **Herribus** (☎ 943 49 18 01).

Day 2: Pasai Donibane to Hondarribia

6–6½ hours, 22.6km

Water is readily available on the moderate walk across Jaizkibel's barren backbone.

From the boat drop, turn left through Pasai Donibane past the plaza and town hall. Continue straight along the maritime walkway passing the church, Basílica de Bonanza, and then five minutes further reach an archway of the **Castillo de Santa Isabel**, which once defended the port (currently it's a private house). In 100m, beyond the archway, take an ascending path to the right along the steep slopes. In 200m leave the path and turn right, following the red-and-white blazes in the trees, heading cross-country uphill for a hard 300m. Return to the footpath just above a young pine grove. Reaching the rocky summit, use a stile to cross a wire fence to a wide trail. At the first fork, turn left. Soon the **Castillo de Lord John** ruins appear, surrounded by a picnic area with a fountain.

Keeping these on the right, continue straight to a gravel road that is soon sealed. Continue for 1km. Reaching the road, turn left. Errenteria (Rentería) is visible below to the right. Follow the road for 700m. After passing a bar, turn right where the guardrail ends and head to the one-time military **watchtower**.

Turning left, the ridge-crest trail begins. Over the next 9km it offers continuous ocean views. The contrast between the tranquillity and solitude of the ocean (on your left) and the hubbub of the urban areas below (right) is striking. The red-and-white marks are less frequent here. If in doubt, choose the trail that most closely follows the ridge crest. During this stretch, the trail passes two more watchtowers. Approximately one hour from the first watchtower, it reaches a group of communications towers. Keep these on your left. At the base of the second one, a **mirador** offers gorgeous views of the Aiako Harria range straight ahead, the Bahía Txingudi surrounded by Hondarribia, Irún and Hendaye,

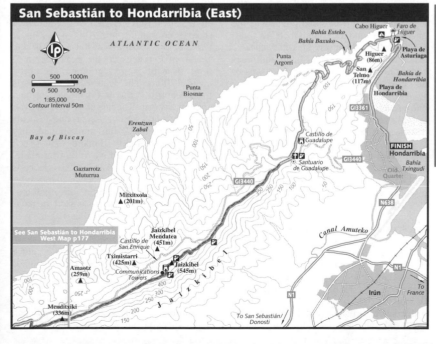

San Sebastián to Hondarribia (East)

and Larrun peak, just over the border in France. Just beyond the third antenna, the ruins of the **Castillo de San Enrique** are on the right. Cross the ruins to **Jaizkibel's** summit (545m). After passing a tiny forestry outpost, the descent begins.

Beyond a rocky area, the trail curves right and crosses a fence via a stile to a pasture. Head for the modern *mirador* visible in the distance (1km). Halfway there, look left for a dolmen. After reaching the **mirador**, the trail passes another defensive tower, crosses another pasture and then passes two more dolmens. After the second of these (the day's halfway point), the trail forks left onto a grassy trail. As you pass the last of the watchtowers (on the right), Hondarribia looms large below. Another stile marks the end of the pasture and the beginning of a steep descent to the road. The **Santuario de Guadalupe** is off to the right. Hondarribia's patron saint, the miraculous Virgin of Guadalupe, allegedly interceded on behalf of the townsfolk during a siege in 1638, when the city successfully defended itself for 69 days. Every 8 September the townspeople process to the sanctuary. Around the church there's a fountain, *mirador* and **bar** serving sandwiches.

The trail crosses the road and continues straight along a concrete trail. The ruins of the large **Castillo de Guadalupe** are to the right. At the first fork, descend left and in 600m reach a crossroads. Turn left onto the asphalt road (towards Artzu). After 10 minutes the asphalt ends at the Agroturismo Artzu and continues on a dirt road. After passing two houses on the right, the descent towards the ocean stiffens. From a T-junction, head right on the dirt road that roughly follows the coastline for 3.5km, crossing a chestnut grove, to a water sanitation station.

Round the station and the trail exits to an asphalt road and the **Camping Faro de Higuer** (☎ 943 64 10 08; *Carretera del Faro; adult/ tent/car €3.50/3.50/3.50*). Its *menú* costs €8. Turn right onto the asphalt past the camping ground, the lighthouse and a **mirador** overlooking the French coast. Continue on the road for 200m and turn left to wind down to Hondarribia's fishing port. Using the walkway, head round the beach to a roundabout.

Turn right following the bike lane past the recreational port to the maritime walkway and Calle Itsasargi, where Hondarribia's famous fishing quarter begins. The historical quarter is straight ahead and up the hill.

GR11: Elizondo to Roncesvalles

Duration	2 days
Distance	42.3km
Difficulty	moderate–demanding
Start	Elizondo (p181)
Finish	Roncesvalles (p337)
Transport	bus, taxi

Summary The GR11's highlight section in the Navarran Pyrenees, taking in enchanting beech woods, airy ridge crests and farmland

The GR11 Pyrenean Traverse starts at sea level from Hondarribia in Euskadi and by day's end reaches Bera in Navarra. The Navarran section of the GR11 is roughly eight stages from Bera to just beyond Isaba (Izaba), continuing into Aragón at Zuriza. Only at this extreme eastern end of the Navarran Pyrenees do the peaks begin to impress with jagged grandeur, reaching up to 1700m. The featured section starts from beautiful Valle de Baztan (202m) and ends in historic Roncesvalles (951m) after making several serious ascents and descents (from 200m to 1260m) on rounded, airy ridges often thickly flanked with beech woods and connected by rolling farmland.

Spain and France share these mountains and many ancient trails once used by smugglers, refugees and simple folk crisscross back and forth. Pilgrims also used the pathways and from Roncesvalles it's easy to link to the Camino Francés as described in the Camino de Santiago chapter (p328).

The Navarran Pyrenees are important for migratory birds (turtledoves, wood pigeons, geese, ducks) and, consequently, hunters. Hunting is prohibited in spring during nesting but is allowed in autumn when birds return to their winter grounds. Blinds, though very expensive, are numerous and common along the walk. For additional information on the GR11 and the Pyrenees see the Pyrenees chapter (p92).

Overnight accommodation on the walk is complicated. From Puerto de Urkiaga at the end of Day 1 the nearest lodging is 12km downhill in Eugi or 7km further in Zubiri. No buses connect to Puerto de Urkiaga from either Eugi or Zubiri. On weekends the area is very popular with walkers and it may be possible to hitch a ride to Eugi or Zubiri. To be on the safe side, either take a tent to bivouac or prearrange transport with a taxi (from Zubiri) before leaving Elizondo; cell phones don't work at Puerto de Urkiaga. Alternatively, continue along the GR11 for a further three hours to Refugio Sorogain (Casa Pablo).

PLANNING
When to Walk
Mist and fog are possible at any time of year and can cause disorientation. The most predictably dry and clear months are July to September. Hunting season runs from October through November. Hunters prize early October mornings and weekends.

Maps & Books
Alpina's 1:40,000 *Alduides Baztan* topographic map covers the walk but has a few errors. Prames' *GR11: Senda Pirenaica* provides 1:40,000 maps plus a guide with skeletal route descriptions. Paul Lucia's *Through the Spanish Pyrenees: GR11* is based on the Spanish version. Buy all maps and books in either Pamplona or San Sebastián.

NEAREST TOWNS
See also Roncesvalles (p337).

Elizondo
Elizondo is the Valle de Baztan's capital and most important urban centre. The **tourist office** (☎ 948 58 12 79; *Casa de Cultura, Plaza de los Fueros; open 10am-2pm Mon-Sat June-Sept, 10am-2pm Mon-Fri Oct-May)* provides local information. The town's bookshop, **Librería Nafarpress** *(Jaime Urrutia 43)* has books on the Baztan valley, local and regional history and some maps.

Pensión Eskisaroi *(☎ 948 58 00 13; Jaime Urrutia 40; doubles with/without bathroom €27/20)* has older, bargain rooms below and newly renovated ones above. The attractive **dining room** overlooking the river is a good place to enjoy an excellent *menú* (€8.40). **Hotel Saskaitz** *(☎ 948 58 04 88; María Azpilikueta 10; singles/doubles with bathroom €31/50)* offers comfort and tranquillity. Elizondo has several **supermarkets** and good restaurants, including **Restaurante Galarza** *(Santiago 1)* and **Restaurante Santxotena** *(Pedro Axular 4)*.

Getting There & Away Elizondo is connected by **Baztañesa** *(☎ 948 58 01 29)* buses with Pamplona (€3.60, one hour, three daily) and San Sebastián (€4.35, two hours, three daily). By car, take the N121-A north from Pamplona or south from Hondarribia and then head east on the N121-B to Elizondo.

THE WALK (see maps p182 & p183)
Day 1: Elizondo to Puerto de Urkiaga
6½–7½ hours, 21.3km
The route beings to the right of Elizondo's Iglesia de Santiago, along Avenida Monseñor Berecochea heading southeast. After 500m without detouring, the last farmhouse and a GR11 information panel appear. Turn right onto an ascending trail. In 150m, head right on a footpath enveloped in young hazels. Within an oak grove, veer slightly left to join an asphalt road. Turn right and upon reaching a farmhouse (on the left), continue along the sealed road or turn right onto a footpath that returns to the road 200m later.

Ten minutes later (having passed another farmhouse on the right), leave the asphalt for a trail heading right (south). In 200m the path opens to a clearing. Where the trail turns hard right, keep straight on a poorly marked trail climbing southeast along the hillside. Cross a concrete road, continue straight and then head left onto a cobbled, wooded lane. After 1km, where the forest clears, reach a T-junction and turn right. As the lane levels out, it also widens then, reaching a left-hand curve, steepens. Soon thereafter shortcut

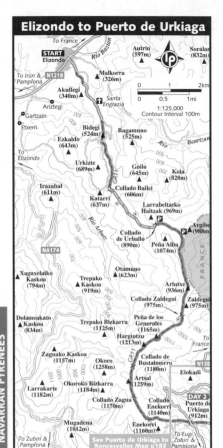

Elizondo to Puerto de Urkiaga

the ground. Reaching a wire fence, turn right (south) and continue parallel to it over the next 3.5km – circumnavigating Peña Alba, crossing another beech wood, ascending a col and finally reaching the hunters' cabin 'Txau-Xilo' and spring in **Collado Zaldegui** (975m). During this section there are numerous hunting blinds and stones (known locally as *mugas*), numbered 128, 129 and 130, that mark the Spain-France border.

From the cabin, continue along the dirt trail passing two more cabins over the next 300m. At the last cabin the track ends. Take a footpath heading northwest that, after climbing a nearby hill, turns left (southwest) to initiate a beautiful section through beech wood. After passing a damp area filled with rushes, the trail exits onto a field. At a hawthorn tree, turn first left (southwest) and then quickly west, and head cross-country up a steep, grassy hill. There are blazes on stones. The trail reappears on the slope below the summit, continues round the peak and then veers left towards a wire fence.

Parallel to the fence, ascend rocky **Peña de los Generales** (1165m). Where the ascent markedly steepens, jump the fence (there's no stile) and continue along the slope, maintaining the same height, until rejoining the fence on its way down the peak. Follow the fence for nearly 1km ascending a hill. At the next saddle, **Collado de Bustalmorro** (1180m), take a footpath to the left that circles the next peak without ascending it. Rejoin the fence and follow it for 1.2km to a gate at the foot of Enekorri (1160m). With the gate on your right, turn left (southeast) and head cross-country through a field leaving a bunker to the right. Round Enekorri and enter a dense beech wood. A new wooden cabin marks the beginning of a pronounced 1.5km descent to Puerto de Urkiaga.

Eugi & Zubiri

Eugi, 12km south of Puerto de Urkiaga on the Eugui reservoir, has a **supermarket** and two *hostales*, **Mesón Quinto Real** (☎ 948 30 40 44; *Carretera Pamplona-Francia; doubles with bathroom €43*) and **Hostal Ezkurra**

right onto a track that in five minutes rejoins the previous lane. In 100m reach a wide dirt road and turn left. At the next two forks, head left to **Collado Bailei** (606m).

Continue ascending along the dirt road for 3km (passing two springs) to **Collado de Urballo** (890m) at the foot of Peña Alba (1074m). Notice the first hunting blinds. Continue straight (east), leaving the first blind off to the left, through a beech forest. Continue along Peña Alba's northern slope, paying close attention to the blazes, first along the rocks and then, after crossing a stream (the halfway point), on posts nailed to

(☎ 948 61 50 80; Asunción 4; doubles with bathroom €36). Both serve meals.

See p339 for information on Zubiri, a further 7km away. A **taxi** *(☎ 948 30 40 67)* from Zubiri can drop you (or, by pre-arrangement, pick you up) at Puerto de Urkiaga. **Montañesa** *(☎ 948 33 05 81)* buses from Pamplona connect to Eugi (€3.50, one hour, one daily Monday to Friday) and Zubiri on the Eugui and Roncesvalles lines.

Day 2: Puerto de Urkiaga to Roncesvalles

6–6½ hours, 21km

Cross the N138 and take an ascending dirt track roughly east through spruce. In 100m leave the road, heading left along a footpath that enters a beech forest. After about 10 minutes the trail returns to the dirt road. Turn left and follow the road, marked with red arrows, for 1.3km. When the road forks veer left onto a dirt path, abandoning it 300m later, when the ascent stiffens, for another path on the right. The path narrows entering the beech wood and ascends to a gate leading to a grassy pass. Here, instead of descending along the trail straight ahead, follow the narrow path that heads off right (south) above

the beech forest to a bowl on the northern face of Adi (1458m). The footpath disappears under the grass. Cross the bowl at the same height, looking for blazed rocks. Head towards the slope dotted with beech straight ahead. The footpath reappears and climbs over **Collado Adatún** (1200m). On the path look right for cypress and a wire fence that descends from Adi's summit.

Use a stile to cross over the fence and pass through a brief section of cypress, then blueberry bushes and finally beech wood initiating a steep descent. During this section it's very important to watch for blazes in the trees. After 1km straight down, the trail crosses various brooks and then veers right to avoid a steep ravine straight ahead. Follow cairns through here as the slashes also disappear. Soon the footpath becomes clearer as the path opens to heather. In another 500m, the trail reaches a beautiful enclave amidst boxwood and beech at the junction of two streams. Curve left, descending parallel to the Arroyo Odia. Crossing the stream twice, the trail begins to follow the Río Sorogain and descends through the ever-widening valley, finally reaching a dirt road. Turn right onto the road and in less

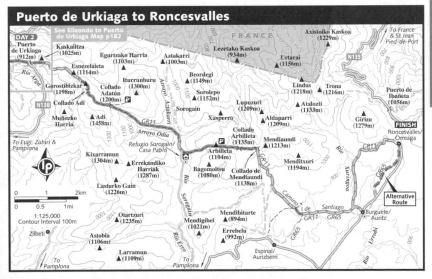

Puerto de Urkiaga to Roncesvalles

than 1km reach the **Refugio Sorogain** (*Casa Pablo;* ☎ *686 41 96 15; dorm beds €7, doubles €24*). The *refugio* serves breakfast (€3), lunch and dinner (€8). There's a fountain 200m beyond the *refugio*.

The route continues behind the *refugio*, crosses a wire fence then ascends left, joining a wider trail that goes left, then immediately turns hard right and continues cross-country, ascending towards a small structure. The trail continues to climb in the same direction, passing a small forest on the right. Reaching a lone beech tree, it follows a small, dry torrent. Pass another forest and wire fence on the right. The trail approaches the wire fence and, at the first summit, runs parallel to it for 1km. Climbing a second summit you'll see the first of the day's hunting blinds. By some wheel tracks in Collado Arbilleta (1135m) at the foot of Mendiaundi (1218m), use a stile to cross the wire fence and continue straight into the forest along a dirt road that descends for more than 2km without deviations.

After passing a gate, the trail gives onto another dirt road. Head left and just after going through a second gate Burguete comes into view in the distance. At the next crossroads, by a cultivated field, turn right at 90 degrees and head through a pasture with trees (on the right) to a stile. Cross over. The GR11 and the GR65/Camino Francés coincide here. Turn left for 1.2km, passing two streams and a gate to a dirt road that leads to a fork. Going right leads to Burguete and then Roncesvalles via the GR65 (see Alternative Route: Via Burguete). Turn left to reach Roncesvalles in 4km via the GR11.

Alternative Route: Via Burguete
45 minutes, 3km
Head right at the fork to see picturesque Burguete, which has **markets**, **restaurants**, **lodgings**, bank and pharmacy. On reaching the highway, turn left and walk through town for 1km. At the last house on the left, turn left down an asphalt road. At the first right veer into the forest, and 20 minutes later the trail opens to the highway and Roncesvalles.

Other Walks

PARQUE NATURAL DE VALDEREJO
Desfiladero del Río Purón
The great attraction of Euskadi's most remote park, in Álava's extreme west (access via A2622), is the Río Purón's impressive gorge. Leaving from Lalastra, by the park's **information centre** (☎ *947 35 31 46*), the short highlight walk passes through the abandoned village of Ribera and then enters the high, narrow gorge; at times the trail is excavated in the rock. The park centre has the free 1:16,000 Valderejo Parque Natural map, as well as information on other walks in the area.

RESERVA DE LA BIOSFERA DE URDAIBAI
Elantxobe to Kanala
Northeast of Bilbao (via Gernika) is the 230-sq-km Urdaibai Reserve, taking in 12km of sandy shore along the Mundaka estuary and the surrounding hills. An attractive 13km, moderate walk begins in Elantxobe, a fishing village that clings impossibly to steep cliffs, and ascends to Cabo Ogoño, whose vertical walls drop 280m to the ocean. Continue to Akorda and then ascend to the grand *mirador* above the reserve, Ermita de San Pedro de Atxarre. Descend to Kanala on the estuary's shore. In summer boats ferry across to Mundaka. Use the GV 1:25,000 map Nos 38-III and 38-IV.

PARQUE NATURAL AIAKO HARRIA
Visible from San Sebastián as a three-pronged crown, Aiako Harria (821m) is Euskadi's only granite massif. Take the GI363 Oiartzun–Irún road to the Alto de Elurtxe. From here a moderate, 14km loop rounds the massif's perimeter via Arritxulegui and Castillo del Inglés. Alternatively, ascend the impressive crest, taking in Irumugarrieta, Txurrumurru and Erroilbide. Enjoy fantastic views of the city and ocean while walking in alpine forest. The IGN's 1:25,000 map No 65-I *Ventas de Irún* is helpful.

PARQUE NATURAL DE ARALAR
Dolmen Circuit
The Sierra de Aralar, forming a natural barrier between Euskadi and Navarra, harbours the popular Santuario de San Miguel, the classic summit of Txindoki (1340m), and the greatest concentration of megalithic monuments in Euskadi (more than 60). The suggested route leaves from Camping de Etxarri-Aranaz (Navarra), west of Pamplona off the N240A, making a 16.5km mod-

erate ridge walk through dense beech and passing 10 dolmens. The town hall of Etxarri-Aranatz publishes a leaflet in Spanish and Euskara called *Ruta de los Dolmenes* with a 1:25,000 map, and route description.

AROUND THE GR11
Cave Walk

North of Elizondo, via the N121B, an exceptional easy–moderate 16km walk starts from Urdazubi. Marked by blue blazes in the shape of *pottoks* (small local horses), it continues to charming Zugarramurdi, crosses the frontier and ends in the beautiful French village of Sare. Particularly fascinating are a number of irresistible caves, all accessible en route. The Urdazubi caves hold unexpected karstic masterpieces while in Zugarramurdi, witches allegedly used the enormous limestone cavern for their covens. The Sare caves impress for their scale and prehistoric remains. Use IGN 1:50,000 map Nos 65 and 66.

Selva de Irati

The 124 sq km of beech and white spruce northeast of Pamplona in the Irati Forest, one of Europe's largest forests, make for great walking. Take the NA178 via Ochagavía. The information centre is at the Casas de Irati, east of the Irabia reservoir. In an area famed for its abundant flora and fauna, there are eight easy, well-marked routes, all less than 6km in length. The highlight? Monte La Cuestión, northeast of the reservoir, shelters a section of forest untouched by human hands during the 20th century – difficulty of access prevented the lumber industry from removing wood. The recommended 1:40,000 *Irati, Valle de Salazar* map is available in many tourist offices, including Pamplona and Casas de Irati.

Cordillera Cantábrica

The Cordillera Cantábrica straddles the regions of Asturias, Cantabria and the Leonese part of Castilla y León. More than 250km long, it stretches from Serra dos Ancares in Galicia to Sierra de Peña Labra on the border between Cantabria and Castilla y León. Towering 2000m peaks rise from the Atlantic Ocean, forming an imposing barrier that separates the sea from the great Castilian plains. Cut through by powerful river systems and low-lying, verdant valleys where villagers still work the land, these spectacular, humid mountains are among Spain's finest.

In Asturias, the walks take in the panoramic Costa Naviega and the Parque Natural de Somiedo, where the sparsely populated villages and ancient highland pastures evoke the hardship and beauty of Spain's rural past. In Cantabria, walkers enjoy the lower mountains and rustic villages of the Parque Natural de Saja-Besaya. The Cordillera's most popular and challenging area lies at its heart: the Picos de Europa, composed of three magnificent limestone massifs. When planning your walks, keep in mind that the times we quote are actual walking times and do not include rest or meal stops.

Palaeolithic cave art is found extensively in and around the Cordillera (see the boxed text 'Europe's First Artists', p187). Man's destructive hand appears in the Neolithic period (4000–2400 BC), with the spread of agriculture and livestock domestication provoking the first forest clearing. Around 2000 BC, immigrants from the north introduced metal technology and copper was actively mined. As the Roman Empire expanded, the Romans eagerly sought to control the Cordillera's wealth of iron, gold and copper and viciously subdued native tribes in campaigns from 29 to 13 BC. The area's 8th-century Arab presence is more legendary than factual, but nonetheless helped justify and initiate the Christian Reconquest of the peninsula. In 722 the Asturian King Pelayo won the first (legendary) battle against the Muslims at Covadonga (Cave of the Holy Mother) in the Picos

JOSE PLACER

The rugged Macizo Central in the Parque Nacional de los Picos de Europa

- Walking in pastures and past ancient abandoned shepherds' cabins in the Parque Natural de Somiedo (p192)

- Following 2000-year-old Roman highways through the forests of the Parque Natural de Saja-Besaya (p197)

- Watching the indefatigable chamois as they leap around the steep and rocky mountain slopes of the Parque Nacional de los Picos de Europa (p201)

- Contemplating the awesome, sheer-walled spectacle of the Garganta del Cares gorge on the Picos de Europa Circuit (p205)

de Europa. Over time, the cave and its magnificent waterfall evolved into a politico-religious symbol and an exceedingly popular pilgrimage site. Though the centuries-old cyclical practice of bringing the flocks from the low winter pastures of Castilla to the high

Europe's First Artists

Imagine stepping back in time to Palaeolithic Europe (35,000–10,000 BC). Bone-chilling cold hits you (snow remains perpetually at 700m to 1000m) and the land is filled with almost mythical creatures – hairy mammoth and rhinoceros – and huge herds of bison, horses and deer: a hunter's paradise. You've arrived at a pivotal moment in human history. Along the Cantabrian coast, in the Pyrenees and southern France, the first and longest-lasting art form, cave painting, is being developed.

Using magnesium or carbon to create black lines and ochre or iron oxides to create brown, red, orange and yellow earth tones, artists filled walls and ceilings with animals, human figures, isolated hands and various symbols. Using the natural relief of the rock to convey a sense of volume, the movement and realism of the naturalistic animal figures richly contrasts with the distortion of faces and abstraction of symbols in these complex works.

West of Santander is Spain's most famous cave, Altamira. The site is virtually closed to visitors, but a complete recreation of the famous artwork, opened in 2001, provides an excellent sense of its grandeur. The many other caves open to visitors include Santimamiñe, 35 minutes from Bilbao towards the coast; El Castillo, one of four caves in Puente Viesgo 30km south of Santander; and El Buxu at the foot of the Picos de Europa just outside Cangas de Onís. Ask for the free brochure *Routes Through Prehistoric Asturian Art* in Asturian tourist offices.

summer pastures continues, transhumance (the oldest continuous economic activity of the Cordillera) is in decline.

Many of the indigenous forests of the lower slopes were felled to supply iron production, construction and fuel needs, opening up the land to new species of conifers and eucalyptus, the latter brought to the Cantabrian coast 160 years ago. The 20th century brought the most aggressive transformation of the landscape as technology made it easier to extract coal, ore and lumber, and to enter ecologically fragile areas – although, thankfully, conservation efforts now protect many areas.

NATURAL HISTORY

Between 360 and 245 million years ago the rich coal deposits of the central Cordillera were formed from decaying ferns and moss pressed between layers of limestone and sand. Fossilised remnants of marine invertebrates – corals, crustaceans and molluscs – are also embedded in the rock. Forty million years ago, the African and European tectonic plates collided. The Iberian subplate, sandwiched between the two, wrinkled and bulged, creating first the Pyrenees and then the Cordillera. Limestone (karstic) landscapes are among the most significant geological features of the Cordillera and are characterised by dramatic, bare, open rocks, great high depressions and mountains riddled with underground waterways, interior vertical cavities and *simas* (caves; see the boxed text 'Caving in the Picos', p201). Glaciers dating from two million to 10,000 years ago created U-shaped valleys, polished walls, and dumped moraine.

The collision of Atlantic and Mediterranean climates as well as dramatic variation in altitude accounts for the Cordillera's wealth of flora and fauna. Up to 500m along the valley floors and riverways, forests include mountain ash, evergreen oak, common oak, beech, linden, chestnut, elm, alder, hazelnut, hawthorn, willow, maple and cherry trees. Shrubs include blackberry, sloe berry, wild roses and honeysuckle. In the wetter, northern valleys of Asturias, expect to see marsh orchids, globe flowers, ragged robins and marsh helleborines. In the more Mediterranean southern valleys, purple orchids and tassel hyacinths fill the meadows and the forests include strawberry trees and cork oaks. From 500m to 1700m the plant life responds to the shorter summers and early frosts. Beech, birch, mountain ash, holly and holm oaks dominate the forests. In the subalpine zone from 1700m to 2300m, you'll find beech and birch trees as well as juniper clinging to rock walls. The alpine area (2300m and above) supports small plants, including glacier fescue, columbine and toadflax.

CORDILLERA CANTÁBRICA

Cordillera Cantábrica

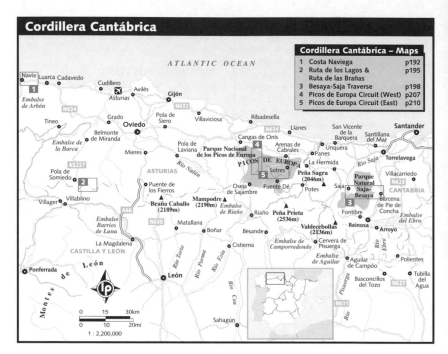

Cordillera Cantábrica – Maps

In the forests, mammal species include brown bears, wild boar, mountain cats, wolves and red and roe deer. Along the river banks, otters and muskrats dwell with kingfishers and wagtails. In the skies goshawks, golden eagles, kestrels, common buzzards, griffon vultures and peregrine falcons dominate. Closer to the trees, listen for green and spotted woodpeckers as well as tawny, horned and barn owls. In rocky areas, tiny birds such as hedge and rock sparrows make their nests.

CLIMATE

Part of the Spanish region called 'España Verde' (Green Spain), the middle and lower elevations of the Cordillera have an Atlantic climate of temperate, wet weather. In winter and spring Atlantic cold fronts and air masses

Oso Pardo, the Brown Bear

Until two centuries ago, the brown bear (known in Spanish as *oso pardo*) inhabited nearly all of the Iberian Peninsula in large numbers, but uncontrolled hunting, habitat destruction and poisoning have caused the bears' progressive decline. Today, counting the 10 bears in the Pyrenees, the Cordillera Cantábrica has the greatest bear population. Their habitat covers 5000 sq km divided into two zones, unfortunately isolated from one another. The eastern zone has between 20 and 25 bears; the western, 50 to 65.

Asturias, in the middle of the protected area, shelters 75% of the population and is the region most committed to the bears' recuperation. It has founded the Bear Foundation of Asturias (Fundación Oso de Asturias) in Casa del Oso in Proaza and established areas of protection, policing hunters. The region also compensates landowners for damage to their land caused by the bears.

bring heavy rain and snow at high elevations. Winds tend to arrive from the northwest. The southern slopes and valleys have a drier, warmer climate, though anywhere in the Cordillera the weather can change rapidly. In general, snow leaves the lower slopes in April and May; at the highest elevations, snow may persist during June.

INFORMATION
Maps
IGN's 1:200,000 *Asturias, Cantabria* and *Cordillera Cantábrica* maps are widely available and useful for orientation.

Map details for the walks are in Maps under Planning for each walk.

Books
Robin Walker's *Walking in the Cordillera Cantábrica* (available in Spanish as *Por la Cordillera Cantábrica*) is worthwhile. Widely available in English within Spain are Tino Pertierra and Eduardo Garcia's interesting cultural guide *Asturias: A Journey into Paradise* and Mike Bent's *Exploring the Cantabrian Coast* (the former in Oviedo and the latter, Santander). In Spanish, the best general guide is Anaya's *Picos de Europa y Cordillera Cantábrica*, by Ramón Martín, with general background information and car and walking routes. For additional route ideas try Juan Luis Somoano and Erik Pérez's *50 Excursiones Selectas de la Montaña Asturiana* and Fernando Obregón's three-volume *50 Rutas en Cantabria*.

Place Names
Bable, the local Asturian dialect, inconsistently appears on signs and maps, especially in the Parque Natural de Somiedo and Picos de Europa. It's easy to match Bable and Castilian names if they vary on maps and signs.

Weather Information
Reports in Spanish are available from park information centres listed under Information Sources later in this chapter.

GATEWAYS
Oviedo (Asturias) and Santander (Cantabria) are the most convenient major cities.

Both make excellent bases for excursions in and around the Cordillera. The city of León (see p354) also can be used as a southern access town.

Oviedo
Oviedo is a charming, slightly inland city. The **tourist office** (☎ 985 21 33 85; w *www .infoasturias.com; Uria 64; open 9am-2pm & 4.30pm-6.30pm Mon-Fri, 9.30am-3pm & 4pm-7pm Sat & Sun*) provides useful information for walkers. Ask for the free 1:75,000 *Picos de Europa* map and the detailed brochure *Mountain Routes*, which gives excellent ideas for walking in the area. The best bookshops are **Librería Cervantes** (*Doctor Casal 9*) and **Librería La Palma** (*Rúa 6*). Overall, the former is better but the latter has a better English-language section.

Places to Stay & Eat In the historical quarter, you'll find decent rooms at **Hostal Los Arcos** (☎ 985 21 47 73; *Magdalena 3; doubles with/without bathroom €39.50/30.50*). Near the train and bus stations is **Hostal Berdasco** (☎ 985 22 54 84; *Fray Ceferino 9, 1st floor; rooms from €30*); the owner enjoys bargaining and will strike a deal. The best value dining is at the **Restaurante Fontàn** (*Plaza Ayuntamiento*), with a varied and economical €6 *menú* (fixed-price meal). There's delicious food and terrace dining at **Restaurante Marcelino** (*Campoamor 17*).

Getting There & Away Buses run by **ALSA** (☎ 902 42 22 42) connect Madrid and Oviedo (€24.75, 5½ hours, 15 a day) as do Renfe trains (€32.65/36.15, 8½/six hours, three a day). By car, take the A6 tollway from Madrid to Benavente (northwest) and then the N630 to León. Continue on the A66 to Oviedo.

Between Santander and Oviedo, **Turytrans** (☎ 942 22 16 85) runs a regular service (€10.70, 2½ hours, nine a day).

Santander
This large seaport city offers all services and last-minute supplies. The **city tourist office** (☎ 942 20 30 00; *Jardines de Pereda*) provides good local information. The **regional tourist**

office (☎ *942 31 07 08;* W *www.turismo.cant abria.org; Plaza Velarde 5; open 9am-9pm daily July–mid-Sept, 9am-1pm & 4pm-7pm daily rest of year)* gives accommodation and transport information as well as free brochures on walking in Cantabria and Liébana (near Potes) and the Picos de Europa.

Librería Estudio *(Avenida Calvo Sotelo 21)* stocks English titles as well as walking guides and maps. The sports shops **Límite** *(Arrabal 20)* and **Eiger** *(Santa Lucía 21)* are helpful and well stocked.

Places to Stay & Eat In the historical quarter, **Pensión La Corza** (☎ *942 21 29 50; Hernán Cortés 25, 3rd floor; doubles with/ without bathroom €45/33)* has good rooms and nearby **Restaurante Versalles** *(Peña Herboso 15)* serves a good €8.50 *menú.* Near the bus and train stations is **Pensión Angelines** (☎ *942 31 25 84; Atilano Rodríguez 9, 1st floor; singles/doubles without bathroom €18/27).*

Getting There & Away Buses run by **Continental** (☎ *942 22 53 18)* connect Madrid and Santander (€21.65/28.75, seven/five hours, six a day) as do Renfe trains (€32/35, eight/seven hours, three a day). **Brittany Ferry** (☎ *942 36 06 11)* connects Plymouth (England) and Santander (€225 return, €390 with car, 24 hours, twice weekly). By car from Madrid, take the A1 to Burgos and then the N623 north.

Costa Naviega

Duration	6–6½ hours
Distance	20.5km
Difficulty	easy–moderate
Start	Km 516 on the N634
Finish	Navia
Nearest Town	Navia (p190)
Transport	bus, train

Summary A coastal walk at the western end of Asturias taking in cliffs, beaches, woodlands and pastures while travelling from village to village

Running parallel to the Cordillera Cantábrica and separated from these mountains by a narrow band of relatively flat plains known locally as *rasas,* the Asturian coast extends east to west for nearly 400km. The coast's jagged cliffs, golden sandy beaches, stony coves and turquoise waters are interspersed with fishing villages laid out attractively around tidal estuaries. On the western fringe the highlight section is the Costa Naviega. Following in the footsteps of medieval pilgrims on their way to Santiago de Compostela, the walk connects the historical whaling and fishing ports of Puerto de Vega and Navia using cliff-side trails and passing through sections of dense woodland, streamways, cultivated pastures and pristine beaches (good for a swim!). The walk also passes by a protected dune area and estuary where the Río Barayo empties into the sea. The rich dune ecosystem around the Playa de Frejulfe merits mention for its diverse flora and as an important habitat for gulls and cormorants.

The walk is rated easy–moderate owing to its length and the need to follow the directions carefully. Sporadically marked with yellow arrows and yellow-and-white slashes, the walk is laid out here from east to west.

PLANNING
When to Walk
Owing to the coast's temperate climate, the walk is feasible year-round. The coast receives heavy precipitation (1000mm to 1300mm per year) and the driest months are July to September.

Maps
IGN's 1:25,000 topographical map Nos 11-III *Navia* and 11-IV *Luarca* cover the route.

Information Sources
Navia's **tourist office** (☎ *985 47 37 95;* W *www.ayto-navia.es)* provides information on local services and a brochure which briefly describes the route. Each June the mountaineering group **Peña Furada** (☎ *985 47 43 68)* organises a group Costa Naviega walk.

NEAREST TOWN
Navia
On the right bank of the Río Navia, Navia has a long history that is best preserved in the

narrow streets of the historical quarter, the fragment of medieval slate wall left standing and its monument honouring the town's emigrants. Some 25% of the population left in the early 20th century seeking their fortune in the Americas. Many came back as wealthy 'Indianos' (the nickname for emigrants to the Americas) and built stately homes.

Navia has all services including a bookshop, **Librería La Villa** (Real 17), and several **markets**. To stay overnight in town both **Pensión Cantábrico** (☎ 985 47 41 77; Mariano Luiña; singles/doubles with bathroom €15/30) and **Pensión San Francisco** (☎ 985 63 13 51; San Francisco; singles/doubles without bathroom €12/24) are centrally located. The latter and **Sidrería La Magaya** (Reguera 18) prepare good set meals for €6.

Getting There & Away Navia lies 118km from Oviedo and 70km from the Asturias airport at Piedras Blancas, northwest of Oviedo. **ALSA** (☎ 902 42 22 42; ⓦ www.alsa.es) buses run between Oviedo and Navia (€8.10, two hours, seven a day) as do highly scenic **FEVE** (☎ 985 47 38 21) trains (€6.15, three hours, three a day). By car from Oviedo, drive west along the N634 to Navia.

GETTING TO/FROM THE WALK

From Navia either take a **taxi** (☎ 985 63 02 18; €8) to the trailhead or get off the bus or the FEVE train in Villapedre. From Villapedre walk east 1.6km along the busy N634 to the trailhead, 600m beyond the Km 516 highway marker (direction Oviedo).

THE WALK (see map p192)

From the N634, the route begins where there's a left-hand detour onto a sealed road with a sign marked 'NV7/Puerto de Vega 3'. Take the asphalt road and in 400m, where the pine grove ends, turn right onto a grassy path. Continue without detours and after descending five minutes, turn left onto a footpath when the trail makes a pronounced right turn. Passing through a mixed wood of pine, eucalyptus and chestnuts, reach and walk around a pasture with a house and fruit trees. The wood thickens and the path descends to the Río Barayo. Follow its course for 10 minutes

until it reaches a dirt road, then turn left. Ascending, pass a **lookout** above the river's mouth and the picturesque Playa de Barayo.

Once above, take a stone trail, adjacent to the car park, and 200m later, when the trail veers left, continue straight on a trail heading towards the coast. For almost 15 minutes continue along narrow trails flanked by ferns, gorse and pastures. After a little pasture look for a solitary, small pine grove to the left and head towards it, taking a wider trail. The trail winds above the small cove of Los Anaos. Instead of continuing straight with the trail, turn right onto another. In 200m the path dies out at a pasture. Cross the pasture and turn right upon reaching a lane. This lane also dies out at a pasture which you cross. Turn right again at the next lane. Five minutes later, above a cove, turn left at a sign marked 'Refugio de Caza'. The trail shortly gives way to another, wider trail flanked (on the left) by a wire fence. In 300m reach a crossroads and turn right. After 5 minutes, where the trail nears the ocean, leave the trail for a left-hand footpath that descends to a stone beach. Continue for 1.3km, along the cliffs, to **Puerto de Vega**.

At the village's first house, turn left onto the cement road, passing the ruins of the defensive walls used to protect the town from pirates in 1586. Descend to the charming port. The ethnographic museum, the Mirador de la Riva (which documents the town's whaling tradition) and the 18th-century Iglesia Santa Marina are worth visiting. Head straight towards the shore dotted with **restaurants** specialising in seafood (try Restaurante La Marina) and turn left up the ascending street. Reaching the Casino, head right onto the NV2 towards Navia. At the next crossroads continue straight. Reaching the last house on the right, turn right onto a dirt lane heading towards the sea. In 400m, after passing a stone wall on the left, take a right-hand footpath and join the cliff-side trail. Soon you will see a small island, Isla de Soirana, just off the coast. Reaching a fork, head left through a eucalyptus grove and, after a gate, turn left and then immediately right onto a dirt lane. After passing a small chapel, the trail joins a sealed road through the houses of Soirana. Continue to

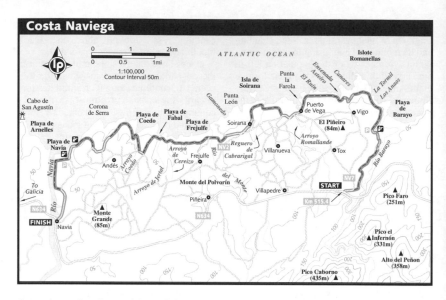

Costa Naviega

the main road and turn right and then right again onto the asphalt road leading to the Playa de Frejulfe.

After 300m, where the asphalt road enters a pine grove, take a left-hand lane that peters out in a pasture. Continue round the pasture's right side and turn right onto the lane which heads to the Playa de Frejulfe. At the extreme left of the dunes, by the beach's car park, take the ascending footpath. After passing a cement-block shed, turn left towards a pine grove. In 15 minutes reach a crossroads and continue straight through pastures until reaching a perpendicular lane. Turn right and head back to the cliffs through the woods. The trail passes above the isolated **Playa de Fabal**. On the beach's western side, the defensive walls of a pre-Roman fort are discernible. Cross a pasture and at the next crossroads, take a left-hand trail that ascends and heads away from the coast through cultivated fields. Reaching a small sealed road, turn right and head towards houses. When the road makes a hairpin left turn, continue straight onto a grassy lane that soon reaches a fork. Veer left, descend to a lane and turn left (turning right leads to the small Playa de Coedo). Ascend

for 200m and where the lane curves left, head right (not straight) through a pasture.

After passing a cove the trail leads to the houses of Andés. Take the sealed road and at the next three crossroads, turn right. By the granary of the first house you come to, leave the sealed road for a right-hand lane. In 300m, turn left and enjoy views of the Faro de Navia lighthouse. At the next fork (in 300m), head right to the **mirador** (lookout) above the Playa de Cascareiras. Continue for 10 minutes along the sealed road enjoying views of the Playa de Navia and the entrance of Navia's estuary to another mirador. Descend to the beach's car park, cross it and then take an elevated pedestrian walkway that in 1.5km leads to the centre of Navia.

Parque Natural de Somiedo

Somiedo, from the Latin *sumetum* meaning 'land of elevated mountains', lies in the southwest corner of Asturias. Established in 1988 and in 2000 named a Biosphere Reserve, the nature park covers some 300 sq km of country featuring lush oak and beech woods, high ancient pastures and low-lying settled valleys. The abrupt relief is typical of the Cordillera, with the highest peak, El Cornón, at 2194m and the lowest valley area, Aguasmestas, at 395m. Glaciers formed the highest valleys, leaving behind the greatest number of glacial lakes in Asturias. All are connected by canals for hydroelectric exploitation. Looking from above, five valleys (Valle de Saliencia, Valle de Lago, Valle del Somiedo, Valle de Perlunes and Valle del Pigüeña) neatly divide the region into zones which also correspond with village organisation.

The park status of Somiedo has helped to save its valuable natural and human resources. Only decades ago, the area's population was 6000. Today 1800 people live in the 35 villages and hamlets of the valleys and some 50 families continue the traditions of transhumance, moving their animals in an annual cycle from low (winter) to high (summer) pastures.

As part of its well-conceived conservation strategy, the park has different zones of usage (indicated on the recommended map). Each of the valleys has routes marked with yellow-and-white markers and wooden signs give route numbers.

Two marked day-walks are presented in this section. Both start from Valle de Lago and ascend to the summer pastures. En route they pass numerous examples of popular architecture: *brañas*, huts of the highland cowherds (who are known locally as *vaqueiros*), *teitos*, thatch-roofed stone cabins (broom is used for the thatch) and abandoned *corros*. The last are circular stone buildings topped with stone and are the shepherds' most ancient form of summer shelter. They were grouped in pairs and the second building was set aside for young animals. In the valleys, *hórreos* and *paneras*, wooden granaries, are typical.

Unusual floral species include the fragile Somiedo centaury *(Centaurium somedanum)* and the *corona del rey (Saxifraga longifolia)*, found only in the Pyrenees and Somiedo (near Valle de Lago). The park is a key sanctuary for the brown bear and the beautiful,

local *vaca roxa*, or red cow, also called the Asturiana de los Valles.

PLANNING
When to Walk
The climate is typical of the Cordillera's north face with high humidity and relatively temperate conditions, and the most stable months are July to September. Snow falls above 1200m from November to April.

Maps & Books
The park's 1:35,000 *Parque Natural Somiedo* topographical map and the Adrados 1:60,000 and 1:30,000 *Somiedo* maps are recommended. Juan Martín's *Somiedo*, available in Pola de Somiedo and Oviedo, is the best Spanish-language guide. Maps are available at the park's information centre and Pola de Somiedo's only bookshop.

Information Sources
The park's **information centre** (☎ 985 76 37 58; open 10am-2.30pm & 4pm-9pm daily mid-June–mid-Sept, 10am-2pm & 4pm-7pm daily mid-Sept–mid-June), in Pola de Somiedo's village centre, has maps and useful leaflets, in Spanish only, describing the park's 12 marked routes. Free guided walks are also available.

ACCESS TOWNS
Pola de Somiedo
With 90 inhabitants, Pola de Somiedo is the area's largest village, boasting a **market**, bank, pharmacy, fountain, ethnographic museum, health centre and public phone. The best accommodation options are **Casa Cesáreo** (☎ 985 76 39 58; singles/doubles with bathroom €15/30), **Pensión Urogallo** (☎ 985 76 37 44; singles/doubles with bathroom €20/36) and **Camping Lagos de Somiedo** (☎ 985 76 34 04; camping per person/tent €3.40/4). All are centrally located in the small village. The Urogallo and **Restaurante Miño** both serve meals – the latter only at midday – for €10 and €8, respectively.

Getting There & Away Buses run by **ALSA** (☎ 902 42 22 42) connect Oviedo and Pola de Somiedo (€5.80, two hours, two daily Monday to Friday, one daily Saturday and Sunday). By car from Oviedo, head west on the N634 to Cornellana and then south, first along the AS15 and then the AS227.

Valle de Lago

Camping Lagos de Somiedo *(☎ 985 76 37 76; camping per person/car/tent €3.50/ 3.50/4)* has a shop the size of a shoebox and a simple **bar-restaurant** as well as maps and information on the park. The management speaks English. Two recommended hostels are **L'Auterio** *(☎ 985 76 38 76; singles/doubles with bathroom €24/36)* and the **Casa Aldea La Corona** *(☎ 985 76 37 11; singles/doubles with bathroom €36/48)* which has excellent views. Local culinary delights include *pote*, a vegetable and meat stew, beef cold cuts and steaks of the *vaca roxa*. Meals are good and economical at **Casa Cobrana** and **La Quintana**; both offer *menús* for under €7. No other services are available in the village.

Getting There & Away Once in Pola, either hitchhike or take a **taxi** *(☎ 985 76 36 71; €12)* with Simón to Valle de Lago 8km away where the routes begin.

Ruta de los Lagos

Duration	6½–7½ hours
Distance	23.6km
Difficulty	moderate
Start/Finish	Valle de Lago (p194)
Transport	taxi
Summary	Verdant pastures, thatch-roofed cowherds' cabins and bare peaks surround the gentle ascent to the isolated Lagos de Saliencia through a region containing the Cordillera's greatest concentration of glacial lakes

This gentle route meanders through the high pastures around Valle de Lago and passes four glacial lakes. An optional finish increases the walk's length. Carry enough water for the day as the only options are in Valle and at a trough en route.

THE WALK (see map p195)
The first segment to the Lago del Valle takes roughly 1½ hours. The route begins at the upper end of Valle de Lago village from a small car park and follows the yellow-and-white slashes of the PRAS15. Walk 800m to the end of Valle de Lago through the houses of L'Auterio and when the road curves sharp left, continue straight along a dirt path through the lush valley past cultivated fields, hazel trees and broom. Soon the first **teito** comes into view. As the valley narrows, ignore a trail (with the sign 'A Lagos de Saliencia') heading left. The walk returns along this trail later. At the next crossroads a sign indicates 'Lago del Valle' (left). Turn left (you'll return from the right on the Alternative Route). After briefly flattening out, the route climbs steeply (along cement) to the valley's high point near a wall and shepherds' hut. From here, you can see the 24-hectare Lago del Valle surrounded by mountains.

Continuing through broom, the route follows the lake's left shore (north). Reaching a low stone wall, turn left (northwest), joining the PRAS15. The trail heads uphill and back towards the Valle de Lago, offering impressive views of the valley as it climbs. On the way, just past an animal trough (with potable water), fork left and five minutes later, at a rocky outcrop, ignore a descending trail. Twenty minutes from the outcrop reach a crossroads and turn right (left returns you to Valle de Lago as described later). The trail ascends northeast to a pass and then turns right and traverses the pastures of **Vega de Camayor**; the trail's exit from the *vega* (pasture or meadow) is clearly visible ahead. Near the *vega*'s limit, the trail ascends through a series of small rocks and then descends to cross a small valley and field. At the field's far end, follow the lane straight ahead (uphill) and ignore a right-hand trail that descends to Lago Cerveriz. On reaching the summit of a rise (marked with signs), turn right along a stony footpath. Follow it southeast for 10 minutes until you have a view of Lago Negro o Calabazosa. Backtrack to the dirt road and turn right; the basin of Lago de la Mina (dry in summer) is below. In five minutes, when the road sharply curves and is hemmed in by a

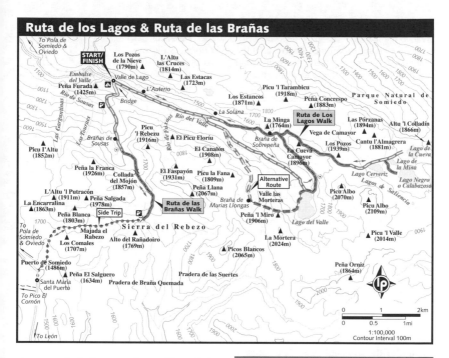

Ruta de los Lagos & Ruta de las Brañas

stone guardrail, there are views of Lago de la Cueva. Traces of iron mining are still apparent along the lake shores.

Retrace your steps back to the crossroads above the valley. Instead of turning left to the lake (and the Alternative Route) continue straight along a wider trail for 1km and then ignore an ascending right-hand trail and descend to the village in a further 4.5km.

Alternative Route: Via Braña de Murias Llongas
2½hours, 4.5km

To add 4.5km to the walk, turn left at the crossroads above the valley and return to the lake, continue along its western shore. Pass the lake's two retaining walls, turn right and follow a low, ascending wall (a feeder canal) to **Braña de Murias Llongas**, a shepherds' hut and *teito*. There is a marked trail on a lower contour but it has no views. Bear right onto a dirt road that passes *teitos* and beech woods to rejoin the main route back to Valle de Lago.

Ruta de las Brañas

Duration	5 hours
Distance	14km
Difficulty	moderate–demanding
Start/Finish	Valle de Lago (p194)
Transport	taxi
Summary	On the remote frontier between Asturias and Castilla y León, discover ancient shepherds' cabins and highland pastures

Beginning in Valle, the route ascends to the Collado del Mojón pass (1857m), an impressive watchtower of the Sierra del Rebezo, and continues to another scenic pass before returning to the starting point. For a harder walk it's possible to proceed on to a *vaqueiro* village, Santa María del Puerto. Both the described walk and the side trip to Santa María are rated moderate–demanding for the challenging, steep ascents. Carry plenty of water; there's only one fountain en route.

CORDILLERA CANTÁBRICA

THE WALK (see map p195)

Head to the information board near the fountain in the centre of Valle de Lago. From the fountain, take the waymarked cement road (the PRAS16 with yellow-and-white slashes) over the bridge, adjacent to a mill, spanning the Río del Valle, and ascend left towards the church. Before reaching it, bear left. The sealed road soon gives way to a dirt lane winding its way among fields.

Ascend along the lane which briefly enters a beech forest before reaching a marvellous, natural balcony with excellent views of the valley below. The high pastures of the valley to the south are your target. Continue on the lane which first passes various shepherds' cabins and then rises to the **Brañas de Sousas** pastures, roughly an hour from the start.

A wooden sign indicates that four hours remain (a generous estimate) to the Puerto de Somiedo. Looking south from the *corros* in the Brañas de Sousas, two peaks dominate the cirque. The trail heads to the base of the right-hand peak. The dirt lane makes a steep ascent southeast among broom, heather and wild roses. After 20 minutes, fork left (the right fork leads to a potable spring) at the summit of the rise and, 400m later, cross a scree section. Now on a path, ignore a left-hand trail. Reward yourself with a view of *corros* and Valle de Lago to the right. In less than an hour, the path reaches the **Collado del Mojón** (Collau del Muñón) pass on the border between Asturias and Castilla y León. *Rebecos* (chamois) often skip through this area.

Heading into Castilla y León, the path crosses a series of depressions and grassy mounds and in 10 minutes reaches a larger, elongated depression framed by the spectacular Sierra del Rebezo. Turn left (southeast) and ascend to a pasture with crumbling huts. Before reaching the ruins, the path veers gently left and then immediately right (south) onto an ascending trail.

Soon you reach a narrow pass with Peña Blanca's elongated ridge extending off to the right (west) and excellent views of a large valley ahead. Here, either turn around and retrace your footsteps or continue for another 1½ hours to Santa María del Puerto (see Side Trip).

Side Trip: Santa María del Puerto

3 hours, 8.6km

To reach the village of Santa María del Puerto (1486m), continue west from the pass along Peña Blanca's southern flank for 35 minutes (1.7km) to a wire fence. Cross the fence and descend steeply into Asturias and Santa María. The village has a **bar**, **shop** and fountain as well as the **Restaurante Hotel El Coronel** (☎ 985 76 37 00; *singles/ doubles with bathroom €23/39*), where meals cost €7.50.

Parque Natural de Saja-Besaya

From Roman roads to shepherds' wild haunts and dense beech forests, the Parque Natural de Saja-Besaya, created in 1988, offers a combination of history and infrequently visited open spaces. Nestled between two of Cantabria's great north–south rivers, the Río Saja and the Río Besaya, the park is a 245-sq-km island in the middle of Spain's largest *reserva nacional de caza* (national hunting reserve), which occupies 30% of Cantabria.

The park's mountains are rounded, unlike the pinnacle-shaped Picos de Europa, and reach their highest at its southern limit: Iján (2084m) and El Cordel (2040m). The J-shaped park contains two sierras (the Sierra de Bárcena Mayor and the Sierra del Cordel) and numerous permanently green valleys formed by the Ríos Besaya and Saja and their tributaries: Argoza/Lodar, Queriendo, Bayones, Cambillas and Bijoz. Park flora and fauna is characteristic of the Cordillera: hill (Atlantic shrubs and oak) and mountain (beech, holly and birch) species (found between 500m and 1600m) dominate the area.

PLANNING
When to Walk

July and August are the warmest and driest months, but May to June as well as September are suitable. Avoid October to January, the hunting season.

Maps

The park itself has no topographic maps. IGN's 1:25,000 map Nos 83-I *Molledo*, 82-II *Los Tojos* and 83-IV *Espinilla* are best for the walk described.

Books

Two Spanish publications are relevant to the area: Juan Miguel Gil and Fernando Obregón's *El Sendero de la Reserva de Saja* details the GR71; Jesús García's *Guía del Parque Natural Saja-Besaya* has an excellent flora and fauna section. In Santander, Librería Estudio publishes guides in Spanish to the Parque Natural de Saja-Besaya.

Information Sources

For information on the area, use W www.saja nansa.com.

Warning

The park lies within a national hunting reserve. Hunting (especially of wild boar) is popular in the late autumn and winter and prohibited in spring and summer. The reserve is divided into sectors which are opened periodically and listed in local newspapers.

Besaya-Saja Traverse

Duration	2 days
Distance	33.1km
Difficulty	moderate
Start	Bárcena de Pie de Concha (p197)
Finish	Saja (p197)
Transport	bus, train

Summary Walk from the Río Besaya to the Río Saja along Roman highways and ancient, stone-paved lanes; cross the Parque Natural de Saja-Besaya through lush forests and tiny villages

This full traverse of the park follows part of the red-and-white waymarked GR71 (Cantabria's first Sendero de Gran Recorrido, or GR, long-distance trail). The GR71 begins its eight-day, 127.5km trajectory from Bárcena

de Pie de Concha (where we begin) and leads to the foot of the Picos de Europa at Potes and west to Sotres. The section of the GR71 that we describe traverses the park in two days and frequently uses *empedrados*, stone-paved lanes that once neatly linked villages. Two recommended side trips head south from Bárcena Mayor village, where Day 1 ends and Day 2 begins, into the park's interior. Both are feasible on a third day.

NEAREST TOWNS
Bárcena de Pie de Concha

This small village (293m) has a **bar-shop**, **market**, pharmacy, bank and public phone. Sleeping and dining options are limited: **Casa Ferrero** (☎ 942 84 13 03; *singles/doubles with bathroom €18/36*) serves meals for €7.

Getting There & Away Fifty-three kilometres south of Santander, Bárcena is easy to access. **García** (☎ 942 36 28 54) buses from Santander to Bárcena (via Reinosa) run frequently (€4.50, one hour, 11 daily Monday to Friday, four daily Saturday and Sunday). Renfe trains connect Santander and Bárcena on the C1 Santander–Reinosa line (€2.50, one hour, 12 a day). By car from Santander, head southwest on the N611 towards Torrelavega and then south towards Reinosa.

Saja

Casa de Labranza Seijos (☎ 942 74 12 23; *doubles with shared bathroom €24*), over the river from the end of the walk, offers clean, ample rooms. Dining is limited to **Restaurante La Florida** 300m out of the village. Set meals cost €9.

Getting There & Away From Saja to Cabezón de la Sal, public transport options are limited but from there it's easy. To Cabezón either hitchhike, take a **Palomera** (☎ 942 70 05 78) bus (€8.50, one hour, every Monday at 8.15am) or a **taxi** (☎ 942 70 05 18) for €20. From Cabezón de la Sal take Palomera's Potes–Santander bus (€2.30, 45 minutes, three daily) to return to Santander. By car, return on the northbound N625 to Cabezón de la Sal and then northeast on the N634 to Torrelavega and finally to Santander via the A67.

THE WALK
Day 1: Bárcena de Pie de Concha to Bárcena Mayor

5½–6½ hours, 20.3km

Water is available in the first villages along the way, but dries up after the route opens up to the ridge crest.

Walk through Bárcena de Pie de Concha following the signs for 'Calzada Romana & Pujayo' and crossing the Río Besaya and the elongated one-street neighbourhood of Pie de Concha. Sporadic GR71 signs (red-and-white slashes) appear and 900m later, the route passes a fountain and a *rollo*, a pillar where punishments were meted out to local malefactors.

In 100m, a left-hand detour leads to Cantabria's best-preserved Roman *calzada* (highway). It runs for 5km from Pie de Concha to Somaconcha further south and retains original stone paving and diagonal drainage canals. Even old carriage-wheel marks are visible. Possibly of military origin, it was used until the 18th century to connect Castilla and Santander.

Continue for 500m and fork right onto a road that reaches **Pujayo** in another 1.5km. From the church head straight and then turn right into the main plaza lined with balconied houses. Every 10 August the village celebrates La Maya, San Lorenzo's feast day. Amid general festivities, the young men of the village cut down a beech limb, mount it in the village square, add grease to the trunk and then compete to scale it.

Cross the plaza, exit left along a street and 100m later reach a fork. Veer right, taking a slowly ascending cement road (that quickly converts to dirt) for 5km up the Barranco de Vaocerezo to a ridge with spectacular views of the valleys and foothills of the Cordillera. Grazing cattle (most likely the area's local breed, *tudanca*, which are grey and black with widely separated horns) and horses roam semi-freely in these pastures.

Reaching the crest, continue ascending 800m to a grassy path on the left that gradually circles around to **Pico de Obios** (1222m) topped with a fire tower and antenna. Continue west along the summit on a descending dirt road and in 500m reach a corral on the right. Take a left-hand trail that undulates for 3.7km (roughly an hour), crossing the **Sierra de Bárcena** to the foot of the conic Pico la Guarda (1085m) and the remnants of a cement-block cabin.

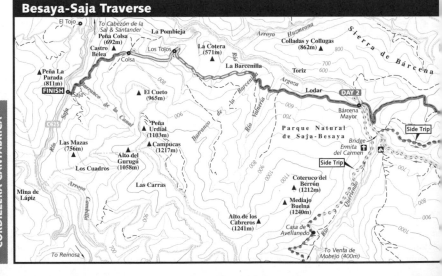

The next portion can be confusing; follow the directions closely. From the base of Pico la Guarda, where the lane curves right, leave the lane along a left-hand (west) track marked with an arrow and 'Bárcena Mayor' (4km is indicated but the distance is closer to 5km). In 400m, before the dirt track reaches a field, take another trail that heads north (right) up a bank. Continue ascending briefly, then leave the trail to descend northwest along a path (which sometimes disappears) parallel to a low stone wall. When the wall turns left, continue straight ahead descending cross-country through grass, gorse and heather to a series of horse trails that cross your path at right angles. Head right (north), taking one of these trails, and aim for the clearing (a round hill) in the oak grove below. Once at the clearing, descend left (west) through the low banks of a narrow and, in summer, dry stream bed which has been made into a makeshift trail that is soon blazed.

The path zigzags through an enchanting beech and oak forest and joins an ancient stone-paved road that, for lack of use and water erosion, is littered with loose stones. Continue 3.5km to **Bárcena Mayor**.

Bárcena Mayor

An EU grant for economically depressed areas gave the picturesque Bárcena a massive face-lift and now tourism is king. The **Albergue de Bárcena Mayor** (☎ 605 14 06 85; dorm beds €9, doubles without bathroom €24) is cheapest and serves a €9 menú. **Venta La Franca** (☎ 942 70 60 67; doubles with bathroom €45) has a good €11 menú. For a meal along the river, try **Mesón El Puente**. There's a free **camping ground** (without showers) 1km south of the village.

Side Trip: Venta de Mobejo

4½ hours, 14.5km
This unmarked forest walk runs partly along an ancient Roman highway, known as the Camino de Reinosa, that connected Castilla to Cantabria and along which, until the 19th century, Castilian wine and wheat were exchanged for Cantabrian carts, barrels and farm tools. Take water with you.

After leaving Bárcena via its only stone bridge, veer left onto a dirt road, passing an information panel which shows the Bárcena Mayor–Ozcaba route via Venta de Mobejo described here.

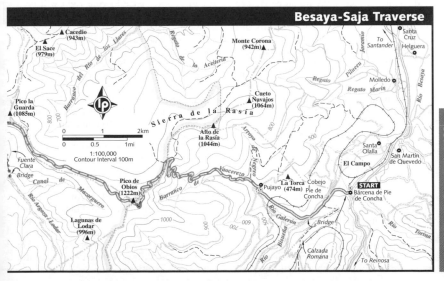

Besaya-Saja Traverse

CORDILLERA CANTÁBRICA

The trail, bordered on either side by high walls, passes a horse stable, huge chestnuts, oaks and a series of crosses (part of a Stations of the Cross). Ignore a left-hand trail at the first cross. After 20 minutes, the trail reaches a sharp, right-hand curve. Keep straight ahead along a dirt road which soon reaches the simple **Ermita del Carmen** chapel.

From the chapel, take the old, southbound stone-paved trail (of Roman origin) that once linked Santander with Castilla. Keep going for 3.5km without detouring (passing through a replanted forest) until the *empedrado* becomes a footpath and continues straight ahead. Reaching a shepherds' hut, turn right onto a path, nearly choked with blackberry brambles and ferns, that leads into a dense holly and beech forest before petering out.

Ascend west briefly through the forest cross-country, following a stone and wire wall that turns left to **Casa de Avellanedo**. From the cabin, take the footpath that undulates around the hillside first through ferns then gorse and heather to the beech forest visible on the next hill. Exit the forest to the fern-flanked hillside trail and then re-enter the beechwood along a cobbled section. Follow the path towards two shepherds' huts on the next hillside. Before reaching the huts, ignore a wide lane turning left in descent, and continue straight along a footpath that in three minutes reaches **Venta de Mobejo**, a medieval wayside inn and stable, in ruins.

Here, either turn around and return to Bárcena Mayor or, if you're looking to stretch your legs further, continue 3km to the C625, before retracing your steps to Bárcena Mayor.

Side Trip: Fuente Clara
2–2½ hours, 6.6km
This circuit walk goes along an open hillside and back along the river. Leave the village, head south along a sealed road. In 800m, after passing a corral on the right, look for the left-hand trail marker. Ascend left along makeshift stairs and enter a pine and chestnut forest soon dominated by pines. The sight and sound of the rapids and pools of the Río Argoza/Lodar are below. The footpath crosses a brook with a small waterfall

and turns left, switchbacking uphill until it levels out and leaves the forest. The trail gently curves southeast around a hill. Using a stile to climb over a wire fence across the footpath, drop down to cross a wooden footbridge over the **Fuente Clara** spring. Visible on the hillside are outcrops with ferns, heather and gorse bushes. Descend towards the Río Argoza below, on the way crossing another wire fence, and cross the river via a wooden bridge. Climb to the dirt road and go northwest for 3km through a rich forest back to Bárcena Mayor.

Day 2: Bárcena Mayor to Saja
4–4½ hours, 12.8km
The last day of the walk undulates through forests and several villages. Leave Bárcena Mayor via its stone bridge and turn right (an information panel incorrectly states 14km to Saja), entering a forest. Immediately fork left, ascending a stone-paved lane which crosses a brook, a wet zone, and two clearings along a footpath. The path heads right, joining a wider path bordered by a wire fence (on the right). Turn left along this wider trail.

After five minutes, fork right at a junction onto a footpath past two large oaks on the left. A barbed-wire fence to your right will be a constant reference during the next 2km. Pass a modern shepherds' cabin and descend to, and cross, a stream. Just before the stream note the huge oak hugging a beech tree; out of their union grow holly and blueberries. From the brook the trail briefly widens and once reaching the crest of the hill, descends in zigzags to a cabin below. Continue descending to the Arroyo de Valnería and cross it.

Continue uphill for five minutes along a wider trail to a fork. Climb steeply along the left fork. After 600m the trail opens to a firebreak for an electricity transmission line. Turn left upon reaching the firebreak and continue for 500m, quickly re-entering the forest, until the village of Los Tojos comes into sight. Twenty minutes later, the dirt lane joins a gravel and earth road that in 2.2km drops you in **Los Tojos** halfway through the day. Tasty **meals** are available in the small village (which has a public phone and fountain).

On reaching Los Tojos, the trail heads left onto the main road, crosses the village and then ascends along the same road for roughly 1km to Colsa (with a fountain). Turn left where the village begins, and at the last house fork right downhill onto a dirt and gravel road. Reaching a monument (on the left), leave the road where it curves right and head straight on the old pathway that reaches Saja in 2.5km. En route pass a beautiful wayside chapel and descend through a luxuriantly leafy forest.

Parque Nacional de los Picos de Europa

The Picos de Europa with their knife-sharp, irregular limestone summits, are the highest, most rugged and awe-inspiring mountains of all the Cordillera. Despite lying only 15km from the Bay of Biscay, the peaks soar dramatically to 2600m. Extending into Asturias (277 sq km), Cantabria (131 sq km) and Castilla y León (94 sq km), the Picos de Europa are 40km long (west to east) and 20km wide. The chain is separated into three massifs by rivers and deep gorges.

The Macizo Occidental (Western Massif), delimited by the rivers Sella and Cares, is the largest and arguably the most beautiful of the massifs, with the greatest variety of landscapes: forests, *majadas* (high pastures with shepherds' huts), gorges, lakes and imposing mountains. Its highest point is the Torre de Santa de Castilla at 2596m.

The Macizo Central (Central Massif), with more rock than flora, lies between the rivers Cares and Duje and includes the highest peak of the Picos, the Torre de Cerredo (2648m). Its rugged and abrupt relief, dotted with rocky bowls known as *jous* in the local tongue Bable (*hoyos* in Spanish), gives it a lunar look. The massif also harbours the Picos' signature peak El Naranjo de Bulnes, or Pico Urriellu (2519m), and Pico Tesorero (2570m), at the region's geographical centre. Finally, the Macizo Oriental (Eastern Massif), demarcated by the rivers Duje and Deva, is the gentlest and lowest massif, though still with wild summits reaching well over 2000m.

On 21 July 1918, at the instigation of Pedro Pidal, Marqués de Villaviciosa, King Alfonso XIII declared the Parque Nacional de la Montaña de Covadonga Spain's first national park. Initially, only the Macizo Occidental fell within the 169 sq km of protected area. During the 1980s and 1990s, campaigns were waged by both Spanish and non-Spanish activists to bring the other two massifs under national protection. Finally, on 30 May 1995 the park limits were extended to 646 sq km.

NATURAL HISTORY

Karstification, the transformation of a limestone landscape by percolating groundwater, is the most outstanding active geological process in the Picos de Europa. Besides causing the area's many cracks and caves, the process of water erosion acting upon lime also creates scree, *jous* and river gorges. Water filters through rocks and springs forth in unlikely spots. These mountains are havens for technical rock climbers as well as for cavers exploring the Cordillera's innards (see the boxed text 'Caving in the Picos').

Caving in the Picos

Walking along the upper reaches of the Picos, it's surprising to learn that underfoot the porous, limestone mountains are riddled with caves hollowed out by the effects of water erosion. Teams from (primarily) Spain, France and England have explored more than 3000 horizontal and vertical Picos cavities.

Caving began here in 1918 but did not take off until the 1960s, culminating in several major feats. In 1985, members of Oxford University's Cave Club descended 1135 spectacular metres into the Macizo Occidental's Sistema del Jito.

On Day 3 of the Picos de Europa Circuit, the trail passes El Farfao, a natural spring that surges out of a fissure in the rock wall. It's believed to be a natural release point for water from the Sima del Trave, the deepest cave (1441m) yet to be explored in Spain and the fourth-deepest in the world. The national park information offices can provide further information on caving permits and speleological clubs.

❋ ❋ ❋ ❋ ❋ ❋ ❋ ❋ ❋ ❋ ❋ ❋ ❋

CORDILLERA CANTÁBRICA

Owing to the lack of topsoil and the large amount of land cleared for pasture, woodlands cover less than 20% of the park. Protected from extremes of climate by deep gorges, Mediterranean species (strawberry, cork and holm oak) cohabit with alder, ash, willow, elm, oak and linden. Mixed deciduous forests of oak, hazel, holly, mountain ash and yew reign at altitudes up to 800m, with birch and beech beyond. Wildflowers are rich: you'll find wood anemone, purple saxifrage, Cantabrian thrift, great yellow gentian, pheasant's eye daffodil and flag iris.

The park's most representative mammal is the chamois, known locally as the *rebeco*. Some 6500 of them skip along on hooves well adapted to the steep, rocky slopes. Wild boar, foxes, wolves (in decline), deer, badgers, martens, hedgehogs, mountain cats and stoats also scrape out a living. Golden eagles, griffon and Egyptian vultures, peregrine falcons and common buzzards can be seen in the skies. Accompanying the walker at the highest altitudes with their unmistakable caws are red-billed choughs and yellow-billed alpine choughs. Also integral to the park are domestic animals including cows (brown *alpina* and *casina* breeds), goats, sheep and Asturian horses (called *asturcón*).

PLANNING
When to Walk
July, August and September are all good walking months, though shepherds agree that September, still clear and warm, is the ideal time as the heat lessens and crowds disappear.

What to Bring
A map and compass are strongly recommended. Especially when fog settles, it's easy to get disoriented. A tent is also vital, particularly in August when *refugios* (mountain huts or refuges) are often full. On Day 7, a tent or bivouac gear is imperative.

Maps
Many Picos de Europa maps are riddled with errors. Adrados's three maps – *El Cornión* and *Picos de Europa: Macizos Central y Oriental* at 1:25,000 and *Picos de Europa y Costa Oriental de Asturias* at 1:80,000 – are outstanding. The park's 1:25,000 topo map, divided into four sheets, contains the routes waymarked in 2002.

Books
Several books in English (original and translated) cover the Picos de Europa, including *In the Picos de Europa: on Foot, on Horseback, by Bicycle, by Car, by 4WD* by V Ena Álvarez. A general book laden with photos is *Picos de Europa: Asturias, León, Cantabria*. FJ Purroy's *The Cares Path: A Walk Along the 'Divine Gorge'* is a lovely, small volume describing this spectacular walk. Finally, for technical climbs, Robin Walker's *Walks and Climbs in the Picos de Europa* is your best bet.

In Spanish, Miguel Adrados has two definitive works: *Picos de Europa. Ascensiones y Travesías de Dificultad Moderada* and *Picos de Europa. Ascensiones a las Cumbres Principales y 20 Travesías Selectas*. With its topographical map, the park also sells a guide to its 30 newly established marked PRs and two GRs. On the park's flora, Modesto Luceño & Pablo Vargas's *Guía Botánica de los Picos de Europa* is best.

Information Sources
The national park maintains three main information centres open year round: in Cangas de Onís (Asturias) at the **Casa Dago** (☎ 985 84 86 14; *Avenida Covadonga 43*); in Posada de Valdeón (León) (☎ 987 74 05 49; *Travesía de los Llanos*); and in Camaleño (Cantabria) (☎ 942 73 32 01; *between Potes & Fuente Dé*). The **Centro de Visitantes Pedro Pidal** (*open 10am-6pm daily Easter–mid-Dec*), within the park near the Lagos de Covadonga, has an audiovisual show and dioramas giving an overview of the park's highlights, as well as selling books. Small, seasonal **information centres** can also be found at Poncebos, Panes, Fuente Dé and Teja Oscura (between Caín and Cordiñanes).

Emergency
The **Grupo de Rescate** (*Mountain Rescue;* ☎ 942 73 00 07; *Cuartel de la Guardia Civil, Obispo 7*) is in Potes – or call ☎ 112 for any emergency.

Permits & Regulations

There are no permits or fees. Camping in the park is permitted only around the *refugios* (which have a 10-tent maximum) and above 1600m wherever you can find relatively flat ground.

Warning

Mist can seriously complicate navigation and rain can increase danger, especially on steep and slippery parts of the trail. You may need to wait out such conditions for a day or two in your tent or at a *refugio* to ensure safety. In addition, water is scarce above 1500m and may only be available at the start and finish of each day.

ACCESS TOWNS

Cangas de Onís is the closest point to the start and finish of the Picos de Europa Circuit, but the walk can be joined (or left) via Arenas de Cabrales (during Day 3), Sotres (Day 4), Potes and Fuente Dé (Day 5) and Posada de Valdeón (Day 3 or Day 7).

Cangas de Onís

Doorway to the Macizo Occidental, Cangas is the busiest and most easily accessed of the Picos towns. Charmingly set along the Río Sella, Cangas can supply all last-minute needs. The **tourist office** (☎ 985 84 80 05; *Jardines del Ayuntamiento; open 10am-10pm daily July-early Sept*) has local and park information. There's also a national park information centre (see Information Sources, p202). **Tuñón** (*Pelayo 31*) has sporting supplies. You'll find maps and books at **Imagen** (*Avenida Covadonga 19*).

Pensión Labra (☎ 985 84 90 47; *Avenida Castilla 1; doubles with bathroom in July & Sept/Aug €25/36*) has good rooms. For something more upmarket, try **Hospedaje Torreón** (☎ 985 84 83 08; *San Pelayo 32; doubles with bathroom in July & Sept/Aug €30/42*). **Camping Covadonga** (☎ 985 94 00 97; *camping per person/tent/car €3.75/3.50/3.25*) has a **supermarket** and **restaurant** and is 4km from Cangas in Soto de Cangas (towards Arenas de Cabrales).

Try *fabada*, a white-bean–based stew made with pork, beef and sausage, and *sidra* (cider; see the boxed text 'Culinary Musts', p204) at either the **Restaurante Los Robles** (*San Pelayo 8; menú €8*), or **Restaurante El Abuelo** (*Avenida Covadonga 27; menú €10*).

Getting There & Away Buses run by **ALSA** (☎ 902 42 22 42) connect Oviedo and Cangas (€4.70, 1½ hours, 14 a day Monday to Friday, eight daily Saturday and Sunday). **Palomera** (☎ 942 88 06 11) buses operate between Santander and Potes (€5.76, 2½ hours, three daily Monday to Friday, two Saturday and Sunday). To reach Arenas and Cangas, change buses in Panes. By car from Oviedo, take the A8 and the N634 east to Arriondas and then the N625 southeast to Cangas.

Arenas de Cabrales

Known best for its pungent cheese, Queso de Cabrales, this small town has banks, a pharmacy, **markets** and a **tourist office**, all on the main street. **La Tienda Nueva** (opposite the tourist office) has Adrados maps, and **Deportes Morán** and **Deportes Cendón** carry sporting goods.

Camping Naranjo de Bulnes (☎ 985 84 65 78; *camping per adult/car/tent €4/3.60/ 3.80, bungalows €40-68; open Mar-Oct*) lies 1km from Arenas (towards Panes), with a nearby **restaurant**, **market** and bar. In town, try homy **Casa Fermín** (☎ 985 84 65 66; *doubles with bathroom in July & Sept/ Aug €24/30*), opposite the tourist office, or nearby **El Castañeu** (☎ 985 84 65 73; *doubles with bathroom in July & Sept/Aug €25/30*). Both the **Restaurante Cares** and **Hotel Picos de Europa** have attractive dining rooms with meals for €10. There's high-quality Queso de Cabrales at **Casa Trespalacios** for €10.50/kg.

Getting There & Away To reach Arenas, you can either connect from Oviedo via Cangas de Onís or from Santander via Panes. **ALSA** (☎ 902 42 22 42) buses connect Cangas and Arenas (€2, 40 minutes, five daily Monday to Friday, two Saturday and

Culinary Musts

With so many milk-producing animals running around the Picos de Europa's high pastures, the cheese-lover will not be disappointed. The most famous cheese, Queso de Cabrales, is produced on the Picos de Europa's north side. Part of the blue cheese family, Cabrales is a semihard, pasty cheese with distinctive bluish-green veins and a pungent smell and taste. The mould (genus *Penicillium*) is crucial to the three- to six-month maturation process. Made with cows', goats' and sheep's milk, the cheese is left in caves with 90% humidity and at a temperature of 8° to 12°C.

The area's rich, steaming stews will satisfy any hunger. *Pote* or *potaje*, named after the dish in which it is cooked, is a stew made with chick peas or white beans, meat, *chorizo* (red sausage), potatoes and leafy green cabbage. *Fabada* is an Asturian variant of *pote* and contains a mixture of pork, beef and sausage – *chorizo* and *morcilla* (blood sausage) – to create a tangy delight to all the senses.

To wash it down, Asturian *sidra* (cider) is a refreshing accompaniment. Dating from at least the 12th century, this lightly alcoholic cider is made from pressed apples fermented in oak barrels. Drunk during fiestas as well as simply on afternoon breaks, *sidra* is widely popular not only for its smooth flavour but for the social atmosphere that accompanies its consumption.

Sunday). By car from Cangas, continue east on the AS114.

Sotres

Sotres is a high-altitude village, located 16km from Arenas. You can sleep and eat well in both **Pensión Perdiz** (☎ 985 94 50 11; singles/doubles with bathroom €24/35) and **Casa Cipriano** (☎ 985 94 50 63; singles/doubles with bathroom €30/48). Both have meals for €8. **Albergue Peña Castil** (☎ 985 94 50 70; dorm beds €7.20) offers simple, mountain accommodation (no cooking is permitted).

Getting There & Away No buses ascend to Sotres from Arenas. Take a taxi (☎ 985 84 50 96) from the stand next to the tourist office (€14), or hitchhike. By car, take the scenic, winding AS264 up through the Garganta del Duje.

Potes

With its well-preserved medieval quarter, Potes is an ideal base for the southern Macizo Oriental and Macizo Central. It has all services including a **tourist office** (☎ 942 73 07 87; Independencia 30), sport shop – **Maratón** (Doctor Encinas 2) – and several bookshops, including **Librería Vela** (San Roque 2) for guidebooks and **Foto Bustamante** (Capitán Palacios 10) for Adrados maps.

The lodging bargain is **El Fogón de Cus** (☎ 942 73 00 60; Capitán Palacios; singles/doubles €15/30). Meals here cost €7. The town's gem is **Casa Cayo** (☎ 942 73 01 50; Cántabra 6; doubles with bathroom €42); some rooms have riverside balconies. It serves excellent local fare from €8.

Getting There & Away See Cangas de Onís (p203) for Santander–Potes connections. By car from Santander, head west on the N634, then south on the N621 via Panes.

Fuente Dé

Sitting literally at the feet of the Picos de Europa at the end of a box canyon, Fuente Dé has few services but unforgettable panoramas. **Camping El Redondo** (☎ 942 73 66 99; camping per person/tent/car €5.30/3.20/3.20, dorm beds €7.50) and **Hotel Rebeco** (☎ 942 73 66 01; singles/doubles with bathroom €45/58) are two lodging options. **Cafetería Fuente Dé**, next to the cable car, serves a wide range of local dishes and a €9.50 *menú*.

Getting There & Away To reach Fuente Dé by road it is necessary to pass through Potes. From 15 July to 31 August only **Palomera** (☎ 942 88 06 11) buses connect Fuente Dé and Potes (€1.21, 30 minutes, three a day). **Taxis** (☎ 942 73 04 00) cost €16.

Refugios in the Picos de Europa

Refugios serve meals, sell basic canned food and most are close to natural springs. Almost all have showers, bathrooms and phones. *Refugio* wardens provide helpful walking information. A standard nightly fee of €3.50/7 for members/nonmembers of federated mountain clubs is charged. Bring your mountain club card from your country of residence to receive the members' rate. Meals work on the same system: breakfast runs at €4/4.50 for members/nonmembers and lunch or dinner costs €9/10.50. Supplies arrive by burro or on foot, which pushes prices up. Meals are not provided at the Refugio de la Terenosa. A new *refugio*, Los Pastores, is expected to open in 2003 at Lago de Enol. For more information on other Picos *refugios*, contact the **Federación de Montañismo del Principado de Asturias** (☎ 985 25 23 62; *Avenida Julian Claveria, Oviedo*) or a national park office. Reserve early, especially if planning an August trip, and always at Refugio Vega d'Urriellu.

location	altitude	spaces	telephone	season
Vega de Ario	1640m	40	☎ 639 81 20 69	open with warden Apr–Nov; call rest of year
La Terenosa	1300m	24	☎ 985 84 59 37	open with warden May–Oct; open without warden rest of year
Vega de Urriellu	1965m	96	☎ 985 92 52 00	open year-round
Jou de los Cabrones	2100m	24	☎ 985 92 52 00	open with warden May–Oct; open without warden rest of year
Cabaña Verónica	2325m	3	☎ 942 73 00 07	open with warden year-round
Collado Jermoso	2046m	28	☎ 616 90 43 53	open with warden May–Oct; call rest of year
Vegarredonda	1470m	58	☎ 985 92 29 52	open with warden Apr–Nov; call rest of year

Posada de Valdeón

Of all the Picos access towns, Posada is closest to León (see p354), south of the park. It has a pharmacy, **supermarket** and bars and **restaurants**. There are two **camping grounds** nearby, in Santa Marina and Soto de Cangas. Inexpensive lodging options in Posada include **Albergue La Cuesta** (☎ 987 74 05 60; *dorm beds €6*) and **Pensión Begoña** (☎ 987 74 05 16; *singles & doubles per person €16*). Begoña has good evening/midday meals for €9/10. You can eat well at **Hotel Posada del Asturiano** and **Casa Abascal** from €9.

Getting There & Away Buses run by **ALSA** (☎ 902 42 22 42) connect León and Posada (€8.50, two hours, one a day) from where you can reach Caín (see Getting to/from the Walk, p206).

Picos de Europa Circuit

Duration	9 days
Distance	91.5km
Difficulty	demanding
Start/Finish	Lago de la Ercina
Nearest Town	Cangas de Onís (p203)
Transport	bus

Summary An unforgettable route covering the Picos de Europa's most extraordinary limestone landscapes – river gorges, alpine lakes, depressions, dense beech woods, narrow canals, cliff-hanging trails and peaks with breathtaking views

This nine-day circuit offers a magnificent overview of the Macizo Occidental and Macizo Central, and includes some of the classic routes of the region. You will visit several

CORDILLERA CANTÁBRICA

villages in the national park, explore the region's greatest gorge, Garganta del Cares, and walk through high, green pastures set against a backdrop of stunning mountain peaks.

The route goes in a clockwise direction for reasons of ease and safety. Some sections we do not recommend doing in reverse. For instance, on Day 5 it's safer to climb up the fixed cable at Horcados Rojos rather than attempt to climb down it.

The circuit is demanding due to the tremendous ascents and descents, the occasionally dangerous sections of scree, and the potential for disorientation, especially if fog sets in.

To complete the loop as described, the best access point is Cangas de Onís in Asturias. Remember the times we give for our walks are actual walking time, without stops. An ambitious, fit walker can undertake the whole walk but the circuit can also easily be divided into shorter sections and day trips. Alternative entry and exit points to the circuit are listed in Getting to/from the Walk, as well as in the walk description at the beginning of each relevant day. Further day excursions are mentioned in Other Walks (p215).

GETTING TO/FROM THE WALK
Cangas de Onís
From July to early September, **ALSA** (☎ 902 42 22 42) runs buses between Cangas and Lago de la Ercina (€1.55, one hour, five a day). To reach the Day 1 trailhead, 24km uphill, by car take the AS114 for 3km and turn right onto the AS262 (towards Covadonga). Continue 12km further to Lagos Enol and Ercina. Taxis to the lakes cost €24. Free multi-day parking is permitted at the Lagos de Covadonga car park below the Pedro Pidal visitors centre; inform the guards of your plans.

Arenas de Cabrales
From here there is easy access to Day 3 of the circuit at the northern end of the Garganta del Cares in Poncebos. To reach Poncebos from Arenas, hitch, walk or take a taxi (€6) 5km uphill. If driving, trailhead parking is available but limited. For information about the funicular connecting Poncebos and Bulnes La Villa see Day 3.

Sotres
To connect to Day 4 of the circuit, walk 5km (two hours) along a 4WD road to the Refugio de la Terenosa via the Collado de Pandébano.

Potes & Fuente Dé
You can hook up with Day 5 by heading through Potes to Fuente Dé. From there a **cable car** (*federated walking club members/ nonmembers €6.75/8 return; open daily 9am-8pm Mar-Dec*) whisks breathless visitors 750m up in less than four minutes to the upper station, known as El Cable. It's possible to walk the same with much greater effort along a spectacular 1½-hour route. From El Cable it's a further two hours' walk to the Cabaña Verónica *refugio*. Take the wide dirt road (north) and turn left at the first crossroads. At a hairpin left turn known as La Vueltona ('the big turn'), veer right onto a footpath through scree and pass below the Torre de los Horcados Rojos to the *refugio*.

Posada de Valdeón
To reach Day 3 of the route at Caín, 9km from Posada, or Day 7 in Cordiñanes, 2km away, walk, hitch or take a **taxi** (☎ 987 74 26 09) for €26/10 to Caín/Cordiñanes.

THE WALK (see maps p207 & p210)
Day 1: Lago de la Ercina to Vega de Ario
2½–3 hours, 7.5km, 630m ascent
A classic Picos de Europa walk, the trail quickly leaves the lakes and climbs through pastures to summits with stunning views of the Macizo Central. The scramble up the impressive Jultayu mountain is unforgettable. There's water at the lakes and at Vega de Ario. A stop at the Pedro Pidal visitors centre before starting the route is recommended.

From Lago de la Ercina (1106m) meadow (Campo La Tiese) near the bus stop, skirt the lake's eastern shore to join an eastbound footpath that ascends above the lake. From the **El Brazu** cabin at the base of Pico Llucia are splendid lake views. With a maximum depth of 2m (550m long, 350m wide), the lake is a breeding ground for coots and waterfowl such as mallards. Teals, pochards and herons make appearances during migration.

An obvious earth-and-stone trail begins to turn away from the lake, ascending southeast through gorse, heather and blue thistles. To the south, beeches cover the hills as the route ascends steeply. The trail levels out at **Vega Las Bobias** pasture, distinctive for shepherds' cabins and livestock. Cross the pasture southeast to a watering trough, where the way abandons the grass and makes an ascent through stones and beeches, following yellow painted trail markers, then descends towards a ravine. Now halfway to Vega de Ario (3.5km, 1¼ hours), cross the Arroyo Llaguiellu to begin a hard ascent with hairpin bends for 15 minutes to the top of the rise.

Once above, continue on a moderate gradient upwards across a succession of small depressions. Limestone boulders carved by water dominate. Forty minutes from the top of the rise, the path reaches a long valley, Las Abedulas, which terminates at a rocky col, **El Jito** (1650m). Cross straight over (southeast). One of the most impressive views of the Macizo Central – jagged peaks sawing the sky – is on the eastern horizon. Closer, to the south, the rounded Jultayu (1940m) appears. On the summit of El Jito, to the right of the trail, is one of three entrances to one of the deepest cave systems in the Picos (see the boxed text 'Caving in the Picos', p201). A bit further on, the path turns left (northeast) and in 15 minutes reaches the lengthy Vega de Ario, **Refugio Vega de Ario** (Refugio Marqués de Villaviciosa) and a **camp site**.

Side Trip: Jultayu
2½ hours, 6km, 330m ascent
To feel on top of the world, try the ascent of Jultayu. From the *refugio*, cross the meadow southeast. At the end of the meadow, near a hut, the path veers right and winds through the rocks, following yellow trail markers. At the oxidised iron sign, turn right (south) towards the mountain. At the base of the peak, 25 minutes from the start, a yellow arrow points down and left (southeast). Ignore this and continue straight (south), ascending 370m to the summit following cairns along the mountain's north face. In less than an hour from the fork you'll reach the natural watchtower. Spread out below are the next

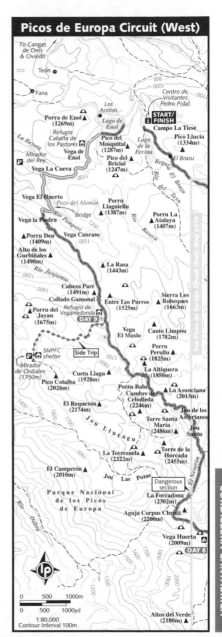

CORDILLERA CANTÁBRICA

days' goals: Caín and the end of the Valle de Valdeón to the south, Garganta del Cares below, and Macizo Central opposite. Vultures and even, with luck, a golden eagle can be seen. Take the same trail back to the *refugio*.

Day 2: Vega de Ario to Caín
4–4½ hours, 9.5km

This day is characterised by a spectacular but hard 1200m descent of the Canal de Trea to Garganta del Cares gorge, a deep, natural dividing line between Macizos Occidental and Central. There's water at the *refugio*, at Fuente El Peyu (in Canal de Trea) and in Caín.

Leave Vega de Ario as though heading to Jultayu (see Side Trip, p207). From the base of Jultayu, follow the southeast descending arrow. After 15 minutes winding through intermittent sections of large rocks and sections of dirt trail (marked with yellow dots), you'll reach a dramatic natural balcony, the entrance to the **Canal de Trea**. Looking straight across to the Macizo Central and down towards the Río Cares, the descent begins. Down the canal, the path is intermittently marked with cairns and red dots. Heading east, the descent steepens through switchbacks and then veers southeast, soon leaving a large rock wall on the left. Further down the scree begins and can be very slippery and unstable. Scree alternates with paths of dirt and stone as the passage narrows and steepens.

Pass a large cavity in the rock wall to the left used to shelter goats, known as **Cuarroble**. Soon the route reaches the halfway point between Vega de Ario and Caín at a spring, **Fuente El Peyu** – a tributary of the Río Cares – rising from below a boulder. Descend along the stream's true left bank for 10 minutes and veer left into an open oak and beech wood. Once among the trees, descend for 40 minutes following the red dots. The last portion uses natural rock stairs and beech roots to drop down to the Senda del Cares trail.

Turn right towards Caín, 2km away. The route soon crosses a suspension bridge, **Puente Bolín**, which offers an unforgettable view of the gorge's depth and greatness. The **Puente de los Rebecos**, 10 minutes later, leads to various tunnels excavated in the rocks, through which the walkway passes. The trail crosses the river twice more before entering **Caín**, over the border in Castilla y León.

Caín

Caín (460m) is surrounded by jagged peaks, mostly over 2000m or more, and its residents honour Gregorio Pérez (1853–1913), a village shepherd who made the first recorded ascent of Naranjo de Bulnes with Pedro Pidal in 1904. From a village where in summer they used to vend linden blossoms, Caín has grown with tourism and has a **supermarket**, public phones in bars, and a tourist kiosk. The fountain is near the church.

You can **camp** in the fields along the river for €2. The fields' owners will collect the money. For somewhere indoors to sleep, try **Casa Cuevas** (☎ 985 74 05 00; doubles with/without bathroom €33/18) or **Hostal La Ruta** (☎ 987 74 27 02; camping free, doubles with/without bathroom €40/27) – ask first before camping here. Both establishments serve good meals for around €8.

Río & Garganta del Cares

The Río Cares springs forth 16km south of Caín, near the Pico Gildar (2078m), and flows through the Valle de Valdeón, Posada de Valdeón, Cordiñanes and numerous low-lying winter pastures. It reaches Caín and the Garganta del Cares at its narrowest point (near the dam) and cuts through the gorge for 10km to Poncebos. Wider and calmer, it descends to Arenas de Cabrales village and continues for another 26km before joining the Río Deva in Panes.

A remarkable engineering feat, the 3m-wide path running the length of the gorge was gouged out of its sheer walls in 1946 to provide access to the Canal del Cares, made by the Viesgo electricity company in 1921. The canal runs from Caín at the top of the gorge to Camarmeña, from where it is funnelled in tubes to the Poncebos hydroelectric plant 230m below. Before the path was hewed into the walls of the gorge, the only way along it was via a trail much higher on the slopes of the Macizo Central – a daring undertaking reserved for the shepherds of Caín.

Day 3: Caín to Bulnes La Villa
5–5½ hours, 13.5km

Perhaps the single most outstanding walk in the Picos de Europa, the Garganta del Cares is undertaken by walkers of all ages. From Poncebos the walk ascends to Bulnes La Villa. Water is available in Caín, Poncebos (in the bar) and Bulnes La Villa. It's possible to join or leave the circuit at both Caín (via Posada de Valdeón) and Poncebos (via Arenas de Cabrales); see Access Towns (pp203–5) and Getting to/from the Walk (p206).

Leave Caín, retracing yesterday's steps. The first section of the gorge is hemmed in by high, sheer walls which slowly open towards Poncebos. After reaching the Puente Bolín, the path stays on the Río Cares' left bank. From the Castilla y León-Asturias border sign, the path remains level for 3km, passing Culiembro, a former seasonal settlement which was nearly destroyed during the construction of the aqueduct. A cabin and a crumbling hut remain.

As you continue, two huts appear; one, converted into the **Bar Espejismo** (Mirage Bar), sells cold drinks in summer, brought in by horse and kept cold in the canal.

After another flat 1km, the wide path narrows as it climbs steeply towards Los Collados. The trail drops down 2.2km to a dirt road. Either continue straight for a bite to eat in Poncebos (Arenas de Cabrales is another 5km downhill) or after 100m along the dirt road, turn right and descend to the Río Cares to initiate the demanding 4.5km ascent to Bulnes La Villa. This ascent can be avoided by taking the seven-minute **Bulnes funicular** *(one way/return €12/15; open daily 10am-12.30pm & 2pm-9pm)* which connects Poncebos to the once isolated village.

In Poncebos you can eat well for €7.20 (or stay) at **Hospedaje la Garganta del Cares** *(☎ 985 84 64 63; singles/doubles €39/51)*.

Cross the Cares over a bridge and a few minutes later cross the Arroyo Tejo over another bridge, ascending along the Tejo's right bank for 2km. At the base of a hill crowned by Bulnes El Castillo, ignore the bridge which leads to it and continue ahead on the gently ascending path, with scree on the left and fields on the right, to Bulnes La Villa (647m). This small village has two lodging options: **La Casa del Chiflón** *(☎ 985 84 59 43; doubles/triples with bathroom €39/45)*, with English-speaking staff, and the **Albergue Peña Maín** *(☎ 985 84 59 39; dorm beds €7)* with 16 bunks. The latter serves an €8 *menú*, as does **Bar Bulnes** *(☎ 985 84 59 34; camping €2, mattress on floor €3.50)*, which permits camping in a nearby field and sleeping on the floor (with no bathroom or toilet). The village spring is upriver on the true left bank.

Day 4: Bulnes La Villa to Vega de Urriellu
5–6 hours, 10km

A constant, 1300m climb through scenic country leads to the base of Naranjo de Bulnes. Water is available in Bulnes, La Jelguera, Refugio de la Terenosa and Vega de Urriellu. It's possible to join or leave the circuit at Refugio de la Terenosa, 5km by road from Sotres (see Access Towns, pp203–5, and Getting to/from the Walk, p206).

Leave Bulnes La Villa via the bridge and turn right, beginning the southeast ascent along the pebble path. Five minutes later, ignore a path on the right and instead continue on a lovely (though treacherous when wet) stone-paved lane through a forest of walnut, linden and hazelnut trees.

A cascade at the foot of Canal de Balcosín (on your right) marks the beginning of a steep and less scenic alternative ascent to Vega de Urriellu via the Collado Camburero and the western scree slopes of the Jou Lluengo.

After 30 minutes of ascent, the first views of the imposing, cubic-looking Naranjo de Bulnes appear off to the right. The lane crosses the Río Tejo twice and reaches a clearing with fields and shepherds' huts. Continue east on the stone-paved lane. After 15 minutes, the lane turns left just before reaching a hut with a walled meadow. Twenty minutes further on, the stone lane ends. After passing a wall with a wooden door, take the dirt path which gently ascends and crosses La Jelguera meadow. Cabrales cheese is sold for €8/kg in several of the cabins; the second on the left also has a fountain. At the meadow's high point, Collado Pandébano, Sotres is visible in

Picos de Europa Circuit (East)

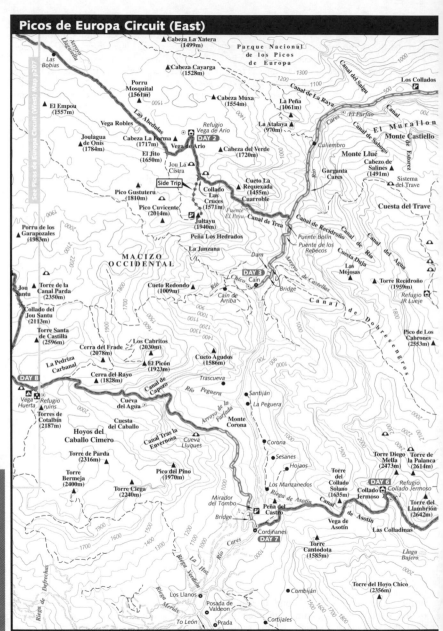

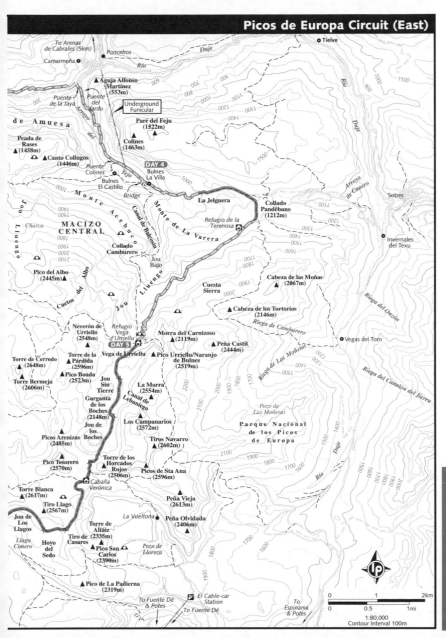

Picos de Europa Circuit (East)

To Arenas de Cabrales (5km)
Camarmeña
Poncebos
Duje
Tielve
Río

Aguja Alfonso Martínez (553m)
Puente de la Jaya
Puente del Jardu
Underground Funicular
d e   A m u e s a
Arroyo del
Paré del Feju (1522m)
Colines (1463m)
Peada de Rases (1458m)
Canto Collugos (1446m)
Puente Colines
Bulnes El Castillo
Bridge
DAY 4
Bulnes La Villa
La Jelguera
Collado Pandébano (1212m)
Sotres
Arroyo de Conero
M o n t e   A c e b u c o
Canal de Balcosin
Monte de La Varera
Refugio de la Terenosa
Invernales del Texu
Jou
Charca
Luenga
MACIZO CENTRAL
Collado Camburero
Jou Bajo
Vegas del Toro
Pico del Albo (2445m)
Cuetos   del   Albo
Jou   Llueng o
Cabeza de las Moñas (2067m)
Cuesta Sierra
Cabeza de los Tortorios (2146m)
Riega del Onzán
Riega de Camburero
Neverón de Urriellu (2548m)
Refugio Vega d'Urriellu
DAY 5
Morra del Carnizoso (2119m)
Peña Castil (2444m)
Riega de Las Moñetas
Vegas del Toro
Torre de Cerredo (2648m)
Torre de la Párdida (2596m)
Pico Boada (2523m)
Vega de Urriellu
Pico Urriellu/Naranjo de Bulnes (2519m)
Torre Bermeja (2606m)
Jou Sin Tierre
La Morra (2554m)
Canal de Lebaniego
Garganta de los Boches (2148m)
Los Campanarios (2572m)
Pozo de Las Moñetas
Parque Nacional de los Picos de Europa
Riega del Canalón del Jierra
Jou de los Boches
Picos Arenizas (2485m)
Tiros Navarro (2602m)
Pico Tesorero (2570m)
Torre de los Horcados Rojos (2506m)
Picos de Sta Ana (2596m)
Río   Duje
Cabaña Verónica
Torre Blanca (2617m)
Tiro Llago (2567m)
Peña Vieja (2613m)
Jou de Los Llagos
Llagu Cimero
Hoyo del Sedo
Tiro de Casares
Torre de Altáiz (2335m)
La Vueltona
Peña Olvidada (2406m)
Pico San Carlos (2390m)
Pozo de Lloroza
Pico de La Padierna (2319m)
El Cable-car Station
To Fuente Dé & Potes
To Fuente Dé
To Espinamá & Potes

0   1   2km
0   0.5   1mi
1:80,000
Contour Interval 100m

the distance to the east. Turn right (southwest) towards several huts, a fountain and **Refugio de la Terenosa** (1315m). If arriving from Pandébano, the shepherd in the first cabin has the keys. You are halfway to Vega de Urriellu.

After the *refugio* the trail continues southwest, above a dense beech forest that cloaks the Monte de La Varera, towards Bulnes La Villa. Further on, the forest disappears and the slope becomes more vertical.

One hour from Refugio de la Terenosa, at the base of a large scree section, the ascent steepens yet again, zigzagging between rocks and scree. Close to the Naranjo de Bulnes, the path curves briefly around its base and then heads towards the northwest face and **Refugio Vega d'Urriellu** (1953m). The first snowfields are visible. The easiest route to the summit, still requiring ropes, is up the southern face along the Vía de los Martínez, opened in 1944. The *refugio* is supplied with water from a spring and nearby is a designated **camp site**.

Day 5: Vega de Urriellu to Collado Jermoso

6½–7 hours, 12km, 660m ascent, 320m descent

This is the most arduous section of the circuit, both for its length and one difficult scramble along a fixed cable. Water is available at Refugio Vega d'Urriellu and at day's end, and can be bought at Cabaña Verónica. Throughout this stage, watch for the cairns, take your time and plant your feet well; erosion has undermined rock stability.

You can join or leave the circuit at Cabaña Verónica via El Cable cable-car station, two hours' walk away above Fuente Dé.

From the *refugio* head southwest along an ascending stone trail. After 30 minutes, ignore a path that heads off right and continue straight to the grand Jou Sin Tierre, an impressive lunar depression. Descend partway into the *jou* and cross its left slope. Take great care with the descent and the steep ascent at the other end. After a brief level section, the path reaches the Jou de los Boches. Cross south via its base and ascend through a scree section to the foot of Torre de los Horcados Rojos, where yellow trail markers

help to indicate the best way out. In ascending the wall, first cross through scree and then through another, more dangerous, section of sheer rock where extreme care is required. Halfway up is a fixed cable leading towards the exit on the right.

From the summit, **Cabaña Verónica** (2325m), a silver-toned igloo adding to the lunar appearance of the landscape, is visible on top of a rocky mound. In Cantabria now, descend to the base of the mound and ascend southwest to the *refugio*. There isn't a fountain (or phone) here but water, meals and expensive canned food are sold (brought in on foot each day during the summer). The *refugio* was once an American aircraft carrier's cannon mount. Several caves nearby have also been prepared for overnight sleeping; ask the warden.

Visible from the *refugio* are: to the southeast, El Cable cable-car station above Fuente Dé; northwest, Pico Tesorero (2570m), where the borders of Asturias, Castilla y León, and Cantabria meet; and south-southwest, the Tiro de Casares, our exit from this desolate spot. Leave the *refugio* and head westsouthwest along the crest of a rocky ridge (shaped like a dyke). After ascending the last part of the ridge, follow cairns and red trail markers that circle around to the left. When you are just opposite the *refugio*, take the trail descending southwest. To the left of the peaks ahead, the exit, a U-shaped saddle, is clearly visible.

Descend to the extreme left of the depression where the trail makes an easy ascent along a nearly vertical 6m-long crack. Once above, detour briefly towards the left and then enter a small gorge along its right side, following the ice fields leading towards the pass at Tiro de Casares. From the crest, descend into the Hoyo del Sedo depression. Once at the base, turn right, following cairns when the trail briefly disappears. Straight ahead (west) look for the exit and ascend to the pass. From here, descend into the Jou de los Llagos along a trail that follows the depression's right-hand slope without going to the bottom. Looking west, in the distance, observe the path zigzagging out of the *jou*.

Having reached the last *jou*, the path sticks close to the right-hand wall, ascending and then crossing a scree section before reaching a grassy col, **Las Colladinas**. Continue along the obvious trail for 10 minutes to the next pass, from which **Collado Jermoso** and **Refugio Collado Jermoso** (Refugio Diego Mella) are visible. Follow a path up a slope to the right of the *refugio* (2046m), a veritable eagle's eyrie. There is also a **camp site** here. All supplies arrive on human backs.

Day 6: Collado Jermoso to Cordiñanes
4–4½ hours, 9km

Leaving behind the high mountains, the walk descends 1200m, first steeply then gently, to low pastures and makes its way through one of the park's most beautiful beech forests before rejoining the Río Cares. Water is available at the beginning and end of the day.

From the *refugio*, head towards the fountain. In a few minutes a sign indicates right to Cordiñanes. Follow the sign to the top of the first steep section of trail (with loose stones). From above, it appears more intimidating than it really is. Once at the bottom, head towards the left wall and in 10 minutes cross a stream that descends from the fountain above. Continue on the cairned path to an area of irregular rocks; a rope has been fixed to make the descent easier. Ten minutes later, after crossing a dry stream bed, follow the sign pointing right to 'Vega de la Sotín' (marked with red dots).

The hillside trail crosses over a high pass and goes directly down a scree slope with protruding rocks at its base. Once at the rocks, turn right following the hillside path that leads to an irregular peak, Torre del Collado Solano. At its base, the path makes a zigzagging descent to the day's halfway point, **Vega de Asotín**. From here, turn right (west) onto a well-defined footpath that first continues above and then enters a majestic beech forest before exiting left to a beautiful hillside trail. Built to help hunters reach the high pastures, the path in some sections has been excavated from the rock.

Cordiñanes village soon appears, surrounded by pastures, the valley and the still small Río Cares. Continue descending to a meadow scattered with rocks and boulders. Turn left onto the pebble road and continue to Cordiñanes (860m). The village fountain is off the first street to the left. Two good sleeping options are **Pensión El Tombo** (☎ 987 74 05 26; singles/doubles with bathroom €23/34) and **Pensión Rojo** (☎ 987 74 05 23; singles/doubles with bathroom €22/32). The former serves lunch and dinner for €9 and €8, respectively. Without a shop in the village, supplies are available from the **supermarket** at Posada de Valdeón, 2km south of Cordiñanes, or in Caín, 6.6km north.

Day 7: Cordiñanes to Vega Huerta
6–7 hours, 10km, 1200m ascent

Hard work gets you up today's 1150m ascent, first through an extraordinarily lush and varied wood and then up steeply to the treeless, rocky heights of the Macizo Occidental. This is the only day without a *refugio*. A tent or bivouac gear is essential. There's water in Cordiñanes as well as late on the route and in Vega Huerta. It's possible to join or leave the circuit in Cordiñanes via Posada de Valdeón (see Access Towns, pp203–5, and Getting to/from the Walk, p206).

Leave Cordiñanes descending towards the Río Cares along a sealed road. Before crossing the new bridge, turn right (past a well-preserved mill) and cross over another bridge to reach the Mirador del Tombo lookout. Ascend on the sealed road for 100m and turn right onto a lane continuing for the next 4km.

At the first fork, ascend left. The path, overgrown but still visible without markers, continues along the slope above Monte Corona and enters a shady forest. Reaching a crossroads, fork left (northwest) and in 15 minutes cross a wooden bridge over the Arroyo de la Farfada. The path abandons the forest. Further along, ascend a grass-covered scree slope to the rock wall in front of you and circle round. Pass through another stretch of beech wood and as you exit, continue on the hillside footpath at the rock wall's base.

The pleasant ascent is now backbreaking as the footpath turns up through the woods (about 30 minutes) and suddenly ends at a sheer wall. This is the halfway point and base of the Canal de Capozo. Below is the Bosque de Corona. Look right for the path bordering the wall and for 45 minutes follow the red-painted trail markers along an ascending stone path that zigzags upwards and crosses a dry stream bed, which it roughly parallel. After abandoning the young hazelnut wood the trail reaches a grassy area and sometimes disappears in the grass. Follow the red dots as the path drifts right. From the next high point, cross (west) the stone-covered base of the ravine and ascend its right slope. At the top of the ravine, the rocky mass of Torre Santa de Castilla (2596m) appears in the northwestern sky. (To get water, head left to a small pasture with a spring.) Head north-west towards the base of the Torre, navigating cross-country as cairns and path give out. Halfway to the Torre you should intersect a trail that ascends west (left) to the crest of a saddle marked by two conical cairns. Past the cairns lie **Vega Huerta** and a **camp site** (2009m). To reach the fountain, take a left-hand path and then go left again at the first fork. It's behind the ruins of a former *refugio*.

Day 8: Vega Huerta to Vegarredonda

5–5½ hours, 10.5km, 400m ascent

An initially hard walk to the most spectacular *jou* of the Picos de Europa is followed by a 5km (600m) descent with unbeatable views of the northern portions of the Macizo Occidental and Asturias. You'll find water at the day's beginning and end.

A clearly marked path leaves Vega Huerta northwest (another heads southwest to Valdeón) and winds among large rocks marked with cairns, yellow slashes and blue dots. In 30 minutes, a tough scree ascent begins. Once above, at the base of Aguja Corpus Christi (2200m), the path reaches a circular depression. Skirt around the *jou* to the right (east) without descending and climb towards a group of rocks where the blue and yellow markers diverge.

The blue dots lead to Vegarredonda via Jou las Pozas, La Torrezuela, Jou Lluengo and Porru Bolu as marked on the Adrados *El Cornión* map.

Follow the yellow trail markers up through the rocks and across another scree section to the northeast. The difficult ascent leads to a type of cirque without any apparent exit. Skirt around its right side and then turn left, seeing (just when you've lost hope) two yellow markers on the wall ahead at the scree's end, which lead over the **La Forcadona** pass. Even though it's necessary to scramble up one of the cracks in the last portion, it's easier than it looks from below.

Once above, ignore the yellow markers ascending to Torre Santa de Castilla, and descend north to cross a year-round snowfield, **El Neverón**. Continue north through a small *jou* containing two snowfields. Climb out of the depression still heading north through rocks. There is no path but there are cairns. From above, one of the depressions to the west which make up the startling **Jou Santu** is visible. You are halfway. Skirt around its right side to meet a path which heads left (west). Once on the path, we recommend leaving your pack and walking back east for five minutes to contemplate, from the col, Jou Santu in its enormous glory.

Continue west on the path around the right-hand side of the diminutive Jou de los Asturianos. After cresting its far lip, the descent begins with superb views of the northern and western valleys and mountains surrounding the Picos, and even Lago de la Ercina and Vega de Enol. In the last 5km, the route descends first on stones and then earth until the black roof of the old *refugio* appears below. You'll find water here and next to the newer **Refugio de Vegarredonda** (1410m). There are **camp sites** around the old *refugio*.

Day 9: Vegarredonda to Lago de la Ercina

3–3½ hours, 9.5km

We highly recommend beginning the day by taking the Side Trip to Mirador de Ordiales (see p215).

To reach Lago de la Ercina, walk through rocks from behind the new *refugio* and turn left (north) onto a path that ascends to a meadow, Collado Gamonal, and then descends past several shepherds' cabins. The path is flanked with stone trail markers and leads over a brook and then to a section bordered by wooden guardrails. Descend to **Vega La Piedra** (with more cabins), named for the large, isolated boulder sitting in its centre. Skirt round the boulder's right side. A bit further down, near a watering trough which has the last potable water until the end of the day, a wider path begins. At the next junction, turn left among beeches. Cross the Río Pomperi to Vega El Huerto, with a pool called the **Pozo del Alemán** (The German's Well) dedicated to Robert Frassinelli (environmental champion of the Picos de Europa) on the centenary of his death in 1987.

Follow a 4WD road that leads north without turn-offs through pastures and huts for 2km to Vega de Enol, where there's a **bar-restaurant**. To reach Lago de la Ercina, continue along the dirt road towards Lago de Enol, veering right to reach the shore and a swimming area. Pick up the lovely footpath that circles the east side of the lake to the sealed road. Turn right and turn then left at the crossroads to reach Lago de la Ercina. To the right of the crossroads is the bus stop.

Side Trip: Mirador de Ordiales

2½ hours, 7.5km

This easy return trip leads to a spectacular lookout and Pedro Pidal's final resting place. Begin the walk west of the new Refugio de Vegarredonda on a stone path. Climbing steadily, the trail crosses a succession of limestone hills and depressions. It's common to see chamois here. After an hour or so, the path reaches a pasture with an abandoned *refugio* of the Sociedad Nacional de Pesca Fluvial y Caza (SNPFC). A last ascent leads southwest to the simple Mirador de Ordiales lookout with views over the peaks, forest, foothills and villages along the Río Dobra.

At the base of the lookout, Pedro Pidal's (1870–1933) remains are interred. Eight years after his death, his final wish – to be buried at this natural balcony – was fulfilled at last. Engraved in a nearby rock are words he wrote (translated here): 'Lover of the Picos, I would love to live, die and eternally rest here in Ordiales. In the enchanted kingdom of the chamois and the eagles...' Return to Vegarredonda on the same path.

Other Walks

PARQUE NATURAL DE SOMIEDO

Five additional marked trails through the Parque Natural de Somiedo appear on the recommended map. The park's office has more information (see Information Sources, p193).

Ruta del Camín Real

Two walks leave from Puerto de San Lorenzo along the Ruta del Camín Real. Once a Roman highway linking Asturias with Astorga, this road was later used by the Muslims on their way to sack Oviedo. The first walk heads southeast to Puerto de la Mesa in 21.5km; the second goes northwest for 6km to Bustariega.

Ruta de la Pornacal

Starting in Villar de Viladas (west of Pola de Somiedo), the route ascends 6km to the *teito*-filled pastures of La Pornacal and Los Cuartos.

Ruta de las Brañas de Arbellales

This walk to Salienca (east of Pola de Somiedo) passes six *brañas* in an easy 6km.

Ruta de El Cornón

This is a day of climbing Somiedo's highest peak, El Cornón (2194m). From Santa María del Puerto, ascend west to the conical summit in 7km (3½ hours). Return the same way or via Collado los Moñones.

PARQUE NATURAL DE SAJA-BESAYA
GR71 Continuation

From Saja, the GR71 continues in daily stages to Tudanca (17km), Pejanda (16km), Cahecho (20km), Potes (8km), Bejes (16.5km) and Sotres (16km). Accommodation is available at the end of each day. For transport and lodging information in Potes and Sotres, see Access Towns (p203–5). The maps in Juan Miguel Gil and Fernando Obregón's *El Sendero de la Reserva de Saja* book are sufficient.

PARQUE NACIONAL DE LOS PICOS DE EUROPA

Using the description of the Picos de Europa Circuit (see p205), a number of day trips are possible. From the Lagos Ercina and Enol, there are several options. A return trip from the Lago de la Ercina to Jultayu (Day 1) is an excellent moderate–demanding walk feasible in seven hours. A return trip from Lago de Enol to the Bosque de Pome via the Mirador del Rey (see Day 9) takes three easy hours. A return trip from Lago de Enol to Mirador de Ordiales (see Day 9) is a walk of moderate difficulty, taking 6½ hours.

Another popular option is to climb to the base of the Naranjo de Bulnes, either from Sotres in nine hours return or, more strenuously, from Poncebos in 10 hours (see Days 3 and 4).

Alternatively, walking the stunning Garganta del Cares gorge from Poncebos can be done in a comfortable seven hours return.

ELSEWHERE IN THE CORDILLERA
Senda Arcediano
In the 17th century this route, possibly a Roman highway, received its name when an archdeacon from Oseja de Sajambre poured money into its improvement. It connected Castilla with Asturias via the Puerto de Beza, avoiding the imposing Garganta de los Beyos gorge created by the Río Sella. We recommend starting in Soto (5km from Oseja) and continuing 15km north to Amieva. Feasible in five to 5½ hours, this moderate route is partially marked with red-and-white trail markers and has stunning views of the Macizo Occidental.

From Soto, ascend to the Portillera de Beza pass and then cross the Valle de Toneyo, La Majada de Saugu, a high summer pasture, and the Collado del Cueta pass to finish in Amieva village. The Adrados 1:25,000 *El Cornión* map and Marta Prieto's booklet *La Senda del Arcediano* cover the area.

Ascent to Treviso
Seventeen kilometres from Potes in the direction of Panes, the Río Urdón flows into the Deva. From here, a literally cliff-hanging path makes a zigzagging ascent more than 800m above the Garganta del Urdón, one of the Picos de Europa's wildest gorges, to the isolated Treviso village. Until the highway from Sotres was constructed, this thrilling path was the only link for the inhabitants of Treviso, who used it to transport cheese by burro to Potes. The footpath slowly zigzags up the nearly vertical slope, passing two natural balconies above the gorge. Vultures are common on this moderate–demanding 2½-hour climb. The Adradros 1:25,000 *Macizo Central y Oriental* map is recommended.

Galicia

Quietly nestled in Iberia's northwest corner, Galicia has a great wealth of natural riches for the walker eager to experiment in this relatively unknown, largely rural, corner of Spain. Plunging sea cliffs and expansive dunes, deep forests and water-fed mountain slopes, are enhanced by fascinating cultural history: prehistoric sites; medieval monasteries, churches and bridges; and surprising vestiges of antique ways of living – thatch-roofed houses, unique stone granaries and yoked oxen driving wooden ploughs.

The chapter's walks explore parts of Galicia's 1200km of coastline along the isolated Costa da Morte (Death Coast) and the Illas Cíes (Cies Islands), which form part of Spain's newest national park. In the Serras dos Ancares and Courel mountain ranges of Galicia's magical, rural interior are rounded crests, river systems and enclosed, lush valleys. Despite these attractions, don't expect excellent walking infrastructure (good trail markers, English-language guides and easy public transport). Galicians are not avid recreational walkers and no agency (public or private) regularly maintains trails. Hopefully, this situation will change.

HISTORY

Megalithic peoples (around 3500 BC) intentionally changed the landscape leaving behind dolmens (burial chambers built with huge stones). Around 600 BC Iron Age peoples (some of them Celts) intensively settled the area, filling Galicia with some 3500 *castros* – permanent, fortified, circular settlements. There are excellent examples of dolmens on the coast and *castros* all over Galicia. Romans arrived in 137 BC and eventually conquered the area in search of mineral wealth. Iberia's oldest (and still functioning!) Roman lighthouse, La Torre de Hércules, protects La Coruña (A Coruña). Roman walls still encircle Lugo.

The 9th-century discovery of James the apostle's tomb in Santiago de Compostela (see History in the Camino de Santiago

Highlights

The village of Laxe is a gateway to the hauntingly beautiful Costa da Morte

- Marvelling at the treacherous beauty of the Costa da Morte (p220) with the ocean lapping at your feet
- Reaching the top of Monte Pindo on the Monte Pindo walk (p221) and seeing the 'end of the earth' amidst the massive blue expanse of the Atlantic
- Sharing the solitary, green ridges of the eastern *serras* with agile deer in the Serra dos Ancares (p231)
- Following a sinuous canyon through timeless villages and ancient chestnut groves on the Río Lor Meander (p239)

chapter, p328) forever put Galicia on the map and the region achieved its maximum glory by the 13th century. The mid–19th-century Rexurdimento, Galicia's political and cultural renaissance, spawned a nationalism which embraced a largely imagined (and romanticised) Celtic past.

Galicia

Galicia – Maps	
1 Monte Pindo	p222
2 Spindrift Walk (East)	p225
3 Spindrift Walk (West)	p227
4 Illas Cíes	p229
5 Ancares Ridge & Piornedo Loop	p234
6 Devesa da Rogueira	p238
7 Río Lor Meander (North)	p240
8 Río Lor Meander (South)	p241

Galicia's economic mainstays have been animal husbandry, agriculture and fishing. When these proved to be inadequate, many Galicians fled to richer areas (such as the Americas and Europe). Emigrants' money, tourism, agricultural efficiency and, somewhat surprisingly, a hugely successful fashion industry all worked to invigorate the weak economy between the 1970s and 1990s. Despite generalised prosperity, young people still seek employment in the urban areas, the fishing industry is currently in grave crisis and an ageing population is left to tend the fields.

NATURAL HISTORY
Split into four provinces (La Coruña, Lugo, Pontevedra and Ourense), Galicia's 29,482 sq km form a complex topography from the coast to the inland mountains. Mainly composed of igneous (granites) and metamorphic rocks (schists and gneiss), Galicia is, geologically speaking, the Iberian Peninsula's oldest area. Tectonic movements were largely responsible for leaving behind a coast of high (500m to 1100m), steep coastal ranges divided dramatically by magnificent, silty *rías*, or tidal estuaries, created by the perpetual battle between ocean waves and river water.

Into the Atlantic pour some 38 rivers and the coast is adorned with more than 50 islands. The interior region undulates well below the level of the coastal ranges before reaching 2000m in the rounded eastern *serras* (Ancares, Courel and Eixe).

Galicia was once densely covered with humidity-loving *carballo*, or common oak, but only 10% of the original oak groves remain. The rest have been largely converted into agricultural land or replanted with fast-growing pines and eucalyptuses. Galicia's best autochthonous, mixed Atlantic forests are found in the Serra dos Ancares. Walkers inevitably encounter scrub characteristic of Galician *monte* (low-hill country) – heather, genista, broom and gorse. Individual walks may feature unique and rare species of flowers; these are covered in the relevant parts of this chapter. Common all over the region are deer, wild boar, hares, foxes, weasels and occasionally otters, pine martens and wolves.

Warning

Eight types of snake inhabit the region. Two are venomous though their bites are rarely fatal. They are small (maximum 50cm to 60cm) and inhabit forest, field and brush habitats. Keys to their identification are their vertical pupils and triangular heads. For a discussion of treatment for snake bites, see Bites & Stings (pp60–1).

CLIMATE

In general, the Atlantic gives Galicia a temperate, wet climate, although its hilly topography makes for numerous microclimates. Precipitation tends to be heaviest on the northern coast and western mountains (up to 3000mm of rainfall annually) and lowest in the southeastern *serra* (600mm annual rainfall). See each walk for local information.

INFORMATION
When to Walk

All walks are feasible from May to October; mid-June to mid-September is best. Outside of these months, rain is common and snow occasionally hits the mountains.

When planning your walks, bear in mind that the times we quote are *actual walking time*.

Maps

For orientation, the following 1:250,000 maps are recommended: Ediciones Sálvora's *Mapa de Galicia* and the Xunta de Galicia's *Mapa Autonómico*. They are widely available in Galician bookshops. The regional tourist office in Santiago de Compostela has the free 1:400,000 *Galicia, North of Portugal* map, which is excellent.

Maps for individual walks are detailed under Planning for each walk.

Books

Galicia, published by Guía Azul (Serie Verde), is a good, general guide (in Spanish) which focuses on the area's natural resources. Walking guides are almost exclusively written in the Galician language.

Purchase maps and books at either **Follas Novas** *(Montero Ríos 37)* or **Abraxas** *(Montero Ríos 50)* in Santiago de Compostela. Maps and books for individual walks can be bought in the Access Towns or Nearest Towns for the walk unless otherwise stated.

Information Sources

In Santiago de Compostela, the regional **tourist office** *(☎ 981 58 40 81; Rúa do Vilar 43; open 10am-2pm & 4pm-7pm Mon-Fri, 11am-2pm & 5pm-7pm Sat, 11am-2pm Sun)* provides regional (and local) transport and accommodation information. Ask for the excellent, free brochures: *Galicia: Natural Paradise*, *Galicia: Its Land and People* and *Galicia: On Foot*. The last, although great in concept (it briefly describes walking routes with simple maps and points of interest), is inadequate; most routes are neither maintained nor consistently waymarked.

Useful websites on Galicia are: W www .turgalicia.es and W www.galinor.es.

Place Names

Road signs are in Galician. City dwellers are primarily Spanish-speakers but Galician is the mother tongue of the rural population (who, if they don't also speak Spanish, at least understand it). In general, maps use Galician place names rather than Castilian. The only exceptions to this rule are some of the older IGN and SGE maps. Differences are minimal enough to be easily recognised in either language.

GATEWAY
Santiago de Compostela

Splendour in stone awaits you in this magnificent medieval city. So does a certain tranquillity: this is a city of nearly 100,000 people whose police have fired their side-arms only twice in the last 10 years – both times at cows running amok. For historical background, see the introduction to the Camino de Santiago chapter (p328). The city **tourist office** (☎ 981 55 51 29; w *www.san tiagoturismo.com*; *Rúa do Vilar 63; open 9am-9pm daily*) has city maps and local information.

Toribio (*Hórreo 5*) and **Piteira** (*Huérfanas 38*), both on Praza de Galicia, are good sports shops for last-minute equipment needs.

Places to Stay & Eat On the city's northeast side is **As Cancelas Camping** (☎ 981 58 02 66; *Rúa 25 de Xullo 35; camping per person/tent/car €4.50/4.20/4*).

Hostal-Residencia Suso (☎ 981 58 66 11; *Rúa do Vilar 65; singles/doubles with bath-room €17/36*) has renovated rooms and is a pilgrims' institution.

An excellent small hotel in the historical quarter is **Costa Vella** (☎ 981 56 95 30; *Porta da Pena 17; doubles from €57*); ask for balconied rooms.

To stay in style, try the five-star parador **Hostal dos Reis Católicos** (☎ 981 58 22 00; *doubles €162*).

Even if you're not buying, the **Praza de Abastos** morning public market is worth a visit; vendors at permanent stalls and local country folk ringing the edges hawk everything from delicious local cheese, pigs' heads and live hens to enormous cabbages and fresh fruit.

For *pinchos* (as tapas are known in northern Spain) head to Rúa da Raíña, where they're free with your drink. Most establishments also serve *bocadillos* (sandwiches),

raciones (main courses) and a *menú del día*, a three-course set meal which comes with a beverage included.

Restaurante 42 (*Rúa do Franco 42; mains €5-10*) does an excellent Galician meal.

For a filling, inexpensive meal head to the pilgrim's hotspot **Casa Manolo** (*Praza de Cervantes; menú €5.50*).

Getting There & Away Santiago de Compostela is connected by **ALSA** (☎ 902 42 22 42; w *www.alsa.es*) buses with Madrid (€34, nine hours, two daily) and, on the same line, Oviedo (€25, six hours, three daily), Santander (€36, nine hours, two daily), Bilbao (€42, 12 hours, three daily) and San Sebastián (€47, 13 hours, two daily). Santiago's **bus station** (☎ 981 58 77 00; *San Caetano*) is east of the centre.

Santiago's **train station** (☎ 981 52 02 02; *Avenida de Lugo*) is a 10-minute walk south from Praza de Galicia. Trains run to and from Madrid (€36, nine hours, twice daily) and, once daily, to Bilbao (€33, 12 hours), Oviedo (€35, 11 hours, change in León) and Santander (€45, 14 hours, change in Palencia).

Santiago is on the A9 tollway off the A6 from Madrid. The N550 is parallel, slow and free. The N634 connects to Oviedo.

Costa da Morte

The Galician coast is broken into three sections: Rías Altas, Costa da Morte and Rías Baixas – the upper and lower *rías* with the Death Coast in between.

Seeing a winter storm batter the Atlantic coast, the meaning of Costa da Morte is immediately clear. Countless ships lost off this rugged coast are mute testimony to its treachery (see the boxed text 'The English Cemetery', p227). The area extends from the cliffs of Malpica, in the northwest around Cabo Fisterra (Finisterre), to the dazzling white dunes of Carnota. Three *rías* (Corme, Laxe and Corcubión) interrupt the coastline, which reaches out to the sea in a series of juts and capes; lighthouses crown seven of these. The *rías* are less windswept, with waveless beaches, dense woods and villages.

Several rare and endangered plants are found almost exclusively on the Galician coast: *herba de namorar*, the 'falling in love plant', a type of thrift, used to enchant the desired partner; *camariña*, which gives Camariñas its name, a small bush that produces a tiny, white fruit; and *angélica*, a 1m-high plant with bright green leaves and umbrella-shaped yellow flowers, unique to this part of the world.

Seabirds thrive on the Galician coast, attracting bird-watchers from around the world. Of particular note are shags (a species of cormorant) that nest in *furnas*, or cliffside caves; the penguin-like guillemot; and the yellow-legged gull. While walking it's common to see dolphins and porpoises playing just offshore.

Wind and clouds from the southwest generally indicate the arrival of rain.

Galician Lace-Making

Observing women *(palilleiras)* swiftly manipulate tens of bobbins *(palillos* or *bolillos)* to slowly produce intricate patterns of delicate lace, known as *encaixe*, is a most impressive sight. Sitting at the doors of their homes or grouped together, *palilleiras* practise an art whose origin is unclear. Some say a Flemish soldier of Carlos I, based on the coast, first imported the lace; others, that it came via the Camino de Santiago (Way of St James). The most romantic version suggests that a strange, foreign woman, saved from a shipwreck by helpful locals, gave them the gift of lace in thanks.

The oblong, pillowed work-board is stuffed with tightly packed hay inside a soft sack. Two wooden sticks project from the top, providing support. Around the board the women wrap the drawn pattern and position countless coloured pins at crucial intersections. Between the pins they skilfully braid linen threads, each attached to walnut *palillos*. Camariñas is the most famous centre of lace-making in the Costa da Morte.

PLANNING

Costa da Morte: Guía Turística-Cultural, by Xan Fernández Carrera, provides excellent historical and cultural information, and has an English translation at the back.

An excellent website on the Costa da Morte is w www.finisterrae.org.

Monte Pindo

Duration	5–6 hours
Distance	16km
Difficulty	moderate–demanding
Start/Finish	O Pindo (p222)
Transport	bus

Summary Ocean views, salty breezes, pine forests, odd granite formations, 360-degree summit views – this loop features a stunning array of natural sculpture on one of Galicia's most celebrated coastal mountains

Rising abruptly out of the Atlantic, rose-gold granitic Monte Pindo is Galicia's Mt Olympus. From its summit, A Moa (627m), there are unbeatable views from Fisterra (north) to Carnota (south). Local legends are extensive: Celts committed mass suicide here rather than submit to Roman colonisation; fertility rites were celebrated on pagan altars on the summit; Moorish treasure is hidden in secret caves. The wondrous moraine and erosion-produced granite formations are a highlight. Semi-wild horses are often spotted on the walk's upper reaches.

Sporadic yellow-and-white slashes mark the trail up to A Moa. The standard descent described is straightforward. A more demanding alternative descent heads down Pindo's backside through the Río Xallas canyon. This section is unmarked and requires a compass (and warrants a moderate–demanding rating). Harnessed since the early 20th century, the river was dammed in 1988 and lost its ecological viability. Spectacular nonetheless, the final 100m waterfall is Europe's longest freshwater-to-ocean drop, forming a 20m-deep pool below.

You'll find water at the trailhead and in Fieiro, 11km into the walk.

GALICIA

Warning

Marine fog makes it easy to get lost on this mountain. Additionally, the dam is opened occasionally for rain overflow in December and January, and on Sundays the rest of the year to show the waterfall in its splendour. There are no warning sirens. If in doubt, take the described road return. Exercise extreme caution descending the canyon; guardrails are not secure and drops are precipitous.

Maps
The IGN's 1:25,000 map Nos 93-I *Brens* and 93-III *O Pindo* cover the route.

NEAREST TOWN & FACILITIES
O Pindo
Set on a hill and the curve of a tranquil, white-sand beach, O Pindo is an attractive fishing town. It has a **supermarket**, ATM and pharmacy.

For accommodation closest to the trail-head **Pensión Sol e Mar** *(☎ 981 76 02 98; singles/doubles with bathroom €16.50/33)* has attractive, new rooms.

A Revolta *(☎ 981 76 48 64; singles/doubles €24/30)* has basic rooms and outstanding coastal fare *(menú €9)*.

From Santiago take an **Arriva** *(☎ 981 58 85 11)* bus to Cee (€7.75, two hours, seven daily Monday to Friday, three Saturday and Sunday) and then transfer to a Cee–Muros bus (€2, 30 minutes, eight daily) and get off at O Pindo. **Castromil** *(☎ 981 58 90 90)* buses connect Santiago to Muros (€4.95, one hour, 12 daily Monday to Friday, six Saturday and Sunday), where you can transfer to the busy Arriva Muros–Cee line.

By car, take the C543 to Noia and then the C550 (for Fisterra) to Muros and O Pindo.

Camping Ancoradoiro
You'll find this place *(☎ 981 87 88 97; camping per person/tent/car €2.85/3.75/2.85)* 15km from the trailhead between Muros and O Pindo, nestled in a seaside pine grove. It has a restaurant serving mains for around €8, but no store. By bus, make

for O Pindo and ask the driver to drop you at the camping ground.

THE WALK
Between O Pindo's church and playground (with fountain), head southeast into the forest, crossing a small stream bed to a narrow path. The dirt and rock trail ascends for 20 minutes through dense foliage, first along a low stone wall and then zigzagging uphill. Where the trail begins to level and veers notably left, look for the **Olimpo Celta** – soon, with some imagination, heads, angels and animals are visible in the granite. During the next 20 minutes the forest thins, the coastal views are outstanding and then the trail steepens, through charred pines, to a T-junction. Looking southwest, **O Pedrullo**, a small peak, is recognisable by the cascade of small rocks at its base. A 10th-century watchtower built here protected the inhabitants from Viking raids. Peasant uprisings in 1467 provoked its destruction.

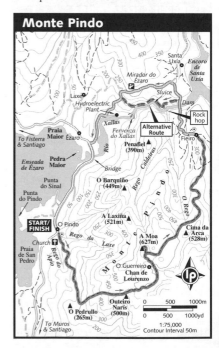

Turn left through the open granite landscape. About 250m after the T-junction don't miss a poorly marked left fork. Continue steadily uphill for 15 minutes through a narrowing canyon. A stone barrier between two huge boulders hems in semi-wild horses. Cross the barrier and continue ascending for another 20 minutes to the surprising alpine plateau, **Chan do Lourenzo** (Lorenzo's Floor). Horses often graze here amidst the heather and broom. Looking left, A Moa's light, rounded summit appears. Carnota's 6km of white beach lie to the south. A wolfram mine, exploited by locals desperate for pesetas during WWI and WWII, lies behind the shepherd's hut.

Go northwest towards A Moa, keeping left to avoid the boggy centre, and in 100m look for 6m-high **O Guerreiro** (the Warrior) sitting with his back to you. Follow the trail on this sentinel's right which, after 20 minutes ascending, leads to a plateau at A Moa's base. About 300m beyond O Guerreiro take a poorly marked left fork. Circle around to A Moa's northeast face and the summit trail. In a saddle where Xallas canyon comes into view, turn left (west) and continue ascending along the easy granite trail to the top. Punctured with erosion pools, the summit offers great views. From right to left is Cabo Fisterra, Illas Lobeiras (last breeding ground of monk seals, exterminated in the 19th century), O Pindo, Quilmas and Carnota.

To avoid navigational difficulties, descend the same way. After 10 minutes, with A Moa's huge granite wall on the right, turn 90 degrees left (east) towards two large granite masses framing a wide tongue of grass that leads down towards a steep ravine. Windmills are clearly visible beyond. At first there is no clear path although cairns mark the route. Search for the trail which steeply descends 50m through brush to the base of the southern (right-hand) granite mass. At the base the trail turns left (east) and descends to a shallow basin studded with young pines. For 10 minutes follow the horse trails along the left side of the basin – the highest peaks are on the left – and aim for a small plateau to the northeast. Cairns mark the trail across the high, open plain. For 250m the trail zigzags down the hill and then continues along the ridge (keep right) to reach a clear forest trail. Avoid descending the ravine. For 25 minutes the trail clearly undulates through forest and open hill, and reaches another horse barrier. The descending trail opens to a wide firebreak. Continue for another 20 minutes to a flat, dirt and stone road. Turn left and in 10 minutes this road brings you to Fieiro.

Turn left onto the sealed road and in 1km the trail crosses the Xallas dam. There are two ways to reach Ézaro from here: either as described here, by 4.5km of sealed road, or through the impressive river gorge (see Alternative Route: Via Río Xallas Gorge).

For the road option, continue on the sealed road and descend the steep hill past Mirador do Ézaro. In 1km fork left onto a cement road and descend towards the hydroelectric plant and then Ézaro. It's possible to detour to the waterfall's base by turning left onto the hydroelectric plant's service road.

Once at the highway, turn left over the bridge and continue to O Pindo.

Alternative Route: Via Río Xallas Gorge

1 hour, 2.5km

This route is about half an hour faster, and 2km shorter, than the descent by the road. It is more spectacular, but is made challenging and dangerous by rock-hopping, the absence of safety features and some precarious drops.

Cross the dam and turn left onto a descending road that peters out at a tunnel. Take a dirt path left, through bushes, to the riverbed. The imposing walls of the dam looms large on the left. Head to the river's left bank where 20 to 30 minutes of rock-hopping leads to a sluice. Depending on the water level it may be easier to access the sluice from the right bank. Cross over the sluice and then climb a ladder to the canal's unforgettable walkway. Vertical drops on your left reveal the magnificent **canyon** with pools and cascades. In 10 hair-raising minutes you'll reach a footpath that passes under water pipes and then ascends to a pumping station. Rejoin the main route on the cement road for the last 1.7km of the descent to Ézaro.

GALICIA

Spindrift Walk

Duration	2 days
Distance	39km
Difficulty	easy–moderate
Start	Laxe (p224)
Finish	Camariñas (p224)
Transport	bus

Summary With the ocean never out of sight, this walk provides an excellent introduction to the often desolate and always hauntingly beautiful Costa da Morte

If the sea is one of your passions, this is your walk. From start to finish, the ocean acts as a constant right-hand companion. Linking the Costa da Morte's two northernmost *rías*, the walk provides peace and isolation; only fishing villages interrupt the otherwise desolate coast. The walk ends in Camariñas, famous for its lace (see the boxed text 'Galician Lace-Making', p221). Make sure to get sufficient water for the short first day in Laxe. On Day 2, water is available in several spots and the trail is sporadically marked with yellow-and-white slashes.

PLANNING
Maps
The IGN's 1:50,000 map Nos 43-IV *Laxe* and 67-II *Muxía* cover the route.

NEAREST TOWNS
Laxe
Laxe's tiny historical quarter still retains remnants of its nobler days, including the 14th-century Gothic church, which boasts excellent sculpted figures. There are several **markets**, ATMs and pharmacies along the main drag.

Hotel/Restaurante Casa do Arco *(☎ 981 70 69 04; Praza Ramón Juega; doubles with bathroom €48)* was once the 15th-century residence of Galician nobility. Meals are good but pricey.

Hostal/Restaurante Beiramar *(☎ 981 72 81 09; Rosalía de Castro 30, 1st floor; doubles with bathroom €39)* has simple, clean rooms. Breakfast is included and food is available *(menú €7.80)*.

Outstanding seafood, especially grilled fish, is prepared at **Restaurante Sardiñeira** *(Rosalía de Castro 51; menú €12)*.

For huge servings done well and inexpensively, head to **Restaurante O Pino** *(Isidro Parga Pondal 19; menú €7)*.

Autos Carballo *(☎ 981 58 88 11)* buses go direct to Laxe via Carballo *(€5.80, 1½ hours, one daily Monday to Friday)*. Additional Autos Carballo buses link Santiago and Laxe via Carballo with transfers daily.

By car from Santiago, take the C545 northwest to Zas, then the AC430 north, and finally the AC422 west to Laxe.

Camariñas
This fishing town has a full range of services. **Hostal/Restaurante Gaviota** *(☎ 981 73 65 22; Rúa do Río 15; singles/doubles with bathroom €22/36)* has quiet, new rooms, and meals *(menú €9)*.

For a homy atmosphere, try **Hostal Plaza** *(☎ 981 73 60 37; Real 12; singles/doubles with bathroom €21/27, singles/doubles with shared bathroom €12/21)*.

You'll eat well, inexpensively and abundantly at both **Restaurante Villa de Oro** *(Areal 7; menú €6)* and **Restaurante O Meu Lar** *(Pinzón 26; menú €6)*. The *caldeirada* (seafood stew) is especially good at the latter.

Arriva *(☎ 981 58 85 11)* buses run between Camariñas and Santiago *(€7.35, two hours, two daily Monday to Friday, three Saturday, one Sunday)*.

By car from Camariñas, take the AC432 to Vimianzo. Continue to Baio to pick up the C545 (via Santa Comba) to head southeast to Santiago.

GETTING TO/FROM THE WALK
To return to Laxe from Camariñas, take a **taxi** *(☎ 981 73 61 69)* from the stand next to Bar Praia on the main street *(€20)* or a bus with transfers. With Arriva buses take the 6.30am Camariñas–Santiago bus and transfer at Ponte do Porto (10 minutes from Camariñas) for Laxe (originating in Muxia). Or take the Camariñas–Carballo line *(€5, five daily Monday to Friday, three Saturday, two Sunday)* and transfer in Carballo (see Laxe) for either Laxe or Santiago.

THE WALK (see maps p225 & p227)
Day 1: Laxe to Camelle
3–3½ hours, 12km

Leave the main Praza Ramón Juega along the quaint Rúa Río. Ascend 600m along the sand and then cement road to the chapel, Santa Cruz da Rosa. Numerous candles burn for fisherfolk and devotion.

From the chapel, take a wide southbound dirt lane, which converts to a narrow grass footpath heading southwest, flanked by stone walls separating fallow fields. The long stretch of gorgeous, rolling coastline lies ahead. After five minutes, as the Praia de Soesto appears, head right (northwest) across the fields over obvious breaks in the low walls. Aim north for the low hill's base to pick up a wide trail leading straight down to the beach. Ignore the yellow-and-white trail markers ascending the low hill. Cross the beach. Take a small footpath bordering the coast – spindrift may brush your skin – and continue for 15 minutes.

Reaching a small stone beach the path becomes a dirt lane. At the next sandy beach, with a fishing hut and several weathering boats, the lane becomes a wide dirt road. Twenty minutes later, when the road turns left and separates from the sea, take a narrow right-hand path first through gorse and then over a grassy plain towards the great stretch (2.5km) of white sand, **Praia de Traba**. Cross the beach. Early in this stretch, a river drains into the sea. Fording it barefoot may be necessary. Halfway down the beach, an optional detour (left) ascends the dunes to Lagoa de Traba, a protected freshwater lagoon. Marsh birds such as coots and grebes thrive. A small bar on the beach's west end shows a photo of an American fighter plane forced to land on the beach in 1944.

At the beach's end, 4km remain to Camelle. Continue on a right-hand dirt lane that promptly forks right onto a narrow access trail (a wider stone trail here rejoins the narrow path). For 30 minutes the trail rolls (sometimes disappearing) through granite boulder fields to a wide dirt lane. With Camelle in sight, the trail veers left, narrows through dense brush and reopens at a stone beach. Either take the sealed road for 500m, turning right down a road to the maritime walkway, or, better, veer right onto a fishing trail that soon disappears. Pick your way along the rocky shore to

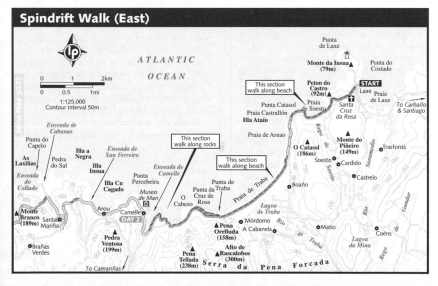

three fishers' sheds, an old sardine-salting factory and the maritime walkway. Both routes curve around the bay of Camelle, leading to its port and commercial centre.

Camelle

In Camelle, **A Molinera** (☎ 981 71 00 02; *Calle Principal 79; 4-person apartments €30)* has four immaculate apartments with bathroom and kitchen. **A Chalana**, several doors away, serves excellent coastal fare for €7.20. **Bar Rotterdam** *(Calle del Muelle 20)* has delicious seafood; mains run from €6. Try the *caldeirada* or paella. There is a **supermarket** and other basic services.

Day 2: Camelle to Camariñas
7–8½ hours, 27km

Leave Camelle's port via Rúa do Porto. Climb for 200m and make a hairpin right turn onto a sealed road leading to Arou (1.8km). In Arou ascend along Rúa Praia and turn right onto Rúa d'Abaixo, which leaves the village as a sealed road. In 1.2km turn left

Man, el Alemán de Camelle

As you approach Camelle eye-catching, coloured circles on the village breakwater seem oddly out of place. Signs for 'Museo' along the maritime walkway lead past salty types chewing the fat over fishing nets to the unexpected museum of Man (Manfred), a German who came to Camelle more than 30 years ago and set himself up on the breakwater, where he stayed until his death in late 2002. Man built a highly creative open-air museum using the flotsam brought by the waves – tree roots, nets, floats, shoes, whale vertebrae, scraps, plastics etc. Pinnacle-shaped sculptures made from stones fixed with cement and several paths covered with local plants completed this fantastical wonder. Man, a true modern-day hermit, explained his vision simply – life is a circle. At the time of printing the future of Man's museum is unclear. It was extensively polluted by the November 2002 *Prestige* oil spill and it is hoped that Man's final public request, for his museum to be left untouched as a reminder of the devastating effects of the spill, is heeded.

onto an ascending 4WD road; 50m later the route heads right onto another 4WD road. A strenuous 30-minute ascent (1km) leads to an even wider dirt road. Turn right. In 1km Santa Mariña fills the steep valley stretching below. Turn right and descend in hairpins through the houses of this lonesome enclave. Descend towards the port and, about 300m above it, turn left down a dirt path that, after a slight dip and ignoring a dirt track on the left, launches into the longest (1.4km) and hardest ascent of the day, straight on. On reaching the summit, head right to the wide road.

In 10 minutes the road skirts Monte Branco (White Mountain), named for its sandy composition. After 30 minutes of easy walking above the dunes and Praia do Trece, veer right at a junction and continue descending 2km to the ocean and the **Cemiterio dos Ingleses** (English cemetery).

Continue along the road for an hour (3.5km). Views of the lighthouse of Cabo Vilán and the islets off the cape dominate the horizon here. Five minutes after a sign (left) describes how wolves *(lobos)* were once trapped, the road begins to ascend and curve left. Take the road, or better, continue straight along a footpath that shortcuts up the steep hillside and returns to the road. Sheep and goats often graze in this area and there's a natural spring. Continue for 30 minutes and, just after the first windmill on the right, take a small footpath to the right that makes a beeline for the lighthouse (1km), crossing the road twice. The majestic **lighthouse** sits 135m above the sea, is 25m high and was the first in Spain (1896) to function with electricity. Ships can see it from 60km away.

From the lighthouse follow the sealed road. Where it curves sharp left (100m below the dirt road), search on the right for an obvious southbound footpath. Follow the coastline for 35 minutes aiming for the hill topped by a chapel. Nearing the hill, the trail veers left and, before reaching a soccer field and granary, turns right. From the hill's base make a five-minute ascent up the well-defined trail to the **Capela da Virxe do Monte**. Excellent views southwest to the Ría de Camariñas, the village of Muxía and Cabo Touriñán are worth the climb.

Spindrift Walk (West)

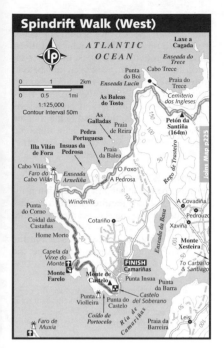

ATLANTIC OCEAN

Laxe a Cagada
Enseada do Trece
Punta do Boi
Cabo Trece
Enseada Lucín
Praia do Trece
Cemiterio dos Ingleses
As Baleas do Tosto
1:125,000
Contour Interval 50m
As Galladas
Praia de Reira
Pedra Portuguesa
Petón da Santiña (164m)
Illa Vilán de Fora
Insuas da Pedrosa
Praia da Balea
Cabo Vilán
Faro de Cabo Vilán
Enseada Arneliña
O Foxo
A Pedrosa
Rego de Trasteiro
Punta do Corno
Windmills
Coidal das Castañas
Cotariño
A Covadiña
Pedrouzo
Xaviña
Home Morto
Monte Xesteira
Capela da Virxe do Monte
FINISH
Camariñas
To Carballo & Santiago
Monte Farelo
Monte de Castelo
Punta Insua
Punta da Barra
Punta Violleira
Punta do Castelo
Castelo del Soberano
Punta da Barra
Faro de Muxía
Coído de Portocelo
Ría de Camariñas
Praia da Barreira
Leis

Johns Map p225

Descend the same way to the base. Before the soccer field, turn right onto a descending sea-access road. After 200m make a hairpin turn left towards the beach. Notice stacks of drying seaweed used to fertilise fields. Skirt the beach and then ascend along stone walls following the beach contour. At the first junction, fork right. Continue for 15 minutes along the coast through fields (of potatoes, beans and cabbage) and forest. At the first house on the right the trail becomes cement. Three minutes later pass between two houses and veer right. In 200m pass the 17th-century ruins of Carlos III's Castelo del Soberano. The castle's stones were used to construct the port and the cannons became mooring posts. Turn left to reach Camariñas.

Illas Cíes

With their crystalline waters and white sand beaches, the Cíes are a very beautiful 9km

breakwater protecting Vigo from the Atlantic's fury. The 434-hectare archipelago consists of five tiny islets and three islands: Monte Agudo, the largest and most rugged; O Faro, linked to Monte Agudo by a white sandy crescent (Praia das Rodas) which forms a lagoon (O Lago); and San Martiño, separated from the other two and only accessible by private boat.

The Cíes were first protected in 1980. In July 2002 they, together with the Ons and Sálvora archipelagos and Illa Cortegada, were declared Galicia's first and Spain's 13th national park, Parque Nacional Marítimo Terrestre de las Islas Atlánticas de Galicia. The park covers 1665 terrestrial and 1135 maritime hectares.

Since pre-Roman times humans have inhabited the islands. During the 14th century each island had a monastery, but pirate raids precluded the establishment of a stable population up until the 19th century; the last inhabitants left in the 1970s.

Owing to the islands' low altitude (maximum 197m) and proximity to the mountainous mainland, rainfall is very low – with a marked summer drought – giving the islands a mixed Mediterranean-Atlantic climate. The granite massifs, shaped by wind and water into steep 100m cliffs on their eastern faces,

The English Cemetery

On 10 November 1890 the British training vessel *Serpent* ran aground off the coast between Cabo Vilán and Praia do Trece. The attempts of nearby villagers to help were futile. Of the 173 hands on board all but three were lost. The humble cemetery at the foot of the rocks shelters their remains. In thanks for the heroics of the local people and the burial of the sailors, the British Admiralty gave a rifle to the priest of nearby Xaviña, a gold watch to the mayor and a barometer to the town hall. In addition, whenever a British military ship passed the area it was to sound cannon in honour of the lost sailors. Within the cemetery walls is a stone cross dedicated to the thousands of nameless *náufragos* (shipwrecked) of the Death Coast.

and gentler, forested and dotted with dunes and beaches on their western sides, harbour excellent examples of rare Galician flora (375 species), as well as a unique species of thrift *(Armeria pungens)* and Mediterranean species such as rockrose, cork oak and wild asparagus. Noticeably absent is heather.

Key populations of marine birds find sanctuary here. The largest colony in the world (22,000 breeding pairs) of the yellow-legged gull is found on the Cíes, and 1000 breeding pairs of shags thrive here. From the two bird observatories that our walks visit you can observe the cliff-side nests of both species. Nesting occurs from January to August; chicks are born in June and July. And, unlike the overfished coastal waters nearby, the protected seabeds teem with life.

PLANNING

There is a limit of 2200 visitors daily, and the islands' only lodging facility, the camping ground, has an 800-person nightly limit. Especially in August, the islands are overwhelmed with visitors; a reduction of permitted maximums is imperative to protect the islands' delicate ecosystems. All the islands' services (ferry, bars and restaurants, camping, Red Cross, ranger service and information) are open at Easter and from 15 June to 15 September. Both walks are easily combined as a single day trip (don't forget your swimsuit!), but to stay longer, plan ahead. The islands have no potable water source. Either bring your own or pay a high price on the islands.

Maps & Books

The IGN's 1:10,000 *Parque Natural Islas Cíes* map covers the walks. The islands' information centres have free self-guided walks with simple maps.

Two accessible books, on sale in the islands' Casa Forestal, are J Luaces and C Toscano's *Islas Cíes* (available in English), giving a general overview, and J Mouriño's *Guía de las Flores de las Islas*.

Information Sources

Two centres on the islands, staffed by park rangers, offer excellent information. The information centre *(open 10am-2pm & 4pm-7.30pm daily)*, in a small hut 100m from the ferry dock, has brochures. Fifteen minutes by foot from the dock, on O Faro island, the 17th-century remains of the San Estevo monastery house the park's permanent **Casa Forestal** *(open 10am-2pm & 4pm-7.30pm daily)*. Two floors of good exhibits here on the islands' flora and fauna include an audiovisual programme. The mainland park office *(☎ 986 80 54 69; Benito Corbal 47, 5th floor)* is in Pontevedra.

Permits & Regulations

Permits are not necessary to visit but a return ferry ticket is required if making a day trip, and reservations at the camping ground if staying longer.

The national park regulations are in the process of being tightened. Meanwhile, the following are prohibited:

- camping beyond established facilities
- disturbing flora and fauna (sea or land)
- entering designated Marine Birds Sanctuary areas
- fires (except Campingaz stoves)
- making excessive noise
- pets

ACCESS TOWN & FACILITIES
Vigo

The major gateway to the Cíes, Vigo, is Galicia's largest port city. The regional **tourist office** *(☎ 986 43 05 77; Rúa do Mestre Mateo; open 9.30am-2pm & 5pm-7.30pm Mon-Fri, 10am-2pm & 5pm-6.30pm Sat & Sun)* is across the street from the Estación Marítima (ferry terminal) on the Muelle de Transatlánticos. In the Estación Marítima there's a **cafetería** and ticket windows for the Naviera Mar de Ons ferry and the **Camping Illas Cíes** *(reservations ☎ 986 43 83 58; open 8.30am-1pm & 2.30pm-7pm daily)*. For more information, see Camping Illas Cíes (p229).

Hostal La Palma *(☎ 986 43 06 78; Palma 7; singles with bathroom €15/25; open mid-June–Sept)* has very good rooms, some with balcony, and does excellent seafood *(menús €6 to €8)*.

Across from the central library, **Hostal Estrella** *(☎ 986 22 63 63; Joaquín Yáñez 1, 4th floor; per person €10)* has sunny rooms.

One street up from the bustling port, the old fishing quarter bursts with **tapas bars** and **restaurants**. The **public market** is on Rúa Pescadería.

From Santiago, **Castromil** (☎ 981 58 90 90) buses connect to Vigo (€5.85, 1½ hours, hourly services). Regular train services run to/from Santiago (€5.50, 1½ hours, hourly services) and Madrid (€36, seven hours, three daily).

By car, the A9 tollway runs to/from Santiago via Pontevedra.

Camping Illas Cíes

Camping Illas Cíes (reception ☎ 986 68 76 30; camping per adult/child/tent €5/3.80/5) is the only lodging option. To camp, it is obligatory to have a tarjeta de acampado (camping voucher), purchased for €6 from the camp's office in the Estación Marítima in Vigo (see Vigo, p228–9). Alternatively, if arriving from Baiona or Cangas, reserve by phone and then pay at the camp's reception upon arrival. When reservations are made, the date and time of departure must be fixed. The return can be modified once there, if necessary.

The camping ground has a self-service **cafetería**, **restaurant** and small **supermarket**. If self-catering, mainland prices are cheaper.

For access, see Getting to/from the Walk.

Illa Do Faro

Duration	2–2½ hours
Distance	7.7km
Difficulty	easy–moderate
Start/Finish	Muelle das Rodas
Nearest Town	Vigo (p228)
Transport	boat

Summary A gentle ascent to a bird observatory and Monte Faro lighthouse offering outstanding views

GETTING TO/FROM THE WALK

Naviera Mar de Ons (☎ 986 22 52 72; ⓦ www.mardeons.com) ferries operate from Vigo (€28 return, 45 minutes, four daily from mid-June to mid-September) to

the Muelle das Rodas jetty on Illa de Monte Agudo. Ferries also leave from Baiona (€28 return, one hour, four daily from late June to mid-September) and Cangas (€28 return, 45 minutes, twice daily from late June to early September). With good weather more ferries are added.

THE WALK

From the boat jetty, walk left down the obvious trail 100m to the information centre. The jetty is fronted by **Bar-Restaurante Playa de Rodas** serving sandwiches (from €2.50) and meals (€10).

Illas Cíes

From the information hut turn left (south) along the obvious trail which circles **O Lago** via a sea wall (built in the 1960s) joining the two islands. Sea life in the pool, clearly visible from the wall, abounds. Continue past the camping ground to the **Casa Forestal**, a two-storey stone building on the right. Another 250m further on, you'll reach a crossroads. Turn right up a clear path that zigzags for around 20 minutes, forking right once, before opening up to a lookout and the hollowed-out 'bell-tower rock' **Pedra da Campá**. A further 100m ahead is the bird observatory, a small blind with space for four to observe birds.

Return the same way to the fork. Veer right and continue on the wide trail for 30 minutes up to the lighthouse crowning **Monte Faro** (172m). Enjoy outstanding views of Illa San Martiño and the mainland. Descend the same way until reaching a trail on the right marked 'Carracido/Faro da Porta'. Descend right, at first steeply, along the dirt firebreak to a T-junction. Turning right leads to the Faro da Porta lighthouse in 10 minutes. Instead, turn left and wind down towards Carracido beach and the port. Sailboats dock here frequently. In 10 minutes pass Fonte de Carracido (of dubious potability) and a beach to reach the crossroads.

Continue straight ahead for 200m and turn right where indicated to 'Praia de Lago/Rodas'. Upon reaching another fork, either turn left along the trail, first past **Casa de Comidas Serafín** *(salads €3, fish & beef €6-9)*, with very pleasant open-air seating, and then back to the start via the camping ground, or alternatively you could head right to descend to Praia das Rodas, and return to the ferry dock via the beach.

Side Trip: Praia da Nosa Señora
25 minutes, 1.4km

From the crossroads, a 10-minute detour leads initially east and down past Praia da Nosa Señora and then a brief rock- and sand-hop leads to the islands' 200-year-old cemetery. Either continue round to make a loop back to the main trail, return the same way to the crossroads, or continue along Praia das Rodas to return.

Illa Monte Agudo

Duration	2–2½ hours
Distance	7.3km
Difficulty	easy
Start/Finish	Muelle das Rodas
Nearest Town	Vigo (p228)
Transport	boat

Summary Outstanding lookouts, crashing waves, cliffs and a chance to end at the island's best beach

GETTING TO/FROM THE WALK
For details of ferry access to the Muelle das Rodas jetty, where the walk starts and ends, see Getting to/from the Walk (p229).

THE WALK (see map p229)
From the jetty, walk 100m left to the information hut and turn right (north) along the pine-lined path; cement tracks run down the centre. The protected **Dunas de Figueiras-Mixueiro**, where many endangered plants survive, are to the right. About 300m from the start ignore the 'Praia de Figueiras' sign (it's the islands' nudist beach). The trail becomes enveloped by eucalyptus trees and progressively ascends, offering fantastic views of the Ría de Vigo. Observe a clearing in the eucalyptus on the right where a few native oaks grow. Continue to a crossroads.

To reach the **Alto do Príncipe** (122m), a magnificent lookout, turn left (west) onto an ascending trail which quickly turns south. Sloe berries, *torvisco* (Mediterranean mezereon) and rockrose flank the trail. Fifteen minutes from the crossroads the trail briefly dips before turning right and ascending to the lookout. Enjoy the excellent views of Monte Faro and its lighthouse as well as the granite rocks and erosion pools. Return to the crossroads.

Turn left (north) towards 'Faro do Peito'. After 400m a wide trail briefly heads left to a lookout before rejoining the main trail. Surrounded by open grassland, continue 15 minutes to a fork. Here, the route makes a short loop. Go left and stay on the main trail for five minutes. Reaching another fork, head left and continue briefly to a granite outcrop and, visible below on a small trail, the bird observatory (Monte Agudo is to the left). Return to the fork and descend left briefly downhill to another fork (marked with a wooden post). Head downhill 250m to the old lighthouse and a large sea cave, **Furna de Monteagudo**, a bit further down the access port ramp. Return to the fork and turn left. In 10 minutes complete the small loop.

Return to the crossroads for the last time. Take the trail to the left marked 'Campo de Traballo'. Descend for 10 minutes through forest. Before reaching some research tents, take a footpath right towards the ocean and the rocky area **O Bufardo**. Keep straight (south) on the narrow forest trail just above the white beach for 10 minutes to **Praia de Figueiras**. Either descend and cross the beach or continue along the obvious forest path. Both trails rejoin at the beach's southern end and in 10 minutes reach the information hut.

Serra dos Ancares

The Ancares range (composed of granite, slate and sandstone) runs for 30km and covers an area of 127 sq km, reaching its maximum heights at Pico Cuíña (1987m) in León and O Mostallar (1935m) in Galicia. In the Ancares, the westward-flowing rivers include the Ser, Rao and Navia while the Cua, Ancares and Burbia head east. Due to its isolation, ruggedness of life and political marginalisation the Ancares were slow to modernise, maintaining their customs and ancient dwellings, the *pallozas*, (see the boxed text 'Galician Vernacular Architecture). In the 1990s the area began to receive EU development grants and the government's tourism branch realised that 'the past' sells. Money has primarily been funnelled into rural guesthouses rather than conservation of the enormous natural assets. Ancares is a *reserva nacional de caza* (national hunting reserve), though area supporters optimistically label it a *parque natural* on signs and stickers.

Not overwhelmed by eucalyptuses and pines, the Ancares woodlands are distinctly Atlantic (oak, birch, laurel, hazel, yew and holly). Chestnut, oak and walnut groves are also an intrinsic part of the landscape. Retaining its leaves and fruit in winter, holly plays a crucial role, providing 50% of the herbivores' nourishment and shelter; it's 5°C warmer under its canopy. Due to human

Galician Vernacular Architecture

Inhabited until the 1980s, *pallozas* are dwellings that were first developed during pre-Roman times and well adapted to the Ancares. Upon an oval floor, 1m-high stone walls rise to meet the conical roof of rye-thatch that prevented the accumulation of snow and water. People shared the inside – separated into various rooms with the hearth at the centre – with their animals, taking advantage of their heat. Constructed with a southern exposure and on a slant to improve drainage, they had small windows but no chimneys; smoke filtered up through the thatch.

Near to the dwellings are *hórreos*, free-standing granaries elevated on columns or solid blocks and used to store the harvest free from humidity. Between the column and the granary's base a projecting horizontal rock prevents hungry rodents from gaining access. Asturian *hórreos* are square with wooden walls and a four-sided tile, slate or even thatch roof. The Galician ones are quite diverse but are usually rectangular and made of stone, with a pitched tile roof often decorated with a cross.

Constructed on riverbanks, *molinos* milled corn and wheat using water power. River water was diverted through a canal then released, dropping onto a turbine that moved a huge stone wheel which ground the grain. Mills either had one owner, who kept a percentage of the flour milled, or several who took turns milling. In the 19th century more than 8200 *molinos* functioned in Galicia.

Cortines, appearing on mountain hillsides near villages, are circular or oval stone walls up to 1.5m high with horizontally projecting stones rimming their tops. These prevented sweet-toothed bears from robbing the beehives kept inside them of their honey. Examples are found in both the Ancares and Courel.

GALICIA

exploitation of the environment (cutting trees for timber and pastures), scrub (including tasty blueberries) covers much of the range. The great yellow gentian is a beautiful companion on the range's heights.

The Ancares woodlands contain rare and endangered mammals such as pine martens, wolves and the *urogallo*, or capercaillie, known locally as the *pita do monte* (mountain chicken). Its spectacular nuptial song once filled the woods in spring. The *urogallo* has been protected from hunting since 1971, but only 10 pairs are believed to survive. Expect to see roe deer, diminutive creatures which skip across scree.

PLANNING

Ancares winters are long, cold and wet (1500mm to 2000mm of rainfall). Autumn colours are particularly appealing for walking. A compass is recommended for navigation here.

Maps & Books

Everest's 1:80,000 *Os Ancares: Mapa de Carretera* is ideal for orientation. For both walks described the IGN's 1:50,000 *Sierra de Ancares* topographic map is best. Cumio's 1:50,000 topographic map and guidebook *Ancares: La gran sierra Galaico-Leonesa* are also good and informative.

Information Sources

Area information is best acquired through the town halls in Pedrafita do Cebreiro or Becerreá (see Access Towns & Facilities). Camping in the wild is frowned upon; ask for permission in the San Román de Cervantes (henceforth known as Cervantes) town hall. Get petrol at access towns as none is available within the Ancares.

ACCESS TOWNS & FACILITIES
Pedrafita do Cebreiro

Straddling the most important pass connecting Galicia to Madrid via the NVI highway (the A6 *autovía* bypasses the town proper), Pedrafita is a gateway to either the Ancares (north) or the Courel (south). You'll find all general services here. A culinary must is the local cow's-milk cheese,

Queixo do Cebreiro. With its original cream cheese–like texture and flavour, it is divine alone or with local honey or cherries.

The **town hall** (☎ *982 36 71 03; open 9am-3pm Mon-Fri*) has basic information on the Ancares.

Hostal Restaurante Pazos (☎ *982 36 70 85; Avenida Castilla 1; doubles with bathroom €36*) and **Casa Garcia** (☎ *982 36 70 21; Camiño da Feira 2; doubles with bathroom €30*) both have simple rooms and serve meals (from €8). Rustic Cebreiro, 5km south on the Triacastela road, also has lodgings (see Cebreiro, p359).

ALSA (☎ *902 42 22 42;* W *www.alsa.es*) runs buses to Pedrafita from Santiago de Compostela (€12.60, three hours, three daily) and Madrid (€23.20, five hours, two daily).

Find taxis from Bar Galicia on the main street or call **Juan Carlos** (☎ *647 84 29 50*), who operates daily from June to August and at weekends the rest of the year. From Pedrafita to Degrada he charges €36 and to Seoane do Courel, €22.

By car from Santiago, take the N634 (towards Oviedo) to Guitiriz and then head for Pedrafita on the A6 via Lugo. From Madrid take the A6 (towards La Coruña).

Becerreá

Nicknamed the 'Gateway to the Ancares', Becerreá offers all general services. The **town hall** (☎ *982 36 00 04; open 8.30am-2pm Mon-Fri, 9am-1pm Sat*) will help you find your bearings.

To overnight here, convenient **Hostal Herbón** (☎ *982 36 00 35; doubles with/without bathroom €24/20*) is across from the bus stop and also serves meals (*menú* €7).

ALSA (☎ *902 42 22 42*) runs daily buses to Becerreá from Santiago de Compostela (€11.05, three hours, three a day) and Madrid (€25, five hours, two a day).

Taxi drivers congregate at Calle Carlos III, **Bar Centro** (☎ *982 36 0016*) or you can contact the local driver on ☎ 689 56 33 93. Tariffs from Becerreá are: to the Camping Os Ancares €10.50, to Degrada €23, and to Piornedo €34.

By car from Santiago, take the N634 (towards Oviedo) to Guitiriz and then head for

Becerreá on the A6 (towards Madrid) via Lugo.

Camping Os Ancares

In Mosteiro 5km south of Cervantes (on the Becerreá–Degrada road) is **Camping Os Ancares** (☎ 982 36 45 56; camping per adult/child/tent/car €3.10/2.80/3.10/2.80).

Piornedo

Both walks end here. The town is nicknamed the 'pre-Roman hamlet' for its fine grouping of *pallozas*; the **palloza museum** *(admission €1)* is a must. Of the four lodgings, the best are **Cantina O Mustallar** *(☎ 982 15 17 17; doubles with/without bathroom from €31.25/19.25)*, which serves excellent home-cooked meals *(menú €7.80)* and runs the museum; and the mountain lodge **Hostal Piornedo** *(☎ 982 15 13 51, 982 16 15 87; doubles with/without bathroom €25/22)*. The latter sells books and maps of the area and has good meals for €10.

Piornedo lies 10km beyond Degrada (see Refuxio dos Ancares). To travel between Piornedo and Degrada (€20) or Becerreá (€40) by taxi contact **Pedrete** *(☎ 982 15 13 59)* in Piornedo. On weekends and afternoons, **Manolo** *(☎ 659 28 64 24)* in Cervantes also runs from Piornedo (€36) and Degrada (€22) to Becerreá.

Ancares Ridge

Duration	5½–7 hours
Distance	19km
Difficulty	moderate–demanding
Start	Refuxio dos Ancares (p233)
Finish	Piornedo (p233)
Transport	taxi

Summary Walking with the clouds; this south–north traverse climbs five high peaks before descending to the hamlet of Piornedo with its pre-Roman–style dwellings

Beginning from Refuxio dos Ancares, just outside Degrada, and ending in Piornedo, this outstanding ridge walk can also be done in reverse; although the Mostallar ascent is taxing.

Carry plenty of water as there are no fountains, other than a natural spring, en route.

NEAREST FACILITIES
Refuxio dos Ancares

Adjacent to the Ancares Ridge walk trailhead, **Refuxio dos Ancares** *(☎ 982 18 11 13; dorm beds €5; singles/doubles with bathroom €20/30)* is 1.5km from Degrada, which is little more than a crossroads with several houses. Food is available *(menú €10)*.

Degrada lies roughly 40km from either Becerreá (9km towards Navia de Suarna then towards Cervantes) or Pedrafita (towards Doiras); both approaches follow seemingly endless winding roads. Hire a taxi from Becerreá or Pedrafita if travelling on public transport.

THE WALK (see map p234)

From Refuxio dos Ancares (1350m), take the sealed road that heads southeast among broom, ferns and heather for 30 minutes (1.3km) until the sealed road converts to dirt track. Over the next easy 5km the trail passes a fountain trough, the Campa de Ortigoso and a holly and oak forest. The track peters out at **Campa de Tres Obispos** (1579m) at the base of Pico Tres Obispos. There are spectacular panoramic views of the *serra's* highest peaks from here. From left to right (northeast to southwest) are Cuíña, O Mostallar, Lagos or Lanzas, Corno Maldito, das Charcas, Penedois, Tres Obispos and, on the far right, the hooked Pena Rubia.

Take the southbound footpath that ascends towards Pico Tres Obispos. For 25 minutes climb steeply through heather and then grass along the ridge towards the peak. Keep along the peak's right slope to a meadow at the base of the summit. Search for a trail on the left that climbs to the rocky summit of **Pico Tres Obispos** (1795m). Views of the *serra* and a good part of León and Lugo provinces are yours from this legendary gathering spot of the bishops of Astorga, Lugo and Oviedo – the shared corner of their dioceses.

Descend briefly southeast. Take the ridge trail northeast, crossing the rocky and irregular peaks of **Os Penedois** (1754m). The trail sometimes disappears underneath the stones.

GALICIA

Ancares Ridge & Piornedo Loop

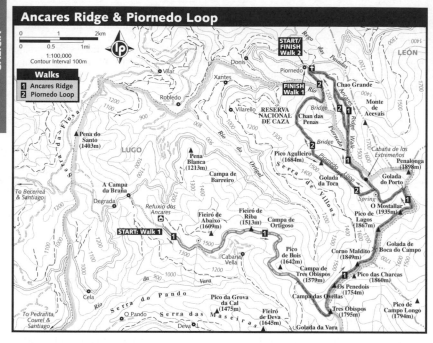

Instead of ascending the next peak, Pico das Charcas (1793m), take a trail from its base and follow its left-hand slope to the base of the conical **Corno Maldito** (Damned Horn).

Circle around the base of Corno Maldito's right slope through open pasture, then turn left (northeast) ascending to the ridge. Once on the ridge, if you want to go to Corno Maldito's summit turn left and in five minutes reach the summit cairn (1849m). Return to the ridge. Follow the left slope of the next hill and descend to the wide saddle, **Golada de Boca do Campo**. A small cirque lies off to the right. You are now halfway through the walk.

Ascend the ridge heading north for 25 minutes to **Pico de Lagos** (Pico de Lanzas; 1867m). From the summit, also cairned, O Mostallar comes into spectacular view to the northeast. Descend towards it along the ridge. Look for a level trail through scree along Mostallar's west face. Once through the scree the trail remains level and converts to

grass before turning sharply and steeply right. This is the only tricky part and you may need to use your hands. Aim for the ridge 30m away. Once on the ridge turn left, quickly reaching the flat-topped and grassy summit of **O Mostallar** (1935m). Continue to the cairn and then head left (north) in descent along a wire fence (a footpath runs parallel to it). Follow this all the way down to the saddle, **Golada do Porto**.

Turn left (west) and descend across the basin (a perfect example of a glacial hanging valley) for 30 minutes to a shepherd's hut, **Cabaña de los Extremeños**. En route, pass a natural spring, cross a stream (the origin of Río Piornedo) and, if you're lucky, ripe blueberries. From the dilapidated cabin take a road descending to the left for 30 minutes to another open valley. Cross the river again via an old wooden bridge. Continue straight ahead, first ascending and then continuously descending (for 3km) to Piornedo along the wide lane. Enter the village past its chapel.

Piornedo Loop

Duration	4½–5½ hours
Distance	13km
Difficulty	moderate
Start/Finish	Piornedo (p233)
Transport	taxi

Summary A varied walk through lush forest, mountain pastures, high valleys and a long ridge crest to the xorigin of the sparkling Río Piornedo

The walk starts and ends in Piornedo. Drinking water is available only at Piornedo's public fountain.

THE WALK (see map p234)

Ascend through Piornedo to the chapel. Take the road on which the Ancares Ridge description ends, and pass through the gate. Ascend for 25 minutes (1.2km). Where the road briefly descends for 200m, and veers right then left before beginning a steep ascent, look for a 3m-high boulder to the right of the road. From here a footpath heads off left (south) along the southwestern slope of the open hillside sprinkled with holly, birch and rowan. Looking right, the valley below is clearly visible, as are the ridge, forest and zigzagging trail that the walk reaches later. After five minutes the footpath enters a dense forest and gently ascends for 20 minutes along an intermittently rocky trail.

As the ascent ends, continue south, keeping left through the high broom and pastures. The trail reaches the second, lower valley described in the Ancares Ridge walk. Cross the wooden bridge and ascend the wide trail for 35 minutes to the shepherd's cabin, **Cabaña de los Extremeños**. Head eastward, towards the Golada do Porto saddle (left of O Mostallar) aiming for the centre of the great basin. Look for the multi-coloured snow-marker. Once you spot it, turn right to face southwest, and look for the only visible path up to the ridge (some sections are open dirt). Aim for this path and ascend steeply for 15 minutes, out of the basin to the ridge, which has outstanding views.

Turn north (right) along the crest of the ridge (if you went left, you would reach Pico de Lagos) and head towards the next peak. After 20 minutes (1km) the trail descends to a narrow saddle, Golada da Toca. Ignore a trail descending steeply to the right, which returns to the wooden bridge. Continue ascending the ridge to the summit of **Pico Agulleiro** (1684m).

On a poorly marked westbound trail, begin the gentle descent on a high open plain for 300m. Turn right (northeast) and descend 200m, going cross-country, towards the forest. Reaching the magical birch forest, look for the clear left-hand (north-northwest) descending trail. It stays close to the edge of the forest. Descend for 20 minutes until the trail reaches another, wider trail. Turn left onto the new trail, which immediately leaves the forest. Turn right, keeping a couple of boulders on your left. A thick tunnel of broom leads to a deep trail that becomes enveloped in holly forest before reaching an open plain surrounded by huge boulders, **Chan das Penas**. The trail peters out here.

Turn right (north-northeast) for 100m along the grass and when the trail reappears continue straight ahead (north) ignoring another trail leading left. The trail makes a serpentine 30-minute descent, primarily in the forest, passing two large, dry oaks on the right, before reaching the valley floor. Cross the stone bridge, spanning the Río Piornedo, and take the dirt road straight ahead which ascends directly to the village (near the chapel) in 20 minutes.

Serra do Courel

Lying on a northeast-southwest axis, the Serra do Courel or Caurel (210 sq km) is divided and demarcated by three mighty rivers – the Lor (west), Quiroga and Sor (east). Its steep, forested hillsides and rounded, open peaks reach a maximum height at Pico Formigueiros (1643m). The iron-rich limestone and slate mountains were the focus of Roman mining operations and evidence of these activities is found throughout the area. The Courel's main attractions are its rustic mountain villages and extraordinary flora.

GALICIA

The soils, orientation, slopes, minimal pollution and the convergence of Atlantic and Mediterranean climate systems have produced more than 1000 floral species that flourish between 400m and 1600m. Remarkably, 40% of Galicia's flora is represented in the Courel, which constitutes only 1% of the total territory. Special forests called *devesas* – humid, north-facing mixed woodlands of *carballo* (common oak), Pyrenean oak, maples, hazel, beech (Spain's westernmost examples), holly, birch, rowan and yew trees – thrive here. Mediterranean species include holm and cork oaks and strawberry trees as well as the aromatic

Chestnuts, Soutos & Sequeiros

Huge *soutos* (chestnut groves) grow thickly around Courel villages. The chestnuts' enormous trunks, often twisted and gnarled, support odd-looking small limbs intentionally cultivated this way for two reasons: to provide lumber without killing the whole tree, and to produce more chestnuts. The carbohydrate-rich fruit, wrapped in prickly husks, was long fundamental to the local diet (before the potato's arrival). Come autumn, the Courel turns rich tones of yellow, and the husks (known locally as *ourizos*, or literally 'hedgehogs') turn brown and fall to the ground. Continuing an ancient cycle, the Courel's signature tree is ready for harvest. Soon the air fills with the delicious scent of roasting chestnuts. Today a *magosto* (chestnut roast) is still celebrated each November in alternating years in Seoane and Folgoso. Roasted, stewed, stuffed in birds, boiled and mashed, or simply raw – chestnuts are integral in regional dishes. For year-round use, chestnuts were dried during a laborious 20-day process in *sequeiros*, stone and slate-roofed drying cabins frequently grouped together. As the old ways die out, some of these buildings as well as the *cabañas* used to store hay – both of which are commonly seen on walks – are being converted into weekend homes.

rockrose and lavender bushes. Wildflowers are particularly rich and include purple orchid, columbine, butterwort, toadflax and purple flag iris.

Bats inhabit the area's limestone caves, and it's possible to encounter rare mountain cats and martens, and to see the endangered golden eagle (only five reproductive pairs remain) in the sky.

GETTING AROUND

Public transport consists only of taxis and inconveniently infrequent summertime **Empresa Courel** (☎ 982 42 82 11) buses connecting Quiroga, on the Courel's southern extreme, with Folgoso do Courel (see p237) and Seoane do Courel.

ACCESS TOWNS

See Pedrafita do Cebreiro (p232).

Seoane do Courel

Hillside Seoane, 25km south of Pedrafita, has a bank (with ATM) and a pharmacy.

Located 1.5km from Seoane (towards Visuña) **Acampamento O Caurel** (☎ 982 43 31 01; camping per person/tent/car €3.20/ 3.20/3.20; 2/4-person bungalows €34/55; open Easter & mid-July–Dec) has a cafetería, telephone and information sheets with details of nearby walks.

Casa Ferreiro (☎ 982 43 30 65; doubles with/without bathroom €30/24) has comfortable rooms and an attractive dining room (meals €8).

Nestled in the woods on the fringe of the village is **Restaurante-Hospedaje Fontiña** (☎ 982 43 31 06; doubles with bathroom €24), where meals run from €8.

Try **Restaurante Anduriña** at the village centre for a meal with great views, or the small **market** for basic foodstuffs.

Empresa Courel (☎ 982 42 82 11) makes runs to Folgoso and Seoane from Quiroga (see p237; €4, one hour, one daily). During July and August this bus runs only Monday, Wednesday and Friday.

The owner of **Bar Hydra** (☎ 982 43 30 81) doubles as the taxi driver. He drives between Seoane and Pedrafita (€18), Moreda (€6), Folgoso (€18) and Vilamor (€18).

By car, head south from Pedrafita (towards Triacastela) on the LU651. Just before Hospital da Condesa, turn left to Seoane.

Folgoso do Courel

Folgoso is the Courel's largest community and serves as the administrative centre. The only information centre actually within the Courel is Folgoso's **town hall** (☎ 982 43 30 01; W caurel.fegamp.es; open 9am-3pm & 5pm-8pm Mon-Fri), which provides the basics in Spanish. There are ATMs, a pharmacy and the area's **health centre** (open mornings only).

O Mirador (☎ 982 43 30 64; doubles with bathroom €24), on the main road towards Vilamor, has the best rooms in town.

Casa Constantino (☎ 982 43 30 05; singles/doubles €9/15), in the upper part of the village, offers simple, budget lodgings and home-style cooking (meals €6).

Bar-Hospedaxe Novo (☎ 982 43 30 07; doubles with/without bathroom €21/18) has comfortable rooms and good meals (€9). For supplies there are **markets** in centre of the village.

Bus access is as for Seoane do Courel (see pp236–7). By car, continue from Seoane for 12km on the LU651. Folgoso's taxi driver, **Alejandro** (☎ 982 43 30 87), makes runs to Pedrafita (€24), Seoane (€9), Vilamor (€6) and Froxán (€9).

Quiroga

If using public transport you will need to spend a night in Quiroga on the range's southern end. The **tourist office** (☎ 982 42 89 46; Rúa Xardíns; open daily) supplies area information, and adjacent **Librería Celia** has books and maps. **Hostal Quiper** (☎ 982 42 84 51; General Franco 62; doubles with bathroom €30) doubles as the bus stop. For a bite to eat, try **Restaurante O Roxo Vivo** (Pereiro 8; menú €7). There's an **Empresa Monforte** (☎ 981 56 42 96) bus between Santiago and Quiroga via Monforte (€9.55, two hours, one daily). **Taxis** (☎ 982 42 89 08) run from Bar Cine on General Franco to Folgoso (€15) and Seoane (€24).

Devesa da Rogueira Loop

Duration	6–7 hours
Distance	19.8km
Difficulty	moderate–demanding
Start/Finish	Moreda (p237)
Transport	taxi

Summary An ascent through magical forest with more than 1000 species to the Serra do Courel's crest, Galicia's only glacial lagoon and a unique natural spring

Initially enveloped in the enchanting *devesa*, this trail breaks through to the open ridge for superb panoramic views of the Courel. The return leg leads down to the rustic village of Moreda. Most of the Courel was once covered by *devesas* but these were nearly logged to death at the turn of the 20th century. Information panels in Spanish accompany the trail for 20 minutes and explain how many of forest's trees were traditionally used. The trail is intermittently marked as the PR50.

The walk ascends 870m through the forest. In spring both the Fonte do Cervo and the glacial Lagoa A Lucenza will be full, while the changing leaves make autumn an attractive time. To shorten the walk by 5km simply descend back through the forest where indicated in the text. Water is available at several natural springs en route.

PLANNING
Maps
The IGN's 1:25,000 map No 157-I *Seoane do Courel* covers the route.

NEAREST TOWN
Moreda
Moreda is laid out on a steep hillside at the base of the Devesa da Rogueira. It has a fountain and a charming, rural guesthouse, **A Casiña da Rogueira** (☎ 982 15 56 23; doubles €27, 5-person house with kitchen €87), near the walk's end.

At the trailhead, 300m down the road, is the **Aula de Natureza** (open 10am-2pm & 4pm-8pm daily), an interpretive centre that is staffed year-round and has a public toilet. Displays on flora, fauna and local life are

GALICIA

worth a run-through. Also available is the excellent free booklet (in Spanish), *Itinerario Ambiental por el Bosque de A Rogueira*.

Moreda is 7km from Seoane. Either take a taxi (see Seoane do Courel, pp236–7) or drive. Travelling towards Folgoso, turn left towards Parada/Moreda.

THE WALK

From Moreda's interpretive centre, head southeast into a chestnut grove. Five minutes later cross a stream adjacent to a *sequeiro* (and, further along, some *cabañas*). For 25 minutes the trail ascends along a trail (ignore

Devesa da Rogueira

field-access trails (left) and enjoy views of the *devesa* and ridge to be climbed). Where the trail crosses a stream, make a hairpin left turn, and five minutes later reach a fork.

Take the right fork and begin a series of switchbacks through forest for 20 minutes. The trail levels and passes a stretch where the stream descends in cascades. Immediately after fording the stream, the trail steepens again and the hardest section begins – 30 minutes uphill through woodland. On reaching a fork go right. Continue ascending to a T-junction and turn right. Five minutes later there's another T-junction – with the upper loop trail. Turn left and in five minutes reach the **Fonte do Cervo**. From the high rock-face two springs flow – one red (rich in iron), the other clear (calcareous). They taste and smell differently and are said to be medicinal.

Continue east, ascending for 30 minutes through forest and then low, often dense shrubs. The narrow trail zigzags to a slate road on the crest of the *serra*. Rounded Formigueiros peak (1639m) is visible to the left during this section. Turn right (southwest) onto the 4WD road, ascending to the summit of **Teso das Papoulas** (1603m). Enjoy superlative views – look for Ancares to the right (northeast). Descend the slate road to a crossroads in a wide saddle, Campa da Lucenza.

To visit the lagoon (visible to the left while descending from Teso das Papoulas), continue straight ahead at the crossroads and veer left onto an unmarked grassy area. A path soon appears and descends to the base of a hill. From here go right on a footpath to reach the shore of **Lagoa A Lucenza** (1376m). Retrace your steps to Campa da Lucenza.

Take the 4WD road straight ahead (northwest) and immediately take a right fork along a road that is level at first, and then descends steeply. Continue for 20 minutes. When the road runs nearly parallel to another road on the left, turn right onto a path that soon reaches a small slate quarry and then enters the *devesa* heading southeast. In 15 minutes the path reaches a familiar junction.

Take the left fork and descend the trail to a junction (three minutes). Instead of turning left along the trail you came up on the ascent (returning this way saves 5km), continue straight on. After 100m ignore a footpath that goes left. During the next hour the obvious trail fords two streams, passes through an area rich in yews, and twists through the forest in gradual descent. It continues by breaking through the forest to an area with hazels, scrub oaks, rowan and birch, and reaches a sealed road hemmed in by pines, near the top of Alto do Couto. Where the forest opens, it's easy to spot the descent route: look north for the *cabañas* and Moreda below.

Turn left down the road; after 100m there's a fountain and water tank. Continue for 1.4km (25 minutes), ignoring dirt roads. Branch left off the sealed road onto a dirt trail that zigzags downhill and in 15 minutes reaches the first cabin. Turn right and descend (ignore two dirt trails left) to pastures and continue straight. *Cabañas* are visible at the foot of a section of scree. Continue through a wet zone and trees and take a descending fork left. The cobbled path widens as it descends steeply in 10 minutes to Moreda Maior, some cabins surrounded by walnuts. Continue for 15 minutes on the clear trail; a chestnut grove indicates Moreda is close. Reaching a fork, head left and, once past some small gardens, enter Moreda via the cement road. At the guesthouse, 100m further on, turn left and in 300m reach the interpretive centre, or turn right down to Moreda's plaza and fountain.

Río Lor Meander

Duration	3 days
Distance	51.5km
Difficulty	moderate
Start	Seoane do Courel
Finish	Vilamor
Nearest Towns	Seoane do Courel (p236), Folgoso do Courel (p237)
Transport	bus, taxi

Summary An outstanding village-to-village walk through the steep-sided canyon of the sinuous Río Lor, passing inhabited villages, *soutos* and a pre-Roman fort

This route invites you to see the Courel through the eyes of the river. Primarily undulating along the canyon of the Lor's true left bank, it uses ancient pathways traversed for millennia by villagers travelling to the foundry, to the *cortines* to get honey (see the boxed text 'Galician Vernacular Architecture', p231), to the *sequeiros* to tend chestnuts (see the boxed text 'Chestnuts, Soutos & Sequeiros', p236), or just to get from place to place. Marked with 'Ruta do Lor' wooden signs and yellow arrows (haphazardly), the recently rehabilitated trail is the work of local people wishing to recuperate a not-so-distant yet abandoned past. If you are short on time, we recommend Day 2 and especially Day 3 as highlights. Parts of the walk may be overgrown, especially during Day 1. Long pants are advised. Water is readily available at village fountains.

PLANNING
Maps
The IGN's 1:25,000 map Nos 157-I *Seoane do Courel*, 156-II *Folgoso do Courel* and 156-IV *Salcedo* cover the route.

THE WALK (see maps p240 & p241)
Day 1: Seoane do Courel to Folgoso do Courel
5–6½ hours, 16.3km

Left of Bar Gloria in Seoane take a descending paved road past houses towards the canyon. After 90m, fork right down the chestnut-flanked trail. At a crossroads continue straight ahead and fork right downhill. On the left, just before the trail passes under a house, is a 19th-century water-powered foundry. Cross over the bridge and continue to a wooden 'Ruta Río Lor' sign 100m ahead. Distances are clearly marked.

Take the ascending trail curving right to a chestnut grove. After passing a house on the right and two impressive vertical boulders, the trail continues for 5km along roughly the same contour while rounding the great flanks of the hill on the left. The trail never reaches the river, although it is audible much of the way. About 20 minutes into the walk take a left fork and 10 minutes later, at a T-junction, go left again and pass some *sequeiros*. Take a fork to the right after a further 100m or so. Just before entering the village there are fantastic views down the canyon. The trail curves left past several houses, becomes a paved road and descends to **Ferreirós de Abaixo**, on the river, and a **bar-restaurant** serving outstanding meals (€8). Don't miss this place! The owner is a true local artist who transforms tree trunks into magnificent pieces of furniture.

Head to the road (the guardrail shows Ruta do Lor distances) and ascend for 300m. After several large chestnut trees marked with yellow arrows, veer right down a footpath. For 30 minutes descend gradually through forest – some sections are overgrown. The gorge narrows to 30m across. During the next 2km (40 minutes) the trail rolls through the forest past a natural spring (on the left), then branches left (ascending away from the Lor past a *sequeiro*) and finally drops to another fork on a wider path. Go left here. (The right fork descends 50m to an old wooden bridge, Ponte do Porto, and a beckoning swimming hole.) Ascend

Río Lor Meander (North)

along an open hillside with the main road above you, and in 10 minutes pass a crumbling *cortín* on the left. Twenty minutes later, when a tower is visible to the southwest (left) on a hilltop, veer right, downhill, at an unmarked fork. Look ahead to the next bend and aim for the trail visible on a contour below yours. You may need to go cross-country in places. At the bend continue on roughly the same contour for 10 minutes, ascending only gradually to meet the trail, marked with yellow arrows, at a big slate outcrop. Briefly ascend, with the arrows, to a curve in a wide slate road. Turn left (uphill) to reach Folgoso; to the right (downhill) the trail continues to Valdomir (see Day 2).

Ascend 3.5km along a zigzagging dirt road. Folgoso is visible most of the time. Either continue to the top along the road, to the tower, and turn right onto the main road to reach Folgoso in 400m, or take an old field-access trail. This small trail ascends straight ahead through mimosas, heather and lavender from the last 180-degree left curve before the tower, when the village is directly ahead and above. A 20m section of blackberry brambles may block your passage. If not, continue for 350m along the open hill to a cobbled lane. In 10 minutes reach the village plaza.

Day 2: Folgoso do Courel to Vilamor
5–6½ hours, 16.2km

Return to the Folgoso–Valdomir juncture along the slate road from the previous day. Continue downhill to a wooden bridge and cross, then veer left. In five minutes cross another wooden bridge, **Ponte de Sudrios**, spanning the Río Loúzara near its confluence with the Lor. Over the bridge turn left and continue for 20 minutes, passing O Touzón (its small chapel, dedicated to San Roque, is worth a peek) and the houses of A Pendella before reaching the main road and a bridge at Valdomir. Cross the bridge to the **Mesón Catuxo**, which is a great spot for a drink or meal (from €7).

From the parking lot, take the trail past the chapel (right) and ascend to the Ruta do

Río Lor Meander (South)

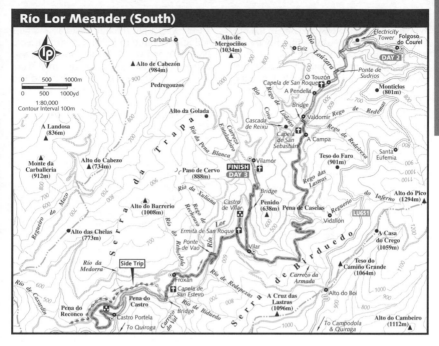

0   500   1000m
0   500   1000yd
1:80,000
Contour Interval 100m

Lor sign. Turn left, reaching an old aqueduct in 150m, and then take a fork to the right uphill along a narrow, steep trail which opens to a *souto*. Look for arrows and ascend straight to a zigzagging trail up to A Campa. Arrows accurately lead left, right, left and right through the maze of houses. From A Campa's last house, Vilamor's church, high on the opposite side of the canyon, dominates. The good trail undulates for 2km: go left at four forks. Where the trail ascends steeply to a wide slate road, go right downhill (the fifth fork) and pass below Vidallón. Visible in the distance are the houses of Vilar, nestled in chestnut trees at approximately the same elevation as you. Mediterranean species suddenly appear on this section: rockrose, cork oaks and strawberry trees. In 10 minutes reach a 'Ruta Castro do Vilar' sign and a *cabaña*. Leave the road and take a narrow but obvious descending trail towards Vilar. The trail is magnificent through here as it winds around

cliffs. In another easy 25 minutes you'll reach **Vilar**.

At the concrete plaza turn left to the fountain or continue straight through a tunnel (formed by a balconied house) to a fork. Immediately to the right is a small **museum** *(admission by €1 donation)* run by a fascinating local man who has salvaged everything from harnesses and saddles to pots and spinning tools from Vilar and neighbouring villages. The route to Froxán (signposted) veers left through the village; today's route veers right, downhill, towards Vilamor. Continue for 20 minutes through Vilar's chestnut grove and then through hillside scrub to the river. Cross the Lor over a wooden bridge. Ascend along switchbacks for 25 minutes to a chestnut grove and a T-junction. Make a sharp turn left and in another 100m reach the sealed road into Vilamor. The church is on a hill to the right. Turn left, and then in 100m turn right into dilapidated Vilamor.

Vilamor

With one foot in the past and one in the present, Vilamor is kept alive primarily by one entrepreneurial family. There are no shops or services, but rooms and outstanding fresh country meals (breakfast €2.50, lunch and dinner €9) are available in the family's home, **Casa Carlos** *(☎ 982 15 56 18; doubles with bathroom €25)*. It also rents two small houses equipped with kitchen and bathroom: **Casa Dosinda** *(€50)* sleeps five and **Casa Comerciante** *(€42)* sleeps three.

No buses reach Vilamor. By car, continue on the LU651 for 6km from Folgoso. **Carlos** *(☎ 982 15 56 18)* of the rural guesthouse drives a taxi from Vilamor to Seoane (€12), Pedrafita (€30) or Quiroga (€20).

Day 3: Vilamor to Castro Portela Return

5½–7 hours, 19km

Return to Vilar the same way. Hairpin right through the village and continue for five minutes through the hamlet, *souto* and gardens. Veer right past the San Roque chapel to the ruined 2nd-century Castro de Vilar upon a rocky spur above the Lor. In spite of the overgrowth, it's possible to discern defensive walls and the ruins of circular dwellings.

Back at the chapel, take the footpath that descends right (west) through chestnuts and then open hillside for 20 minutes to the Río Lor. Cross the wooden bridge, **Ponte de Vao** (the last PR51 sign), and ascend left along a wider path. Where it levels out look for cork oaks. At the next fork veer left, entering Froxán, a hamlet of medieval appearance, and continue to its plaza. The village fountain is up to the right. Veer left from the plaza down past the houses. After the last house turn left and immediately go right on a cobbled lane that descends to a sealed road on the banks of the Lor in 10 minutes.

Cross the Río Lor on the road and continue for 1km. Turn right onto a descending lane that appears when the road makes its first left turn, initiating the 2.5km loop of Castro Portela. Continue straight, ignoring a descending trail right, for 15 minutes on a hillside trail among chestnuts above the Lor. After the trail descends and curves left,

passing a restored *sequeiro*, it curves right to a fork. Veer right through pastures and huts and after 300m turn left in ascent to Castro Portela. Wend your way up through the village, past a fountain, to the sealed road. Turn left, return to the bridge along the road and continue to Vilamor via Froxán and Vilar.

Side Trip: Lor Continuation

1½ hours, 5km

Exploring the Lor's true right bank below Castro Portela, this walk offers the longest continuous section along the river.

From the bridge over the Lor near Castro Portela, take the sealed road towards Froxán and in 400m you will reach cork oaks and a *cortín*. Turn left along an ancient lane that once linked the villages and descend towards the river. The path parallels the river, offering spectacular views for 2km until it reaches some cabins in a field surrounded by chestnuts. Return the same way.

Other Walks

Parque Natural Fraga do Eume

Under the lush shelter of Galicia's last great Atlantic woodland, this circuit walk descends along the Río Eume's canyon, continuing along its river bank to reach the Caaveiro monastery. This easy–moderate 12km walk is accessed via Pontedeume, starts at the Camping Fraga do Eume and is intermittently marked as the GR50. Use the IGN's 1:25,000 map Nos 22-III *Pontedeume* and 22-I *Fene*.

SANTIAGO DE COMPOSTELA
Monte Pedroso

A must if staying in Santiago, this easy 10km return walk leaves from the Praza do Obradoiro and ascends Monte Pedroso (Rocky Hill) to the north. Panoramic views of Santiago and the surrounding countryside are exceptionally fine. From the parador, descend the ramp to the Carmen de Abaixo church. Turn right immediately after the bridge. Veer left up the first road until it converts to dirt, winding to the top.

Sobrado dos Monxes

North of Melide, but reached from Arzúa, is one of the best conserved (and still functioning) monasteries of Galicia, Sobrado dos Monxes. Around the monastery is a 12km loop. Leaving from the Barrio de Alvariza the trail covers the monastery's lands, a lagoon, oak woods and various hamlets. IGN map Nos 71-III *Sobrado* and 71-IV *As Cruces* cover the walk.

SERRA DOS ANCARES
Picos Cuíña & Penalonga

East of Piornedo, accessible by car and just within León's borders, is the Porto dos Ancares. From here a trail (at first poorly marked) heads south (constantly veering right) and ascends two large hills before reaching the summit of Pico Cuíña (1998m), the highest peak in the Ancares. From its base, a trail leads right to the summit of Penalonga (1898m). This hard return trip takes seven hours. Use the IGN's 1:50,000 *Sierra de Ancares* map.

Campa de Brego Loop & Pico Pena Rubia

This 15.5km easy–moderate walk starts at Refuxio dos Ancares (Degrada) and descends to tranquil valleys within the most well-preserved and beautiful forest in the range. The loop initially uses the same trail as the Ancares Ridge walk, then detours at Campa de Tres Obispos descending to the Golada de Vara and back via Cabaña Vella. A 4.5km detour ascends to Pena Rubia (1822m) from the *golada*, adding challenge and views to the walk. Use IGN's 1:50,000 *Sierra de Ancares* map.

SERRA DO COUREL
Courel Ridge

Ten kilometres from Seoane, along the highway from the camping ground (heading towards Visuña) at the Alto do Couto, a dirt road turns off right. Over the course of 10km, the track snakes along the crest of the *serra*, passing Formigueiros, Mallón, Pía Paxaro, Cobaluda and ending at the Alto do Boi (10km from Folgoso). Use IGN's 1:25,000 map Nos 157-I *Seoane do Courel* and 156-IV *Salcedo*. This 20km return trip is feasible in a day.

Valencia

Without a 'star' mountain range, Valencia doesn't immediately spring to mind when thinking about walking in Spain. Most visitors link the region with images of sun, sea and sangria, but much of Valencia's interior is rugged, extremely beautiful and well covered by long- and short-distance footpaths.

On the northwestern fringes of the Comunidad Valenciana (region of Valencia), close to Aragón and Catalunya, the end of the Sistema Ibérico forms a complex of ravines and craggy summits known as Els Ports ('the region of the mountain passes'). The walled city of Morella is the gateway to this area of seemingly endless rolling sierras (mountain ranges). In the south closer to Alicante the rocky, arid mountains of La Marina tower above the Mediterranean, tempting walkers to explore thin gullies and narrow ridges.

With a variety of terrain and a long walking season the region's mountains are a great alternative to the skyscrapers and sun lounges of the Costa Blanca. Keep in mind when planning your walks that the times we give are *actual walking time* and do not include rest stops.

HISTORY

Valencia's Iberian peoples were already trading with Greek and Phoenician merchants by 800BC, and the Mediterranean coast ensured prosperity for Valencian communities through Roman, Visigoth and Muslim occupations.

Muslim influence on the region was considerable between the conquest in AD 709 and 1238 when the Christian armies of Jaime I of Aragón captured the city of Valencia. By 1245 the Christian Reconquista (Reconquest) of Valencia was complete, but Valencia retained considerable political and legal independence. The marriage of Fernando II of Aragón and Isobel I of Castilla in 1469 unified Castilla and Valencia, with other counties of the Aragonese crown following suit in 1479.

Despite the Reconquista thousands of Muslims remained, not least in order to tend

Highlights

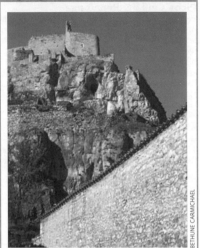

BETHUNE CARMICHAEL

A hilltop castle crowns the historic walled city of Morella

- Walking under the huge, overhanging limestone cliffs leading to the Portell de l'Infern, on the Els Ports Loop (p247)

- Looking out across waves of remote mountain ranges from the medieval walled city of Morella (p249)

- Eating excellent Valencian cuisine in the mountain restaurant of El Trestellador, overlooking the Valle de Guadalest, on the Ruta La Marina Alta walk (p258)

- Climbing down to the warm waters of the Mediterranean after spectacular ridge walking on the Serra de Bérnia Traverse (p262)

the irrigation systems that watered the terraced *huertas* (market gardens). The final Muslim expulsion began in 1609 and was an economic disaster that the region didn't recover from until the 19th century. While tourism is now the region's biggest money

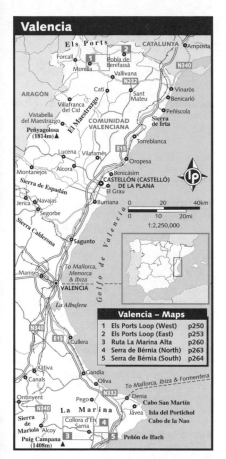

Valencia

Els Ports — CATALUNYA — Amposta
Forcall — **1** — Pobla de Benifassà — N340
Morella — Vallivana
— N232
ARAGÓN — Catí — Sant Mateu — Vinaròs
— Villafranca del Cid — Benicarló
Vistabella del Maestrazgo — Peñíscola
Peñyagolosa (1814m)▲ — COMUNIDAD VALENCIANA — Sierra de Irta
— Torreblanca
Lucena — Vilafamés — E15
— Oropesa
Montanejos — Alcora — Benicàsim
Sierra de Espadán — CASTELLÓN (CASTELLÓ) DE LA PLANA
— El Grau
Jérica — Navajas — Burriana — 0 20 40km
Segorbe — 0 10 20mi — 1:2,250,000
Sierra Calderona — Sagunto

Manises — To Mallorca, Menorca & Ibiza
VALENCIA
La Albufera
N340 — E15 — Cullera
— Xàtiva — Gandía
Canals — Oliva — To Mallorca, Ibiza & Formentera
Ontinyent — Pego — N332 — Denia
La Marina — Cabo San Martín
Sierra de Mariola — Collora d'En Sarria — Jávea — Isla del Portichol
Alcoy — **4** — Cabo de la Nao
Puig Campana (1408m)▲ — **3** — **5** — Peñón de Ifach

Valencia – Maps
1	Els Ports Loop (West)	p250
2	Els Ports Loop (East)	p253
3	Ruta La Marina Alta	p260
4	Serra de Bérnia (North)	p263
5	Serra de Bérnia (South)	p264

spinner, Valencia's fertile lands produce vast amounts of fruit (oranges are big here), vegetables, cereals and rice.

The Comunidad Valenciana was established in 1982 and includes the provinces of Castellón, Valencia and Alicante.

NATURAL HISTORY

Away from the resorts Valencia has a diverse coastline containing *salinas* (salt pans; at Santa Pola, close to Alicante, you'll see flamingos), freshwater lagoons teeming with bird life, towering cliffs and rugged outcrops as well as miles of beautiful beach.

Move west, inland across the *huertas*, and sierras covered in *sécanos* (orchards) become common. Further west the *meseta* (high tableland of central Spain) begins, although on the border with Murcia are areas of semidesert.

Valencia's mountains are contrasting. The relatively low, arid peaks in the south (such as the red and white limestone massifs of La Marina) are offshoots from the Sistema Bético that rises up in Andalucía. In the northwest El Maestrazgo is an extension of the Sistema Ibérico and the mountains are higher and wetter.

These different habitats support contrasting fauna and flora and 12 *parques naturales* (nature parks) and three *parques marinas* (marine parks) have been established since 1982. However, Valencia's wildlife has suffered from agricultural and tourist development.

CLIMATE

Valencia has a mild Mediterranean climate. When it rains (around 400mm to 500mm per year) it does so in downpours, and mostly between September and December, with another burst from April to June.

Average maximum temperatures are 13°C in winter and around 29°C in summer. Generally speaking, the mountains of the south are warmer than those in the north, which are snow-covered in winter.

INFORMATION
Maps

Three IGN 1:200,000 Mapa Provincial sheets cover Valencia. The *Alicante* map covers La Marina while the *Castellón* map covers Els Ports. Michelin's map No 445 *Central & Eastern Spain* (1:400,000) covers the whole region.

Buying Maps The best map shop in the region is Valencia's **Librería Patagonia** (☎ 96 393 60 52; ⓦ *libreriapatagonia.com; Calle Santa Amalia 2*), beside the Pont de Fuster tram station.

In Alicante **Librería International** (☎ 965 21 79 25; *Rafael Altamira 6*) carries an excellent range of 1:25,000 maps covering the La Marina region.

VALENCIA

Books

Few books in English cover walking in the Valencia region and none cover Els Ports. Readers of Spanish will have a better choice, including the comprehensive *Montañas Valencianas* series, by Rafael Cebrían.

Lonely Planet's *Valencia & the Costa Blanca* provides great insight and covers many areas (with good walking) not mentioned in this book.

Information Sources

The best place for walking information is the **Centre Excursionista de Valencia** *(☎ 96 392 31 47, fax 96 391 16 43;* **w** *www.redestb.es/cev; Plaza Tavernes de Valldigna 4; open Mon-Fri 5pm-9pm)*, which has a library and café. The organisation runs excursions, expeditions and also publishes a list of Valencian footpaths plus other general walking literature. Many Valencian towns have a *centro excursionista* or *grupo excursionista* – tourist offices and **w** www.andarines.com (in Spanish) have details.

Leaflets promoting rural tourism cover many popular walking areas (they provide a good overview) and are available from most tourist offices. Information on rural tourism is also available on **w** www.comunitat-valenciana.com and **w** www.gva.es.

Place Names

Since the end of Franco's dictatorship, Valenciano (a Catalan dialect), like many regional languages in Spain, has become increasingly popular. It was common a few years ago for names of geographical features to appear in Valenciano on local signs, but in Castilian on maps. However, the new IGN 1:25,000 map series has switched to Valenciano in some instances. We have tried to keep to the map reference, but luckily Valenciano is not *too* different from Castilian, eg *font* instead of *fuente*, *serra* instead of *sierra*.

Accommodation

All accommodation should be booked in advance by a week or more. The walking season doesn't correspond with the tourist high season and consequently many places close if they don't have bookings.

A limited selection of *casas rurales* (rural houses or farmsteads with rooms to let) can be booked through local tourist offices, but there are a host of private companies offering the same services (many also offer walking trips) in the region. These include:

Csnatura (☎ 96 472 48 45, **w** www.csnatura.com)
Escapada Rural (☎ 96 416 01 26, **w** www.escap adarural.com)
Turistrat (☎ 902 19 31 19, **w** www.turistrat.es)

See Guided Walks (p249) for contacts to help with renting a *casa rural* in the Els Ports region.

GATEWAY
Valencia

The prosperous capital of the region, Spain's third-largest city, has great nightlife, fantastic historical buildings and a contemporary architectural masterpiece, the Ciudad de las Artes y de las Ciencias (City of Arts and Sciences). If you are around for the festival of Las Fallas in mid-March you'll experience one of Europe's wildest street parties.

Information The main **tourist office** *(☎ 96 398 64 22;* **e** *touristinfo.Valencia@turisme .m400.gva.es; Paz 48)* has *some* good walking material, plus lots of background information. The town hall and Estación Norte also have offices.

Supplies & Equipment Close to the tourist office, **Base Deportes Altarriba** *(☎ 96 392 21 99; Calle Paz 11)* is a good central choice for outdoor and camping gear. If they don't have it, **Deportes Aitana** *(☎ 96 391 55 22; Calle Borrull 16)* probably will.

There's no shortage of supermarkets and specialist food outlets – **Mercado Central** *(Plaza Mercado; open daily until 2pm)* is impressive.

Places to Stay & Eat Barrio del Carmen, midway between the train and bus stations, has plenty of accommodation.

Hostal El Rincón *(☎ 96 391 79 98; Calle de la Carda 11; singles/doubles with bathroom €14/24)* is one of Valencia's oldest hostels and is good value. Lock-up parking is available here.

Hôme (☎ 96 391 62 29; W www.likeath ome.net; Calle Lonja 4; dorm beds/singles/ doubles/triples €14/21/30/43) is more expensive, but well equipped (laundry €4) and on the young, hip side of Valencia's accommodation market. Another **Hôme** (Calle Cadirers 11) is just around the corner.

Hostal Antigua Morellana (☎/fax 96 391 57 73; Calle En Bou 2; singles/doubles €29/ 42) is a lovely little place in the old heart of the town.

Close to the train station, **Meliá Plaza** (☎ 96 352 06 12, fax 96 352 04 26; W www.meli aplaza.solmelia.com; Plaza del Ayuntamiento 4; doubles weekends/weekdays €85/164) is one of Valencia's smartest hotels.

Off Plaza de la Virgen in La Seu is **Las Cuevas** (Calle Samaniego 9), a subterranean bar with a cracking range of tapas. Nearby, the good-value **Restaurante El Generalife** (Calle Caballeros 5; menú del día €9) packs 'em in.

Inventive and with a great lunch menu is **Seu-Xerea** (☎ 96 392 40 00; Calle Conde Almodóvar 4; lunch €15). **Café de las Horas** opposite is good fun, while for authentic paella take a tram to Las Arenas to the beachside **restaurants** (3-course meals under €15).

Getting There & Away Valencia is the region's main transport hub and is well served by a variety of transport options.

Air Valencia's **Aeropuerto de Manises** (☎ 96 159 85 00) is 10km west of the centre. Regular flights connect Valencia with Madrid, Barcelona, Palma de Mallorca and Ibiza, and there are daily scheduled flights to London, Paris, Milan, Lisbon, Zurich and Basel. There are no cut-price carriers, however, so if your budget's tight, fly to/from Alicante, which has several cheapo charter flights daily to major European cities.

Train Of the 10 Alaris services from **Estación Norte** (☎ 96 352 02 02) to Madrid (€35.50, 3½ hours), two originate in Castellón de la Plana (€38.50, 4½ hours). *Cercanías* (short-range suburban trains) also head to Castellón

(€3.20, 1¼ hours, hourly). Fast *Euromed* trains whiz north to Barcelona (€29 to €41, three to five hours, five daily), there are direct services to Vinaròs (€7 to €17, 1½ to two hours, eight daily) and Alicante (€8.80 to €21.50, 1½ to 2½ hours, nine daily), plus one train to both Granada (€39, eight hours) and Seville (€40.50, 6¾ hours).

Bus From the **bus station** (☎ 96 349 72 22; Menéndez Pidal) **Alsa** (☎ 902 42 22 42) buses go to Barcelona (€20 to €24.50, 4¼ to 5¾ hours, 17 daily), Granada (€22 to €27.50, six to eight hours, eight daily) and Alicante (€13, 2½ hours, nine daily).

Auto-Res (☎ 96 346 62 66) operates services to Madrid (€18.50 to €21.50, four hours, 20 daily) and **Bilman Bus** (☎ 96 347 89 89) has services to Santander (€27.50, 10¼ hours, one daily) and Pamplona (€18.50, 7½ hours, two daily)

Hife (☎ 902 119 814) buses to Castellón are slower and less frequent than train services.

Boat Ferries are run by **Trasmediterranea** (☎ 96 367 65 12; W www.trasmediterranea .com) between Mallorca (Palma) and Valencia (€25.30, 4¼ to 7½ hours, one daily).

Balearia Lines (☎ 902 19 10 68; W www .balearia.com) runs ferries (mostly via Ibiza) to Palma (€44 to €55, five to nine hours, twice daily) from Denia (80km south of Valencia).

Els Ports Loop

Duration	6 days
Distance	106.5km
Difficulty	moderate
Start/Finish	Morella (p249)
Transport	bus
Summary	From the medieval walled city of Morella, this flexible walk loops through a remote landscape along walled paths, crossing through spectacular gorges and over narrow passes

Generally speaking, walking in this area is not about peak-bagging, but wandering along ancient tracks and walled lanes, negotiating

(side margin) **VALENCIA**

deep gorges and travelling along beautiful river valleys. This walk leads into the heart of Els Ports.

Handily, this sparsely populated region contains a great network of trails, including the GR7 long-distance route, the red-and-white trail markers of which are followed between Morella and Refugi de Font Ferrera. The second half of the walk follows various PRV routes. These *senderos de pequeño recorrido valencianos* are basically shorter footpaths marked with yellow-and-white trail markers.

Many communities en route offer accommodation and the walk can be lengthened and shortened to suit. In particular, Day 3 could be skipped or done only in part. Refugi de Font Ferrera is a good launching point for walks northeast across Els Ports, an area well worth further exploration.

HISTORY

Thanks to its location beside an important pass on the route from the coast to Zaragoza, the town of Morella has long dominated the cultural and economic landscape of Els Ports. It's one of Spain's oldest towns in one of the country's earliest inhabited regions. Prehistoric cave paintings can be seen at Morella la Vella and evidence of Mediterranean man (from around 6000 BC) has been found in the Ríu de la Sénia gorge, where archaeologists believe the trail snaking up to Bellestar has been used since 300BC.

After the Reconquista, Monasterio Santa María de Benifassà in La Tinença de Benifassà (known as the 'Seven Settlements of Benifassà') exerted considerable power and influence over the region, but the contemporary picture has been one of rural dereliction, followed by a huge EU/national programme of renovation and rejuvenation seeking to boost rural tourism. However, housing is often inherited and many houses in Els Ports are now second homes for city dwellers.

NATURAL HISTORY

It's the eastern fringes of the Sistema Ibérico that form the heavily eroded network of jagged limestone peaks and deep gorges in Els Ports. This decidedly un-Mediterranean landscape is a habitat more typical of Aragon, with original pockets of holm, gall and kermes oaks still found in remote valleys. A small pocket of boxwood trees remains near El Boixar (the village that bears their name), the rest having been used by craftsmen to make ploughing equipment and tableware.

This wild, remote area has an abundance of unique plants and you're more likely to see pardel lynx, wildcats or red squirrels here than anywhere else in Valencia. Wild boar and Spanish ibex often forage near mountain villages. Birds to look out for include the golden eagle, the tawny vulture, numerous falcons, robins, coal tits and nightingales.

El Cid

Rodrigo Díaz de Vivar, popularly known as El Cid, was born in the Christian kingdom of Castilla in 1043 and was put in control of the kingdom's army at the tender age of 22. Exiled for an unauthorised raid on the Muslim kingdom of Toledo (supposedly under the protection of Castilla at the time!), El Cid subsequently travelled through Els Ports before working for al-Mu'tamin, the Muslim ruler of Zaragoza. For nearly a decade El Cid served him and his successor, gaining knowledge of Hispanic-Arabic politics and Islamic law. He enhanced his reputation as a great military commander by inflicting devastating defeats on the Muslim king of Lérida in 1082 and the Christian army of Sancho Ramírez of Aragón in 1084.

Then in 1092 he saw an opportunity to take over the Muslim kingdom of Valencia when Ibn Jahháf, Valencia's chief magistrate, murdered the city's ruler, al-Qádir. El Cid besieged the city until Ibn Jahháf surrendered in the mistaken belief that his safety was guaranteed. El Cid had him burned at the stake.

El Cid ruled Valencia until his death in 1099, acting as a magistrate for both Christians and Muslims. On hearing of his death, Muslim armies besieged the city, only to flee in terror when his body, propped on a horse, was led out through the city gates. His body was finally taken to the monastery of San Pedro de Cardeña in Castilla, where it became the centre of a lively tomb cult.

PLANNING
When to Walk

Els Ports experiences more variable weather, harsher winters and more rain than elsewhere in the region. Compared with Valencia, Morella is 5.5°C cooler (11.5°C is the average daytime temperature) and has 200mm more rainfall. Some higher communities are snowbound in winter.

Walking is possible from spring to late autumn, although both ends of the season are susceptible to occasional snow and June to September is very hot. Between November and April the rivers and *barrancos* (gullies or ravines) flow. Late April to June is the best time to walk.

Maps

Piolet's 1:40,000 *Els Port* map illustrates the northeast corner of this route well, but was out of print at the time of writing. Similar, but elusive, is the Institut Cartogràfic de Catalunya (ICC) 1:30,000 *El Port* map. Llibrería Altaïr in Barcelona (see pp96–7) may be the best place to get these maps.

The IGN's 1:25,000 map Nos 545-I *Morella*, 545-II *Vallibona*, 520-IV *Herbés*, 521-III *Fredes* and 546-I *La Sénia* cover the walk in good detail.

Books

Good Spanish-language walking guides include *Els Ports de Morella y Benifassá – Ports de Beceite* and *Els Ports – 40 Rutas de Senderisme,* by Joan Tirón Ferré.

Information Sources

Morella's **tourist office** (☎/fax 964 17 30 32; W www.morella.net; Torre de San Miguel) has a little information about walking in the area.

Guided Walks

The following companies offer walking trips and also act as agents for *casas rurales* in the Els Ports region:

Casas de Morella (☎ 964 17 31 17, W www.morella.net)
El Sports (☎ 964 17 31 71, fax 964 17 31 31)
Gubiana dels Ports (☎ 977 51 05 99, W www.gubiana.com)

NEAREST TOWN
Morella

Perched on a hilltop, crowned by a castle and completely enclosed by a wall, Morella is an impressive sight. The walk begins and ends here, but spend at least a day exploring town (the Gothic **Basílica de Santa María la Mayor** is stunning) and sampling local restaurants.

Morella is an excellent place for specialist cheese, meats and other foods. Several small **supermarkets** offer more mundane supplies.

A number of ATMs are found in the centre of town and a few local IGN 1:25,000 maps are available from local newsagents.

Places to Stay & Eat There's a free **camping ground** north of the castle beside the municipal swimming pool (which has hot showers).

The cheapest place to stay (and eat) is the always-full **Fonda Morena** (☎ 964 16 01 05; Calle San Nicolás 12; doubles €15). The *menú del día* (fixed-price meal) costs €7.50.

Hostal El Cid (☎ 964 16 01 25; singles/doubles €24/38), just inside Portal de Sant Mateu, has good rooms. The bar is often full of retired men playing cards and there's a reasonable restaurant (the *menú* costs €7.50). **Pensión La Muralla** (☎ 964 16 02 43), just around the corner, is a little cheaper and prices include breakfast.

Built in the 16th century as the cardinal's palace, **Hotel Cardinal Ram** (☎ 964 17 30 85; e hotelcardenalram@ctu.es; Cuesta Suñer 1; singles/doubles €37.50/59) is well worth a splurge. The restaurant is also good.

For a gastronomic blowout the town's best restaurant, **Restaurante Casa Roque** (☎ 964 16 03 36; Cuesta San Juan 1; lunch menú €9, full meals €25), offers regional specialities such as *sopa morellana con buñuelos* (broth with dumplings) and *gallina trufada* (chicken with locally dug truffles).

Getting There & Away Morella is easily reached via Castellón and Vinaròs, which both have good train connections south and north (see Getting There & Away for Valencia, pp246–7).

From Castellón **Autos Mediterráneo** (☎ 964 22 05 36) buses leave from Calle

Maestro Ripollés (€6.75, 2½ hours, two daily Monday to Friday, one daily Saturday) passing through the bus station (beside the train station) a few minutes later. From Vinaròs (€4.70, 1½ hours, two daily Monday to Friday) buses leave from Plaza Primero de Mayo (returning services pass the train station) and connect with a Morella service in Sant Mateu.

On Monday, Wednesday and Thursday (and other weekdays in July and August) there's an Autos Mediterráneo bus between Alcañiz and Morella. There are bus connections to Zaragoza from Alcañiz.

In Morella there's one **taxi company** (☎ 659 48 78 61) but rates are high.

THE WALK
Day 1: Morella to Villibona
4–4½ hours, 17.5km

Go through Portal de Sant Mateu and head left down a cobbled alley to a sealed road. Turn left, off the GR7 (which somewhat

boringly follows sealed roads for the next 3km), and head down to the N232. Turn right, then after 25m turn left (southeast) down a dirt road. This route, poorly marked with green trail markers, crosses a stream at **Masía San Vicente** – a mill with a 600-year-old *fuente (*spring) – and up and over the hill to a dirt track in about 30 minutes. Turn right down to the N232, turn left, rejoining the GR7 (which has with red-and-white markers), and walk east to the N232's Km 59 marker. Fork left down a 4WD track before a bridge over the Ríu Bergantes, then ford right across the river 10 minutes later beneath a grove of poplars. Follow the course of the river on the true left bank for another 15 minutes before recrossing it and following the riverside track upstream past a beautiful waterfall and deep pool, then along a 4WD track to a sealed road.

Turn left, then after 100m fork right (east) up a farm track climbing steadily (look back for great views of Morella) past Masía

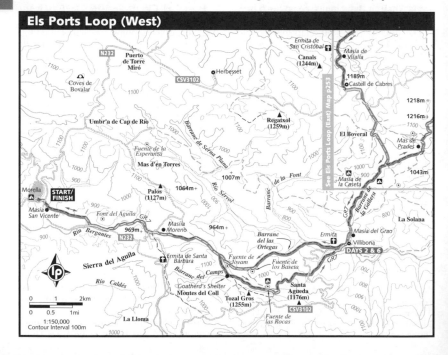

Els Ports Loop (West)

Moreno (a farm) and up to the edge of holm oak woodland. Continue roughly east along a wide, walled lane before bearing right (east) through sparse woodland to a gate and up the northern side of a gully in a slightly surreal landscape of **juniper trees** that look like escapees from an ornamental garden.

Upon reaching a 4WD track turn right (east), then fork left up to great views of Morella, a small shrine, a gate and a junction of trails. Pass through the gate and turn right onto a narrow, often faint path that leads southeast (left) along a ridge. Five minutes after passing through a gap in the ridge-top wall the trail makes a sharp left (east) before winding past a goatherds' shelter and climbing to a fence.

The summit of Tozal Gros (1255m) can be reached by continuing along the ridge (southeast), but from the fence the GR7 bears left off the ridge and southeast. After a 20-minute stroll through oak woodland, **Fuente de las Rocas** (a possible camp site) and a 4WD track are reached. Head east a little way, then fork left (north) down a spur before turning right off this 4WD track and following the GR7 east around a couple of gullies, through a group of houses and northeast to the CSV3102. Cross and pick up a well-worn path that zigzags down an oak-wooded gully back to the CSV3102. Turn right, cross the Río Sérvol and fork left up into **Villibona**.

Hostal-Restaurante La Carbonera (☎ *964 17 20 00; Plaza Sant Antoni; singles/doubles €14/28)* has good rooms and a so-so restaurant. **Bar Sant Antoni** across the square is often more lively and also does food. Villibona has a few **grocery shops** and loads of **casas rurales**; ask around, or see Guided Walks (p249) for contact information.

Day 2: Villibona to Refugi de Font Ferrera

6½–7 hours, 23km

Turn right out of the hostel and then right onto the higher of the two roads leading north into a gorge. Ford Barranc de la Gallera then loop around and up the gorge's eastern side (the GR7 takes a short cut) to emerge west of Masía del Grao (a farm). Here an alternative route that allows walkers

to avoid wet feet between November and April, when the river is swollen, leads northeast along a well-used dirt road to Mas de Prades in about two hours (stay south and east of the peaks on the ridge).

The main route continues north across the grass to a dirt road. Turn left, then right (north), following the GR7 upstream beside Barranc de la Gallera along a faint 4WD track that crisscrosses the small section of permanently flowing river into a beautiful narrow gorge. Some 20 minutes later the 4WD track disappears and so (except in winter) does the water. A narrow trail now leads upstream, climbing up the true left bank in about 35 minutes to avoid a set of waterfalls (and past the 4WD track descended on Day 5). Continue northeast for 30 minutes to the head of the valley (which is extensively terraced) and bear right up to a dirt road (the alternative route to Villibona) and **Mas de Prades**, a farmhouse perched on a saddle. To the east, in a dramatic gorge, is Arroyo de Bel.

Head north along the dirt road for 100m, then bear right onto a trail that zigzags up the pine-covered slope past another farmhouse to a 4WD track. Turn right onto it, then right again at the next junction (a *fuente* is reached in 15 minutes by turning left), avoid the next left and climb roughly northeast for 10 minutes to another junction. Continue straight ahead, then after 80m peel off right with the GR7, heading northeast across a clearing, left of a low wall and out into a large bowl. Meadows and a muddy spring lie to the south (a beautiful **camp site** if clean water could be found).

Continue northeast, then turn right onto a 4WD track that should be followed for 30 minutes as it zigzags between the summits of Cerro de Aguila (1249m) and La Devesa (1224m) and winds roughly north past a wonderful, igloo-shaped, dry-stone **goatherd shelter** (possible camp site) to the Km 25 marker on the CSV3102. Turn right, then walk 200m down the road before bearing left up the slope and northeast along a scrub-covered ridge to **El Boixar** (Bojar). For accommodation and other services see Day 4 (pp253–4).

Head south across CSV3102 down to the old clothes washrooms and *fuente*, then turn

VALENCIA

left, heading east down to a T-junction. Bear right, then continue north along a 4WD track and across a stream. Trail markers now lead downstream along the true left bank, but it's best to turn right into the adjacent field before cutting back to the trail on easier ground just before it meets a 4WD track and the Arroyo de la Canal is crossed. Continue northeast along the rocky track for around 10 minutes until, just after crossing a small stream (and with an old farmhouse and some good **camp sites** 150m north), the GR7 cuts up right through a gate and northeast beside Arroyo de la Pascuala. Cross the stream after about 15 minutes then bear right (northeast) up the slope, through an area of terracing, before traversing east to an excellent **viewpoint** above the head of the valley.

Follow the trail roughly east for a couple of minutes to a 4WD track at the edge of a stunning **canyon**. Turn right and then, after 50m, bear left onto a faint track leading to a shallow gully. Stay on the southern side of it until the GR7 bears off left (north) following power lines to a dirt road. Turn right and head northeast to **Fredes**, reached about 1¼ hours after leaving El Boixar.

Fredes has one *casa rural*, **Casa Nuri** (☎ 977 72 91 02; *accommodation per person* €12-15); they're used to short-stay walkers. For the nearby beautiful **Mas del Pitxon** camp site, see Day 4 (pp253–4).

Bar Santa María (☎ 977 72 90 22; *open Tues-Fri)* serves up hearty rather than cordon bleu cuisine.

Walk for a further 1½ hours (6km) northeast along the GR7, which winds around the gullies and cliff tops of Roca Blanca before cutting north to a dirt road. Bear right for 100m, then turn right (east) up a 4WD track leading to a trail that descends into the Reserva Nacional de Caza and, at 1220m, **Refugi de Font Ferrera** (*refugi* ☎ 647 84 71 05, *office* 977 26 71 10; **W** *www.feec.es; dorm beds* €10.75; *open daily mid-July–mid-Sept & most weekends year-round).* The *refugi* (mountain hut or refuge) has space for 40, hot showers and a small guest kitchen, and hearty meals are available (book in advance). The *refugi* may be open more often

than the official opening hours suggest; call ahead.

Day 3: Refugi de Font Ferrera to Fredes

4½–6 hours, 12.5km

This day could be cut down to a simple two-hour loop to Montenegrelo or done as a long day walk from Fredes.

From the *refugi* walk east to the 4WD track, turn left, and then right (east) at the T-junction. Follow this dirt track for 15 minutes, then bear right onto a narrow trail (still the GR7) just after another T-junction. A 20-minute traverse brings you onto a small saddle where a trail turns right (south) off the GR7 and climbs to a wonderful cliff edge east of **Montenegrelo** (1345m). Turn right and follow the trail past a weather station to the peak. As well as eagles and vultures swirling around the summit you may also see magnificent, solitary male ibex.

Head west from the peak along a 4WD track. Continue straight ahead (southwest) at a switchback (to the right) reached after 15 minutes along the ridge, until reaching a crossroads of trails just beyond two large boulders. Turn right (west), descending to another junction in about eight minutes. Refugi de Font Ferrera is 10 minutes away (northwest), but cut back left (southwest) following the yellow-and-white trail markers up and over the ridge to a 4WD track. Turn right and head down southwest for 15 minutes before turning left and descending sharply to another 4WD track. Turn right, ignore a right turn a few minutes later and continue east to Mas de Peraire, an area of grassy terraces and a **water depository** (like a big natural tank formed in the rock).

The trail begins a steep 45-minute descent through dramatic rock outcrops to the **Barranc del Salt**. Cross the stream and turn right, scrambling along the rocky trail through a dramatic gorge to a beautiful set of falls. The trail now climbs for 35 minutes to a 4WD track and a tricky junction (keep an eye on the trail markers). Take the second right switchback, then climb steeply west to another 4WD track. Turn right and right again onto a track leading west to Fredes 10 minutes later.

Day 4: Fredes to El Boixar

6½–7 hours, 22.5km

Retrace your steps along the last 10 minutes of Day 3 and then continue east along the PRV75.16 that soon bears left off the track onto an old, rocky trail. This trail heads southeast, up to and across a 4WD track, then down to **Mas del Pitxon**, a beautiful ruined farmhouse (and fine camp site) with a fantastic view.

Cut east into the Reserva Nacional de Caza (unmarked on all maps) and then southeast along a long spur below overhanging cliffs (one containing a *fuente*) and through the **Portell de l'Infern** ('gate to hell'). The landscape here is just splendid and this short traverse is probably the most stunning section of the walk.

Zigzag down south, then southeast across more open ground below the pinnacles of Punta Sola d'en Brull, before ducking right down along the southern side of a narrow gully that opens out. Head southeast below

the towering cliffs and then continue down to a cluster of houses beside Embalse de Ulldecona about an hour from Portell de l'Infern.

Turn right and walk for 2.2km along the lakeside road (past a free **camp site**) to the CSV3102 and a dam. Beside the dam is **Mesón-Hotel Molí l'Abad** (☎ 977 71 34 18), which has a large self-service restaurant-bar.

From the restaurant head west along the road, then 1.6km later turn left down the driveway of Vivers Forestals Forn del Vidre, a forestry nursery. **Monasterio de Santa María de Benifassá** (open 1pm-3pm Thurs) is further along the road.

Follow the trail markers down the driveway, ford the Ríu de la Sénia, then fork left through metal gates and loop right (west) around the old mill. Recross the river and then follow it upstream for 30 minutes before crossing to the true right bank and continuing upstream to Fuente Canaleta. The track soon becomes a trail that winds west beneath sandstone cliffs. Then, 1¼ hours from the

VALENCIA

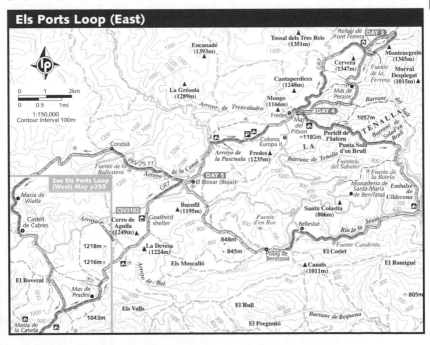

Els Ports Loop (East)

forest nursery, bear right (northeast) up the side of the gorge on an ancient path leading to **Bellestar**. It's a stunning, timeless arrival.

The most reliable place for food and drink is **Mesón Bellestar** (☎ *977 72 90 92*), but phone ahead in winter.

West of the village, trail markers lead to **Pobla de Benifassá**, which has a grocery shop and a couple of bar-restaurants (try Fonda la Morena). **Hotel Tinença de Benifassá** (☎/fax *977 72 90 44; doubles €59-79*) provides accommodation and **Auberge la Font Lluny** (☎ *977 72 91 25; dorm beds from €9*) is a cheaper place to stay.

From the western end of Calle Mayor follow the PRV75.4 northwest past Auberge la Font Lluny along a dirt road. Fork left after 10 minutes, keeping parallel to a stream that is soon crossed. Turn right at the T-junction and climb northwest for an hour to a cliff-top sealed road. **El Boixar** is a further 1km northwest along a flat road.

Casa-Refugi El Boixar (☎ *977 72 90 71;* e *mglp@tinet.fut.es; Carrer Mayor; half-board per person €21.50-26.50*) offers excellent accommodation, and operates a *casa rural* costing €15 per person. The *refugi* sometimes closes on Sunday night, but the *casa rural* remains open. Down on the CSV3102 is a small **bar**, which serves meals.

Day 5: El Boixar to Villibona
6–7½hours, 15.5km

Turn right out of the *refugi*, then right (north) again onto the PRV75.11, which leads down a concrete track, across the road and northwest, down into a gully. Cross the stream and continue northwest for 20 minutes to the head of a small stream before zigzagging up to a tarmac road. Turn left then, at a sign (which gives some confusing instructions), cut back right 50m up a 4WD track. Turn right at the crest of a hill, then 20m later bear left on a trail that heads north then west for 10 minutes to a junction. Bear right off the (now 4WD) track and continue to a saddle below a 1245m peak. Turn left (west) and descend to a meadow and Fuente de la Ballestera before heading north across to, then along, a tarmac road. A trail soon

bears off right leading across to **Coratxà** (Corachar).

Hostelería Sant Jaume (☎ *977 72 91 90; Plaça Mayor; singles/doubles €38/49*) is a very pleasant place to stay, with flash rooms and a great restaurant.

Follow the concrete road west from Plaça Mayor, then after 20m turn left (north). Take the next left fork onto a 4WD track that leads west through a shallow valley. After 20 minutes fork left (west) onto a faint track just as the main track climbs northwest. Bear left on a track just past a *fuente* and head southwest before cutting up and over the ridge. It's now gentle descent to **Ermita de San Cristóbal** (1248m). Perched on the edge of Sierra de los Aragoneses, this once magnificent religious retreat affords 270-degree views. To the north you can see as far as Alcañiz.

Head back east to a large cairn, then descend southeast on a marked trail towards Masía de Vilalla, a sturdy farmhouse (behind it is Font Juana), before turning right (south) and working west around the northern side of a saddle. Cut down south below the saddle and then traverse east beneath a row of cliffs on an ancient trail that zigzags down across a 4WD track to a stream. After crossing it, traverse west to a 4WD track and signpost 15 minutes later. Follow the PRV75.8 (the trail markers are sketchy in places) roughly south, past a grave, down through a gully and up to a sharp ridge. Turn right (southwest) and begin the 30-minute, snaking climb up to an amazing set of **terracing**. From the terracing continue south to a ridge and then around the 1189m peak overlooking **Castell de Cabres**.

Bar-Restaurante La Espiga (☎ *977 72 90 25*) serves up some decent fare, but **Casa El Cuartel** (☎ *964 17 31 17; accommodation per day €69*) and **Casa La Mestra** (☎ *964 17 31 17; accommodation per day €89*), let as complete houses, are the only places to stay.

Turn left onto the CSV3102, then at the Km 31 marker pick up a short cut leading southeast to a junction back on the CSV3102. Head southeast down the dirt road, following it right after 15 minutes, up to a three-way junction by a water depository. Turn left (south) and take a switchback right a few minutes later. Shortly after passing a *fuente*, fork left, then take the next right following the 4WD track south to Barranc de la Gallera and the GR7. Turn right and follow the trail south back to Villibona retracing the outward route on Day 2 (see pp251–3).

Day 6: Villibona to Morella
4–5 hours, 15.5km

The return leg to Morella is made more interesting by bearing right off the CSV3102 20m down from the Telefónica building southwest of Villibona onto a trail that traverses west, high above the Río Cérvol, to an *ermita* (hermitage) and then slopes down to the river. Cross below a fine, walled gully and head upstream, crossing two small streams before bearing left up a muddy slope into the mouth of the gorge formed by Barranc de las Ortegas.

Continue southwest through the gorge, past Fuente de los Baseta, and then after 30 minutes cross to the true left bank of the gorge and continue southwest past a set of overhanging cliffs and livestock pens. Fork right (west) at the end of the gorge and follow the trail markers through oak woodland to a wide, walled lane. To the northwest is a grand-looking farmhouse, but continue west through sparse oak woodland for 10 minutes to a 4WD track. Turn right and follow the trail markers through a short cut before climbing northwest up to the signpost and shrine on the Tozal Gros ridge. From here it's simply a matter of retracing your steps to Morella, as per the outward route on Day 1 (see pp250–1).

La Marina

North of the high-rise blocks, sun lounges and all-night discos of Benidorm are the beautifully rugged, arid mountains of La Marina. Made up of numerous east–west ridges, the range is divided into *baja* (lower) and *alta* (higher) regions and occupies a huge headland that juts out into the Mediterranean between Alicante and Valencia.

These mountains are not giants – the highest peak is Aitana at 1557m – but the area has a variety of interesting terrain and the village hospitality is first class. Dry, rocky *montebajo* terrain is common, but good trails and a network of forestry tracks crisscross the region allowing for dramatic ridge walks, traverses down precipitous gullies and peak-bagging. Despite the tourist hordes a stone's throw away, for nine months of the year it's perfectly possible to pick up your pack, disappear into the mountains and not speak to another person for days on end.

HISTORY

The greatest historical and cultural influence on La Marina, which has been occupied since about 5000BC, came from the period of Muslim occupation. Mozarabic trails (see the boxed text 'Mozarabic Trails', p261), irrigation systems and terraced hillsides remain as evidence of the collective industry of the times, while ruined hill forts are a sign of the struggle between Christians and Muslims. Also found in the mountains are watchtowers built to warn of piracy and raiding parties – common in the 17th century when Valencia lacked stability and strong leadership.

Before the tourist boom Benidorm was a poor fishing village and agricultural production dominated La Marina's economy. More recently agriculture on the more marginal lands has been abandoned and old terraces have fallen into disrepair following great urban migration to the coast.

NATURAL HISTORY

Scarred by fissures and crags, the rocky, arid limestone slopes of La Marina are called *montebajo* terrain and provide habitats for lime-tolerant plants such as the spring-blooming yellow anthyllis, and early summer-blooming black, vanilla, mirror, frog and Bertoloni's bee orchids. Local specialities include the rusty foxglove, found on scree, and the tiny rush-leaved daffodil. The scent of sage, thyme, rue, curry plant and cotton lavender fills the air during the intense heat of summer when pink century and red valerian bloom.

Rabbits, hares and foxes are found in the mountains, but you'll be lucky if wildcats and wild boar cross your path. You may see the bold, brown-and-black hoopoe (said to bring bad luck if hunted), along with eagles, many species of harriers and warblers, colourful rollers and bee-eaters, and you'll often startle partridges in long grass.

Lataste's viper, which is yellow with a triangular head and a wavy line down the spine, is the only poisonous viper found here. The caterpillar of the pine processionary moth (see the boxed text 'The Pine Processionary Caterpillar', p32) can also be seen here.

CLIMATE

The coastal regions enjoy a mild winter, but on the higher peaks you should be prepared to walk in 7°C, regular frosts and occasional snowfalls. Cold, wet winds occasionally blast the mountains from October until June.

PLANNING
When to Walk

Few people are crazy enough to walk from July to September, when temperatures can soar above 35°C, even at altitude. Much of the region's annual 490mm of rainfall descends during the *gota fría*, a stormy period in September and October, but mild winters mean that the walking season runs from October to June. March to May, when many wildflowers bloom, is ideal.

What to Bring

In late spring you could easily get away with sleeping out under the stars, but don't skimp on walking boots suited to rocky terrain.

Maps

There are no regional maps specific to the La Marina area; it is covered by those mentioned in Maps under Information (p245). For large-scale maps see the Planning sections of individual walks.

Books

Landscapes of the Costa Blanca, by J Oldfield, and the excellent *Mountain Walks on the Costa Blanca* and *Costa Blanca Mountain Walks* (volumes 1 and 2), by Bob Stansfield, are good and intended for the day-walker.

Warning

If you must walk during summer, when most of the rivers and streams dry up and many lesser *fuentes* (springs) are unreliable, set off at dawn and beware of sunstroke, sunburn, heat exhaustion and cramp. Carry plenty of water (5L to 6L on a long, hot walking day) and keep your salt levels up. Rehydration sachets are an excellent idea.

Also be aware that much of the rock here is friable: safe-looking holds can sometimes crumble or come away in your hand.

Information Sources

The website W www.marina-alta.com is worth a look as it has some reasonable background to the region.

Guided Walks

The Costa Blanca Mountain Walkers have been exploring La Marina for more than 10 years and walkers are welcome to join them on numerous trails around the region. Details of their walks are published in the weekly *Costa Blanca News*.

The following companies operate walking trips in La Marina:

Bikes and Hikes (☎ 96 587 86 00, W www .bikes-and-hikes.com). It runs mainly guided day walks and cycle trips.
Terra Ferma (☎/fax 96 589 03 92, W www.ter raferma.net). This is a well-respected climbing and walking outfit.

ACCESS TOWNS
Alicante

Benidorm has the access to La Marina, but Alicante is a pleasant city and with so many cheap flights arriving at **Aeropuerto El Altet** (☎ 96 691 91 00) you may have to spend a night here.

The main **tourist office** (☎ 96 520 00 00; *Rambla de Méndez Núñez 23*) offers a wealth of information for walkers while **K2 Esports** (☎ 96 520 65 62; *Calle Belando 5*) and **El Corte Inglés** (☎ 96 592 50 01; *cnr Ave Maisonnave & Calle Churruca, 6th floor*) are the best places for walking and camping equipment.

Top Left: Spring wildflowers are a feature of mountain walking in Valencia. **Top Right**: Not for the faint of heart – an exhilarating section of ridge walking on the Serra de Bérnia Traverse. **Bottom**: At the start of the Ruta La Marina Alta, Confrides nestles amid the sierras of La Marina.

DAVID TOMLINSON

INGRID RODDIS

Top: Island delights – even if you've partied the night away, Mallorca sunrises are enough to entice anyone to hit the trail at dawn. **Bottom**: The fascinating early-19th-century ruins of Monestir de Sa Trapa, near Sant Elm, are undergoing gradual restoration.

Places to Stay & Eat In El Barrio (the old town) **Hostal Les Monges Palace** (☎ 96 521 50 46, fax 96 514 71 89; Calle San Agustín 4; singles €16-22, doubles €33-49) has nice rooms in a lovely building so book in advance.

Hostal Portugal (☎ 96 592 92 44; Calle de Portugal 26; singles/doubles €16.25/25.25) is an old place opposite the bus station.

There are dozens of cheap restaurants in **El Barrio**.

Getting There & Away Buses run the 12km from the airport to Plaza del Mar in Alicante (€1.05, every 40 minutes) via the bus station, from where there are **Alsa/Entacar** (☎ 902 42 22 42) buses to Madrid (€21.50 to €33, 4½ to 5½ hours, 11 daily), Valencia (€13, 2½ hours, nine daily) and Benidorm (€2.75, one hour, every 30 minutes).

From **Estación de Madrid** (☎ 902 24 02 02) Altaria trains leave for Madrid (€34, 3½ to four hours, seven daily) and Valencia (€8.80 to €21.50, 1½ to two hours, nine daily); regionales are the cheapest.

From **Estación de la Marina** (☎ 96 526 27 31) the trenet, a small local train, runs along the narrow-gauge railway between Alicante and Denia via Benidorm (€2.85, hourly).

Benidorm

Tacky tourism at its most heinous? Perhaps, but a lot of people look down their noses at Benidorm without ever having been there. Don't believe the hype. With good bus links into La Marina, it's the most sensible place to stay before or after the walk. The old town is an enjoyable place to spend an evening and, weirdly, the place grows on you. Honest.

Information The main **tourist information office** (☎ 96 585 13 11; w www.beni dorm.org; Martínez Alejos 16) does not have much information for mountain walkers.

Supplies & Equipment The best place for walking equipment is **Beni-Algar Sports** (Intersport; ☎ 96 585 77 20; Calle Mercado 3), and the covered **market** close by is a good place for supplies. **Supermarkets** are easy to find.

A limited selection of IGN 1:25,000 maps can be obtained at **Librería Francés** (☎ 96 585 15 01; Ruzafa 4).

Places to Stay & Eat The more expensive hotels sometimes offer winter deals; it is always worth asking.

A great camping ground is **Camping Villasol** (☎ 965 85 04 22; w www.camping-villa sol.com; Avenida Bernat de Sarrià; camping per person/tent €5.90/6.40).

Hostal les Roques (☎ 96 585 26 65; Calle Alicante 28; singles/doubles €18/36) is not stunning value and its charm is of the frosty, boarding-house variety, but it always seems to have vacancies.

Hotel Bilbaíno (☎/fax 96 585 08 04; e bilbaino@arrakis.es; Avenida Virgen del Sufragio 1; singles €31-50, doubles €50-90), overlooking Playa del Levante, is one of the oldest hotels in Benidorm.

Calle Santo Domingo and **Plaza de la Constitución** in the old town are the best areas for (Spanish) food and drink. **La Cava Aragonesa** (☎ 96 680 12 06) has a magnificent selection of tapas and juicy canapes and a good Basque restaurant in the basement. Not far away, **Bar de los Monstros** (off Plaça Sant Jaume) is worth a look.

Getting There & Away Buses run by **Alsa** (☎ 96 680 39 55) to Madrid (€24 to €36, 5½ to 6½ hours, eight daily), Valencia (€10, 3½ hours, seven daily) and Alicante (€3, one hour, every 30 minutes) all leave from Avenida Europa.

The trenet to Alicante (€2.85, hourly) leaves from the FGV station north of town.

Callosa d'En Sarriá (Callosa)

Once the most important towns in La Marina, Callosa is a historic little place with just enough of interest for a pre-walk diversion – visit the **Casa de Cultura** (☎ 96 588 02 62; Calle Sellesos) for information.

Places to Stay & Eat The nearest **camping ground** (camping per person €4.05) is 3km east of town in El Algar, 700m past the famous Fonts de l'Algar. It's well equipped, but stark, and some facilities close in the low season. A bunch of nearby bars and restaurants cater for the tourist crowds drawn to the gorges and waterfalls of Fonts de l'Algar. Extensive roadworks at time of writing prevented bus transport between Collosa and the camping ground; taxis are available.

Fonda Galiana *(☎ 96 588 01 55; Calle Collon; singles/doubles €15/30)* has simple rooms, shared facilities and a restaurant specialising in local cuisine.

Hostal Avenida *(☎ 96 588 00 53; Carretera Alicante 9; singles €12, doubles with/without bathroom €24/30)*, opposite the bus stop, is a simple, friendly and functional place with a popular bar.

El Repós del Viater *(☎ 96 588 23 22; Calle Mayor 3; singles/doubles €30/48)* is a far more upmarket place and includes breakfast.

Mesón San José *(Carretera de Bolulla)* is good for regional cuisine.

Getting There & Away Buses run by **Ubesa** *(☎ 96 680 39 55)* leave Avenida Europa in Benidorm for Callosa (€1.60, almost hourly).

Another option is a **taxi** *(☎ 629 67 12 18)*. The fare to Bolulla or Fonts de l'Algar is about €8, while Confrides costs around €20.

Ruta La Marina Alta

Duration	4 days
Distance	49km
Difficulty	moderate
Start	Confrides
Finish	Bolulla
Nearest Towns	Collosa (p257), Confrides (p258)
Transport	bus, taxi

Summary This S-shaped exploration of La Marina Alta includes the region's highest ridge, the intriguing ruins of Muslim castles, a number of ridge walks and La Marina's best restaurant

Forestry tracks and marked paths lead across the Sierra de Aitana, through Valle de Guadalest, over the Serra de Serrella and around the Serra d'Aixorta. The major decision comes at Puerto del Castillo, from where routes to Bolulla via Castell de Castells or to Callosa after a walk along Serra d'Aixorta bear off. A highly recommended day walk (see Serra de Serrella, p265, under Other Walks) joins the route here.

It's possible to do the walk staying in village accommodation, but equally possible to break it up and sleep in the mountains. You can spin the walk out to seven nights if you prefer to take your time. The short first day allows for the fact that the bus arrives in Confrides in the afternoon.

Determined walkers could link this walk with the Serra de Bérnia Traverse (see the boxed text 'Bolulla to Fonts de l'Algar Link', p263).

PLANNING
Maps
The IGN 1:25,000 map Nos 821-IV *Castell de Castells*, 822-III *Parcent*, 847-II *Relleu* and 848-I *Altea* cover the walk.

NEAREST TOWNS
See Collosa d'En Sarriá (Collosa), p257.

Confrides
Spending the night in Confrides allows the first two days to be walked in one.

There are a few small **grocery shops**, as well as some *casas rurales*, including **Casa a Faragulla** *(☎ 965 28 65 19, 654 665 054; Plaza del Nogal 8; accommodation per person €15)* and **Casa Can Llorens** *(☎ 677 34 03 77; Calle En Medio 1; accommodation per person €10-20)*.

You could also stay at **El Pirineo** *(☎ 96 588 58 58; doubles €36)*. This *pensión* has a cracking *menú* for €9.

GETTING TO/FROM THE WALK
From Callosa catch an **Alsa** *(☎ 96 680 39 55)* bus to Confrides (€1.40, 45 minutes, two daily) from opposite Hostal Avenida.

If you're not walking the alternative finish to Callosa you'll need to take a taxi there from Bolulla or you could walk to Fonts de l'Algar at the end of the walk (see the boxed text 'Bolulla to Fonts de l'Algar Link', p263).

Neveras: the Original Fridges

Neveras are deep, cylindrical pits, usually constructed on the northern slopes of high mountains, once used to make ice from snow. Normally about 15m deep and 10m wide, the larger ones had supporting beams and wooden tiled roofs. Smaller *neveras* had domed, dry-stone roofs.

In winter, the pits were filled with snow which was compacted into ice, insulated with straw and left until the summer months when local men *(nevaters)* would come up from the villages at night to cut the ice into usable blocks, transporting it by mule down to the valleys before sunrise.

Neveras were mainly used during the 17th and 18th centuries, but older men in the village of Confrides maintain that the practice continued into the early part of the 20th century. *Neveras* fell into decay with the introduction of electric refrigeration, but good examples remain below the cliffs of Aitana.

THE WALK (see map p260)
Day 1: Confrides to Fuente Forata
3–3½ hours, 11.5km

Walk up Calle San Antonio, opposite El Pirineo, past the *fuente* and take the first switchback right (west) and then fork right following the sign for the PRV22. Once high above the village, bear right with the tarmac road which continues southwest (eventually turning to dirt) for the best part of 1½ hours before turning southeast (giving views of the antennae and radar domes on the summit of Sierra de Aitana) to the shaded Fuente Arbols (also known as Font de l'Arbre or Fuente Aitana) at Casas de Aitana – a possible **camp site.**

From the *fuente*, zigzag south up the well-made forestry track, then follow it east below the cliffs, passing *neveras* (see the boxed text 'Neveras: the Original Fridges') on the left after 30 and 45 minutes. Five minutes after the second *nevera* there's a sharp left turn. Ignore it and fork left a few minutes later onto a minor track, which leads to **Fuente Forata**, a beautiful camp site. A *forat* (hole through the rock) is clearly visible to the southeast and there are stunning views across Valle de Guadalest to the Serra de Serrella and north to the Serra de Bérnia.

Day 2: Fuente Forata to Benimantell
3–4 hours, 10km

From Fuente Forata a well-worn path leads southeast around a scree slope to a boulder-strewn gully. Clamber up the gully, bearing left halfway (just below a yew tree), and climb up through **Puerto de Tudos** (or 'Fat Man's Agony'), a very narrow pass leading to the summit ridge of Sierra de Aitana. Once through, traverse left (east) above a large fissure down to a marked, chest-high rock face and trail junction. The summit of Aitana (1557m), the highest peak in La Marina, is within the military radar station to the west, but before the boundary fence a lesser **summit** (1549m) gives uninterrupted views of La Marina. Particularly impressive is Puig Campana (1408m) to the southeast.

Back at the junction head south, then east, to Peña Alta (1505m), the beginning of an enjoyable, 50-minute ridge walk east to Paso Mulero (1254m). Cross the forestry road linking Benifato and Sella, then continue east up and over **Peña Mulero** (1306m) on a 4WD track. The views of Alto de la Peña de Sella (1105m; a great place for a ridge walk) and El Realet, a jagged barrier between Sella and Puig Campana, are excellent.

Descend east to a small saddle (1043m) about 35 minutes from Paso Mulero and cut back left through the small rock gateway. Descend northwest to an old 4WD track leading to a major forestry road. Those wishing to camp discreetly at **Fuente Partagas** should turn left (it's a 50-minute walk). For the main route turn right, then 30 minutes later right again onto a sealed track that zigzags down past Font Moli to a tarmac road on the edges of Benimantell. Head north along the tarmac road, fork right, and 250m later a right turn leads to **Pensión El Trestellador** *(☎ 96 588 52 21; singles/doubles €31/42)*, which offers truly excellent Valencian cooking.

Alternatively, a 45-minute walk west in Benifato is **Hostal Sant Miquel** *(☎ 96 588 53*

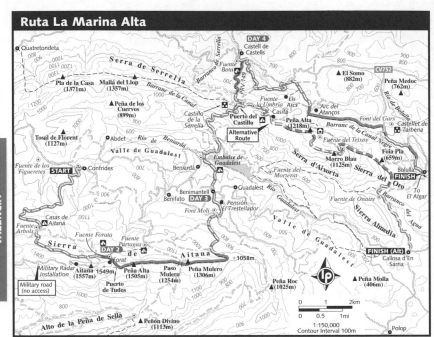

Ruta La Marina Alta

50; *Calle Sant Miquel 12; singles/doubles €24/40)*, which offers spotless rooms and includes breakfast.

Benimantell is 20 minutes north of Pensión El Trestellador and 20 minutes west of **Guadalest**. Both villages have bars, restaurants and grocery shops. The latter is also something of a tourist trap, but has bus connections to Callosa (€0.80, four daily) and the wonderful Castillo de San José.

Day 3: Benimantell to Castell de Castells
4–4½ hours, 11km

From Plaça Mayor in the centre of Benimantell head northwest around the church. Past the school fork right, heading down a 4WD track past the cemetery and zigzagging roughly north towards Embalse de Guadalest. After 25 minutes fork left (west) off the ridge and then make a right and cut back left in quick succession, bringing you to the lake and a possible **camp site**.

The track performs a loop around a gully up to the tarmac road north of Beniardá. Go right, passing a *fuente* before crossing the Río de Beniardá and turning right along a tarmac road around the edge of the lake to a gully, Barranco de les Coves, and a T-junction in 30 minutes. Go straight (north), forking right, then left, to begin the 75-minute climb to **Puerto del Castillo**, a high pass.

At the pass is a crossroads. To the right (east) a track leads onto Serra d'Aixorta

Níspero

Níspero or loquat trees grow by the thousand under vast netting systems (for protection against spring storms) that cover the slopes around Callosa. The climate and soil around Callosa particularly suit *níspero* trees, which produce a yellow, tangy, apricot-like fruit, most of which are exported to the Far East.

(see Alternative Finish: Collosa); to the left (west) are the ruins of Castillo de la Serrella, one of the last Muslim strongholds in La Marina. About 40 minutes away, the ruins can easily be reached by heading west along the dirt road from the pass, then climbing up. Be wary if you climb to the exposed lookout – the walls are 500 years old and the southern cliffs sheer.

For the main route descend straight ahead for a couple of minutes to a T-junction. Turn left and loop (west) around to the ridge of a spur, then turn right onto the PRV149, which follows an old Mozarabic trail (see the boxed text 'Mozarabic Trails') down to **Camping El Castellet** *(4-bed cabins €24)*. Camping is free and cabins include mattresses and a wood-burning stove. The **camp guardian** *(☎ 96 551 82 61; Calle San Antonio 16, Castell de Castells)* has keys for hot showers and the cabins, which can also be reserved through **Silvoturismos** *(☎ 676 49 07 01;* e *arco@ stl.logiccontrol.es)*.

Pensión Castells *(☎ 96 551 82 54;* w *www.darburn.com; Calle San Vicente 18; singles/doubles €25/50; open Sept-June)* is 20 minutes away in Castell de Castells. Rates include breakfast and the owners have extensive knowledge of walks in the area.

Casa Pilar *(☎ 96 551 81 57;* e *casapilar@grupobbva.net; Calle San José 2; singles/ doubles €27/49)* is a beautifully renovated village house.

Three good local **bar-restaurants** and a couple of **grocery shops** are found close to the village church.

Alternative Finish: Callosa

6½–8 hours, 23km

From Puerto del Castillo ascend east on a well-made forestry track past beautiful, overhanging cliffs (a possible **camp site**) reaching a well-kept *casita* (small farm shack) with a well in 30 minutes. Turn right off the road here and head south, forking left onto an old 4WD track that climbs for 25 minutes past a ruined farmhouse and along a series of goat tracks to a large threshing circle at El Pas del Xic (a saddle). Bear left (northeast) past another ruin to the start of a rocky channel. Turn right and head east up the channel, then

Mozarabic Trails

During the early centuries of southern Spain's Islamic occupation a large percentage of the local population converted to Islam. Those who chose to remain Christian were not persecuted, but given full legal protection secured by the payment of tax. Christians mixed freely with Muslims and the two slowly became indistinguishable in appearance, causing the Christians of northern Spain to name them the *mozárabes*, the 'Arabised' or Arab-like. Elements of Arab culture (such as craft and building skills, which in turn filtered into the northern Christian kingdoms) were also adopted by the *mozárabes*, who even built churches in an Arabic style.

Ancient stepped tracks through the mountains of Valencia (and Andalucía) are also the work of the *mozárabes*. Typically, these cobbled trails zigzag across the steepest slopes and down into the deepest ravines, making navigable once treacherous routes. It's also likely that many of these trails were constructed by the Mudéjars, Muslim settlers who stayed after the Reconquista and converted to Christianity.

Many of these paths are still in quite good condition, testament to the merits of solid construction and skill of *mozárabe* and Muslim craftsmen.

traverse to a narrow col. **Peña Alta** (1218m) is a rocky scramble northwest from here (the views are worth the climb) and a left turn leads west to Fuente de Teixos (dry at the time of writing) where there's a large, simple **refugi** with a wood-burning stove.

Head southeast from the col across a meadow to a 4WD track that leads to the weather station on **Moro Blau** (1125m) in about 25 minutes. As 270-degree viewpoints in La Marina go, this is one of the best. Continue east following the looping road down to the head of Barranc Negra. Turn right down a wide track past a *fuente* in an old bath and follow the cairn-marked trail (soon with yellow-and-white trail markers) east down an impressive gully for about 20 minutes until the trail moves off southeast,

VALENCIA

crossing the head of another gully and over a spur to a goat shed and 4WD track (leading down to Bolulla) at Foia Pla (659m).

Turn right, then after 20m turn left onto a narrow, winding trail that leads down to a tarmac road in about 40 minutes. Turn right and follow the road for an hour to Callosa.

Day 4: Castell de Castells to Bolulla

6½–7 hours, 16.5km

Head east along the CV752, then 50m beyond the turn-off to Camping El Castellet turn right, climbing up the dirt road leading to Puerto del Castillo. After 20 minutes turn left (south) then fork right four minutes later and follow the track east for about 20 minutes to a T-junction. Turn right, heading up and around a gully to a ridge to meet a 4WD track coming from the CV752. Go right, and right again 700m later at a T-junction. Follow the 4WD track southeast between a couple of hills, past the turning for the PRV151 and Els Arcs (a double rock arch well worth a 30-minute return detour southwest) and on to another T-junction. Turn left, following a well-used 4WD track downhill through a number of zigzags and past a farmhouse to a flat area of cleared land beyond which the road passes between two pines.

Proceed southwest across the clearing to an old track that soon swings southeast for a 25-minute climb into and along the western side of a narrow gully with **Arc del Atanços**, a small natural rock arch, on its eastern side (it's best seen from inside the gully). Once beside the stream cross and head straight up (east) through the pines on a cairn-marked path that crosses a level area crisscrossed with stone walls, and continues due east to the head of Barranc de la Canal Negre and a magnificent narrow valley. Continue east, sticking to the northern side of the valley and arriving at a saddle and dirt road in 1¼ hours.

Due east, on a precipitous peak, are the ruins of **Castellet de Tárbena** (Penya del Castellet on the IGN 1:25,000 map). It's a tricky scramble up there and the ruins are dangerous. Just north of the pass is an area of pasture that could make a great **camp site** (finding water is a bit of a hike) and it's

worth walking this way for a few minutes just for the views east to the row of dramatic cliffs and ravines that line the upper reaches of Río de Bolulla. From here the PRV49 forks right off the 4WD track on a loop around El Somo (886m) – a great day walk.

Back at the pass turn right (south), descending to a right-hand bend where the tarmac begins. Bear off straight ahead (south), cutting a loop out of the road, and then, 10 minutes after rejoining the tarmac and 30m after a switchback left, turn right onto a narrow Mozarabic trail that winds south down the side of ridge to a 4WD track. Follow it south for 50m before bearing left onto a trail leading beside (and through) the Río Bolulla. 10 minutes later, back on the 4WD track, turn left, walking up to a concrete road that leads in about 15 minutes down to **Bar la Era** (a good place to eat and drink) in Bolulla.

Atelier Capelletes (☎ 96 588 04 52; [e] capelletes@ctv.es; Partida Capelletes 2; singles/doubles €33/42) is just south of the village; rates include breakfast.

Serra de Bérnia Traverse

Duration	9–10½ hours
Distance	16km
Difficulty	demanding
Start/Finish	Fonts de l'Algar
Nearest Town	Callosa (p257)
Transport	private
Summary	A hard, but extremely enjoyable ridge walk requiring nerve and agility, but offering excellent views across La Marina mountains and down to the coast at Benidorm

This exhilarating traverse of the jagged western ridge of Serra de Bérnia begins at the popular tourist spot Fonts de l'Algar (or Fuentes del Algar), 3km from Callosa. Initially following ancient drovers' paths, the well-marked route, with 976m of ascent, is not beyond the average walker prepared for a few simple climbing moves and some exposed sections.

If you have transport it's possible to start the walk in Bérnia, thus saving three hours.

Bolulla to Fonts de l'Algar Link

A simple 45-minute route leads 2.5km from Bolulla along sealed tracks through *níspero* orchards to the start of the Serra de Bérnia Traverse.

Cross into the large car park opposite the centre of Bolulla, turn right and pick up the road (marked as a *pista* on the recommended IGN 1:25,000 map Nos 848-I *Altea* and 822-III *Parcent*) that leads happily southeast and then south, down through a couple of zigzags, to the restaurants of El Algar at Fonts de l'Algar.

❋ ❋ ❋ ❋ ❋ ❋ ❋ ❋ ❋ ❋ ❋ ❋ ❋ ❋

The route can be split by camping at Bérnia or Fortaleza de Bérnia, but walking the ridge with a large pack is far from ideal.

There's also the possibility of heading south off the ridge to L'Olla on the coast.

PLANNING

It's a good idea to bring swimming togs for a refreshing post-walk dip in the waterfalls and gorges of **Fonts de l'Algar** *(admission €1.65-2.35)*.

Maps

The IGN's 1:25,000 map Nos 848-I *Altea* and 822-III *Parcent* cover the walk.

GETTING TO/FROM THE WALK

At the time of writing extensive road works meant no buses were going to Fonts de l'Algar from Callosa; take a taxi from Callosa (see p258).

From L'Olla, the alternative finish, catch a No 10 bus via Altea (€0.80, five daily) or the FGV *trenet* (€1.20, seven daily) back to Benidorm or Alicante.

THE WALK

From the main entrance to Fonts de l'Algar head southeast up the road, turn left at the T-junction and commence the 1.1km climb southeast up the sealed road through the *níspero* groves to a switchback left. Here the PRV48 (with yellow-and-white trail markers) zigzags on a 45-minute climb up the lower slopes of La Campana (Penya Severino; 792m), past Cova del Bardalet (a *cester* or livestock shelter), where the trail turns east to a ruined farmhouse and threshing circle. Pick up the wide track heading east and then bear off left onto a narrow track that leads up to **Fortaleza de Bérnia** in about 20 minutes.

The fort was built for King Felipe II in 1562, but subsequently occupied by Muslims escaping persecution and expulsion. Felipe III had it dismantled in 1612 to deny the fugitives the use of it, but substantial sections remain and provide good shelter. East of the fort is **Font del Fort**, a not-very-private camp site.

From the ruins head northeast, zigzagging up a scree slope. About 20m below the cliff wall a red arrow and various red dots (markers that illustrate the whole ridge walk) lead left (northwest). Traverse across the wide ledge and around the western buttress of Serra de Bérnia to an exposed ledge. From here scramble/climb east up onto the main ridge, from where it's a 30-minute scramble (exposed in places) to **Bérnia peak** (1126m).

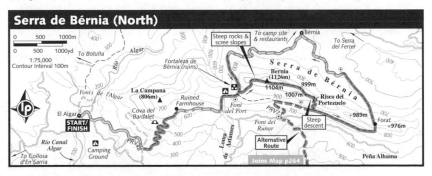

Serra de Bérnia (North)

It's a stunning viewpoint (Ibiza is visible on a clear day) and from here the trail leads across a lesser peak and up to the 1104m peak 20 minutes after the main summit.

Care is needed for the next section as the trail drops steeply from the main ridge (stick to the northern side) to a col (999m), before which a few climbing moves are required to complete a traverse (a little exposed) across a rock face and around a tree. After this crossing the trail cuts back to the southern side of the ridge and it's a simple walk up to the 1007m peak. On the southern side of the peak a trail leads to **Risco del Portezuelo** – an impressive col. Again, it's very steep, but like big steps and not too unnerving.

At the col red dots lead northeast back onto the main ridge (the trail reportedly covers the whole range), but instead turn right (south) down a steep, but manageable scree slope to a well-worn trail. Here you could turn right (west) and head down to L'Olla on the coast (see the Alternative Finish) or back to Fortaleza de Bérnia in about 40 minutes. However, the main route turns right (east) on a *forat*, a narrow 25m-long tunnel leading through the *serra*. Once through pick up the obvious trail leading northwest down to a *fuente* and 4WD track. Turn left for Bérnia, reached about an hour from the *forat*.

Bérnia has three restaurants, but none open in the evening during the week (or during the week out of the tourist season – June to September). **Restaurant Serra Bérnia** *(mains €4-6; open Sun-Fri)* is open year-round for lunch and is the closest to the trail-head, serving good, simple food. There's an unloved and untidy free **camp site** with no facilities about 1.5km north of the restaurant.

Upon meeting the tarmac road 50m south of Restaurant Serra Bérnia turn left, following the wide, rocky track up to a saddle between the Bérnia massif and Serra del Ferrer. Fortaleza de Bérnia and the route back down to Fonts de l'Algar lies just south of here, about 45 minutes from Bérnia.

Alternative Finish: L'Olla
3–3½ hours, 9km
South of Risco del Portezuelo turn right. Upon reaching a large boulder 20 minutes

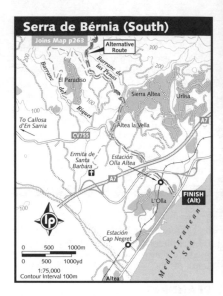

Serra de Bérnia (South)

later, turn left onto the PRV7 (with yellow-and-white trail markers) heading down past Font del Runar, along a tarmac road, south-east through a parking area and onto a narrow trail that descends to a dirt road in about an hour. Follow this road south, passing a few houses, to a T-junction. Turn left (northeast) following the tarmac southeast for 100m before turning left onto a rough track by an electricity substation just before a round-about. Drop through the woods to another tarmac road, turn right and continue south to Altea la Vella. Turn left onto the CV755 and after 800m turn right onto a tarmac track that leads under the motorway (A7) and across a bridge. Turn left, then bear left, heading south to Olla-Altea FGV station (and the pleasant **Barbacoa Bar**). Alternatively, continue south across the N332 to a couple of **restaurants** on the pebble beach of Playa L'Olla.

Other Walks

ELS PORTS
Chiva de Morella & Surrounds
These two simple day walks take in interesting local history while giving a taste of the surrounding countryside. The first walk heads north then

northwest from Morella, passing a 13th-century aqueduct on the way, to the picturesque village of Chiva de Morella and the Santuario de Roser. The second walk heads northwest to the prehistoric cave paintings close to the farmhouse of Masía de Morella la Vella. Both walks are covered by the IGN 1:25,000 map No 545-I *Morella*.

Morella to Forcall
There are two routes to Forcall. The first follows the PRV2 from the western side of Morella while the new PRV116 (the route more commonly used) leads off from the GR7 a couple of kilometres from town and heads northwest across Mola de la Garumba (1144m) to Forcall – a 15km walk of four hours. In Forcall there are a couple of places to stay and a bus back to Morella on weekday mornings. IGN 1:25,000 map Nos 545-I *Morella* and 544-II *Forcall* cover the walk.

Ascent of Caro
Leaving from Refugi de Font Ferrera (see Day 2 of the Els Ports Loop, p251), this walk heads northeast to the summit of Caro (1442m) on the GR7, returning to Fredes on a string of PRV routes via Embalse de Ulldecona and the Portell de l'Infern. There are *refugis* at Les Casetes and south of Caro there is **Refugio Caro** (*☎ 977 26 71 28)*. Allow three days to complete this route comfortably. Piolet's 1:40,000 *Els Port* map and the ICC 1:30,000 *El Port* map cover the whole walk.

LA MARINA
Serra de Serrella
As an add-on to the Ruta La Marina Alta walk (see p258) it's a great idea to spend a day exploring the Serra de Serrella. From the village of Quatretondeta climb the PRV24 to Pla de la Casa (1371m). After this popular peak head east past Malla del Llop (1357m) and along the magnificent trough of Barranc de la Canal (the north of which is lined by a row of *agujas* or *aiguilles* – narrow pinnacles of jagged rock) to Castillo de la Serrella. Use the IGN 1:25,000 map No 821-IV *Castell de Castells*.

Taxis to Quatretondeta can be arranged in Castell de Castells at **Bar Venecia** (*☎ 96 551 80 81, 646 48 07 07; Ave de Denia 3)*.

Puig Campana
At 1408m, the second-highest peak in La Marina is a big brute of a mountain and begs to be climbed. Most ascents begin from Finestrat, which has a few

places to stay and eat – **Travellers Rest** (*☎ 647 25 89 01; singles/doubles €18/25)* and **Restaurant Font Moli** are nearest to the trailhead. Catch the No 12 bus from Benidorm (€0.80, two daily).

The route leads off from a 4WD track just above Font Moli onto a simple trail that leads up to a saddle between the two peaks (turn right for the summit). North of the saddle a 300m scree run leads to a climbers' hut and some interesting routes towards Sella and Polop (which is serviced by regular Ubesa buses from Benidorm) as well as routes around the base of the mountain back to Finestrat.

The IGN's 1:25,000 map Nos 847-IV *Villajoyosa/La Vila Joiosa* and 847-II *Relleu* are required.

Sierra Helada
This 6km-long range of tall cliffs separating Benidorm from El Albir is not a bad place to escape the madness of Benidorm and a pleasant warm-up for things to come. It's a pretty comfortable traverse. Use the IGN 1:25,000 map No 848-III *Benidorm*. A comprehensive booklet about the range (in English) is available from the tourist office in Benidorm.

Sierra de Mariola
This range of mountains is little visited by foreign tourists, but contains some great walking trails and beautiful scenery. Alcoy is a good place to be based and the GR7 snakes through the region, linking the summits of Menejador (1352m), Montcabrer (1390m) and Sant Jaume (956m). Other PRV trails crisscross the region. The IGN covers this region with 1:25,000 maps.

LA SERRANÍA
The GR37
This newly established long-distance footpath encircles La Muela (1546m), the highest peak in La Serranía, an arid region of orchards, cereal fields and rugged gorges northwest of Valencia. The 62km trail follows ancient *vías pecuarias* (drovers' roads) that link the villages of Aras Alpuente, Titaguas (which has bus links to Valencia) and Alpuente, passing numerous *verónicas* (small chapels) on the way. There's accommodation in at least five of the villages en route allowing for a comfortable walk with plenty of diversions.

For further information contact the Centre Excursionista or the main tourist office in Valencia (see p246–7), where a good leaflet on the GR37 is available.

VALENCIA

Mallorca

Mallorca is the largest of the Islas Baleares (Balearic Islands), an archipelago of four inhabited and several smaller, deserted islands that spangle the Mediterranean off Spain's eastern coast.

Measuring 75km from north to south and 100km from east to west, it receives over 10 million visitors each year. However, most visitors are packed into the beach resorts of the south and northeast, while the upland areas of the northwest remain magically unspoiled and underpopulated. Here, the imposing Serra de Tramuntana dominates, its abrupt cliffs plunging into the sea. And here is where the good walking lies…

HISTORY

Over the centuries, Mallorca was occupied by wave after wave of invaders, and Phoenicians, Carthaginians, Romans, Visigoths and Arabs have all left their mark.

The Arabs built the first water channels for irrigation and introduced the *noria* (water wheel) to raise water from wells and underground reservoirs. They also constructed the island's earliest banks of terracing, which increased cultivable space on the flanks of the steep valleys. Then, in 1229, the Catalan army of Jaume I, king of Catalunya and Aragón, put an end to more than three centuries of Muslim occupation.

After the 'discovery' of the Americas, Spain's attention was drawn increasingly to its transatlantic possessions, to the neglect of its offshore Mediterranean islands, which were repeatedly battered by raiding Barbary pirates and Turkish warships.

Mass tourism, which began as a trickle in the 1950s and has gushed in greater volume with every subsequent year, has been the economic saviour of the islands but at considerable environmental cost.

Throughout recent Mallorcan history the Serra de Tramuntana was mainly the preserve of olive farmers, charcoal-burners and *nevaters*, or snow-collectors (for more about *nevaters*, see the boxed text 'Neveras: the

Highlights

INGRID RODDIS

Walkers make the steep descent down Torrent de Pareis

- Rewarding yourself with an ice cream at day's end at Sa Fabrica de Gelats in Sóller (p269)

- Savouring the views of the Sóller valley, way below, from the Mirador d'en Quesada on the Barranc de Biniaraix & Embassament de Cúber walk (p275)

- Enjoying the superb seascapes from the Camino del Archiduque on the Valldemossa Loop (p277)

- Clambering down Mallorca's deepest gorge, the Torrent de Pareis (p282)

Original Fridges', p259). Nowadays, the major part of the range, which is classified as Áreas Naturales de la Serra de Tramuntana, enjoys a degree of environmental protection.

There's no longstanding tradition of walking for pleasure among Mallorcans. Until relatively recently life was hard for

Mallorca

0   50   100km
0   25   50mi

Menorca

Maó

Palma
de Mallorca   Artá

Mallorca

Ibiza   Cabrera

ISLAS BALEARES
(BALEARIC ISLANDS)

Ibiza

Formentera

See Main Map

0   20   40km
0   10   20mi
1:2,000,000

Mallorca

Pollença   To Menorca

Sa Calobra   Alcúdia

Port de Sóller   Sóller

Valldemossa   Inca   Artá

Sant Elm   Palma de
Mallorca

Andratx   Manacor

Felanitx
Llucmajor

To Denia,
Valencia &
Barcelona   To Menorca

To Ibiza

most and leisure time limited. You walked for a purpose, to get where you needed to be, and not for the intrinsic pleasure of the journey. To this day, many walks follow ancient paths between villages and most walkers on the trails are foreign visitors.

NATURAL HISTORY

Mallorca is a continuation of the Andalucian mountains, also known as the Baetic Plate, on the Spanish mainland. Limestone, uplifted from the sea floor by tectonic forces some 150 million years ago, constitutes the core of the Serra de Tramuntana.

There, north-facing crags and cliffs are much steeper than those facing south, in many places making access to the coast impossible from the landward side.

Evergreen oak *(carrasca)*, its leaves waxy and shiny to reduce evaporation in the heat of summer, is common. Its subspecies, the holm oak, once the charcoal-burners' favourite, thrives at lower altitudes. Seeds of the carob or locust bean, formerly fed to livestock, are now mainly used as a substitute for chocolate and as a guaranteed, flush-you-through laxative.

At higher levels pines predominate, surviving up to about 1000m. Most common is the Aleppo pine, which, despite its name, may have originated in the Balearic Islands and only later become established in the Levant.

The main cultivated trees are olive trees (some veterans are reputed to be over 1000 years old), fig trees – pendulous and often supported by sturdy poles – and almond trees, whose blossoms tint the countryside pink in spring. Orange and lemon orchards proliferate, especially in the mild Sóller valley.

In springtime the hills blaze yellow with broom. Aromatic rosemary, with its characteristic blue flower, and wild rockroses stay in flower longer. Asphodels colonise land low in nutrition and somewhere, sometime, you're bound to get your boots tangled in *callitx*, a type of grass with long, sharp-edged leaves.

Migratory birds use the islands as a staging post in spring and autumn. You're certain to spot raptors such as red kites, kestrels, black vultures, hawks and both Eleanor's and peregrine falcons.

Keen bird-watchers can contact fellow enthusiasts at the **Grupo de Ornitología Balear** *(GOB; ☎ 971 72 11 05, fax 971 71 13 75)*, also known as the Grup Balear d'Ornitologia i Defensa de la Naturalesa, in Palma.

CLIMATE

The major rains fall between late October and February. But even December, the dampest month, has an average of only eight days' rain, a statistic that walkers from soggier climes regard with envy.

MALLORCA

INFORMATION
When to Walk
The best period for walking is from late February to May, when the countryside is green and blossoming and temperatures moderate, or September and early October, after the summer crowds have gone but before the rains arrive. This said, winter walking, when the average daily temperature rarely drops below 10°C, can be splendid and many aficionados actually prefer it.

Between late June and August, daily average temperatures are around 25°C and hiking the tops without even a bush for shade can be a sticky experience. But if summer – when there's no rain to speak of – is the only time you can get away, don't despair. Make an early enough start and you can be cooling off in the sea by the time the sun reaches its zenith.

When planning your walks, bear in mind that the times we quote are *actual walking time*, and do not include rest stops.

Maps
The best overall map of the island for outdoor enthusiasts is Kompass' 1:75,000 *Mallorca*, with walking and mountain bike routes superimposed. For driving and general orientation, the free *Las Islas Baleares* map, available from any tourist office, is quite adequate.

Discovery Walking Guides (also known as Warm Island Walking Guides) publishes three reliable walking maps of the island, based on IGN 1:25,000 originals, together with a detailed route description in English. Their 1:40,000 *Mallorca Mountains Walking Guide* presents 19 enticing walks around Sóller and Port de Sóller. *Mallorca North & Mountains Tour & Trail Map* at the same scale covers almost all the Serra de Tramuntana. This map, like the Freytag & Berndt 1:50,000 *Mallorca Tramuntana* map, covers all the walks in this chapter except the Monestir de Sa Trapa walk.

Foment del Desenvolupament de Mallorca (Fodesma), a branch of the Consell Insular (the island's governing body), has produced a number of good walking brochures. In addition to a large-scale plan of the walk, each contains a wealth of background information. Unfortunately – and absurdly – they're only in Catalan.

Books
Walking in Mallorca, by the late June Parker, describes more than 50 walks on the island. It's solid on background and extremely well researched and written, its only deficiency is the spindly monochrome maps.

Mallorca, by Valerie Crespi-Green, in the Sunflower series is, by comparison, thin beer. Even so, it describes several worthwhile hikes and the 1:40,000 colour maps are easy to follow.

Birdwatching in Mallorca, by Ken Stoba, is worth slipping into your pack. *Wild Flowers of Majorca, Minorca and Ibiza*, by Elspeth Beckett, the best guide for amateur botanists, is no longer easy to obtain.

Tourist offices carry a free pamphlet *20 Walking Excursions in Mallorca*. It gives pointers but needs to be supplemented with a good map.

Information Sources
You'll find gigabytes of information about the island at Ⓦ www.visitbalears.com.

GATEWAYS
All the walks in this chapter, except Monestir de Sa Trapa, are accessible by public transport from Sóller or Port de Sóller, so it makes sense to base yourself in one or the other. Palma de Mallorca is the logical base for the Monestir de Sa Trapa walk – and you may find yourself spending a night there on your way to or from the other trails.

Palma de Mallorca
The islands' only true city this is an agreeable, albeit crowded, spot to pass through.

Information The Consell de Mallorca's **tourist office** (☎ 971 71 22 16; Plaça de la Reina 2; open 9am-8pm Mon-Fri, 10am-2pm Sat) covers the whole island.

　　La Casa del Mapa (☎/fax 971 22 59 45; Carrer Sant Domingo 11) has a comprehensive selection of large-scale Mallorca maps. **Librería Fondevila** (☎ 971 72 56 16; Costa *de la Pols 18)* also carries a good stock of maps and guidebooks.

The **Grup d'Excursió Mallorqui** *(GEM;* ☎ *871 94 79 00;* W *www.gemweb.org; Carrer Doctor Andreu Feliu 20; open 7pm-9pm Mon-Fri)* has friendly members and a good library.

Supplies & Equipment A good range of walking gear, and a smaller selection of walking books, are available at **Es Refugi** *(Vía Sindicat 21)* and **Foracorda** *(Carrer Miquel Marquès 20).*

Places to Stay & Eat Central **Hostal Apuntadores** *(☎ 971 71 34 91;* e *apunta dores@ctv.es; Carrer Apuntadors 8; dorm beds €14, singles/doubles/triples €21/33/45, doubles/triples with shower €37/49)* is a travellers' favourite. **Hostal Ritzi** *(☎/fax 971 71 46 10; Carrer Apuntadors 6; singles/doubles €23/34, doubles with shower/bathroom €37/49),* next door, is equally popular. If you want to be fresh for the next day's walking, ask for a room away from the street.

Carrer Apuntadors and adjacent streets seethe with restaurants. Nearby, **La Boveda** *(☎ 971 71 48 63; Carrer Boteria 3; mains €8-12.50),* just off Plaça de la Llotja, is enormously popular, offering excellent food at reasonable prices. Veggies should head for **Bon Lloc** *(☎ 971 71 86 17; Carrer Sant Feliu 7; meals €20-25; open Mon-Sat, lunch only Mon & Tues).*

Getting There & Away There's a daily stream of charter flights into Palma from Europe, especially from the UK and Germany, for details see Air (pp370–2).

Iberia, Air Europa and Spanair operate scheduled flights from major Spanish cities. Cheapest and most frequent are those from Barcelona and Valencia (€70 to €90 one way).

Trasmediterranea *(☎ 902 45 46 45;* W *www .trasmediterranea.com)* runs daily sea transport between Palma and both Barcelona (3¾ to seven hours) and Valencia (4¼ to 7¼ hours). Duration and price (€25.30 to €47.70) to/from each depend upon the kind of vessel.

Mallorca's Blocked Passages

Until quite recently you could do a magnificent circuit round the lip of the bowl of mountains in which Sóller nestles – until a farmer up on the tops erected a series of locked gates to bar the way. It *is* possible to cross his territory but only as part of an organised group with a guide who pays the proprietor. It's not what walking, wild, free and harming no one, should be about.

Another favourite walk used to be the Puig Roig circuit, much of it following an old corniche path once used by smugglers. But here, too, property owners have blocked the route, allowing access on Sunday only. On another trail near the Monestir de Lluc the landowner exacts a €3 toll.

Unfortunately, there's little tradition of walking for walking's sake on the island. So there's no pressure group with the clout of, say, the admirable Ramblers Association in the UK which, at the click of a barred gate, can drum up a posse of walkers to challenge closed footpaths and militate for freedom of access.

Palma's train station is on Plaça d'Espanya. The bus station is on Carrer Eusebi Estada, just northeast of the train station. Tourist offices and both stations carry a pamphlet listing bus times and routes throughout the island, and Palma–Sóller train times.

Sóller

Don't worry about the daytime crowds which more than double Sóller's population of around 11,000 as the train from Palma and the rickety tram from Port de Sóller decant their passengers. Come nightfall, when they've all retreated, calm returns to one of the island's most Mallorcan of pueblos.

Information The **tourist office** *(☎ 971 63 80 08;* W *www.sollernet.com; Plaça d'Espanya; open 9.30am-2pm & 3pm-5pm Mon-Fri, 10am-1pm Sat & Sun, closed Sun Nov-Feb)* is in an old train carriage beside the station.

MALLORCA

Librería Calabruix (☎ 971 63 26 41; Carrer Sa Lluna) stocks a limited range of walking maps and guidebooks.

Forn de Campos (Calle Jeroni Estades 8) bakery has a couple of Internet points.

Places to Stay & Eat The cheapest option is **Hostal Nadal** (☎/fax 971 63 11 80; Carrer Romaguera 29; singles/doubles/triples €16/ 24/32, singles/doubles/triples with bathroom €20/32/41). The mood when we visited ranged from lugubrious to bickering but the rooms are just fine.

Casa Margarita (☎ 971 63 42 14; Carrer Real 3; singles/doubles/triples/quads €18/ 30/35/46) has seven rooms with big old beds and bags of character.

Hotel El Guía (☎ 971 63 02 27; singles/ doubles with bathroom €46/66; open Apr-Oct) is beside the train station. Rates include breakfast. It's the most comfortable option and does a good-value menú (fixed-price meal) at €16.

All three are popular walkers' haunts so it's advisable to book ahead – except, paradoxically, between July and September, when most visitors to Mallorca are stretched out on the beaches.

Celler Cas Carrete (☎ 971 63 03 64; Plaça de America 4; mains €6-13) occupies an old cart workshop, and does good weekday menús at €7.70 and €8.30.

Refresh yourself on the shady terrace of **Sa Fabrica de Gelats** (☎ 971 63 20 56; Plaça del Mercat) with one of its scrummy ice creams, many varieties made with local fruit. It also does generously topped pizzas (€3 to €5.30), to eat in or take away. **Café Sóller** (☎ 971 63 00 10; Plaça Constitucio 13), German run, is a good choice for a drink or a pasta-based meal.

Forn de Campos (Calle Jeroni Estades 8) does great coffee and cakes, and bakes a variety of good breads.

Getting There & Away Four trains (☎ 971 75 20 51) daily (€2.40) and one tren turístico (tourist train; €4.80) make the rattling 80-minute journey between Palma and Sóller.

An express bus runs hourly between Palma and Port de Sóller (€2.10, 45 minutes).

It calls by Sóller's Plaça de América about 10 minutes before it arrives in Port de Sóller.

For a taxi, call **Radio Taxi Sóller** (☎ 971 63 84 84). Prices to/from Sóller include Port de Sóller €6, Deià €15.50, Embassament de Cúber €20, Valldemossa €24 and Sa Calobra €38.50.

Port de Sóller

Port de Sóller has a fairly wide choice of hotels. It's essential to reserve in high summer.

Information There's a small **tourist office** (☎ 971 63 30 42; Carrer Canonge Oliver 10; open 9am-1pm & 2.30pm-5pm Mon-Fri, 10am-1pm Sat Mar-Oct).

Places to Stay & Eat A 45-minute walk from Port de Sóller, beside the lighthouse, is **Refugi Muleta** (☎ 971 63 42 71, fax 971 63 47 69; dorm beds €7.50). Recently established, it also provides meals. Toni, the warden and a qualified mountain guide, is a mine of information about walking in the Tramuntana.

Hotel Brisas (☎ 971 63 13 52, fax 971 63 21 46; Camí del Far 15; singles/doubles with bathroom €30/45), on the lighthouse road, is small by Port de Sóller standards and family run.

The whole sweep of the bay is bordered by restaurants and cafés for every palate and pocket. One block back, **Sa Paella** (☎ 971 63 44 62; Carrer Esglesia 2; open Tues-Sun) does a good range of takeaway dishes. For fresh fish, head for the 1st-floor terrace of **Sa Llotja des Peix** (☎ 971 63 29 54; Moll Pesquer), on the quayside overlooking the small fishing port.

Getting There & Away A rumbly tram (€0.75), with regular departures about every half-hour between 7am and 9pm, runs between Sóller and Port de Sóller. There's also an express bus that runs hourly between Palma and Port de Sóller (€2.10, 45 minutes) via Sóller's Plaça de América. See also Getting There & Away for Sóller (pp269–70).

Monestir de Sa Trapa

Duration	4–4½ hours
Distance	12km
Difficulty	easy–moderate
Start	Sant Elm
Finish	S'Arracó
Nearest Town	Palma de Mallorca (p268)
Transport	bus, taxi

Summary A robust ascent from the coastal resort of Sant Elm to the ex-Trappist monastery of Sa Trapa is followed by a gentler inland return to the village of S'Arracó

The coastal stretch of this walk, where over 80 bird species have been recorded, is particularly rich for ornithologists; that's why local ecological group, the Grup Balear d'Ornitologia i Defensa de la Naturalesa, purchased the dilapidated monastery of Sa Trapa in 1980. It's gradually renovating the monastery, the intricate system of irrigation, fed by a single stream, and the fine stone terracing.

The first part of the walk offers superb seascapes to compensate for the huffing and puffing. You stand a good chance of seeing red kites, kestrels, alpine swifts and maybe even a hawk or peregrine falcon. Once you reach the *mirador* (lookout point) at Cap Fabioler, it's flat or downhill all the way home, though the route is indistinct in a couple of places.

PLANNING
What to Bring
It's well worth slipping your binoculars into your day pack.

Maps
The whole of the area is covered by the SGE 1:50,000 map No 37-27 (697) *Andratx*, though by no means all of the route is indicated.

GETTING TO/FROM THE WALK
Bus No IB32 between Palma and Andratx (pronounced an-**dratch**; €2.90, 30km, 1¼ hours) leaves Palma every 45 minutes from Plaça d'Espanya, beside the train station.

Bus No L5 leaves Andratx for Sant Elm via S'Arracó (six daily). Convenient buses head back to Andratx from Sant Elm (two daily), calling by S'Arracó about 10 minutes after departing Andratx. The service may vary in winter. For the current schedule, ring **Autocares Andratx** (☎ 971 20 45 04).

Radio Taxi Andratx (☎ 971 13 63 98) will run you from Andratx to Sant Elm for about €9. At the end of the walk, ring them from S'Arracó and they'll be round in two shakes to pick you up (€6 to return to Andratx).

THE WALK (see map p272)
From Sant Elm's bus terminus in Plaça Mossen Sebastia Grau, head northeast up Avinguda de Sa Trapa. After 15 minutes, when you reach the farm of Ca'n Tomevi and a four-way junction with a signboard, go straight ahead along a narrow path and *not* right, as the sign indicates. Both ways lead to Sa Trapa. The one we recommend makes for a rather tougher ascent but offers more shade and more spectacular views. (If you

Monestir de Sa Trapa

Expelled from France in 1791 in the wake of the French revolution and its anticlericalism, a small group of Trappist monks (hence the name, Sa Trapa) found their way to Tarragona, on the Catalan coast south of Barcelona. A few years later, when France invaded Spain, they had to flee again and found their way to Mallorca. At the desolate southwest tip of the island, they founded a monastery.

Never numbering more than 40, the monks returned to the mainland in 1820. But during their 10 short years of occupation they built a small monastery, channelled the intermittent stream which flows down the San Josep valley into a network of irrigation canals, established agriculture and constructed a corn mill, threshing house and banks of terraces with dry-stone walls, all of which remain to this day.

After many years of neglect, the property and its land were acquired by Grup Balear d'Ornitologia i Defensa de la Naturalesa, in whose trust the complex remains.

MALLORCA

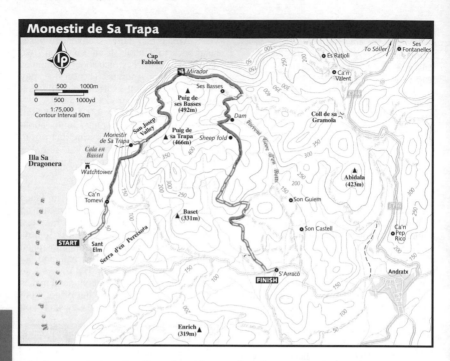

Monestir de Sa Trapa

only fancy a short outing from Sant Elm, you can ascend to Sa Trapa by one of these alternatives and return by the other.)

As the intermittently cairned path comes out of the woods and onto a cliff, the steep stuff begins in earnest, as do the great views of the coast and the uninhabited island and nature reserve, Illa Sa Dragonera.

At the top of the last rocky crag, watch out for the red arrows directing you right and up a series of large, steep boulders. Miss these and you'll find yourself facing a sheer drop to the sea.

Once over the brow, you see the ruins of the **Monestir de Sa Trapa** below, less than 10 minutes' walk away. The once-rich setting which induced a group of Trappist monks to establish their self-contained community here (see the boxed text 'Monestir de Sa Trapa', p271) is now bleak as a result of a devastating fire in 1994 which left most of the pines no more than twisted black fingers. Despite extensive replanting, and even

though grasses and *montebajo* (scrub) are reasserting themselves, it will be a generation before the valley fully recovers. Below the monastery, the old cereal mill and the circular threshing area is a *mirador* with a simple plaque to one Joan Lliteras, who fell to his death when only 18.

Retrace your steps along the well-defined track and continue beyond the junction with the path from Sant Elm. At a steep hairpin, where a sign indicates S'Arracó and Sant Elm to the right, take instead the narrow path heading north, away from the bend. You're now at the heart of the area devastated by the fire, much of it replanted with young pines encased in chicken wire to protect them from feral goats, their principal threat.

After an undemanding ascent to 400m, the route again levels out, letting you maintain a steady clip. At a giant cairn about 45 minutes from La Trapa, don't miss the brief (precisely 2½ minutes brief!) diversion left (west) to the **mirador** at Cap Fabioler. This, with its sweeping views of sea and coast, makes an agreeable rest stop.

Only a few metres beyond the cairn, you finally kiss goodbye to Illa Sa Dragonera, now in your wake, as the views open out to reveal the rocky coastline and the Serra de Tramuntana range, the southwestern extremity of which you're walking. Aim eastwards towards the first significant clump of live trees since you entered the area of the fire's devastation. Within this copse is Ses Basses, 25 to 30 minutes beyond the *mirador* and the first intact building since Sa Trapa. Written records reveal a building on this site as early as 1389.

At a hairpin bend a few minutes beyond Ses Basses, you have a choice. Continuing along the wide main track leads in about an hour to the Coll de Sa Gremola at the Km 106 marker on the C710 road running between Andratx and Sóller. From here, you can walk a further 5km down an old cart track to Andratx. The descent via the Torrent Gore d'en Betts to S'Arracó that we describe takes 1½ to two hours. It's more varied, though you do have to cast around for the route at a couple of points.

For the Torrent alternative, take the narrow, sandy track to the right, which briefly doubles back before swinging southeast. The track ends beside a small dam. Take the path which veers away right over a small bluff, following an ancient wall. Stick with it as, by now well cairned, it runs west up the flank of a side valley to curl around its top. About 20 minutes beyond the dam, you reach a sheepfold, where the path all but disappears briefly under yet more burnt pines. However, if you keep the building on your right, you'll soon pick it up again.

After dropping gently southwestwards for some 10 minutes, you enter the welcome semi-shade of a pine grove with a small, neglected almond orchard to your right. Just beyond, the path runs parallel with a terrace wall, still heading southwards, to become a wide, rocky track that steadily descends. Ruined farmsteads and abandoned cultivation give way to chic, renovated second homes as you approach your destination, S'Arracó.

Sóller to Deià

Duration	3–4 hours
Distance	10km
Difficulty	easy
Start	Sóller
Finish	Deià
Nearest Town	Sóller (p269)
Transport	bus

Summary An undemanding, well-signed walk beside olive groves and pasture, with a coastal path to Cala de Deià and an ascent by an ancient track to Deià

The walk links two interesting communities on Mallorca's northwest coast. The optional cut-out to Deià at the end of the Camí de Castelló saves 3km and can make a good warm-up walk after a midday arrival in Sóller.

HISTORY

Until Sóller–Deià road was thrust through in the 19th century, the Camí de Castelló was the main thoroughfare between the two villages. Superseded and neglected, it became the preserve of hunters, charcoal-burners and shepherds. Recently restored, it's now a well-signed and popular track for walkers.

The Camí de la Mar, less well defined nowadays, also has a long history. In late medieval times, for example, it was deliberately sabotaged in places to make access more difficult for Arab coastal raiders.

PLANNING
When to Walk

Reasonably shady, the route can be walked comfortably even at the height of summer, when you can also dunk yourself in one of the small coves or at the Cala de Deià.

What to Bring

Pack your swimming kit if you fancy cooling off in one of the coves.

Maps

Discovery Walking Guides' 1:40,000 *Mallorca North & Mountains Tour & Trail Map* and the Freytag & Berndt 1:50,000 *Mallorca Tramuntana* map cover the route.

MALLORCA

GETTING TO/FROM THE WALK

Buses run between Deià and Sóller, and Port de Sóller (three daily Monday to Saturday, one daily Sunday).

THE WALK

From Sóller, head for the Repsol petrol station on the bypass road that goes to Port de Sóller. If you take Carrer de Bauçà from the main Plaça de sa Constitució and keep heading west as directly as the turnings allow, you won't miss it.

Cross the bypass to a sign, Camí del Rost, which also marks the beginning of the Camí de Castelló. After about 15 minutes, the sealed road narrows to a footpath that, once over a stream bed, becomes a fine stone stairway.

Just over the half-hour, the cobbles stop and you descend briefly among olive trees, ignoring both a potential fork and a manifest turn to the right. The way is now a wide cart track.

A little under an hour out, you arrive at a minor crossroads, signed for Deià. Soon, a couple of giant fig trees overhanging the path offer juicy refreshment as you skirt the estate of C'an Carabasseta.

At a junction beside a small 17th-century chapel, now sadly ruined, mount the less obvious cobbled path to the left of the chapel. It's indicated by the first of the GR signs that help what's already easy navigation until you reach the C710 (it's the inaugural section of what, a few years down the road, will be the Ruta de Pedra en Sec, a grand long-distance trail traversing the whole Tramuntana).

The path ascends to **Son Mico**, also known as Ca'n Prohom, a large farmhouse with roots at least as deep as the 15th century. There, you can fortify yourself with fresh orange juice and cakes. Queen Isabel II, who's reputed to have spent the night here when she visited Sóller in 1888, enjoyed, no doubt, more sumptuous fare.

Some 200m beyond Son Mico, leave the track and turn sharp left just before an electricity pylon to mount a clearly signed cobbled track.

Once the cliffs of the Cala de Deià come into view, there's a clearly signed potable spring, the Font de ses Mentides, in a gully just off route.

Over the brow of an incline, you're in sight of Lluc Alcari, a cluster of coastal houses. About two hours into the walk, turn

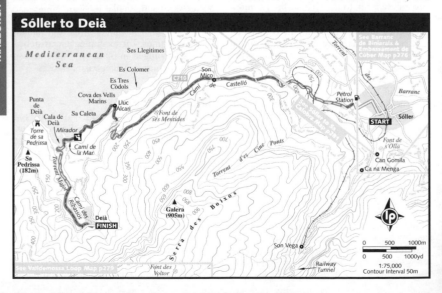

Sóller to Deià

Mediterranean Sea

Ses Llegitimes

Es Colomer

Son Mico

C710

Es Tres Còdols

Cova des Vells Marins

Lluc Alcari

Camí de Castelló

Punta de Deià

Sa Caleta

Font de ses Mentides

Petrol Station

Barranc

Cala de Deià

Torre de sa Pedrissa

Mirador

START

Sóller

Font de s'Olla

Sa Pedrissa (182m)

Camí de la Mar

Can Gomila

Ca na Menga

Torrent d'es Cinc Ponts

Galera (905m)

Torrent des Bóixos

Camí des Ribassos

Deià
FINISH

Son Vega

Serra des

Railway Tunnel

0   500   1000m
0   500   1000yd
1:75,000
Contour Interval 50m

See Valldemossa Loop Map p279

See Barranc de Biniaraix & Embassament de Cúber Map p276

Font des Voltor

right at a T-junction to follow a sealed driveway and cobbled lane to meet the C710 main road. Here, you can either cut out to Deià by walking west for about 30 minutes or turn east to continue the walk via Lluc Alcari, as described here.

After a little less than 10 minutes of roadwork, go left at the Lluc Alcari turn-off (signed Hotel Costa d'Or) then right at a fork (the left option leads to the hotel). After a bend, look for a narrow path on the right, its entry probably half masked by bushes. Follow it for some 200m above an olive grove then bear left to thread your way downhill.

When you intersect with Camí de la Mar, the coastal path, turn left to follow the coastline. Although debris from recent logging (the clear-up after a particularly destructive storm) makes the path indistinct in places, wayfinding is, in general, uncomplicated.

From a **mirador**, reached 20 minutes after having hit the coast, you can pick out the 17th-century Torre de sa Pedrissa, a defensive tower on the headland beyond Cala de Deià. The latter's pebble beach, reached after around three hours' walking, may well be crowded but the water is clean and inviting.

There's only one way out of the tight valley; head inland along a dirt track that soon becomes a narrow sealed road. After 10 minutes, cross the bed of the Torrent Major by a wooden bridge onto the true left (west) bank to ascend an excellent, recently restored cobbled path. You're now following the Camí des Ribassos, another ancient pathway linking Deià with its small sea outlet. Turn left where it joins a well-defined track. From the Cala to the village is about 40 minutes.

Deià

Deià is an attractive cluster of some 75 houses on the lower slopes of the Puig des Teix. It can be massively crowded during the day as convoys of tourist coaches deposit their cargo. Then, like Sóller, it becomes itself again each evening as the buses pull out.

The village has a high proportion of expats, a longstanding tradition, going back to the days when it was a thriving artist colony with the late Robert Graves its most famous denizen.

Barranc de Biniaraix & Embassament de Cúber

Duration	3½–4 hours
Distance	11km
Difficulty	easy–moderate
Start	Sóller
Finish	Embassament de Cúber
Nearest Town	Sóller (p269)
Transport	bus

Summary An ascent of the tight Barranc de Biniaraix valley to the small upland plateau of l'Ofre; crossing a col to descend through woodland and on to the Embassament de Cúber reservoir

This classic walk follows part of an old pilgrim route which ran between Sóller and the Monestir de Lluc. The earliest documented evidence of its use as a pilgrim route is a letter dated AD 1438 from the local bishop to his priest in Sóller, granting an indulgence of 40 days to those who helped to maintain the track.

NATURAL HISTORY

Few evergreen oaks, the valley's original cladding, remain. They've been superseded by olive and orange groves, carob trees and, in the upper reaches, pine trees and juniper bushes. In the humid areas near the banks of the Torrent des Barranc is a rich variety of ferns, some of them endemic to Mallorca.

PLANNING
Maps

Discovery Walking Guides' 1:40,000 *Mallorca North & Mountains Tour & Trail Map* and the Freytag & Berndt 1:50,000 *Mallorca Tramuntana* map cover the route.

GETTING TO/FROM THE WALK

The later of the twice-daily buses linking Pollença and Port de Sóller via Sóller passes by Embassament de Cúber reservoir, at the end of the walk, between 5.05pm and 5.20pm. Miss it and you've one helluva hike home. If you opt to do the route in reverse – an easier but less fulfilling option – take the morning bus which leaves Port de Sóller at

9am, calling by the Repsol petrol station on the Sóller bypass at 9.10am, and get off at the reservoir.

THE WALK

From Plaça de sa Constitució in Sóller head northeast along Carrer de sa Lluna, which becomes Carrer de l'Alquería del Comte. Continue straight onto Carrer d'Ozones. After 15 minutes, cross a bridge onto the true right bank of the Torrent des Barranc – the stream that you'll be following to its source. At **Biniaraix**, an attractive little village that merits a brief stop, go up a flight of steps beside a telephone box and turn right up a cobbled street to emerge in Plaça de la Concepció, about 25 minutes from Sóller. Beyond it is a wash house and – mercifully upstream – a drinking-water fountain.

Take the track to the right, signposted 'A l'Ofre'. From here on, navigation is made simpler by fresh GR signs at strategic points, marking a completed section of the Ruta de Pedra en Sec long-distance trail (see the Sóller to Deià walk, p273). After five minutes, cross the stream bed and begin the long haul up well-maintained cobblestone steps.

The lower reaches of the stream will probably be dry, its waters siphoned off farther upstream. Higher up, you walk beside waterfalls and enticing pools and over stepping stones. Throughout the valley, even in its steepest, most inhospitable sections, there are tight terraces of olive trees above neat dry-stone walls, superbly constructed and maintained.

Pass beneath the russet Coves d'en Mena, a huge scar on the precipitous cliff face that's clearly visible from Sóller, now in sight way below, together with the lighthouse and upper buildings of Port de Sóller.

As you pass through a green gate, ignore for once the sign saying 'l'Ofre, Propiedad Privada'. The area proclaims itself a private property at every turning, but you're grudgingly allowed through. Pay heed, however, to the bull sign, although it's debatable whether the bull – if he exists – is there primarily to serve the cows or the farmer's interests in keeping walkers out.

The track dwindles to a narrow pathway, easily followed and still progressing southward. From it, the way to the splendid **Mirador d'en Quesada** (see Side Trip, p277) branches off.

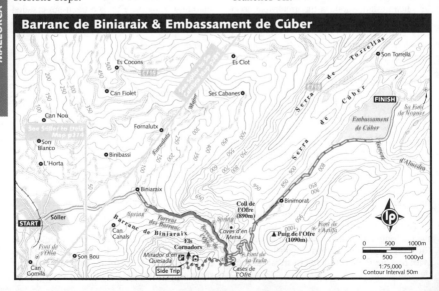

Barranc de Biniaraix & Embassament de Cúber

To continue to l'Embassament de Cúber, go through a green gate to bypass the farm with its sign emphasising 'no entry'.

The path soon joins a wide forest track. Around 20 minutes beyond the Mirador d'en Quesada turn-off, avoid a bend or two in the track by turning left (northeast) up a rocky path that debouches at the **Coll de l'Ofre** (890m) some 15 minutes later.

From the pass, 2½ to 2¾ hours' walking from Sóller, there are fine views eastwards to the cone of Puig de l'Ofre (1090m), the reservoir glinting below and, beyond it, Puig Mayor – at 1443m, the highest point on the island and crowned by telecommunication aerials.

Shortly after the col, take another short cut on the left to rejoin the track at the lone building of Binimestir. Leave the less than welcoming l'Ofre land by the lower of two gates after about three hours' walking.

When you reach the reservoir minutes later, follow its east bank over the dam head until you hit the main road, which today's travellers use, with much less effort but correspondingly less satisfaction, to get from Sóller to the Monestir de Lluc.

If you've time on your hands before the bus is due, drop down the road for less than five minutes to Sa Font de Noguer, a shaded picnic area with a delightfully cool spring. The bus will happily stop to pick you up here if you signal.

Side Trip: Mirador d'en Quesada
1–1¼ hours, 3km
From the sign 'Mirador d'en Quesada', about two hours out of Sóller, head right just below a concrete cistern. As you climb, there's only one point where you might go astray; at a sharp bend where the track turns west, go with the turn and disregard the smaller path heading away from it. At a col about 35 minutes from the turnoff, take a signed path up to the right (northeast). After passing a stone *refugio* (mountain hut or refuge), this leads you to the *mirador*.

Once you've savoured the magnificent, expansive views of the entire Sóller basin and the coast beyond, retrace your steps back to the cistern.

Valldemossa Loop

Duration	5¼–5¾ hours
Distance	15km
Difficulty	moderate
Start/Finish	Valldemossa
Nearest Towns	Sóller (p269), Port de Sóller (p270)
Transport	bus

Summary A steepish ascent leads to the plateau of Es Pouet, the Mirador de ses Puntes, the splendid Camino del Archiduque, a detour to the summit of Es Teix and home via the Vall de Cairats

This is a pick-and-mix day; if you don't want to do the whole walk there are two points where you can take a significant short cut. You can also omit the ascent to the summit of Es Teix. Do any of these and the difficulty of the walk becomes easy– moderate; you'll still enjoy some splendid coastal views from the main section of the Camino del Archiduque.

Both landowner and villager have made their contribution to the landscape. Walkers have Archduke Ludwig Salvator of Habsburg, (see the boxed text 'El Archiduque', p278), to thank for laying out the *camino* (way), a dramatic trail which follows the clifftops.

HISTORY
In the late 19th century, Archiduque Luis Salvador built a series of paths through his estate of Miramar. In the spirit of high Romanticism, these private bridleways allowed him to ride his lands – and to impress his constant stream of visitors with spectacular coastal views and seascapes. The finest of these are from what is known today as the Camino del Archiduque.

PLANNING
Maps
Discovery Walking Guides' 1:40,000 *Mallorca North & Mountains Tour & Trail Map* and the Freytag & Berndt 1:50,000 *Mallorca Tramuntana* map cover the route (don't attempt the path traced on the latter linking Coll de s'Estret de Son Gallard and Deià; it's no longer walkable).

MALLORCA

El Archiduque

Archduke Ludwig Salvator (Luis Salvator in Spanish) of Habsburg, Lorraine and Bourbon was much more than just another romantic, northern European aristocrat doing the Grand Tour. Captivated by the Islas Baleares, and Mallorca in particular, he bought the estate of Miramar in 1872 and made it his home for more than 40 years – notwithstanding spells at his castle outside Prague and other homes at Ramleh in Egypt and Zinis, near Trieste, plus visits to the imperial court in Vienna and long Mediterranean cruises in his prized yachts, *Nixe 1* and *Nixe 2*.

Polymath and ecologically sensitive before the term had even been invented, he restored decaying farmhouses and dwellings, created a magnificent garden of indigenous plants and shrubs at Miramar, bought up trees that farmers were about to fell and entertained a constant procession of visitors – while still finding time to write more than 70 books and scientific treatises, of which the most famous is *Les Balears Descrites per la Paraula i el Gravat* (The Balearics in Words and Images).

What to Bring

The broken rocks and stones used to repair and improve the *camino* are, paradoxically, potential ankle-twisters. While most of the walk is fine if you're wearing runners, this major stretch makes boots advisable.

GETTING TO/FROM THE WALK

Bus No 14 runs between Valldemossa and Port de Sóller, passing by Sóller's Plaça de América (three daily, one daily on Sunday).

THE WALK (see map p279)

From the bus stop in Valldemossa, walk towards Palma and take Carrer de la Venerable Sor Aina, the first road on your left. Turn right along Carrer de Joan Miró, the first intersection. Go straight ahead up a flight of steps beside a school then zigzag left-left-right at the rear of the school along Carrers Alzines, des Ametlers and de les Oliveres. At the end of this cul-de-sac, take the track heading northwest beside a sign which says, alarmingly, in English, 'Danger: Big Game'. The more trustworthy Spanish version merely warns that you're entering a hunting zone!

Take the path beside the sign. A couple of minutes later, where the broad track is blocked by a fence, turn left (north) up a rocky path, which was once an old charcoal-burners' track. Pass through gateposts, then over a stile, to maintain a generally north-northwest bearing, ignoring any side trails, through, for the most part, shady oaks.

A little under 45 minutes from Valldemossa, go through a gap in a dry-stone wall to emerge onto a small plateau. Disregarding tracks to right and left, continue straight ahead through spindly oak trees, passing beside a *sitja* (charcoal-burners' circle) to reach the well of Es Pouet (don't drink from its murky depths).

For a short cut, you can follow the dominant track to the right (bear initially north, then east) to bypass the *mirador*, save yourself around an hour of walking and rejoin the route at Coll de s'Estret de Son Gallard. Mind you, if you do, you'll miss out on a spectacular panorama…

For the Mirador de ses Puntes, take the minor path which heads initially straight ahead (north) then very soon turns west. Climbing at first, then gently descending through pine, oak and scrub, you skim the southwestern flanks of Povet and Veiá to arrive, something over the hour from Valldemossa, at the **Mirador de ses Puntes**. From here, there are spectacular views of the village of Puigpunyent, squat on top of the first hill to the west, the Tramuntana chain trailing away westwards and, to the south, the suburbs of Palma.

Here, with an initial hairpin east, the **Camino del Archiduque** begins. After 15 minutes you pass alongside the knoll of Veiá (867m), clearly identifiable by its trig marker. Ten minutes later the trail arrives at a crumbling stone shelter from where you can see the next hour or so of the route snaking before you. As you leave the ruins, the path heads briefly towards the sea before resuming its easterly progression.

Valldemossa Loop

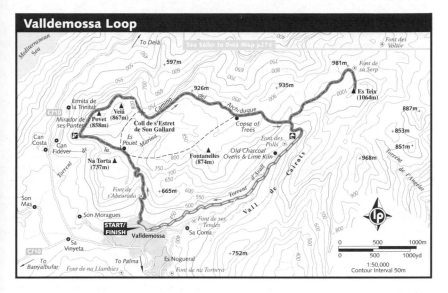

After around 1¾ hours of hiking you arrive at the **Coll de s'Estret de Son Gallard** with a welcome stone bench. To the right (south) is that short-cut path coming up from Es Pouet.

A 15-minute ascent from the col leads to the most spectacular portion of the causeway, with sheer drops to the seaward side. After 2½ hours of walking in total, you skirt a copse of trees, isolated on the bleak plateau. This is about the only shaded picnic stop until you reach the Vall de Cairats towards the end of the walk. To its right, a narrow path heads back to Es Pouet and offers a slightly shorter return to Valldemossa.

Thirty minutes later, take the turn-off left (east) at a large cairn to bag the peak of **Es Teix** (1064m), marked by two iron crosses (allow 45 minutes to one hour for the round trip). Es Teix means the yew tree in Catalan – though most of the yews were felled long ago. Bountiful, Es Teix furnished local villages with water and ice for the hotter months. It was also a provider of firewood for the hearth, of charcoal – and of stones that, once crushed, fed the kilns to produce lime.

For views toward Sóller and Ses Cornadors, be sure to climb Es Teix's left-hand

(easterly) summit, not the one with multiple crosses – otherwise you'll see nothing new. Some 10 minutes from the cairn is a small plain with a spring, the Font de sa Serp, where for most of the year you can replenish your water bottles.

Return to the junction with the main path at the head of the Vall de Cairats. Some 4¼ hours into the day, you reach the end of the archduke's path as the track widens and steepens to plunge down past a *casa de sa neu* (ice pit).

Just below is a shelter, originally the bunkhouse for the *nevaters*, or snow collectors. With benches and a hearth, it's pleasantly cool and dark on a hot day. But resist the temptation to lunch here if you've held out this far because in under 10 minutes you reach the **Font des Polls** (Spring of the Poplar Trees) with water and shaded benches (don't confuse it with the stagnant cistern a couple of minutes below the *refugio*). As you continue to descend, you pass several charcoal-burning circles with their characteristic green moss or sward and a lime kiln, where rock from Es Teix used to be crushed and slow fired to make lime for whitewashing houses.

MALLORCA

About 4¾ hours into the walk, cross a large stile beside a locked gate to leave the estate of the eponymous archduke. Continue along the track and, at a fork, bear right over a cattle grid. Once you hit a sealed road about 15 minutes from the stile, bear right, then first left to drop to the main road and turn right for Plaça Campdevànol and the bus stop – an anticlimactic final 15 minutes of blacktop at the end of an exhilarating day.

Sóller to Sa Calobra

Duration	6¼–7¼ hours
Distance	18km
Difficulty	moderate
Start	Sóller
Finish	Sa Calobra
Nearest Towns	Sóller (p269),
	Port de Sóller (p270)
Transport	bus, boat

Summary A steepish, optional climb leads to the Mirador de ses Barques, from where the route descends to the Vall de Bàlitx and rises to the Coll de Biniamar to follow the cliffside corniche to Cala Tuent and pass over the col to Sa Calobra

A warm-up stroll through the Sóller valley is followed by a fairly hard slog up to the Mirador de ses Barques (which you can omit – as many walkers do – by taking the morning bus to this point). Woods give way to cultivation as you descend to the pleasantly fertile Vall de Bàlitx. Just after the Coll de Biniamar, a detour to the abandoned farm of Sa Costera (which you could omit, and save 45 minutes, if pushed for time) makes for a pleasant lunch stop. The great views of the bay of Racó de sa Taleca continue as you walk the cliff path.

At Cala Tuent, you can take time out for a swim, and also, in summer, catch a boat back to Port de Sóller. If you're continuing to Sa Calobra – as you must between October and May – allow yourself plenty of leeway to catch the last boat back to Port de Sóller. The short sea trip, with spectacular views of the cliffs you recently walked, isn't the least of the day's pleasures.

If you begin at the *mirador*, deduct around 45 minutes from the total walking time. If you finish at Cala Tuent, knock off about an hour.

PLANNING
Maps
Discovery Walking Guides' 1:40,000 *Mallorca North & Mountains Tour & Trail Map* and the Freytag & Berndt 1:50,000 *Mallorca Tramuntana* map cover the route.

GETTING TO/FROM THE WALK
To begin the walk at the Mirador de ses Barques, take the morning bus for Pollença, which leaves Port de Sóller at 9am, calling by the Repsol petrol station on the Sóller bypass at 9.10am.

You need to catch the last boat back from Sa Calobra to Port de Sóller (€3, 45 minutes). This leaves at 3pm from November to January, 4pm from February to mid-May and 5pm from mid-May to the end of October; miss it and you're in trouble. The service is run by **Tramontana Cruceros** (☎ 971 63 31 09; �W *www.tramontanacruceros.com*). From Monday to Friday between June and September, the boat also puts in at Cala Tuent at around 5.10pm.

Thrush Netting

Mallorca is rich in bird life, but it could be a whole lot richer. In spite of the efforts of local environmental groups such as Grup Balear d'Ornitologia i Defensa de la Naturalesa, many islanders still think that if it's got wings, it's up there to be brought down and eaten.

One particularly cruel practice is thrush netting. In October and November flocks of *tords* (thrushes) migrating from Europe to warmer African climes briefly drop in on Mallorca to feed and fortify themselves for the next leg.

Special nets, called *filats*, are slung between the olive trees. In them, the thrushes are entrapped and struggle to exhaustion. 'It's better than being slowly poisoned by insecticides', aficionados will tell you, but that really doesn't wash if your other option as a thrush is to be up there flying, wild and free.

THE WALK

Leave Plaça de sa Constitució in Sóller by Carrer de Sa Lluna. Take the second left onto Carrer de la Victoria 11 Maig and bear right beside a small bridge to follow the sign for Fornalutx. After about 10 minutes, turn right just before the high wall of the village football stadium. Take the left tine at a three-way fork onto Carrer ses Moncades to meet a sign directing you towards Tuent and Sa Calobra. The trail, zigzagging quite steeply, crosses the sealed C710 road and continues northwards to the **Mirador de ses Barques**, reached around 45 minutes after leaving Sóller.

Leave the *mirador* by the steps on the upper, northeast side of the car park at a sign for Bàlitx, Sa Costera and Tuent. The path passes over a hillock to join a track, which you take to the left. Soon after, this merges with a wide cart track that runs beside an extensive olive plantation. About 25 minutes from the *mirador*, at the entrance to the farm of Bàlitx de Dalt, veer right through a gateway to enter the richly cultivated **Vall de Bàlitx**. Savour the twisted, gnarled olive trees – some of them reputed to be over 1000 years old. Ahead, on the valley's wooded northern flank, you can make out the winding path that will lead you up to the Coll de Biniamar.

About 300m into the valley, leave the main track at a hairpin bend to go straight ahead and down some cobbled steps. Just off route is the Font de Bàlitx, a reliable source of water except towards the end of summer in particularly dry years. Rejoin the wide cart track just before the forlorn, abandoned Bàlitx d'es Mig. Continue to a sign 'Agroturismo, Bàlitx d'Avall'. Don't follow it; turn left to take the more direct pedestrian route to the farm, down several flights of stone steps. This finely engineered way descends to **Bàlitx d'Avall** (also known as Bàlitx d' Abaix) to complete approximately 1¼ hours of walking from the mirador. It's well worth pausing at this substantial farm to down a glass of fresh orange juice, squeezed from the fruit of the surrounding orchards.

The track crosses the Torrent d'es Llorés stream bed to begin climbing in earnest. Blue trail markers stay with you as you toil until,

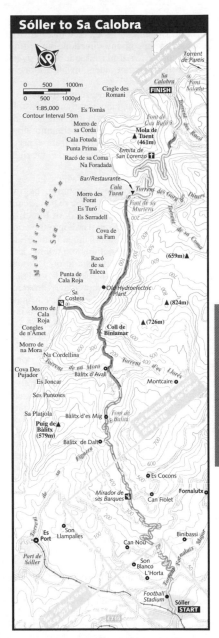

Sóller to Sa Calobra

35 to 40 minutes from the farm, you reach the Coll de Biniamar. Thick tree foliage at first obscures views in any direction, but within five minutes a red-blazed side trail, overgrown in places, meanders off left to lonely **Sa Costera**.

This former farm overlooks the bay of Racó de sa Taleca, tantalisingly inaccessible some hundreds of metres below. The grounds themselves make an excellent picnic stop, with year-round water available from a spring in a cave on the terrace behind and to the right of the house.

Return to the main trail, which narrows soon after the wooded vegetation begins to dwindle and becomes an exposed but quite safe walk along the flank of the cliff. Though it appears to run parallel to the contour lines, there's a surprising amount of up and down work, yet nothing too taxing, and the views are positively inspirational. About 35 minutes from the col, pass a side trail that drops to an abandoned shoreline hydroelectric plant. Continue along this fine corniche route through successive stone gates, until it meets a wide track and a lone farm about 1¼ hours beyond the Coll de Biniamar and three hours from the *mirador*. Turn left and, after only 20m on a newly graded track, don't miss the flight of steps leading downwards to the left. After a brief stretch on another new road, drop left again down a path signed 'Tuent es Vergaret', then turn left yet again at a gravel road to take a path, marked by two cairns, down through the wood.

The path ends beside a **bar-restaurant**, perched on a knoll overlooking Cala Tuent, reached after about 3¼ hours from the *mirador*. From here, it's easy to drop down to the beach of sand and pebbles for a swim or a laze. (Here, in summer, you have the option of catching a boat back to Port de Sóller; see Getting to/from the Walk, p280).

To continue to Sa Calobra, take the sealed road which leads via a series of bends to Ermita de San Lorenzo (Sant Llorenç), a 13th-century chapel clearly visible at the breach in the saddle to the northeast. As you follow the winding road up to the pass, resist the temptation to short-cut the hairpins; the distance saved is outweighed by the energy

you'll expend clambering over boulders and forging your way through the scrub. Instead, resign yourself to this stretch of very lightly trafficked road and enjoy the changing perspectives of Cala Tuent below you.

Once at the col, go through a gate just beyond the *ermita* and take an ancient paved track, now sadly overgrown, its steps and stones ill-maintained, yet still discernible. At its end, turn left at the first house you meet, then left again when you hit the sealed road for an easy 15-minute descent to the clamour of Sa Calobra, teeming with day-trippers. Reward yourself with a drink at one of the **café terraces** as you wait for the boat to arrive.

Allow a generous 90 minutes to reach Sa Calobra from Cala Tuent. This gives you enough leeway to catch the late afternoon boat back to Sóller.

Torrent de Pareis

Duration	4–4½ hours
Distance	6km
Difficulty	moderate–demanding
Start	Escorca
Finish	Sa Calobra
Nearest Towns	Sóller (p269), Port de Sóller (p270)
Transport	bus, boat
Summary	A steep descent along a switchback trail leads to the even steeper gorge of the Torrent de Pareis, Sa Calobra and the sea

It's downhill all the way and it's only a little more than 6km. But you'll expend as much energy as you would on a full-day hike when you negotiate the Torrent de Pareis, Mallorca's deepest canyon – mostly by walking but sometimes scrambling and bringing all four limbs into play.

NATURAL HISTORY

The Torrent de Pareis, believe it or not – and it is difficult to credit for much of the year, when it's reduced to a few residual pools – is the island's principal watercourse. Over the millennia rainwater has gouged a narrow

Warning

After a rainstorm, or if a cloudburst is predicted, there's a real risk of flash floods.

Ring the **Grup d'Excursió Mallorqui** (☎ 871 94 79 00) – see also Palma de Mallorca, (p268) – to ask about conditions in the gorge. Even if the descent is practicable, the rocks can be treacherously slippery until they dry.

gorge, in places more than 200m deep, through the soft limestone. The side valley of Sa Fosca, leading to the Torrent des Gorg Blau, is a Mallorcan mecca for cavers.

PLANNING
When to Walk

This is the one walk on Mallorca that's better done in summer. In winter, you may have to wade through pools. In the hotter months, although the first part of the walk down from the plateau is unshaded, the sun only fleetingly penetrates to the depths of the ravine.

What to Bring

Consider packing a pair of runners – lighter than boots and providing a better grip when you're scrambling over boulders or stretched at full length. After rain (see the Warning) you may need to take a length of rope.

Maps

Discovery Walking Guides' 1:40,000 *Mallorca North & Mountains Tour & Trail Map* and the Freytag & Berndt 1:50,000 *Mallorca Tramuntana* map both cover the route but you don't really need them.

GETTING TO/FROM THE WALK

For Escorca, take the morning bus for Pollença, which leaves Port de Sóller at 9am, calling by the Repsol petrol station on the Sóller bypass at 9.10am. Ask the driver to drop you off – Escorca, at the milepost signed 'Km 25', is only a couple of houses and is easily overrun. To return, you need to catch the last boat back from Sa Calobra to Port de Sóller (for details see Getting to/from the Walk for the Sóller to Sa Calobra walk, p280).

THE WALK

Drop down the steep path opposite Restaurante Escorca. You can take lightly the litany of warnings on the adjacent sign; the advice to pack a wet suit seems particularly like overkill. Follow the level path that runs along the boundary of Ses Tanques de Baix, a series of sheepfolds.

After a little more than five minutes, take a sharp left through a metal gate and continue straight to the lip of the gorge, from where a well-defined path, rocky in places, makes a zigzagging descent (look out for its beginning about 10m before a natural hole in the rock face overlooking the valley).

After 25 minutes, you reach a small, round terrace with close-cropped sward. This former charcoal-burners' site is an ideal spot to pause and savour the view, where the only other evidence of humanity is the distant farm of Son Colomí on the opposite flank.

Soon after, the trail improves as you negotiate a series of long switchbacks. A lone fig tree marks around 45 minutes of unremittingly downhill hiking from the lip. Twenty metres beyond it, a seasonal spring drips from the rocks and a narrow trail, briefly much steeper and more of a clamber, begins its descent through rock and long grass to the bed of the Torrent de Lluc. Angle up onto its true left bank to find a path. This, though heavily overgrown with sharp grasses, is less taxing than battling your way over the boulders in the riverbed.

After passing between two giant, perpendicular cliffs and feeling pretty small, return

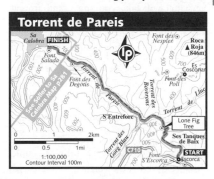

Torrent de Pareis

to the stream bed; 20 minutes beyond the fig tree you'll reach S'Entreforc, the confluence where the smaller Torrent des Gorg Blau (Blue Ravine) joins the main valley from the southwest. Here begins the true Torrent de Pareis ('Pareis' meaning 'pair' in the Mallorcan dialect of Catalan).

On a large rock are four very faded, painted arrows labelled: 'Lluch' (Lluc), pointing back upstream; 'Sa Fosca', left; 'Calobra', straight ahead; and *Millor no anar* (Better not go), pointing at the sheer, unassailable cliff wall on your right. Ho, ho!

Though the Torrent des Gorg Blau is for experienced cavers only, it's well worth briefly detouring to explore the first few hundred metres, known as Sa Fosca (The Darkness), an apt name for this narrow canyon, where the sun rarely penetrates to the base of its near-vertical walls.

Continue along the main gorge by taking a path on the true right bank, signalled by a green arrow, in order to avoid a jumble of boulders. This threads back to the riverbed after little more than five minutes.

Now the fun really begins as you climb down the first of the three areas of giant boulders, easing yourself through a pair of narrow chimneys. Take care as the rock is slippery from the rubbing of so many boots and bums – and particularly treacherous after rain. Then comes a brief easy stretch where you can stride out along the unencumbered stream bed before the valley narrows drastically.

When you're about 1¼ hours from the confluence, look for a path on the true left bank that will take you above and around another boulder-strewn defile. Work your way around the right face of a huge monolith then left of another giant (aided by a rope anchored around the rock). Your reward is the **Font des Degotis**, a spring where water drips from the fronds on the rock wall. Here you can quench your thirst and even take a natural shower.

Two hours from the confluence you must again take evasive action, this time up the true right bank to bypass a pair of monoliths and what, in summer, may still be a couple of late-season pools.

Soon after, the gorge at last opens out. A final flat stretch takes you to the small beach of Sa Calobra's eastern cove where, if you can find a spare square metre, you can relax on the shingle and cool off in the sea. A pedestrian tunnel leads to the thronged port and the boat to Port de Sóller.

Other Walks

Some good walks radiate out from the hamlet of Lluc (also spelt Lluch), east of Sóller and at the eastern limit of the most exciting stretch of the Tramuntana. The village has at least three places to eat and you can stay in the austere 18th-century monastery, **Santuari de Lluc** (☎ *971 87 15 25, fax 971 51 70 96; singles/doubles/triples with bathroom €24/29/32.50*).

Discovery Walking Guides' 1:40,000 *Mallorca North & Mountains Tour & Trail Map* covers the first two walks. The Freytag & Berndt 1:50,000 *Mallorca Tramuntana* map includes all three.

Lluc to Embassament de Cúber

This 14km, 4¼- to 4¾-hour walk interlinks with the route between Sóller and the Embassament de Cúber described earlier in the chapter. It continues the old pilgrim route and will, in the course of time, be a fitting conclusion to the proposed long-distance trail along the Tramuntana. Make an early-ish start so that you can pick up the return bus to Lluc that passes by the dam head at about 3.30pm.

Lluc to Torre de Lluc

You'll have to plan ahead for this one since access is only permitted on Sundays (see the boxed text, 'Mallorca's Blocked Passages', p269). The route (19km, 4½ to five hours one way) leads from the monastery to a magnificent coastal viewpoint beside an old watchtower. About 1¾ hours of walking bring you to the cave houses of Coscona while a little over 15 minutes beyond are the ruins of an old customs house, unattractive in themselves but offering great views (you can always make this more easily accessible spot your goal for the day).

Lluc to Pollença

This route takes you from the Monestir de Lluc to the attractive inland town of Pollença, following the old *camino*, now little travelled and superseded by the modern highway. It's an undemanding 20km walk that will take you between 4½ and five hours - and you don't have to be up with the dawn to arrive in time to catch the 4.20pm bus back from Pollença to Lluc.

Andalucía

Andalucía – the south of Spain, a stone's throw from Africa – is famous for many things including its vibrant, fiesta-loving people, its great Islamic architecture, its passionate flamenco music, song and dance, and its pretty, white villages. Less known to the outside world are Andalucía's natural attractions – large tracts of beautiful, rugged mountain country, gorgeous green river valleys, abundant wildlife and long stretches of dramatic coast that are a far cry from the packaged Costa del Sol. Half of Andalucía is hills or mountains, including mainland Spain's highest peak, Mulhacén (3479m).

Northerners might imagine Andalucía is too hot for much walking; in fact, for about half the year the climate is ideal. But trail marking here is still relatively sparse, so there is ample opportunity to use your navigational skills. Walking for pleasure took off much later in Andalucía than in northern Spain, and you'll rarely encounter anything like a crowd on any walk. Remember the walk times we give do not include stops, so allow extra time to look at maps, chew your *bocadillo* (long sandwich) and gaze at all those gorgeous Andalucian panoramas!

HISTORY

In AD 711 the Muslim general Tariq ibn Ziyad landed at Gibraltar with 10,000 men. Somewhere on the Río Guadalete in western Andalucía, his forces decimated the Visigoth army, and within a few years the Muslims had overrun most of the Iberian Peninsula.

The Andalucian cities Córdoba (756–1031), Seville (1040–1248), then Granada (1248–1492) took turns as the leading city of Muslim Spain or, as it was called, Al-Andalus (from which Andalucía is derived). At its peak in the 10th century Córdoba was the biggest, most cultured city in Western Europe. Andalucía's Islamic heritage is one of its most fascinating aspects. This is not only a matter of great buildings, such as Granada's Alhambra and Córdoba's Mezquita, but also of gardens, food, music and more. Many

of the villages you walk through preserve their labyrinthine Muslim street layout, and the irrigation and terracing of much of the Andalucian countryside have similar roots.

Andalucía fell to the Christian Reconquista in stages between 1214 and 1492. The Muslims soon faced a variety of repressive measures, which sparked revolts in Andalucía in 1500 and 1568. They were finally expelled from Spain between 1609 and 1614.

ANDALUCÍA

Andalucía

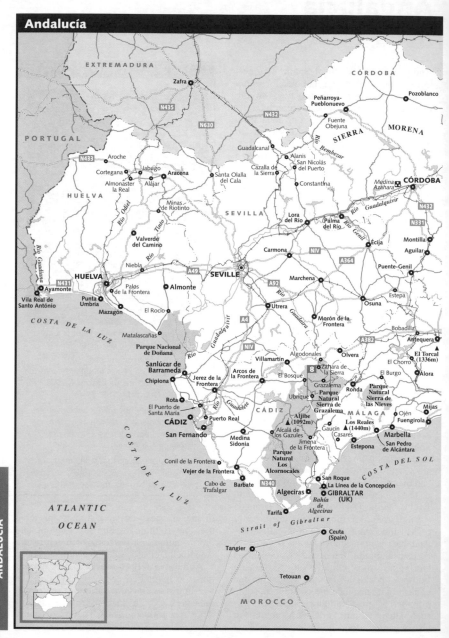

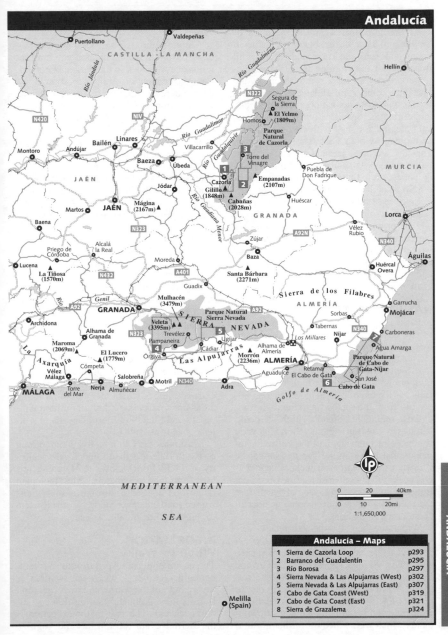

Andalucía

Columbus' 'discovery' of the Americas in 1492 brought great wealth to the ports of Seville and, later, Cádiz, but the Andalucian countryside sank into a profound decline, with noble landowners turning formerly productive food-growing land over to sheep. By the late 19th century rural Andalucía – especially the west – was a hotbed of anarchist unrest, and during the Spanish Civil War Andalucía split along class lines, with savage atrocities committed by both sides. The hungry years after the war were particularly hungry here, and between 1950 and 1970 1.5 million Andalucians left to find work in industrial northern Spain and other European countries.

Since the 1960s a coastal tourism boom, a series of community works schemes, better welfare provisions, massive EU subsidies for agriculture and tourism-driven construction have made a big difference. Andalucía's major cities today are bright, cosmopolitan places and its people increasingly well educated and prosperous.

NATURAL HISTORY

In basic geographic terms, Andalucía consists of two east-west mountain chains separated by the valley of the Río Guadalquivir, plus a coastal plain. Of the two mountain chains, the low Sierra Morena rolls along Andalucía's northern borders, while the higher Cordillera Bética is a mass of rugged ranges that broadens out from the southwest to the east; it includes mainland Spain's highest peak, Mulhacén (3479m), in the Sierra Nevada southeast of Granada, and the collection of ranges that make up the Parque Natural de Cazorla in northeast Andalucía, where several peaks top 2000m. Much of the Cordillera Bética is limestone, the erosion of which over the millennia has produced some wonderful karstic rock formations.

With more than 80 protected areas, covering some 15,000 sq km (well over half of all the environmentally protected land in Spain), Andalucía has huge appeal for nature lovers. Its vast range of plants (around 5000 species, some 150 of them unique) is largely due to the fact that the last Ice Age was relatively temperate at this southerly latitude, allowing plants which were killed off further north to

survive. The mountains harbour much of the variety.

Among animals, the ibex numbers perhaps 12,000 in Andalucía and you may see it on several walks. In the Parque Natural de Cazorla, chances are high of spotting fallow deer, and reasonable for red deer, wild boar and mouflon, a wild sheep.

Andalucía is a magnet for bird-lovers, with 13 resident raptor species and several summer visitors from Africa. The Sierra de Grazalema has a large population of griffon vultures. Andalucía is also a haven for water birds, mainly thanks to extensive wetlands along the Atlantic coast. The beautiful greater flamingo can be seen in large numbers in several places including on the Cabo de Gata Coast walk.

CLIMATE

Andalucía is the most southerly and, overall, warmest part of peninsular Spain. On the coast it's temperate in winter and hot in summer. Inland, temperatures are more extreme and the climate can be cold and inclement from November to February but sizzling in July and August. Daytime temperatures in these hottest months reach 36°C in inland cities, and about 30°C on the coasts. From December to February it regularly gets down to near-freezing at night in Granada.

You must subtract several degrees for the extra altitude at which many of the walking areas are set. Average daily minimum temperatures in the high Sierra Nevada in winter get as low as -9°C.

Most places get 400mm to 500mm of rain a year (a little less than London), the majority of it falls from October to March; there's little from June to September. Most mountain ranges get at least a dusting of snow most winters, and the upper Sierra Nevada is white for eight or nine months a year.

INFORMATION
When to Walk

The best months are April to June, September and October – when the weather is warm, but not too warm, and the vegetation is at its most colourful (spring flowers, autumn leaves). The one major exception is the Sierra Nevada (best in July and August).

Top: The arid Cabo de Gata promontory offers stretches of blissful isolation and Andalucía's finest coastal walking. **Bottom**: The majestic Sierra Nevada provides the backdrop to the Alpujarran villages of Bubión and Capileira.

WAYNE WALTON

DAVID PEEVERS

WAYNE WALTON

Top Left: The Holy Grail – Santiago de Compostela's Catedral de Santiago is the goal of the 30-day Camino Francés. **Top Right**: You're on the right track – walkers on the pilgrim routes follow trail markers depicting the stylised, yellow scallop shell. **Bottom**: Enough to melt a heart of stone? Pilgrim statues greet Santiago de Compostela from the hills above.

Maps

Michelin's 1:400,000 *Southern Spain* map, is good for overall planning. It's widely available in and outside Andalucía.

Published large-scale maps of Andalucía should be regarded as approximations to reality – useful, but never fully to be trusted. They're OK on contours, courses of rivers and other natural features, but when it comes to paths and tracks, they show a lot that don't exist, and ignore many that do exist. See the Planning sections of individual walks for specific recommendations.

Buying Maps Most recommended maps are fairly easily obtained in the walk areas, but it's always worth visiting map and bookshops in cities on the way, such as the Gateways and Access Towns in this chapter.

Books

Lonely Planet's *Andalucía* fills out the picture for those who want to experience the region's cities, culture and nightlife as well as its wilder places. *Walking in Andalucía,* by Guy Hunter-Watts, has detailed descriptions and maps of 32 good day walks. Among Spanish-language walking guides, we recommend the two-volume *Excursiones por el Sur de España,* by Juan Carlos García Gallego. Volume I includes Las Alpujarras and the Sierra Nevada; volume II covers the Parque Natural de Cazorla.

For historical, cultural and social background, the erudite but irreverent *Andalucía,* by Michael Jacobs, is hard to beat. Naturalists will find *A Selection of Wildflowers of Southern Spain,* by Betty Molesworth Allen, and *Where to Watch Birds in Southern & Western Spain,* by Ernest Garcia, Andrew Paterson and Christopher Helm, useful, but will want a field guide with pictures to complement the latter. See Planning (p300) for further book recommendations.

GATEWAYS
Málaga

This central port city is the region's chief international arrival point and has good connections with Madrid and other Andalucian cities. There's a useful regional **tourist office**

(☎ 95 221 34 45; *Pasaje de Chinitas 4; open 9am-7pm Mon-Fri, 10am-2pm Sat & Sun*) off the central Plaza de la Constitución. IGN maps are available at the **CNIG** (☎ 95 221 20 18; *Calle Ramos Carrión 48*). A good central outdoor equipment shop is **Deportes La Trucha** (☎ 95 221 22 03; *Calle Carretería 100*). You can stock up on food supplies at the colourful **Mercado Central** (*Calle Atarazanas; open early-1pm Mon-Sat*).

Places to Stay & Eat The city's HI hostel, **Albergue Juvenil Málaga** (☎ 95 230 85 00; *Plaza Pío XII No 6; under 26 yrs/others €12.90/17.25 mid-June–mid-Sept, €10.90/15.20 rest of year*), is 1.5km west of the centre and a couple of blocks north of Avenida de Andalucía. It has 110 places, most in double rooms.

Two friendly, central *hostales* (budget hotels) are **Pensión Córdoba** (☎ 95 221 44 69; *Calle Bolsa 9; singles/doubles with shared bathroom €14/25*) and **Hostal Derby** (☎ 95 222 13 01; *Calle San Juan de Dios 1; singles/doubles €27/36*). The Derby has spacious rooms. **Hostal Victoria** (☎ 95 222 42 24; *Calle Sancha de Lara 3; singles/doubles €50/60*) has modern rooms in a handy location.

The city centre is peppered with eateries. The barn-like **La Posada** (*Calle Granada 33; mains €8-16*) is great for a meat feast. Friendly **El Vegetariano de la Alcazabilla** (*Calle Pozo del Rey 5; mains around €6-8; open 1.30pm-4pm & 9pm-11pm Mon-Sat*) concocts spectacular vegetarian dishes.

Getting There & Away Many international carriers, including no-frills airlines, fly direct to Málaga: see Air (pp370–2). Flying daily nonstop to/from Madrid, Barcelona, Bilbao and Valencia is **Iberia** (ⓦ *www.iberia.com*). **Spanair** (ⓦ *www.spanair.com*) flies from Barcelona and Madrid, and **Air Europa** (ⓦ *www.air-europa.com*) from Madrid: they're well worth checking for special deals.

The **bus station** (☎ 95 235 00 61; *Paseo de los Tilos*) is 1km west of the centre. Buses come from Madrid (€16.30, six hours, at least seven daily), Granada (€7.50, 1½ hours, 16 or more daily), and a few from Barcelona (€52, 15 hours) via Valencia.

ANDALUCÍA

The **train station** (*Explanada de la Estación*), around the corner from the bus station, has services to/from Madrid (€30 to €52, four to 7¾ hours, at least seven daily), and to/from Valencia and Barcelona (€65 to €68, 13 to 14 hours, three daily). For Granada there are no direct trains, but you can get there in 2¼ hours for €11.50 with a transfer at Bobadilla.

Granada

Home to the world-famous Alhambra palace, Granada is, for many, Andalucía's most magical city. The **Oficina Provincial de Turismo** (☎ 958 24 71 28; *Plaza de Mariana Pineda 10; open 9.30am-7pm Mon-Fri, 10am-2pm Sat*) is very helpful. **Cartográfica del Sur** (☎ 958 20 49 01; *Calle Valle Inclán 2*), just off Camino de Ronda, is an excellent map shop. Nearby is mountain equipment supplier **Deportes Sólo Aventura** (☎ 958 12 53 01; *Camino de Ronda 1*). IGN maps are also sold by the **CNIG** (☎ 958 29 04 11; *Avenida Divina Pastora 7 & 9*).

Places to Stay & Eat Just a short walk from the bus station and 2.5km northwest of the centre is **Camping Sierra Nevada** (☎ 958 15 00 62; *Avenida de Madrid 107; camping per person/tent/car €4.25/4.25/5.00*). It has big clean bathrooms and a laundrette.

Albergue Juvenil Granada (☎ 958 27 26 38; *Calle Ramón y Cajal 2; under 26 yrs/ others €12.90/17.25 Mar-Sept, €10.90/ 15.20 Oct-Feb*), the HI hostel, is 1.7km west of the centre, with 89 comfy double and triple rooms, all with bathrooms.

Three friendly, clean and central *hostales* are **Hostal-Residencia Lisboa** (☎ 958 22 14 13; *Plaza del Carmen 27; singles/doubles €17/26, with bathroom €29/38*), **Hostal Sevilla** (☎ 958 27 85 13; *Calle Fábrica Vieja 18; singles/doubles €14/20, with bathroom €17/29.50*) and **Hostal Zurita** (☎ 958 27 50 20; *Plaza de la Trinidad 7; singles/doubles/ triples without bathroom €17/29/41, doubles/ triples with bathroom €36/50*).

The Plaza Nueva area is a fruitful food-hunting ground. The bar **Bodegas Castañeda** (*Calle Almireceros; raciones from €5*) does magnificent tapas and *raciones* (meal-sized servings of tapas): seafood, omelettes, cheese, ham, pâtés – you name it. The labyrinthine old Muslim area, the Albayzín, has some great eateries too: **Samarcanda** (*Calle Caldería Vieja 3; mains around €5.40*) cooks up excellent Lebanese cuisine.

Getting There & Away Daily flight services to/from Madrid and Barcelona are provided by **Iberia** (ⓦ *www.iberia.com*).

The **bus station** (*Carretera de Jaén*), nearly 3km northwest of the centre, has services to/from Madrid (€12.45, five hours, nine daily) and Barcelona (€50, 12 hours, at least one daily) via Valencia. The **train station** (*Avenida de Andaluces*), 1.5km west of the centre, has two daily services to/from Madrid (€26.50 to €32.50, six hours) and one or two to/from Barcelona (€47, 12 hours) via Valencia.

Parque Natural de Cazorla

The Parque Natural de las Sierras de Cazorla, Segura y Las Villas (to give it its full title), in Jaén province in northeast Andalucía, is, at 2143 sq km, the largest protected area in Spain. It's a crinkled, pinnacled region of several complicated sierras (mountain ranges) – not extraordinarily high, but memorably beautiful – divided by high plains and deep river valleys. Much of the park is thickly forested and – a big attraction – wild animals are abundant and visible.

The park stretches 90km from north to south, with most of its ranges aligned roughly north-south. The Guadalquivir, Andalucía's longest river, rises in the south of the park, between the Sierra de Cazorla and Sierra del Pozo, and flows 60km north into the Embalse del Tranco de Beas reservoir, where it turns west towards the Atlantic.

It's in the south of the park, where millions of years of erosion of limestone and dolomitic rocks have created the most marvellous karstic mountainscapes, that we have chosen the three day-walks in this section. They're separate walks, not one circuit, because in this

Cazorla Wildlife

The big five animal species here are the ibex, mouflon, wild boar, red deer and the smaller fallow deer. All are subject to controlled hunting: indeed the fallow deer and the mouflon (a large, reddish-brown, wild sheep) were introduced here in the 1960s specifically for hunting.

The ibex lives mainly on rocky heights but we have also seen it on the Río Borosa and Barranco del Guadalentín valley walks. It numbers a few thousand. The other four big animals prefer forests – as does the fairly common red squirrel.

The likelihood of seeing wildlife improves as you get further away from the beaten track. The chances are also higher early and late in the day – deer are most likely to emerge onto open grassy areas at these times. While walking it's very likely you'll come across areas of upturned earth where wild boar have rooted for food.

Some 140 bird species nest in the park. Rocky crags are the haunt of golden and Bonelli's eagles, griffon and Egyptian vultures and peregrine falcons. Something of an emblem of the park, but one you'd be very lucky to see, is the lammergeier, Europe's largest bird of prey. It disappeared from the park, its only Spanish habitat outside the Pyrenees, in 1986, but an attempt is being made to reintroduce it.

southern area the only bus service and all the places to stay – including the camping grounds, which are the only places you are allowed to camp – are along the Guadalquivir valley. Thus anywhere more than half a day's walk from the Guadalquivir or from the park's fringe towns is out of reach for people without a vehicle. The *ideal* way to explore the park is with a vehicle to reach day walks in some of its more remote areas.

HISTORY

In the 18th century these sparsely populated sierras were turned over to the Spanish navy, which had many of the native oaks and black pines floated downriver to be made into ships at Cádiz or Cartagena. In 1960, 710 sq km in what's now the southern part of the park were declared a *coto nacional de caza* (national hunting reserve). This greatly increased the numbers of larger animals by subjecting hunting to strict controls, reintroducing species that had been hunted to extinction here such as the red deer and wild boar, and introducing new species.

The *parque natural* (nature park) was created in 1986 in response to a surge in tourism that was threatening the area's ecological balance. The park attempts to conserve the environment while promoting compatible economically beneficial activities, such as responsible forestry, agriculture and tourism.

NATURAL HISTORY

The Parque Natural de Cazorla has Andalucía's biggest forests, with pine species predominant. The tall black pine, with its horizontally spreading branches typically clustered near the top, generally likes the higher terrain above 1300m. The other two main pine species, introduced here for timber, are the maritime pine, with its typically rounded top, growing at elevations up to about 1500m, and the Aleppo pine, with a bushy top and separated, often bare branches, predominant at warmer, drier levels up to 1100m.

PLANNING
When to Walk

The walking is best from April to June and in September and October. At these times temperatures are moderate and the number of other visitors (except in Semana Santa – Easter Week) should be well below the summer holiday peak.

Maps

The Editorial Alpina 1:40,000 *Sierra de Cazorla* map is the best for all three walks. You should be able to find it in Cazorla town if you haven't obtained it beforehand.

Information Sources

The park's main visitors centre is the **Centro de Visitantes Torre del Vinagre** (☎ 953 71 30 40), on the A319 16km northeast of Empalme del Valle and 33km northeast of

ANDALUCÍA

Cazorla. The centre's hours vary from season to season, but you can rely on it being open from 11am to 2pm daily, and two or three additional afternoon hours (except perhaps on Monday and Tuesday from September to June). Tourist information offices in Cazorla town can also be useful.

ACCESS TOWN
Cazorla

This attractive and historic old town stands on the western border of the *parque natural*. The **Oficina de Turismo Municipal** (☎ *953 71 01 02; Paseo del Santo Cristo 17; open Apr-Oct*) is 200m north of Plaza de la Constitución where buses stop. Privately run **Quercus** (☎ *953 72 01 15; Calle Juan Domingo 2; open 10am-2pm & 5pm-8pm daily, to 9pm in summer*), just off Plaza de la Constitución, provides some tourist information as well as selling maps, guidebooks and park excursions. You can stock up on supplies at plenty of **bakeries** and **shops** around the centre.

Places to Stay & Eat The a spick-and-span youth hostel **Albergue Juvenil Cazorla** (☎ *953 72 03 29; Plaza Mauricio Martínez 6; under 26 yrs €8.50-12.90, others €11.50-17.25*) is 200m uphill from the central Plaza de la Corredera.

Pensión Taxí (☎ *953 72 05 25; Travesía de San Antón 7; singles/doubles with shared bathroom €18/33*) is a friendly spot just off Plaza de la Constitución.

Hotel Guadalquivir (☎ *953 72 02 68;* [e] *info@hguadalquivir.com; Calle Nueva 6; singles/doubles €31/41.30*), just off the short main street Calle Doctor Muñoz, is a cheerful place with pretty rooms boasting bathroom, TV, air-con and heating – a step up in quality.

Mesón Don Chema (*Calle Escaleras del Mercado 2; mains €7-9*), down a lane off Calle Doctor Muñoz, serves up excellent local fare including venison, pork and the sizzling *huevos a la cazorleña*, a mixed stew of sliced boiled eggs, sausage and vegetables.

La Forchetta (*Calle de las Escuelas 2; pizzas €3.60-5.40*), just down from Plaza de la Constitución, serves tasty pizzas, plus pasta at similar prices.

Getting There & Away Buses run by **Alsina Graells** (☎ *958 18 54 80*) head to Cazorla from Granada (€11.65, 3½ hours, two daily) stopping in Jaén, Baeza and Úbeda. The main stop in Cazorla is Plaza de la Constitución; Quercus has timetable information.

Sierra de Cazorla Loop

Duration	6½ hours
Distance	17km
Difficulty	easy–moderate
Start/Finish	Cazorla (p292)
Transport	bus
Summary	A panoramic loop in the Sierra de Cazorla combining mountain and woodland scenery

This walk takes you right round the hills that rise impressively to the south and east of Cazorla town. Take water for the whole walk.

THE WALK (see map p293)

Leave Cazorla's handsome Plaza de Santa María by Camino de San Isicio, between the 400-year-old Fuente de las Cadenas and the Restaurante La Cueva de Juan Pedro. Five minutes from the plaza veer left up a concreted track. One minute later, at a one-spout fountain, go left up an unpaved track that winds past little farms. Ten minutes from the fountain take the upward, left fork with a red-and-white trail marker post; shortly after fork left again. Cazorla's upper castle, the Castillo de Cinco Esquinas, soon appears up to your left. About ten minutes after the castle appears follow a footpath climbing ahead to the southwest where the main track does a sharp left bend. After a few minutes you rejoin the main track: follow it to the left, uphill, and within 15 minutes you reach the 17th-century **Monasterio de Montesión** in a beautiful fold of the hills. The monastery is currently inhabited by just one monk of a hermitic order.

From the leftward (southeast) bend where the monastery came into view, take a lesser track up to the east. After a few minutes turn right along the second track crossing this. Immediately bend left and wind up through

Sierra de Cazorla Loop

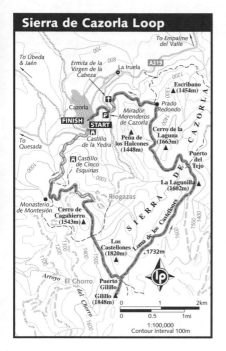

To Empalme del Valle

To Úbeda & Jaén

Ermita de la Virgen de la Cabeza

La Iruela

A319

Escribano ▲(1454m)

Cazorla

Mirador Merenderos de Cazorla

Prado Redondo

FINISH START

Cerro de la Laguna (1663m) ▲

To Quesada

Castillo de la Yedra

Peña de los Halcones (1448m) ▲

Puerto del Tejo

Castillo de Cinco Esquinas

La Lagunilla ▲(1602m)

Riogazas

Monasterio de Montesión

Cerro de Cagahierro (1543m) ▲

Los Castellones (1820m) ▲

+1732m

Arroyo

El Chorro Puerto Gilillo

Gilillo ▲(1848m)

0   1   2km
0   0.5   1mi
1:100,000
Contour Interval 100m

Coto

You see this word scrawled over every part of the Spanish countryside. On rocks, signs, walls, on the ground, by roadsides, in forests. With a variety of companion words – Coto Privado, Coto Nacional, Coto Deportivo de Caza, Coto Municipal San Isidro, Coto X4204, Coto Torrox – but most mysteriously on its own, over and over again: COTO, COTO, COTO.

Is it a football team? A political movement? The latest teen music sensation? No. Like so many things in the Spanish countryside, it's to do with *la caza* (hunting). One – perhaps the original – meaning of *coto* is cairn or boundary marker, but it has come to mean an area on which hunting rights are restricted to a certain person or group – be they private individuals *(coto privado)*, a municipality *(coto municipal)*, or even the nation *(coto nacional or reserva nacional de caza)*. *Cotos privados* are often also signalled by small, rectangular signs divided diagonally into a black triangle and a white triangle. Publicly owned hunting rights are normally shared out, by methods including lottery, among individuals who apply for them for a season. So that there will still be animals and birds to be hunted the following year, there are complicated rules and regulations, even on *cotos privados*, about which animals can be shot, where and when.

As for plain old *coto* on its own, the only thing you can be sure of is that – even if you were inclined to – *you* can't shoot nothin' in there.

pines to emerge on a broad vehicle track after 15 minutes. Go left along this for nearly 10 minutes, then take a path turning sharp right (almost doubling back on yourself) at a map showing park walking routes. After about 15 minutes, turn left (south) onto a lesser path at a small cairn. This soon becomes an excellent, clear path, climbing gradually through the pine woods. After about 25 minutes you emerge from tree cover and start to enjoy ever better views of the crags above and the sea of olive trees rolling over the plains below (Jaén province produces 10% of the world's olive oil). A further 20 minutes upward brings you to the 1750m **Puerto Gilillo** pass, where fine eastward views open out. There's a small stone shelter just below the pass.

To cap **Gilillo** (1848m), the highest peak in this area of the park (just over 1000m higher than Cazorla), head 15 minutes south up from the pass. Back at the pass, take the northward path from the left-hand (west) side of the stone hut. This wends along the **Loma de los**

Castellones ridge, with alternating eastern and western panoramas. Griffon vultures like to cruise the air currents along here. The path is mostly clear but after 15 minutes, going down the far (north) side of the hump marked 1732m on the Editorial Alpina map, you need to fork left at a faint green arrow on a rock; you're soon continuing in the same direction as before. Ignore a right turn by three cairns around 15 minutes later, and after another 20 minutes cross a grassy basin to join a track coming from the right. A further 10 minutes along you reach the **Puerto del Tejo** pass (1556m), with a three-way path junction.

ANDALUCÍA

Go left and follow the path as it winds around Cerro de la Laguna and descends northward. Around an hour from Puerto del Tejo you reach the *cortijo* (farm) **Prado Redondo**, an enchanting spot. From the western corner of the Prado Redondo building head 60m west-southwest to a red-and-white trail marker among trees (be careful: this is not the only trail marker post here). Turn right at the marker post. The path bends left (southwest) and descends into a gully, around seven minutes from Prado Redondo: follow it down the gully right. Soon after it curves westward out of the gully to pass above the Knights Templar castle in La Iruela village. **Ermita de la Virgen de la Cabeza** chapel, with views over Cazorla town below, is reached around 30 minutes from Prado Redondo. Head down from the chapel to emerge on the paved La Iruela–El Chorro road opposite the Mirador Merenderos de Cazorla. A path down to the right of the *mirador* (lookout) heads down into Cazorla and you'll reach the town centre in 20 minutes.

Barranco del Guadalentín

Duration	5 hours
Distance	16km
Difficulty	easy–moderate
Start/Finish	Empalme del Valle–Campos de Hernán Perea road, Km 25.5
Nearest Town	Cazorla (p292)
Transport	private

Summary Beautiful valley and gorge scenery, and abundant wildlife, in the little-visited eastern part of the Parque Natural de Cazorla

The highlight of this beautiful walk is the two-hour stretch following the valley, which becomes a gorge, of the Río Guadalentín. Wild animals such as ibex, fallow and red deer, wild boar and mouflon are plentiful in this remote area and you'll be very unlucky if you don't see some.

Take enough water for the whole walk. You walk beside several streams and rivers but there's no certainty they'll be fit to drink.

Warning

The 35-minute stretch of the walk down the gorge from the Arroyo de San Pedro could be risky if there has been a lot of rain. Turn back if you think the river looks dangerously high or strong.

NEAREST TOWNS & FACILITIES
See Cazorla (p292).

Complejo Puente de las Herrerías
Worth considering if you're motorised is the Complejo Puente de las Herrerías (☎ 953 72 70 90; camping per person/tent/car €4/3.60/ 3.60, doubles with bathroom €45, 2-person cabins €42.80), in the Guadalquivir valley 24km from Cazorla and about 15km from the start of the walk. This camping ground has room for 1000 people, and there are also an 11-room hotel, self-catering cabins and a restaurant.

GETTING TO/FROM THE WALK
The start/finish is just over one hour's drive from Cazorla: follow the A319 to Empalme del Valle (17km), then continue east where the A319 turns north. You cross the Río Guadalquivir after 3.5km, then climb through forest for 7km, the road surface changing from smooth to rough 4.5km beyond the river. The walk starts where the track to the Cortijo del Vado de las Carretas forks down to the right, a few hundred metres after the Km 25 marker.

THE WALK (see map p295)
Start by following the road in the Campos de Hernán Perea direction (initially northeast) for just under 5km. There's hardly any traffic and the scenery en route is dramatic. After 2km you pass the strange rock formations of the **Estrecho de los Perales** on the left.

About one hour from the start, turn sharp right down a track which has a chain to bar vehicles round its first bend. This descends in 25 minutes to the Río Guadalentín at the bottom of its steep, wooded valley, then turns southwest to follow the bubbling river, with

Barranco del Guadalentín

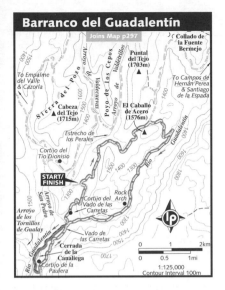

Joins Map p297

To Empalme del Valle & Cazorla

Sierra del Pozo

Cabeza del Tejo (1715m)

Puntal del Tejo (1703m)

Collado de la Fuente Bermejo

El Caballo de Acero (1576m)

To Campos de Hernán Perea & Santiago de la Espada

Estrecho de los Perales

Cortijo del Tío Dionisio

START/ FINISH

Río Guadalentín

Rock Arch

Cortijo del Vado de las Carretas

Arroyo de los Tornillos de Gualay

Arroyo de San Pedro

Vado de las Carretas

Cerrada de la Canaliega

Cortijo de la Paulera

0   1   2km
0   0.5   1mi

1:125,000
Contour Interval 100m

pinnacled crags rising high on both sides. To the east is the Sierra de la Cabrilla, the highest range in the park. Look out for deer around a ruined house by the track after 15 minutes. Around 40 minutes later, there's a big natural **rock arch** up to the right (you can get up to it in 15 minutes). A further 20 minutes along, after the track has crossed the river twice, a stone wall runs along the left side of the track. On a left-hand bend, 80m past the wall, take the broader, leftward, downhill fork: the right-hand option had a *'prohibido el paso, perros sueltos'* sign (no entry, loose dogs) when we last passed here. At a track junction ten minutes later turn right, following the perimeter fence of the Cortijo del Vado de las Carretas, away from the Vado de las Carretas, a ford. After just 30m, head 40m left (west) over to a small bridge over the Arroyo de San Pedro. Over the bridge, turn left along a path following the *arroyo* (stream) downstream. The *arroyo* almost immediately joins the Río Guadalentín. The old fishers' path you're following initially involves some pushing through bushes, though its course is clear. As the valley narrows, to assume gorge dimensions after 20 minutes or so, you crisscross the river a few

times and the beautifully constructed path takes to purpose-built ledges and stepping-pillars to progress downriver.

The Arroyo de los Tornillos de Gualay joins the Guadalentín from another gorge on the right, around 35 minutes from the bridge over the Arroyo de San Pedro. You are now in the **Cerrada de la Canaliega**, a beautiful spot where the deep, green river is hemmed in by tall rock walls.

You can return upriver the way you came down, but for a different return route go 40m downstream from the meeting of gorges and cross the river where stone pillars suggest there was once a bridge. From the far end of the ex-bridge, head to your right (south) into a faint gap in the bushes. This is the start of a soon-clear path winding up the hillside. Fork left after a minute or so, and 15 minutes later you reach the top, to be confronted by the perimeter fence of Cortijo de la Paulera. Follow the fence round its southern end and up onto an unpaved vehicle track. Head left (north) along this and in 30 minutes you'll be fording the Guadalentín at the Vado de las Carretas. Across the ford, fork left and follow this track for 35 minutes up the valley, with a dense holm oak forest on its western side, to return to your starting point on the Campos de Hernán Perea road.

Río Borosa

Duration	6–7 hours
Distance	24km
Difficulty	easy–moderate
Start/Finish	Centro de Visitantes Torre del Vinagre
Nearest Town	Cazorla (p292)
Transport	bus
Summary	Exquisite valley and mountain scenery as you ascend a tributary of the Guadalquivir, via a narrow gorge and two tunnels, to two beautiful mountain lakes

The Cazorla park's best known walk follows the Río Borosa (also called Aguas Negras) upstream through scenery that progresses from the pretty to the majestic.

PLANNING

Try to avoid the times when there will be large numbers of other people on the route: Easter, July, August and fine spring and autumn weekends.

The route is dotted with good trackside springs, the last of these at the Central Eléctrica. Carry a water bottle that you can fill there with enough water to take you to the top of the walk and back (about three hours). A torch (flashlight) is comforting, if not essential, in the tunnels.

NEAREST TOWNS & FACILITIES

See Cazorla (p292).

Around Torre del Vinagre

While Cazorla is an adequate base for this walk there's also a variety of places to stay on and near the A319 within a few kilometres of Torre del Vinagre. All the following can be reached by the Cazorla–Coto Ríos bus service (see Getting to/from the Walk).

Hotel de Montaña La Hortizuela (☎ 953 71 31 50; singles/doubles with bathroom €35.30/47), 2km north from Torre del Vinagre, then 1km up a side road, is a cosy small hotel in a tranquil setting, with a good restaurant offering a €9 menú del día (fixed-price meal). There are boar in the surrounding woods.

A further 1km north on the A319 is **Hostal Mirasierra** (☎ 953 71 30 44; singles/doubles with bathroom €28.90/34), with **Apartamentos El Pinar** (☎ 953 71 30 68; 4–8-person apartments €57-102) adjoining.

Further north by 2km is **Camping Chopera Coto Ríos** (☎ 953 71 30 05; camping per person/tent/car €3.15/3.25/2.25), with a rather cramped but shady site by the side road into Coto Ríos. From October to April it's worth ringing to confirm it's open.

GETTING TO/FROM THE WALK

The start and finish point is the Centro de Visitantes Torre del Vinagre (see Information Sources, p291). Using the Cazorla–Coto Ríos bus service, which stops at Torre del Vinagre, you can do the walk in a day trip from Cazorla.

Carcesa (☎ 953 72 11 42) runs buses from Cazorla's Plaza de la Constitución to Coto Ríos via Torre del Vinagre (€2.40, one hour, two daily Monday to Saturday). You should confirm times with the company or with Quercus in Cazorla.

THE WALK (see map p297)

Opposite the Centro de Visitantes Torre del Vinagre, take a road east off the A319 signed 'Central Eléctrica'. This crosses the Guadalquivir and, 1.5km from the A319, passes a *piscifactoría* (fish farm), with parking areas close by. The road then crosses the Río Borosa. Turn right here and follow the track along the north side of the river.

The first section is along a dirt road which twice crosses the tumbling, trout-rich river as you move up the narrow, lush valley. After 40 minutes, where the road starts climbing to the left, take a path forking right. This leads through a beautiful, 20-minute section where the valley narrows to a gorge, the **Cerrada de Elías**, and the path briefly takes to a wooden walkway to save you from swimming.

You re-emerge on the dirt road and reach the Central Eléctrica, a small hydroelectric transformer station, 40 minutes later.

A path passes between the power station and river to a 'Nacimiento de Aguas Negras, Laguna de Valdeazores' sign directing you upwards. The karstic mountainscape begins to look like a Chinese landscape painting as the river beside you descends a series of high rock steps in **waterfalls**. Unfortunately the flow here is sometimes diminished because some of the waters have been diverted for the power station. Around 40 minutes from the power station, the path turns left to cross below a cliff, then within 10 minutes turns sharp right to enter a **tunnel** inside the cliff. Water for the power station passes through the tunnel too: your narrow path is separated from the watercourse by a fence. The tunnel is dimly lit by a few openings in the rock wall for most of its five-minute length.

Then there's five minutes in the open air before you enter a second tunnel, one minute long. From this you emerge just below the dam holding back the **Laguna de Aguas Negras**, a picturesque little reservoir surrounded

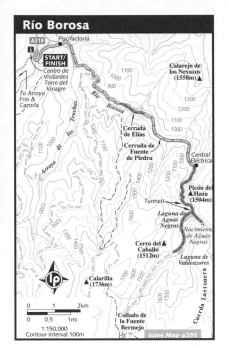

Río Borosa

A319 Piscifactoría
START/FINISH
Centro de Visitantes Torre del Vinagre
To Arroyo Frío & Cazorla
Río Borosa
las Truchas
Arroyo de
Calarejo de los Nevazos (1558m)▲
1100
1000
900
1300
1200
1100
1000
Cerrada de Elias
Cerrada de Fuente de Piedra
Central Eléctrica
Picón del ▲Haza (1504m)
Tunnels
Laguna de Aguas Negras
Nacimiento de Aguas Negras
Cerro del ▲ Caballo (1512m)
Laguna de Valdeazores
▲Calarilla (1736m)
Cuerda Lastonera
Collado de la Fuente Bermejo
Joins Map p295

0 — 1 — 2km
0 — 0.5 — 1mi
1:150,000
Contour Interval 100m

by hills and trees. You have ascended 550m from the Río Guadalquivir to reach this point. A few minutes up the valley to the southeast is the **Nacimiento de Aguas Negras**, where the Borosa wells out from under a rock. A 15-minute walk south from the reservoir brings you to a similar-sized natural lake, the **Laguna de Valdeazores** – altogether about 3½ hours walking from Torre del Vinagre.

Return the way you came, unless you happen to have vehicle support, in which case you could continue 4km southwest to be picked up at the Collado de la Fuente Bermejo.

Sierra Nevada & Las Alpujarras

A casual visitor to the Alhambra in Granada will see, except perhaps from July to October, an imposing line of snow-topped mountains to the southeast. This is the western end of the

Sierra Nevada, which includes mainland Spain's highest peak, Mulhacén (3479m), and many others over 3000m.

On the south side of the Sierra Nevada lies one of the oddest, most picturesque crannies of Andalucía, the 70km-long jumble of valleys called Las Alpujarras, or La Alpujarra. Here, arid hillsides split by deep ravines alternate with oasis-like villages set by rapid streams and surrounded by vegetable gardens and groves of olives, figs, almonds, chestnuts, holm oaks and other useful trees.

The two walks in this section – the five-day Alpujarras Tour and the three-day Sierra Nevada Traverse – can be linked to each other, since one starts where the other ends, in the high Alpujarras village of Trevélez. A snag however is that their optimum seasons differ (see the Planning section of each walk): the second half of June and the first three weeks of September are the least uncomfortable crossover times. The Alpujarras Tour is easily divisible or extendable.

The upper parts of the Sierra Nevada form the 862-sq-km Parque Nacional Sierra Nevada, Spain's biggest national park, created in 1998. Surrounding this on the lower slopes of the range, and including many Alpujarras villages, is the separate, 848-sq-km Parque Natural Sierra Nevada, less stringently protected.

PLANNING
Information Sources
In the Alpujarras village of Pampaneira, the **Punto de Información Parque Nacional de Sierra Nevada** (☎ 958 76 31 27; Plaza de la Libertad; open 10am-2pm & 5pm-7pm Tues-Sat Easter–mid-Oct, 10am-2pm & 4pm-6pm Tues-Sat rest of year, 10am-3pm Sun & Mon year-round) has information on the Alpujarras and Sierra Nevada, including maps for sale, and can inform you on walks and *refugios* (mountain huts or refuges). Pampaneira is the starting point of the Alpujarras Tour and this is also the nearest information office to the start of the Sierra Nevada Traverse.

GETTING THERE & AROUND
Alsina Graells (in Granada ☎ 958 18 54 80, in Lanjarón ☎ 958 77 00 03, in Almería

Alpujarras Villages

Travellers who have been to Morocco may notice a resemblance between villages in the Alpujarras and those in Morocco's Atlas mountains, from where the Alpujarran style was introduced in Muslim times by Berber settlers. The huddled white houses seem to clamber over each other in an effort not to slide down the hillsides. Streets too narrow for vehicles ramble between them, decked with flowery balconies.

Somewhere in most villages stands a solid 16th-century *mudéjar* church – one built by Muslims living under Christian rule in medieval Spain. Most houses have two storeys, with the lower one used for storage and/or animals. The characteristic *terraos* (flat roofs), with their protruding chimneypots, consist of a layer of *launa* (a type of clay) packed onto flat stones, which are themselves laid on wooden beams. Nowadays there's often a layer of plastic between the stones and the *launa* for extra waterproofing.

❀ ❀ ❀ ❀ ❀ ❀ ❀ ❀ ❀ ❀ ❀ ❀ ❀ ❀

☎ 950 23 51 68) runs buses to the Alpujarras. From Granada, buses travel to Lanjarón (€3.25, one hour, three daily), Órgiva, Pampaneira (€4.25, two hours), Bubión (€4.50, 2¼ hours), Capileira (€4.65, 2½ hours) and Pitres (€5.10, 2¾ hours). The last two each day continue to Trevélez (€5.25, 3¼ hours) and Bérchules (€6.25, 3¾ hours). Return buses start from Bérchules at 5am and 5pm, and from Pitres at 3.30pm. Alsina also runs a twice-daily Granada–Ugíjar service (€7.60, four hours) via Lanjarón, Órgiva, Cádiar, Yegen and Válor, a Málaga–Lanjarón service (daily except Sunday), and daily buses from Almería to Bérchules (€6.75) and Ugíjar (€ 4.70).

A taxi between Trevélez and any of the Barranco de Poqueira villages costs around €30.

ACCESS TOWNS
Trevélez

Trevélez, set in a deep gash in the Sierra Nevada's southern flank, is a frequent starting point for ascents of the high Sierra Nevada peaks. It's famous for producing some of Spain's best *jamón serrano* (mountain-cured ham), with hams trucked in from far and wide for curing in the dry mountain air.

Along the main road you're confronted by a welter of ham and souvenir shops, but an exploration of the upper parts reveals a lively, typically Alpujarran village. La General bank just above the main road has an **ATM**. There's a **Coviran** supermarket on the street approaching Hotel La Fragua from the Plaza del Barrio Medio.

For transport information see Getting There & Around (pp297–8).

Places to Stay & Eat A kilometre south of Trevélez along the GR421 road towards Busquístar is **Camping Trevélez** (☎ 958 85 87 35; camping per person/small tent/car €3/ 2.40/2.70). It's set on a terraced and treed hillside and has a good-value restaurant.

Hotel La Fragua (☎ 958 85 86 26; Calle San Antonio 4; singles/doubles with bathroom €19/30) has pleasant rooms near the top of the village and is popular with walking groups – some of whom may rise earlier, and more noisily, than you'd like to!

Mesón La Fragua (mains €5-10), just along the street from Hotel La Fragua, does excellent meals ranging from some good vegetarian dishes to wonderful *solomillos* (pork steaks).

Restaurante González (☎ 958 85 85 31; Plaza Francisco Abellán; singles/doubles/ triples with shared bathroom €15/25/35) is by the main road at the foot of the village, with basic rooms in a separate building down a nearby side-street. The good-value restaurant (mains €5-9) serves trout, ham, *plato alpujarreño* and other local fare.

Capileira

The highest of the three Barranco de Poqueira villages, Capileira offers the easiest access to day walks in the valley and to the high Sierra Nevada. There is a **supermarket** here for supplies. For transport information see Getting There & Around (pp297–8).

Hostal Poqueira (☎/fax 958 76 30 48; Calle Doctor Castilla 6; singles/doubles

Mountain Meal

The *plato alpujarreño*, found on almost every Alpujarras menu, consists of fried potatoes, fried eggs, sausage, ham and maybe a black pudding, usually for around €5.

€18/24), just off the main road, is a friendly place with decent-value rooms.

Hostal Atalaya *(☎ 958 76 30 25; Calle Perchel 3; singles/doubles €15/28, exterior doubles €30)*, 100m down the main road, offers pleasant, modernised rooms with breakfast included.

Cortijo Catifalarga *(☎ 958 34 33 57; singles €40, doubles €55.30-79.35, apartments from €72.10)* is a charmingly renovated farmstead. Its 500m driveway begins 750m up the Sierra Nevada road from the top of the village.

Bar El Tilo *(Plaza Calvario; raciones €3-5)* serves good-value *raciones*.

Alpujarras Tour

Duration	5 days
Distance	90.5km
Difficulty	moderate
Start	Pampaneira (p300)
Finish	Trevélez (p298)
Transport	bus

Summary Linking many of this unique region's picturesque Berber-style villages, this route features a variety of landscapes from lush river valleys to arid, eroded *ramblas*, from orchards and vegetable gardens to mountain oak and pine forests

The old paths connecting the intriguing villages of Las Alpujarras pass through constantly changing scenery. Though tourism here, especially in the western villages, is ever-increasing, the area remains a world apart, with a rare sense of timelessness and mystery. Reminders of the Muslim past are ubiquitous in the form of the Berber-style villages and the terracing and irrigation of the land.

Several villages along our route – including those at the start and finish, all those with overnight stops, and Bérchules on the long fifth day – are hubs of good day-walk routes. With rarely more than two hours between villages, and plenty of food, water and lodgings along the way, there's infinite scope for subdividing and varying the stages of our route. With plenty of time, you could spend more than one night in some places and explore local areas on day walks. Most of our recommended places to stay can furnish local route information.

The walk begins in the Barranco de Poqueira, one of the deepest of many gashes in the southern flank of the Sierra Nevada. The Poqueira villages – Pampaneira, Bubión and Capileira – are three of the most picturesque (albeit most touristed) in Las Alpujarras. If you have time, it's rewarding to spend a day or two exploring the Barranco de Poqueira, which reaches close up beneath the Sierra Nevada's highest peaks. You can obtain information on local walking routes from the information office in Pampaneira (see Information Sources, p297).

For several stretches our route follows the GR142 or GR7 long-distance footpaths. The well-marked GR142 runs 140km from Lanjarón in the western Alpujarras to Fiñana on the north side of the eastern Sierra Nevada; the more erratically marked GR7 runs the length of Spain from Andorra in the north to Tarifa in the south, and is part of the European E4 route from Greece to Andalucía.

HISTORY

In Muslim times Las Alpujarras grew prosperous supplying the textile workshops of Almería, Granada and Málaga with silk thread, spun from the unravelled cocoons of the silk moth. Together with irrigated agriculture, this activity probably supported a population of more than 150,000 before the fall of Granada in 1492.

Christian promises of tolerance for the conquered Muslims soon gave way to forced mass conversions and land expropriations, and in 1500 Muslims rebelled across Andalucía. Afterwards, they were given the choice of exile or conversion to Christianity.

Most converted – to become known as *moriscos* – but the change was barely skin-deep. A new revolt in Las Alpujarras in 1568 led to two years of vicious guerrilla war, and ended only after the rebel leader Aben Humeya was assassinated by his own cousin.

Almost the whole Alpujarras population was then deported to other parts of Spain, and some 270 villages and hamlets were repeopled with settlers from northern Spain. More than 100 others were abandoned. Over the following centuries the silk industry fell by the wayside and swathes of Alpujarras' woodlands were lost to mining and cereal growing.

PLANNING

The best times are April to mid-June and mid-September to early November. The summer months can be stiflingly hot, especially in the low-lying easterly parts of the route, and winter is often cold in the higher villages.

It's best to ring ahead for rooms in your preferred lodgings. The larger villages have banks with ATMs. All Alpujarras villages have fountains where you can drink and fill water bottles. If in any doubt about water quality, just ask a local *'¿Es potable?'* ('Is it safe to drink?').

Maps & Books

The IGN 1:50,000 *Sierra Nevada* map covers the whole route but is hard to obtain locally. Try for it at CNIG offices or specialist map shops such as Cartográfica del Sur in Granada (see p290). Editorial Alpina's 1:40,000 *Sierra Nevada, La Alpujarra* map and Editorial Penibética's 1:50,000 *Sierra Nevada* map are fairly good but cover only about half and three-quarters of our route, respectively. The Alpina and Penibética maps come with booklets, available in English or Spanish, describing various walking routes in Las Alpujarras and the Sierra Nevada.

South From Granada, by Englishman Gerald Brenan, who settled in the Alpujarras village of Yegen, is a fascinating and amusing picture of an isolated corner of Spain in the 1920s.

Another Englishman, Chris Stewart, settled as a sheep farmer near Órgiva in the 1990s: his *Driving over Lemons* tells entertainingly of modern life as a foreigner in Las Alpujarras.

GR142 Senda de la Alpujarra, by Mariano Cruz Fajardo and Ramón Fernández del Real, and *GR7 Senda Granadina,* by Mariano Cruz, Jesús Espinosa and Natalio Carmona, are fine Spanish-language trail guides, full of fascinating local background. The Punto de Información in Pampaneira (see Information Sources, p297) sells the best selection of maps and books locally. You'll also find some in shops in Trevélez.

NEAREST TOWNS

See Trevélez (p298).

Pampaneira

This attractive Barranco de Poqueira village has the area's most useful information centre (see Information Sources, p297), as well as a **supermarket**. For transport information see Getting There & Around (pp297–8).

Two good-value *hostales* face each other at the entrance to the village: **Hostal Pampaneira** (☎ 958 76 30 02; *Avenida Alpujarra 1; singles/doubles €20/30*), with one of the cheapest restaurants in the village (*menú del día €7.25*), and **Hostal Ruta del Mulhacén** (☎ 958 76 30 10; *Avenida Alpujarra 6; singles/ doubles €27/32*).

Casa Diego (*Plaza de la Libertad 15; mains €4.50-7.50*), with a pleasant upstairs terrace, is a good choice from the three restaurants just along the street.

THE WALK (see maps p302 & p307)
Day 1: Pampaneira to Ferreirola
3 hours, 9km

This first stage is short, but its eight villages invite exploration, and there's a lot of up-and-down between them. (It's also a nice lead-in to Days 2 and 3, which are long!)

From Pampaneira's central square (1055m) take the uphill street beside Taberna Narciso. At each division or meeting of streets, take the most upward option (follow Calle Príncipe at the one junction where this distinction is not obvious). Turn right up Calle Castillo on the village edge, at an information board for the blue Barranco de Poqueira walking route. Fork left 40m from the sign-board, then right after another couple of minutes, following marker posts for the blue route. The path winds up among orchards, poplars and chestnuts to **Bubión** (1300m). Work your way up to the main road passing through the village and, 70m down the main road from the Teide restaurant, turn up Calle Ermita (with a GR7 signpost 'Capilerilla 1 hr'). This street becomes a narrow dirt road, climbing through chestnuts and holm oaks. Once clear of the village it makes a sharp left turn followed by a sharp right: a few minutes later, at a fork, continue straight on, *not* sharp left. A few metres further up, your track *does* turn sharp left: just around this bend turn right up a path with an easily missed red-and-white marker post for the GR7 – look for the 'X' (wrong way) sign on another post just past the turning. From here, your path follows red-and-white paint markers up the fairly steep hillside to cross the ridge by an electricity pylon.

The path dips and crosses a broader track running north-south. Continue following red-and-white posts and paint markings. The path crosses the upper **Barranco de la Sangre** (Ravine of Blood; scene of a battle during the 1568–70 rebellion). Follow the GR7 sign for Pitres and Capilerilla at a crossroads among pines. This is where the Alternative Start (see p304) joins the route. Follow a red-and-white GR7 post at a downward right fork a little further along. Another 15 minutes along this path (no longer the GR7), a small 'Capilerilla, Pitres' signpost sends you down into the hamlet of **Capilerilla**. Follow the path downwards and you emerge on the plaza of Pitres, the next village, around 10 minutes later (1¼ hours from Bubión).

Pitres (1245m) is not quite so picturesque nor as touristed as the villages in the Barranco de Poqueira. **El Jardín** (*Calle Escuelas Viejas; mains €6.30-7.20; open 6pm-10pm Tues-Thur, 1pm-10pm Fri-Sun, Easter to late autumn)* is a fine British-run vegetarian restaurant with a lovely shady garden, 200m east of Pitres' plaza. **Camping El Balcón de Pitres** (*☎ 958 76 61 11; camping per person/tent/car €3.85/3.85/2.90, 2-person*

cabins & cottages from €30.05) is just above the GR421 main road on the western side of Pitres and has an inexpensive restaurant. **Refugio Los Albergues** (*☎ 958 34 31 76; dorm beds €7; open 16 Feb–14 Dec)* is a friendly little German-owned walkers' hostel in a beautiful setting 200m (signposted) down a path from the GR421 on the eastern side of Pitres. It has a kitchen and hot showers.

The five hamlets in the valley below Pitres are grouped with Pitres and Capilerilla in the *municipio* (municipality) of La Taha, a name that recalls the Muslim Emirate of Granada, when the Alpujarras was divided into 12 administrative units called *tahas*. Today these tranquil lower hamlets form a tiny world almost of their own, where the air seems thick with accumulated centuries. The tinkle of running water is ubiquitous, and ancient paths wend their way through lush woods and orchards.

Take the street down beside Restaurante La Carretera on the main road below Pitres' plaza. This becomes a partly cobbled old *camino real* (state-maintained path) which will have you down in **Mecina** in 15 minutes. Two places to stay and eat here may prove useful if the lodgings in Ferreirola are full.

Hotel Albergue de Mecina (*☎ 958 76 62 54; Calle La Fuente; singles/doubles with bathroom €47.10/58.85)* is a tasteful, modern 21-room hotel with a restaurant.

L'Atelier (*☎ 958 85 75 01; Ⓦ www.ivu.org/ atelier; Calle Alberca; singles €30, doubles with bathroom €36-42)* is a welcoming French-run vegetarian guesthouse, serving gourmet international meatless meals. Rates include breakfast.

From Mecina head down the road past the church to **Mecinilla**, the second hamlet. At **Bar Aljibe** (which serves good-value *raciones*), continue straight on down, by streets and then an old path. Entering **Fondales**, the lowest Taha village, take the first street down to the right after a single-spout fountain. Bear left to pass a four-spout fountain at the foot of the village and head on down to the Río Trevélez ravine at the bottom of this deep valley. The path reaches an old **Muslim bridge** over the gorge, with a ruined Muslim mill beside it.

Sierra Nevada & Las Alpujarras (West)

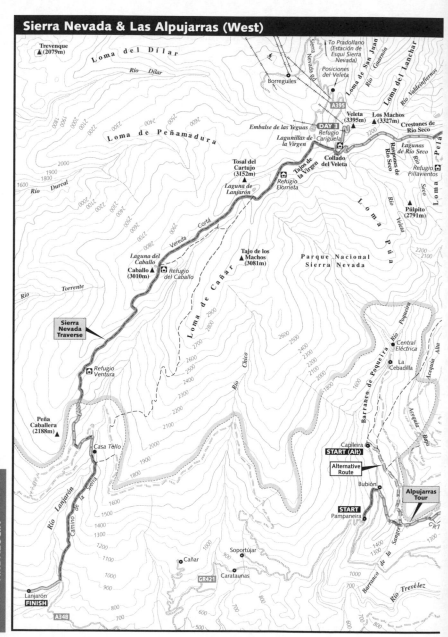

Trevenque
▲ (2079m)

Loma del Dílar

Río Dílar

To Pradollano
(Estación de
Esquí Sierra
Nevada)

Sierra Nevada Rd.

Borreguiles

Posiciones
del Veleta

Loma de San Juan

Río Guarnón

Loma del Lanchar

Río Valdeinfiernos

A395

Loma de Peñamadura

Embalse de las Yeguas

Lagunillas de
la Virgen

DAY 3
Refugio
Carigüela

Veleta
(3395m) ▲

Los Machos
▲ (3327m)

Crestones de
Río Seco

Raspones de
Río Seco

Lagunas
de Río Seco

Refugio
Pillavientos

Loma Pua

Tosal del
Cartujo
(3152m) ▲

Laguna de
Lanjarón

Refugio
Elorrieta

Tajo de
la Virgen

Collado
del Veleta

Río Veleta

Seco

Púlpito
(2791m) ▲

Río Durcal

Vereda

Cortá

Tajo de los
Machos
▲ (3081m)

Parque Nacional
Sierra Nevada

Laguna del
Caballo

Caballo ▲
(3010m)

Refugio
del Caballo

Loma de Cañar

Río Torrente

Sierra
Nevada
Traverse

Río Chico

Barranco de Poqueira

Río Poqueira

Central
Eléctrica

La
Cebadilla

Acequia Alta

Refugio
Ventura

Acequia Baja

Peña
Caballera
(2188m) ▲

Casa Tello

Río Lanjarón

Camino de la Sierra

Capileira

START (Alt)

Alternative
Route

Bubión

Alpujarras
Tour

START
Pampaneira

Barranco de la Sangre

GR7

Soportújar

Cañar

GR421

Carataunas

Río Trevélez

Lanjarón
FINISH

A348

Sierra Nevada & Las Alpujarras (West)

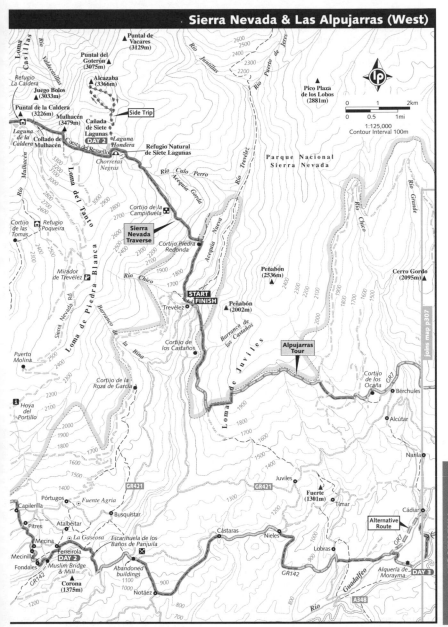

You have descended 420m in 45 minutes from Pitres to reach this marvellous spot.

Take the eastward path along the river's north bank, immediately crossing a side-stream and forking left up its far bank. After 10 minutes you come out onto another path. Turn right, and in five minutes you enter Ferreirola.

Alternative Start: Capileira
45 minutes, 3.2km
Starting in Capileira (see pp298–9) avoids the steep uphill first hour from Pampaneira through Bubión. Walk southeast up the Sierra Nevada road from Capileira for 2km, then branch right along a track signed 'Cortijo Prado Toro'. Some 600m south down this track, fork left at another 'Cortijo Prado Toro' sign. In another 600m you reach a crossroads among pines. Turn left here to join the main route, following the same GR7 sign to Pitres and Capilerilla.

Ferreirola
Set amid lush vegetation, Ferreirola is perhaps the most beautiful Taha village. Your path brings you up between its church and a fountain. A sign here points up the street to **Sierra y Mar** (☎ 958 76 61 71; W *www.sierraymar.com; Calle Albaicín; singles/doubles with bathroom €25/45*). This charming guesthouse (rates include breakfast) has nine highly individual rooms set around multiple patios and gardens, and its multi-lingual Danish and Italian hosts are both welcoming and highly knowledgeable about walking in the area. For an evening meal, you need to walk back to Mecina or Mecinilla – just over 1km by road.

Day 2: Ferreirola to Alquería de Morayma
6 hours, 17.5km
From Ferreirola's central fountain, follow the street down past Villa Kiko. On the east edge of the village, follow the GR142 signpost to Busquístar. In a few minutes you reach **La Gaseosa**, a spring with tiles around its water spout. The water is mildly fizzy and good to drink. At a fork 10 minutes later, take the broader, right-hand option (with a red-and-white paint X, indicating that you are leaving the GR142). The path descends to a ruined mill beside a bridge over the Río Trevélez, then zigzags up the south side of this steep valley by an ancient, part-cobbled path, the **Escarihuela de los Baños de Panjuila**. The path becomes wider and less steep 20 minutes from the bridge, and winds around in a further 15 minutes to a small group of houses where a vehicle track joins it from the right. Go left (east) along the track and in 150m you emerge on a paved road. Go left along this for 15 minutes to a junction amid a scattering of buildings. The **abandoned buildings** nearby mark the former departure point of an aerial conveyor system carrying iron ore from the Conjuro mines, just northeast of here, to Rules, 20km west. The mines and conveyor functioned from 1955 to 1968. Take the right-hand option, signposted 'Cástaras', at the road junction, and after five minutes turn down a path to the right with a GR142 signpost to Notáez. The narrow path – very well marked with red-and-white marker posts and paint stripes – leads downhill for 30 minutes to the pretty, quiet village of **Notáez**. As you enter Notáez a GR142 signpost to Cástaras indicates your onward direction, but it's worth having a little look round the village before you press on.

From Notáez follow the GR142 for one hour, mostly upward, to **Cástaras**, another pretty village, set on a rock outcrop with greenery all around. Take the street signposted 'Nieles, Jubiles' along the left wall of Cástaras church. The street soon turns right and becomes the road to Nieles, 40 minutes east. Take the first path down to the right after Nieles church, with a GR142 signpost to Lobras. After 1¼ hours winding down into and up out of two valleys, you emerge on a tarmac road just south of Lobras village. Go right (south), following a GR7 (not GR142) signpost to Cádiar. After about 220m, just past a building enshrouded in foliage, an easily missed post with faded red-and-white rings marks the start of a path on the left. This descends in 10 minutes to cross two *ramblas* (seasonal watercourses) in immediate succession (between the two you cross the GR142, here following a separate, longer route to Cádiar). Cross the second *rambla* and follow red-and-white paint dashes ahead. After 100m the path turns uphill to the right. Fifteen minutes later it crests a ridge, crosses a vehicle track and starts descending towards the verdant Río Guadalfeo valley. About 20 minutes from the ridge, on a rightward bend of the GR7, is a sign to the **Alquería de Morayma** (☎/fax 958 34 32 21; w www.alqueriamorayma .com; doubles & apartments €50-63) down to the right off the GR7. A great place to stay, this old *cortijo* has been lovingly renovated in meticulous *alpujarreño* fashion. Excellent, medium-priced food is available, and there's a library and fascinating art and artefacts everywhere. To reach it, follow the short signposted path (at times muddy and/or rather overgrown) from the GR7, cross the Guadalfeo (more a stream than a river) and head about 80m upstream to a path heading up to the right with an 'Alquería de Morayma 400m' sign: in fact, it's more like 600m.

The more budget-conscious should continue on the GR7 at the turn-off to the Alquería de Morayma and head to Cádiar (see Alternative Accommodation).

Alternative Accommodation

For cheaper but much less salubrious lodgings, continue on the GR7 for another 2km up the Guadalfeo valley to Cádiar, a metropolis for these parts with around 2000 people. **Pensión Montoro** (☎ 958 76 89 00; Calle San Isidro 20; singles/doubles with bathroom €10/20), 250m from the church, has plain, basic rooms.

In the morning take the street heading uphill from the more southerly of the town's two bridges over the Río Guadalfeo, then turn down a path to the right after 150m. After 40m fork left alongside an irrigation channel. In about 15 minutes the path crosses the channel and goes up to the left. Turn left when you meet a vehicle track after 150m, right at a track junction after another 150m, and left at another after 100m. This takes you through the tunnel under the A348, where you join the main Day 3 route.

Day 3: Alquería de Morayma to Mairena
8½ hours, 29km

The 8.5km stretch along the Río Yátor on this stage can be impassable after a lot of rain. To avoid it, you can road-walk or take a bus between Cádiar and Ugíjar, or try the alternative route via the Yátor–Ugíjar road mentioned later in this day's description.

From the Alquería de Morayma, walk up the driveway to the A348 and turn left. At a junction after 600m, go left towards Cádiar. Follow the GR142 onto a track on the left of the road after 150m, then onto a footpath on the right after another 450m. The path descends and passes eastward through a tunnel under the A348.

At a junction of vehicle tracks 80m beyond the tunnel, follow the red-and-white paint markings of the eastbound GR142, which our route now stays with for 18km to Las Canteras. After 350m you pass the ruined Venta de Cuatro Caminos at a crossroads. For the first half of the 7km from here to the largish village of Jorairátar, the GR142 follows the Rambla del Repenil, a usually dry watercourse. Then it winds up to the right, with increasingly fine panoramas to the north, before descending gradually over the final 2.5km to **Jorairátar**, which is reached about 2½ hours from the Alquería de Morayma.

Follow the street ahead through the village: at a plaza with a phone box, fork left down to the Hogar del Pensionista bar and take the street down the right-hand side of this, soon passing a GR142 'Los Montoros' signpost. The path descends to the Arroyo Jorairátar, climbs and descends again to the Río Yátor, 30 minutes from Jorairátar. Now the GR142 simply follows the Río Yátor downstream for 8.5km, about 2¼ hours. (If there has been a lot of rain, which will make it impossible to walk along the Río Yátor, we're told that as an alternative you can cross the river at the point where you first reach it – assuming it's not too deep or swift – and walk up the Barranco de las Cañadas, opposite, for about 1km to a track which in another 500m reaches the Yátor–Ugíjar road. Then turn right and walk 10km to Ugíjar. In suitable conditions, however, the Río Yátor is a lovely walk on which you may not see another soul. There's no point trying to keep dry feet, as you have to cross the river several times. In the early stages you need to push through a couple of spots of thick vegetation, but downstream the watercourse broadens out and the going is easy. A good spot for a break is the broad leftward bend around the ruined Venta Pampana on the left after 1¼ hours (5km).

You'll pass the hamlet of Los Montoros, then when the Río Ugíjar enters from the left 3.5km later (there are GR142 signs to Los Montoros, Las Canteras and Darrical at the confluence), turn left and go up it, passing Las Canteras hamlet after 10 minutes. This river is usually dry, but if there has been any significant rain this is likely to be the least pleasant part of your entire walk, because the river will probably be carrying foul-smelling effluent either from Ugíjar's sewers or from the large greenhouses near the town. Hope for dry weather, and 20 minutes up from Las Canteras, bear right where the watercourse forks (the left option has a dam a short distance upstream). Around 20 minutes later, to avoid a somewhat overgrown section, head up to a small ruined *cortijo* on a rise to the left, take the path heading westward uphill behind it, turn right at a track junction after a few minutes, and follow this track down through an area of greenhouses till it peters out back beside the river 10 minutes later. Cross to the east bank to pick up another northward track, which after a few minutes switches back to the west bank, then, five minutes later, emerges on the Yátor–Ugíjar road. Turn right and in 15 minutes you reach a T-junction in approximately the middle of the unexciting town of Ugíjar.

If you're very weary, or your budget is too tight for Las Chimeneas in Mairena (at the day's end), **Hostal Vidaña** (☎ 958 76 70 10; *Carretera de Almería; singles/doubles with bathroom €20/30)*, at the T-junction, has reasonable rooms, and an inexpensive restaurant. Otherwise, turn left (west), then right after 250m, immediately above Ugíjar's church. This street runs some 500m up through the town, ending at another T-junction with a brick-topped wall facing you. Go left, then

first right, following the wall. At the top of this street, go left. Where the street soon bends 90 degrees to the right, go straight on (north-northwest) along a broad unpaved area with some buildings on both sides. Take the lane out of the far end of this, passing an electrical pylon on a concrete base. Descend to cross a river bed, then start climbing towards Mairena. The clear route passes a water storage pond on the right after 30 minutes. Around 20 minutes later, just after a small *cortijo* above the left side of the road, the track forks. The Alternative Route: Via Válor–Mairena road diverges here. The main route (quicker, but harder to follow) goes right, passing a pond on the left after 100m. Your track descends, crossing a gully a few minutes later. Turn left up a lesser vehicle track 70m past the gully, and left again (almost doubling back) after another 60m. This path soon curves to the right, climbing, and within five minutes, after a short steep section, you emerge in an olive grove. The path runs left along the edge of the cutting you have just walked up. It soon becomes much clearer, continuing upward. Soon, just past a pond on the right, you fork left along the lip of a slope, descending for perhaps half a minute. A couple of minutes later, fork right along a clear footpath with a wall on its right side. This soon turns sharply right uphill and in a further 15 minutes you emerge at the foot of Mairena, across the road from **Las Chimeneas** (☎ 958 76 03 52; W www.moebius.es/contourlines; Calle Amargura 6; rooms or self-catering apartments for up to 3 people €50-60). This excellent guesthouse is a just reward for your day's exertions. It has great views and large, spotless rooms, serves good dinners (€15) and has helpful young British owners who are full of information on this little-visited area and its walks.

Alternative Route: Via Válor–Mairena road
1 hour, 4km

If the final half-hour or so up to Mairena, described above, seems too complicated, the longer but easier-to-follow option from the fork above the small *cortijo* is to go straight ahead towards Mairena, which is visible above you. This track soon bends left and in 20 minutes emerges on the Válor–Mairena road. Mairena is nearly 3km uphill to the right. Virtually the first house you reach, on the left of the road, is Las Chimeneas.

Day 4: Mairena to Yegen
3½ hours, 10km
This is a short stage sandwiched between two long ones. Walk northwest along the road from Las Chimeneas, soon crossing a bridge. Shortly after, on a right-hand bend, take a track turning sharp right uphill. Past a 'Parque

Natural' sign, fork right, and one minute later, a GR7 marker post indicates a narrow path up to the left. This soon becomes a broad track winding across the terraces. After 10 minutes go straight on up a narrower path where the main track bends left. In one minute you emerge on a broader track heading northwest. Cross a gully around five minutes later, and in another minute or so fork left along a narrow path, with white-and-red paint dashes on the first tree along.

You come down into a gully 10 minutes later: turn left down a path marked by a cairn and red-and-white paint stripes on the rock

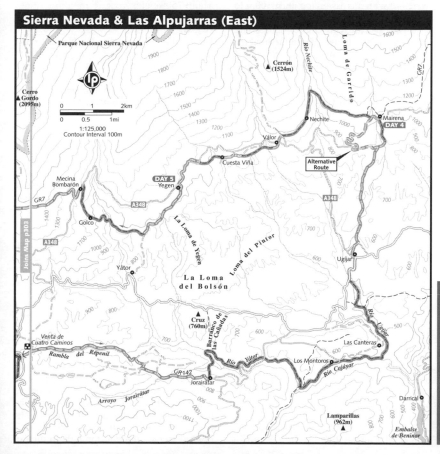

Sierra Nevada & Las Alpujarras (East)

behind it (the paint stripes may be obscured by vegetation). In 25 minutes this path descends to and crosses the **Río Nechite**, in its pretty valley. About 10 minutes beyond the river, at a fork with a signpost pointing back to Mairena, take the lower, left-hand option. Entering the small village of **Nechite** five minutes later, follow the street to the left, then go left, downhill, at the first fork, then right at a T-junction. Turn right at the bottom of this street, passing the Santa Lucía fountain, and follow the street up to Nechite's church. Go back 60m along the street from the church, then 70m uphill (left) from a white hut with a cross on top, then 100m to the right. Here, at a fork of the road, turn left up a path indicated by a GR7 signpost to Válor. After 10 minutes veer to the right off the path as it heads down to the left, onto a broader track. Five minutes later a GR7 post tells you to fork right. For a few minutes your path is joined by an irrigation channel, until the channel diverges left, downhill. Five minutes later you emerge at the top of **Válor**, one of the larger Alpujarras villages. Turn left down the road and go right at the first fork. You emerge on the main road through Válor, beside **Restaurante El Puente** (*bocadillos* €2-2.50, *mains around* €5), a fine spot for a bite of lunch. **Hostal Las Perdices** (☎ 958 85 18 21; *Calle Torrecilla; singles or doubles with bathroom* €26), a few hundred metres to the left (east) along the main road, has clean, straightforward rooms.

Take the street downhill opposite Restaurante El Puente, and turn right along the back of the large church to a plaza which you exit by its far (southwest) corner. Turn right at the bottom of the street, then left along a whitewashed stone wall. Just before the end of the wall, fork left, down to a smaller church. The street along the right side of this church leads you out of the village by the ancient **Puente de la Tableta** bridge.

Follow the road uphill from the bridge but don't miss a GR7 post directing you to turn sharp left after a few minutes. Go right at forks 10 and 15 minutes later, and left down a tarmac road after a further five minutes. In five minutes this brings you into the hamlet of **Cuesta Viña**, at the far end of

which is a green-tiled enclosure with a concrete arch, containing half a dozen ferruginous (iron-bearing) springs – all worth a sip as each has a different strength.

Walk up past the right side of the springs building. Just past the top of a shabby picnic area, a GR7 post indicates your path bending up and leftward. Ten minutes up, just after an abandoned two-storey *cortijo*, head up to the right (northwest) following red-and-white paint markings. In 10 minutes, cross the Válor–Yegen road. A few minutes later, turn left along a vehicle track to rejoin the road after 60m. Turn right and you reach Yegen within 15 minutes.

Yegen

This is the village made famous by writer Gerald Brenan, whose house, just off Yegen's fountain plaza, has a plaque. Local walks include a 2km Sendero Gerald Brenan: you can pick up a leaflet on them at the **Café-Bar Nuevo La Fuente** (☎ 958 85 10 67; *Calle Real 38; singles/doubles* €12/24), on the fountain plaza, a friendly place with eight very clean rooms.

El Rincón de Yegen (☎ 958 85 12 70; *singles/doubles with bathroom* €22/36), the first building you reach as you enter Yegen on our walk, has the village's most comfortable rooms and a good, medium-priced restaurant.

Day 5: Yegen to Trevélez

7½ hours, 25km

Head past the Brenan house, then fork right. Pass a supermarket down a street to the left, then a church on the right, before reaching a long plaza which you leave by the street at its far end, signed 'Camino a Montenegro'. A few minutes from the village edge, follow the concrete road bending left past a GR7 marker post on the right. The track passes the village cemetery, then winds downhill in an overall southwesterly direction. After 20 minutes turn right at a GR7 signpost to Golco. The track becomes a footpath. After two or so minutes take the lower, left option at a fork; a minute later pass a GR7 post on the left as you walk up a stream bed. The path then climbs a little indistinctly in a northwesterly direction through an area of boulders: watch for another GR7 post a few minutes after the last one.

The path becomes clear and leads down to a river crossing beside a poplar grove 20 minutes later. Veer left on the far bank and the path soon bends right, uphill. Five minutes later fork right (indicated by a GR7 post) on a rightward bend of the track. In three more minutes turn right along a semicobbled path. In 10 more minutes you reach Golco village: turn right at a GR7 signpost to Mecina Bombarón, then straight on along a path marked by a GR7 post where the road bends sharp left. Your path climbs up across the terraces and in 20 minutes brings you up onto the main street of Mecina Bombarón. The terrace tables and chairs of **Restaurante El Portón** (Calle Iglesia Vieja; raciones €3.50-7), just below the main street, are hard to resist.

Walk left along the main road for around five minutes, then turn right up a concrete road with a 'Ruta Pintoresca' sign. You soon reach Mecina's upper plaza, Plaza Vieja. Turn left up the street signed 'Bérchules 2h' and follow this round to the left at an almost immediate fork. After 10 minutes, soon after a radio mast, ignore a broad track turning right. Around five minutes later curve left, ignoring a straight-on option. At another fork 10 minutes later, go upward to the right. You pass through a pine wood and, 10 minutes after the fork, go left (downhill) at another fork, following a 'Cortijo Cortes' sign. Bérchules comes into view ahead but the track turns right (north) up the Bérchules valley. After 10 minutes heading northward, just past a fenced plantation on the left, take a faint path down to the left on the far side of a single chestnut tree opposite a small ruined building. Follow the line of a fence on your right and look for red-and-white paint stripes on a stone on the ground, five minutes from the chestnut tree. The now-clearer path bends right and descends more sharply towards the valley bottom. Within 30 minutes from the chestnut tree you cross the Río Guadalfeo by a little bridge beside a ruined mill, and in 20 minutes more (fairly steeply uphill) you enter **Bérchules**. Go left along the street, fork right at a fountain after two minutes, and soon you enter Plaza del Ayuntamiento, also called Plaza Abastos,

where the friendly **La Posada** (☎ 958 85 25 41; e laposadaberchules@wanadoo.es; Plaza del Ayuntamiento 7; B&B per person €15; open mid-Aug–mid-July) provides simple but comfortable walkers' lodgings in a sturdy 18th-century inn. Your hosts can provide vegetarian food, and speak some English. For more comfortable rooms head almost 1km down to the main road at the foot of the village, where **Hotel Los Bérchules** (☎ 958 85 25 30; Carretera de Bérchules 20; singles/doubles with bathroom €24/36) has Bérchules' best restaurant, and English-speaking hosts.

Finding your way out of Bérchules can be tricky. If in doubt, ask anyone you meet for the camino a Trevélez (path to Trevélez). Head up Calle Fuente Iglesia, 60m north from the church. Opposite Bazar Angelita, fork right up Calle Platera. Five minutes from the church, turn right to pass house No 28, then continue up the street left. Immediately before house No 44, turn right up steep Calle Fuentecilla, passing a house with a white turret. Fork up to the left (north-northwest) after a few minutes, and shortly after go left at a dirt road. Around 10 minutes later, 80m beyond a small square building beside an electricity pylon, fork left to pass Cortijo de los Ocaña. At another fork around five minutes later, go straight (not down to the left). The track curves right and a view of Cádiar and Narila opens out in the valley below. Pass a cortijo left and bend left round a gully, 10 minutes from the last-mentioned fork; 150m after the gully, take a narrow path right. When this soon meets the road again, take another track heading west up the slope. Within 10 minutes you reach a firebreak along the edge of a pine wood. Follow this upward, crossing straight over a good dirt road after 10 minutes; 600m beyond, go left along another dirt road through the trees. One hundred metres along this, fork left along a lesser track which passes through a clear area, then a second pine wood. Follow another firebreak up this wood's far edge for 200m, then veer left through a gate.

The dirt road you're on soon starts to climb steadily along the edge of the national park, across a rather bleak moor with superb eastward views. After 40 minutes, you reach the Loma de Juviles ridge at 2000m, with a firebreak running down it. Walk 120m south down the firebreak, then turn right (west) down another firebreak. Keep going down this and turn 90 degrees left with it after about 15 minutes. Around 10 minutes later the firebreak, now a vehicle track, meets another track: turn right (north-northwest) along this, which, as a marker post at the junction indicates, is our old friend the GR7! After about 15 minutes, take the left-hand, downward option at a fork of tracks. Trevélez soon comes into view on the far side of the valley. Your track narrows to a footpath but cairns and red-and-white GR7 posts and paint marks guide you down to Trevélez in a further 1¼ hours. Keep your eyes peeled for markers where the track occasionally becomes indistinct.

Sierra Nevada Traverse

Duration	3 days
Distance	45km
Difficulty	moderate–demanding
Start	Trevélez (p298)
Finish	Lanjarón (p313)
Transport	bus

Summary A strenuous but rewarding route across the higher reaches of the Sierra Nevada, a spectacular wilderness with surprising animal and plant life; includes mainland Spain's highest and third-highest peaks

The upper Sierra Nevada provides, in many ways, Andalucía's ultimate walking experience, for its altitude and climatic conditions and also for its forbidding, wild aspect – large tracts are a rugged wilderness of black mica schist rock and stones, with plenty of sheer faces and jagged crags.

The Sierra Nevada's *tresmiles* (peaks higher than 3000m) – the only ones in peninsular Spain outside the Pyrenees – are strung along a serpentine stretch of its main ridge between Cerro Pelao (3179m), 11km north of Trevélez (the nearest village to the high summits), and Caballo (3010m), 15km west of Trevélez. Our route heads straight up from

Trevélez to the heart of the *tresmil* zone, takes in Mulhacén and Veleta, the two highest peaks in the range (with Alcazaba, the third-highest, as an optional side trip), then traverses southwest before descending to the spa town of Lanjarón. For some shorter options in the Sierra Nevada, see the boxed text 'Short Walks in the Sierra Nevada' (p312).

NATURAL HISTORY

During the Ice Ages Europe's most southerly glaciers formed in the Sierra Nevada, the last of them surviving into the early 20th century. Many of the tarns (alpine lakes) here lie in glacially deepened basins, or cirques. For a visual guide to some of the most recognisable glacial landforms, see the boxed text 'Signs of a Glacial Past', (p23).

The Sierra Nevada's combination of high altitude and southern latitude gives it unique botanical variety. Among its 2100 plant species are 66 endemics – including its own species of narcissus, poppy, crocus, monkshood and gentian. Receding snows in the summer uncover much of this variety; most endemic species are found on rocky crags and cliffs above 2800m. Damp, grassy areas around the tarns, called *borreguiles*, also harbour many tiny flowering plants.

Pre-eminent among animals is the ibex, which numbers about 5000 (more than anywhere else in Andalucía) in the Sierra Nevada. In summer you stand an excellent chance of seeing ibex anywhere above 2800m.

PLANNING
When to Walk

July, August and early September are best but even at these times the weather can change quickly. Try to pick a spell of settled, clear weather and keep a careful eye on any clouds that begin to settle on the mountains. Even under clear summer skies, the heights of the range can be blasted by strong, cold winds, and nocturnal temperatures can fall close to freezing. By late September, expect it to get very cold at night above 2500m, perhaps with snow and storms. Year-round, the temperature on the summits averages 14°C less than in the highest Alpujarras villages. The first major snowfall is usually

Maps

Because of its larger scale, Editorial Alpina's 1:40,000 *Sierra Nevada, La Alpujarra* map just about gets the nod over Editorial Penibética's 1:50,000 *Sierra Nevada* map and the IGN 1:50,000 *Sierra Nevada* map.

around mid-October. The high ground begins to thaw in May. In June there's often plenty of snow still on the ground.

What to Bring

You'll need warm gear up here even if the skies are a cloudless blue and you've been sweltering down in the valleys. This means plenty of clothing layers – including head covering and gloves – and a warm sleeping bag. You need food for three days, and a tent.

There's plenty of water from springs, streams and tarns, but there are also quite a lot of animals in the Sierra Nevada, so purification tablets are advisable. Start Day 1 with enough water to reach the Cañada de Siete Lagunas.

Permits & Regulations

Overnight camping in the Sierra Nevada is permitted only above 1600m, at least 50m from high-mountain lakes and at least 500m from staffed *refugios* and vehicle tracks. It's advisable to check the latest regulations through a park information office such as the one in Pampaneira (see Information Sources, p297). At the time of writing you were required to give prior notification of all camping by email, fax or letter to the **Director-Conservador del Parque Nacional Sierra Nevada** *(fax 958 02 63 10; e pn .snevada@cma.junta-andalucia.es; Carretera Antigua de Sierra Nevada Km 7, 18191 Pinos Genil, Granada)* stating the name and identity card/passport number of the person responsible, the location and the number of people and tents.

The Sierra Nevada Road

Construction of the road over the Sierra Nevada from Granada to Capileira began in the 1920s for tourist purposes. A paved section to the top of Veleta (3395m) from the Granada side, touted as the highest road in Europe, was completed in 1935. In the 1960s this road was joined below the Veleta summit, at about 3250m, by a dirt road constructed from Capileira, thus creating a road right over the sierra – albeit one whose upper reaches would be blocked by snow for all but two or three months each year. A 7km dirt spur reaching to within 800m of the top of Mulhacén was added in 1974. This brought the two highest summits in the Sierra Nevada within reach of anyone with a car.

Growing concern for the alpine environment tolled the road's death knell as a public highway. In the mid-1990s, a permit system was introduced. Today, there are barriers on both sides of the range to stop drivers altogether, unless they have permits (very difficult to obtain). The southern barrier is at Hoya del Portillo (2150m), 12.5km above Capileira, and the northern one is at Hoya de la Mora (2475m), 3km up from the ski resort at Pradollano. From about late June to the end of October the Sierra Nevada national park operates **information offices** *(open approximately 8.30am-2.30pm & 3.30pm-7.30pm daily)* at Hoya de la Mora and Hoya del Portillo.

The national park also runs a bus service providing access to the upper reaches of the range during the same periods. Details of these services are subject to change but at the time of writing a shuttle bus ran 16km up the Sierra Nevada Road from Capileira (to Puerto Molina, 3km above Hoya del Portillo, at 2400m) and about 6km up from Hoya de la Mora (to the Posiciones del Veleta, at 3020m). Tickets (€4/6 one-way/return on either route) were sold at the Hoya de la Mora information post and at the Altas Cumbres office beside the main road in Capileira. One or two early and late runs from Capileira continued beyond Puerto de Molina as far as the Mirador de Trevélez at about 2670m.

Short Walks in the Sierra Nevada

The following are a few of the many possible ways to experience the Sierra Nevada in one or two days. Routes using the national park shuttle bus are of course dependent on bus schedules and departure points. Times and distances given for these walks assume the shuttle bus goes to Mirador de Trevélez. For more information on the shuttle bus see the boxed text 'The Sierra Nevada Road' (p311). The Editorial Alpina 1:40,000 *Sierra Nevada, La Alpujarra* map is recommended.

Trevélez-Mulhacén-Trevélez
(10–11 hours, 18km)
Follow the Sierra Nevada Traverse from Trevélez to the Cañada de Siete Lagunas and on to the summit of Mulhacén, then go back down again!

Trevélez-Mulhacén-Capileira
(7½ hours, 14km)
Follow the Sierra Nevada Traverse from Trevélez to the summit of Mulhacén, descend southward to the Sierra Nevada Road and the Mirador de Trevélez. Catch the shuttle bus to Capileira.

Trevélez-Mulhacén-Capileira
(2 days, 22km)
Follow the Sierra Nevada Traverse to the summit of Mulhacén, then descend to Refugio La Caldera and Refugio Poqueira (see Day 2 of the Sierra Nevada Traverse, pp314–15). Sleep at Refugio Poqueira and descend to Capileira in four hours the next day via Cortijo de las Tomas and Barranco de Poqueira trail No 3, with yellow marker posts (shown on the recommended map).

Trevélez-Mulhacén-Veleta-Capileira
(2 days, 36km)
Follow the Sierra Nevada Traverse to Mulhacén and continue the same day to Refugio Carigüela, a strenuous 8½ hours' walking. The next day ascend Veleta and return to Refugio Carigüela and Refugio La Caldera (three hours), then either head southeast along the Sierra Nevada Road to pick up the shuttle bus to Capileira (this saves 5km), or descend to Refugio Poqueira (1¼ hours) and from there to Capileira (four hours) as per the preceding walk.

Capileira-Mulhacén-Capileira
(4 hours, 10km)
After taking the shuttle bus to Mirador de Trevélez, walk to the top of Mulhacén and return the same way.

Capileira-Mulhacén-Capileira
(2 days, 18km)
After taking the shuttle bus to Mirador de Trevélez, walk to the top of Mulhacén, descend to Refugio Poqueira and sleep there. The next day descend to Capileira as per the two-day Trevélez-Mulhacén-Capileira route.

Capileira-Mulhacén-Alcazaba-Trevélez
(2 days, 24km)
Take the shuttle bus, walk to the top of Mulhacén, descend by the Cuesta del Resuello (see Day 2 of the Sierra Nevada Traverse, pp314–15) to the Cañada de Siete Lagunas and camp there. The next day ascend Alcazaba (see Side Trip: Alcazaba, pp313-14), return to the Cañada de Siete Lagunas and descend to Trevélez.

NEAREST TOWNS
See Trevélez (p298).

Lanjarón
Numerous places to stay and eat are strung along Lanjarón's lengthy main street. The town's bright lights and vaguely festive air in summer and autumn certainly make a change from the black, windswept heights of the sierra.

Some of the first lodgings you come to, about 1km from the bridge at the east end of town where the Camino de la Sierra emerges, are among the cheapest, including **Hostal Dolar** (☎ 958 77 01 83; *Avenida de Andalucía 5; doubles with shared bathroom €25*), **Hostal Astoria** (☎ 958 77 00 75; *Avenida Alpujarra 5; doubles with private bathroom €27*) and **Hostal Continental** (☎ 958 77 00 57; *Avenida Alpujarra 7; doubles with shared/private bathroom €24/30*).

The main bus stop is opposite the Hostal Dolar. See Getting There & Around (pp297–8) for transport information.

THE WALK (see map p302)
Day 1: Trevélez to Cañada de Siete Lagunas
3½ hours, 7km, 1300m ascent
Around 4m up the street from Trevélez's Hotel La Fragua, turn right under an arch to a junction where you take the uphill option. Fifty metres up, turn left into a path indicated by a yellow arrow, various paint dashes and a wooden marker post with an arrow. This leads you up through cultivated areas to an outlying farmlet, Cortijo Piedra Redonda, with one stone building on each side of the path, 2km (40 minutes) from Trevélez. At a fork 100m beyond, a 'Campiñuela, Siete Lagunas' sign points you up to the left. In a couple of minutes you pass through a fence with your route confirmed by a green paint blob. In another two minutes go left at a fork of paths. Continue upwards, keeping to the right of a fence and helped by the occasional national-park path marker post. Around 30 minutes from Cortijo Piedra Redonda the path swings northward to parallel the Acequia Gorda irrigation channel. It crosses the channel after 10 minutes and angles up through a

pine plantation. You pass through another fence 40 minutes from the Acequia Gorda, cross another irrigation channel and continue upward to **Cortijo de la Campiñuela** (2400m), composed of a ruined stone building, a threshing floor (a flat area paved with stones) and a tumbledown corral.

A clear path now climbs more gently northwest towards the Chorreras Negras, two waterfalls tumbling over black stones. After 30 minutes, cross the Río Culo Perro and climb a path which soon heads for the **Chorreras Negras**. The path crosses the foot of the right-hand waterfall, 30 minutes from the river crossing, then makes a steep 20-minute climb up beside the left-hand waterfall. At the top (2850m) you emerge suddenly in the Cañada de Siete Lagunas glacial basin. A shallow tarn, **Laguna Hondera**, stretches before you. The rock mass of Mulhacén looms ahead, with the crags of Alcazaba to its right. Laguna Hondera and several of the six other tarns in the basin are surrounded by grassy areas – good **camp sites**, but as alpine tarns are fragile environments, your camping habits should be impeccable – don't forget the national park rule banning camping within 50m of mountain lakes. On a rise just southeast of Laguna Hondera is the so-called **Refugio Natural de Siete Lagunas**, a trio of shelters formed by rock walls around a boulder, with room for about 10 people to stretch out. There are also a number of low **rock enclosures** providing some wind shelter.

Side Trip: Alcazaba
3–3½ hours, 6km
If you have reached the Cañada de Siete Lagunas by lunchtime and have reserves of energy, it's a fine idea to devote the afternoon to Alcazaba (Fortress). The name is entirely apt for this 3366m rock massif protected by awesome crags and precipices on every side but the southeast. Compared with neighbouring Mulhacén, barely a trickle of walkers tackle this giant.

Begin by walking up the ridge forming the northeast flank of the Cañada de Siete Lagunas. As you pick your way carefully over its first lot of crags, about 1¼ hours from Laguna Hondera, Alcazaba's pyramid-shaped summit cairn appears just west of north. You can walk to the right of and below the remaining crags of the ridge before veering right (north) up the Alcazaba summit ridge (with a precipice on its west side). From the **peak** itself, two hours from Laguna Hondera, steep walls drop away to the north and west. There are great panoramas just about every way you look.

To return, you can – after retracing your steps most of the way southward down Alcazaba's summit ridge – descend the stony valley on the north side of the ridge that you ascended from the Cañada de Siete Lagunas. Make for a discernible pass in this ridge, southeast from Alcazaba's summit. Once there (30 minutes from the summit), you find that you're on a more northerly spur of the ridge than the one you ascended. Head south for 20 minutes, losing little height, to return to your original spur, from where it's a simple 30-minute descent to Laguna Hondera.

Day 2: Cañada de Siete Lagunas to Refugio Carigüela
6 hours, 13km
This day takes you to the Sierra Nevada's two highest summits, Mulhacén (3479m) and Veleta (3395m).

From the southeast end of Laguna Hondera, a path climbs to the east end of the Cuesta del Resuello (Cuerda del Resuello on some maps), the rocky ridge forming the southwest flank of the Cañada de Siete Lagunas, then follows the ridge upwards. As you climb, you'll understand how the Río Culo Perro (Dog's Arse River), flowing out of Laguna Hondera, got its name. Mulhacén's summit is around 630m higher than Laguna Hondera, and the altitude may slow you down. Where the path up the Cuesta del Resuello fades, spots of yellow paint and small cairns show the way, keeping towards the north side of the ridge.

Two hours from Laguna Hondera, you emerge on a path 400m south of the summit. Turn right, and in 10 minutes you're standing on the highest rock in peninsular Spain. The **summit** supports a small shrine, a roofless stone chapel and a couple of small stone shelters. Immediately behind the summit is a near-perpendicular 500m drop to the Hoya de

Mulhacén basin. In clear weather the views take in such distant ranges as the Sierra de las Nieves, Sierra de Cazorla and even the Rif Mountains of Morocco.

Head back down the summit path but after 150m turn right at two small cairns to descend Mulhacén's steep west slope. About 20 minutes down, fork right to the **Collado de Mulhacén** (or Collado del Ciervo), where there are great views of Mulhacén's perpendicular north face, Alcazaba and the Hoya de Mulhacén. It's then a straightforward 15 minutes down to the **Refugio La Caldera**, 40m or 50m above Laguna de la Caldera, identical to Refugio Carigüela at the end of this day's walk. Another similar shelter, **Refugio Pillavientos**, is 20 minutes southwest along the Sierra Nevada road from Refugio La Caldera. A further accommodation option, 1¼ hours from Refugio La Caldera, is **Refugio Poqueira** (☎ 958 34 33 49; *dorm beds* €7.80), a modern staffed *refugio* in the upper Poqueira valley. Breakfast (€3.50) and dinner (€10) are available. To reach it, follow the Río Mulhacén downhill for 2.3km to the 2500m level, then follow a path veering 750m southeast to the *refugio*.

To continue our route from Refugio La Caldera, take the path crossing the slope above the north side of Laguna de la Caldera, to reach the Loma Pela (or Loma Pelada) ridge after 20 minutes. Fine views unfold ahead. Descend 10 minutes to the Sierra Nevada road and continue westward along this between the **Crestones de Río Seco** crags and the Lagunas de Río Seco tarns. The road passes through a nick in the rocks where the Crestones and the equally jagged **Raspones de Río Seco** meet. A few minutes later a gap in the Crestones gives dramatic views down into the Valdeinfiernos valley.

Passing under the almost sheer southeast side of Veleta, the road zigzags up to the 3200m **Collado del Veleta** (or Collado de la Carigüela del Veleta) pass. A tremendous westward panorama opens out, with the jagged Tajos de la Virgen ridge snaking west-southwest and Granada 25km northwest. A few metres above the pass, two hours from Refugio La Caldera, is **Refugio Carigüela**. This simple shelter, maintained in good condition, is free, always open, and has boards for 12 people to spread out sleeping bags, plus a table and benches.

From the *refugio* it's 30 minutes to the top of **Veleta**. A footpath up from the Collado del Veleta soon joins the paved Veleta summit road, which passes the top lifts of the Sierra Nevada ski station. The summit area is disfigured by a line of aerials and a small concrete building.

Day 3: Refugio Carigüela to Lanjarón

7½–8½ hours, 25km

From the Collado del Veleta, a path heads west-northwest 25 minutes down to the **Lagunillas de la Virgen**, a group of tarns about 250m lower. This northern side of the sierra can retain substantial snow cover well into the summer, in which case the tarns may appear as patches of snow or even be invisible.

From the southernmost of the *lagunillas* (small tarns), which is visible (snow permitting) as you descend, an excellent path climbs southwest across the boulder-strewn slopes of Tajos de la Virgen. About 50 minutes up you reach **Refugio Elorrieta**, on the ridge southwest of the Tajos de la Virgen crags. This multi-chambered *refugio* has great views but is a sorry mess inside.

Refugio Elorrieta stands above the Laguna de Lanjarón (or Laguna de las Tres Puertas) at the head of the Lanjarón valley, a typical stony, high Sierra Nevada wilderness. Crossing into this valley you have crossed the watershed between waters flowing to the Atlantic and waters destined for the Mediterranean.

From Refugio Elorrieta follow the southwest path along the western side of Loma de Cañar. After 10 to 15 minutes this heads down right. Fork left about five minutes down, then right after a further five minutes. Your path leads down across the Río Lanjarón. Across the river the **Vereda Cortá** (Cut Path) rises along the craggy northwest flank of the valley. Around 30 minutes along is the feature that earns this path its name – a steep (but not very wide) gully slicing down across the path. This requires an all-four-limbs scramble to the path's continuation, a metre or two

higher on the far side of the gully, with the aid of a length of cable fixed in place as a handhold. Another half-hour or so brings you to the little **Refugio del Caballo**, even more of a last resort than Refugio Elorrieta. This *refugio* stands just above Laguna del Caballo and below the most westerly *tresmil* in mainland Spain, Caballo (3010m).

If you're not happy about the gully manoeuvre on the Vereda Cortá you have two alternatives, both involving an extra descent of about 200m and ascent of 150m. One is to go left at the second fork as you descend the Loma de Cañar, and cross the Río Lanjarón at any convenient spot about 1km down. The other is to backtrack a couple of minutes from the gully and descend the stony slope to the valley floor. In either case you then walk southwest along the valley, picking up a path which after about 15 minutes starts to climb towards Caballo. You'll reach the Refugio del Caballo around 30 minutes later.

A clear path across the left side of Caballo leads into a steady southwest descent. A stream 1¼ hours down, just after a pine plantation, is probably the last drinkable water before Lanjarón. Fifteen minutes later, fork left down to a concrete irrigation channel and, beyond, the **Refugio Ventura** (of similar standard to the Refugio del Caballo) among some grey rocks.

From Refugio Ventura continue down on a path heading south-southwest in and out of pines. At the foot of a brief straight-downhill section, the path steers to the right and becomes a dirt road. This winds downhill through pines, passing a small meteorological station 25 minutes from Refugio Ventura. From a southbound leg of the zigzag 40 minutes later, zip left down a steep firebreak. At the bottom of the firebreak, go 350m left (northward) along a dirt road, then turn right down a path which in 10 minutes emerges on a broader track, where you again turn right. In 15 minutes this winds down to a group of semi-derelict forestry buildings, **Casa Tello**. From the west end of Casa Tello take a path diverging westward from the track you came in on. Go left at a fork after 60m and follow this trail 15 minutes down (with the aid of red paint dashes) to a footbridge over the Río

Lanjarón. Just upstream, opposite two inviting waterfalls, is a **picnic spot** too good to pass.

Follow the path up the east side of this valley, forking right beside a small irrigation channel after five minutes, and choosing right (downhill) at a junction after another 10 minutes, with a stone *cortijo* to your left. The track you are following is the **Camino de la Sierra**, an old *camino real*. You pass a long *cortijo* on the right about 45 minutes from the last-mentioned junction. Shortly after turn right down a side-track, then immediately left into a path marked by a red paint dash. After another 40 minutes, 40m past a small stone hut on the right and almost within spitting distance of the Lanjarón rooftops, diverge to the right down a path marked by another red paint dash. You emerge on the A348 road at the east end of Lanjarón 10 minutes later. The town centre is 1km to your right.

Cabo de Gata

Andalucía's 700km coast isn't all packed throngs of pink bodies à la Costa del Sol. Far from it. The most spectacular coastal scenery of all is around the arid Cabo de Gata promontory east of Almería.

The combination of a dry, desert climate with the cliffs of the volcanic Sierra del Cabo de Gata plunging towards the azure and turquoise Mediterranean waters produces a landscape of stark grandeur. Between the cliffs and headlands are strung some of Spain's best and least crowded beaches – and no large towns.

CLIMATE

With just 100mm of rain in an average year, Cabo de Gata is the driest place in Europe, and one of the hottest.

NATURAL HISTORY

Cabo de Gata, especially the *salinas* (salt-extraction lagoons) south of El Cabo de Gata village, is renowned for its birds. In spring many migratory birds call at the *salinas* while in transit from Africa or Doñana in western Andalucía to breeding grounds further north. A few flamingos (and many

other birds) stay to breed, then others arrive in summer; by late August there can be 1000 flamingos here. Autumn brings the biggest numbers of migratory birds as they pause on their return south. In winter the *salinas* are drained after the autumn salt harvest.

Cabo de Gata's dry climate and poor soil yield an unusual vegetation including the dwarf fan palm, Europe's only native palm, a bush usually less than 1m high with fans of lance-shaped blades. You'll also come across areas of prickly pear cactus and of sisal, a cactus-like plant with thick spiky leaves, both of which are grown commercially here – sisal for rope-making, prickly pear for food.

PLANNING
Information Sources

The main information office of the Parque Natural de Cabo de Gata-Níjar, which covers Cabo de Gata's 60km coast plus a thick strip of hinterland, is the **Centro de Visitantes Las Amoladeras** (☎ 950 16 04 35; *open 10am-2pm & 5pm-9pm daily mid-July–mid-Sept, 10am-3pm Tues-Sun rest of year*), 8km north of El Cabo de Gata village.

ACCESS TOWN
Almería

The provincial capital is dominated by a fine 10th-to-15th-century fortress, the **Alcazaba**, which, along with the 16th-century **cathedral**, shouldn't be missed if you're passing through. You can stock up on food supplies at the **covered market** (*Rambla del Obispo Orbera*).

Information For information on places around Almería province, the **Patronato Provincial de Turismo** (☎ 950 62 11 17; *Plaza Bendicho; open 10am-2pm & 5pm-8pm Mon-Fri*) is probably the pick of the city's three separate tourist offices. **El Libro Picasso** (*Calle Reyes Católicos 17 & 18*) stocks a vast range of books and maps.

Places to Stay & Eat Clean and well kept, the **Albergue Juvenil Almería** (☎ 950 26 97 88; *Calle Isla de Fuerteventura; under 26 yrs/others €12.90/17.25 mid-June–Aug & holiday periods, €10.90/15.20 rest of year*) is 1.5km east of the centre; take bus No 1

('Universidad') from Rambla del Obispo Orbera in the centre.

Hostal Americano (☎ *950 28 10 15; Avenida de la Estación 6; singles/doubles €21/36, with private bathroom €26/42)*, near the combined train and bus station, has decent-sized, but slightly drab rooms.

Hostal Sevilla (☎ *950 23 00 09; Calle de Granada 23; singles/doubles with private bathroom €27/40.25)*, in the centre, is a cheerful place with clean, air-con rooms.

Cafetería Central *(Avenida de Federico García Lorca; platos combinados or main dishes €5.70-11)* is a big, bright eatery not far from Hostal Americano.

Restaurante Alfareros *(Calle Marcos 6; fish & meat mains €7)* is an economical, no-nonsense place in the centre.

Getting There & Away Almería's airport receives some international charter flights, and scheduled services from Barcelona and Madrid.

The combined bus and train station is on Plaza de la Estación, about 1km southeast of the city centre. Buses come from Málaga (€12.40, 3¼ hours, at least eight daily) and Granada (€10, 2¼ hours, at least five daily). Trains run to/from Granada (€11.10, 2¼ to three hours, four daily). There are also direct trains to/from Madrid and buses to/from Valencia and Barcelona.

Cabo de Gata Coast

Duration	3 days
Distance	51km
Difficulty	easy–moderate
Start	El Cabo de Gata (p318)
Finish	Agua Amarga (p318)
Transport	bus
Summary A coastal walk along southern Spain's most spectacular seaboard	

This walk follows the coast through a beautiful *parque natural*, combining paths, dirt roads and occasional sections of paved road.

Given the locations of the accommodation options, it's impossible to divide the walk into three approximately equal days. We've opted for a short third day, giving a chance to linger at some of the more secluded beaches late in the walk or to head off from the final destination, Agua Amarga, in good time. The walk *could* be done in two long days, but that leaves little time to enjoy Cabo de Gata's inviting beaches and coves. In fact we recommend allowing at least one extra day for just that purpose!

PLANNING
When to Walk

You *can* walk here almost any time of year. But July and August are too warm for some people (there's hardly any shade); in these months you would need to take it slowly and cool off at beaches along the way. It *can* be very hot right through from June to September. September and October have the advantage that the sea is still warm (it's warmer in October than June).

What to Bring

There's never more than 3½ hours between villages, so you only need to carry picnic food – but take plenty of water on each stage.

Maps

Editorial Alpina's 1:50,000 *Cabo de Gata Níjar* map is best. The information offices at Las Amoladeras and San José normally have copies.

Permits & Regulations

Camping in the *parque natural*, and therefore along the walk route, is only allowed in the few organised camping grounds.

NEAREST TOWNS

You should call ahead for accommodation during Easter, July, August and September.

Warning

It's not advisable to do the Lobos to Cala del Bergantín or San Pedro to Cala del Plomo sections in mist or cloud – you might step over the edge of a cliff.

ANDALUCÍA

El Cabo de Gata Village

Officially called San Miguel de Cabo de Gata, this is the main village on the western side of the promontory. Though still a fishing village, it is now more a cluster of holiday chalets and apartments – an amiable, low-key place, set on a long, sandy beach. A bank on Calle Iglesia has an ATM.

Camping Cabo de Gata (☎/fax 950 16 04 43; camping per 2 people & tent €15) is 1km from the beach, 2.5km north of the village by dirt roads. It has a restaurant.

Hostal Las Dunas (☎ 950 37 00 72; Calle Barrio Nuevo 58; singles/doubles with bathroom €38.50/55), at the northern end of the village, has well-kept, modern rooms.

Hotel Blanca Brisa (☎/fax 950 37 00 01; Calle Las Joricas 49; singles/doubles €38.50/64.30) is a modern hotel, with comfortable rooms and a decent restaurant, at the entrance to the village.

Pizzeria Pedro (Calle Islas de Tabarca 2; open Easter-Nov), round the corner from the Blanca Brisa, serves fine pizzas and pasta at middling prices.

Alsina Graells (☎ 950 23 51 68) runs buses from Almería bus station to El Cabo de Gata (€1.80, 55 minutes, four or more daily).

Agua Amarga

This is a pleasant fishing-cum-tourist settlement stretched along a straight, sandy beach.

Hotel Family (☎ 950 13 80 14; Calle La Lomilla; singles/doubles with bathroom €50/55, with sea views €80/85) has nine lovely rooms. Prices include a big breakfast, and an excellent four-course menú (€16) is served nightly at 7pm. You pass Calle La Lomilla at the end of the walk.

Hostal Restaurante La Palmera (☎ 950 13 82 08; Calle Aguada; rooms with bathroom €48-84), at the eastern end of the beach, has 10 pleasant rooms: prices depend on the views. Food is available (meat and fish mains cost €6.60 to €15).

Autocares Bergarsan (☎ 950 26 42 92) runs buses from Agua Amarga to Almería (€4, 1½ hours) at 6.15am Monday and Friday only. A taxi from Agua Amarga costs around €50 to Almería or €40 to El Cabo de Gata village. **Manuel Gordillo Moreno** (☎ 950 36

68 94, 649 12 90 68) and **Fernando** (☎ 950 36 71 96, 678 42 41 31) operate taxi services throughout the Cabo de Gata region.

THE WALK (see map p319)
Day 1: El Cabo de Gata to San José
5½–6 hours, 21km

South of the village, you can choose between walking along the beach, the main road or a dirt road parallelling it inland. Just inland of the dirt road are the **Salinas del Cabo de Gata**, salt-extraction lagoons that are famous for their water birds (see Natural History, p316). There's a **bird-watching hide** in a fenced area 3km south of the village.

Ten minutes past the hide, the village of **La Almadraba de Monteleva** has a curious towered church at its north end. The salt from the *salinas* is piled up in great heaps here. South of La Almadraba, pass through the hamlet of La Fabriquilla, then you must resort to the road for the 45-minute section of steep coast round to the **Faro del Cabo de Gata** lighthouse at the peninsula's southern tip.

A path from the lighthouse joins the road for the 15-minute climb up to the **Torre Vigía Vela Blanca**, an 18th-century watchtower, 213m above sea level. You can avoid the road's long last hairpin by short-cutting up a gully. From the top, the eastward views along the next stretch of coast are magnificent. The road becomes dirt here and is barred to vehicles by a gate. It winds 25 minutes down to a similar barrier stopping traffic from the San José direction, then passes behind the enticing sandy beaches **Cala Carbón, Cala de la Media Luna** and **Playa Mónsul**, all reachable by short tracks.

Five minutes past the Mónsul car park, take a path to the right towards the nudist beach Playa del Barronal. Before reaching the beach, bear left at a fork of sandy paths and spend 10 minutes working your way up to the little pass just left (north) of the highest of the hillocks rising to the east. From the pass head on down to El Lance del Perro, the first of a string of gorgeous, isolated, sandy beaches, the **Calas del Barronal**, along this bit of the coast. El Lance del Perro has striking **basalt rock formations**, including a set of

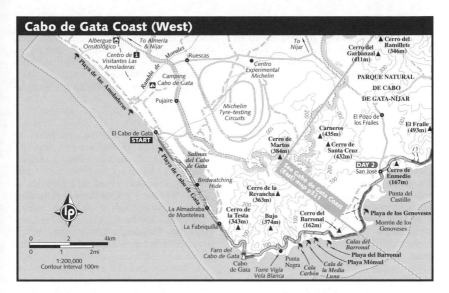

Cabo de Gata Coast (West)

Albergue Ornitológico
To Almería & Níjar
To Níjar
Centro de Visitantes Las Amoladeras
Ruescas
Rambla de Morales
Cerro del Garbanzal (411m)
Cerro del Ramillete (346m)
Playa de las Amoladeras
Centro Experimental Michelin
PARQUE NATURAL DE CABO DE GATA-NÍJAR
Camping Cabo de Gata
Michelin Tyre-testing Circuits
Pujaire
El Pozo de los Frailes
El Fraile (493m)
El Cabo de Gata
START
Carneros (435m)
Cerro de Santa Cruz (432m)
Salinas del Cabo de Gata
Cerro de Martos (384m)
DAY 2
San José
Cerro de Enmedio (167m)
Playa de Cabo de Gata
Birdwatching Hide
Cerro de la Revancha (363m)
Punta del Castillo
See Cabo de Gata Coast (East) map p321
Playa de los Genoveses
La Almadraba de Monteleva
Cerro de la Testa (343m)
Bujo (374m)
Cerro del Barronal (162m)
Morrón de los Genoveses
La Fabriquilla
Calas del Barronal
Playa del Barronal
Faro del Cabo de Gata
Cabo de Gata
Torre Vigía Vela Blanca
Punta Negra
Cala Carbón
Cala de la Media Luna
Playa Mónsul
0   2   4km
0   1   2mi
1:200,000
Contour Interval 100m

basalt columns sticking out of the sand towards its east end. Tides permitting (they normally do), you can walk round the foot of the cliffs to the next three beaches, **Cala del Barranco**, **Cala Grande** (with abandoned workings where the basalt was once quarried for paving stones) and **Cala Chica**. (If, tiresomely, the tides don't permit, you have to make your way over the intervening hills from beach to beach.) Leave Cala Chica by the path climbing to the right across the hillside to the east. This curves left and, 10 minutes from the beach, crests a ridge where a marvellous view of the broad, 1km-long Playa de los Genoveses opens before you. Head down to and along **Playa de los Genoveses** and, 100m before its northern end, go 100m inland to the start of an avenue between pines. At a crossing of tracks 170m along the pine avenue, turn right. The path leads 1km northeast to an old windmill where you rejoin the road towards San José.

San José

Entering San José follow 'Centro Urbano' signs, which bring you onto the main street, Avenida de San José, opposite the **tourist office & park information office** (☎ 950 38 02 99; *open 10am-2pm & 5pm-7pm or later Mon-Sat, 10am-2pm Sun*). Calle Cala Higuera, straight on, leads in 10 minutes to the youth hostel and Camping Tau. One block to the right along the main street is San José's central intersection where you'll find an **ATM**. There are three **supermarkets** on Avenida de San José.

San José becomes a chic little resort in summer, but out of season it's almost deserted. It's a pleasant place, with no high-rise development.

Camping Tau (☎ 950 38 01 66; *camping per person/tent/car €3.50/3.50/3.50; open Apr-Sept*) has a shady little site some 300m back from San José beach.

Albergue Juvenil de San José (☎ 950 38 03 53; *Calle Montemar; dorm beds €8; open Apr-Sept*) is a friendly youth hostel run by the local municipality. To find it, head along Calle Cala Higuera towards Camping Tau but turn right after crossing a dry river bed.

There are a dozen or more *hostales* and hotels. **Hostal Bahía** (☎ 950 38 03 07; *Avenida de San José; singles/doubles with bathroom €36/48*), at the central intersection, has attractive rooms in bright, modern buildings.

ANDALUCÍA

Hostal Ágades (☎ 950 38 03 90; Calle Sidi Bel Abbes 1; singles/doubles with bathroom €39/50), by the Almería road on the edge of town, has pleasant rooms and may have vacancies when more central places don't.

Restaurante El Emigrante (Avenida de San José; mains €6-12), at the central intersection, is an excellent-value eatery with a wide-ranging menu.

Day 2: San José to Las Negras
5½ hours, 19km

Head past Camping Tau and turn right at the T-junction at the end of the street. At a three-way junction after a few hundred metres, take the middle option signed 'Playa'. Ignore a second 'Playa' turning 250m down this track, and continue 550m to the back of a house called La Atalaya. Here take a smaller track up to the left, which in five minutes joins a higher track. Follow this to the right, rounding the corner of the hillside, and continue for 1¾ hours to Los Escullos. There's a good cliff-top section at the start, after which it's a winding route, mostly away from the coast. You pass beneath El Fraile (493m), the highest peak on Cabo de Gata. The road becomes paved a few minutes before **Los Escullos**, which has two small places to stay close to the beach – **Hotel Los Escullos** (☎ 950 38 97 33; rooms €51-60), and **Casa Emilio** (☎ 950 38 97 32; singles/doubles €39/48), both with average-priced restaurants – and the large **Camping Los Escullos** (☎ 950 38 98 11; camping per 2 people & tent €16), 900m back from the beach and with a cheaper restaurant.

Head north along Playa del Arco. For the 1km to the tiny village of La Isleta del Moro, you can continue by the water's edge except for a couple of brief sections. **Hostal Isleta del Moro** (☎ 950 38 97 13; singles/doubles €21/43) has rooms with bathroom and a restaurant with fresh seafood. **Casa Café de la Loma** (☎ 950 52 52 11; singles/doubles €30/42) on a small hill just above the village, is a friendly place with a summer part-vegetarian restaurant.

From the north end of La Isleta's Playa del Peñón Blanco, a path heads inland, initially following white posts. Unless you want to

visit **Cala de los Toros**, a small black-sand beach backed by a splash of green trees, you should continue northeast cross-country to meet the road. Go uphill with the road to the **Mirador Las Amatistas** lookout, 1¼ hours from Los Escullos. You need to stay with the road as it heads inland towards the former gold-mining village of Rodalquilar and then bends northeast.

Northeast of Rodalquilar you pass the Hotel de Naturaleza, then a turning marked 'La Polacra' (see Alternative Route: Lobos). About 300m along the road past the La Polacra turning, turn right along a level track. The track passes the **Castillo de Rodalquilar**, which served as a refuge from 16th-century pirates, and 2km from the main road reaches **Playa del Playazo**, a good, sandy beach stretched between two headlands (1¼ hours from the Mirador Las Amatistas).

At the north end of Playa del Playazo pick up the track heading north and follow the sign 'Sendero a Las Negras', which steers clear of the 18th-century Batería de San Ramón fort (now a private home) for an enjoyable 30-minute walk over the rocks to **Camping Náutico La Caleta** (☎ 950 52 52 37; camping per 2 people & tent €11.40), in its own cove. This camping ground has little shade but a nice pool, restaurant and shop.

A paved road heads 1km north to reach Las Negras.

Alternative Route: Lobos
1¾ hours, 6.5km

It's worth the detour up 265m **Lobos** for magnificent views (adding about 1¼ hours to your day's walk). From the 'La Polacra' turning a paved road runs right to the top (3km, 50 minutes), with a gate barring vehicles about halfway. Lobos is topped by an 18th-century watchtower converted into a lighthouse.

From Lobos you can head northward down to the bay Cala del Bergantín, then on to Playa del Playazo by the pass between Cerro del Romeral and Cerrico Romero. There's no real path as far as Cala del Bergantín: just steer away from the cliffs, which have quite an overhang in places, and in one spot curve unexpectedly far inland.

Las Negras

Set on a pebbly beach stretching towards an imposing headland of volcanic rock, Cerro Negro, the village of Las Negras attracts a vaguely trendy holiday clientele.

Hostal Arrecife (*☎ 950 38 81 40; Calle Bahía 6; singles/doubles with bathroom €26/38*), on the main street, with 11 rooms, is the only hotel. Other accommodation is mostly holiday apartments and houses to let, but you may find a few signs offering rooms by the night. Some **apartments** are available for one or two nights: try calling ☎ 950 38 80 75, ☎ 950 38 80 88 or ☎ 950 23 73 95.

Pizza y Pasta (*open Mar-Nov; mains €5-6*), just down from the main street, is a bright, friendly place serving exactly what the name suggests.

Day 3: Las Negras to Agua Amarga

3½ hours, 11km

A path climbing beside the last house at the north end of Las Negras beach joins a dirt road from the back of the village. Follow this round the back of Cerro Negro for 25 minutes. It then becomes a path high above the sea for another 25 minutes to **San Pedro**. This isolated hamlet, with a fine beach, was abandoned by its Spanish inhabitants some years ago; today a small floating population of travellers and others hang out here in tents, abandoned buildings and the odd cave.

There's no way out of San Pedro by land except up. A good path climbs from the round tower on the east side of the valley. You climb steeply for 25 minutes, then gently for another 15, during which you suddenly find you're walking along the top of a cliff – take care! The path is clear most of the way; where it's not, cairns guide you. You come down to **Cala del Plomo**, a beach of sand and pebbles with a tiny hamlet around 1½ hours from San Pedro. Five minutes along the track back from the beach, take a path to the right with a 'Cala de Enmedio' sign 30m along it. In a few minutes this meets the Barranco de los Calares and follows it down to its meeting with the Barranco de la Cala, 15 minutes from the 'Cala de Enmedio' turning. Continue a few minutes downstream if you wish

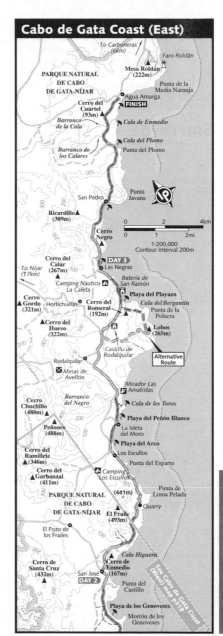

Cabo de Gata Coast (East)

ANDALUCÍA

to visit the nice little Cala de Enmedio beach; for Agua Amarga, take an uphill path northward at the meeting of *barrancos*, marked by a small cairn by two fig trees. This winds up and over a small hill and will have you removing your boots on the beach at **Agua Amarga** in 40 minutes.

Sierra de Grazalema

The Cordillera Bética gives a final flourish west of the little white hill town of Grazalema before fading away to the coastal plains of Cádiz province. The Sierra de Grazalema – actually several small sierras – is not particularly high or extensive but it encompasses a great variety of beautiful landscapes, from pastoral river valleys to precipitous gorges, from dense Mediterranean woodlands to rocky summits atop perpendicular cliffs.

The Grazalema hills and some surrounding lowlands comprise the 517-sq-km Parque Natural Sierra de Grazalema. Within the park is a 30-sq-km *área de reserva* (reserve area) occupying most of the triangle between Grazalema, Benamahoma and Zahara de la Sierra. This contains much of the park's most spectacular territory and some of its finest walks. We certainly recommend these walks, but as entry to the reserve area is only allowed with a permit from the park office in El Bosque, which can be a little complicated to obtain, we focus instead on two equally fine walks outside the reserve area. You'll find information on walks in the reserve area under Sierra de Grazalema – Área de Reserva (p327) under Other Walks.

HISTORY

In the 13th to 15th centuries, this area was a Muslim-Christian frontier zone, which gave rise both to the area's livestock-raising tradition (animals being easier to move from conflict than crops) and the way villages huddle into the rocky hillsides for protection. In the 19th century, with land ownership concentrated in the hands of a few, the area was renowned for banditry and poaching. Zahara de la Sierra was a noted hotbed of anarchism.

In the mid-20th century swathes of forest were levelled for fuel and a big slice of the population departed in search of a more prosperous life elsewhere: you'll see many abandoned *cortijos* on your walks.

NATURAL HISTORY

Climbing El Torreón provides the best chance of spotting some of the park's 500 ibex. However, you will see a lot of domesticated animals, among them plenty of Iberian pigs, the black or dark brown breed that is turned into Spain's best ham, especially when (as it has ample opportunity to do here) it has eaten lots of acorns. The star of the bird population is the griffon vulture. Around 100 pairs live in the Garganta Verde and Garganta Seca gorges south of Zahara de La Sierra.

Much of the area is covered in beautiful Mediterranean woodland of holm, gall and cork oak, olive, *acebuche* (wild olive) and *algarrobo* (carob). The north flank of the Sierra del Pinar between Grazalema and Benamahoma supports a famous 3-sq-km *pinsapar*, the country's best preserved woodland of the rare Spanish fir *(pinsapo)*. This handsome, dark green tree survives in significant numbers only in pockets of southwest Andalucía and northern Morocco. Growing up to 30m high and able to live 500 years, it's one of 10 species around the Mediterranean that are relics of the extensive fir forests of the Tertiary period (which ended about 2.5 million years ago).

CLIMATE

The Sierra de Grazalema is the first major elevation encountered by prevailing warm, damp winds from the Atlantic. Consequently, this is one of the wettest parts of Spain (Grazalema town has the highest measured rainfall in the country at an average of 2153mm a year), and one of the greenest parts of Andalucía. Snow is fairly common in late January and February.

PLANNING
When to Walk

May, June, September and October are best. July and August can be unpleasantly hot.

Maps

We prefer the Junta de Andalucía/IGN 1:50,000 *Parque Natural Sierra de Grazalema* map, though it omits some good and obvious trails. More widely available locally is the Libros Penthalon 1:50,000 *Plano Topográfico del Macizo de Grazalema*, a revamp of some ancient SGE maps.

Information Sources

The nature park's main information office, the **Punto de Información El Bosque** (☎ *956 72 70 29; Avenida de la Diputación; open 10am-2pm daily year-round, 6pm-8pm Fri, Sat & holidays Apr-Sept, 4pm-6pm Fri, Sat & holidays Oct-Mar)* is in El Bosque. There are further information offices in Grazalema and Zahara de la Sierra (see p326).

ACCESS TOWN
Grazalema

This neat, pretty little town nestles into a corner of beautiful mountain country. Grazalema's **tourist office** (☎ *956 13 22 25; Plaza de España; open 10am-2pm & 5pm-8pm Tues-Sun approx Easter-Oct, 10am-2pm & 4pm-6pm Tues-Sun rest of year)* is very helpful with information on the area. The smattering of **shops** will furnish food and drink supplies.

Places to Stay & Eat At the top of the village beside the A372 to El Bosque is **Camping Tajo Rodillo** (☎ *956 71 62 75; camping per person or tent €3.60)*. In winter you may only find it open at weekends.

Casa de las Piedras (☎ *956 13 20 14; Calle Las Piedras 32; singles/doubles with shared bathroom €9.50/19, with private bathroom €27/39.50)* is a good-value *hostal* with a restaurant serving hearty medium-priced meals.

Hotel Peñón Grande (☎/fax *956 13 24 35; Plaza Pequeña 7; singles/doubles €35/50)* is an excellent small hotel, with large, rustic-style but very comfortable rooms.

Among several places to eat on Calle Agua, off the central Plaza de España, is the excellent-value **Bar La Posadilla** (*Calle Agua 19; platos combinados €2-6)*.

Restaurante Cádiz El Chico (*Plaza de España 8; mains €6-13)* is good for a more

expensive meal, with excellent meat, egg dishes and fish.

Getting There & Away Buses run by **Los Amarillos** (*in Málaga ☎ 95 235 00 61)* travel between Málaga and Grazalema (€8.70, three hours, twice daily), via Ronda.

Grazalema Loop

Duration	6 hours
Distance	20km
Difficulty	easy–moderate
Start/Finish	Grazalema (p323)
Transport	bus

Summary A walk through surprisingly remote valleys and passes, green woodlands and impressive limestone scenery

There are several routes across the higher country between Grazalema and Benaocaz, 8km southwest as the crow flies. This walk follows one outward and another returning to Grazalema, with a total ascent of 1000m. Carry enough water for the whole of each leg of the walk.

Warning

Grazalema cattle always seem to have long, sharp horns pointing in your direction. It makes sense to walk near some cover (walls, fences, trees, rocks, thick undergrowth) that you could resort to if necessary.

THE WALK (see map p324)

From Camping Tajo Rodillo walk a couple of minutes up the A372, then turn left along a path with a 'Camino Peatonal' (pedestrian path) sign. This climbs gradually westward below the road. After 30 minutes it reaches a picnic shelter, the Merendero del Boyar, by a bend in the road. Go through a gate 50m to the right of this, with a sign 'Paso a Pie Salto del Cabrero'.

A dirt track leads 25 minutes southwest down to a white *cortijo*. Just before the *cortijo*, assorted signs direct you down to the

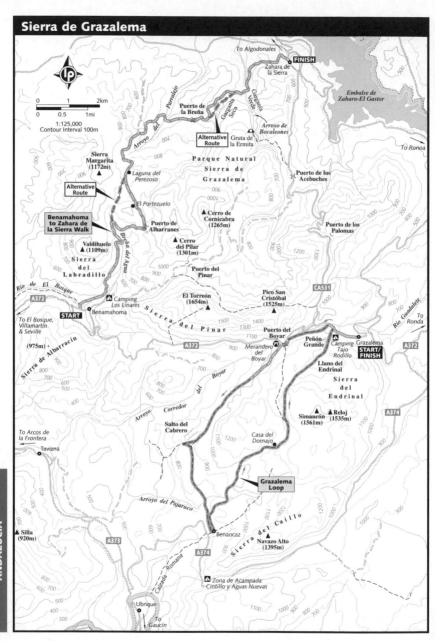

Sierra de Grazalema

To Algodonales

FINISH

Zahara de la Sierra

Embalse de Zahara-El Gastor

0   1   2km
0   0.5   1mi
1:125,000
Contour Interval 100m

Garganta Verde

Garganta Seca

To Ronoa

Puerto de la Breña

Alternative Route

Gruta de la Ermita

Arroyo de Bocaleones

Arroyo del Parralejo

Sierra Margarita (1172m)

Laguna del Perezoso

Alternative Route

El Portezuelo

Benamahoma to Zahara de la Sierra Walk

Puerto de Albarranes

Valdihuelo (1109m)

Sierra del Labradillo

Breña del Agua

Parque Natural Sierra de Grazalema

Puerto de los Acebuches

Cerro de Cornicabra (1265m)

Cerro del Pilar (1301m)

Puerto de los Palomas

Puerto del Pinar

Río de El Bosque

A372

Camping Los Linares

START

Benamahoma

To El Bosque, Villamartín & Seville

(975m) +

Sierra de Albarracín

El Torreón (1654m)

Pico San Cristóbal (1525m)

CA531

Río Guadalete

To Ronda

Puerto del Boyar

Merendero del Boyar

A372

Peñón Grande

Camping Tajo Rodillo

Grazalema

START/ FINISH

A372

Llano del Endrinal

Sierra del Endrinal

Sierra del Pinar

Sierra del Boyar

Arroyo Corredor

Salto del Cabrero

Simancón (1561m)

Reloj (1535m)

A374

Casa del Dornajo

Grazalema Loop

To Arcos de la Frontera

Tavizna

Arroyo del Pajaruco

Sierra del Caíllo

Silla (920m)

Benaocaz

Navazo Alto (1395m)

A373

A374

Calzada Romana

Zona de Acampada Cintillo y Aguas Nuevas

Ubrique

To Gaucín

left, through a gate and onto a path marked by a couple of green paint arrows. This descends through a **gall oak wood**.

Thirty minutes from the *cortijo* the path starts to climb in a southwesterly direction. Just before the top of a rise, the path veers to the right between rocks, indicated by the odd green paint splodge or arrow, then bends left through a gate. It goes straight ahead after the gate, then veers right through terrain studded with limestone rocks. You descend to a flat, grassy area and curve westward through a gap between rocky ridges to the edge of the **Salto del Cabrero** (Goatherds' Leap) – a sloping fissure perhaps 500m long and 100m across, where the earth simply seems to have slipped 80m or 100m downwards – one hour from the white *cortijo*.

Return to the flat, grassy area and veer right to leave it by its south corner. Cross a small rise and head south towards **Benaocaz**, which soon becomes visible. You'll reach it in roughly an hour from the Salto del Cabrero, passing the Hostal San Antón as you walk up into the village. For food, continue about half a kilometre along the street to **Las Vegas** *(Plaza de las Libertades; mediaraciones €4.50)*.

The footsore have the option of returning to Grazalema by a Los Amarillos bus from Ubrique which passes through Benaocaz at 3.10pm (3.40pm Saturday, Sunday and holidays). Otherwise head back to Hostal San Antón and follow the street along its righthand (east) side. At the top of the street take the path passing the left-hand (west) side of Restaurante-Bar El Parral. This soon bends right (northeast) to pass through a gate five minutes from El Parral. You now stay with this path for 1¼ hours as it winds its way up to the Casa del Dornajo, an abandoned farmstead high in a holm-oak–strewn valley northeast of Benaocaz. Yellow paint arrows provide indispensable assistance along the way. Twenty minutes from the gate the route turns left through a gate between two brick pillars. Fifteen minutes later look for a yellow arrow on the ground, pointing north, when you arrive in a small clearing with paths going every which way. Twenty minutes after that, you go through another gate:

initially head north-northeast up the valley ahead but after 300m the path veers up the right (northeast). Ten minutes later you reach a bath serving as an animal drinking trough: look for a yellow arrow 25m uphill, pointing left (northeast). Follow this and soon you reach the **Casa del Dornajo** – less impressive than your exertion in reaching it deserves, but still worth a breather beneath its trees!

From Dornajo start out northeast and almost immediately you're following blue paint arrows against the direction they point in. The path bends northward across the lower slopes of Simancón (1561m), and 25 minutes from Dornajo you crest a rise where the Grazalema–Benamahoma road comes into view. The path descends to a gate about 15 minutes away. From the gate head 150m north, still against the blue arrows, then turn sharp right at a path junction. This takes you over a rise past two cairns. Head northeast down to the bottom of the valley in front of you, which takes 30 minutes. At first there's a maze of sheep tracks, but a decent path materialises just right of centre after a few minutes. This switches to the left side of the valley about halfway down. Just after a water trough by the corner of a small pine plantation at the bottom of the valley, take a lesser path up to the left. This passes beneath the rock-climbers' crag **Peñón Grande** to emerge at the car park outside Camping Tajo Rodillo, 30 minutes from the trough.

Benamahoma to Zahara de la Sierra

Duration	5 hours
Distance	14.5km
Difficulty	easy
Start	Benamahoma (p326)
Finish	Zahara de la Sierra (p326)
Transport	bus
Summary	A beautiful walk through limestone hills, native oak woods and olive groves to the region's most spectacularly sited village

This walk takes you across some surprisingly remote country of thick woodlands and high pastures just outside the *área de reserva*. If you're doing some of the walks in the reserve area (see Sierra De Grazalema – Área De Reserva under Other Walks, p327), this is one way of getting from the end of the Pinsapar walk to the jumping-off point for the Garganta Verde. Carry enough water for the whole walk.

NEAREST TOWNS
Benamahoma

This small, attractive village is 13km west of Grazalema and 4km east of El Bosque, on the A372.

Camping Los Linares (☎ 956 71 62 75; *camping per person/tent/car €4/4/3.25, 4-person cabins €69; open daily June-Sept, Sat & Sun Oct-May)* is 600m up Camino del Nacimiento at the back of the village. There are several **places to eat** in the village.

The Grazalema–El Bosque bus, departing Grazalema at 5.30am Monday to Saturday, stops in Benamahoma (€1.35, 30 minutes).

Zahara de la Sierra

Topped by a crag with a ruined castle dating back to the 12th century, Zahara has a superb setting above the Zahara-El Gastor reservoir. The Grazalema park's **Centro de Visitantes Zahara de la Sierra** (☎ 956 12 30 14; *Plaza del Rey 3; open 9am-2pm daily & 4pm-7pm Mon-Sat)* is in the village centre.

Hostal Los Tadeos (☎ 956 12 30 86; *Paseo de la Fuente; singles/doubles/triples with bathroom €24/37/50)*, down on the south-west edge of the village, is friendly with good rooms and a small restaurant.

Hostal Marqués de Zahara (☎/fax 956 12 30 61; *Calle San Juan 3; singles/doubles with bathroom €28/40)*, a converted mansion in the village centre, has comfy rooms.

You won't go wrong eating at either of two neighbouring establishments on Calle San Juan: **Restaurante Los Naranjos** (*meat & fish mains €5.40-10.80)* or **Bar Nuevo** (*menú €8)*.

Comes (☎ 95 287 19 92) operates buses between Zahara and Ronda (€3, one hour, two daily Monday to Friday). Ronda is on the Málaga–Grazalema bus route. There's no bus service available between Zahara and Grazalema.

THE WALK (see map p324)

Turn north by the Venta El Bujío bar at the bottom (west) end of Benamahoma. The side road crosses the Río de El Bosque and immediately divides. Take the left option, then turn right after 70m. Ignore a right fork opposite a pillared gate after a few minutes, but almost immediately turn 90 degrees to the right. Go through a gate, ignore a left turn soon afterwards, and the dirt road you are now on leads all the way to Zahara de la Sierra. However, a few worthwhile variations from the basic route are detailed in what follows.

The track soon starts climbing fairly steeply, with a few zigzags. Around 35 minutes from the last gate mentioned, with the track now more level, you pass through another gate as you head up the west side of the Breña del Agua valley. In a further 30 minutes there's a fenced enclosure on the left. Just 100m beyond this, a path branches left (north) shortly before the main track makes a sharpish right bend. Here you have a choice.

If you stay with the main track (passing a *cortijo* after 10 minutes or so, going left at a junction at the Puerto de Albarranes 15 minutes later, and passing the *cortijo* El Portezuelo after another 10 minutes), you'll enjoy views of the Cerro del Pilar (1301m), Sierra del Pinar and Cerro de Cornicabra (1265m).

An alternative route is offered by the path, which saves you a few minutes and passes through some lovely woodlands. The path is not very clear at the start, but soon becomes so as it climbs 15 minutes to a little pass (925m). Descending, it bends a little to the right before emerging in a grassy upland valley with Sierra Margarita (1172m) rising from its west side. Head for the gate in the fence across the middle of the valley, where you rejoin the main track descending from El Portezuelo.

Just through the gate is the so-called **Laguna del Perezoso**, a shallow, stone-walled depression that collects rainwater but is often dry. The track continues ahead for five minutes, then begins a winding, 50-minute descent to the Arroyo del Parralejo (often dry). From the *arroyo* there's a 20-minute ascent through perhaps the loveliest woods of the whole walk (mainly holm oaks and olives) to the Puerto de la Breña (600m).

Then it's downhill for 50 minutes to the Arroyo de Bocaleones issuing from the Garganta Verde. As you descend, you can see, to your right, some of the cliffs of the gorge, which is home to a large vulture colony. After passing Puerto do la Breña you could choose to pick up the Alternative Route (see Alternative Route: Colada de la Breña). From the Arroyo de Bocaleones you have around 40 minutes of up-and-down through olive groves to Zahara.

Alternative Route: Colada de la Breña
35 minutes, 1.2km
It's possible to follow the old **Colada de la Breña** livestock route and avoid some of the main track's curves. Take the driveway down towards a *cortijo* on the right, a few minutes after the Puerto de la Breña. Turn left off the drive and follow a broad swathe northeast downhill for 10 minutes. Pass just to the right of another *cortijo*, then immediately veer to the left downhill. Pick up a clear trail running along for 20 minutes above the Garganta Scca stream, to rejoin the main track a few minutes before the Arroyo de Bocaleones.

Other Walks

SIERRA DE GRAZALEMA – ÁREA DE RESERVA
These walks are among the best in the Grazalema park, but access is controlled. The rules change from time to time, so it's well worth seeking advance information from a park information office or local tourist office, such as in El Bosque (see Information Sources, p323) Grazalema (see p323) and Zahara de la Sierra (see p326). At the time of writing you need a free permit from the El Bosque park office for any of these walks. You can call or visit El Bosque up to 15 days in advance for

this, and it's advisable to do so, as the number of people allowed on each route is limited; you can arrange to collect permits at the Zahara visitors centre or Grazalema tourist office. For map advice see Planning (pp323–4).

In July, August and September, when fire risk is high, some routes are wholly or partly closed, or you may be required to go with a guide from an authorised local company. Such companies – which offer guided walks year-round – include **Horizon** (☎ 956 13 23 63; *Calle Corrales Terceros 29, Grazalema*), with English-speaking guides, **Pinzapo** (☎ 956 13 24 36; e *pinzapo@wana doo.es*), also in Grazalema, and **Al-qutun** (☎ 956 13 78 82; w *www.al-qutun.com; Calle Zahara de la Sierra*) in Algodonales.

Grazalema to Benamahoma via the Pinsapar
After a couple of steepish ascents in the initial third of this 14km walk, it's downhill most of the way. You walk up from Grazalema to a parking area by the Zahara de la Sierra road, just under 1km up from the A372. Here starts the footpath that leads across the northern slopes of the Sierra del Pinar. The thickest part of the *pinsapar* comes in the middle third of the walk, below the Sierra del Pinar's precipitous upper slopes.

El Torreón
The highest peak of the Grazalema region, El Torreón (1654m) tops the Sierra del Pinar between Grazalema and Benamahoma. The ascent starts 100m east of the Km 40 marker on the Grazalema–Benamahoma road. It's about 2½ hours up and 1½ hours down.

Garganta Verde
The 'Green Gorge', 100m and more deep, has been carved out of the limestone south of Zahara de la Sierra by the Arroyo de Bocaleones. This beautiful walk begins 3.5km from Zahara on the Grazalema road. Before descending into the gorge itself, the path passes a viewpoint overlooking a large colony of griffon vultures. Then comes a steep descent of 300m. In the bottom of the gorge visit the Gruta de la Ermita, a large cavern hollowed out of the rock wall by water action. Retrace your steps back up again.

ANDALUCÍA

Camino de Santiago

The Camino de Santiago (Way of St James) originated as a medieval pilgrimage. For more than 1000 years Europeans have taken up the Camino's age-old symbols – the scallop shell and staff – and set off on the adventure of a lifetime, risking life and limb to reach the tomb of James, the apostle, in the Iberian Peninsula's far northwest. Today, this magnificent long-distance walk, spanning 783km of Spain's north from Roncesvalles, on the border with France, to Santiago de Compostela in Galicia, attracts walkers of all backgrounds and ages, from about 60 countries. No wonder. Its laundry list of assets (culture, history, nature, infrastructure) is impressive, as are its accolades: Europe's Premier Cultural Itinerary and a Unesco World Heritage Site. To feel, absorb, smell and taste northern Spain's diversity, for a great physical challenge, for a unique perspective on rural and urban communities, to meet intriguing companions, as well as for the opportunity to immerse yourself in a continuous outdoor museum, this is an incomparable walk.

HISTORY

In the 9th century a remarkable event occurred in the poor Iberian hinterlands: following a shining star, Pelayo, a religious hermit, unearthed the tomb of the apostle James the Greater (or, in Spanish, Santiago). The news was confirmed by the local bishop, the Asturian king and later the Pope. Its impact is hard to truly imagine today, but it was instant and indelible: first a trickle, then a flood of Christian Europeans began to journey towards the setting sun in search of salvation. Europe and the incipient Spain would never be the same.

In that age, saintly relics were highly valued, traded as commodities and even invented with great vigour to further ecclesiastical and monarchical interests. Relics were believed to have their own will, legally justifying many cases of 'sacred thievery'. To see and, even better, touch a relic was a way to acquire some part of its holiness. The church

Highlights

A long-awaited sight for triumphant walkers – the Catedral de Santiago

- Appreciating warm, animated conversation, intriguing walking companions and welcome rest in simple *albergues* after long days of walking

- Revelling in the solitude on Castilla's flat plain, with the wind combing endless fields of wheat that roll off into distant nothingness

- Admiring the sun filtering through the countless stained-glass windows in León's beautiful cathedral, creating a divine kaleidoscope (p354)

- Completing the epic journey and reaching Santiago's cathedral square after walking 783km in one month

cultivated the value of relics by offering pilgrims indulgences – a remittance of sins committed in this life. Pilgrimage was by parts devotion, thanks and penance as well as an investment for one's future permanent retirement.

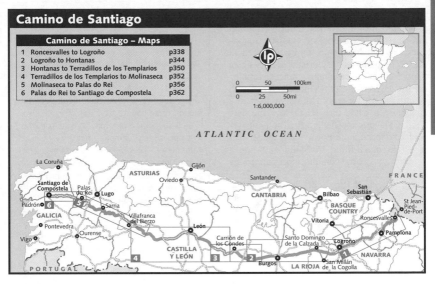

Camino de Santiago

Camino de Santiago – Maps

1	Roncesvalles to Logroño	p338
2	Logroño to Hontanas	p344
3	Hontanas to Terradillos de los Templarios	p350
4	Terradillos de los Templarios to Molinaseca	p352
5	Molinaseca to Palas do Rei	p356
6	Palas do Rei to Santiago de Compostela	p362

0   50   100km
0   25   50mi
1:6,000,000

ATLANTIC OCEAN

Compostela became the most important destination for Christians after Rome and Jerusalem. Its popularity increased with an 11th-century papal decree granting it Holy Year (Año Santo or Año Jacobeo in Spanish, and Xacobeo in Galician) status: pilgrims could receive a plenary indulgence – a full remission of one's lifetime's sins – during a Holy Year. These occur when Santiago's feast day (25 July) falls on a Sunday (which happens at intervals of 6, 5, 6 and then 11

What's in a Name?

All the derivations of 'Santiago' (Sant Iago) can be confusing. The original Latin Iacobus became Jakob in German, James in English, Jacques in French, Jaume in Catalan, Jacopo in Italian, Xacobe in Galician and even Diego (as in San Diego).

The origin of 'Compostela' is another etymological conundrum. Some theorists argue that it means 'starry field' in Latin, referring to the hermit's discovery, while others suggest the more sedate Latin *compostium*, or burial ground.

years): the last Año Santo was in 1999; the next will be in 2004 and 2010.

An obvious question persists: What were the remains of Santiago, martyred in Jerusalem in 44 AD, doing in northwest Iberia? Here, medieval imagination and masterminding take over. The accepted story suggests that two of Santiago's disciples secreted away his remains in a stone boat, set sail in the Mediterranean, passed through the Straits of Gibraltar and moored at present-day Padrón (see the boxed text 'The Scallop Shell', p342). Continuing inland for 17km, they buried his body in a forest named Libredon (present-day Compostela). All was forgotten until Pelayo saw the star.

The story's veracity is irrelevant. The fact that it was believed led to the mass movement of millions of pilgrims; the Camino's birth; the subsequent taming of the Iberian wilderness, unseen since the Roman colonisation; the spread of Romanesque and Gothic art styles (see the boxed text 'Romanesque & Gothic Art & Architecture', p348); and a major influx of settlers and of religious orders that established pilgrims' *hospitales* (wayside guesthouses) and monasteries.

These factors helped to safeguard and re-populate the northern territories gained through the Christian Reconquista (reconquest) of Muslim Spain. Directly linked to the Reconquista as the Christians' holy hero, Santiago made several appearances at major battles as Matamoros (Moor-Slayer). With sword raised, he would descend from the clouds on a white charger to save the day. Santiago is thus apostle, pilgrim (both images are found throughout Europe) and the violent moor-slayer (limited to Spain and South America, where the conquistadors carried his image).

The 11th and 12th centuries marked the pilgrimage's heyday. The Reformation was devastating for Catholic pilgrimages and by the 19th century the Camino nearly died out. In its startling late 20th-century reanimation, which continues today, it's most popular as a personal-cum-spiritual journey of discovery rather than one primarily motivated by religion.

NATURAL HISTORY

Starting in the low western Pyrenees (1057m) of Navarra amid thick, well-maintained deciduous forests (beech, hazel and linden), the Camino drops onto rolling plains. Wild roses, stinging nettles, broom and blackberries appear on the first and nearly every other day. Navarra's rich cultivated fields produce cereals, red wine grapes and white asparagus.

In La Rioja the chalky, clay and alluvial silt soils support vineyards that produce excellent red wines – Spain's best-known abroad. Common riverbank species include black poplar, which is used for paper production, common alder and willow. Wildflowers (best in May and June) include mallow, milfoil, rue, thistles, cornflower and bellflower. Cereal fields are often red with poppies.

The *meseta* (high tableland) dominates the landscapes of Castilla y León (Burgos lies at 860m and León at 829m). Cereal crops roll endlessly and evergreen oaks sparsely shade the plains. North–south river systems (Ríos Carrión, Pisuerga, Cea, Bernesga and Órbigo) cut across the Camino and once made the pilgrimage much more challenging than it is now. The Camino returns to the mountains

Medicinal Plants

The great variety and richness of flora growing beside the way proved crucial for pilgrims and the staff of the hospices. For example, herb robert came in handy for blisters; its crumbled, fresh leaves were mixed with honey and the compound was applied over the wound three times a day.

Dull-sounding common ragwort (or even less appealingly named stinking willy) – its Latin name *(Senecio jacobaea)* proves its connection to the pilgrimage – known in Spanish as *hierba de Santiago*, was fried in oil and then applied between the toes to soothe broken, irritated skin.

Fennel boiled in milk was the equivalent of a modern-day power drink used to counteract low energy. To treat flatulence and indigestion it was boiled in water and drunk after meals. A remedy for sore, inflamed feet – as common among walkers centuries ago as they are today – is a footbath of cool water, vinegar and salt. Many *albergues* keep buckets on hand just for this purpose.

in western León, where Mediterranean aromatic thyme, lavender, rockrose and sage grow by the wayside. In the El Bierzo region, nestled between two mountain systems, cherry trees, red pepper plants and red wine grape vines thrive.

Forests and endless hills return in Galicia: chestnuts, oaks, then pines and, finally, eucalyptuses. The land is perpetually green along the undulating descent to Compostela, the Camino's lowest point (260m). In this rich dairy and farming country, common crops include potato, corn, cabbage and *grelos*, the leafy green that makes the soup *caldo gallego* distinctive. Inheritance practices here led to the continual division of land and its demarcation by unending stone walls and innumerable hamlets, a marked contrast to the *meseta*'s larger, widely scattered settlements.

Birds are the most common visible wildlife. The most obvious is the white stork (see the boxed text 'Storks', p344), found from Navarra to El Bierzo.

CLIMATE

Navarra and La Rioja have wet and blustery springs, hot summers and fairly mild winters, with snow in the higher elevations of Navarra. Castilla y León has relentlessly hot summers and cold, snowy winters. Cold northern winds, off the Cordillera Cantábrica, often sweep the *meseta*. In Galicia, expect rain at any time of year and mild temperatures. People should expect cold conditions and snow from December to May in any of the mountainous areas of Navarra, León and Galicia.

INFORMATION
Maps

The IGN's 1:600,000 *Mapa del Camino de Santiago* is available in the bookshops of the route's major cities.

Books

Countless reams of paper and parchment are dedicated to the Camino. A fascinating text is the 12th-century *Liber Sancti Jacobi* (Book of St James), a five-chapter manuscript detailing the pilgrimage. The fifth chapter is a fascinating guidebook to the way, describing the places, the rivers, the relics and the people encountered (the description of whom gets downright obscene!). It's available in English as *The Pilgrim's Guide to Santiago de Compostela*, translated by William Melczer.

Michael Jacobs' *Northern Spain: The Road to Santiago* is a decent, compact architectural guide. David Gitlitz and Linda Davidson's *The Pilgrimage Road to Santiago: The Complete Cultural Handbook* is an outstanding source of information covering art, architecture, history, folklore, flora and fauna (though not ideal for weighing down your backpack).

Pilgrim Stories: On and Off the Road to Santiago, by Nancy Frey (coauthor of this chapter), brings to life the Camino's present popularity, focusing on individual experiences. Among modern travellers' accounts, try Jack Hitt's *Off the Road* for a hilarious personal account of his 1993 journey, and Lee Hoinacki's *El Camino* for a spiritual perspective.

The **Confraternity of Saint James** (☎ 020-7928 2844; Ⓦ *www.csj.org.uk*; *27 Blackfriars Rd, London, SE1 8NY*) in the UK publishes basic, straightforward guides for walking the pilgrim roads and trails in Spain (and France) including *Camino Francés*, *Camino Mozárabe*, *Los Caminos del Norte*, *Finisterre: Guide for Walkers*, *Madrid to Sahagún*, *Camino Inglés* and the *Camino Portugués*.

Information Sources

Tourist offices along the Camino usually provide free local, regional and Camino-specific brochures. Since the 1980s a number of 'Friends of the Camino' associations have formed worldwide. Many publish members' bulletins, provide information to prospective walkers and even produce their own Pilgrim's Credential, valid along the route.

Australia Amigos del Camino de Santiago, c/o Bill and Lorna Hannan, 20 Shiel St, North Melbourne, VIC 3051
Canada (☎ 416-778 8349, Ⓦ www.santiago.ca) Little Company of Pilgrims of the Way of St James, c/o Barbara Cappuccitti, 138 Langley Ave, Toronto, ON M4K 1B5
UK (☎ 020-7928 2844, Ⓦ www.csj.org.uk) Confraternity of Saint James, 27 Blackfriars Rd, London, SE1 8NY
USA (Ⓔ dgitlitz@aol.com, Ⓦ www.geocities .com/friends_usa_Santiago) Friends of the Road to Santiago, c/o Linda Davidson, 2501 Kingstown Rd, Kingston, RI 02881

Thousands of Camino-related websites cover topics from history to practical advice and personal experiences. Useful sites with many links are Ⓦ www.jacobeo.net and Ⓦ www.xacobeo.es.

Pilgrim's Credential

Most people who walk, even if not religious, carry the Credencial del Peregrino (Pilgrim's Credential/Passport). An accordion-fold document, it gives bearers access to the well-organised system of *albergues* or *refugios* (pilgrims' hostels) along the route – see the boxed text 'Albergues along the Camino Francés' (pp332–4). You can obtain

[Continued on page 335]

Albergues along the Camino Francés

The Camino has an extensive system of pilgrim *albergues* and all stages end at one. Other day-end accommodation options are also listed.

Run by parishes, local governments, Camino associations and private owners, *albergues* or *refugios* generally have bunks without sheets in communal dorms, toilets, showers (sometimes sex-segregated) and kitchens. They maintain opening hours (usually 3pm to 10pm, closed after 8am) and the vast majority do not take reservations. Some rely on pilgrims' donations (denoted by 'D' in this table) to operate while others charge a fee (from €3 to €6). Help with cleaning the facilities is appreciated. Some are staffed by a *hospitalero voluntario* (volunteer attendant) who may spend part of a vacation, or may even work full-time, looking after pilgrims. To stay, present the Credencial to the *hospitalero*.

The following list indicates facilities that provide accommodation for pilgrims walking (or cycling) the route. In July and August local and regional governments frequently make additional facilities (eg, *polideportivos* or gymnasiums) available to walkers. Inquire at the local *albergue*.

Since space is limited in summer, it's common, unfortunately, to encounter a 'refugio race' mentality: getting up very early to reach the next *refugio* and queue up for hours in order to ensure a bed space, instead of enjoying the walk. Resist the rat race.

town	spaces	fee	kitchen	km to next	other
Roncesvalles	76	€7	no	22.6	
Zubiri	22	€3	no	6	
Larrasoaña	37	€5	yes	11	
Arre	33	€3	yes	4.8	
Pamplona (Calle Ansoleaga 2)	20	€4	yes	5	
Cizur Menor (Maribel Roncal)	35	€5	yes	17.7	
Cizur Menor (Orden de Malta)	25	€3	yes	17	open June–15 Sept
Puente la Reina (Padres Reparadores)	72	€3	yes	22.7	
Puente la Reina (Albergue)	54	€6	no	21.7	
Estella	114	€3	yes	9.5	
Villamayor de Monjardín	28	€5	no	13	
Los Arcos (Casa Romero)	30	€6	yes	8.6	
Los Arcos (Municipal)	72	€3	yes	8	
Los Arcos (Casa Alberdi)	20	€8	yes	8	
Torres del Río	36	€6	no	11.2	
Viana	54	€4	yes	9.6	
Logroño	90	€3	yes	13	
Navarrete	40	D	yes	6.4	
Ventosa	30	€6	yes	11.2	
Nájera	56	D	yes	6	
Azofra (Parish)	16	D	yes	15.7	
Azofra (La Fuente)	12	€6	no	15.7	
Santo Domingo de la Calzada (Cofradía)	125	D	yes	7.3	
Santo Domingo de la Calzada (Cofradía)	32	D	yes	7.3	open May–Aug
Grañón	29	D	yes	5	
Redecilla del Camino	44	D	yes	12.2	
Belorado (Parish)	60	D	yes	12	
Belorado (Cuatro Cantones)	20	€7	no	12	

Albergues along the Camino Francés

town	spaces	fee	kitchen	km to next	other
Villafranca Montes de Oca	23	€2	yes	12.6	
San Juan de Ortega	83	D	no	6.5	communal dinner
Atapuerca	20	€4	yes	22	
Burgos	96	D	no	5.5	
Villalbilla	11	D	no	3.5	
Tardajos	12	D	no	2.5	
Rabé de las Calzadas	18	€6	yes	7.8	
Hornillos del Camino	24	€4	yes	6	
Arroyo Sanbol	12	€4	yes	4.8	open May–Oct
Hontanas	50	€3	yes	5.5	
Convento San Antón	16	D	no	4	open June–Sept
Castrojeriz (Resti)	32	D	no	9.3	
Castrojeriz (Municipal)	50	D	no	9.3	
Puente Fitero	12	D	no	1.8	open mid-June–Sept
Itero de la Vega	20	€3	yes	9	
Boadilla del Camino (Maison)	48	€4	no	6	open Apr–mid-Oct
Boadilla del Camino (Municipal)	12	€3	no	6	open July & Aug
Frómista	55	€3	no	3.4	
Población de Campos	16	€3	yes	11.2	
Villalcázar de Sirga	24	D	yes	6.4	
Carrión de los Condes (Santa Clara)	30	€7	yes	17.5	
Carrión de los Condes (Parish)	54	€3	no	17.5	
Calzadilla de la Cueza	100	€4	no	6.2	
Ledigos	50	€4/7	yes	3.2	
Terradillos de los Templarios	30	€4/6	no	13.4	
Sahagún (Municipal)	64	€3	yes	5	
Calzada del Coto	24	D	no	6.2/8.3	distance to Bercianos/ Calzadilla
Calzadilla de los Hermanillos	18	D	yes	27.2	distance to Mansilla de las Mulas
Bercianos del Real Camino	16	D	yes	6.8	
El Burgo Ranero	26	D	yes	11.3	
Reliegos	44	D	yes	6.6	
Mansilla de las Mulas	46	€3	yes	18/17.5	
León (Madres Carbajalas)	44	D	no	21.5/21.8	distance to Villar/ Villadangos
León (Municipal)	64	€3	no	22/22.3	distance to Villar/ Villadangos
Villar de Mazarife (Ramón)	60	D	yes	15	distance to Hospital
Villar de Mazarife (Loli)	14	€6	no	15	distance to Hospital
Villadangos del Páramo	36	€3	yes	3	
San Martín del Camino	60	€3.50	no	8	
Hospital de Órbigo (Parish)	80	D	yes	5	
Hospital de Órbigo (Municipal)	20	€3	yes	5.5	
Santibáñez de Valdeiglesias	26	€3	yes	12	
Astorga (Calle Matías Rodríguez 28)	30	€3	no	5	
Astorga (Plaza de los Marqueses)	106	€3	no	5	
Murias de Rechivaldo	20	€2	no	4.5	

CAMINO DE SANTIAGO

Albergues along the Camino Francés *(continued)*

town	spaces	fee	kitchen	km to next	other
Santa Catalina de Somoza	18	€3	no	4	
El Ganso	16	D	no	7.8	no running water
Rabanal del Camino (Gaucelmo)	57	D	yes	6	open Apr–Oct
Rabanal del Camino (Pilar)	72	€4	yes	6	
Rabanal del Camino (Municipal)	40	€3	no	6	
Foncebadón	20	D	no	4.5	
Manjarín	20	D	yes	7	no running water
El Acebo (Mesón)	38	€4	no	3.6	
El Acebo (Municipal)	10	€2	no	3.6	ask for key in Mesón
Riego de Ambrós	50	€3.50	yes	5.8	
Molinaseca	30	€4	yes	5.4	
Ponferrada	80	D	yes	17.2	
Cacabelos (Hogar Peregrino)	17	D	no	7	ask police for key
Cacabelos (Municipal)	72	€3	no	7	open June–Sept
Villafranca del Bierzo(Ave Fenix)	50	€4	no	5.8	
Villafranca del Bierzo (Municipal)	78	€4	yes	5.8	
Pereje	30	€5	yes	4.4	
Trabadelo	40	€3	yes	6.3	
Vega de Valcarce (Sarracín)	50	€4	no	3.1	
Vega de Valcarce (Municipal)	50	D	yes	2.2	
Ruitelán	34	€3	no	5.3	
La Faba	30	€3	yes	5.3	
Cebreiro	96	D	yes	4.5	
Hospital da Condesa	18	D	no	14.5	
Triacastela (Xunta)	80	D	no	10/13.7	distance to Samos/ Calvor
Triacastela (Aitzenea)	38	€7	yes	9.5/13.2	distance to Samos/ Calvor; open May–Oct
Samos	90	D	no	15.6	distance Samos to Sarria
Calvor	22	D	yes	5	distance Calvor to Sarria
Sarria	40	D	yes	4.7	
Barbadelo	18	D	yes	9.5	
Ferreiros	22	D	yes	9.5	
Portomarín	90	D	yes	8.4	
Gonzar	20	D	yes	4	
Ventas de Narón	22	D	yes	4.7	
Ligonde	18	D	yes	1.3	
Airexe	20	D	yes	7.7	
Palas do Rei	50	D	no	6	
Casanova	20	D	yes	3.7	
Leboreiro	18	D	no	6	
Melide	130	D	yes	11.3	
Ribadiso	62	D	yes	3.2	
Arzúa	60	D	yes	17	
Santa Irene (Xunta)	36	D	yes	2.7	
Santa Irene (Private)	15	€9.10	no	2.7	
Arca	80	D	yes	16.2	
Monte do Gozo	800	D	no	4.5	
Santiago (Belvís)	280	€5	no	1.5	

[Continued from page 331]

the Credencial (which costs €0.25) upon starting in Roncesvalles (see p337) and in major cities along the way: in the Burgos *albergue*; in the León *albergue* of the Madres Carbajalas; in Santiago de Compostela at the **Oficina del Peregrino** (☎ *981 56 24 29;* W *www .archicompostela.org; Rúa do Vilar 1).* Alternatively, contact one of the pilgrim associations abroad (see Information Sources, p331).

The Compostela certificate, obtained from the Oficina del Peregrino in Santiago de Compostela, is proof of completing the journey. To receive the Compostela, the Credencial must be ink-stamped twice each day (eg, in *albergues* or churches) of the walk. It's imperative to complete the last 100km to Santiago de Compostela (a cumulative 100km done piecemeal is not accepted). At the Oficina del Peregrino, you will be asked to affirm that the journey was made for spiritual or religious motives. Iberia Airlines and Spanair offer reduced-price one-way tickets from Santiago de Compostela's international airport to pilgrims who present the Compostela.

Place Names
In Navarra the Spanish and Basque names for settlements appear together, whereas in Galicia local signs and village names are in Gallego. We do the same.

Warning
Dogs are usually leashed and more bark than bite. Nonetheless, some people complain about aggressive, wild dogs and carry a stick for protection.

Guided Walks
On Foot In Spain (☎ *686 99 40 62;* W *www .onfootinspain.com)* runs all-inclusive 12-day cultural walking tours from Roncesvalles to Santiago. **Bravo! Adventures** (☎ *1800 938 9311;* W *www.caminotours.com)* offers 9-day León to Santiago walking tours. For 14-day walking and sightseeing tours of the Camino also try **Saranjan Tours** (☎ *1800 858 9594;* W *www.saranjan.com).*

GATEWAY
Pamplona
Pamplona (Iruña), the capital of Navarra and location of the raucous San Fermín festivals in early July, is an ideal launching point. Its highlights include the cathedral and its museum, Calle Estafeta, where the running of the bulls takes place, and the bars and cafes around Plaza del Castillo. The **tourist office** (☎ *948 20 65 40;* W *www.cfnavarra.es/turis monavarra; Plaza de San Francisco)* has excellent brochures.

Supplies & Equipment On the town's outskirts, **Decathlon**, a sports superstore open from 10am to 10pm daily, is best reached by taxi. In the historical district, try **Basati Kirolak** *(Plaza de Recoletos 5)* for outdoor gear, and for books, **Xalbador** *(Calle Comedias 16).*

Places to Stay & Eat You'll find **Camping Ezcaba** (☎ *948 33 03 15; Eusa-Oiricain; camping per person/tent/car €4/3.55/3)* 5km from Pamplona on the Pamplona–Irún (N121) highway.

Pensión Ascaray (☎ *948 22 78 25; Calle Nueva 24, 1st floor, IZQ; singles/doubles €17/34)* has low-end rooms.

Comfortable **Hostal Bearán** (☎ *948 22 34 28; Calle San Nicolás 25; singles/doubles with bathroom €36/42)* and the upmarket **Hotel Maisonnave** (☎ *948 22 26 00; Calle Nueva 20; singles/doubles with bathroom €63/85)* are very central.

For *pinchos* (finger foods) head to Calles San Nicolás (especially **Bar-Restaurante Baserri**, which also has an outstanding *menú* – fixed-price meal – going for €10) and Estafeta. There's also a vibrant **public market**, open mornings, just off Plaza del Ayuntamiento.

Getting There & Away Regular **Conda** (☎ *948 22 10 26;* W *www.condasa.com)* buses connect Madrid and Pamplona (€20.95, five hours, four daily). To/from Barcelona (€20.85, six hours, four daily) take **Vibasa** (☎ *948 22 09 97;* W *www .vibasa.es)* buses. **ALSA** (☎ *902 42 22 42;* W *www.alsa.es)* runs buses to/from Bilbao

(€10.15, two hours, five daily), Santander (€14.45, four hours, twice daily) and to/from Santiago de Compostela (€41, 11 hours, one daily, transfer in Vitoria).

Trains run between Pamplona and Madrid (€52, 4½ hours, three daily), Barcelona (€28, five hours, three daily), Bilbao (€44, four hours, six daily) and Santander (€37, nine hours, twice daily).

Camino Francés

Duration	30 days
Distance	783km
Difficulty	moderate–demanding
Start	Roncesvalles (p337)
Finish	Santiago de Compostela (p220)
Transport	bus, train

Summary A magnificent route that traverses the north of Spain along back roads, forest tracks and agricultural fields through more than 1000 years of Spanish history, art and culture

There are actually many Caminos de Santiago. Medieval pilgrims simply left home and picked up the closest and safest route to Compostela. Many of these became established in and outside Spain (see Other Pilgrim Walks, p364). We describe the most popular, the Camino Francés, from the Pyrenees to Santiago de Compostela in 30 stages. Walking daily for a month is demanding; schedule at least five weeks to allow for rest days, cultural visits or to break up longer stages. Depending on your pace and goals, the walk is feasible in fewer or more stages.

To divide the route into shorter sections, in two weeks the stretch from León (from Day 14) can be safely entertained. With a week the beautiful Galician portion, beginning in Cebreiro (from Day 24), offers a scenic introduction. The initial week in Navarra, from Roncesvalles to Logroño, in the region of La Rioja, is a true highlight. If you crave solitude and desolation or have never walked in a seemingly horizonless landscape, then try walking from Burgos to Hontanas (Day 11) or Castrojeriz (Day 12).

The distances given here will vary from those in other guidebooks: ours are from *albergue* to *albergue* for consistency and to avoid the frustration of reaching the town gate and realising that the *albergue* is 1km further. All times given are actual walking time and do not include rest stops.

The route regularly passes through villages and cities. In the walk description, settlements are either referred to as having a bar and/or restaurant, or all services, signifying a bar, restaurant, pharmacy, bank, market, shops etc. Potable water is readily available in bars or from treated village fountains. Many restaurants offer an inexpensive *menú del día*, which usually includes three courses, wine or water and bread. All prices given are for high season (usually Easter and July to mid-September).

Trail markers (from bright-yellow painted arrows on trees, rocks and houses, or blue metal signs with stylised yellow shells, to ceramic shells and cement blocks) are frequent and easy to follow, making detailed maps and a compass superfluous. The Camino Francés corresponds to the GR65 long-distance trail throughout Navarra; red-and-white slashes join the yellow arrows. The walk is essentially one-way (east to west) and the yellow arrows reflect that. Local economic interests can influence the yellow arrows' direction through or around villages (for example, unnecessarily passing a particular bar). Sometimes it's necessary to choose between two diverging paths. We describe the best (the most attractive, those with the highlights) and summarise the alternatives.

PLANNING
When to Walk
The walk is feasible year-round, but the best months are May, June, September and October. Spring offers long days and visual splendour – rivers are full, hillsides burst with wildflowers and the *meseta*'s cereal crops sway green. Anticipate some showers and cool mornings. The unbearable heat and crowds of July and August diminish by September and October, and shades of brown dominate the landscapes. Be prepared to encounter snow at higher elevations and on

the *meseta* any time from November to early May.

July is Santiago de Compostela's month of celebration. The 25th is the Feast of Santiago and Galicia's 'national' day. The night before, Praza do Obradoiro comes alight with Os Fogos do Apóstolo, a spectacular light, music and fireworks show that dates back to the 17th century and culminates in a mock burning of the Mudéjar (an Islamic-influenced style of the 12th and 13th centuries) facade to commemorate the city's razing by Muslims in 997. The town authorities organise processions, numerous concerts, notably in Praza da Quintana, and other cultural activities.

What to Bring

Many people, expecting hardship, carry too much. All supplies are readily available in towns and villages. A sleeping bag, though, is essential. Some *albergues* have coin-operated washing machines.

Walkers frequently suffer blisters (*ampollas* in Spanish) and various pains (knee, back or tendons). Pharmacies stock necessary supplies, but bring any favourite remedy. Stiff, alpine walking boots are not recommended. The variety of surfaces and long stretches of gently rolling terrain require more flexible, all-round, sturdy walking shoes or boots.

NEAREST TOWNS

See Santiago de Compostela (p220).

Roncesvalles

Nestled quietly in the woods, Roncesvalles (Orreaga; 960m) is one of the pilgrimage's oldest way stations and is linked to the great medieval epic *The Song of Roland*. Roland, Charlemagne's most loyal knight, and the rearguard were ambushed and killed here while returning to 8th-century France through the Pyrenees. Worth a visit are the Royal Pantheon containing the remains of Navarra's 13th-century King Sancho El Fuerte (the Strong), the 14th-century cloister, the museum and the Silo of Charlemagne. In the restored Gothic church a 12th-century pilgrims' blessing is read at the 8pm (6pm on Saturday and Sunday)

mass. There is also a **tourist office** (☎ 948 76 03 01).

People beginning in Roncesvalles often arrive a day ahead and get the Credencial (€1) at the **Oficina del Peregrino** (☎ 948 76 00 00) below the arch at the entrance to the monastery. After it opens at 4pm, the attendant requests statistical information and then explains the **albergue**. During our research the *albergue* was closed for renovations and due to reopen in 2004. In the meantime, the **Albergue Juvenil** (☎ 948 76 03 02; *dorm beds* €7) in the cloister left of the church fills the gap. **La Posada** (☎ 948 76 02 25; *singles/doubles with bathroom* €36/45; *closed Nov*) and **Casa Sabina** (☎ 948 76 00 12; *doubles with bathroom* €42) provide additional accommodation. Both offer a €6 pilgrims' *menú* when you present the Credencial, pay and reserve ahead.

Getting There & Away From Pamplona **La Montañesa** (☎ 948 22 15 84) runs buses to Roncesvalles (€3.90, 1½ hours, one daily Monday to Saturday). Taxis from Pamplona's Plaza del Castillo to Roncesvalles cost €40. By car from Pamplona, take the N135 (towards France) to reach Roncesvalles at the 47.6km post.

GETTING TO/FROM THE WALK

You can reach all the cities of the Camino using buses or with **Renfe** (☎ 902 24 02 02; [w] *www.renfe.es*) trains from Madrid and Barcelona.

THE WALK
Day 1: Roncesvalles to Zubiri

6–7 hours, 22.6km

Walk 100m down the N135 (towards Pamplona), cross and enter a tree-lined path for 15 minutes. Where the forest opens, veer left, continuing to the N135 and Burguete (Auritz; all services), famous for its white *caseríos* (farmhouses) with red shutters and as Hemingway's trout-fishing getaway in *The Sun Also Rises*. From the plaza, dominated by the San Nicolás de Bari church, continue 100m and turn right down a dirt road leaving Burguete. Cross the stream over a wooden bridge to a wide, paved then

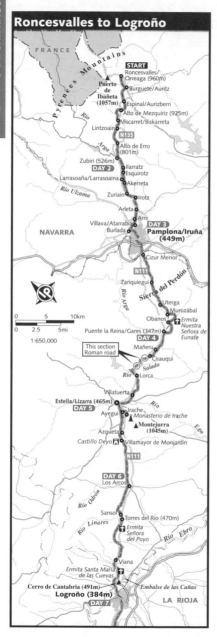

dirt lane through pastures to a gate and stream. Cross this and then another stream soon thereafter. The path rolls through woods (hawthorn is abundant) making a 10-minute ascent. Descend 1.5km to Espinal (Aurizberri; all services), a picturesque hamlet founded in 1269.

Turn left and, just past mid-village and a curious fountain (potable water), left again onto an ascending paved road which 400m later converts to dirt. Fork right onto a dirt trail, soon entering a spruce and then a beech wood. Climb the wooden stairs and turn right 90 degrees, enjoying great field and valley views (left). Descend to the N135 at the Alto de Mezquíriz (925m), cross and continue straight ahead.

Viscarret (Biskarreta; with fountain) is 3km from here. The rocky trail descends steeply through a beech wood and parallel to the N135, opening to it after 1.5km. Continue 20m along the road and turn right up a boxwood-enveloped trail that leads to a paved road and Viscarret.

Walk through Viscarret, over the N135, and then turn left down an imitation-stone path that converts to dirt after 400m. At the N135, cross onto a dirt path that leads to Lintzoain. Note the *frontón*, a court on which *pelota vasca* (or *jai alai* in Basque) – a type of handball popular in Navarra and the Basque Country (País Vasco, known as Euskadi or Euskal Herri to the Basque people) – is played. Past the fountain (a long trough), turn right up a street that becomes a 5km undulating path through pine, oak, box, and beech to the **Alto de Erro** (801m). Cross the highway and continue descending on the forest and dirt path (passing the crumbling Venta del Puerto, once an inn for pilgrims and now a cow stable) to Zubiri (526m). Enter across the **Puente de la Rabia**, so nicknamed because livestock were circled three times around the central pillar to cure rabies. The magnesite factory, clearly visible on descent, sustains the local economy. To reach the **albergue** continue to the main road (aka Avenida Roncesvalles), passing the church and a fountain. Cross the road, turn right and in 175m reach the nondescript building on the left.

Zubiri

Immaculate **Pensión Goikoa** (☎ 948 30 40 67; Avenida Roncesvalles 8; singles/doubles €23/26) and **Hostería de Zubiri** (☎ 948 30 43 29; Avenida Roncesvalles 6; singles/doubles with bathroom from €44/55) have comfortable rooms. **Gau Txori** (☎ 948 30 40 76; Avenida de Roncesvalles, Km 21; menú €9) next to the petrol station has meals and rooms. Zubiri has a small **market**.

Day 2: Zubiri to Pamplona

5½–6½ hours, 21.3km

Cross back over Zubiri's bridge and turn right up a cement lane. After 150m the trail converts to dirt and rolls for 1km to a sealed road. Veer left, ascending the road for 500m, and continue along this unpleasant section, above the factory, before descending to the right on a trail. The winding footpath passes two hamlets – Ilarraz and Esquirotz (fountain) – before reaching **Larrasoaña**, which has a **bar-restaurant**, fountain and **albergue**.

To continue, head left towards Akerreta. The path narrows through a pine and oak forest, slowly approaching the Río Arga. Cross it at Zuriain (with fountain). Turn left at the N135 and continue for 600m. Turn left down a paved road towards Ilurdotz. Cross the bridge and turn right onto a dirt path that leads to an abandoned mine. The trail turns right, ascending to Irotz (with fountain) and then the hamlet of Zabaldika straddling the N135. Turn left onto the N135 and cross at a picnic spot (with fountain and toilet). The path ascends and skirts the hillside – passing a restored house – to the highway (Carretera de Irún). Cross via a tunnel and turn right up the road that winds down to the Río Ultzama, an Arga tributary. Cross the **Romanesque bridge** to Trinidad de Arre (currently a boys' seminary) **monastery** with **albergue**. Continue left.

The Camino makes a beeline through Villava (Atarrabia; home town of five-times Tour de France winner Miguel Indurain), first along the Calle Mayor and then the Avenida de Serapio Huici for 2km to Burlada's Calle Mayor. Near the end of Burlada, by Talleres Garysa, turn right onto a pedestrian crossing over the Francia–Irún highway. Continue

along the acacia-lined footpath and then a narrow road to the 14th-century Magdalena bridge. A modern *cruceiro* (cross), dedicated to Santiago, marks the foot of the bridge. Cross and veer right through the park, circling briefly below the city's ramparts before ascending to Pamplona's impressive, stone-gated northern entrance, the **Portal de Francia**. The way through the old quarter is well marked with blue-and-yellow trail markers. Take Calle del Carmen, turning right onto Calle de Mercaderes. Fork right onto the Antigua Rúa del Mentidero to the Plaza Consistorial (town hall). Just beyond is the **San Saturnino** (also San Cernín) church and **albergue** (see also Pamplona, pp355–6).

Day 3: Pamplona to Puente la Reina

6–7½ hours, 27.9km

The described route goes via Eunate; to reduce the walk by 3.5km take the Alternative Route (see p340) once you reach Muruzábal.

With San Saturnino church on the left continue straight, then fork left onto Calle Mayor. Continue on Calle Bosquecillo to Avenida Navas de Tolosa. Cross the city park along a stone path skirting the 16th-century defensive Ciudadela. Turn hard right and cross Calle Vuelta del Castillo and Avenida Sancho el Fuerte to Calle Fuente de Hierro, descending past the Universidad de Navarra. Reaching a T-junction, turn right and cross the wooden footbridge.

Continue 4.8km to Cizur Menor, with a **bar-restaurant**. Up the hill to the right is the **albergue** and the Romanesque **Iglesia de San Miguel**. Continue straight through the village crossroads and then veer right (a medieval fountain is on the left) onto a footpath past a *frontón* and through a housing development. Reaching a sealed road, head right and after 700m, turn hard left onto a trail through wheat fields.

Aim for windmill-studded Sierra del Perdón, 8.5km ahead. The trail becomes a lane and in 4.6km reaches Zariquiegui (with fountain) and a Romanesque church. En route, hilltop Galar village (left) and the ruins of Guendulain (right) are visible. The more pronounced ascent of the sierra begins. Near the summit the dry **Fuente Reniega** (Renounce-ment Fountain) is part of a pilgrim legend. The Devil tempted a dehydrated pilgrim to renounce his faith in exchange for water. He refused and in return Santiago appeared and led him to a spring. At the **summit** (780m), a wind-power company has mounted a sculpture depicting medieval pilgrims and saying: 'Where the Way of the Stars and the Way of the Wind meet'. The phrase refers to the ancient linking of the Milky Way (*vía láctea* in Spanish) with the Camino, as they roughly parallel. According to legend, Charlemagne was the first pilgrim to Compostela; he found his way by following the Milky Way.

The next 10km are laid out in a sweeping westward view. Cross the road and descend the initially steep, loose-stone path through an oak and boxwood forest. Continue through rolling fields to Uterga (with fountain). Exit the village heading left on a downhill dirt path. At the bottom, take a path to the right, passing cultivated fields, almond trees and vineyards to Muruzábal, with fountain and **bar**.

From the small plaza, turn left past a 16th-century palace. Descend out of town along a sealed then dirt road for 2.5km to the highway and the octagonal, 12th-century, Romanesque **Ermita Nuestra Señora de Eunate** (with fountain). Possibly a Knights Templar construction (See the boxed text 'Knights Templar', p358), it was also a pilgrims' cemetery.

Cross the car park to the picnic area and take a dirt path for 800m to the highway. Either continue 1.4km along the road or cross the highway (recommended), reaching Puente la Reina via Obanos in 3km, ascending to the cemetery and then descending back to the highway. Cross and in 2.1km reach Puente la Reina (347m) at the convent and Iglesia de Crucifijo (both on the left) and the **albergue Padres Reparadores** (right).

Alternative Route: Via Obanos
1–1½ hours, 4.3km
Leave Muruzábal along the main road and turn right on a descending path for 1km to Obanos (with fountain and all services). Obanos' fame resides in the legend of

fratricide between two saints, Felicia and Guillermo. The Iglesia San Juan Bautista houses the ghoulish relic of Guillermo (his cranium covered in silver) in the sacristy. Pass under the arch to the left of the church and descend (right) to Puente la Reina. On the N111 a modern pilgrim statue marks the historic junction of the Camino Francés and Camino Aragonés.

Puente la Reina
An example of a *sirga* (one-street village), Puente la Reina is famous for its magnificent 11th-century **bridge** spanning the Río Arga, sponsored by, most likely, Doña Mayor (wife of the Navarran king Sancho III, El Grande). The diamond-shaped pillars strengthen the bridge by reducing resistance.

The second **albergue** is at the end of the bridge. On Calle Mayor, along with the **Iglesia de Santiago**, you'll find the charming **Hotel Bidean** (*☎ 948 34 11 56; Calle Mayor 20; doubles with bathroom €51*), the fine restaurant **Lorca** (*Calle Mayor 54; menú €9.65*), **Bar-Restaurante Joaquín** (*Calle Mayor 50; menú €8*), and several small **markets**.

Day 4: Puente la Reina to Estella
5–6 hours, 22.7km
Walk through Puente la Reina, cross the bridge and turn left for 100m. Cross the highway and turn right onto a dirt path that narrows to an ascending trail. Snake up the embankment to the summit where Mañeru's church steeple appears. Continue to Mañeru (with fountain), crossing through the village and exiting via Calle Forzosa. Soon you'll pass the cemetery, hemmed in with white walls and planted with cypress. Cemeteries in this region (and, later, in Castilla y León) are on the outskirts of town, in contrast to Galicia, where they are in the churchyards.

Passing between vineyards, cereals and olive trees, the dirt trail winds pleasantly for 2.7km to the compact and labyrinthine **Cirauqui** (a Basque word meaning 'nest of vipers'). The village retains some medieval walls, the arched portal, a hub-shaped urban plan and the **Iglesia de San Román** – justifiably famous for its 13th-century lobed-arch

Mudéjar portal. At the columned plaza, deviate from the arrows and turn right to ascend to the church. The fountain is by the church's main door. Descend steeply left from the church plaza, turning sharply right once out of the village.

Cypress trees flank the impressive stretch of nearly 2000-year-old **calzada romana** (stone-paved Roman road) that descends over a **Roman bridge** and up to the N111. Cross the highway. Turn left onto a dirt road that descends to a medieval bridge and continues nearly 2km along the Roman *calzada* to the N111 again. Turn right onto a smaller, sealed road passing under a modern aqueduct to the Río Salado. The 12th-century *Pilgrim's Guide* narrates a grim story: Several Frankish pilgrims, arriving at the river bank, asked two Navarrese men sharpening their knives on the other side if the water was safe for their horses. They assented. The Frankish horses drank deeply and collapsed, dead, and the knife-wielders had fresh horse skins. The Franks were not in a position to argue. Cross the bridge and ascend to Lorca (with fountain).

Villatuerta (with fountain) lies 4km away along paths through cereal fields and plastic-covered rows of white asparagus. Pass Villatuerta's church and take the main street to the road. Cross and keep straight along a dirt path running parallel to the N111 and passing the Ermita de San Miguel. Descend along stairs to a picnic area, cross the road and take a sinuous trail to the Río Ega, crossed via a wooden bridge. After 1km of lane, head right along a cement road that reaches Estella (Lizarra; 465m) and the **albergue** on Rúa Curtidores in 1km.

Estella

Continue down Curtidores to the tourist office, housed in the Camino's finest example of Romanesque civil architecture. The Romanesque cloister of the **Iglesia de San Pedro de la Rúa** (opposite the tourist office) and the Romanesque portal of the **Iglesia de San Miguel** are must-stops.

Both **Pensión San Andrés** (☎ 948 55 41 58; Plaza de Santiago 1; singles/doubles/ triples/quads per person from €12) and near-

by **Hostal Izarra** (☎ 948 55 06 78; Calderería 20; doubles €24) offer simple, clean rooms, and food (menú €7.85). For a meal, try the Izarra or **Restaurante Casanova** (Wenceslao de Oñate 8; menú €8.40).

Day 5: Estella to Los Arcos
5½–6 hours, 22.4km

Carry plenty of water for the long stretch between Villamayor and Los Arcos. Leave Estella via Rúa Curtidores and Calle San Nicolás. After the second roundabout and petrol station, ascend right onto a dirt road. After 1.2km either fork left (recommended) to Azqueta via the 12th-century Monasterio de Irache, or veer right downhill directly to Azqueta (via Hotel Irache).

To pass the monastery, fork left downhill, cross the highway and ascend a lane to the ingenious red wine and water fountain installed by Bodegas Irache (the adjacent winery) in 1991. Continue past the monastery, following the stone wall to a fork (a longer route continues straight along the base of 1045m-high Montejurra to Luquín). Turn right, cross the highway and head left passing behind **Hotel Irache**. As you walk past a housing development, castle-topped **Monjardín** (894m) fills the western sky. Continue 3.2km to Azqueta, first through oak forest and then turning sharply left uphill, bordering cereal fields. Azqueta's fountain is in the tiny plaza. Pablito, famous for giving pilgrims staffs of hazel wood (chosen because it is both strong and flexible), lives in the last house on the right side of Azqueta's first street on the right.

Leaving the village, veer right down a dirt lane and circle a cow stable. The route gently climbs to the base of Monjardín, passing the restored 13th-century Fuente de los Moros (questionably potable water) below the ruins of the Roman-based Castillo de Deyo. Continue to the quiet village of Villamayor, which has an **albergue**, fountain and **bar-restaurant**. Head off left downhill through red-soil vineyards to an agricultural track. Reach Los Arcos in 12km through wheat and asparagus fields and an odd series of rounded hills studded with conifers. Los Arcos (444m) suddenly

The Scallop Shell

An important symbol since at least the 11th century, the scallop shell appears on a backpack, hat or tunic in nearly all images of Santiago or his followers from the 12th century onwards. The symbol's origin remains a mystery. The most colourful legend explains that when the martyred James arrived on the Galician coast in his stone boat a pagan wedding almost turned to disaster when the bridegroom and his horse crashed into the sea (upon seeing the strange sight) and began to drown. James demonstrated his goodwill by saving them from the waves; when they arose, scallop shells covered their bodies.

The Roman *Finis terrae* (end of the earth), today Fisterra, lies 90km west of Santiago and was the site of an important sun cult; souls were believed to live on an island somewhere beyond. *Finis terrae* became a popular post-Santiago destination for pilgrims. Roman influence also left a Venus cult; its prime symbol was the scallop shell. The scallop served as a talisman against evil as well as a symbol of fertility, rebirth and rejuvenation. Most likely these pre-existing pagan beliefs became fused with the Santiago pilgrimage, and the shell, with its rich symbology and abundance on the coast, was quickly incorporated. Originally, it was only worn by pilgrims after reaching Santiago. Today, most people wear it from the start.

appears. Enter the village and continue straight ahead, passing **albergue Romero**, then turn right to the main square, dominated by the **Iglesia de Santa María**. Pass under the only remaining arch and cross the road to the **albergue municipal** (on the right) and **albergue Alberdi** (left).

Los Arcos

Weathered **Hostal Ezequiel** (☎ *948 64 02 96; Ruta Bilbao-Zaragoza, Km 9; singles/doubles per person from €18)*, just out of town, and centrally located **Hotel y Restaurante Mónaco** (☎ *948 64 00 00; Plaza de Coso; doubles €24)*, renovated in 2002, offer lodging. **Suetxe**, known locally as La Sidrería, does

the best local food. It's on a small, unnamed street just off the main road, Avenida Sancho El Sabio, to the right. There are several small **markets** off the main plaza.

Day 6: Los Arcos to Logroño
7½–9 hours, 28.8km

From the *albergue municipal*, turn right onto a dirt road, passing the cemetery on your right. A macabre statement etched in the archway reads: 'I was what you are. You will be what I am.' A mostly flat and straight 6.7km remain to Sansol. After 3.7km, near a hut, veer right onto a marked dirt road that continues left to a sealed road. Sansol is clearly visible. Turn left onto the road and in 1.3km reach Sansol. The yellow arrows zigzag through the streets without ascending to the church. Outstanding panoramic views of Torres del Río below make the effort to ascend worthwhile.

Descend out of town and cross the highway (at a dangerous blind curve!) to a descending footpath. The water from the fountain at the bottom is not potable. A steep ascent through Torres' streets leads to the **Iglesia de Santo Sepulcro**, another 12th-century octagonal masterwork linked to the Knights Templar. At the time of our research, Torres had an **albergue** which served meals (from €8.30). The owners, however, were hoping to leave, and its future was in doubt.

Leave Torres, heading straight up from the church to its highest point, and exit past the cemetery. The rural road runs parallel to the highway and then crosses it, ascending left along a path to the **Ermita Señora del Poyo**, where the Virgin of Le Puy appeared, leaving behind a statue which refused to be moved – thus the chapel.

Over the next kilometres pay careful attention to the arrows. Descend to the road and continue along it briefly before turning right onto a footpath. After 600m the footpath reaches a road. Turn left on the road and briefly continue before veering onto a clay road. Immediately fork right (it's unmarked). Viana's bell tower is visible on the horizon. Descend through the Barranco Mataburros (literally, 'donkey-killing ditch') following the graded lane to the highway.

Cross and ascend on a dirt trail. Viana's church appears, still 3km away.

At the foot of this historic frontier town, the trail crosses the highway and ascends to the **Plaza de los Fueros**. Here you'll find a fountain, all services and an **albergue**. The adjacent **Iglesia de Santa María**, with its concave Renaissance portal and soaring Gothic interior, is especially interesting.

Logroño lies 9km from Viana, but is partially hidden behind a flan-shaped hill (Cerro de Cantabria, with pre-Roman, Roman and medieval remains). Leave Viana, skirting the ruins of **Iglesia de San Pedro**, and walk down past apartments. Follow several well-marked zigzags out of Viana through a housing development and veer left with the arrows onto a path through gardens. Cross a sealed road and then walk parallel to the N111 (towards Logroño). Cross and turn left onto a sealed road that reaches the Ermita Santa María de las Cuevas. Continue on a dirt road past the Embalse de las Cañas. Head right up to and cross the highway, continuing to a crossroads at the Navarra-La Rioja border. Take the red asphalt trail (passing under two tunnels) around the Cerro de Cantabria's north side, finally reaching Logroño's cemetery. Enter the city over the Río Ebro via the **Puente de Piedra**. The first street to the right, Rúa Vieja, leads to the **albergue** in 200m.

Logroño

The capital of the major wine-producing region of La Rioja, Logroño (384m) has long been a strategic and hotly contested city along the pilgrims' way. Just 18km south of town is Clavijo, the legendary site of Santiago's first appearance as Matamoros. The facade of the **Iglesia de Santiago** has an excellent Matamoros image. The city has a population of 135,000, many of whom are immigrants who have settled here and continue to do backbreaking agricultural work. The **tourist office** (☎ 941 29 12 60; Paseo del Espolón; open daily) has excellent city and regional information.

The recently renovated **Hostal-Residencia Numantina** (☎ 941 25 14 11; Calle Sagasta 4; singles/doubles with bathroom €28/43) and the clean but aged **Fonda Bilbaína** (☎ 941 25

42 26; Calle Capitán Gallarza 10, 1st floor; doubles from €21) are in the historical quarter. For mouthwatering pinchos, head to Calle Laurel in the historical quarter. **Café Moderno** (Plaza Carnicería) does good set meals for €8.

Day 7: Logroño to Nájera

7½–9 hours, 30km
Six kilometres of cement start the day. Follow the paving-stone scallops through the cobbled old quarter along the Rúa Vieja past the pilgrim's fountain in the Plaza de Santiago to Calle Barriocepo. Where it ends turn right to exit via the remnant of the city's medieval walls. Cross the car park and continue round the Plaza Alférez Provisional to the long Calle Marqués de Murrieta. Reaching two petrol stations (on either side of the road), turn left onto Calle Entrena, passing an industrial zone, and continue through a tunnel below the highway. Continue 2.4km along a flat cement footpath to the agreeable surprise of the Embalse de la Grajera reservoir.

Circling to the right, the trail ascends through vineyards to a sawmill. The large billboard bull on the hill once advertised Osborne sherry. Turn left along the highway for 300m and then cross it, descending along a path that affords views of hilltop Navarrete. Make a beeline to the village via an overpass and past the 12th-century ruins of Hospital de San Juan de Acre. One of its portals now serves as Navarrete's cemetery door on the other side of town.

Navarrete has all services and an **albergue**. Wrapped liked a blanket round the hill, Navarrete retains its medieval character with its cobbled, narrow streets and labyrinthine layout. Alfarerías, pottery shops, where the area's red clay soil is worked, have been fundamental to the local economy since Roman times. The magnificent Baroque altarpiece of the **Iglesia de la Asunción** merits a stop.

There are no fountains or villages in the next 16km to Nájera. Follow the trail markers out of Navarrete down to the N120 (towards Burgos). Follow the N120 for 500m to the cemetery. The dirt trail runs parallel to the N120 for 300m until the path veers left through vineyards, olives and fruit trees,

Logroño to Hontanas

BURGOS

See Hontanas to Terradillos
de los Templarios Map p350

Montes de Oca

N1

San Juan
de Ortega
(1000m)

DAY 11

Alto de la
Pedraja
(1150m)

Orbaneja Atapuerca Agés
Villafría Villalval
Cardeñuela

Mostelares
(900m) DAY 13 Tardajos
Hontanas Hornillos del Rabé de las Villalbilla
(930m) Camino Calzadas Castañares N120
Itero
de la
Vega Ermita de
San Nicolás Sanbol Burgos
(860m)
Castrojeriz Convento de
San Antón DAY 12 Río Arlanzón

reaching a sealed road at the Vitivinícola de Sotes building. Turn left, descending along the road to the N120. Take the dirt trail parallel to the highway for 1.5km to a fork. Either continue straight (recommended) or turn left and make a 500m detour through Ventosa (with **albergue** and fountain).

From the fork continue 2.5km to where cairns mark the initially rocky ascent to the Alto de San Antón (670m), offering great views of Nájera, still 7.5km away. The track descends, crosses the highway, and skirts round two telecommunications antennae and a gravel works. Cross a footbridge and continue to Nájera (485m). Cross the Río Najerilla and enter the old quarter, built directly into the huge, red walls rising behind the town. Parallel to both the river and the

wall is the fascinating Benedictine **Monasterio de Santa María la Real**; adjacent to it, on the right, is the **albergue**.

Nájera

There are attractive, quiet rooms at **Hostal Hispano** (☎ 941 36 36 15; *Calle La Cepa 2; singles/doubles with bathroom €24/34*), before you cross the river. Ask for rooms in the adjacent **Bar-Restaurante Hispano** (*Paseo San Julián*), which has great meals for €9. Or try renovated **Hotel San Fernando** (☎ 941 36 37 00; *Plaza San Julián; singles/doubles €27/48*). Near the *albergue*, you can eat well and economically at both **Mesón La Amistad** (*Calle La Cruz 6; menú €7.50*) and **La Judería** (*Calle Constantino Garrán 13; menú €8.50*). There are small **markets** in the old town.

Day 8: Nájera to Santo Domingo de la Calzada
4½–5½ hours, 21.6km

Follow the road that curves round the monastery (right) and continues uphill (10 minutes) on first a sealed road, then a red dirt road flanked by pines and cliffs. Descending through a ravine, the way flattens past vineyards to a sealed road and continues 5km to Azofra, which has a fountain, two **albergues** and all services.

Leave Azofra down the main street to the road. Turn right and after 100m turn left onto a dirt lane passing a large *rollo* (a medieval juridical pillar used to hang villains) converted into a cross. Climbing a small hill, the lane descends close to the N120, turns left and then parallels the highway to a sealed

Storks

In spring and summer you'll inevitably see and hear the elegant *cigüeña* or European white stork, which, after passing the winter in North Africa, flies to the Iberian Peninsula to reproduce. White storks almost always settle near human populations, in contrast to their shy black relatives, which hide in the woods. They construct or reinhabit huge, complex nests perched in high places, such as water pumps, telephone poles or chimneys. Church bell-towers are a preferred nesting site and a single tower is sometimes crowded with three or four heavy nests. The distinctive chatter of clapping beaks is frequently heard.

Logroño to Hontanas

road. Cross the sealed road to pick up the dirt lane again. For 700m the path cuts across wheat fields rolling away on either side and then ascends. At the top, the trail flattens to Cirueña (with fountain). A golf course is under construction. Entering the village, take the main road to the right; in 150m, with hops to the right, the path turns left and undulates for 6km to Santo Domingo de la Calzada. At the main highway, turn left along the footpath, entering the historical quarter along Calle Mayor, which houses both **albergues**.

Santo Domingo de la Calzada

The founder of the town, Santo Domingo (1019–1109), was a religious hermit who lived on the banks of the Río Oja when it was still wild woodland. Rejected by the local monastery due to his humble origins, he worked independently, constructing a church and pilgrims' *hospital* – now a *parador* (state-run luxury hotel) – and built bridges and highways from Logroño to Burgos. A bizarre legend makes the village and the saint famous (see the boxed text 'Of Saints & Chickens').

Just outside the old town, **Hostal Miguel** (☎ 941 34 32 52; Avenida Juan Carlos I 23; singles/doubles/triples/quads per person from €18) has impeccable rooms. **Hostal El Río** (☎ 941 34 02 77; Calle Alberto Etchegoyen 2; singles/doubles €15/24) offers simple, worn lodgings, as well as meals (*menú* €7). There are numerous small **markets**, and you'll find a good evening meal at **Mesón del Abuelo** (Plaza Alameda; menú €7.75) or **Restaurante La Taberna** (Calle Mayor 54; menú €7.60).

Of Saints & Chickens

As you enter Santo Domingo de la Calzada cathedral's south door, you'll see a pair of live white chickens (exchanged for a fresh pair every 15 days) that are kept in an elevated chicken coop on the western wall. This odd custom traces back to the famed miracle of Santo Domingo. A young pilgrim, travelling with his parents to Santiago, was accused of pilfering silver from a local tavern. In reality the barmaid, her amorous advances rejected, had angrily slipped the silver into his knapsack and notified the authorities. To his parents' horror, the pilgrim was strung up on the gallows. Praying, they continued to Santiago and then returned. Surprisingly, rather than encounter his decomposing body, they found him well – yet still hanging, with the saint supporting his feet. They ran to the judge who, having just sat down to eat roast chicken, refused to be bothered. When the pilgrims insisted, the judge exclaimed that if their son were innocent the chickens would rise from his plate and crow. And they did, giving the town its motto: 'Donde la gallina cantó después de asada' (Where the hen crowed after being roasted).

In the cathedral it's considered good luck to find a chicken feather or to hear them crowing; five chicks were born inside the elegant henhouse in 2001. Look also for the wooden fragment of the gallows hanging on the wall above the south transept and, in town, don't miss the 'hanged pilgrim' pastries found in many bakeries.

Day 9: Santo Domingo de la Calzada to Belorado

5½–6½ hours, 23.4km

Entering Burgos province within Castilla y León, the way rolls through valleys surrounded by high tablelands. Continue straight along Calle Mayor to the N120. Cross the Río Oja (giving La Rioja its name) using Domingo's refitted bridge. Take a path right and in 1.3km return to the N120 and cross to a dirt road parallel to the N120 on its left. Continue 2.5km to a fork. Either go left on a dirt lane (recommended), reaching Grañón's back door in 2.3km (a sign indicates 3.2km but that distance includes an unnecessary detour), or continue straight for 1.9km along the dangerous N120.

After 1.5km of gentle ascent along the lane, a sign suggests two ways to enter Grañón (with fountain and **bar**). Ignore the long right-hand option and continue straight on, passing the cemetery before reaching Grañón's highest point. To enter the village, turn right down its main street. Once fully walled, it had two monasteries and a pilgrims' *hospital*. The restored main altar of the **Iglesia de San Juan Bautista** is a masterpiece of 16th-century Renaissance art. Find the curious **albergue**, built into the church's southern wall; pilgrims wash laundry on top of the vault!

From the high point continue straight, cross a sealed road and then pass between the *frontón* and the fountain, leaving the village on a dirt track for 350m (turn right at the T-junction, then immediately left). Reaching a farm, head right, cross the bridge and then turn left on the second dirt road. In 2.7km reach Redecilla. En route a sign marks the border between La Rioja and Castilla y León. Redecilla, straddling the highway, has a fountain, **albergue** and **bar-restaurant**. Cross the N120 and turn left through the village. The **Iglesia Virgen de la Calle** contains an exceptional Romanesque baptismal font resting on eight columns.

At Calle Mayor's far end, take a dirt road that parallels the N120's left side, detouring to Castildelgado (with fountain). Continue on the sealed road to Viloria (the fountain's water is not potable) and then Villamayor

del Río (with a fountain). At the entrance to Belorado (770m), cross the highway and enter along the dirt path which veers right, below the cliffs, past the **parish albergue** and nearby Iglesia Santa María. The other **albergue** is off the main plaza.

Belorado

Filling the Río Tirón valley, Belorado's southern cliffs and caves once housed medieval hermits – including San Caprasio, who is venerated in the Iglesia San Nicolás. Iglesia San Pedro is off the circular Plaza Mayor, where all services are available.

Try comfortable **Camas Toñi** (☎ 947 58 05 25; Calle Redecilla 7, 1st floor; singles/doubles with bathroom €18/33) or, at the far end of town, **Hotel Belorado** (☎ 947 58 06 84; Avenida Generalísimo 34; singles/doubles with bathroom €21/36; menú €7.50). Meals at **Etoile** (Plaza Mayor 6; menú €7) are the best on the plaza. There's a **market** several doors right of Etoile.

Day 10: Belorado to San Juan de Ortega

7–8 hours, 24.8km

Get supplies in Villafranca Montes de Oca as San Juan de Ortega has no shop. Descend across the Plaza Mayor and turn left onto Calle Hipólito Bernal and continue along Avenida Camino de Santiago. Leave Belorado, following the convent wall to the N120. Cross the road and the Río Tirón along a wooden footbridge. Follow a dirt trail parallel to the N120. After passing the petrol station, cross the highway and pick up the dirt trail which leads to Tosantos (with fountain) in 5km. Nuestra Señora de la Peña, the eye-catching church excavated into the hill on the right just before reaching Tosantos, contains another miraculous Romanesque image. In less than 2km the trail reaches deserted-looking Villambistia (with fountain). Typical of rural Castilla y León, these are adobe villages. Follow the trail markers to the highway and Espinosa del Camino (with fountain).

Leave the tranquil village along a dirt road. En route an overgrown pile of rocks on the right are the vestiges of **San Felices** – a great

9th-century Mozarabic monastery (Mozarabic design incorporated Arabic elements or techniques into Christian structures and was pre-Romanesque). Continue to the highway and turn right to Villafranca Montes de Oca, which has a fountain, **bar-restaurant** and **albergue**. This 'Village of Franks' is named after the traders, artisans and settlers who took advantage of the reduced taxes and privileges offered by monarchs to repopulate Muslim territories gained during the Reconquista.

Leave Villafranca (948m) by walking right (and steeply upwards) behind the **Iglesia de Santiago**, and for 12km wind through the desolate **Montes de Oca** among oaks and conifers to San Juan (1000m). The only fountain en route, **Fuente Mojapán**, is 1.5km from Villafranca at a lookout with picnic benches (near the top of the long initial ascent). The climb then gently ascends through oaks and flattens before reaching its highest point, **Alto de la Pedraja** (1150m), at a cross commemorating Spanish Civil War victims. The wide trail descends and then ascends the steep gully initiating a fairly flat stretch of 7.5km, shadeless despite the trees, that eventually leads to the monastery (which suddenly appears). The **albergue** is in the monastery complex.

San Juan de Ortega

San Juan, Santo Domingo de la Calzada's disciple, founded the monastery on this once inhospitable stretch. His tomb is in the Romanesque and Gothic **church**. Every year thousands of visitors flock to see the 'Miracle of the Light' on the vernal and autumnal equinoxes, when a shaft of light illuminates a Romanesque capital depicting the Annunciation.

An adjacent monastery has a long-standing tradition of hospitality, serving delicious *sopas de ajo*, a bread-based garlic soup. Pilgrims often share from their packs for a communal dinner. **Taberna Marcela** serves simple meals (*menú* €7) and sandwiches (€2.60).

Day 11: San Juan de Ortega to Burgos

7–8 hours, 28km

It's 26km to the cathedral in Burgos and a further 2km, away from the city centre, to the *albergue*. Burgos merits a leisurely visit, thus we give city lodging options. The described walk avoids 7km of industrial mess and busy streets following the Río Arlanzón's peaceful, though paved, course.

Leave the monastery, walking along the road to a crossroads. From here, continue straight for almost 3km on a flat, dirt path enveloped in a thick forest of oak and conifers. Reaching a meadow, pass through the wire shepherd's gate and descend to Agés (with fountain). Cross the village and continue 2.5km along a paved road to Atapuerca, which has a fountain, **albergue** and **bar**.

Nearby, in Sierra de Atapuerca, archaeologists actively work on hugely important excavations of human remains dating from 800,000 years ago as well as a potential predecessor of *Homo sapiens* and a Neanderthal, dubbed *H. antecessor*. An **information office** (☎ 947 43 04 73; e info@paleorama.es; *open during good weather*) in Atapuerca organises visits to the excavation sites.

Leaving the village, turn left, after the fountain on a dirt path, ascending 2km to the **summit** (1060m). Enjoy exceptional views to Burgos. The path descends to the valley, reaching a dirt road. Turn left onto the road and 300m later fork right (even if the arrows are painted out) to reach Orbaneja on a trail that winds pleasantly through wheat fields. (The left fork to Orbaneja is 1.5km longer, paved and passes through Villalval (**bar**) and Cardeñuela).

From Orbaneja (with fountain and **bar**), follow the road heading west (right) for 700m to a bridge. Cross the *autovía* (highway). Immediately afterwards, by an abandoned military outpost, turn left onto a footpath skirting the outpost. After 1.3km the path circles an airfield following the cyclone fence until the trail veers left to Castañares. Turn right onto the trail paralleling the highway. Continue 1.5km to the Metal Ibérica factory (on the right), and turn left, crossing the highway. This turn is easy to miss! Take a dirt lane that soon converts to asphalt and passes through Villayuda (Ventilla; with fountain) and leaves under the train's pedestrian tunnel. It soon reaches Capiscol, a suburb of Burgos.

Romanesque & Gothic Art & Architecture

The medieval Romanesque and Gothic art and architectural styles arrived on the Iberian Peninsula via the Camino de Santiago. Christian Europe's first 'international' style, Romanesque, was developed at the beginning of the 11th century as an expression of feudal thought and as a post-millennium gesture of gratitude for the world's survival. It was spread via religious orders and pilgrimages across Europe. Solid and permanent, buildings constructed in this style used thick, squared-stone walls, massive columns, semicircular arches and barrel vaults, and had few windows. Churches had three or five naves, a Latin cross floorplan, a cupola above the crossing, one or more semicircular apses and a pilgrims' ambulatory. Romanesque sculpture (incorporated into the building) and painting (which covered the interior walls completely!) accomplished a didactic, rather than decorative, function; the illiterate devout 'read the Bible' through the images, which sought to stimulate piety and fear of the Church. A common representation was Pantocrator (Christ) as powerful king and inflexible judge, seated on his throne and surrounded by the evangelists (Matthew, Mark, Luke and John) symbolically represented as an angel, lion, bull and eagle.

The Gothic style surfaced in the 12th century in conjunction with a general socioeconomic shift of power from the country to the city. Using the pointed arch and the ribbed vault, buildings, especially cathedrals, strove for height and luminosity (representing the light of God). The basilica (rectangular) floorplan, wider at the transept, also had an ambulatory and chapels behind the altar. The high walls incorporated stained-glass and rose windows inside and flying buttresses and needle-like pinnacles on the outside. The painting and sculpture sought realism and beauty rather than present a message to be read. The Virgin Mary appears more frequently and Christ as judge is substituted for Christ as man who suffers on the cross. Sculptures are found on portals, chorus seats, gargoyles and altars, while painting (on wood) appears principally on altarpieces. Both reflect a greater preoccupation with light, movement, perspective and naturalism.

At the road either turn left (recommended) for the river route (3.3km to the cathedral) or follow the road (4.2km to the cathedral) right to the N1 (Calle Vitoria) by a petrol station, rejoining the conventional, waymarked city trail.

To follow the river, turn left. Head right, following the walkway to the **Puente El Cid**. Continue through the sycamore-shaded **Espolón** to the **Puerta de Santa María**, the dramatic stone gateway which leads to the cathedral plaza. To reach the **albergue** (with fountain) continue along the river walkway for 2km to a stone bridge. Cross the bridge and then cross the road to the El Parral city park (to the brown barracks).

Burgos

In the 15th century Burgos (860m), long associated with the pilgrimage, boasted 32 pilgrims' hospitals. Must-stops are the Gothic **cathedral** (which is a Unesco World Heritage Site), considered one of Spain's masterworks for its interior and exterior opulence, the Gothic **Iglesia de San Nicolás**, and the *mirador* (lookout) below the castle ruins. The **tourist office** (☎ 947 20 31 25; *Plaza Alfonso Martínez 7; open daily)* has excellent local and regional information.

Pensions, though numerous, tend to be run-down. **Pensión Peña** (☎ 947 20 63 23; *Calle Puebla 18, 2nd floor; singles €12, doubles with bathroom €19)* is the diamond in the rough. **Hostal Manjón** (☎ 947 20 86 89; *Calle Gran Teatro 1, 7th floor; doubles with/without bathroom €40/33)* has well-maintained rooms (some with cathedral views).

You can eat well and economically just steps from the cathedral at **Don Nuño** (*Plaza de la Catedral; meals from €8)*. The best local tapas are on Calles Sombrerería and San Lorenzo. If staying at the *albergue*, buy supplies in town. **Restaurante Miguel** (*Calle Serramagna 3; menú €6)* serves good meals near the *albergue*.

Day 12: Burgos to Hontanas

8–9½ hours, 29.8km

After the initial 10km of mostly sealed roads, the way enters a magnificent no-man's-land; the meaning of *meseta* becomes vividly clear. Get supplies in Burgos or Tardajos (much more limited) as neither Hornillos nor Hontanas has a market.

From the *albergue*, follow the trail (left) that leaves the park and reaches the Hospital del Rey (today a university building). Continue straight along the footpath parallel to the main road for 700m to a roundabout and head right onto Calle Pérez Galdós. The street becomes dirt and winds between poplars and fields to Villalbilla (with fountain and **albergue**). Skirting the village, reach its small train station and veer right through agricultural fields to the highway. Cross and take a dirt lane that parallels the highway to Tardajos, complete with all services, fountain and an **albergue**. Cross through the village, leaving via a paved road that veers left, reaching Rabé de las Calzadas (with fountain) in 2km.

Leave Rabé on a dirt road passing an **albergue** (right) and a chapel and cemetery (on the left). The way climbs a small hill, flattens out and continues for a seemingly endless 8km to Hornillos del Camino (825m). There's a fountain to the right of the trail 2.4km from Rabé. For some, this stretch (and the next to Hontanas) is mentally fatiguing as the horizon stretches to infinity. Others feel liberated, far from the sights and sounds of 'civilisation'. Hornillos has a fountain, **albergue** and **bar** (which serves sandwiches).

Leave Hornillos, forking right to take a dirt road (past cellars tunnelled into the hillside) for 600m. Ascend to the crossroads marked with white limestone field stones and veer left. The path flattens and rolls off into nothing. Crossing two minor dirt roads, continue to an unanticipated dip marked with a red Santiago cross. Off to the left a small, solitary structure (painted with a red Knights Templar cross) is the small oasis of Sanbol, which has an **albergue** (with no bathroom facilities) and a fountain with very cold water. The way continues without turns for 5km to Hontanas (930m). The church's bell tower suddenly pierces the

sky, signalling your arrival. Past the church on the right you'll find the **albergue**.

Hontanas

The women who run the *albergue* prepare evening meals for €6. The small, greasy **Bar Vitorino** (☎ 947 37 70 24; *main street*) has cheap meals and beds, but the scrupulous should definitely stay away.

Day 13: Hontanas to Boadilla del Camino

8–9½ hours, 29.6km

Buy supplies for the day's end in Castrojeriz or continue for an additional 4.5km to Frómista (see Day 14). Leaving Hontanas, cross the highway (towards Castrojeriz) onto a path that rejoins the road 4km later. Another 5km remain to Castrojeriz. Countless poplar, linden and elm leaves rustle musically along the way. Outside Castrojeriz, the road reaches the lamentable ruins of the Gothic **Convento de San Antón**. When ergotism, or St Anthony's Fire (a gruesome disease causing reddened extremities, burning skin boils and eventually gangrene), broke out across Europe in the 10th and 11th centuries, the saint's order blessed pilgrims with their symbol, the Greek letter tau, as insurance against the malady. The west rose window has the tau woven into the tracery. There is an **albergue** here.

The road continues to Castrojeriz (808m), a *sirga* wrapped round the hill's southern slope and topped with a castle, still impressive despite its ruined state. Entering town, pass the churches of the Virgen del Manzano, Santo Domingo (with a small museum) and San Juan. All services are available, including two **albergues**. Descend out of town, crossing the highway to a dirt road, and over the medieval stone then wooden bridge.

Steeply ascend the imposing hill for 1.2km to the summit of **Mostelares** (900m); an unexpected botanic garden greets you. The dirt path continues for 500m along the high mesa before abruptly descending to flat farmland and finally reaching a picnic area, Fuente del Piojo (Louse Fountain). Continue along the paved road for 1km and turn left onto a field road which descends past the **Ermita San Nicolás**, a small

Hontanas to Terradillos de los Templarios

Romanesque church converted by an Italian Camino association into a simple **albergue**. Cross the 11-arch medieval bridge spanning the Río Pisuerga, the natural border between Burgos and Palencia provinces.

Head right on the wide dirt road to the village of Itero de la Vega (with fountain and an **albergue**). Leave Itero via a paved road and continue on a wide dirt-and-stone road for a long 8km to adobe Boadilla (795m). A shady, wheeled fountain on the left offers welcome respite. Follow the arrows to reach both **albergues**.

Boadilla del Camino

The adobe village eye-catchers are the 16th-century Iglesia de la Asunción and the flamboyant 15th-century Gothic **rollo** (gibbet) where criminals were strung up. Typical in these arid climes are *bodegas*, cold-storage cellars dug into the hillside; and *palomares*, dovecotes, usually cylindrical or cubic adobe structures topped by a small tower. Adobe, made of dirt, hay and water, can last for 75 to 100 years.

Ask at the private *albergue* (Maison) about rooms in the **casa rural** *(rural guesthouse;* ☎ *979 81 02 84; doubles €24)* and for evening meals *(menú €7)*. **Bar Dori** *(meals from €4.50)* has a small **shop** and serves meals and sandwiches.

Day 14: Boadilla del Camino to Carrión de los Condes

7½–8½ hours, 27km

Leave Boadilla via the marked dirt road. Reaching a large barn and *palomar*, turn left

and continue on the flats until gently rising to the Canal de Castilla. Designed for irrigation, transport and grain milling, the 240km of these waterways are primarily used today for irrigation. Continue for 4km along the canal's left shoulder to the sluice gate (above the locks) and cross it via the footbridge.

Continue straight along the road to Frómista, which has all services and an **albergue**. Frómista's highlight is the **Iglesia de San Martín**, a fine example of Romanesque architecture, famous for its 100 interior capitals and 315 exterior stone-sculpted figures (called corbels) gracing the eaves.

Leave Frómista along a sycamore-flanked walkway towards Carrión de los Condes. Once beyond the overpass, turn right onto the Senda de Peregrinos (Pilgrims' Path) running parallel to the highway. In 3km reach Población de Campos, with a fountain, **bar** and **albergue**.

From Población to Villalcázar there are two options: either roughly follow the Río Ucieza's course (recommended) or walk 9km along the Senda de Peregrinos. The former is more scenic, tranquil and 1.3km longer.

To reach the river, at the end of Población turn left before reaching the road leading to the Senda de Peregrinos. Veer right onto a dirt road that soon turns left then reaches Villovieco (with fountain) in 3.5km.

Continue past the village, cross over a bridge and immediately turn right onto a dirt trail which parallels the river. In 1.3km reach a dirt road and another bridge to the right (do not cross the bridge). A sign suggests turning left to Villarmentero and the

Senda, but we recommend continuing straight along the river using the wide, flat trail. Follow the river for 3.7km to a sealed road and turn left. Passing the large Ermita Virgen del Río, continue for 1.8km to Villalcázar de Sirga. It has all services, a fountain and an **albergue**. This is one of the few villages with a documented Templar presence, and the central remnant of their powerful past is the magnificent 13th-century **Iglesia de Santa María la Blanca** (see the boxed text 'Knights Templar', p358). The carved southern facade, the chapel of Santiago with the seated Virgen Blanca (south transept) and the altarpiece of Santiago (north transept) are especially noteworthy.

Continue on the Senda de Peregrinos, the only option now, for 6km to Carrión (830m). Walk up the main street past, first, the private **albergue** of the Clarisas (on the left) and then the parish **albergue** behind the Iglesia Cristo del Tiempo.

Carrión de los Condes

The Romanesque facade of the **Iglesia de Santiago** in the main square has fine carvings. **Hostal La Corte** (☎ 979 88 01 38; Calle Santa María 34; singles/doubles/triples from €15/27/45) has immaculate, recently renovated rooms and tasty meals (menú €7). Charming **Hostal Santiago** (☎ 979 88 10 52; Plaza de los Regentes 8; singles/doubles/triples with bathroom €18/29/42), which opened in 2002 behind the Iglesia de Santiago, caters to pilgrims. **Cervecería JM** (Calle Santa María 1) serves great food from €5. The town has several **supermarkets**.

Day 15: Carrión de los Condes to Terradillos de los Templarios

7½–9 hours, 27km
On the flat, shadeless 16km stretch between Carrión and Calzadilla, studded with oaks and a few poplars, there's one fountain.

Descend to and cross the Río Carrión, passing the **Monasterio de San Zoilo**, now converted into a beautiful hotel. Continue straight through two consecutive crossroads (towards Villotilla). Three dreary kilometres of highway lead to and pass the Abadía Benevivere, founded in 1085 and now a farm. Cross the new bridge and after 700m reach and cross the highway heading straight onto a flat stone-and-dirt path – a Roman highway that connected Bordeaux to Astorga. In 2km, next to a tall poplar and a concrete marker which reads 'Hospital de Don García', is the fountain. In 10km more, always straight and crossing a road once, reach Calzadilla de la Cueza, with a fountain, **bar-restaurant** and albergue.

Trail markers lead to the N120 where an information panel explains four alternative routes to San Nicolás del Real Camino. Initially we describe 'Ruta 4' to Ledigos and then from there 'Ruta 3: Al Palomar' because it's the most scenic and tranquil.

Turn right onto the N120 and after crossing the Río Cueza take the Senda, which parallels the highway's left shoulder. At a fork, 200m later, take 'Ruta 4' and continue 5.3km to Ledigos, which has a fountain, **bar** (which serves sandwiches but no meals) and **albergue**. Cross the highway to the sealed road (towards Población de Arroyo) and in 300m turn right onto an agricultural road. A large, circular *palomar* sits on the left. In 500m make a sharp left onto a path that leads to Terradillos de los Templarios (880m) in 2km. At the village entrance, veer right to find the **albergue** 100m further along on the left.

Terradillos de los Templarios

The name suggests a Templar past, most likely from the 13th century. The *albergue* runs a small **shop** and does meals for €7. There's a small **bar**, open after 10pm and all day Saturday and Sunday, on the tiny plaza, and a **minimarket** on Calle de la Iglesia.

Day 16: Terradillos de los Templarios to Burgo Ranero

9–10½ hours, 32km
Castilla y León's wheat fields have been both Spain's breadbasket and a wool-industry centre. Large flocks are a common sight on the *meseta* walks.

Leave Terradillos on the first dirt road going left (west), to the right of an electricity tower, after entering the village. Ignore the uphill arrows; they return to the highway and the Senda. Continue 1.4km to the

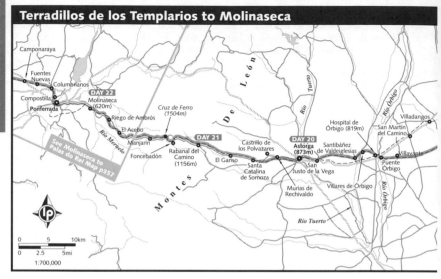

Terradillos de los Templarios to Molinaseca

sealed road. Turn left and after 400m, veer right down a dirt lane passing a hand-pump fountain. Medieval Villaoreja once existed here. Continue to Moratinos (with fountain) and 2.5km later San Nicolás del Real Camino (with fountain) appears.

Cross the quiet village to a small poplar grove. The arrows diverge: turn right to the Senda, which runs parallel to the highway to reach Sahagún in 5.8km, or continue straight (west) along the unmarked dirt-and-gravel lane for 7.3km to Sahagún; the latter (recommended) is more tranquil and scenic. At the first junction, continue straight on the dirt track; at the second, make a right-angled turn right. Trail markers begin again. After a gentle ascent to a barren plateau, Sahagún appears ahead. Descend to an unmarked T-junction and turn right to the N120, then left onto the Senda. After 300m, cross a bridge and either continue straight on the Senda or cross the N120 (recommended) to the agricultural road that leads to the Mudéjar-style **Ermita Virgen del Puente** – note the brick construction and horseshoe arches – surrounded by poplars. Continue under an overpass and enter Sahagún de Campos, which has all services

and an **albergue** – in the restored Trinidad church. Sahagún's monuments are excellent examples of Mudéjar architecture. Celebrated examples include the San Tirso, San Lorenzo and La Peregrina churches.

Leave Sahagún via Calle Rey Don Antonio. With the neoclassical **Arco de San Benito** on the right, cross the 11th-century bridge over the Río Cea. To the right, the legendary Field of the Lances acquired its name when 40,000 of Charlemagne's Christian soldiers died here fighting to free the north of Muslim influence and make the pilgrimage road safe. It's now a municipal **camping ground**.

Take the Senda parallel to the road and in 3.6km cross the N120 to rejoin the Senda straight ahead. After 250m reach another crossroads with two options. Straight ahead leads to Calzada del Coto (which has an **albergue**) on a rugged, desolate, poorly marked alternative that reaches Mansilla de las Mulas after 35.5km along the Via Traiana. Exceptionally hot in summer, during one 25km stretch the route lacks food, water or accommodation opportunities; only Calzadilla de los Hermanillos breaks the monotony.

Instead, at the crossroads, take the Senda de Peregrinos, marked with a cross, which

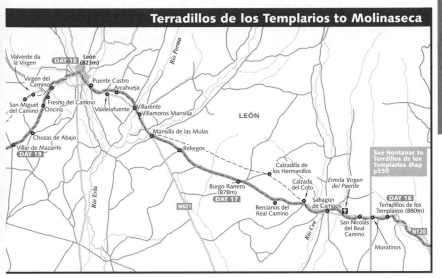

Terradillos de los Templarios to Molinaseca

heads west for 32km to Mansilla de las Mulas. Take the Senda reaching Bercianos del Real Camino in 5.5km, which has a fountain and **albergue**, and 8km later Burgo Ranero (878m). The **albergue** is across the street from the Hostal El Peregrino.

Burgo Ranero
The area surrounding this simple adobe village was once full of ponds, lagoons and – consequently – numerous frogs, giving the town its name (*rana* in Spanish means frog). **Hostal-Restaurante El Peregrino** (☎ 987 33 00 69; singles/doubles €15/20, doubles with bathroom €20/35) has mediocre rooms, good in a pinch, and serves food (*menú* €8). The village has a small **market** and pharmacy.

Day 17: Burgo Ranero to León
10–11½ hours, 37.7km
This long, often windy, stage is easily divided by stopping in Mansilla de las Mulas, a sizable town with *albergue* and all services, after 19.3km.

Next to a pond at the west end of Burgo Ranero, the Senda de Peregrinos begins again. After 12.5km of solitary, uninterrupted, barren plains (crossing the railway

tracks once) the way reaches sleepy Reliegos, which has a fountain, **bar-restaurant** and **albergue**. Leave Reliegos, passing the *frontón* to the Senda de Peregrinos, and 6km later enter Mansilla de las Mulas via the Puerta de Santiago gateway, passing a modern monument to the tired pilgrim. The **albergue** is along the pilgrim's route. Mansilla's odd coat of arms depicts a *mano* (hand) over a *silla* (saddle). The name Mansilla, though, probably derives from the town's beginnings as a Roman *mansionella* (way station).

Leave town, crossing the bridge over the Río Esla, and walk parallel to the N120 on a dirt trail for 4km to Villamoros de Mansilla. Continue through the village and take the Senda parallel to the N120, crossing a 20-arch bridge to the footpaths of Villarente, with fountain and all services. At the end of Villarente, after passing the petrol station, turn right onto a dirt trail that ascends to Arcahueja (with fountain). Descend to a junction: continue straight (recommended) to Valdelafuente (with fountain) or turn left to the highway route. In 1.5km from the fork, the dirt road ends at a sealed road. Turn left to reach the N120 and in 600m reach the **Alto del Portillo** (890m). Descend along the left side of the N120 for 2km and turn left to enter the León suburb of Puente Castro.

Continue straight, crossing a footbridge, and 1km further on, at the end of Avenida de Madrid, the paths to the two *albergues* diverge. To reach the **albergue municipal**, on the city's outskirts, turn left onto Avenida Fernández Ladreda, then left again on Calle Monseñor Turbado to the Colegio Huérfanos Ferroviarios (CHF) building. It's also a youth hostel. To reach the **albergue Madres Carbalajas** in 1.2km, and the historical quarter, continue straight on Avenida Alcalde Miguel Castaño, turning right onto Calle Barahona just after Plaza Santa Ana. Barahona converts to Puerta Moneda. Turn right onto Calle Escurial and 100m later you'll find the convent on the right, across from Plaza Santa María.

León

The most important inheritance of León (823m), originally a Roman garrison town, is its fine Romanesque and Gothic monuments. Highlights include the **San Isidoro** church; the **Panteón Real**, nicknamed the 'Sistine Chapel of Spanish Romanesque' for its exceptional Romanesque ceiling paintings; and the **Santa María de la Regla** cathedral, a French-influenced Gothic masterpiece with 2000 sq metres of stained-glass windows. The **tourist office** (☎ 987 23 70 82; *open daily*) is on the cathedral plaza. Leaving town, you'll pass the shell-covered **Monasterio and Hostal de San Marcos** (now a luxury hotel), abutting the Río Bernesga, which was once the seat of the powerful religious-military Order of Santiago.

Near the cathedral and off the newly refurbished **Plaza Mayor** are **Pensión Berta** (☎ 987 25 70 39; *Plaza Mayor 8, 2nd floor; singles/doubles €15/20*) and **Pensión Puerta Sol** (☎ 987 21 19 66; *Calle Puerta Sol 1, 2nd floor; singles/doubles €11/20*), both good budget options. Two rooms at the Puerta have cathedral views. Rooms at centrally located **Hostal Guzmán El Bueno** (☎ 987 23 64 12; *Calle López Castrillón 6; singles/doubles/triples with bathroom €28/43/57*) are excellent. Head to Plaza San Martín for delicious tapas, and for sit-down meals try **La Ruta Jacobea** (*El Cid 18; menú €8*) or **Casa Pozo** (*Plaza San Marcelo 15; menú €9*).

Day 18: León to Villar de Mazarife

5½–6½ hours, 21.5km

As Villar de Mazarife is very small, buy supplies in Virgen del Camino.

From Calle Puerta Moneda continue straight to Calle Herreros, which merges with Calle La Rúa. Turn right on Calle Ancha and continue uphill, turning left into the cathedral's Plaza Regla.

From the plaza take the first left down Sierra Pambley to Dámaso Merico to Recoletas and finally turn right onto Calle El Cid. Continue to Plaza San Isidoro and turn left down the stairs to Calle Ramón y Cajal. Turn right and then left onto Calle Renueva, which becomes Avenida Suero de Quiñones. Continue past the Hostal de San Marcos and over the medieval bridge to the N120.

Continue 1.5km through houses and highrises to a small plaza where the trail crosses the train tracks via a pedestrian walkway before rejoining the N120. Veer left to avoid a dangerous curve before returning to, and crossing, the N120. Take Calle La Cruz, which ascends past the entrances to subterranean *bodegas* on the left. After the road flattens, continue straight for 1.2km to the N120. Take the parallel sealed trail past the petrol station to enter Virgen del Camino, which has a fountain and all services. The facade of the church, built in 1961, is the work of José María Subirachs (sculptor of stylistic and expressionist modern art) and contains 13 bronze statues (12 apostles – Santiago points to Compostela – and the Virgin Mary).

After the church, cross the N120 and descend along the sealed road. Two options rejoin in Hospital de Órbigo: the isolated, dirt roads via Villar de Mazarife (recommended) after 28.6km, or the Senda and highway via Villadangos after 24.3km. Along the latter, the route enters the villages of Valverde de la Virgen, San Miguel del Camino and, 14km beyond Virgen del Camino, Villadangos, which has all services and an **albergue**. The next 10km parallel the N120, passing San Martín del Camino (with **albergue**) and Puente Órbigo before reaching Hospital.

The clearly marked way to Villar de Mazarife undulates along dirt trails and minor roads past Fresno del Camino (with fountain), Oncina (with fountain), Chozas de Abajo, and after 13.5km reaches Mazarife. **Albergue Ramón** is on the left 150m after the first houses and **Albergue Loli** is next to the church.

Villar de Mazarife

An unexpected highlight of simple Villar de Mazarife is the **museum** of the eccentric local artist, Monseñor, who makes excellent Romanesque replicas. **Señora Loli** (☎ 987 39 05 17; per person €12) lets rooms behind the church (ask in the Bar Torre) and will open an *albergue* in 2003. **Mesón Rosa** and **Bar La Torre** do meals and sandwiches.

Day 19: Villar de Mazarife to Astorga

8–10 hours, 32km

To shorten this long stage you could stop in the *albergue* of either Hospital de Órbigo (after 15km) or Santibáñez (after 20km). Santibáñez has no services.

Leave Mazarife, following the straight sealed road for 6km to a crossroads. Continue straight onto a dirt road and in 3.5km pass two canals and reach Villavante. Continue straight without entering Villavante (ignore arrows leading to the village). Cross the train tracks and the highway over a bridge to an industrial park that soon reaches the N120. Cross the highway and enter Puente Órbigo, aiming for its church adorned with massive stork's nests.

Turn left over the long stone bridge spanning the dammed Río Órbigo. Its 19 arches date from the 13th to the 19th centuries. Dubbed the **Paso Honroso**, the bridge gained fame in 1434 when Don Suero de Quiñones challenged all-comers to a jousting tournament to assuage the torments of an unrequited love. Dispatching some 300 knights over the course of one month, Suero triumphed and later made a pilgrimage to Santiago in thanks. Hospital de Órbigo has all services and two **albergues** (the parish one on the main street and the municipal one 500m through the poplar forest right (north) of the bridge).

Leave Hospital following its long main street (crossing a busy road once) to a fork.

Either head straight for 1.5km to the road and an additional 9km parallel to the main road where the two options rejoin at the Crucero de Santo Toribio, or turn right (recommended) and for 11.5km enjoy tranquillity and rural life.

Turning right, walk a very flat 2km through cultivated fields to Villares de Órbigo (with fountain and **bar**). Turn left and then right past a *lavadero* (place to wash clothes) and fountain. Continue straight, crossing a sealed road and bridge, to a dirt footpath that turns left, ascending along the hillside (look for fragrant lavender and thyme) to a sealed road. Turn right, descending to Santibáñez de Valdeiglesias (with fountain and *albergue*). Reaching mid-village, before its subterranean fountain, turn right up the street and veer right out of the village for 7km to the **Crucero de Santo Toribio** (905m), ascending and descending through fields and forest.

Framed by mountains, Astorga spreads out majestically below. Descend to and pass through San Justo de la Vega, which has a fountain and all services. After crossing the bridge, turn right and then immediately left along a dirt track that in 1.8km leads to the main road. Turn right (crossing the train tracks) and turn left down the first road and then right. At the T-junction turn left and then make a hairpin right turn to ascend steeply into Astorga (873m). On the right, 50m further along, are the remains of a Roman villa complete with intact mosaic flooring. The **albergue municipal** is on a parallel street off to the left.

Astorga

Once a strategic Roman way station linking the ore-rich mountains with the southbound transport route (the Vía de la Plata), Astorga retains numerous Roman artefacts. Today, the town is known for its *mantecadas* and *hojaldres*, rich sweets enjoyed with coffee. The spacious Gothic cathedral and Catalan architect Antoni Gaudí's early 20th-century **Bishop's Palace** (with an outstanding museum) are especially interesting.

Both **Hostal-Restaurante La Peseta** (☎ 987 61 72 75; Plaza San Bartolomé 3; singles/ doubles with bathroom €37/48; menú €8) and **Pensión García** (☎ 987 61 60 46; Bajada Postigo 3; singles/doubles €18/28) have serviceable rooms. **Restaurante La Berciana** (Magín G Revillo 4) has an extensive pilgrims' menú (€6); for the local specialty cocido Maragato (huge platters of every pig part imaginable served with potatoes, cabbage and broth) head to **Las Termas** (Santiago 1; mains €15). There are several **supermarkets** handy in the old town.

Day 20: Astorga to Rabanal del Camino
5–6½ hours, 21.1km
Leave Astorga along Calle San Pedro and cross the NVI to the descending sealed road (towards Castrillo de los Polvazares). After 3.5km reach Murias de Rechivaldo, which has a fountain, **albergue** and **bar-restaurants**. Note the stone-and-wood construction, distinctive door jambs, balconies and slate roofs typical of the Maragatería – the area west of Astorga reaching the summit beyond Foncebadón. Leave Murias along a dirt track. In 2.6km cross the road and continue along a Senda parallel to the road to reach Santa Catalina de Somoza, which has a fountain and **albergue**, in 1.8km. Cross the village and then continue along the Senda to El Ganso (with fountain and **albergue**). The last 7km to Rabanal del Camino (1156m) is a continuous ascent along Senda and road. Be sure not to veer right to Rabanal el Viejo. At the base of Rabanal, either fork left to reach the **albergues municipal and Pilar** or fork right (immediately passing a tiny **market** and **guesthouse** on the left) to the **albergue Gaucelmo**.

Rabanal del Camino
Next door to albergue Gaucelmo and opposite the church is a small Benedictine monastery renovated in 2001. The monks hold an evening Mass with chant.

Enjoy traditional Maragata cuisine (menú €8) and simple rooms in **Mesón-Hostal El Refugio** (☎ 987 69 18 26; Camino Real; singles/doubles with bathroom €27/48). **La Posada de Gaspar** (☎ 987 76 10 79; Calle Real 27; singles/doubles with bathroom €33/48) has handsome accommodation in traditional style, as well as meals (menú €9).

Day 21: Rabanal del Camino to Molinaseca
7–8 hours, 26.5km
Fountains en route are unreliable. Get water in Rabanal, El Acebo (17km) and Riego de Ambrós (20.5km).

Ascend Calle Real, taking a trail to the paved road, and ascend the road for 4.2km to Foncebadón, a small village with a few seasonal residents. Fork left and ascend through the village, past the recently renovated church. The 12th-century hermit Gaucelmo ran a pilgrims' hospital here and an **albergue** is expected to open in 2004. Veer left onto a lane that soon ascends round the hill to the road. Cross and take the parallel trail that soon ends at the summit of **Monte Irago** (1504m) and the **Cruz de Ferro** (Iron Cross).

A highly emblematic monument of the Camino, the simple iron cross rises out of a long, wooden trunk planted in a milladoiro (huge mound of stones). The Romans called these cairns 'mountains of Mercury' in

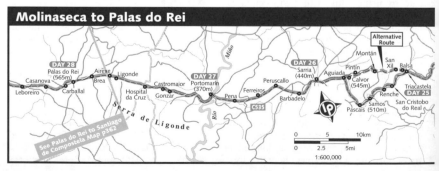

Molinaseca to Palas do Rei

honour of the walkers' deity. Continuing an age-old tradition, many pilgrims throw stones (some brought from home), which represent symbolic weights or sins, onto the pile.

The route runs parallel to the paved road for 2.2km to the largely abandoned, yet still inhabited, village of Manjarín. A bell may be rung in greeting as you approach Tomás, a modern-day Knight Templar, who runs a simple **albergue**.

Continue on the undulating highway before descending 12.5km to Molinaseca. The way alternates between stretches of highway and dirt paths, passing two villages. El Acebo has a fountain, **bar-restaurant** and two **albergues**. Riego de Ambrós has a fountain, **bar-restaurant** and an **albergue**. Note the slate roofs and overhanging wooden balconies with external staircases that are typical of the area.

Leaving El Acebo, an iron bicycle commemorates the death of a German pilgrim killed en route to Compostela. Continue along the road and veer left through broom to Riego de Ambrós. From Riego the path zigzags downhill through chestnut groves and open scrub to the road. Walk 100m along the road and turn right onto a dirt track. Descend to Molinaseca (620m), a beautiful village on the banks of the Río Meruelo, crossing the Romanesque bridge. To reach the municipal **albergue** continue walking 1km through Molinaseca on the main street and then the main road.

Molinaseca

Just off the bridge, **El Palacio Casa Rural** (☎ 987 45 30 94; Calle Palacio; doubles with/ without bathroom €33/43) has superb rooms and superb-value meals (pilgrims' menú €6.50). **Babel Casa Rural** (☎ 987 45 30 64; Calle Real 42; doubles with bathroom €36) is also very comfortable and has a kitchen. **Mesón Puente Romano** (Calle La Presa; menú €6) offers extensive variety. The village has all services.

Day 22: Molinaseca to Villafranca del Bierzo

7–8 hours, 29.6km

Leave Molinaseca along the highway. After 2km of gentle ascent, Ponferrada comes into sight. Either continue along the highway (recommended) or take a trail to the left that makes a long (1.8km) unnecessary detour via Campo. Continuing on the highway, cross the Río Boeza and enter Ponferrada (meaning Iron Bridge) along Avenida de Molinaseca. At the first crossroads, turn left onto Avenida del Castillo and 400m later, next to the Iglesia del Carmen, you'll find the **albergue**. Continue straight to the famed **Castillo de los Templarios**, finished in 1282. The knights used it only until their disbandment 30 years later. The mammoth complex overlooking the Río Sil has been extensively modified since then; now, fortunately, the town is renovating it.

Turn right uphill to reach the tourist office (in a stone building on the left) and the Plaza de la Encina with **bars** and the **Virgen de la Encina** church. From the plaza entrance, turn left and descend the stairs. Turn left, crossing the bridge, and then right on Calle Río Urdiales. Turn right onto Avenida Huerta del

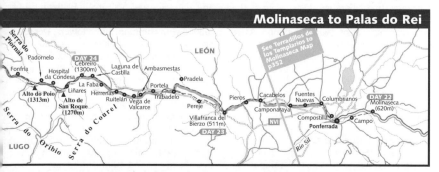

Molinaseca to Palas do Rei

Knights Templar

Beginning in the 11th century as a consequence of the crusades, religious-military orders developed to combat the Muslims, and recuperate and defend holy places and the roadways interconnecting them. Spain, thanks to the active Reconquista (Reconquest) and the Camino de Santiago, had its share of these orders. The most famous were the Knights of the Temple of Solomon (or Knights Templar) founded in Jerusalem in 1118. Despite poor beginnings, the order soon achieved great power, with numerous possessions; it became the most established bank of the period. Not surprisingly, the order attracted various enemies, among them Phillip IV of France. In 1307 he ordered the detention of the Knights Templar, tortured many and confiscated their wealth, basing his actions on unfounded accusations including devil worship. The order was finally suppressed in 1312.

Sacramento and 1km later, turn right at Avenida de la Libertad. Passing mountains of coal, take the first left turn through Compostilla, passing the villages of Columbrianos, Fuentes Nuevas and Camponaraya (with all services) over the next 7km.

After Camponaraya, turn left along a dirt road next to the Cooperativa Viñas del Bierzo. After crossing the bridge, continue through vineyards along a dirt track for 2.5km to a sealed road. Descend along the road 1.5km to Cacabelos, which has all services and two **albergues**. Depart across the Río Cúa and continue 4.5km along the highway, passing Pieros (with fountain). After the Km 406 highway sign, turn right onto a dirt trail that leads through vineyards and fruit trees in 2.8km to Villafranca (511m). Immediately on the right is the **albergue municipal** and on the left, past the Romanesque **Iglesia de Santiago**, is the stone **albergue** of Jesús Jato, built by and for pilgrims.

Villafranca del Bierzo

Overlooking the town is the Santiago church. Pilgrims too sick to continue to Compostela could pass through its northern portal, the **Puerta del Perdón**, and receive dispensation for their sins.

Walk down into town for additional lodging, including clean and economical **Hostal Comercio** (☎ 987 54 00 08; Puente Nuevo 2; singles/doubles/triples €15/18/21; meals for lodgers €7.50) and upmarket **Hotel San Francisco** (☎ 987 54 04 65; Plaza Mayor 6; singles/doubles with bathroom €35/48). Good options for a meal are **Mesón Ancares** (Calle Yedra 1; menú €8), just off the Plaza Mayor, or **El Padrino** (Doctor Aren 17; menú €8). On or just off the main plaza you'll find all services. The **tourist office** (☎ 987 54 00 28) is past the Monasterio-Hotel San Nicolás.

Day 23: Villafranca del Bierzo to Cebreiro

8–9 hours, 30.8km

This stage is the most physically challenging of the Camino with a total ascent of 1280m. The conventional route leaves Villafranca and follows a highway for 10.5km to Trabadelo (and to Portela after 14.4km). We describe a more difficult but far safer and more beautiful way to Trabadelo. There are various *albergues* en route to break up the stage if necessary.

Drop down into Villafranca, head towards the river and exit via the medieval footbridge and then a car bridge over the Río Burbia to a fork. Fork left for the highway option (passing Pereje, with **albergue**) to Trabadelo in 9km, or fork right initiating a long ascent of 480m (towards Pradela), first on the paved street and then a dirt-and-stone track. Enjoy increasingly excellent views of Villafranca and the Valle del Valcárcel. Flattening out along the ridge, the way heads towards a hill topped with communication towers. Descend among chestnuts (Pradela comes into sight off to the right) and at the first fork, bear left. After 600m, fork left again through chestnuts and descend for 3km. Cross a sealed road several times until finally descending into Trabadelo (which has an **albergue** and **bars**) from behind along an ancient access trail. Turn right and join the NVI in 1km.

Continue along the highway for 2.2km to Portela (with **bar**). In 400m, turn left at the petrol station, and 400m further along veer left onto the road towards Vega de Valcarce. Continue 5.5km to the Herrerías fork, along the way passing Ambasmestas (with fountain and **bar-restaurants**); Vega de Valcarce (with all services and two **albergues**); and Ruitelán (with a **bar** and **albergue**).

In 1km from Ruitelán, where the sealed road forks, turn left, descending to Herrerías (with fountain). Pass through the village and ascend the sealed road for 1km. Watch for the fork and descend left along a Galician *corredoira* (stone-cobbled lane). Ascend steeply for 1.5km to La Faba, with fountain, **albergue** and a sporadically open **bar**. Continue through the village, returning to the *corredoira*, which ascends through pastures and rolling hills to Laguna de Castilla (with fountain), the last village of León, in 2km. Around 150m beyond the village fork left onto a lane that reaches Cebreiro (1300m) in 2km. Soon after, spot the entry into Galicia and the first cement trail marker indicating that 153km remain to Santiago de Compostela. The countdown begins: every 500m another marker appears. Cebreiro's **albergue** is at the far western end of the small burgh.

Cebreiro

The hamlet of Cebreiro retains nine thatched *pallozas* (see the boxed text 'Galician Vernacular Architecture', p231); one contains an ethnographic museum. The 14th-century Miracle of Cebreiro occurred during a mass at Cebreiro's church, when, or so the Church holds, the wine and host literally turned into the blood and flesh of Christ.

Despite its diminutive size Cebreiro has numerous guesthouses and watering holes. Both **Hospedería San Giraldo** (☎ 982 36 71 25; singles/doubles with bathroom €30/36), adjacent to the church, and **Habitaciones Frade** (☎ 982 36 71 04; singles/doubles with bathroom €30/36) have comfortable rooms with rustic charm. Meals at the former (*menú* €8) and at **Venta Celta** are highly recommended. Frade runs a small **grocery**.

Day 24: Cebreiro to Triacastela
5–6 hours, 19km

In Galicia, green and grey tones predominate, rain is a constant possibility and the

Galician language, *gallego*, is commonly spoken. Rural Galicia with its countless hamlets connected by *corredoiras*, granite churches, stacked-tomb cemeteries and unending hills is bound to enchant.

Leave Cebreiro on the main road (towards Triacastela) and in 2.5km reach Liñares (with **bar**), founded as a linen plantation. Ascend to the **Alto de San Roque** (1270m) either via the highway or by turning right down a sealed road that after 100m converts to a footpath and ascends to the pass. A large, dramatic pilgrim statue braces against the elements at the top. Turn right onto a path that descends 1km to Hospital da Condesa, which has a fountain and an **albergue**. Traverse the hamlet and rejoin the highway for 600m. Turn right onto a sealed road (towards Sabugos) and in 200m take a dirt trail that ascends to Padornelo (with fountain). Climb steeply to **Alto do Poio** (1313m). Two **bar-restaurants** mark the summit – the Camino's last high point. Walk along the highway for 700m and then veer right onto a lane that reaches Fonfría in 2.5km.

The next 9km to Triacastela follow rural lanes past Viduedo, up Monte Caldeirón, and then descending continuously to Filloval and through forests of chestnut and oak on a dirt lane to As Pasantes (reached via a tunnel below the road) and Ramil, before finally entering Triacastela (665m). Immediately on the left is the **albergue Xunta** and straight ahead, in town, is the **albergue Aitzenea**.

Triacastela

Straight ahead is the village. **Bar-Fonda O'Novo** (☎ 982 54 81 05; Avenida Camilo Jose Cela 14; doubles with/without bathroom €35/18) has rooms in two different houses and a *menú* for €7. **Pensión García** (☎ 982 54 80 76; Rúa do Peregrino 8; singles/doubles €15/30) also lets adequate rooms. The village has all services including two **markets**. **Parrillada Xacobeo** (Calle Cadorniga Carro 4; meals from €7) has the best local food.

Day 25: Triacastela to Sarria
6½–7½ hours, 25.5km

To reach Sarria from Triacastela (where the trail splits at a T-junction) there are two options: left via Samos or right via San Xil. The former (the highlight is Samos) is described here and the latter (its charm is rural) in the Alternative Route.

Turn left along the highway and continue parallel to the Río Oribio for 3.4km. Veer right down the marked, paved lane through San Cristobo do Real, over the Oribio and ascend past the hamlet's cemetery to a beautiful rural lane flanked with chestnuts and oaks. Keep straight on, crossing the Oribio again (near an in-use water mill) and then steeply ascend along a sealed road through Renche to the highway. Walk briefly along the road and descend (right) and reach Freituge in 1km. Mid-hamlet, fork right onto a rural lane that crosses the Oribio in 500m. Steeply ascend along the sealed road through a highway tunnel. Veer left onto a dirt lane that descends to Samos (510m).

Founded in the 6th century (the date is confirmed by a Visigothic tablet), the Samos **monastery** has a 9th- to 10th-century chapel and a wealth of Renaissance and baroque art. The Benedictine monks run tours. The village has all services and a monastic **albergue**.

From Samos, 15km remain to Sarria. Walk through and veer left out of the village, keeping the Oribio on your left. After the last houses, a footpath (left) parallels the road to the Teiguín river park (with fountain). After 150m, passing a bridge and water mill on the left, cross the main road and ascend a steep, sealed road. Continue 800m to Pascais. Just before its first houses, turn left onto a descending dirt lane. In 400m, after a farm, there's an unmarked fork. Fork left, skirting round the church and descending along a dirt lane to a sealed road. Continue 1.5km to a bridge (over the Río Frollais) guarded by an enshrined praying saint. The inscription reads: 'This bridge was made in the year 1840, those who cross entrust themselves to the souls of purgatory.' Soon thereafter, turn left onto a sealed road (towards Sivil) that is level and then climbs to Aguiada in 3.4km.

From Aguiada take the dirt Senda to the right of the road for 4km to Sarria (440m). In Sarria, cross the river, turn right on the street and then make a quick left, ascending a flight of penitential steps (Escalinata Maior) to Rúa Maior and the **albergue** at No 79.

Alternative Route: Via San Xil
4½–5 hours, 18km
Fork right and follow the sealed road, turn left after crossing the highway, and in 1.7km reach long Balsa. Cross its bridge and ascend right through woods to a sealed road. Turn right and soon reach San Xil (with fountain). In 2km ascend to the Alto de Riocabo (905m) and then descend to Montán. In 3km reach Pintín after passing through Fontearcuda. Continue, passing another hamlet, to Calvor, which has an **albergue**. The path runs parallel to the road for 350m until it turns right onto a sealed road (towards Aguiada). In 250m the two routes reunite in Aguiada.

Sarria
The budget option is **Pensión Mar de Plata** (☎ *982 53 07 24; Calle Jose Antonio 39; per person €10; menú €8)*. **Hotel Roma** (☎ *982 53 22 11; Calle Calvo Sotelo 2; singles/doubles with bathroom €28/40; menú €10)* is 1km from the centre but is the best offering. Both do great meals. Sarria is a large town with all services and numerous **markets**.

Day 26: Sarria to Portomarín
6–7 hours, 23.7km
Today's walk passes through 23 hamlets. Continue ascending along Rúa Maior past the Santa Marina (on the right) and Salvador (on the left) churches to a fountain. With the castle ruins ahead, turn right onto Avenida de la Feria, ascending to the Magdalena monastery (on the right).

Turn left, descending past the cemetery to a road. Turn right and in 150m turn left over a medieval bridge. The path runs parallel to the train tracks, crosses them and then after a wooden footbridge ascends through a dense chestnut forest. Ruins of a chestnut-drying hut are on the right. The path ascends to Vilei and then Barbadelo, which has an **albergue**. Barbadelo's church is a fine example of rural Galician Romanesque sculpture.

The Camino winds and bends along dirt, stone and sealed lanes through numerous signposted crossroads and hamlets, including Rente, Peruscallo (with **bar**), Lavandeira, Brea (100km to go!), Morgade (with fountain and **bar**), Ferreiros (with **albergue** and **bar**), Mirallos, Pena (with fountain), Rozas, Pena dos Corvos (spectacular views and the first appearance of Galician pines), Moimentos, Mercadoiro, Montras, Parrocha and Vilachá. Finally, the route descends steeply to Portomarín (350m).

Cross the bridge over the Río Miño. Old Portomarín, submerged below, was sacrificed in 1956 to construct a dam. Turn right, ascending along the footpath below the city park. Turn left and in 150m you will reach the **albergue**.

Portomarín

The fortress-like **San Nicolás church**, dominating the main plaza, was moved stone by stone to its present location before the inundation. There are quiet rooms, great meals (*menú* €6.50) and reservoir views at **Restaurante-Hostal Pérez** (☎ 982 54 50 40; *Plaza Aviación Española 2; doubles €24*). **Taberna O Pelegrín** (☎ 982 54 51 76; *Benigno Quiroga 6; doubles €20; menú €7*) has simple rooms which share bathrooms.

Day 27: Portomarín to Palas do Rei

6½–7 hours, 26km

Cross the main plaza, descend along the columned main street to the main road and turn left. In 150m turn right and then cross the footbridge over the reservoir. Ascend Monte de San Antonio for 2km through forest to the highway at a brick factory. Cross to the Senda de Peregrinos, continuing for 1.6km to Toixibó and 3.8km further to Gonzar, which has an **albergue**.

Past the *albergue*, turn left to Castromaior where the first eucalyptus trees appear. Continue on the sealed road to the highway, walking parallel to it before descending left in 2.8km to Alto do Hospital, which has a fountain, **bar-restaurant** and **albergue**.

Leave Alto, crossing the highway over a bridge, and turn left, then 100m later turn right onto a sealed road (towards Ventas de Narón). Over the next 11km or so you'll pass through Ventas de Narón (with fountain), over the gentle Sierra de Ligonde (756m), then downhill through Previsa, Lameiros, Ligonde (with fountain and **albergue**), Airexe (with fountain and **albergue**), Portos (**bar**), Lestedo, Valos and, finally, Brea. The path runs parallel to the highway for 1.4km to Rosario and veers left past the camping ground and gym, entering Palas do Rei (605m) by the **albergue**, opposite the town hall.

Palas do Rei

Without doubt, **Hostal Vilariño** (☎ 982 38 01 52; *Avenida Compostela 16; singles/doubles with bathroom €24/36*) has the best rooms and food (*menú* €7.30). Rooms at **Hospedaje Guntina** (☎ 982 38 00 80; *Travesía del Peregrino 4; singles/doubles with bathroom €18/24*) are clean and economical. Try **Casa Curro** (*Avenida Orense 15; menú €7*) for a good meal. Palas has all services, including a **supermarket**.

Day 28: Palas do Rei to Ribadiso

6½–7½ hours, 27km

Ribadiso has no services other than an *albergue* but Arzúa, 2.5km further uphill, does. Along the way, shop in Melide for supplies.

Descend to the N547 and follow it to the Palas city limits. Before entering Carballal, cross the highway and climb through the village (with fountain) back to the N547. The route soon veers left on a descending trail to San Xulián do Camiño (with fountain). Cross a river and wind through an oak grove to Casanova, which has an **albergue**. In 2.5km the way reaches the border between Lugo and La Coruña. Turn left at the next crossroads along a dirt path to Leboreiro (with fountain); its Romanesque church has a simple image of the Virgin carved in the tympanum, and erotic corbels. Leave the village over its curious bridge to a path bordered by poplars and plains across Melide's industrial park (with fountain) for more than 2km. Descend to Furelos (with fountain). Cross the four-arch medieval bridge and continue for 1km to **Melide**, which has all services and an **albergue**.

Cross the town via Calle Principal to its main plaza. On fair days streetside *pulperias* (vendors of octopus boiled in copper pots and served *a la feria* on wooden plates with olive oil, red pepper and marine salt) provide a tempting excuse for a break. The **ethnographic museum** *(admission €2; open 10am-2pm & 4pm-8pm daily)*, next to the town hall, packs in innumerable tidbits of Galicia 'as it was'. The **Iglesia de San Roque** and the 14th-century **cross** (to the left), considered Galicia's oldest, merit visits.

Follow the trail markers out of Melide past the cemetery and along a walled path to the highway. Cross the N547 and take the sealed road (towards San Martiño) for 200m before turning right (past the Romanesque **Iglesia de Santa María**). Over the next 5km pass Carballal, Parabispo and A Peroxa. In Boente (with fountain and **bar**), cross to the church and turn left through the village. Descend through eucalyptus groves and then ascend steeply to Castañeda, location of the 12th-century lime ovens used to make cement for Santiago de Compostela's cathedral. Pilgrims once carried stones from Triacastela to these ovens. Before reaching the N547 200m later, turn left towards Río, then veer right downhill. The way climbs a hill, descends, crosses the highway via an elevated bridge and then descends steeply to riverside Ribadiso. Two hundred metres above Ribadiso there's a **bar**. Cross the medieval bridge to the **albergue**, a restored 15th-century pilgrims' hospital. The closest alternative accommodation options are 2.5km and 3km further on, in Arzúa.

Arzúa

Arzúa has all services. **Pensión Rúa** *(☎ 981 50 01 39; Avenida Lugo 130; singles/doubles with bathroom €24/36)* has excellent, new rooms. **Hostal Teodora** *(☎ 981 50 00 83; Avenida Lugo 38; singles/doubles €21/33)* serves great meals (*menú €7*) and has comfortable rooms.

Day 29: Ribadiso to Arca
6–6½ hours, 23km

Alternative lodgings are available 1.5km before Arca, in Rúa. From Ribadiso, ascend towards the highway and turn left to pass through a tunnel under the N547. A footpath parallel to the highway reaches the centre of Arzúa (385m) in 2km.

Before reaching the main plaza, veer left down Calle Cima do Lugar (past the **albergue**) and go straight, leaving Arzúa via the stone-paved Rúa do Carme. Descend past the Fuente de los Franceses, and ascend through oaks past the Pazo As Barrosas (a country mansion). The dirt-and-stone lane reaches a stream, parallel to the path, and climbs to Pregontoño. The path forks right out of the hamlet, through a tunnel and past three houses.

In A Peroxa (not to be confused with the one on Day 28) fork left onto the dirt road flanked by oak and fruit trees. Over the next 8km wind through the sleepy hamlets of Tabernavella, Calzada, Calle (with fountain), Boavista and, finally, Salceda (with fountain), where the path and highway run side by side. Just before Salceda, under a large chestnut tree, sits a rectangular stone

mortar where apples were crushed for the fermented beverage, *sidra*.

Continue for 450m parallel to the N547, past a small **shop-bar**, and turn right onto a forest track. After a 200m climb, a pair of bronzed shoes unexpectedly commemorates the spot where a 63-year-old German pilgrim took his last steps in 1993. After Xen, Ras and Brea the path joins the highway at Rabiña and runs parallel to it to a pass and two roadside **restaurants**. Turn sharp right onto a dirt track flanked with eucalyptus that soon passes the **albergue Xunta** in Santa Irene (the private **albergue** is across the N547). Continue downhill 850m through eucalyptus forest. Cross the highway to Rúa and continue downhill for 1.5km on a paved road to Arca (290m; also called Pedrouzo). Turn left onto the N547 and reach the **albergue** in 150m. Arca has three **markets**, and meals are available in **Restaurante Compás** by the petrol station and **Restaurante Regueiro** in town.

Rúa

At Rúa's first house, turn right towards the highway to reach lovely **Hotel O Pino** (☎ 981 51 10 35; *Rúa de Arca 5; singles/doubles with bathroom €24/36; menú €7.50*). Continue straight in Rúa to **Bar-Casa Rural O Acivro** (☎ 981 51 13 16; *Rúa de Arca 23; doubles with bathroom €36, apartments €84; menú €6*), which has rustic charm.

Day 30: Arca to Santiago de Compostela

5½–6 hours, 20.7km

Follow the N547 to Arca's tiny main plaza (1km) and turn right at the Casa do Concello. Fifty metres past the school, turn left into the eucalyptus forest. Continue for 3km to the N547 at Amenal. Cross and continue straight, entering a natural tunnel of rich vegetation and deep, dirt walls. Ascend for 2km, finally veering right to a roundabout on the main road. Turn left and look for two cement waymarks. You discover that up till now the distances given have been incorrect: there are 15km, not 12km, left to Santiago! Continue straight ahead, skirting the signal lights of the airport, and cross a sealed road.

Descend to San Paio, known for the saint born in Pontevedra, martyred in Córdoba and popular throughout Galicia. Depart to the left and climb to a dirt road and eucaplypt forest, reaching the first houses of Lavacolla (with **bar-restaurant**). The fame of Lavacolla is etymological – its name (literally, 'washing one's loins') describes medieval pilgrims' pre-arrival ablutions.

Pass Lavacolla's church, cross the N547 and in 150m reach the famed but nondescript Río Lavacolla. The last 10km to the cathedral square are sealed. Ascend for 5km through Vilamaior, past the large Galician and Spanish television stations, and then turn left into San Marcos. From here medieval pilgrims sprinted to the nearby summit of Monte do Gozo (Mount Joy), dubbing the first to arrive 'king'. The cathedral's three spires are now in sight (barely!) for the first time. The summit's modest San Marcos chapel is overshadowed by the pilgrim sculpture in honour of the Pope and the 800-bed **albergue**, camp, **bar-restaurant** and amphitheatre.

Five kilometres of city streets remain. Descend straight, cross the highway bridge and round the left side of the roundabout. Continue straight to Rúa dos Concheiros. Turn left down the cobbled street to a roundabout. Cross to Rúa San Pedro, which leads to Porta do Camiño, one of the seven original entrances to the walled medieval city (the walls no longer exist). Granite flagstones lead up to the Praza de Cervantes and descend right through the Azabachería – the zone of the jet (petrified wood) artisans – then passes the Catedral de Santiago's north entrance and descends a flight of stairs to the grand Praza do Obradoiro.

Upon arrival, pilgrims usually mark the end with several rites: adding their hand imprint to the marble stone column at the cathedral's west end, hugging the large, Romanesque statue of Santiago and visiting the crypt containing his remains at the main altar. In Holy Years (see History, pp328–30) the great *botafumeiro* (incense burner) is swung every day at the Pilgrims' Mass at noon, and is a sight to behold, especially from the north or south transept. To request the Compostela, head to the **Oficina del**

Peregrino (☎ *981 56 24 29;* W *www.archi compostela.org, Rúa do Vilar 1).*

The only **albergue** in Santiago (and always threatened with closure) is the **Seminario Menor de Belvís**, 1km from the centre and accessed via Calle de las Trompas. Pilgrims are permitted to stay three nights. See also Santiago de Compostela (p220).

Other Pilgrim Walks

Though 91% of pilgrims walk the Camino Francés, some other historical pilgrimage routes are briefly described here. For guides to these routes see Books (p331). Galicia's regional tourist offices have free *Roads to Santiago* brochures describing all except the Camino Aragonés.

Camino Aragonés

Using the higher Somport Pass in the Pyrenees, walk 146km through Aragón, joining the Camino Francés at Puente la Reina (see p340). This quiet, more rugged route reveals the Pyrenees as peaks rather than lumps and descends gently through fertile valleys rich in monuments. The distance, intermittently waymarked, can be covered in five or six days. Canfranc, Jaca, Undués, Sangüesa and Monreal have *albergues*.

Caminos del Norte

Pilgrims crossed the France-Spain border to Irún, reaching the Basque Country, and took the coastal route via San Sebastián, Bilbao and Santander to Ribadeo (Galicia) or headed inland via the Túnel de San Adrián (1443m) to La Rioja and the Camino Francés. Those sailing from the north landed (eg, in Santander or Gijón) and continued along the coast to Galicia or south to Fonsagrada and León via Oviedo. In Asturias there are 22 *albergues* and in Galicia Ribadeo, Lourenzá, Mondoñedo, Vilalba, Baamonde, Sobrado dos Monxes, Fonsagrada and O Cadavo have them. See W www .gawthorpe40.freeserve.co.uk for information.

Vía de la Plata

From Seville, the Vía or Ruta de la Plata (Silver Way) runs 690km north to meet the Camino Francés at Astorga (see pp355–6) via Zafra, Mérida, Cáceres, Salamanca and Zamora. Partly marked with yellow arrows, the route's infrastructure progressively improves. Passing through large cities and lengthy, desolate stretches, water and people are scarce. Be prepared to carry supplies. Heat in Extremadura in July and August is unbearable, often more than 30°C. There are *albergues* in A Gudiña, Verín, Monterrei, Sandiás, Ourense, Cea, Silleda, Vilar de Barrio and Xunqueira.

Fisterra & Muxía

The 80km rural walk from Santiago de Compostela to the sea is feasible in three days passing through Negreira (with *albergue* and lodging), Olveiroa (with *albergue*), Cee and Corcubión (both with lodging), and Fisterra (with *albergue* and lodging). Continue another 30km north along the coast to Muxía, the legendary site of an encounter between Santiago and the Virgin Mary. Buses return daily from Fisterra and Muxía to Santiago.

Camino Portugués

From Lisbon a coastal route (via Porto and Tui) and two interior ones (via Braga and Verín or Ourense) reach Santiago. The coastal route is waymarked from Porto to Santiago and from the border at Tui. It's feasible in five days and there are *albergues* in Tui, Redondela, Pontevedra, Padrón and Teo. The interior routes join a Vía de la Plata variant in Verín and share the same *albergues*.

Camino Inglés

British pilgrims sailed to the ports of Ferrol or La Coruña and walked roughly 100km to Santiago. The two paths unite in Bruma (with *albergue*). The longer Ferrol section passes through the historic towns of Pontedeume and Betanzos, and there are *albergues* in Neda and Miño.

Travel Facts

TOURIST OFFICES
Local Tourist Offices
All cities and many smaller towns have an *oficina de turismo* or *oficina de información turística*, as do many tiny villages in walking areas during the summer months. Look for a sign with a large 'i' on it.

In general, the more important tourism is to a region the better informed the staff. Some of the small summer-only offices in walking areas are only as good as the brochures they carry. All are reliable for information on accommodation and local transport and, increasingly, those in popular walking areas will have a booklet on local walks.

National parks and many nature parks have visitor centres where the information, sometimes supported by a video or display panels, is usually much more useful for walkers – but don't expect to find too much in English.

Tourist Offices Abroad
Spanish national tourist offices include:

Canada (☎ 416-961 3131, |e| toronto@tour spain.es) 2 Bloor St West, 34th Floor, Toronto, M4W 3E2
France (☎ 01 45 03 82 50, |e| paris@tourspain .es) 43 rue Decamps, 75784 Paris, Cedex 16
Germany (☎ 030-882 65 43, |e| berlin@tour spain.es) Kurfürstendamm 180, 10707 Berlin; branches in Düsseldorf, Frankfurt am Main and Munich
Netherlands (☎ 070-346 59 00, |e| lahaya@ tourspain.es) Laan Van Meerdervoort 8a, 2517 AJ The Hague
UK (☎ 020-7486 8077, brochure request ☎ 09063-640630, |e| londres@tourspain.es) 22–23 Manchester Square, London W1M 5AP
USA (☎ 212-265 8822, |e| nyork@tourspain.es) 666 Fifth Ave, 35th Floor, New York, NY 10103; branches in Los Angeles (☎ 213-658 7188), Chicago (☎ 312-642 1992) and Miami (☎ 305-358 1992)

VISAS & DOCUMENTS
Passports
Citizens of European Union (EU) member states and Switzerland can travel to Spain simply on their national identity card. If you're from an EU country – such as the UK – that doesn't issue ID cards, you need a valid passport, as do all other nationalities.

Spaniards wouldn't venture as far as the corner shop without their Documento Nacional de Identidad (DNI). By law you too are supposed to carry identification at all times. In practice, you'll only need to flash your ID sometimes when paying by credit card and when registering at a hotel or camping ground – the latter, simply so that they can spell your name correctly without losing face.

Visas
EU citizens and nationals of many other countries, including Australia, Canada, Israel, Japan, New Zealand, Switzerland and the USA, don't need a visa for tourist visits of up to 90 days. If you're from elsewhere, check with a Spanish consulate.

Travel Insurance
Buy a policy that covers you for medical expenses, theft or loss of luggage and tickets, and for cancellation of delays in your travel arrangements. It may be worth taking out cover for mountaineering activities and the cost of rescue. Check your policy doesn't exclude walking as a dangerous activity.

Buy travel insurance as early as possible to ensure you'll be compensated for any unforeseen accidents or delays. If items are lost or stolen get a police report immediately – otherwise your insurer might not pay up.

If you're from an EU country, pick up an E111 form from your local health authority before you leave (see Medical Cover, p56).

Driving Licence
All EU member states' driving licences are recognised in Spain. Other foreign licences should be accompanied by an International Driving Permit (IDP). In practice, your home licence should suffice for rentals or dealing with traffic police. The IDP is available from automobile clubs around the world.

Copies

All important documents (passport, credit cards, travel insurance policy, driving licence etc) should be photocopied before you leave home. Leave one copy at home and keep another with you, separate from the originals.

✶ ✶ ✶ ✶ ✶ ✶ ✶ ✶ ✶ ✶ ✶ ✶

Travel Discounts

Hostel Cards You'll need a Hostelling International (HI) card or youth hostel card from your home country to stay at most HI-affiliated youth hostels in Spain. If you aren't carrying one, you can buy it in instalments at most Spanish HI hostels, paying €3 on top of the nightly rate, up to a total of €18.05.

Student, Teacher & Youth Cards These cards can get you worthwhile discounts on travel and reduced prices at some museums and sights. The International Student Identity Card (ISIC), for full-time students, and the International Teacher Identity Card (ITIC), for full-time teachers and academics, are issued by more than 5000 organisations worldwide. If you're under 26, the International Youth Travel Card (IYTC; previously called the GO25 card) and Euro<26 card (w www .eyca.org) confer similar advantages.

EMBASSIES
Spanish Embassies

Among Spanish embassies abroad are:

Australia (☎ 02-6273 3555, w www.embas pain.com) 15 Arkana St, Yarralumla, Canberra, ACT 2600
Canada (☎ 613-747 2252, e spain@docuweb .ca) 74 Stanley Ave, Ottawa, Ontario K1M 1P4
France (☎ 01 44 43 18 00, e ambespfr@mail .mae.es) 22 avenue Marceau, 75008 Paris, Cedex 08
Germany (☎ 030-254 00 70, e embesde@mail .mae.es) Schoneberger Ufer 89 6th floor, 10785 Berlin; moving to Lichtensteinallee 1, 10787 Berlin in 2003
Ireland (☎ 01-269 1640, e embespie@mail.mae .es) 17A Merlyn Park, Ballsbridge, Dublin 4
Netherlands (☎ 070-302 49 99, e embespnl@ mail.mae.es) Lange Voorhout 50, 2514 EG The Hague

UK (☎ 020-7235 5555, e empespuk@mail.mae .es) 39 Chesham Place, London SW1X 8SB
USA (☎ 202-452 0100, w www.spainemb.org) 2375 Pennsylvania Ave NW, Washington, DC 20037

Embassies in Spain

Embassies in Madrid include:

Australia (☎ 91 441 60 25, w www.spain .embassy.gov.au) Plaza del Descubridor Diego de Ordas 3–2, Edificio Santa Engracia 120
Canada (☎ 91 423 32 50, w www.canada-es .org) Calle Nuñez de Balboa 35
France (☎ 91 423 89 00) Calle del Marqués Ensenada 10
Germany (☎ 91 557 90 00, w www.embajada -alemania.net/madrid/de/home/index.html) Calle Fortuny 8
Ireland (☎ 91 436 40 93, e irlmad@ibm.net) Paseo de la Castellana 46
Netherlands (☎ 91 353 75 11, w www.emba jadapaisesbajos.es) Avenida Comandante Franco 32
New Zealand (☎ 91 523 02 26) Plaza de la Lealtad 2
UK (☎ 91 700 82 00, e presslibrary@ukin spain.com) Calle Fernando el Santo 16
USA (☎ 91 587 22 00, w www.embusa.es) Calle Serrano 75

CUSTOMS

For duty-paid items bought in one EU country and taken into another, guidelines are up to 90L of wine, 10L of spirits, unlimited perfume and 800 cigarettes (or 200 cigars or 800g of tobacco). Sadly, you'll only manage to squeeze a fraction of this into your backpack. Since taxes on booze and tobacco remain relatively low in Spain, you'll normally find it's cheaper to buy from a local shop or supermarket than airport duty-free shops.

Visitors entering Spain from outside the EU can bring in duty-free 1L of spirits, 2L of still wine, 60mL of perfume and 200 cigarettes (or 50 cigars, or 250g of tobacco).

MONEY
Currency

Spain uses the euro, divided into 100 centimos.

Exchange Rates

For the very latest exchange rates check out the currency converter on w www.oanda.com.

Talking Euros

Now that the euro is common currency, the Spanish have settled on three ways of referring to centimos.

If bartenders want to tell you your beer costs €1.50, they may say:

'uno coma cinquenta' (one, comma, 50)
or *'uno con cinquenta'* (one with 50)
or simply *'uno cinquenta'* (one fifty)

❋ ❋ ❋ ❋ ❋ ❋ ❋ ❋ ❋ ❋ ❋ ❋ ❋ ❋

Exchange rates as this book went to press were:

currency	unit		euros
Australia	A$1	=	€0.57
Canada	C$1	=	€0.64
Japan	¥100	=	€0.82
New Zealand	NZ$1	=	€0.50
UK	UK£1	=	€1.58
USA	US$1	=	€1.00

Exchanging Money

You can change major first-world currency notes at most banks and exchange offices (though the New Zealand dollar tends to be greeted with a blank gaze). Most banks have a *cajero automático* (cashpoint, ATM), which will accept all major credit and debit cards. Credit cards are widely accepted in larger shops and restaurants and for train and long-distance bus travel.

Don't necessarily go for a bank or exchange office with the sign 'No Commission' in the window; they're in business too and usually compensate by offering a poorer exchange rate. At exchange offices, which generally offer quicker service than banks, both exchange rates and commission can differ quite markedly from one to another. For bank opening hours see Business Hours (p369).

The exchange rate for travellers cheques is usually a little better than for cash. Very few places allow you to use them like money and make purchases.

On the Walk

The safest way to travel is with a credit card, perhaps supplemented by a fallback stash of travellers cheques. Carry enough euros to live modestly for at least a week in the mountains and more isolated areas. Here, ATMs are rare, confined to towns and larger villages, and banks are even rarer.

Costs

A Spanish walking holiday needn't break the bank. Cost of living and internal transport in Spain is cheaper than in much of Northern Europe. To get to Spain, several low-cost airlines and charters (see Air, pp370–2) link major cities in Spain and, particularly, the UK.

You can live like a monarch of the mountains on €50 a day and for less than €25 a day if you're camping and self-catering. As everywhere, two can travel more cheaply (per person) than one.

Here are some typical costs for basic items:

item/service	cost
camping ground (tent & one person)	€6–9
pensión or *hostal* (per person sharing)	€10–15
refugio	€10–15
refugio with dinner and breakfast	€26–30
dinner in a modest restaurant	€12–20
lunch of filled baguette or breadstick	€3–5
glass of wine or beer	€1.50
can of soft drink	€0.50

Tipping & Bargaining

Most people leave some small change if they're satisfied with the service: 5% of the bill would normally be adequate and 10% generous. Many locals leave a couple of coins at bar or café tables. Taxi drivers don't have to be tipped but a little rounding up won't go amiss.

Bargaining is rare. Try it and you risk being regarded as a skinflint.

Taxes & Refunds

Value-added tax (VAT) on goods and services is known as Impuesto sobre el Valor Añadido (IVA; pronounced **ee**-ba). The rate varies from 7% on accommodation and restaurant prices to 16% on retail goods and car hire. In restaurants and modest accommodation it's usually included in quoted prices. Medium and top-range hotels frequently slap it on as a separate item.

Visitors are entitled to a refund of the 16% IVA on purchases costing more than €90 if they are taking them out of the EU within three months. Ask the shop for a Cashback refund form showing the price and IVA paid for each item and identifying the vendor and purchaser. Present the refund form to the customs booth for IVA refunds at the airport, port or border from which you leave the EU. The officer will stamp the invoice and you hand it in at a bank at the departure point for the reimbursement.

POST & COMMUNICATIONS
Post

The creaking *correos*, the Spanish postal service, is worse than that of many a third-world country. Letters routinely take up to a week to other EU countries, 10 days or so to North America and as long as two weeks to Australia and New Zealand. So mail your postcards on day one of your visit! Mail is normally quite safe but speed is a word yet to enter the postal service's vocabulary unless you pay premium rates.

Post your mail in a yellow *buzón* (post box) on the street or at a post office. Stamps are sold at every *oficina de correos* or *correos* (post office), most *estancos* (tobacconist shops; look for the yellow-on-brown 'Tabacos' sign) and some newsagents. Even quite small villages have a post office, though its opening hours may be very restricted.

For poste restante ask for letters to be addressed to 'Lista de Correos' and your family name to be written in capitals. If a postcode isn't specified the letter will go to the main post office in the addressed city. For post office opening hours see Business Hours (p369).

Postal Rates A postcard or letter weighing up to 20g costs €0.25 to post within Spain, €0.50 to other European countries and €0.75 to the rest of the world. Corresponding prices for letters between 20g and 50g are €0.40, €1.15 and €1.65.

Telephone

Roadside pay phones are blue, distinctive, abundant and easy to use for both domestic and international calls. You have the option of using coins or a phonecard issued by the national phone company Telefonica, or, in some cases, a credit card. Calls from pay phones, whether using coins or a card, cost about a third more than from private lines. Coin pay phones inside bars and cafés normally cost a little more than street pay phones. Phones in hotel rooms are frequently a lot more expensive.

Calls except those to mobile phones are cheaper between 8pm and 8am (6pm to 8am for local calls), and all day Saturday and Sunday.

Domestic Calls Dial all nine digits of a telephone number, wherever within Spain you're calling to. For internal directory inquiries call ☎ 1003; this is a free call from pay phones.

International Calls The access code for international calls from Spain is ☎ 00. Dialling from abroad, Spain's country code is ☎ 34. Follow this with the full nine-digit number you are calling. For international directory inquiries, dial ☎ 025 and be ready to pay about €1. Andorra's country code is ☎ 376.

Phonecards A *tarjeta telefónica* (phonecard) comes in denominations of €6 and €12. Phonecards are sold at post offices and *estancos*.

Lonely Planet's ekno Communication Card, aimed at travellers, provides competitive international calls (but avoid using it for calls to other EU countries or within Spain), messaging services and free email. Visit ⓦ www.ekno.lonelyplanet.com for information on joining and accessing the service.

Mobile Phones Use of the *teléfono móvil* (mobile phone) has mushroomed in recent years. Spain uses GSM 900/1800, compatible with the rest of Europe and Australia but not with the North American GSM 1900 or the totally different system in Japan (this said, some North American GSM 1900/900 phones do work here). If you have a GSM phone, check with your service provider about using it in Spain and beware of calls being routed internationally (very expensive for a 'local' call).

In a decreasing number of rural areas, yet in most of the high mountains, there's no coverage – just when you could probably do with it most!

Fax

A fax is useful for guaranteeing accommodation: some hotels may insist upon receiving one before confirming a reservation.

Most main post offices have fax service. The first page and subsequent pages cost €1.90/0.60 within Spain. You'll often find cheaper rates at shops or offices showing 'Fax' signs.

Email

Increasingly, even quite small towns will have an Internet point. Within walking chapters, we list Internet cafés and other public access points. Prices generally vary between €2.50 and €5 per hour with some places insisting on a minimum log-on of 15 minutes.

TIME

Spain, like most of Europe, is on GMT/UTC plus one hour during winter and uses GMT/UTC plus two hours during daylight-saving time (from the last Sunday in March to the last Sunday in October). Britain, Ireland and Portugal are one hour behind.

Spanish time is normally USA Eastern Time plus six hours and USA Pacific Time plus nine hours. Subtract eight hours from Australian Eastern Standard Time to get Spanish time; subtract 10 hours from Australian Eastern Summer Time.

Timetables, as in most of Europe, usually follow the 24 hour clock.

ELECTRICITY

The electric current in Spain, like elsewhere in mainland Europe, is 220V, 50Hz. Plugs have two round pins.

WEIGHTS & MEASURES

Spain uses the metric system (see the conversion tables on the inside-back cover of this book). Like other mainland Europeans,

the Spanish indicate decimals with commas and thousands with a dot.

BUSINESS HOURS

Generally, people work from about 9am to 2pm and then again from 4.30pm or 5pm for another three hours, Monday to Friday. Shops and travel agencies usually open these hours on Saturday too, although some may skip the evening session. In summer, many people work a *jornada intensiva* (intensive working day), starting as early as 7am and finishing by 2pm.

Big supermarkets and department stores often stay open from about 9am to 9pm without a break, Monday to Saturday. A lot of government offices don't bother with afternoon opening. Main post offices in cities and towns are usually open from about 8.30am to 8.30pm Monday to Friday and around 9am to 1.30pm Saturday. Banks are generally open from 8.30 or 9am to 2pm weekdays and until 1pm on Saturday. However, in the peak summer months you'll be lucky to find any bank open on a Saturday morning.

Don't expect to come down from the hills and top up on provisions at the village shop between 2pm and 5pm, when they normally close. On the other hand, shops, supermarkets and visitors centres usually stay open until at least 7pm and often 8pm. For restaurant hours see Food (pp42–4).

PUBLIC HOLIDAYS & SPECIAL EVENTS

Check in advance for public holidays (Spain has one of the world's most generous allocations) that might fall within your walking dates. On those days, Spain takes to the roads and trails, it's often difficult to find a bed and public transport operates a reduced Sunday service.

The two main Spanish holiday periods are Semana Santa (the week leading up to Easter Sunday) and the month of August. At these times and during much of July, pressure on accommodation, including *refugios*, is intense and it's important to reserve in advance.

Every region of Spain has at least 14 official holidays a year, some observed nationwide, others (to compound your planning problems), observed only locally. When a public holiday nudges near a weekend, Spaniards observe the excellent tradition of *el puente* (literally 'bridge') – and take the intervening day off too. The seven national holidays, which are supplemented by those 'bridges' and locally observed holidays, are:

Año Nuevo (New Year's Day)	1 January
Viernes Santo (Good Friday)	March/April
Fiesta del Trabajo (Labour Day)	1 May
La Asunción (Feast of the Assumption)	15 August
Día de la Hispanidad (National Day)	12 October
La Inmaculada Concepción (Feast of the Immaculate Conception)	8 December
Navidad (Christmas)	25 December

To supplement these, each regional government decrees an additional seven days a year. Other commonly observed holidays include:

Epifanía (Epiphany) or **Día de los Reyes Magos** (Three Kings' Day)	6 January – children receive presents
Día de San José (St Joseph's Day)	19 March
Jueves Santo (Maundy Thursday, the day before Good Friday)	March/April
Corpus Christi	June (variable)
Día de San Juan Bautista (Feast of St John the Baptist)	24 June – King Juan Carlos' saint's day
Día de Santiago Apóstol (Feast of St James the Apostle)	25 July – Spain's patron saint's day
Día de la Constitución (Constitution Day)	6 December

Getting There & Away

As one of Europe's top holiday destinations, Spain has excellent air, rail and road links with other European countries.

If you're travelling to Spain from within Europe, flying is not only the quickest option, but is almost certainly less expensive and it's easy to hire a car on arrival, if you want to. If

Warning

The information in this chapter is particularly vulnerable to change: Prices for international travel are volatile, routes are introduced and cancelled, schedules change, special deals come and go, and rules and visa requirements are amended. You should check directly with the airline or a travel agent to make sure you understand how a fare (and ticket you may buy) works and be aware of the security requirements for international travel.

The details given in this chapter should be regarded as pointers and aren't a substitute for your own research.

travelling from outside Europe, check the cost of flying via a major European hub such as London, Amsterdam, Milan or Frankfurt against that of a direct flight; the former is frequently less expensive.

AIR
Airports

The main gateways to Spain for scheduled flights are Madrid's **Aeropuerto de Barajas** (☎ 91 393 60 00, flight information ☎ 902 35 35 70) and Barcelona's **El Prat** (☎ 93 298 38 38). However, most holidaymakers arrive via the principal charter flight destinations of Málaga (for Andalucía), Alicante (for the Costa Blanca and Valencia region) and Palma de Mallorca. If you plan to walk in Andorra or the Catalan Pyrenees, Barcelona and Toulouse (in France) are the handiest points of arrival.

Baggage Restrictions

Airlines impose tight restrictions on carry-on baggage. No sharp implements of any kind are allowed onto the plane, so pack items such as pocket knives, camping cutlery and first-aid kits into your checked luggage.

If you're carrying a camping stove, remember that airlines also ban liquid fuels and gas cartridges from all baggage, both check-through and carry-on. Empty all fuel bottles and buy what you need at your destination.

The high season for air travel to Spain – and for ticket prices – is July and August, Easter and Christmas. Additionally, flights from the UK are normally fully booked and prices at a premium during British school half-term holidays, usually for a week during November and March.

You can get flight information online for all Spanish airports at [W] www.aena.es.

Departure Tax

On both scheduled flights and charters, airport taxes are factored into ticket prices. However, it's not always as clear when you're ringing around for the best quote, so do ask.

The UK

The two flagship airlines linking several airports in the UK and Spain are:

British Airways (BA; in the UK ☎ 0845-773 3377, in Spain ☎ 902 11 13 33, [W] www.british -airways.com)
Iberia (in the UK ☎ 0845-601 2854, in Spain ☎ 902 40 05 00, [W] www.iberia.com)

Of the two, BA is more likely to have special deals that are lower than the standard scheduled fares.

Other airlines' regular scheduled flights and destinations include:

Air Europa (in the UK ☎ 0870-240 1501, in Spain ☎ 902 40 15 01, [W] www.air-europa. com) flies from London (Gatwick) to Madrid.
British Midland (in the UK ☎ 0870-607 0555, in Spain ☎ 902 10 07 37, [W] www.flybmi.com) flies from London (Heathrow) to Madrid and Palma de Mallorca.
Monarch (in the UK ☎ 0870-040 5040, in Spain ☎ 96 691 94 47, [W] www.fly-crown.com) flies from London (Luton) to Alicante and Málaga.

No-frills, web-based budget airlines fly between an ever-increasing number of UK and Spanish airports. Potentially, they're your cheapest option as long as you are organised enough to book early – the price goes up steeply as a flight fills.

BMI Baby (☎ 0870-264 2229, ☎ 902 10 07 37, [W] www.bmibaby.com) flies from East Midlands and Cardiff to Alicante, Barcelona, Málaga, Murcia and Palma de Mallorca.

Best-Value Air Ticket

For short-term travel, it's usually cheaper to travel mid-week and take advantage of short-lived promotional offers. For 'no-frills' airlines, the earlier you book, the (substantially) cheaper the flight. On scheduled flights, return tickets are usually cheaper than two one-ways. Nowadays, booking via airlines' websites is generally the cheapest way to buy tickets for Spain.

Buying tickets with a credit card should mean you get a refund if you don't get what you paid for. Go through a licensed travel agent, who should be covered by an industry guarantee scheme.

Whatever your choice, make sure you take out travel insurance (see p365).

❀ ❀ ❀ ❀ ❀ ❀ ❀ ❀ ❀ ❀ ❀ ❀ ❀

Buzz (in the UK ☎ 0870-240 7070, in Spain ☎ 917 49 66 33, [W] www.buzzaway.com) flies from London (Stansted) to Girona, Murcia (for Alicante) and Jerez de la Frontera (Andalucía).
easyJet (in the UK ☎ 0870-600 0000, in Spain ☎ 902 29 99 92, [W] www.easyjet.com) flies from Bristol, East Midlands, Liverpool and London (Gatwick, Luton and Stansted) to Alicante, Barcelona, Bilbao, Madrid, Málaga and Palma de Mallorca.

Virgin Express (☎ 020-7744 0004) flies from London (Heathrow) to its hub in Brussels, from where it operates cheap flights to Spain (see Mainland Europe).

Ireland

Compare what's available direct to Spain and from London; passing through London may save you money.

Aer Lingus (☎ 01-868888; [W] www.aerlingus.ie) and **Iberia** (☎ 01-407 3017 [W] www.iberia.com) fly to Madrid and Barcelona. **CityJet** (☎ 01-844 5566; [W] www.cityjet.com) has direct flights from Dublin to Málaga.

Mainland Europe

Principal carriers linking mainland Europe and Spain, in addition to Iberia, are:

Belgium
Virgin Express (in Belgium ☎ 070-35 36 37, in Spain ☎ 91 662 52 61, [W] www.virgin-express .com)

France
Air France (in France ☎ 08 20 82 08 20, in Spain ☎ 901 11 22 66, W www.airfrance.com)
Germany
Lufthansa (in Germany ☎ 018030-803 803, in Spain ☎ 902 22 01 01, W www.lufthansa.com)
Italy
Alitalia (in Italy ☎ 8488-65643, in Spain ☎ 902 10 03 23, W www.alitalia.com)
Netherlands
Basiq Air (in the Netherlands ☎ 0900-227 47 24, in Spain ☎ 902 11 44 78, W www.basiq air.com)
easyJet (in the Netherlands ☎ 023-568 48 80, in Spain ☎ 902 29 99 92, W www.easyjet.com)
KLM (in the Netherlands ☎ 020-474 77 47, in Spain ☎ 902 22 27 47, W www.klm.com)

The USA & Canada
Spain's **Iberia** (☎ 212-644 8841; W www .iberia.com) and **Air Europa** (☎ 212-921 2381; W www.air-europa.com) fly nonstop from New York to Madrid. You can often get better deals with other airlines by travelling via another European city.

Australia & New Zealand
There are no direct flights from Australia or New Zealand. However, there are numerous possibilities for travel to another European city, where you can connect with flights to Spain. Lufthansa and Air France/Qantas from Australia and Thai International from New Zealand have some of the best deals.

LAND
Bus
Buses run by **Eurolines** (in the UK ☎ 0870 514 3219, in Barcelona ☎ 93 490 40 00, in Madrid ☎ 91 528 11 05; W www.eurolines.com) and its affiliates crisscross Europe. For schedules and online bookings check out the website.

From the UK, it's a long and masochistic haul that will scarcely save you a centimo and may even work out more expensive than a budget air-hop.

Train
The UK From the UK, you have to take Eurostar and change in Paris, and probably at the Spanish border as well. It *is* possible to take the cheaper ferry route across the Channel but you can't book all the way through to Spain that way. Consequently, taking the train to Spain, though a more comfortable option than the bus, may take almost as long – and it's more expensive.

Rail Europe Travel Centre (☎ 08705-848848; W www.raileurope.co.uk; 179 Piccadilly, London W1V 0BA), a subsidiary of SNCF, the French national railways company, offers an efficient reservations service.

For information and bookings on Spanish railways from the UK, you can approach **Prestige International UK Ltd** (☎ 020-7409 0379; Berkeley Square House; Berkeley Square, London W1J 6BS).

France Go to W www.raileurope.com for timetables and reservations. For bookings within France, ring **SNCF** (in French ☎ 08 36 35 35 35, in English ☎ 08 36 35 35 39). Within Spain, call ☎ 01 547 84 42.

Car & Motorcycle
The main crossings from France into Spain are the highways to Barcelona and San Sebastián. If you want to walk in the Pyrenees some convenient passes are: Roncesvalles (Roncevaux in French), which links St Jean Pied-de-Port in France with Pamplona; the new Túnel de Somport, north of Jaca in the Aragonese Pyrenees; Puerto de Portalet, near Sallent de Gállego, the Túnel de Bielsa; the Túnel de Vielha, which links the Vall d'Aran with the rest of Spain; and l'Hospitalet, on the border between Andorra and France.

SEA
The UK
P&O European Ferries (☎ 08702-424 999; W www.poportsmouth.com) sails from Portsmouth to Bilbao twice a week. **Brittany Ferries** (☎ 08703-665 333; W www.brittanyferries.co.uk) operates between Plymouth and Santander mid-March to mid-November. Both carry cars; sailings take 24 to 30 hours.

Getting Around

AIR
Internal flights within Spain are quite costly and it's far more sensible to make use of the

efficient and considerably less expensive train or bus services. The one exception here is the Balearic Islands, to where, if you're on the mainland, you might want to take a flight in preference to travelling by ferry. For details, see Palma de Mallorca (pp268–9).

Iberia (☎ 902 40 05 00; W www.iberia.es) and its subsidiary, **Iberia Regional-Air Nostrum**, have an extensive network covering all Spain.

Competing with Iberia are **Spanair** (☎ 902 13 14 15; W www.spanair.com) and **Air Europa** (☎ 902 40 15 01; W www.air-europa.com). Air Europa, the bigger of the two, has regular flights between Madrid and Barcelona, Palma de Mallorca, Málaga and a host of other mainland Spanish destinations.

BUS

The bus is usually cheaper, if less comfortable, than the train. The biggest carrier with a nationwide network is **Alsa** (☎ 902 42 22 42; W www.alsa.es).

In most larger towns and cities, buses leave from a single bus station, the *estación de autobuses*, usually located in the heart of town. In smaller places, buses tend to stop at a set street or plaza, often unmarked. Locals will know where to go. Usually a specific bar sells tickets and has timetable information.

On most short runs between towns and villages, the ticket you buy is for the next bus due to leave and can't be used on a later one. For all longer trips (such as Barcelona–Valencia), you can (and should) buy your ticket in advance. On some routes you have the choice between express and all-stops services, the former sometimes costing more.

Rural Services

Rural bus services have been sliced to the bone and some villages rely on only two or three buses a week. Where a morning or evening run serves primarily to transport children to school from outlying villages, the service may only operate during the school year. Even frequent weekday services can drop off to a trickle at weekends. Many rural services don't operate at all on Sunday. We strongly advise you to check the current schedule before setting out on a walk.

In the Pyrenees and parts of rural Galicia, enterprising car owners in villages without public transport run an informal, on-demand taxi service. If you're stuck, ask at the local shop or bar.

TRAIN

Renfe (Red Nacional de los Ferrocarriles Españoles; ☎ 902 24 02 02; W www.renfe.es) operates the national rail network. Call them for information (in Spanish); you can also reserve on line.

For short hops, bigger cities have a local network known as *cercanías*. From Madrid, for instance, *cercanía* trains cover the entire Comunidad de Madrid region. The slowest and very much the cheapest of the *largo recorrido* (long-distance) trains are called *regionales*. These are generally all-stops services between provinces within the one region.

Train timetables are posted at most stations. *Llegadas* (arrivals) tend to be listed on white posters and *salidas* (departures) on yellow ones. Often separate information on specific lines is also posted. Leaflets with timetables for specific lines are generally available free of charge at stations.

You can book trains at stations, Renfe offices and through many travel agencies. Some sample one-way fares (from cheapest to most expensive) are:

from	to	hours	fare
Madrid	Barcelona	6½–9½	€31–56
	Granada	6–9½	€27–43
	Valencia	3½–5½	€19–55
Barcelona	Bilbao	8½–9	€32–43
	Pamplona	6–7	€27–37

CAR & MOTORCYCLE

A car can save hours of waiting around for buses. If you're in a group doing a linear or multiday walk, someone can cut short their walk, or miss out altogether, and play taxi driver.

Be sure to pack your driving licence if you intend to hire a vehicle.

Road Rules

The speed limit in built-up areas is 50km/h. This rises to 100km/h on major roads and 120km/h on *autopistas* (tolled dual-lane highways) and *autovías* (dual-carriage highways which are toll-free). Motorcyclists must use headlights at all times and wear a helmet if riding a bike of 125cc or more.

Spanish truck drivers often have the courtesy to use their right indicator to show that the way ahead of them is clear for overtaking (and the left one if it's not and you're attempting this manoeuvre).

Vehicles already in roundabouts have right of way. Seat belts must be worn – both front and rear – if fitted.

Car Rental

All major airports have car-rental facilities. Local operators normally work out cheaper than the multinationals. To hire, you need to be at least 21 years old and have held a driving licence for a minimum of a year (sometimes two years). It's easier, and with some companies is obligatory, to pay by credit card.

HITCHING

Hitching is never completely safe and we don't recommend it. Women travelling alone should be extremely cautious about hitching anywhere. This said, in less populated areas you may well find yourself exercising your thumb as the only practical alternative

Language

Spain has one official national language, Spanish, and three official regional languages, Basque, Catalan and Galician.

As the country's national language, Spanish (often referred to as *castellano*, or Castilian) is understood by everyone and spoken fluently by nearly all. In global terms it's the most widely spoken of the Romance languages – the group of languages derived from Latin which includes French, Italian and Portuguese.

Like Castilian, Catalan (*català*) is a Romance language; including the dialects spoken in the Balearic Islands (Islas Baleares), Andorra and much of the Valencia region (where it's usually referred to as *valenciano*), Catalan is the most widely spoken of Spain's three regional languages. It has a rich literary history and culture; you'll even find a substantial volume of writing about trekking and mountaineering, many titles unavailable in any other language. Signs in Catalunya are frequently only in Catalan – fortunately, the written forms of Catalan and Spanish are very similar.

Galician (*galego*) is also a Romance language. It is very similar to Portuguese – in fact, up until the 13th century they were pretty much identical. The debate over the status of Galician as a dialect of Portuguese or a separate language still rages today.

Basque (*euskara*) has long been a conundrum for linguists. Bearing no relation to any neighbouring – or, indeed, any other – language, its origins remain obscure. It's spoken by a minority in the *País Vasco* (Basque Country – called *Euskadi* in Basque) and in Navarra.

Wherever these regional languages are spoken, people will generally be happy to converse with you in Spanish. Away from the main tourist areas and big cities, English isn't as widely spoken as many visitors seem to expect. It's therefore a good idea to try to gain some knowledge of simple conversational Spanish before you travel. It

isn't difficult to pick up, particularly if you have even the most basic grounding in French, Italian or Portuguese. Being able to communicate at any level with the people you meet will prove both useful and rewarding – even when they reply in English, they'll have appreciated the effort you made.

Take a reference book with you. Lonely Planet's pocket-sized *Spanish phrasebook* is a goldmine of information and practical phrases for coping with everyday situations; it has a two-way dictionary and includes special sections covering Basque, Catalan and Galician.

If you need to ask for something in English in an out of the way place, your best bet is often to approach someone under 20 – anyone who's been through the education system since about 1985 will have studied four to five years of English.

Gender in Spanish

As in all Latin-based languages, Spanish nouns and adjectives are marked for gender. Where two optional endings (for example *soy diabético/a* are given in the following words and phrases, the first variant is for a male speaker, the second for a female speaker.

Pronunciation

Spanish pronunciation isn't too difficult; apart from a few throat-rasping exceptions, many Spanish sounds resemble their English counterparts. There's also a very clear and consistent relationship between pronunciation and spelling; if you can read it, you can say it. Stick to the following rules and you'll have few problems making yourself understood.

Vowels

Unlike English, each of the vowels in Spanish has a uniform pronunciation, which doesn't vary. For example, the letter 'a' has one pronunciation rather than the numerous variations we find in English, such as in 'cake', 'care', 'cat', 'cart' and 'call'. Many words have a written acute accent. This accent (as in *días*) usually indicates a stressed syllable – it does not change the sound of the vowel. Vowels are pronounced clearly even if they are in unstressed positions or at the end of a word.

a	somewhere between the 'a' in 'cat' and the 'a' in 'cart'
e	as in 'met'
i	somewhere between the 'i' in 'marine' and the 'i' in 'flip'
o	similar to the 'o' in 'hot'
u	between the 'u' in 'put' and the 'oo' in 'loose'

Consonants

Some Spanish consonants are the same as their English counterparts. The pronunciation of others varies according to which vowel follows. The Spanish alphabet also contains the letter **ñ**, which isn't found in the English alphabet. Until recently, the clusters **ch** and **ll** were also officially separate consonants, and you're likely to encounter many situations – for example in lists and dictionaries – in which they're still treated that way.

b	soft, as the 'v' in 'van'; also (less commonly) as in 'book' when word-initial or preceded by a nasal such as **m** or **n**
c	as in 'cat' when followed by **a**, **o**, **u** or a consonant; before **e** or **i** as the 'th' in 'thin'
ch	as in 'choose'
d	as in 'dog' when word-initial; elsewhere as the 'th' in 'thin' – or not pronounced at all
g	as in 'go' when followed by **a**, **o**, **u** or **a** consonant; before **e** or **i**, a harsh, breathy sound, like Spanish **j**
h	always silent, as in 'honest'
j	a harsh, guttural sound similar to the 'ch' in Scottish *loch* or a discreet clearing of the throat
ll	similar to the 'y' in 'yellow'

ñ	a nasal sound like the 'ni' in 'onion' or the 'ny' in 'canyon'
qu	(they always occur together) as the 'k' in 'kick'
r	a rolled or trilled sound; longer and stronger when initial or doubled
s	as in 'send', never as in 'fusion', 'mission' or 'miser'. Often not pronounced at the end of a word
v	pronounced the same as **b**
x	as the 'x' in 'taxi' when between two vowels; as the 's' in 'so' when it precedes a consonant
z	as the 'th' in 'thin'
y	on its own (when it means 'and') it's pronounced as 'i'; elsewhere its sound is somewhere between the 'y' in 'yonder' and the 'g' in 'beige', depending on the region – pronounce it as 'y' and you'll be understood everywhere

Greetings & Civilities

Good morning.	*Buenos días.*
Good afternoon.	*Buenos tardes.*
Hello.	*Hola.*
Goodbye.	*Adios.*
See you later.	*Hasta luego.*
Yes.	*Sí.*
No.	*No.*
Please.	*Por favor.*
Thank you.	*Gracias.*
That's OK/ You're welcome.	*De nada.*
Excuse me.	*Perdón/Perdona.*
Sorry/Excuse me.	*Lo siento/Discúlpeme.*

Useful Phrases

What's your name?	*¿Cómo te llamas/Cómo se llama usted?* (informal/polite)
My name is ...	*Me llamo ...*
What's the time?	*¿Qué hora es?*
Please wait for me here.	*Espérame aquí, por favor.*
Do you speak English?	*¿Habla inglés?*
I understand.	*Entiendo.*
I don't understand.	*No entiendo.*
Please speak more slowly.	*Por favor, habla más despacio.*

Just a minute.	*Un momento.*
Could you write it down, please?	*¿Puede escribirlo, por favor?*
How do you say ...?	*¿Cómo se dice ...?*
What does ... mean?	*¿Qué significa ...?*

Getting Around

When does the ... leave/arrive?	*¿Cuándo sale/llega el ...?*
boat	*barco*
bus/intercity bus	*autobus/autocar*
train	*tren*

next	*próximo*
first	*primer*
last	*último*
timetable	*horario*

I'd like a ... ticket.	*Quisiera un billete ...*
one-way	*sencillo*
return	*de ida y vuelta*

Where's the bus stop?	*¿Dónde está la parada de autobús?*
I want to go to ...	*Quiero ir a ...*
Can you take me to ...?	*¿Puedes llevarme a ...?*

I'd like to hire a ...	*Quisiera alquilar ...*
car	*un coche*
taxi	*un taxi*

Directions

ahead/behind	*mas adelante/detrás*
below/above	*debajo/encima de*
before/after	*antes/después (de)*
up/down	*arriba/abajo*
flat/steep	*llano/empinado*
ascent/descent	*subida/bajada*
near/far	*cerca/lejos*
on the other side of	*al otro lado de*
towards/away from	*hacia/desde*
north/south	*norte/sur*
east/west	*este/oueste*

Go straight ahead.	*Siga todorecto/derecho.*
Turn left.	*Gire a la izquierda.*
Turn right.	*Gire a la derecha.*

Signs

Entrada	**Entrance**
Salida	**Exit**
Información	**Information**
Abierto	**Open**
Cerrado	**Closed**
Prohibido	**Prohibited**
Comisaria	**Police Station**
Servicios/Aseos	**Toilets**
Hombres/Caballeros	**Men**
Mujeres/Damas	**Women**

Around Town

I'm looking for ...	*Estoy buscando ...*
a bank	*un banco*
a chemist/ pharmacy	*una farmacia*
the market	*el mercado*
the police	*la policía*
the post office	*los correos*
a telephone	*un teléfono*
the tourist office	*la oficina de turismo*

What time does it open/close?	*¿A qué hora abren/cierran?*

Accommodation

I'm looking for ...	*Estoy buscando ...*
a camping ground	*un camping*
a hotel	*un hotel*
a guesthouse	*una pensión*
the youth hostel	*el albergue juvenil*

What's the address?	*¿Cuál es la dirección?*
Do you have any rooms available?	*¿Tiene habitaciones libres?*

I'd like ...	*Quisiera ...*
a bed	*una cama*
a single room	*una habitación individual*
a double room	*una habitación doble*
a room with a bathroom	*una habitación con baño*

Where is the bathroom?	*¿Dónde está el baño?*

How much is it ...?	¿Cuánto cuesta ...?
per night	por noche
per person	por persona
per tent	por tienda

Shopping

Where can I buy ...?	¿Dónde puedo comprar ...?
I'd like to buy ...	Quisiera comprar ...
How much is it?	¿Cuánto cuesta/ Cuánto vale?

Time, Days & Numbers

What time is it?	¿Qué hora es?
today	hoy
tomorrow	mañana
in the morning	de la mañana
in the afternoon	de la tarde
Monday	lunes
Tuesday	martes
Wednesday	miércoles
Thursday	jueves
Friday	viernes
Saturday	sábado
Sunday	domingo

0	cero	17	diecisiete
1	uno, una	18	dieciocho
2	dos	19	diecinueve
3	tres	20	veinte
4	cuatro	21	veintiuno
5	cinco	22	veintidós
6	seis	30	treinta
7	siete	31	treinta y uno
8	ocho	40	cuarenta
9	nueve	50	cincuenta
10	diez	60	sesenta
11	once	70	setenta
12	doce	80	ochenta
13	trece	90	noventa
14	catorce	100	cien/ciento
15	quince	200	doscientos
16	dieciséis	1000	mil

one million	un millón

Health

I'm ill.	Estoy enfermo/a.
I need a doctor.	Necesito un doctor.

Help!	¡Socorro!/¡Auxilio!
Call a doctor!	¡Llame a un doctor!
Call the police!	¡Llame a la policía!
There's been an accident.	Ha habido un accidente.
Go away!	¡Váyase!
Where is the toilet?	¿Dónde están los servicios/aseos?

I'm ...	Soy ...
diabetic	diabético/a
epileptic	epiléptico/a
asthmatic	asmático/a

I'm allergic to ...	Soy alérgico/a a ...
antibiotics	los antibióticos
penicillin	la penicilina

antiseptic	antiséptico
aspirin	aspirina
condoms	preservativos/condones
contraceptive	anticonceptivo
diarrhoea	diarrea
medicine	medicamento
nausea	náusea
tampons	tampones

WALKING
Preparations

Where can we buy food supplies?
  ¿Dónde podemos comprar comida?
Can I leave some things here?
  ¿Puedo dejar algunas cosas aquí ?
I'd like to talk to someone who knows this area.
  Quisiera hablar con álguien que conozca esta zona.
Where can we hire a guide?
  ¿Dónde podemos alquilar un/una guía?
We are thinking of taking this route.
  Pensamos tomar esta ruta.
Is the walk very difficult?
  ¿Es muy difícil el recorrido?
Is the track (well) marked?
  ¿Está (bien) señalizado el sendero?
Which is the shortest/easiest route?
  ¿Cuál es la ruta más corta/más fácil?

Is there much snow on the pass?
¿Hay mucha nieve en el collado?
We'll return in one week.
Volverémos en una semana.

Clothing & Equipment

altimeter	*altímetro*
rainjacket	*anorak/chubasquero*
backpack	*mochila*
batteries	*pilas*
cooking pot	*cazo*
bootlace	*cordón de bota*
boots	*botas*
camp stove	*hornillo*
candle	*vela*
canteen/	*cantimplora*
water bottle	
compass	*brújula*
crampons	*crampones*
gaiters	*polainas*
gas cartridge	*cartucho de gas*
ice axe	*piolet*
kerosene	*keroseno*
methylated spirits	*alcohol de quemar*
pocketknife	*navaja*
provisions (food)	*comida*
rope	*cuerda*
runners/trainers	*zapatillas*
sleeping bag	*saco de dormir*
sleeping mat	*colchoneta aislante*
sunblock	*protector solar*
sunglasses	*gafas de sol*
tent	*tienda*
torch/flashlight	*linterna*
walking poles	*palos telescópicos*

On the Walk

How many kilometres to ...?
¿Cuántos kilómetros hay hasta ...?
How many hours' walking?
¿Cuántas horas hay caminando?/
Hace cuántas horas de marcha?
Does this track go to ...?
¿Va este sendero a ...?
How do you reach the summit?
¿Cómo se llega a la cumbre?
Where are you going to?
¿A dónde vas?
Can you show me on the map where we are?
¿Puedes señalarme en el mapa dónde
estamos?

Walking Signs

Camino Particular	Private Road
Camping	Camping Ground
Campo de Tiro	Shooting Range
Coto Privado de Casa	Private Hunting Area
Cuidado/Ojo con el Perro	Beware of the Dog
Finca Particular	Private Farm
Proibido el Paso	No Entry
Propriedad Privada	Private Property
Toro Suelto	Loose Bull

What is this place called?
¿Cómo se llama este lugar?
We're doing a walk from ... to ...
Estamos haciendo una excursión
desde ... a ...

bridge/footbridge	*puente/pasarela*
to carry	*llevar*
circuit	*circuito*
climb/to climb	*escalada/escalar*
fence	*cerco/alambrado*
firebreak	*cortefuego*
to fish	*pescar*
to follow	*seguir*
mountain guide	*guía de montaña*
mountaineer	*montañero*
park ranger/	*guarda*
refugio warden	
path/trail	*sendero/senda*
refuge/mountain hut	*refugio*
route	*ruta*
short cut	*atajo*
signpost	*señal/marca*
ski field	*pista de esquí*
traverse	*traversía*
village	*pueblo/aldea*
a walk	*una excursión*

Map Reading

altitude difference	*desnivel*
contour lines	*curvas de nivel*
map	*mapa*
metres above sea level	*metros sobre el nivel del mar*
spot height	*cota*

Weather

What will the weather be like?
¿Qué tiempo hará?
Tomorrow it'll be cold.
Mañana hará frío.
It's going to rain.
Va a llover.
It's windy/sunny.
Hace viento/sol.
It's raining/snowing.
Está lloviendo/nevando.
It's clouded over.
Se ha nublado.

cloud/cloudy	*nube/nublado*
fog/mist	*neblina/niebla*
ice	*hielo*
rain (to rain)	*lluvia (llover)*
snow (to snow)	*nieve (nevar)*
wind	*viento*
clear/fine	*despejado*
high/low tide	*altamar/bajamar*
spring melt/thaw	*deshielo*
storm	*tormenta*
summer/autumn	*verano/otoño*
winter/spring	*invierno/primavera*

Camping

Where's the best place to camp?
¿Dónde está el mejor lugar para acampar?
Can we put up a tent here?
¿Podemos montar una tienda aquí?
Is it permitted to make a fire?
¿Está permitido hacer fuego?
I have a gas/petrol stove.
Tengo un hornillo a gas/a gasolina.
I'm going to stay here (two) days.
Voy a quedarme (dos) días aquí.

bivouac	*vivac*
to camp	*acampar*
campfire/fireplace	*hoguera*
camp site	*sitio de acampar*

Difficulties

Careful!	*¡Cuidado!*
Is it dangerous?	*¿Es peligroso?*
Can you help me?	*¿Puedes ayudarme?*

I'm thirsty/hungry.	*Tengo sed/hambre.*
I'm lost.	*Estoy perdido/a.*
Can you repair this?	*¿Puedes arreglarme ésto?*

Features

avalanche	*alud*
branch or tributary of lake	*afluente*
cairn	*hito*
canyon/gorge	*cañón/barranco*
cave	*cueva*
cliff	*acantilado*
coast, shoreline	*costa*
confluence	*confluencia*
creek/small river	*arroyo*
crevasse	*grieta*
fjord/sound	*ría*
frontier/border	*frontera/límite*
glacier	*glaciar*
hill	*colina*
island	*isla*
lake	*lago*
landslide	*desprendimiento*
lookout	*mirador*
moraine	*morrena*
mountain	*montaña*
mountain chain	*cordillera/sierra*
névé/permanent snowfield	*nevero*
pass	*collado*
plain/flat terrain	*llanura/planicie*
plateau/tableland	*meseta*
range/massif	*sierra/macizo*
rapids	*catarata*
ridge/spur	*espolón/cresta*
river	*río*
riverbank/shoreline	*orilla*
slope/rise	*cuesta/pendiente*
spring	*fuente/manantial*
stream/brook	*riachuelo*
summit/peak	*cumbre/cima/pico*
thermal springs	*aguas termales*
tide	*marea*
torrent	*torrente*
valley	*valle*
waterfall	*cascada*
wood/forest	*bosque*

Glossary

Unless otherwise indicated, glossary terms are in Castilian Spanish *(castellano)*. Other languages are listed in brackets and are abbreviated as follows: Aran = Aranese, Arag = Aragonese, Bas = Basque *(euskara)*, Cat = Catalan, Eng = English, Gal = Galician. Words which appear in italics within definitions have their own entries.

abrigo – shelter
acequia – irrigation channel
agua potable – drinking water
aiz – (Bas) rock, spur
albergue – shelter or refuge
albergue juvenil – youth hostel
alde – (Bas) neighbourhood
aldea – hamlet
alpujarreño – from Las Alpujarras
área de acampada – free camping ground, usually with no facilities
área de reserva – reserve to which access is restricted
arroyo – stream, brook or creek
autonomía – autonomous region: Spain's 50 *provincias* are grouped into 17 such units
autopista – tollway
autovía – toll-free, dual-carriage highway
ayuntamiento – district or town council; town hall

bable – Asturian language
bahía – bay
balneario – spa or health resort
barranc – (Cat) *barranco*
barranco – gully or ravine
barrio – district or area
bide – (Bas) path
bocadillo – long sandwich
bodega – old-style wine bar; wine cellar
borda – (Cat) mountain hut used in summer by shepherds and cowherds
bosque – forest
braña – stone hut or cabin found in the Cordillera Cantábrica

cabaña – cabin, hut
cabo – cape, promontory

cala – cove, small bay
calle – street
calzada – roadway
calzada romana – stone-paved Roman road
camí – (Cat) *camino*
camino – footpath, track, path, trail or road
camino real – state-maintained *camino*
campa – (Gal) treeless land or meadow
cañada – drovers' road
capilla – chapel
carrer – (Cat) *calle*
carretera – public road or highway
carta – menu
casa – house or building
casa de labranza – *casa rural* in Cantabria and Asturias
casa de pagès – *casa rural* in Catalunya
casa rural – rural house or farmstead with rooms to let
cascada – waterfall or cascade
castellano – Castilian; a term often used in preference to 'español' to describe the national language
castillo – castle
castro – fortified circular village, usually pre-Roman
català – (Cat) Catalan language; a native of Catalunya
caza – hunting
cervecería – beer bar
charca – pond or pool
charco – pool or puddle
circo – *cirque*
cirque – (Eng) *corrie* or bowl at the head of a valley, typically formed by glaciation
CNIG – Centro Nacional de Información Geográfica: it distributes *IGN* maps
col – (Eng) mountain pass
coll – (Cat) *col*
collada – (Arag) *col*
collado – *col*
coma – (Cat) *cirque*
comú – local authority (Andorra)
comunidad autónoma – *autonomía*
concha – shell
cordillera – mountain range
corniche – (Eng) coastal road or path

corredoira – (Gal) stone-cobbled rural lane connecting hamlets in Galicia
corrie – (Eng) *cirque*
cortijo – farm or farmhouse, especially in Andalucía
costa – coast
coto – area where hunting rights are reserved to a specific group of people; also cairn, boundary or boundary marker
couloir – (Eng) gully
cruceiro – (Gal) stone cross marking crossroads
cuesta – slope or hillside

dehesa – woodland pasture
devesa – in Galicia, woodland combining Atlantic and Mediterranean species
desfiladero – gorge, defile or narrow pass between mountains
DNI – Documento Nacional de Identidad; Spanish identification card

embalse – reservoir or dam
ermita – wayside chapel or hermitage
erratic – (Eng) a solitary rock different from those around it
erreka – (Bas) stream
estación de autobuses – bus station
estación de tren/ferrocarril – train station
estanh – (Aran) *estanque*
estanque – pool, small lake or tarn
estany – (Cat) *estanque*
etxe – (Bas) house
Euskadi – (Bas) Basque Country

faro – lighthouse
finca – building or piece of land, usually rural
font – (Cat) *fuente*
fonte – (Gal) *fuente*
forau – (Arag) cave or pothole
fuente – spring, fountain or water source

gallego – Galician language; a native of Galicia
garganta – throat; also gorge or ravine
golada – (Gal) *col* or pass
GR – Gran Recorrido (Long-Distance), a classification of some walking routes; also the prefix of some road numbers in Granada province
guía – guide

harri – (Bas) spur
hito – cairn; also landmark
hondartza – (Bas) beach
hórreo – granary in Galicia and Asturias
hospital – literally, hospital; also wayside guesthouse
hospitalero – *albergue* or *refugio* attendant on pilgrim route
hostal – inexpensive hotel
hoyo – hole, pit; *bable* word for *jou*

ibaia – (Bas) river
ibón – (Arag) small lake or *tarn*
iglesia – church
IGN – Instituto Geográfico Nacional, producing countrywide maps
illa – (Cat & Gal) *isla*
isla – island
iturria – (Bas) fountain
IVA – Impuesto sobre el Valor Añadido, or Value-Added Tax (VAT)

jou – hollow or pothole in Asturias

karst – (Eng) characteristic spiky landforms of a limestone region
kasko – (Bas) summit, peak
koba – (Bas) cave

lago – lake
laguna – pool or lagoon
lagunillo – small lake; *tarn*
lepoa – (Bas) pass
librería – bookshop
llano – plain
loma – low ridge

macizo – massif
madrileño/a – native of Madrid
mapa – map
marisquería – seafood restaurant
mendatea – (Bas) mountain pass
mendia – (Bas) mountain
mendikatea – (Bas) range
menú del degustación – fixed-price sampler of local dishes
menú del día – fixed-price, usually three-course, meal which often includes a drink
mercado – market
merendero – picnic spot
meseta – high tableland of central Spain

mesón – simple eatery with home-style cooking
mirador – lookout
mojón – boundary marker or large cairn
monasterio – monastery
montebajo – scrub or undergrowth
moraine – (Eng) rock debris swept down by glaciers and dumped as the ice melts
morisco – Muslim converted to Christianity in medieval Spain
mudéjar – Muslims living under Christian rule in medieval Spain; their characteristic style of architecture
muga – border marker or boundary

nava – high plain in Andalucía
nevera – pit or building used for making ice from snow
nevero – permanent, high-level snowfield

oficina de turismo – tourist office

palloza – thatch-roofed stone dwelling in the eastern sierras of Galicia
parador – luxury state hotel; many occupy historic buildings
parque nacional – national park
parque natural – nature park
pensión – boarding house or guesthouse
peregrino – pilgrim
pic – (Cat) *pico*
pico – peak or summit
piedra – stone or rock
pinsapar – woodland of Spanish firs
pista – trail or track
pla – (Cat) *llano*
plan – (Arag) *llano*
plato combinado – fixed-price dish with three or four items served on the same plate
playa – beach
port – (Cat) *puerto*
potable – (Eng) safe to drink
pozo de nieve – snow-storage pit
prado – meadow
praia – (Gal) *playa*
prat – (Cat) *prado*
presa – dam
pueblo – village or small town
puente – bridge
puerta – gate or door
puerto – port; also pass

ración – serving of food larger than *tapas*
rambla – seasonal watercourse; also avenue
refugi – (Cat) *refugio*
refugio – mountain hut or refuge
Renfe – Red Nacional de los Ferrocarriles Españoles, the national railway network
reserva nacional de caza – national reserve, where hunting is permitted but controlled
ría – estuary in Galicia and Asturias
río – river
riu – (Cat) *río*
rúa – (Gal) street
ruta – route

senda – path or track
sendero – footpath
serra – (Cat & Gal) *sierra*
SGE – Servício Geográfico del Ejército, producing countrywide maps
sierra – mountain range
sima – pothole, sink hole or fissure

taberna – bar or tavern
tapas – bar snacks
tarn – (Eng) small mountain lake or pond
tasca – bar, particularly specialising in *tapas*
teito – thatch-roofed stone cabin
tienda – shop; also tent
torrente – beck, mountain stream or narrow valley
tree line – (Eng) altitude above which trees can no longer survive
tresmil – peak higher than 3000m
true left/right bank – (Eng) side of the riverbank as you look downstream
tuc – (Cat) peak, summit

ugalde – (Bas) river
urbegia – (Bas) spring

vado – ford
vall – (Cat) *valle*
valla – fence or barrier
valle – valley
vega – pasture or meadow
vía pecuaria – drovers' road
vivac – bivouac
volcán – volcano

zona de acampada – *área de acampada*
zubi – (Bas) bridge

LONELY PLANET

You already know that Lonely Planet produces more than this one guidebook, but you might not be aware of the other products we have on this region. Here is a selection of titles that you may want to check out as well:

Spain
ISBN 1 74059 337 5
US$24.99 • UK£14.99

Madrid
ISBN 1 74059 174 7
US$14.99 • UK£8.99

Spanish phrasebook
ISBN 0 86442 719 0
US$7.99• UK£3.99

Barcelona
ISBN 1 74059 341 3
US$14.99 • UK£8.99

Andalucía
ISBN 1 74059 279 4
US$17.99 • UK£10.99

Valencia & the Costa Blanca
ISBN 1 74059 032 5
US$17.99 • UK£11.99

Western Europe
ISBN 1 74059 313 8
US$27.99 • UK£16.99

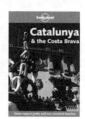

Mediterranean Europe
ISBN 1 74059 302 2
US$27.99 • UK£16.99

Catalunya & the Costa Brava
ISBN 1 74059 315 7
US$17.99 • UK£11.99

Cycling France
ISBN 1 86450 036 0
US$19.99 • UK£12.99

Walking in France
ISBN 0 86442 601 1
US$19.99 • UK£12.99

Walking in Italy
ISBN 1 74059 244 1
US$19.99 • UK£12.99

Available wherever books are sold

Index

Text

For a list of walks see the Table of Walks (pp4–7).
For individual mountains, ranges and peaks, see under the heading 'mountain ranges & peaks'.

Bold indicates maps.
For a full list of maps, see the
    map index (p8).
For a full list of walks, see the
    walks table (pp4–7).

Bold indicates maps.
For a full list of maps, see the map index (p8).
For a full list of walks, see the walks table (pp4–7).

Boxed Text

LONELY PLANET OFFICES

Australia
Locked Bag 1, Footscray, Victoria 3011
☎ 03 8379 8000 fax 03 8379 8111
email: talk2us@lonelyplanet.com.au

USA
150 Linden St, Oakland, CA 94607
☎ 510 893 8555 TOLL FREE: 800 275 8555
fax 510 893 8572
email: info@lonelyplanet.com

UK
10a Spring Place, London NW5 3BH
☎ 020 7428 4800 fax 020 7428 4828
email: go@lonelyplanet.co.uk

France
1 rue du Dahomey, 75011 Paris
☎ 01 55 25 33 00 fax 01 55 25 33 01
email: bip@lonelyplanet.fr
www.lonelyplanet.fr

World Wide Web: www.lonelyplanet.com _or_ AOL keyword: lp
Lonely Planet Images: www.lonelyplanetimages.com